Counseling
An Introduction

Counseling
An Introduction

Second Edition

John J. Pietrofesa
Wayne State University

Alan Hoffman
Wayne State University

Howard H. Splete
Oakland University

HOUGHTON MIFFLIN COMPANY BOSTON
Dallas   Geneva, Illinois   Hopewell, New Jersey   Palo Alto

Cover photograph by Ann McQueen.

5, 33, 104, 190, 443   Angelo Boy and Gerald Pine, *Client-Centered Counseling: A Renewal* (Boston: Allyn and Bacon, 1982). Reprinted by permission.

6, 9, 11, 189   Gary Belkin, *An Introduction to Counseling* (Dubuque, Iowa: Wm. C. Brown, 1980). Reprinted by permission.

34, 58, 263, 448   Bruce Shertzer and Shelley C. Stone, *Fundamentals of Counseling*, 3rd ed. (Boston: Houghton Mifflin, 1980). Reprinted by permission.

65, 185, 193, 201–202, 285   Gerard Egan, *The Skilled Helper*, 2nd ed. (Monterey, Calif.: Brooks/Cole, 1982). Reprinted by permission.

213, 214, 217, 245, 246   Sidney M. Jourard, *The Transparent Self* (Princeton, N.J.: D. Van Nostrand, 1964 [rev. ed., 1971]). Reprinted by permission.

442, 444   Copyright © 1983 Houghton Mifflin Company. Reprinted by permission from *The American Heritage Dictionary of the English Language, Second College Edition.*

443   Merle Ohlsen, "Professional Commitment," in William Van Hoose and John Pietrofesa, eds., *Counseling and Guidance in the Twentieth Century* (Boston: Houghton Mifflin, 1970). Reprinted by permission.

465   The lines from "voices to voices, lip to lip" from *is 5,* poems by E. E. Cummings, are reprinted by permission of Liveright Publishing Corporation and Granada Publishers Ltd. Copyright 1926 by Horace Liveright. Copyright renewed 1953 by E. E. Cummings.

This edition is dedicated to—

Diana, John David, and Paul Pietrofesa
Marjorie Susannah Hoffman (1911–1982)
Marlene Splete

Contents

PART II   *Theoretical Foundations* 71

Part III The Counseling Relationship 181

Part IV The Counseling Process 257

Part V   Professional Interests and Trends 439

Preface

In *Counseling: An Introduction,* Second Edition, we have tried to present what we believe to be the fundamentals of counseling in a systematic, comprehensive framework that is both readable and practical. Because counselors today function in a variety of settings—prisons, industry, schools, community mental health centers, vocational/career centers, and substance abuse and crisis intervention centers (to name but a few)—we have designed this book for counselors in all settings who deal with clients with diverse backgrounds and experiences.

Throughout this book, we have integrated counseling theory, professional issues, practice, and research. It is our belief that all counselors should have extensive background in each area to enable them to make appropriate professional decisions.

Audience

Counseling: An Introduction is intended for use as a basic text in introductory counseling courses taught at either the graduate or undergraduate level. It can also be used as a supplement in counseling internship or practicum classes. Related programs in social work, psychology, marriage and the family, and pastoral counseling may also find this book helpful to their students.

Coverage

The book is organized around five major topics: counseling foundations, theoretical foundations, the counseling relationship, the counseling process, and professional issues and trends. *Part I* on counseling foundations includes chapters on the meaning and history of counseling, the counselor, the client, and goals and

expectations of counseling. *Part II,* dealing with the theoretical foundations of counseling, includes chapters on affective, behavioral, and cognitive theories of counseling, in addition to providing a conceptual model for the content of counseling that allows for a variety of personalized counseling styles. *Part III* on the counseling relationship contains chapters on regard and respect, authenticity, and empathy. *Part IV* describes the techniques of counseling. It looks at specific counselor behaviors that can enhance client growth. Included in this section are separate chapters that discuss group and family counseling and specialized counseling concerns such as alcoholism counseling, substance abuse counseling, holistic counseling, sex counseling and therapy, and career counseling. *Part V* covers the profession of counseling, research in counseling, and significant issues and trends.

Features of the Revision

This edition of *Counseling: An Introduction* contains a number of changes from its predecessor. A considerable expansion of coverage has taken place. There are new chapters in *Part I* on the counselor, the client, and expectations and goals of counseling. *Part II* presents a greatly expanded treatment of the basic affective, cognitive, and behavioral counseling theories. *Part III* has been reduced in length but hopefully still conveys to the reader the importance of a good counselor-client relationship and what makes for it. *Part IV* now includes two new chapters: one on group, couple, and family counseling and one on specialized counseling concerns. Finally, *Part V* contains a new section on evaluation and examines many new professional issues and trends. Of course, throughout the book, all statistics and research studies have been thoroughly updated where appropriate.

Pedagogical Features
A variety of features have been included to help readers better comprehend the material.

Chapter Organizers Each chapter begins with an organizer that outlines the material within that chapter. Several questions are asked to help the reader address the major issues raised therein. The overall aim of the chapter is identified in a concise statement.

Counseling Dialogues In numerous chapters, counseling dialogues are incorporated within the text to serve as illustrations of what and what not to do during counseling. Discussion usually precedes or follows each dialogue and tries to highlight what the reader should look for.

Chapter Summaries At the end of each chapter, a detailed summary highlights the key points of that chapter.

Chapter References Extensive references appear at the end of each chapter. These references may be used by students to pursue interest areas, to develop projects, or to do research in the counseling area.

Appendices Several appendices follow the text. Perhaps the most important of these is the Code of Ethics of the American Association for Counseling and Development. Every counselor should be familiar with this ethical code that guides his or her daily conduct within the profession.

Acknowledgments

We are grateful for the help of a large number of wonderful people. We would like to acknowledge particularly the contributions made by Diana Pinto as a co-author of the first edition. In addition, a number of reviewers made key contributions to the organization and content of the book, most notably:

John H. Childers, University of Arkansas
Glenn E. Clark, Oregon State University
James Firth, Oregon State University
Janet Franzoni, Georgia State University
J. C. Heddesheimer, George Washington University
Paul Johnson, East Texas State University
Wayne Lanning, University of Wyoming
Robert Micali, University of New Mexico
Wendell A. Osorno, University of Northern Colorado
Larry Palmatier, University of San Francisco
Leo Remacle, University of Wisconsin, Oshkosh
William Rogge, Governors State College
Eldon E. Ruff, Indiana University at South Bend
James M. Seals, Oklahoma State University
Donald Smith, Florida International University
Lennis D. Smith, Jackson State University
Kenneth W. Wegner, Boston College
A. Paul Winans, Central Missouri State University
Michael T. Yura, West Virginia University

Finally, appreciation is expressed to Pam Saenz who helped in the preparation of this manuscript, and, of course, to the editorial staff of Houghton Mifflin.

J. J. P.
A. H.
H. H. S.

PART I

Counseling Foundations

CHAPTER 1

Counseling: An Overview

Chapter Organizer

Aim of the Chapter

This chapter will provide the reader with a brief overview of the counseling field.

Chapter Preview

1. *Counseling* is defined as a relationship between a professionally trained, competent counselor and an individual seeking help with a personal concern.
2. Counseling can be described by at least seven basic characteristics.
3. The similarities of counseling and psychotherapy are more important than their differences.
4. The four types of counseling are (1) crisis, (2) facilitative, (3) preventive, and (4) developmental.
5. Counseling has been influenced by five major historical forces.
6. Counseling is a needed service in our society.

Relevant Questions

The following are several questions to keep in mind while reading this chapter:

1. What is an adequate definition of counseling?
2. What factor or factors seem to have been most influential on the development of counseling?
3. Which type of counseling is most needed? Why?

Introduction

The purpose of this book is to provide a basic introduction to counseling—a fundamental process used by mental health professionals. The five major sections of this book cover the foundations of counseling, counseling theories, the counseling relationship, the counseling process, and professional issues and trends in the field.

Part I, "Counseling Foundations," comprises four chapters. Chapter 1 provides an overview of counseling, including definitions of the term *counseling,* a description of the types of counseling available, and a discussion of the development of counseling. Chapter 2 focuses on counselor qualities and client perceptions of the counselor. Characteristics of clients are described in Chapter 3. Chapter 4 concludes the first part of the book with a discussion of the expectations and goals of counseling.

Concepts of guidance and counseling have existed since the beginning of human society. In prehistoric times, people aided one another to survive physically as individuals and as members of a group. In modern society, counseling can be viewed as a process of helping individuals to understand themselves and their world and to act on that understanding.

In the past, "guidance and counseling" was often used as a single phrase. Of the two terms, *guidance* was most often identified with educational settings. As Crow (1982) states, "Guidance services are concerned with the study, understanding and adjustment of every learner in school" (p. 1). *Counseling* was seen as one of a number of guidance services. However, with the increased emphasis on providing effective mental health services to clients in a variety of settings other than schools, interest has increasingly been focused on the specific practice of individual counseling.

To set the stage for our review of counseling, we need first to present a working definition of the term *counseling* and describe its characteristics, second to outline four basic types of counseling, and third to describe the background and development of formalized counseling.

Counseling Defined

Aspects of Counseling   *Counseling* is difficult to define. It is not a single activity but seems to be a component of several professions. The term is further muddled by its use by professionals not really engaged in counseling, such as rug counselors, counselors-at-law, pest control counselors, and financial counselors. Nonetheless, the following seven characteristics of *counseling,* as we use the term, can be identified.

1. *Counseling is a professional service offered by a competent counselor.* Counseling denotes a professional relationship in which counselors take the

responsibility for making their efforts aid the client in a positive manner. It is not a "casual incident designed to 'adjust' or 'straighten' out the client" (Pietrofesa et al., 1978, p.4). The counselor needs to be able to use effective techniques and skills that have been gained through education and training. Boyd (1978) indicates that successful counselors grow personally and professionally and become increasingly competent through ongoing counseling experiences and supervision. A major element of counseling, then, is that the counselor has a particular expertise not found in typical relationships. Generally, social conversations or a "friend lending an ear" are devoid of such expertise.

2. *Counseling is a process in which the counselor-client relationship is basic.* Rogers (1952) emphasizes "the process by which the structure of the self is relaxed in the safety of the relationship with the therapist, and previously denied experiences are perceived and then integrated into an altered self" (p. 70). Brammer and Shostrum (1982) state, "The heart of the therapeutic process is the relationship established between counselor and client" (p. 143). Boy and Pine (1982) support the importance of this relationship: "When a counselor has an authentic caring relationship with a client, that client responds to the relationship by becoming fully involved in the counseling process" (p. 3). Effective counseling is based on this counselor-client relationship. Counseling does not take place in a casual relationship with, for example, a bartender or a stranger on a plane, where conversation is often too glib or superficial to be meaningful.

3. *Counseling is concerned with decision-making skills and problem resolution.* As Ivey and Simek-Downing (1980) indicate, "The counselor's task is to generate alternatives, aid the client in loosening and breaking old patterns, facilitate the decision-making process, and find viable solutions to problems" (p. 29). Carkhuff and Anthony (1979) present a counseling process in which decision making and goal setting are crucial steps. Problem definition and strategies for problem resolution need to be carried out continuously during counseling according to Cormier and Cormier (1979). Counseling teaches the client skills that can be applied in new situations. Without the development of decision-making tools, the client will be dependent on the counselor indefinitely.

4. *Counseling involves the client learning new behavior or formulating new attitudes.* Stefflre (1970) stated that "counseling is a learning-teaching process, for the client learns about his life space. . . . if he is to make meaningful and informed choices, he must know himself the facts of his present situation, and the possibilities . . . as well as the most likely consequences of the various choices" (p. 253). Krumboltz and Thoreson (1976) emphasize that "counselors are people who help their clients to learn" (p. 3). Counseling strategies often focus on client recognition of behaviors to be changed and appropriate steps to change them. Client

action and behavior change are crucial outcomes of the counseling process.

5. *Counseling is a mutual enterprise on the part of counselor and counselee and, as such, is based on respect for the individual.*   Boy and Pine (1982) indicate that an effective counseling relationship is one in which the client and counselor engage each other as equals. Both the client and counselor jointly are involved in the counseling process. Counseling goals are selected and refined by the counselee as well as by the counselor. It is not enough to depend on the counselor's expertise to choose client goals, but, on the other hand, that expertise is necessary to help the client accomplish whatever ends are chosen.

6. *Counseling cannot be specifically defined since it is a changing entity, but there are skills common to all such facilitative relationships.*   Belkin (1980) speaks of counseling as "a growing, evolving, continually changing concept, responsive to a nexus of interlocking pressures and concerns" (p. 20). Skills, because of their very quality, can however be defined in specific terms that may be applied in all counseling settings. Such counseling skills as attending, listening, responding, and behavior-change abilities will be discussed in later chapters.

7. *Counseling is a way of life.*   Pietrofesa et al. (1978) write, "Counseling, furthermore, becomes a way of life for the counselor, and is not turned on or turned off like the kitchen faucet. A counselor acts in a facilitative manner—and in contrast to what some may think—a manner that is unpredictable since it is authentic and not contrived" (p. 6). While it may be unpredictable, *it is always facilitative*—that is, it fosters growth in others. It is not hurtful and is certainly never done with malicious intent.

Counseling then, as used in this book, is defined as a relationship between a professionally trained, competent counselor and an individual seeking help in gaining greater self-understanding and improved decision-making and behavior-change skills for problem resolution and/or developmental growth. Counseling is provided in a professional setting by a counselor committed to counseling as a way of life.

Counseling and Psychotherapy   Counseling literature is replete with discussions of the differences between counseling and psychotherapy. Counselors often contend that such distinctions exist, yet counseling and psychotherapy are both concerned with essentially the same process. Any differences that do exist and can be identified are more superficial than substantial.

Differences   Psychotherapy has been distinguished from counseling by the fact that it (1) deals with the more "serious" problems of the "mentally ill," (2) places more emphasis on the past than on the present, (3) emphasizes insight more than change, (4) requires the therapist to conceal rather than reveal personal values and feelings, and (5) requires the therapist to work as an "expert" rather than as a sharing partner with the client.

We would like to qualify the basic nature of such differences. The concept of mental illness is being discarded, even by some psychiatrists, who increasingly find themselves conducting so-called growth groups. Behavioral and rational-emotive therapies, often considered to be more representative of psychotherapy than counseling, focus on the present and the future and on changing behavior as much as, or more than, the client-centered approach, which is considered to be more representative of counseling than psychotherapy. Therapist and counselor differences based on value or moral systems cannot be justified. We would agree that the notion of "patient" is foreign to counseling, but we would also suggest it might be better changed in psychotherapy also. We accept the notion that counseling focuses more on developmental-educational-preventive concerns, whereas psychotherapy focuses more on remediative-adjustive-therapeutic concerns, but neither to the exclusion of the other.

A number of authors have outlined differences between counseling and psychotherapy. Ivey and Simek-Downing (1980) contend that "counseling is a more intensive process concerned with assisting normal people to achieve their goals or function more effectively"; in contrast, "psychotherapy is a longer term process concerned with reconstruction of the person and larger changes in personality structure" (pp. 13–14). This view is shared by Brammer and Shostrom (1982), who indicate that "psychotherapy emphasizes intensity and length of involvement and is more concerned with alleviating severe problems in living" (p. 8). Yet both sets of authors agree that the therapeutic process of both counseling and psychotherapy is similar and that professionals often use the terms interchangeably.

Although some differences do exist between counseling and psychotherapy, we feel they are quantitative—a difference in degree—rather than qualitative. The similarities are far more important.

Similarities   Essentially, goals for both psychotherapy and counseling are the same: self-exploration, self-understanding, and action or behavior change. There is the common concern of trying to eliminate self-defeating behaviors in the client. Both counseling and psychotherapy put a great deal of emphasis on helping the client to develop decision-making and planning skills. The importance of the relationship between the client (or patient) and counselor (or therapist) is accepted as an integral part of both processes.

We believe that the therapeutic process, common to both counseling and psychotherapy, may have these similar effects:

1. The client gains a more positive view of self.
2. The client accepts self and others and becomes more open.
3. This greater openness allows for increased acceptance of one's strengths, weaknesses, and potential.

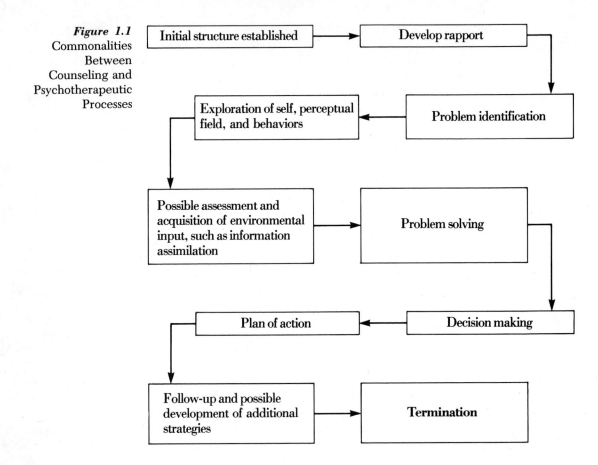

Figure 1.1
Commonalities
Between
Counseling and
Psychotherapeutic
Processes

4. Decision making on the client's part improves, and goals, aspirations, and plans become more realistic.
5. This realism increases the likelihood of successful achievement of goals.
6. Positive behavior change occurs.

Figure 1.1 shows common attributes of both the counseling and psychotherapeutic processes.

Types of Counseling

Our definition of counseling specifies that a person seeks the help of a counselor in order to deal with a specific concern. Resolution can be immediate, or it can take a relatively long period of time. We also recognize that counseling can be classified in a number of ways (for example, social, personal, educational, or vocational) and that a wide variety of counseling techniques or approaches can be employed. At this time, however, it is appropriate to give a broad overview of four general types of counseling situations and to indicate how a counselor might be involved in them. These four counseling types are crisis, facilitative, preventive, and developmental, as presented in Table 1.1.

Crisis Counseling　　Brammer (1973) states: "Crisis is a state of disorganization in which the helpee faces frustration of important life goals or profound disruption of his life cycle and methods of coping with stress" (p. 114). These situations often call for specific responses on the part of the counselor to aid the incapacitated client.

Belkin (1980) further discusses types of crises: "All of us, at some time in our lives, have witnessed or experienced crisis-situations—loss of a loved one, drug-induced crisis, inability to cope with life situations, a family crisis, an interpersonal crisis with one we love or care about, and so on. When a crisis reaches the stage where it is immobilizing and prevents one from consciously controlling oneself, then it becomes the type of crisis for which a person seeks treatment" (p. 330).

Crisis situations can be related to suicide attempts, unwanted pregnancy, death of loved one, divorce, hospitalization, job relocation, new family member, loss of job, imprisonment, infidelity, retirement, drug addiction, or financial problems. Regardless of the nature of the crisis, the counselor needs to accept the situation and maintain personal poise and self-assuredness. This type of confidence can help to reduce the anxiety on the part of the client, as the counselor models responsibility for the client at this time. By reassuring the client and expressing hope, the counselor can deal with this immediate situation and then, in the future, aid the client in a developmental sense.

Belkin (1980) has made some suggestions for counselor behavior in crisis intervention counseling:

Do's
1. Remain calm and stable. Prepare yourself psychologically for the turbulence of emotion which is soon to flow from the client.
2. Allow the client full opportunity to speak. Attempt to determine the type of crisis, its precipitating forces and its severity. Interrupt only when it is for the client's benefit, never to relieve yourself of distressing feelings being induced by the client.
3. When indicated, ask object-oriented questions. These should, if asked properly, have a calming effect upon the client. If they fail to have such an effect, the counselor should consider the possibility that he or she is asking ego-oriented questions.
4. Deal with the immediate situation rather than its underlying, unconscious causes that may be left for later. "In the crisis period," Brockopp (1973) points out, "the person is open to change; the sooner we can work with him the more likely we are able to minimize the possible deterioration of the personality and to develop an effective solution which will improve the personality functioning of the individual."

| | | | Possible Counselor |
Type	*Time Lines*	*Possible Concerns*	*Activities*

Crisis	Immediate	Suicidal
		Drug anxiety
		Rejection by lover
			Personal support
			Direct
			  intervention
			Gather additional
			  support
			Individual
			  counseling or
			  refer to
			  appropriate
			  clinic or agency

Facilitative	Varies
	(short to long
	  term)
		Job placement
		Academic
		  problems
		Marriage
		  adjustment
			Individual
			  counseling
			  including:
			reflection of
			  content and
			  feelings
			informing
			interpreting
			confronting
			directing activities

Preventive	Specific time span
	(depending on the
	  program)
		Sex education
		Self and career
		  awareness
		Drug awareness
			Information giving
			Referral to
			  relevant
			  programs
			Individual
			  counseling
			  regarding
			  program content
			  and process

Developmental	Continuous (over
	  life span)
		Developing
		  positive self-
		  concept in the
		  elementary
		  school
		Mid-career change
		Acceptance of
		  death and dying
			Aiding values
			  clarification
			Reviewing
			  decision making
			Individual
			  counseling
			  regarding
			  personal
			  development in
			  conjunction with
			  significant others
			  and environ-
			  mental
			  placement

Table 1.1
General Types
of Counseling
Situations

5. Have readily available local resources to assist the counselor: community, medical, legal, etc.

Don'ts

1. Don't try to "cheer up" the client, to tell him that his or her problems are not as bad as they seem, to reassure him or her unless he or she specifically requests these types of interventions (which is, by the way, the exception rather than the rule).
2. Don't ask the suicidal client to abandon his or her plans. Always make such a request a temporary delay.
3. Don't attempt to solve the total personality adjustment difficulty. Some counselors make the error of minimizing the crisis itself and attempting to get the client to speak about the more "fundamental" things (p. 345).

Facilitative Counseling

In our viewpoint, facilitative counseling is the process of helping the client to clarify a concern; then, through self-understanding and acceptance, to devise a plan of action to work on the concern; and finally to act on it in a self-responsible manner. This type of counseling is often labeled "remedial" or "adjustive," as if one were correcting a fault or an undesirable behavior. Remedial counseling is often thought of as aiding an individual to progress from a deficient stage to a functional one. Facilitative counseling can do this and more. We prefer to consider this approach in a positive light, as persons at all stages of their development may gain from continued growth through facilitative counseling.

The basic procedure is the generally accepted format for what most people consider counseling today. When we speak of the one-to-one helping relationship in facilitative counseling, we agree with Carkhuff (1983) that the counselor aids the client through the cyclical process of exploration, understanding, and action. Regardless of the type of approach, on the continuum from nondirective to rational-emotive therapy, the counseling goal is client action on the clarified concern.

Concerns in facilitative counseling include choosing academic options; planning a career; getting along with family members, fellow workers, or classmates; and identifying individual strengths, interests, and aptitudes. Regardless of the concern or the counseling approach employed, professionally trained and competent counselors can help individuals to gain self-understanding and change their behavior through the general framework of facilitative counseling.

Throughout this book, we shall be reviewing counseling, primarily as it can be practiced in this facilitative manner.

Preventive Counseling

Preventive counseling differs from the other three types of counseling mentioned here in that it is primarily programmatic; it is, in addition, usually related to a specific concern. Such counseling could involve, for example, an elementary school sex education program having the purpose of alleviating future anxieties about sexuality and sexual relationships. Pietrofesa (1976) and Kelly (1976) support the efforts of counselors working with youth to help them understand themselves in relation to sexual concerns so that they are better prepared to handle them in the future.

Another programmatic approach, as outlined by Carkhuff and Friel (1974), focuses on self-awareness as it relates to future career choices and career preparation. Drug awareness, retirement options, and communication skills are other areas that can be approached systematically by counselors.

In preventive counseling, the counselor may present information to a group or refer individuals to relevant programs. The counselor may also continue to work individually with clients—either on a group or a one-to-one basis. Thus, in the area of preventive counseling, we often find the counselor's work with individual clients being complemented by clients' involvement in other relevant programs.

Developmental Counseling

Developmental counseling is an ongoing process that occurs throughout an individual's entire life span. This type of counseling focuses on helping clients to achieve positive personal growth at any stage of their lives. Havighurst (1980) indicates that developmental counseling helps the individual learn how to achieve healthy growth in our society. We believe that counselors can aid individuals at all age levels and wholeheartedly support the concept of child counseling, which is essential in the developmental process.

Dinkmeyer and Caldwell (1970) describe developmental counseling in the elementary school as follows:

Developmental counseling, which can be contrasted with adjustment or crisis counseling, is not always problem-oriented in terms of assuming that the child has some difficult problem. Instead, the goals are the development of self-understanding, awareness of one's potentialities, and methods of utilizing one's capacity. Developmental counseling truly focuses on helping the individual know, understand, and accept himself. This type of counseling, then, becomes personalized learning, not individualized teaching. The child learns not only to understand himself but to become ultimately responsible for his choices and actions. (p. 84)

Erikson (1968), Havighurst (1953), Kohlberg (1969), and Piaget (1952) have all discussed stages of individual development. Sprinthall (1971) makes the following point, as it relates to personal growth and development:

Identity has early roots in initial experience and is gradually reformed in successive episodes. Whether the personal identity so formed is positive, proactive, and competent will be determined by the degree of success at each of these developmental sequences. (p. 15)

Counselors can help individuals to have these necessary success experiences.

A client can attain self-understanding, improved decision-making skills, and positive behavior change through developmental counseling. Pietrofesa and Splete (1975) point out that individual counseling is an integral part of one's career development and formation of decision-making abilities. Sinick (1976) indicates that counseling, as it occurs throughout the life span and includes working with young and old alike, is truly developmental.

More recognition is being given to older adults in our country as they continue to grow in numbers and to contribute significantly to our society. The process of counseling these persons in an ongoing developmental mode is receiving a great deal of attention.

The application of counseling skills as they relate to the development of adults is described by Schlossberg, Troll, and Leibowitz (1978). According to Van Hoose and Worth (1982), counselors with an understanding of life's phases can effectively aid persons as they progress through various stages and transitions in adult life.

Concerns that are ongoing include developing and maintaining a positive self-concept, finding an appropriate lifestyle as it relates to use of working and leisure time, learning and using decision-making skills, clarifying one's current values and interests, understanding and accepting changes, and developing an understanding of the life process from birth to death.

Brammer (1973) provides an illustration of developmental counseling as it relates to grieving and the acceptance of death:

The normal course of grief work consists of: (1) accepting the grief work process; (2) expressing the feelings of grief; (3) dealing with the memory of the deceased; (4) readjusting to the new environment without the deceased; (5) building new relationships. An important element in the helping process is to enable the bereaved to accept and work through this grief process. (p. 119)

Individual counseling to aid a person who is dealing with grief over personal loss can be considered crisis counseling in the sense that the grief may be overpowering at first, but it fits into the developmental framework as the client learns to cope and adjust. Persons at all ages can benefit from working through such "crisis" concerns with the aid of competent counselors.

In developmental counseling, as in the other types of counseling, a counselor can effectively help people through individualized counseling. In developmental counseling, the counselor may be working closely with significant others in conjunction with the one-to-one counseling relationship (for example, in helping a client with a mid-life change).

A professional who has been conducting ongoing developmental counseling is better prepared to work with concerns that arise in preventive, facilitative, and crisis counseling situations. One would hope that, in the future, professionals will be able to expend as much time and effort in developmental and preventive counseling as they now do in the crisis and facilitative areas.

Influences on the Development of Counseling

Counseling in the United States has been shaped by five major historical forces: (1) social reform, (2) vocational guidance, (3) individual assessment, (4) psychological practices, and (5) societal changes. The following is a brief sketch of these influences. For a more detailed review, the reader is referred to Aubrey's 1977 article in the *Personnel and Guidance Journal.*

Social Reform Movement

The closing decade of the nineteenth century found many Americans, particularly in industrialized urban areas, victims of poverty, unemployment, and injustice. Muckrakers, such as Ida Tarbell and Jacob Riis, helped focus the public's concern on needed social reforms. As a result of this concern for human needs, charities were organized, settlement houses were established, and general education was improved.

Clifford Beers, a social activist, directed public attention to the plight of the mentally ill. His book, *A Mind That Found Itself,* describing his experiences and observations in mental hospitals, was an influential best seller. In addition to fostering needed changes in mental health institutions, this focus on the mentally ill provided support for new psychological practices, such as Freud's psychoanalytic approach and Adlerian therapy.

Vocational Guidance Movement

The concept of social reform was further evidenced in the vocational guidance movement. Borow (1964) spoke of Jesse B. Davis, a Detroit educator and counselor, in this fashion: "One of the first American practitioners of vocational guidance, Davis was a product not of an emerging applied psychology or of vocational education but of the social reform movement which dominated his era." He continued, "Almost without exception, the earliest pioneers of vocational guidance were social workers" (p. 49).

Frank Parsons, often called "the father of guidance," established the Vocational Bureau of Boston in 1908 and authored the book *Choosing a Vocation.* Parsons believed that youth could best choose an occupation by analyzing their abilities, reviewing jobs and using that data to match themselves with a job. Largely due to the efforts of Parsons and his supporters, vocational guidance programs and vocational education courses became relatively common public school offerings.

Individual Assessment Movement Another important influence on the counseling movement was the increased use of individual assessment. In addition to the assessment of vocational traits, as initiated by Parsons, mental ability testing became standardized and widely used. Alfred Binet's intelligence test was developed in France and then adapted and used in the United States. The Army Alpha, a verbal mental ability test, and the Army Beta, a nonverbal mental ability test, were devised for testing and screening purposes in World War I. Other quantitative tools were developed to measure interests, aptitudes, and abilities; the use of these assessment instruments provided respectability to the guidance and counseling movement.

The end of the nineteenth century witnessed the implementation of another aspect of individual assessment, the observation and clinical study of individuals. Based on the work done in Wilhelm Wundt's experimental laboratory in Germany, G. Stanley Hall founded a psychology laboratory at Johns Hopkins University and then initiated the child study movement through his work at Clark University. The child study movement stressed the need for factual information about individuals and led to more rigorous methods of observation and data gathering.

Both the development of assessment instruments and the emphasis on the study of individual behavior provided support for the development and practice of various psychological schools of thought.

Psychological Theories and Approaches The formulation of various psychological counseling theories and approaches influenced counselors and the counseling movement. A major influence on counseling practice has been Freud's psychoanalytic approach. In the early 1900s, both functionalism—which attempted to study perception, attention, and emotional responses—and behaviorism—which attempted to study actual behaviors, as opposed to conscious recognition or recall—became well-known psychological theories.

Later, two other major psychological approaches, Gestalt and humanistic, came into being. The Gestaltists believed that here-and-now behaviors and experiences are parts of one's whole being and that individuals are responsible for themselves. Humanistic psychology, as promoted by Carl Rogers, indicated that individuals' subjective perceptions are most important in determining their behavior and that clients ought to be treated with the utmost dignity and respect.

Individual counselors tended to identify with one of these approaches or theories and to follow its precepts as they worked with their clients. Part II of this book will examine various counseling theories in detail.

Societal Changes Societal changes have influenced the counseling movement. Economic conditions, war and its aftermath, scientific and technological advances, changing family and marriage patterns, and population shifts and decline are some of these societal influences.

During periods of large-scale unemployment, vocational counseling has been provided by many agencies, including the U.S. Employment Service.

With companies and businesses cutting back or closing down in recessionary times, counselors have been called on to provide "out-placement counseling," which aids workers in finding other jobs or in preparing for early retirement.

The need for screening and placement of both military and civilian personnel has been met by counselors during periods of war. After the conclusion of wars, counselors, such as those in the Veterans Administration, have helped returning service persons readjust as they dealt with vocational, educational, and mental health concerns.

Scientific and technological advances have affected our society and its counselors. After the Russians launched "Sputnik" in 1957, the federal government placed more emphasis on education and funded counseling programs at the secondary and elementary school levels through the National Defense Education Acts. Naisbett (1982) points out that our current society is becoming increasingly technological. With this "high tech," there is a corresponding need for "high touch," which counselors can and do provide through increased recognition of and response to human needs.

With the decreasing school populations, there seems to be a diminution of support for school counseling programs and positions. On the other hand, with the increase of family, marital, and personal problems in our society, more emphasis seems to be placed on the provision of mental health counseling services in public and private clinics. This trend is illustrated in the 1983 name change of the American Personnel and Guidance Association to the American Association for Counseling and Development.

Many factors have combined to foster an accepting environment for the counseling movement. These factors seem to be interrelated and, regardless of their independent emphasis, focus on helping individuals to attain better and more fulfilling lives.

A key concept of the counseling profession is the belief in the dignity and worth of each human being. Particularly in the United States, we have seen an increasing desire on the part of individuals to control their own destiny. Counselors support this "rise of the individual" and are helping their clients as they work toward establishing self-respect and finding self-fulfillment.

The need for counseling is evident. Therefore, it is crucial that current and future counselors develop and upgrade their personal and professional skills in order to effectively aid their clients. This book will provide a thorough overview of the counseling relationship and process as they apply to counselors working with individuals in a professional and competent manner.

Summary

We have defined *counseling* and discussed its various dimensions. Although this book deals primarily with the counselor's work in a one-to-one facilitative counseling situation, we also described three other types of counseling situations—crisis, preventive and developmental. Examples of significant influences on the development of counseling were provided.

The major points of this chapter were as follows:

1. Counseling is a relationship between a professionally trained, competent counselor and an individual seeking help with a personal concern.
2. There are seven characteristics of counseling. It is
   a. a professional service offered by a competent counselor.
   b. a process in which the counselor-client relationship is basic.
   c. concerned with decision-making skills and problem resolution.
   d. a process that involves the client in learning new behaviors or formulating new attitudes.
   e. a mutual enterprise on the part of the counselor and counselee.
   f. difficult to specifically define.
   g. a way of life.
3. There are more commonalities than differences between counseling and psychotherapy.
4. Helping professionals have become an integral part of the American way of life and provide crisis, facilitative, preventive, and developmental counseling.
5. Formalized counseling has been developing only over the past one hundred years and has been influenced by social reforms, vocational guidance, individual assessment, psychological practices, and societal change.
6. There is an obvious need for counseling services in our country today. Counselors are meeting this need based on their belief in the dignity and worth of each human being.

References

Aubrey, Roger. "Historical Development of Guidance and Counseling and Implications for The Future," *Personnel and Guidance Journal* 55 (1977):288–295.

Belkin, Gary. *An Introduction to Counseling.* Dubuque, Iowa: Wm. C. Brown, 1980.

Borow, Henry, ed. *Man in a World at Work.* Boston: Houghton Mifflin, 1964.

Boy, Angelo, and Gerald Pine. *Client-Centered Counseling: A Renewal.* Boston: Allyn and Bacon, 1982.

Boyd, John. *Counselor Supervision: Approaches, Preparation, Practices.* Muncie, Ind.: Accelerated Development Inc., 1978.

Brammer, Lawrence M. *The Helping Relationship, Process and Skills.* Englewood Cliffs, N.J.: Prentice-Hall, 1973.

———, and Everett Shostrom. *Therapeutic Psychology—Fundamentals of Counseling and Psychotherapy.* Englewood Cliffs, N.J.: Prentice-Hall, 1982.

Brockopp, G. W. "Crisis Intervention: Theory, Process, and Practice." In D. Lester and G. W. Brockopp, eds., *Crisis Intervention and Counseling By Telephone.* Springfield, Ill.: Charles C Thomas, 1973.

Carkhuff, Robert. *The Art of Helping.* (5th ed.) Amherst, Mass.: Human Resource Development Press, 1983.

———, and William Anthony. *The Skills of Helping.* Amherst, Mass.: Human Resource Development Press, 1979.

———, and Theodore Friel. *The Art of Developing a Career.* Amherst, Mass.: Human Resource Development Press, 1974.

Cormier, William, and L. Sherilyn Cormier. *Interviewing Strategies for Helpers.* Monterey, Calif.: Brooks/Cole, 1979.

Crow, Lester D. *Principles of Guidance.* Dublin, Ind.: Printit Press, 1982.

Dinkmeyer, Donald, and Edson Caldwell. *Developmental Counseling and Guidance—A Compre-*

hensive School Approach. New York: McGraw-Hill, 1970.

Erikson, Erik. *Identity, Youth and Crisis.* New York: W. W. Norton, 1968.

Havighurst, Robert. "Life-Span Developmental Psychology and Education." *Educational Researcher,* November 1980, pp. 3–8.

————. *Human Development and Education.* New York: David McKay, 1953.

Ivey, Allen, and Lynn Simek-Downing. *Counseling and Psychotherapy: Skills, Theories, and Practice.* Englewood Cliffs, N.J.: Prentice-Hall, 1980.

Kelly, Gary. *Learning About Sex, the Contemporary Guide for Young Adults.* Woodbury, N.Y.: Barrons Educational Series, 1976.

Kohlberg, Lawrence. *Stages in the Development of Moral Thought and Action.* New York: Holt, Rinehart and Winston, 1969.

Krumboltz, John, and Carl Thoresen. *Counseling Methods.* New York: Holt, Rinehart and Winston, 1976.

Naisbett, John. *Megatrends: Ten New Directions Transforming Our Lives.* New York: Warner Books, 1982.

Piaget, Jean. *The Origins of Intelligence in Children.* New York: International Universities Press, 1952.

Pietrofesa, John J. "The School Counselor in Sex Education." *Personnel and Guidance Journal* 54 (1976):358–361.

————, **G. E. Leonard, and William H. Van Hoose.** *The Authentic Counselor.* Chicago: Rand McNally, 1978.

————, **and Howard Splete.** *Career Development: Theory and Research.* New York: Grune & Stratton, 1975.

Rogers, Carl R. "Client-Centered Psychotherapy." *Scientific American* 187 (1952):66–74.

Sinick, Daniel. "Guest Editor's Introduction —Counseling over the Life Span." *Personnel and Guidance Journal* 55 (1976):100–101.

Schlossberg, Nancy, Lillian Troll, and Zandy Leibowitz. *Perspectives on Counseling Adults: Issues and Skills.* Monterey, Calif.: Brooks/Cole, 1978.

Sprinthall, Norman A. *Guidance for Human Growth.* New York: Van Nostrand Reinhold, 1971.

Stefflre, Buford. "Counseling in the Total Society: A Primer." In W. Van Hoose and J. Pietrofesa, eds., *Counseling and Guidance in the Twentieth Century.* Boston: Houghton Mifflin, 1970. Pp. 251–265.

Van Hoose, William, and Maureen Worth. *Counseling Adults, A Developmental Approach.* Monterey, Calif.: Brooks/Cole, 1982.

CHAPTER 2

The Counselor

Chapter Organizer

Aim of the Chapter

This chapter will provide an overview of counseling, paying particular attention to the characteristics of the counselor and their influence on counseling dynamics.

Chapter Preview

1. Helping skills are important, but equally important is the counselor as a person.
   a. There is a substantial research base to suggest that the personality characteristics of good helpers distinguish them from nonhelpers.
   b. A counselor's personality should display high nurturance and affiliation needs.
   c. Client-counselor cognitive congruence does affect counseling success.
2. Counselor expertise influences the counseling process.
   a. The client may place some worth on degrees and diplomas, particularly during the early stages of counseling.
   b. Presession information emphasizing the counselor's skills, similarity to the client, and eagerness tend to result in higher client estimates of counselor expertise.
   c. A positive relationship exists between perceived counselor attractiveness and client assessment of improvement.
   d. Counselor race and gender will not compensate for a nonhelping orientation.
3. Client and counselor values affect the process of counseling.
   a. Values help to mold the decision-making process of the client.
   b. The focus in counseling often involves value contradictions.
   c. Values frequently affect actions and behaviors of clients.

Relevant Questions

The following are several questions to keep in mind while reading this chapter:
1. How does the counselor's philosophy of helping affect the counseling process?
2. What personal qualities of the counselor are essential in the helping relationship?
3. To what degree is counseling education? How is the counselor like a teacher?
4. What role do the counselor's values play during counseling? Do counselor values allow for the refusal to see a particular client? If so, under what circumstances?

Introduction

There has been much confusion about counseling. Much of the confusion relates to the fact that counseling has just begun to flower as a discipline. We are only starting to recognize that counseling is both an art and a science—even though some writers emphasize one aspect and ignore the other. In this chapter we move from a discussion of helping to a clarification of the impact of counselor characteristics on counseling. Within this framework we will specifically address counselor personality, intelligence, expertise, attractiveness, gender, and race. We will also examine the place of values—particularly those of the counselor—in the counseling enterprise. Later in the book we will emphasize the importance of skill development, but in this chapter we attempt to make a more fundamental point—that no amount of skill can conceal a nonfacilitative personality.

Counseling: An Art and a Science

Counseling is both an art and a science. It is a science in the sense that we now know many things about the differences between effective counseling and ineffective counseling. Research has pointed to very specific attributes of good and poor counselors. There are specific types of behavior that can be used by counselors to foster growth in the client. On the other hand, counseling is also an art: There are certain unaccountable and immeasurable dimensions to counseling. Furthermore, counselors add certain "artistic" variations, which are the products of personal flair. The artist in counselors is also expressed in the personalized application of techniques and methods. Each counselor applies in a unique manner what is known about counseling. If applications were made in a mechanistic and detached fashion, counselors would find little success. Much of this crucial dimension is not "science" and does not lend itself to simple measurement or training in an academic setting. Counseling must bring together both the scientific and the artistic. People cannot engage in counseling without being aware of research, but they must also apply the research in a natural fashion according to a basic humanistic orientation. The following is a statement made by a client to a beginning counselor, who was following a skills-training approach in a rather mechanistic fashion. Yet, the unspoken elements of caring and interest still came through.

In most instances I knew you were going to say "You feel such and such." At first I was annoyed. I wanted much more than just feelings. I wanted you to tell me what to do, or yell at me, or tell me what I had done wasn't so bad. But you knew I didn't really need those things. After a while I started to appreciate the fact that you were really listening to me and *caring for me.* That made up for your limited responses. In later sessions, you did do other kinds of things, but it always was what occurred on a deeper basis which mattered.

Qualities of an Effective Counselor

The Counselor as Helper Helping is a unique process in which a helper facilitates growth in the helpee. Brammer (1977) states that helping "means assisting other persons to reach goals that are important to them. In the context of the specialist helper, it means facilitating personal growth in the direction chosen by the person being helped, as well as toward the helper's own model of an effective person" (p. 303). It is designed to foster within the helpee greater self-understanding, to increase his or her openness to the world, and to initiate more effective behavior. Helping is a broad concept in that it does not necessarily imply a counseling relationship or even a professional one, but there are some basic differences, at least in degree, between a professional helping relationship and a "friendship" relationship. Egan (1975) states:

> There is an important difference, especially in the helping that is carried out by professionals and paraprofessionals rather than the helping that is woven into the fabric of everyday human relating. Everyday interpersonal relationships are characterized by more mutuality than is the helping or counseling process. Friends help each other, while, in more formalized helping relationships, roles are more clear-cut: one is the helper or counselor and the other is the helpee or client. The helper might find deep satisfaction in his helping, but he is not being helped by the client, nor is he ordinarily establishing a friendship. (p. 11)

While later chapters discuss various theories and substantiating research and specific counseling skills, we believe that the helper, or the counselor in this case, can be far more crucial in successful counseling than the theory or skills. It is not hard to teach someone who reflects positive counselor attributes some basic counseling skills and produce an effective counselor. On the other hand, it is unlikely that one can teach helping skills beyond the most superficial to a person who is basically a nonhelper. Through practice, the latter may well be able to mimic the basic skills, but in a crisis situation where facades crumble, the nonhelper will resort to various ineffective methods that reflect negative attitudes toward self and others. Belkin (1981) implies this when he says that counselor understanding is "through the heart," rather than through the intellect (p. 177). Basically, the counselor's inner being will speak far more loudly than words uttered or skills imitated.

It is important that helpers utilize themselves and the strength of their humanness in their work. Combs et al. (1969) and Combs et al. (1971) write at length of the self-as-instrument concept. They note: "Effective helping relationships will be a function of the effective use of the helper's self in bringing about fulfillment of his own and society's purposes" (Combs et al., 1969). The helper uses his or her own feelings, thoughts, or actions to help the client change.

Combs and his associates deemphasize counseling "methods" and stress instead the importance of the helper's perceptions of world, self, and others as crucial to effective helping. Theoretical orientation, also, is less important than the personal characteristics of helpers; methodology and/or theory will not compensate for nonhelping attitudes and beliefs. These researchers note that a characteristic of helping professions is the inevitable necessity of an "instantaneous response," which cannot be programmed. In such instances, self becomes more important than technique. While some interpret Combs to say that basic counseling skills per se are unimportant, we feel that this is not the essential implication of the self-as-instrument approach. For example, the quality of being "enough" would certainly motivate the good helper to be as skilled as possible.

Personality Characteristics

The writings and research of the Combs group suggest that certain personal characteristics distinguish helpers from nonhelpers. Such characteristics include beliefs about the helpee, the self, and the basic purposes to be achieved through helping. (See Table 2.1.) Patterson and Eisenberg (1983) indicate that effective helpers are

1. skillful at reaching out.
2. able to inspire feelings of trust, credibility, and confidence in people they help.
3. able to reach in as well as to reach out.
4. willing to communicate caring and respect for the persons they are trying to help.
5. respectful of themselves and do not use the people they are trying to help to satisfy their own needs.
6. knowledgeable about some area that will be of special value to the person being helped.
7. able to understand the behavior of the people they try to help without imposing value judgments.
8. able to reason systematically and to think in terms of systems.
9. contemporary and have a world view of human events.
10. able to identify behavior patterns that are self-defeating and help others change their self-defeating behaviors to more personally rewarding behavior patterns.
11. skillful at helping others look at themselves and respond nondefensively to the question, "Who am I?" (pp. 13–17).

To some degree personality determines the counseling theory selected and techniques employed. The therapeutic relationship underlies growth-producing counseling. Perhaps the most quoted of all research that

Table 2.1
Personal Characteristics that Distinguish Helpers from Nonhelpers

A. Good counselors will be more likely to perceive:

1. From an internal rather than from an external frame of reference. The frame of reference can be described as internal rather than external. Helpers are sensitive to and concerned with how things look to others with whom they interact, and they use this as a basis for adjusting their own behavior. They are concerned with perceptions of others as well as with their overt behavior.

2. In terms of people rather than things. Central to the thinking of counselors is a concern with people and their reactions rather than with things and events.

B. Good counselors will perceive others as:

1. Able, rather than unable. Helpers perceive others as having the capacities to deal with their problems. They have faith that others can find adequate solutions as opposed to doubting the capacity of people to handle themselves and their lives.

2. Dependable rather than undependable. Helpers regard others as being essentially dependable rather than undependable. They show confidence in the stability and reliability of others and do not need to be suspicious of them.

3. Friendly rather than unfriendly. Helpers see others as being friendly and enhancing. They do not regard them as threatening but, instead, see them as essentially well-intentioned rather than evil-intentioned.

4. Worthy rather than unworthy. Counselors tend to see other people as being of worth rather than unworthy. They see them as possessing a dignity and integrity that must be respected and maintained rather than as unimportant people, whose integrity may be violated.

5. Helpful rather than hindering. Helpers view people as potentially fulfilling and enhancing rather than impeding or threatening. People are not seen as important sources of frustration and suspicion.

6. Internally rather than externally motivated. Helpers see people as internally motivated rather than conceiving behavior as a product of external events. People are seen as creative and dynamic, rather than passive.

C. Good counselors will perceive themselves as:

1. Identified with people rather than apart from people. Counselors tend to see themselves as a part of all mankind. They see themselves as identified with people rather than as withdrawn, removed, apart, or alienated from others.

2. Enough rather than inadequate. Counselors generally see themselves as enough; as having what is needed to deal with their own problems. They do not see themselves lacking or unable to cope with problems.

3. Worthy rather than unworthy. Helpers see themselves as having dignity, consequence, integrity, and respect.

4. Trustworthy rather than untrustworthy. Helpers trust their own organization and see themselves as essentially dependable and having the potential to deal with events.

D. Good counselors will perceive their purposes as:

1. Freeing rather than controlling. Helpers' purposes are essentially freeing and facilitating rather than controlling, dominating, coercing, or manipulating.

2. Altruistic rather than narcissistic. Helpers appear to be motivated by feelings of altruism rather than narcissism. They are concerned about others, not merely about self.

3. Concerned with larger rather than smaller meanings. Counselors tend to view events in broad rather than narrow perspective. They are concerned with larger connotations of events, with larger, more extensive implications than the immediate and specific. They are not exclusively concerned with details but can perceive beyond the immediate to future and larger meanings.

Table 2.1 (cont.)

4. Self-revealing rather than self-concealing. Counselors are self-revealing rather than self-concealing; that is, they are willing to disclose themselves. They see their feelings and shortcomings as important and significant rather than hiding them or covering them up. They are willing to be themselves.

5. Involved rather than alienated. Helpers are personally involved with the people they work with. They have made a commitment to the helping process and are willing to enter into an interaction.

6. Process-oriented rather than goal-oriented. Helpers see their role as one of encouraging and facilitating the process of search and discovery as opposed to promoting or working toward a personal goal or preconceived notion.

Source: Adapted from Combs et al. *Helping Relationships*. Boston: Allyn and Bacon, 1971, pp. 10–17.

substantiates this notion is the Fiedler (1950) study. Comparing the quality of the therapeutic relationship among psychoanalytic, nondirective, and Adlerian therapists, he reports that the relationship established by the "experts" of each school resembles the relationship created by the "experts" of other schools more than it resembles the relationship created by the "nonexperts" in the same school. Theoretical orientation had less to do with the quality of the relationship than did the "expertness" of the practitioners. Seeman (1948) and McGowan (1954) supported the notion that counselors develop their own styles, which may not be related to theoretical beliefs. Effective counselors may well discard so-called prescriptive and mechanistic performance standards and come to rely on themselves more as they gain in experience.

It should not be assumed that simply because a person wants to be a counselor that he or she possesses helping characteristics. There are many other reasons for entering into the profession, including advancement, recognition, and sometimes a need for self-therapy.

In addition to the Florida studies (Combs et al., 1971) of the helping professions, Jackson and Thompson's (1971) study tends to substantiate the preceding suppositions. They found that the most effective counselors are more positive in their attitudes toward self, clients, and counseling than the least effective counselors. Furthermore, female counselors tend to be more positive than their male counterparts. Effective counselors (and all female counselors) view "the self as more identified than unidentified, enough rather than not enough, and revealing rather than unrevealing. The most effective counselors were more positive in viewing most people and most clients as friendly, able, and worthy while viewing counseling as freeing, altruistic, and important" (p. 252). They stress the fact that "whether or not counselors view and act toward most people and most clients as being friendly or unfriendly, able or unable, worthy or unworthy is related to a counselor's effectiveness" (p. 252). Mezzano (1969) stresses that persons low in dogmatism are the most effective counselors. Other studies have shown that counselors have higher needs for intraception (the need to look at the motives of others), nurturance, and affiliation than do comparative groups, such as administrators (Kemp, 1962; Polmantier, 1966). Pietrofesa and Van Hoose (1969) found that counselors emphasized understanding of others and acceptance of people, whereas administrators stressed evaluative or value-setting dimensions.

Additional studies have attempted to identify personality characteristics of counselors, although not all researchers have looked at both characteristics and effectiveness. Cottle and Lewis (1954) found that male college counselors ranked significantly high on the Guilford-Zimmerman Scales of restraints, sociability, emotional stability, objectivity, friendliness, personal relations, and masculinity. Counselors who create successful communicative counseling relationships are more tolerant of ambiguous material in the counseling interview than are less successful counselors (Brams, 1961). Tuma and Gustad (1957) found that counselors were above average on dominance, sociability, and social presence and that the closer the counselor and client on these variables, the better the client's learning. Counselor trainees most frequently chosen by their peers as most effective had a higher degree of confidence, were normal on the MMPI (Minnesota Multiphase Personality Inventory), and displayed a higher degree of interest in social service and in persuasive, literary, and scientific activities than those not chosen (Arbuckle, 1956). Finally, counselors most competent in the counseling practicum were less prone to manipulate, were more kindly, sympathetic, and demonstrative of love than less competent counselors (Coutts, 1962).

Counselor Intellectual Ability and Cognitive Congruence

A question often raised is, "How important is intellectual ability in contributing to counselor effectiveness?" The relationship between the two factors has not been clearly established. Studies have reported conflicting results. For example, McGreevy (1967) found no relationship between counselor effectiveness and intellectual ability, while Dole (1964) noted that the two variables were related. The inconsistency in findings may be a result of two difficulties found in such research. First, intellectual ability is a controlled variable—the subject population is certainly not random. Second, the criteria of effectiveness has not been equitable from study to study. Measures used in such studies have ranged from supervisor to peer ratings.

One recent study by Felker (1973) indicated that counselor effectiveness in communication was significantly correlated with two measures of intellectual ability (i.e., undergraduate grade-point average [GPA] and MAT scores).

The counselor's intellectual ability as compared with the client's intellectual ability—that is, the cognitive congruence between counselor and client—is also important. Cognitive performance is obviously affected by the counseling relationship. As early as 1959, Luria noted a movement in the successful client's semantic framework toward that of the therapist's semantic framework. Going one step further, Axelrod (1952) obtained a positive relationship between counselor-client similarity in ideation and progress in therapy. Edwards and Edgerly (1970) assessed counseling outcome when clients and counselors were matched on semantic criteria. They found that counselor-client congruence did produce significant change in the cognitive area but little or no change on measures of noncognitive adjustment. It would appear that counselor intelligence is at least minimally related to counseling effectiveness and, furthermore, cognitive congruence between counselor and client is related to client change in the cognitive realm.

A related question has to do with the cognitive complexity and cognitive style of the counselor. Lichtenberg and Heck (1979) studied groups of counselors with differing levels of cognitive complexity and found that they structured their counseling sessions differently. They reported that different counselor cognitive styles influence the character of the counseling process. Heck and Davis (1973) reported that more cognitively complex counselors demonstrate significantly higher levels of empathy. Blaas and Heck (1978) noted that counselor cognitive complexity did relate significantly to counselor subrole, verbal mode, and accurate empathy. These three studies suggest that counselor cognitive factors are involved in counseling, but the relationship between the two may only be understood if counselor "intelligence" is not the sole focus of research; such an understanding may require researchers to look at counselor cognitive patterns as well.

The Client's Perceptions of the Counselor

We have discussed the influence of the counselor's personality and intelligence on the counseling process. Now we will examine how the client perceives the counselor and what effects those perceptions have on the ability of the counselor to influence the client.

Counselor Expertise   It appears that simply having the title "counselor" places one in a position of being an expert and, as such, becomes an influence variable. On the other hand, greater degrees of expertness can play a role in determining how favorably a client views a counselor. Expertness may be a far more important dimension in "influence" counseling approaches or counseling that emphasizes providing direction or answers, diagnosis or advice-giving. The greater the expertise attributed to the counselor by the client, the more likely the counselor's opinion will be sought by the client (Senour, 1982). In view of his or her status as an expert, the counselor will have to avoid pronouncements, meaning "an unqualified statement or declaration of expertise" (Mawson, 1978, p. 71). Expertness is not reflected through glib generalities. Note that expertness does not diminish the importance of counselor "attractiveness," for "expertness" in and of itself will not maintain a continuing contact. On the other hand, counselor expertise may influence the client toward goal attainment.

Social-influence theorists stress the importance of counselor expertise on the client's acceptance of communication from the counselor. Client behavior change is viewed as a function of the strength of therapist social power, which impels compliance and changes forces resisting compliance within the client. One of the counselor's potential social power bases is client perception of the counselor as an expert. If this is the case, then the counselor's attire, certificates, or diplomas or perceived expertise may influence client perceptions.

Opinion-change research tends to suggest that an "expert's" communication is more likely to change opinion than a "nonexpert's" opinion (Aronson et al., 1963; Bergin, 1962). Browning (1966) related the effects of therapist expertness to client acceptance of interpretation and found that a significantly greater number of large-discrepancy interpretations were accepted by counselees in high-prestige conditions than in low-prestige ones. Strong (1968) discussed how diplomas, certifications, certificates of membership, and shelves filled with books attest to expertise. Research by Siegel (1980) and by Heppner and Pew (1977) also supported the idea that diplomas and awards significantly influence initial perception of counselor expertness. Strong (1968) continues:

Less obvious, but perhaps more important, are the evidences of expertise in the counselor's behavior. Most counselors pay considerable attention to structuring the interview. They point out the roles and requirements of the client and the counselor in the interview, the sequences of the process, and events likely to occur as they work toward problem solution. Such structuring, whether explicit or implicit, gives evidence of the counselor's expertness. Since the client must perceive that the counselor knows what he is doing, explicit structuring may be more effective than implicit structuring. (p. 221)

Strong and Schmidt (1970) studied the effects of perceived counselor expertness on counselor influence. The expert-inexpert roles were defined in light of attending and structuring variables. The results of the study supported the idea that perceived expertness exerts some control over counseling influence. Students experiencing expert conditions changed self-ratings more between first and third assessments than did students experiencing nonexpert conditions. Subjects of "expert" interviewers recall more of the problem-solving process (Merluzzi et al., 1977); in addition, perceived interviewer expertness influences subjects to engage in certain limited self-help activities (Heppner and Dixon, 1978). Claiborn and Schmidt (1977) found that presession information emphasizing the counselor's knowledge, skills, and reputation as a successful counselor resulted in significantly higher scores of perceived expertness than did presession information emphasizing the counselor's similarity to the client and the counselor's eagerness to help. Perceived attractiveness in this study made little difference. In another study (Tinsley et al., 1980), factor analysis of client expectations revealed that expertise has an important bearing on the interpersonal influence process. The writers suggest that "it is important to keep in mind that clients expressing strong expectancies of counselor expertise may believe that all he or she needs to do is answer the counselor's questions and he or she will be helped in a couple of sessions and never need help again" (p. 568). Such expectancies then may well impede the progress and flow of counseling.

Atkinson and Carskaddon (1975) obtained ratings of a counselor's video-taped performances, which were differentiated by level of professional jargon and degree of a prestigious introduction. The counselor's knowledge of counseling was rated higher when the language employed was "abstract" rather than "concrete" (lay terminology). Subjects preferred to see someone for counseling if they were given a high-prestige introduction rather than a low-prestige one. This was not true, however, for all populations. Drug-abuse inmates preferred the low-prestige counselor on knowledge of psychology and comprehension of problem. This may well reflect a distrust of people with credentials who also have had dissimilar experiences.

A study by Price and Iverson (1969) examined the effect of counselor status and certain verbal behaviors on client reaction in an initial interview. They found that relatively positive impressions developed toward helpers who conformed to the counseling-role specification. These impressions were enhanced in reactions to a head counselor, with high ascribed status. Price and Iverson concluded, "These relationships indicated that helpers in general and counselors in particular, are no less bound than other personages by the principle that in order to be favorably received by others upon initial contact, one must be role compliant. And it helps to have high status" (p. 473). High commitment was important. A lack of commitment led to a downgrading in the impression of others.

Counselor verbal and nonverbal behaviors do make a difference. Profane language, for example, detracts from perceptions of all counselor attributes, including competency (Paradise et al., 1980; Heubusch and Horan, 1977). Dell (1973) found that structured questioning contributed to perceptions that the counselor was an expert. Claiborn (1979) further noted that the use of interpretation was perceived as more expert than restatement, while responsive nonverbal behavior was seen as more expert than unresponsive nonverbal behavior. Attractiveness was more clearly related to nonverbal than to verbal behavior, while expertness and trustworthiness were related to both.

Merluzzi et al. (1978) studied perceptions of counselor expertise and their relationship to disclosure level. They found that counselors introduced as experts were rated higher than counselors introduced as nonexperts. Low self-disclosing counselors were rated higher in expertise than high disclosers. This was interpreted as fitting traditional stereotypes of psychologists as aloof and distant. On the other hand, high-disclosing experts were highest in attractiveness. Sex differences deserved attention. Merluzzi et al. state, "It is possible that being a woman makes it more important to have the traditional trappings," that is, credentials and office that reflect counselor expertness. Women who were seen as less expert were viewed as far less competent than their nonexpert male counterparts.

Schmidt and Strong (1970) obtained ratings of counselor expertness that were inversely related to counselor training and experience. They further attempted to identify behaviors and characteristics of expert and nonexpert counselors. The experts were viewed as relaxed, friendly, attentive, confident, not stuffy, not arrogant, fluent, lively, informed, able to make recommendations and suggest solutions. The nonexperts were seen as awkward, tense, uneasy, nonconfident, dressed too casually, slouching, deadpan, abrupt, and confused. Barak and Dell (1977) reported a significant positive relationship between perceived counselor expertness, attractiveness, and trustworthiness and willingness to refer oneself to the counselor for a variety of counseling problems. Expertness ratings were consistent with actual counselor training and experience.

Studies by Sprafkin (1970) and Guttman and Haase (1972) suggest that the counselor expertness variable is still open to question under certain conditions. Sprafkin found that regardless of the level of counselor expertise, subjects responded to advocated change. This might well indicate that the title "counselor" per se indicates a certain degree of expertness in terms of help that can be provided. Guttman and Haase noted that clients responded more favorably to a counselor who was introduced as a nonexpert, but that informational recall was greater for clients interviewed by the expert counselor. Global ratings of effectiveness did not differ between expert and nonexpert counselors. They speculated that college-age clients felt more at ease with a nonexpert counselor, who was seen as being more like themselves.

Dell (1973) found that expert counselors were described as being experienced and as more knowledgeable than likeable. They, however, were not seen as totally unattractive. Preferred counselors were described as more likeable than knowledgeable, as perceiving things in a similar fashion, and as understanding the person's experiences. At the same time, preferred counselors were not seen as completely inexpert.

Counselor Attractiveness

Physical attractiveness appears to affect counseling relationships and, consequently, perceptions of counselor expertness. Significant positive relationships exist between perceived counselor attractiveness and client assessment of improvement, counselor likeability, perceived counselor competence, and reactions to counselor self-introductions (Cash et al., 1975; McClernan, 1973; Shapiro et al., 1973; 1976). Cash and Salzbach (1978) found that non-self-disclosing, unattractive counselors elicited less desirable behavioral attributions and counseling expectations than did attractive counselors. Carter (1978) reported that attractiveness alone did not have "main effects" on impressions of counselors, but attractiveness and sex of counselor interacted to produce higher competency ratings for female counselors. Lewis and Walsh (1978) studied the effects of female counselor physical attractiveness on the perception of male and female subjects. The attractive counselor was perceived more favorably by the female observers, particularly with regard to competence, professionalism, interest, relaxation, and her ability to help with problems of anxiety, shyness, career choice, sexual functioning, and anxiety, as compared to the unattractive counselor. Vargas and Borkowski (1983) noted that physical attractiveness of the counselor accounted for more than 50 percent of the variance in perceived effectiveness and future expectancy in the client. Zlotlow and Allen (1981), however, remind us that beauty is in the eye of the beholder, thus making physical attractiveness a complex variable. Physical attractiveness may well have the greatest influence during the early, get-acquainted stage of counseling; after that other variables assume proportionately greater roles in making a counselor attractive. Generally, perceptions of counselor characteristics of expertness, trustworthiness, and attractiveness are related to satisfaction of clients (Heppner and Heesacker, 1983, p. 37).

Counselor Gender   How does counselor gender affect client perceptions? One might assume that counselor gender would influence counselor credibility in the client's eyes. Lee et al. (1980) hypothesized that a female counselor would be more credible than a male counselor on two issues—child rearing and sexual molestation. However, the study found no significant differences between the perceived credibility of male and female counselors. In two earlier studies, in a somewhat contradictory vein, Fuller (1964) had found that female clients with personal-social concerns expressed preferences significantly more often for female counselors, whereas Boulware and Holmes (1970) found that university women preferred older male therapists for vocational concerns but preferred older female therapists for personal concerns. Preference for a particular counselor gender in the latter two studies was related to the presenting problem of clients.

Johnson (1978) carried out an analogue study (a content analysis of counseling dialogues) to explore male and female counselors' responses to male and female clients who expressed anger and depression. Female counselors rated themselves as more empathic than did males, while female counselors were rated by judges as angrier than male counselors. This may well reflect the stereotype that females are more nurturant than males; because their anger is unexpected, it is seen as more extreme.

Highlen and Russell (1980) had university women rate counselor descriptions, representing feminine, masculine, and androgynous sex roles, for counselor preference. Counselor ratings were not influenced by counselor gender or subject sex role. Counselor sex role, however, did affect ratings. Androgynous and feminine counselors were rated higher than the masculine counselor. These findings seem not to be consistent with studies that report more effective therapeutic results with opposite-sex counselors. Janda and Rimm (1977) found that female clients in assertiveness training changed more when seen by a male counselor than when seen by a female counselor. Geer and Hurst (1976) reported that male counselors, using desensitization techniques with female clients, achieved significantly better results than did female counselors. Feldstein (1979) obtained a number of interesting results in her study of the effects of counselor gender and sex role, finding that (1) male subjects indicated greater satisfaction and higher counselor regard with "feminine" counselors than with "masculine" counselors, regardless of counselor sex, (2) female subjects indicated greater satisfaction and higher counselor regard with "masculine" counselors than with "feminine" counselors, regardless of counselor sex, and (3) male subjects talked most about themselves with feminine female counselors and least about themselves with masculine female counselors, while female subjects talked most about themselves with feminine male counselors and least about themselves with masculine male counselors. The inconsistencies and contradictions found in research to date suggest that further study is needed. It may well be that counselor gender interacts with other counselor characteristics to make it difficult to isolate the effects of gender alone. Currently, we can conclude that there is little evidence to suggest that a particular gender counselor would be more effective with a particular gender client.

Counselor Race   Several early studies suggested that, when clients judge the effectiveness of counselors, racial considerations may weigh more heavily than counselor skills and qualities. Banks et al. (1967), Gardner (1971), Grantham (1973), and Wolkon et al. (1973) found that black clients preferred black counselors. Harrison's (1975) review of the literature concluded that "all things being equal" black clients would prefer black counselors and disclose more information to them. In an interesting study of the effects of race and counselor climate, Gamboa et al. (1976) found that delinquent girls experienced the strongest attraction to a counselor when counseling was educationally oriented and that white subjects preferred the black counselor over the white counselor when personal/social problems were the concern. In a more recent study, Sladen (1982) studied the effects of race and socioeconomic status on the perception of process variables in counseling. He found that both black and white subjects "gave highest counselor empathy ratings, client-counselor attraction and cognitive similarity ratings, and client improvement ratings to matchings in which the counselor and client were similar over race and social class, and they gave lowest ratings when the counselor and client were dissimilar over and social class" (p. 560). He concluded, "Findings suggested, then, that a client's preference for a counselor of similar race or socioeconomic background rather than one of dissimilar background may not rest solely on actual differences in empathic skills between the counselors but instead may also be based on the client's biased estimate of differences" (p. 564). Finally, Merluzzi and Merluzzi (1978), trying to determine whether racial labels contributed to counselor assessment of clients, found a reverse bias present. Black-labeled client cases were rated significantly more positive than those labeled white or those that had no label. The researchers felt that counselors seemingly overcompensated to avoid negative professional bias. A fair assessment of the research suggests again that "all things being equal" clients may prefer a counselor of a particular race. On the other hand, race of the counselor will not compensate for ineffective counseling. Counselors should also be careful that racial bias not influence their assessment of client concerns or the direction of counseling.

Values in Counseling

Values are another fundamental consideration in the counseling enterprise. First, values are basic components of the "content" of counseling. Second, the values of the counselor enter into the "process" of counseling.

Values can be described as multifactor or behavioral biases, which mold and dominate the decision-making power of a particular individual (Peters, 1962, p. 373). They can be seen as conceptualized and/or operational. Conceptualized values are verbalized and may serve as an ideal toward which the client would like to move. Operational values are observed through the client's behavior. These two types of values may not be consistent with each other. A client may often state one value and then behave in a way that reflects a totally different value. Often, counseling will focus on these contradictions in values, which create conflict for the client.

Belkin (1981) noted the complexity of the value phenomena. He states, "Whenever we attempt to look at a person's values, it is always helpful to consider those values in terms of how they evolved (development), what they encourage or discourage the individual to do (behavior), and how they make the person feel (affect)" (p. 220).

Values affect decisions as well as actions. Egan (1975) emphasizes the importance of the relationship between values and action by stressing that "a value is a value only to the degree that it is translated into some kind of action" (p. 94). Peterson (1970) describes values as hypothetical constructs providing criteria for judgments, giving a sense of what "ought" to be done, and acting as a motivational force in living.

While values of the client are important in counseling, so too are the values of the counselor. The following statements by Boy and Pine (1982) reflect the relationship between client and counselor value systems.

It is the client's searching and processing of values that characterizes the client's involvement in counseling. . . .

Counseling, then, is a relationship in which the counselor provides the client with a communicating atmosphere that gives the client the opportunity to become involved in the discovering, processing, and synthesizing of values. (pp. 80–81)

Counselors must also be aware of their own value orientation in counseling:

The therapist usually conceives of himself and is often represented as the detached dispassionate scientist. A more realistic view would see him as an involved participant with an interest in the outcome, following a sectarian psychotherapeutic doctrine or combination of doctrines, the selection and practice of which are tinctured by his own basic philosophy of life. (Walters, 1958, p. 249)

Values clarification and change are legitimate counseling goals. Counselor intervention in the client's values is an actuality and a necessary part of the counseling process. Egan (1975) states that "The skilled helper both knows what his own 'real' values are and can help others discover, define, and implement theirs" (p. 10).

There is some research available on the impact of counselor values. Rosenthal (1955) suggested that "counselor values are communicated to the client and that the clients who improved most in therapy revised their values in the direction of the counselors' values, while the values of the unimproved clients became less like the therapists." Schrier (1953) found evidence of a positive relationship between improvement and identification, on the part of the client, with the therapist's need system. Farson (1961), investigating the possibility that the personality of the therapist is introjected by the client, reported that if introjection occurs, it is most likely to occur with less competent and less adjusted therapists. Cook (1966) placed clients in high-, medium-, and low-similarity value groups to their counselors. Clients in the medium-similarity group achieved greater therapeutic success than the low- or high-similarity groups. The research suggested that when the values of counselor and client are too similar or too different, therapeutic outcome is affected negatively.

Another factor, however, may be present. Some counselors may approve of their clients' becoming more like themselves and see this change as progress. Initial diagnoses by clinicians may also reflect such bias. Lee (1968) suggested that social-class bias affected psychiatric residents' diagnoses of patients. Fitzgibbons and Shearn (1972) reported that the professional background of therapists influenced their determination of schizophrenia.

The professional background of school counselors certainly may affect the counseling relationship. Shertzer and Stone (1980) stress that subtle values communication may take place unbeknownst to the counselor. The values thus communicated may contradict other school values. The authors state, for example, that "counselors, in one sense, sometimes contribute to this value conflict, for at the same time that the administrator and the teacher talk about the values inherent in knowledge for its own sake counselors display charts comparing the lifetime salaries of those who do and do not go to college" (p. 161). Such subtle conflicts may arise in any number of economic, social, and political areas. Another potential conflict may be seen between democratic values espoused in schools, and counselors who are viewed as part of an authoritarian, institutional structure.

There is no question that counselors' values are on display during counseling, and properly so. At certain times, it is appropriate for them to share their values with the client. At other times it is not. Counselors own their own value systems, do not conceal them, and are consciously aware of their own valuative responses during the counseling process. On the other hand, counselors should not impose their values on the client, as if theirs were right and his or hers, wrong. Counselors who subtly manipulate the client to certain predetermined values, perhaps to justify their own lifestyle, are being most destructive to progress. The marriage counselor who has been divorced many times and holds marriage in low esteem seems to find that "all my clients end up getting divorces." Conversely, the counselor who goes to any lengths to keep a marriage together is behaving just as inappropriately. Such subtle manipulations, conscious or not, should be foreign to the authentic counseling relationship, which is predicated on the counselee's freedom to choose—a freedom to choose differently from what the counselor might choose. Perhaps, Benjamin (1981) best summarizes our position on the place of counselor values.

The more we become aware of what our values are and the less we need to impose them on the interviewee, the more we may help him become aware of his own values and retain, adapt, or reject them as he sees fit. Knowing my own values, I can state them. If I can accept them as a changing part of my changing self, I may be able to accept his as a changing part of his changing self. Some of these values of mine may remain constant for me, and some may for him; but I shall not be afraid to expose mine, nor shall I fear being exposed to his. (p. 98)

Values should be creative, not static, continually emerging and growing.

Summary

Counseling is a relationship between a professionally trained, competent counselor and a person seeking help. Problem-solving and decision-making skills are used to help the client grow in self-understanding and to behave in a more effective manner. This chapter briefly described several counselor attributes.

The major points of this chapter were as follows:

1. Who the counselor really is—"deep down inside"—is a crucial factor in helping. Superficial counseling skills cannot hide a noncaring personality.
2. Counselor intellectual ability affects counselor performance, and just as important, cognitive congruence should exist between counselor and client.
3. Counselors perceived as experts are viewed by clients more favorably on a number of dimensions, including being more knowledgeable and experienced.
4. Counselor race and gender will not compensate for inadequate counselor skills or a nonhelping orientation in the counselor.
5. Counselor values are on display during counseling. It may be appropriate at times for the counselor to share these values, but it is inappropriate at any time to impose them on the client.

References

Arbuckle, D. S. "Client Perception of Counselor Personality." *Journal of Counseling Psychology* 3 (1956):93–96.

Aronson, E., J. Turner, and J. M. Carlsmith. "Communicator Credibility and Communication Discrepancy as Determinants of Opinion Change." *Journal of Abnormal and Social Psychology* 67 (1963): 31–36.

Atkinson, Donald R., and Gaye Carskaddon. "A Prestigious Introduction, Psychological Jargon, and Perceived Counselor Credibility." *Journal of Counseling Psychology* 22 (1975):180–186.

Axelrod, J. A. *Evaluation of the Effect on Progress in Therapy of Similarities and Differences Between the Personalities of Patients and Their Therapists.* Dissertation Abstracts 12 (1952):329.

Banks, G., G. B. Berenson, and R. R. Carkhuff. "The Effects of Counselor Race and Training upon Counseling Process with Negro Clients in Initial Interviews." *Journal of Clinical Psychology* 23 (1967):70–72.

Barak, Azy, and Don M. Dell. "Differential Perceptions of Counselor Behavior: Replication and Extension." *Journal of Counseling Psychology* 24 (1977):288–292.

Belkin, Gary S. *"Practical Counseling in the Schools."* Dubuque, Iowa: Wm. C. Brown, 1981.

Benjamin, Alfred. *The Helping Interview.* Boston: Houghton Mifflin, 1981.

Bergin, A. E. "The Effect of Dissonant Persuasive Communications upon Changes in a Self-Referring Attitude." *Journal of Personality* 30 (1962): 423–438.

Blaas, Charles D., and E. J. Heck. "Selected Process Variables as a Function of Client Type and Cognitive Complexity in Beginning Counselors." *Journal of Counseling Psychology* 25 (1978):257–263.

Boulware, D. W., and D. S. Holmes. "Preferences for Therapists and Related Expectancies." *Journal of Consulting and Clinical Psychology* 35 (1970):269–277.

Boy, Angelo V., and Gerald J. Pine. *Client-Centered Counseling: A Renewal.* Boston: Allyn and Bacon, 1982.

Brammer, Lawrence M. "Who Can Be a Helper?" *Personnel and Guidance Journal* 55 (1977):303–308.

Brams, Jim. "Counselor Characteristics and Effective Communication in Counseling." *Journal of Counseling Psychology* 8 (1961):25–30.

Browning, G. J. "An Analysis of the Effects of Therapist Prestige and Levels of Interpretation of Client Response in the Initial Phase of Psychotherapy." *Dissertation Abstracts* 26 (1966):4803.

Carter, Jean A. "Impressions of Counselors As a Function of Counselor Physical Attractiveness." *Journal of Counseling Psychology* 25 (1978):28–34.

Cash, Thomas F., P. J. Begley, D. A. McGowan, and B. Weise. "When Counselors Are Heard but Not Seen: Initial Impact of Physical Attractiveness. *Journal of Counseling Psychology* 22 (1975): 273–279.

———, **and Ronald F. Salzbach.** "The Beauty of Counseling: Effects of Counselor Physical Attractiveness and Self-Disclosures on Perceptions of Counselor Behavior." *Journal of Counseling Psychology* 25 (1978):283–291.

Claiborn, Charles D. "Counselor Verbal Intervention, Nonverbal Behavior, and Social Power." *Journal of Counseling Psychology* 26 (1979):378–383.

———, **and Lyle D. Schmidt.** "Effects of Presession Information on the Perception of the Counselor in an Interview." *Journal of Counseling Psychology* 24 (1977):259–263.

Combs, Art W., Donald L. Avila, and William W. Purkey. *Helping Relationships.* Boston: Allyn and Bacon, 1971.

———, **Daniel W. Soper, Thomas Gooding, John A. Benton, Jr., John Frederick Dickman, and Richard H. Usher.** *Florida Studies in the Helping Professions.* Gainesville: University of Florida, 1969.

Cook, T. E. "The Influence of Client-Counselor Value Similarity on Change in Meaning During Brief Counseling." *Journal of Counseling Psychology* 13 (1966):77–81.

Cottle, W. C., and W. W. Lewis. "Personality Characteristics of Counselors II." *Journal of Counseling Psychology* 1 (1954):27–30.

Coutts, R. L. *Selected Characteristics of Counselor Candidates in Relation to Levels and Types of Competency in the Counseling Practicum.* Doctoral Dissertation. Florida: Florida State University, 1962.

Dell, D. M. "Counselor Power Base, Influence Attempt, and Behavior Change in Counseling." *Journal of Counseling Psychology* 20 (1973):399–405.

Dole, A. A. "The Prediction of Effective School Counseling." *Journal of Counseling Psychology* 11 (1964):112–121.

Edwards, Billy C., and John W. Edgerly. "Effects of Counselor-Client Cognitive Congruence on Counseling Outcome in Brief Counseling." *Journal of Counseling Psychology* 17 (1970):313–318.

Egan, Gerard. *The Skilled Helper.* Monterey, Calif.: Brooks/Cole, 1975.

Farson, Richard E. "Introjection in the Psychotherapeutic Relationship." *Journal of Counseling Psychology* 8 (1961):337–343.

Feldstein, JoAnn C. "Effects of Counselor Sex and Sex Role and Client Sex on Clients' Perceptions and Self-Disclosure in a Counseling Analogue Study." *Journal of Counseling Psychology* 26 (1979): 437–443.

Felker, Sally A. "Intellectual Ability and Counseling Effectiveness: Another View." *Counselor Education and Supervision* 13 (1973):146–150.

Fiedler, F. E.   "A Comparison of Therapeutic Relationships in Psychoanalytic, Nondirective, and Adlerian Therapy." *Journal of Consulting Psychology* 14 (1950):436–445.

Fitzgibbons, D. J., and C. R. Shearn.   "Concepts of Schizophrenia Among Mental Health Professionals: A Factor Analysis Study." *Journal of Consulting and Clinical Psychology* 38 (1972):288–295.

Fuller, F. F.   "Preferences for Male and Female Counselors." *Personnel and Guidance Journal* 42 (1964):463–467.

Gamboa, A. M., D. J. Tosi, and A. J. Riccio.   "Race and Counselor Climate in the Counselor Preference of Delinquent Girls." *Journal of Counseling Psychology* 23 (1976):160–162.

Gardner, L. H.   "The Therapeutic Relationship Under Varying Conditions of Race." *Psychotherapy: Theory, Research, and Practice* 8 (1971):78–87.

Geer, C. A., and J. C. Hurst.   "Counselor-Subject Sex Variables in Systematic Desensitization." *Journal of Counseling Psychology* 23 (1976):296–301.

Grantham, R. J.   "Effects of Counselor Sex, Race, and Language Style on Black Students in Initial Interviews." *Journal of Counseling Psychology* 20 (1973):553–559.

Guttmann, Mary A. J., and Richard F. Haase.   "Effect of Experimentally Induced Sets of High and Low 'Expertness' During Brief Vocational Counseling." *Counselor Education and Supervision* 19 (1972):171–178.

Harrison, D. K.   "Race as a Counselor-Client Variable in Counseling and Psychotherapy: A Review of the Research." *Journal of Counseling Psychology* 5 (1975):124–133.

Heck, E. J., and C. S. Davis.   "Differential Expression of Empathy in a Counseling Analogue." *Journal of Counseling Psychology* 20 (1973):101–104.

Heppner, P. Paul, and David N. Dixon.   "Effects of Client Perceived Need and Counselor Role on Clients' Behaviors." *Journal of Counseling Psychology* 25 (1978):514–519.

———, and M. Heesacker.   "Perceived Counselor Characteristics, Client Expectations, and Client Satisfaction with Counseling." *Journal of Counseling Psychology* 30 (1983):31–39.

———, and S. Pew.   "Effects of Diplomas, Awards, and Counselor Sex on Perceived Expertness." *Journal of Counseling Psychology* 24 (1977):147–149.

Heubusch, N. J., and J. J. Horan.   "Some Effects of Counselor Profanity in Counseling." *Journal of Counseling Psychology* 24 (1977):456–458.

Highlen, Pamela S., and Bettina Russell.   "Effects of Counselor Gender and Counselor and Client Sex Role on Females' Counselor Preference." *Journal of Counseling Psychology* 27 (1980):157–165.

Jackson, Mozelle, and Charles L. Thompson.   "Effective Counselor: Characteristics and Attitudes." *Journal of Counseling Psychology* 18 (1971):249–254.

Janda, Louis H., and David C. Rimm.   "Type of Situation and Sex of Counselor in Assertive Training." *Journal of Counseling Psychology* 24 (1977):444–447.

Johnson, Marilyn.   "Influence of Counselor Gender on Reactivity to Clients." *Journal of Counseling Psychology* 25 (1978):359–365.

Kemp, C. G.   "Counseling Responses and Need Structure of High School Principals and Counselors." *Journal of Counseling Psychology* (1962):326–328.

Lee, S. D.   *Social Class Bias in the Diagnosis of Mental Illness.* Doctoral dissertation. University of Oklahoma, 1968.

———, E. T. Hallberg, and L. Jones.   "Effects of Counselor Gender on Perceived Credibility." *Journal of Counseling Psychology* 27 (1980):71–75.

Lewis, Kathleen N., and W. Bruce Walsh.   "Physical Attractiveness: Its Impact on the Perception of a Female Counselor." *Journal of Counseling Psychology* 25 (1978):210–216.

Lichtenberg, James W., and Edward J. Heck.   "Interactional Structure of Interviews Conducted by Counselors of Differing Levels of Cognitive Complexity." *Journal of Counseling Psychology* 26 (1979):15–22.

Luria, Z.   "A Semantic Analysis of a Normal and a Neurotic Therapy Group." *Journal of Abnormal and Social Psychology* 58 (1959):216–220.

McClernan, J. L.   "Implications of Sexual Attraction (Feeling) in the Counselor-Client Relationship." Unpublished doctoral dissertation. University of Southern Mississippi, 1973.

McGowan, J. F.   "Client Anticipation and Expectancies as Related to Initial Interview Performance and Perception." Unpublished doctoral dissertation. University of Missouri, 1954.

McGreevy, P.   "Factor Analysis of Measures Used in Selection and Evaluation of Counselor Education

Candidates." *Journal of Counseling Psychology* 14 (1967):51–56.

Mawson, Carol D. "Educational Interventions in Counseling: The Need to Avoid Pronouncements." *Personnel and Guidance Journal* 57 (1978):70–73.

Merluzzi, Bernadette H., and Thomas V. Merluzzi. "Influence of Client Race on Counselors." *Journal of Counseling Psychology* 25 (1978):399–404.

Merluzzi, T. V., P. G. Banikiotes, and J. W. Missbach. "Perceptions of Counselor Characteristics: Contributions of Counselor Sex, Experience, and Disclosure Level." *Journal of Counseling Psychology* 25 (1978):479–482.

———, B. H. Merluzzi, and T. J. Kaul. "Counselor Race and Power Base: Effects on Attitudes and Behavior." *Journal of Counseling Psychology* 24 (1977):430–436.

Mezzano, Joseph. "A Note on Dogmatism and Counselor Effectiveness." *Counselor Education and Supervision* 9 (1969):64–65.

Paradise, L. V., B. Cohl, and J. Zweig. "Effects of Profane Language and Physical Attractiveness on Perceptions of Counselor Behavior." *Journal of Counseling Psychology* 27 (1980):620–624.

Patterson, Lewis E., and Sheldon Eisenberg. *The Counseling Process.* Boston: Houghton Mifflin, 1983.

Peters, Herman J., ed. *Counseling: Selected Readings.* Columbus, Ohio: Charles E. Merrill, 1962.

Peterson, J. A. *Counseling and Values.* Scranton, Pa.: International Textbook, 1970.

Pietrofesa, J. J., and W. H. Van Hoose. "The Need Structure of Graduate Students Entering a Counselor Education Program." Speech presented at American Personnel and Guidance Association, Las Vegas, 1969.

Polmantier, P. C. "The Personality of the Counselor." *Vocational Guidance Quarterly* 15 (1966): 95–100.

Price, Leah Z., and Marvin A. Iverson. "Students' Perception of Counselors with Varying Statuses and Role Behaviors in the Initial Interview." *Journal of Counseling Psychology* 16 (1969):469–475.

Rosenthal, D. "Changes in Some Moral Values Following Psychotherapy." *Journal of Consulting Psychology* 19 (1955):431–436.

Schmidt, Lyle D., and Stanley R. Strong. " 'Expert' and 'Inexpert' Counselors." *Journal of Counseling Psychology* 17 (1970):115–118.

Schrier, H. "The Significance of Identification in Therapy." *American Journal of Orthopsychiatry* 23 (1953):585–604.

Seeman, J. "A Study of Preliminary Interview Methods in Vocational Counseling and Client Reaction to Counseling." Unpublished doctoral dissertation. University of Minnesota, 1948.

Senour, Maria N. "How Counselors Influence Clients." *Personnel and Guidance Journal* 60 (1982):345–349.

Shapiro, A. K., E. L. Struening, H. Barten, and E. Shapiro. "Prognostic Factors in Psychotherapy: A Multivariate Analysis." *Psychotherapy: Theory, Research and Practice* 10 (1973):93.

———, E. L. Struening, E. Shapiro, and H. Barten. "Prognostic Correlates of Psychotherapy in Psychiatric Outpatients." *American Journal of Psychiatry* 133 (1976):802–808.

Shertzer, Bruce, and Shelley C. Stone. *Fundamentals of Counseling.* Boston: Houghton Mifflin, 1980.

Siegel, Jeffrey C. "Effects of Objective Evidence of Expertness, Nonverbal Behavior, and Subject Sex on Client-Perceived Expertness." *Journal of Counseling Psychology* 27 (1980):117–121.

Sladen, Bernard J. "Effects of Race and Socioeconomic Status on the Perception of Process Variables in Counseling." *Journal of Counseling Psychology* 29 (1982):560–566.

Sprafkin, Robert P. "Communicator Expertness and Changes in Word Meanings in Psychological Treatment." *Journal of Counseling Psychology* 17 (1970):191–196.

Strong, Stanley R. "Counseling: An Interpersonal Influence Process." *Journal of Counseling Psychology* 15 (1968):215–224.

———, and Lyle D. Schmidt. "Expertness and Influence in Counseling." *Journal of Counseling Psychology* 17 (1970):81–87.

Tinsley, H. E. A., K. R. Workman, and R. A. Kass. "Factor Analysis of the Domain of Client Expectancies About Counseling." *Journal of Counseling Psychology* 27 (1980):561–570.

Tuma, A. H., and J. W. Gustad. "The Effects of Client and Counselor Personality Characteristics on Client Learning in Counseling." *Journal of Counseling Psychology* 4 (1957):136–141.

Vargas, A. M., and J. G. Borkowski. "Physical Attractiveness: Interactive Effects of Counselor and

Client on Counseling Processes." *Journal of Counseling Psychology* 30 (1983):146–157.

Walters, Orville S.   "Metaphysics, Religion and Psychotherapy." *Journal of Counseling Psychology* 5 (1958):243–252.

Wolkon, G. H., S. Morwaki, and K. J. Williams. "Race and Social Class as Factors in the Orientation Toward Psychotherapy." *Journal of Counseling Psychology* 20 (1973):312–316.

Zlotlow, Susan F., and George J. Allen.   "Comparison of Analogue Strategies for Investigating the Influence of Counselors' Physical Attractiveness." *Journal of Counseling Psychology* 28 (1981): 194–202.

CHAPTER 3

The Client

Chapter Organizer

Aim of the Chapter
This chapter will describe client characteristics that can influence the counseling process.

Chapter Preview
1. Counselees differ from noncounselees, particularly if the former reflect personal adjustment problems.
    a. Counselees are more likely to have been first-born children and to have been somewhat more unhappy while growing up than noncounselees.
    b. Noncounselees tend to be more peer independent.
2. Clients may be attractive to counselors on a number of variables.
    a. Clients whom the counselor finds attractive talk more, are more spontaneous, and are less resistant.
    b. Counselors are attracted to younger, more conforming clients.
    c. Client race and sex have some subtle effects on client perceptions of the counselor, and conversely, perceptions of the client by the counselor.
3. Before client growth will occur in a nonvoluntary or resistant client, the counselor must eliminate the client resistance and help the client to participate voluntarily in counseling.

Relevant Questions
The following are several questions to keep in mind while reading this chapter:
1. How do counselees differ from noncounselees?
2. What makes one client more attractive to a counselor than another client?
3. What impact does client race or sex have on counselor behavior during counseling.
4. What can be done to defuse a client's belligerence?

Introduction

As seen in the previous chapter, counselors have certain characteristics that affect counseling dynamics. The same is true of clients. How do clients differ from nonclients? What makes some clients easier to deal with than others? This chapter looks at client characteristics, not to pigeonhole or label clients, but to emphasize that the counselor must fully understand the client in order to be most helpful.

The personal characteristics of clients can determine the success or failure of counseling. A client's personality, experiences, and resistance affect his or her interaction with the counselor, and subsequently the counseling outcomes. This chapter discusses client characteristics that directly influence the counseling process. (For a look at client developmental and age characteristics from the perspective of counseling content, see Chapter 7.)

Counselees and Noncounselees Compared

A variety of studies have been concerned with the question "Do people who seek counseling differ from those who do not?" One of the first such studies was conducted by Williamson and Bordin in 1940. They found that differences did exist. Students receiving counseling were better adjusted and obtained higher grade-point averages than students who were not counseled. Schneidler and Berdie (1942) noted that counseled students were representative of noncounseled students. Berdie and Stein (1966), looking at socioeconomic, personality, ability, and achievement variables, found no differences between counseled and noncounseled students. Smith (1977) studied counselees and noncounselees in a university setting. She found no differences among several personality types. Campbell's (1965) study at the University of Minnesota pointed out the following statistically significant differences: Students receiving counseling, as opposed to those who were not, were (1) more likely to have been first-born children and (2) somewhat more unhappy while growing up. Further, clients marked significantly more problems on the Mooney Problem Check List than did nonclients (Doleys, 1964).

Other studies have shown different results. Cooke and Kiesler (1967) reported that students seeking counseling appear to be more psychologically disturbed than those who do not. The former group has been found to be lower in academic achievement, vocationally unsure, and less involved in extracurricular activities (Meadows and Oelke, 1968). They are less judgmental and feeling-oriented but are more introspective and intuitive than nonclients (Mendelson and Kirk, 1962). Rossmann and Kirk (1970) found the differences to be somewhat sex-based. Male counselees had had more family difficulties and had more personal discomfort than nonclients.

Women who used counseling facilities had higher quantitative scores, were lower on spontaneous expression, came from families with lower incomes, and were more likely to plan on full-time work than female noncounselees. Simono (1968) concluded that differences in level of anxiety between those individuals who seek counseling and those who do not are more a function of stable personality characteristics than somewhat severe but fleeting problems.

It has been suggested that the conflicting results might well be caused by the types of problems studied. Counselees with personal adjustment problems seem to display different personality characteristics than noncounselees, while counselees with career and educational problems do not display different characteristics than noncounselees (Goodstein et al., 1960; Gaudet and Kulick, 1954; Minge and Bowman, 1967).

Several studies have looked specifically at this phenomenon. Apostal's (1968) study compared counseled students with vocational problems with noncounselees "whose particular circumstances satisfied a definition for having a vocational problem." The groups were compared on ability achievement, personality, and socioeconomic variables. Noncounseled students were found to have a higher peer-independence orientation; that is, the noncounselees displayed more autonomy and self-sufficiency in doing something about their problems than did the counseled group. More specifically the noncounselees were:

1. More autonomous in relation to peers.
2. Less concerned about how their behavior appears to other students.
3. Less likely to consult with acquaintances about personal matters.
4. Less conforming to prevailing peer norms; less sociable, extraversive, or other-directed. (p. 409)

A conclusion drawn by Apostal was that counselors might well want to concentrate on attempts to increase self-directiveness in clients. The vocational problem should not become the only focus of the counseling sessions.

Galassi and Galassi (1973) compared alienation level in college students seeking personal adjustment or vocational-educational counseling with non-seekers. Significant results did appear between the counseled and non-counseled groups, but the differences were primarily a function of elevated scores of the personal adjustment group. The counselees in this group reflected feelings of powerlessness, isolation, and self-dissatisfaction and were disenchanted with cultural values and ideals. Finally, Sharf and Bishop's (1973) findings substantiated the aforementioned studies. They noted that students with personal adjustment concerns did differ significantly in social and emotional adjustment—were less well-adjusted—than those who did not seek counseling. This finding did not apply to students with vocational-educational concerns.

Characteristics of Clients

Several client characteristics have a bearing on the counseling process. Counselors can increase their effectiveness by understanding how client characteristics influence the counseling relationship.

Client Attractiveness   Clients may be attractive to counselors on a number of levels—for example, physical, attitudinal, or interpersonal. The degree of client attractiveness to the counselor does make a difference in counseling (Corrigan et al., 1980). Studies by Goldstein (1973) and Goldstein and Simonson (1971) noted that when the counselor found the client attractive, the client talked more, was more spontaneous, and was less resistant.

The factor most often found to affect client attractiveness is the degree of similarity between counselor and client. Byrne (1971) suggested a strong attraction to individuals holding similar attitudes, while Davis et al. (1977) found significant degrees of attractiveness related to client conceptual level. In the latter study the following statement appeared:

> . . . since the counseling-relevant characteristics of low SES [socioeconomic status] clients are not desirable for counseling, counselors may develop a negative expectation for counseling outcome with these clients. If so, such clients would not be attractive to counselors presumably because counselors are motivated to be successful in the counseling situation. (p. 475)

Lewis et al. (1981) investigated the effects of client age, physical attractiveness, and in-session behavior on client attractiveness. Counselor "subjects" were significantly more attracted to younger clients and to clients who demonstrated "good" rather than "bad" in-session behaviors. Physical attractiveness had no significant impact. They concluded, however, that counselors tended to favor young, attractive, verbal, intelligent, and successful clients, although some of those characteristics were more potent than others. Jennings and Davis (1977) also stressed that good client verbal behavior increased the counselor's attraction to the client.

Willis (1978) noted that (1) the counselor's perception of client characteristics played an important role in counseling, (2) the counselor's perceptions coalesced into a stable working image during the early stages of counseling (sessions one to four), and (3) early counselor impressions of the client are significantly related to impressions at the end of counseling. Given the preceding findings that particular clients may be more attractive to counselors than other clients, counselors have to be aware of such predispositions and free themselves of any biases in working with clients.

Client Gender   Client gender can affect the counseling interaction. The sex of the client does appear to influence receptiveness to a helping relationship and also to helpers themselves. Counselors, in kind, respond in a variety of ways to the sex of the client.

Male Clients   Male clients may find that they are trapped by their early learnings within the parameters of constricted sex roles that prevent them from seeking or responding to help. Too often men have learned that they should be self-sufficient—be able to take care of their own problems—and should avoid emotional intimacy in their relations with others. Asking for help of counselors may be difficult for them. This may not be peculiar to counseling, but may relate to asking for help generally; for example, men are also less likely to visit a physician when sick (Goldberg, 1976). It appears that a gender generalization might be that men are less sensitive to themselves, and also to others, than women are. This low self-awareness, insensitivity to others, guarded openness, and avoidance of intimacy contributes to what Jourard (1971) calls the "lethal aspects of the male role." These factors contribute to an earlier death for men. The average American white male can expect to live 70.0 years, while his female counterpart's life expectancy is 77.7 years (Meinecke, 1981).

Men are more reluctant clients than women (Graff and Horne, 1973; King et al., 1973). Carlson (1981) writes, "Because male gender identity is threatened by intimacy and relatedness, the male is unlikely to select therapy as a solution to a problem. He is more likely to try to tough it out and attempt to remain unaffected . . . (p. 229). It has been our experience, for example, that even in the clinical practice of marriage or family counseling, it generally is the woman who initiates therapy for the unit. In an excellent article, Scher (1979) points to several counseling considerations for the counselor of the male: "The counselor should consider the cost to the self-esteem of the male who has to admit he cannot deal with his life and must enlist the aid of another to straighten things out" (p. 253). He also stresses that male clients are "productivity" oriented and will "demand" the same of the counselor. He notes further that male clients, feeling under the counselor's control, may also increase competitive behaviors during counseling. In fact, Toomer (1978) felt that male clients "often enter treatment with expectations of male therapists as experts who will help them polish competitive skills and defenses" (p. 24). These are qualities that can make men difficult to work with, but they are also qualities that, if employed constructively, enable men to make maximal use of therapeutic help. Scher (1981) develops this further when he states that "The primary task with men in counseling is dealing with desires for power, intimacy or reduction of pain" (p. 201). These qualities in client-counselor interaction are essential determinants of the success of therapy.

Sex-role issues may be found throughout the male lifespan. Marlowe (1981) discusses gender-identity issues during the childhood period, while Coleman (1981) elaborates on common problems of the male adolescent. Collison (1981) summarized the potential issues for adult men as follows: vocation, intimacy, family life, community, and inner life. The problems of the man in his middle years are often forgotten. Collison writes, "Often such men experience a general state of anxiety, depression, or other symptoms that may not be cause specific. A counselor using the male focus would help the client identify the gender-role issues involved (e.g., achievement status, control dimensions) and could use a male development model to direct inquiry" (p. 221).

Heilbrun (1961) in an often-cited work noted that the closer both sexes conformed to their sex role, the more likely they were not to stay in counseling. He notes that for men, the more independent, "masculine" male would find it difficult to stay in counseling as a counselee with subordinate status. For the male who is more identified with female characteristics, there would be a greater acceptance and identification with a male counselor. It would also appear that the possibilities of a dependency relationship could more easily develop.

Men, it has been found, disclose less and are more likely to disclose to women and high-status interviewers than are women (Brooks, 1974). Johnson (1978) reported that male students expected counselors to be less masculine than did female students, but did prefer a same-sex counselor. Stokes et al. (1980), summarizing a number of studies, concluded:

The results of these studies suggest that men might have difficulties engaging in productive personal counseling or psychotherapeutic relationships, since these relationships require intimate self-disclosure. They further suggest that problems in intimacy or lack of intimate relationships might be a productive area to explore in counseling, especially for men. (p. 197)

Their research did substantiate the findings that men were more willing to disclose to strangers and acquaintances and less willing to disclose to intimates than were their female counterparts. (See section on self-disclosure in Chapter 9.)

Social and educational changes that have occurred during the past decade have altered counseling concerns in a variety of ways. The employment interests of men, for example, have broadened, and these changes have serious implications for career counseling. Lunnenborg and Gerry (1977) noted that college men, perhaps as a result of their education, were turning away from realistic and enterprising areas toward artistic areas. We would, however, expect to see, as a result of the recession of the early 1980s, that future studies report a return to an emphasis on the first two interest areas.

Scher (1981) suggests seven guidelines for counselors of men:

1. Since men are often encapsulated in their roles, counselors can help male clients by pointing out how role expectations are constraining.
2. While men are particularly resistant to change because they feel that their social rewards are high, counselors can help clients change and be supportive during the process.

3. Male clients can be helped to become more sensitive and to develop greater awareness and expression of their feelings.
4. Men can be helped to understand that asking for assistance is not unmanly.
5. Clients can learn to nurture themselves, i.e., to relax, and even be indulged.
6. Men have been raised to be constrained, and, as a result, expect the same of others. Males can learn a sense of personal freedom which can then be extended to others.
7. Finally, because the world of work may be a hostile environment, males have to acquire a sense of judiciousness in the application of counseling insights and behaviors in the work place.

Female Clients   Compared to males, females are more likely to seek out counseling and to feel free to explore their feelings. They are less likely to respond defensively or competitively to the counselor (Thames and Hill, 1979). Females "expect to be more open, more highly motivated, and to accept more responsibility for their behavior in a counseling situation" (Hardin and Yanico, 1983, p. 296). Studies by Heilbrun (1961; 1974) suggested that female clients who did not stay in counseling conformed most closely to the cultural stereotype of their sex. Such female clients, compared to females who stayed in counseling, were less achieving, autonomous, and dominant, and more deferent and abasing. Termination was related, however, to the fact that the nondirective interviews served as a cathartic relief to the dependent, self-disclosing females. Feeling relief, they were less likely to return for a second session. Brooks (1974) reported that female interviewees disclosed more, were more likely to disclose to males, and disclosed more to low-status interviewers than did male interviewees. Female students do expect counselors to be more "masculine" than male students; it was speculated that women students who equate "femininity" with weakness expect an assumedly healthy counselor to be a stronger person (Johnson, 1978).

Much has been written about how the fact that the client is female affects counselor behavior. Research has supported the contention that mental health specialists accept sex-role stereotypes and reflect sex bias against females during counseling. Broverman et. al. (1970) in their landmark work found that clinicians, male and female, are significantly less likely to attribute traits that characterize healthy adults to women than they are to men. Thomas and Stewart (1971) reported that counselors, regardless of sex, evaluated female clients with so-called deviate career goals to be more in need of counseling than those with conforming goals. Pietrofesa and Schlossberg (1970) found that counselors held a bias against women who were interested in entering a so-called "masculine" occupation. Leonard and Collins (1979) state: "Much of psychological and vocational theory is built on hypotheses and data which relate primarily to males" (p. 6). Hare-Mustin (1983) goes even further by stating that clinical theories of development generally are inadequate in terms of the female experience.

More recent research suggests varying degrees of change in counselors working with females. Hill et al. (1977) concluded that counselors' reactions to female clients did fluctuate according to problem type, counselor sex, and client age. They suggested that women should not be used as a "general, single category in research" (p. 65) and feel that counselors today may be quite sensitized to appearing "sexist" and refrain from expressing biased statements. Although it was expected that college women would differ from women in general in their vocational interests, Lunnenborg and Gerry (1977) found few significant differences. These results reinforce the conclusion that sex-role stereotypes are very resistant to change. Finally, Helms (1978) reported that male counselors working with female clients required half as many counseling sessions as female counselors and that something had occurred during counseling to inhibit the male counselor–female client dyad from reaching the identified ideal. In summary, it still appears that a great deal of bias exists in counselors, both male and female, toward female clients. While change has occurred over the years in counselor bias and in female client self-perception, the process has been slow. A great deal of further sensitivity to women's issues is necessary. Nutt (1979) summarizes:

Biased theories and stereotyped attitudes of therapists have led to the development of what has been termed feminist therapy, which may serve as a model for non-sex-role-biased therapy. Feminist therapy has been an outgrowth of the consciousness raising movement . . . and encourages a woman to examine how the culture has worked to keep her in traditional roles that may not be functional for her, learn to be assertive in going after what she wants, own her own anger, challenge normative sex roles, learn that a complex life is possible, understand self-defeating feelings, enhance her self-confidence and feelings of personal power, learn to nurture herself, recognize that she has choices, resist the status quo, and learn to trust other women to be sources of support. (p. 19)

Although this may seem to be an extraordinary effort, Nutt concludes by saying: "In reality, the goals of feminist therapy are really no different than the goals of any humanistic, growth enhancing therapy" (p. 20). Counselors have to develop a commitment to providing such counseling.

Client Race   While many studies examine the impact of client gender on counseling and counselor behavior, little research has been done on the influence of client race on counseling. Yet, one might imagine that race and ethnic origins could well influence counseling. Helms (1979) alerted counselors to the potential pitfalls of sexual or racial stereotyping: "Counselors must disavow the sex and race biased assumptions, beliefs, and attitudes absorbed from societal stereotyping and attempt to discover and accept who the woman is and what her particular needs are" (p. 41). She recommended that counselors of black women cultivate the following knowledge, skills, and attitudes:

Knowledge: 1.   Counselors/therapists are familiar with Black history and contemporary politics as they affect Black women.

2.   Counselors/therapists are knowledgeable about myths, overgeneralizations, and stereotypes about Black women.

Skills: 1.   Counselors/therapists need no unique skills other than flexible use of basic counseling skills.

Attitudes: 1.   Counselors/therapists are aware of personal attitudes toward Blacks.

2.   Counselors/therapists believe that racially different is not necessarily "disadvantaged."

3.   Counselors/therapists are willing to abandon middle-class values and moralistic judgments. (p. 41)

Client Ethnicity   Ethnic differences between client and counselor could well present language, cultural, and valuative conflicts that impede the counseling process. The potential for miscommunication and misunderstanding increases if socioeconomic differences are also present. Ethnicity in counseling can be conceptualized as a general issue, but different ethnic groups have to deal with common issues, for example, oppression. Nonetheless, every ethnic group has its own unique cultural features that must be considered. While it is beyond the scope of this book to discuss the impact of specific ethnic membership, several of the more generalized concepts will be broached.

An ethnic sense centers around the belief in a common ancestry and collectivity and is experienced intellectually and emotionally by members of the group. At times the collectivity and "union" may be more fiction than fact historically; for example, regional differences in culture and language are quite dramatic in Italy, and yet "Italians" are seen as a collective ethnic group in America. Ethnic background may explain responses of individuals to their environment; these responses will in some cases be at odds with broader cultural values and behaviors. For example, the attitude of "machismo" in some Latino males may clash with new, emergent male sex-role behaviors. Certainly, language has come to be one way in which an ethnic identification and culture can be maintained; it may, at the same time, interfere with attempts by counselors to understand and help their clients. Social class, the stratification of groups based on economic factors, is another complicating variable throughout this process. Awareness of the impact of ethnicity on client attitudes, values, and behaviors has to be accomplished within the prevailing understanding of life-cycle development. Ethnic influence changes with each stage of development. Superficial and glib generalizations drawn by counseling theoreticians and practitioners are therefore untenable. It appears that because of the complexities involved, a task-centered, problem-solving approach that demonstrates respect for cultural values and attitudes may be most fruitful in working with clients of various ethnic groups. Such an approach would allow for maximization of counseling effectiveness while avoiding attendant discriminatory features.

The Nonvoluntary Client

Voluntary participation by the client is basic to effective counseling. Forcing clients into counseling denies their freedom of choice and decision-making responsibilities. Growth and behavior change will not occur when there is resistance in a client. Although clients do enter counseling, even when highly motivated, with some degree of self-protectiveness (Brammer, 1979), voluntary participation by the client promotes effective counseling and movement toward client goals.

Nonvoluntary clients present a difficult situation for the counselor because they demonstrate greater resistance than voluntary counselees. Most clients present some degree of resistance to counseling, resistance that may take the form of defensiveness. Pietrofesa et al. (1978) state: "Regardless of its manifest symptoms, resistance is essentially a drawing in, the raising of a protective shield, and a denial, at least for the time being, of growth forces" (p. 81). Nonvoluntary clients, though, may offer, not only a defensive, but also a hostile posture. Patterson and Eisenberg (1983) do not see the reluctant client as pathological but rather as a "person who, if given the choice, would choose not to be in the presence of a counselor and who would prefer not to talk about self" (p. 153).

Beier (1952) identifies the nonvoluntary client as the "individual in whom resistance toward giving up symptoms and substitute gratifications is greater than his desire for help" (p. 332). Reluctant clients are found in a great many settings; they include educational, marital, correctional, personal, and even vocational counseling scenarios. Reluctance, which pervades the counseling spectrum, is displayed in many forms—superficial content, silence, anger, compliance, or placing the counselor on a pedestal are among them.

Counseling voluntariness is obviously related to motivation for growth. This motivation would be related not only to counseling but other areas of life as well. Bednar and Weinberg (1970) suggested that underachieving students who volunteer for treatment show subsequent academic improvement in almost all treatment programs. They noted that volunteers are more highly motivated than nonvolunteers and that such motivation contributes to the effectiveness of the treatment program. Several studies have suggested that counseling is more effective with voluntary underachievers than with nonvoluntary underachievers (Marx, 1959; Redding, 1971), but at least one study suggests that the motivation of the students is more crucial than the counseling itself (Gilbreath, 1971). Redding (1971) did conclude: "However, counseling appears to be more beneficial in terms of the improvement of scholastic achievement and the attainment of educational goals to those students who utilize the counseling service at their own initiative" (p. 25).

The point becomes not whether we should ever see reluctant clients—sometimes we have no choice—but rather how they can be made into nonreluctant clients. Counselees must want to be counseled, and helping them arrive at this state of mind involves many steps. As counselors, we must first deal with our own feelings about ourselves. Reluctant clients can easily elicit in us feelings of uncertainty, hostility, and resentment. As a result of such feelings, some of us might resort to sarcasm and ridicule. Yet, Lauver et al. (1982) stresses the importance of avoiding the "rhetoric of warfare" in counseling and emphasizing the "rhetoric of caring." One way to avoid negative responses, such as sarcasm or ridicule, is to recognize that the client's resistance is not necessarily the counselor's fault. The basic responsibility for lack of client participation lies with the client, not with the counselor. Benjamin (1981) states:

Not everyone wishes to be helped and not everyone can be helped in the helping interview. To have a sincere offer of help rejected is painful, but we must learn to accept this. We may even eventually learn to accept the fact that in situations in which we have 'failed,' another interviewer can succeed. (p. 108)

Once we have appropriately responded to our own feelings, we can proceed to provide the fundamental conditions for growth in our clients. Counselors have to express concern and a sincere interest in helping them. We should provide "authentic" responses, which will force our clients to deal with us as "real" people. Larrabee (1982) suggests reducing resistance through affirmation techniques that emphasize equality between client and counselor. She lists (1) establishing initial rapport, (2) affirmation through paraphrasing, (3) affirmation through reflection of feeling, and (4) affirmation through open-ended questions or leads. There are no easy solutions in dealing with the reluctant client. Riordan et al. (1978), for example, described the available literature on client reluctance as "leaning heavily on inspiration and falling short of systematizing what we know regarding human behavior" (p. 7). Following are several broad guidelines, which allow for individual variations.

1. Accept the responsibility for helping the counselee recognize and deal with feelings of reluctance.
2. Continue to provide a therapeutic atmosphere characterized by warmth, understanding, acceptance, and genuineness.
3. Do not bring forth highly threatening material, which would only increase the counselee's resistance. It is best not to resort to interpretation or confrontation, either of which (a) may be seen as an attack or (b) may encourage the counselee to intellectualize.
4. Respond primarily at the "feeling" level, for this will encourage self-exploration. (Note: The statement, "You resent having to come for counseling," is considered to be a feeling response, not an interpretation.)
5. Give the counselee the opportunity to lead. An interested silence might well accomplish this end (Pietrofesa et al., 1978, p. 90).

6. In order to make the client more comfortable, a "safe" subject may well be broached (e.g., an interest the client might have).

Smaby and Tamminen (1979) discuss belligerent counselees, many of whom "resented our even attempting to form a positive relationship, let alone trying to help" (p. 506). They suggested that it was possible to help such clients by integrating moral reasoning and behavior contracting into the counseling process in order to establish an improved counselor-client relationship. Their proposal involves using counseling and contracting "to establish a mutually respectful working relationship to identify ways of improving the counselee's situation, and to involve the counselee actively in formulating goals, changing behaviors, and evaluating outcomes" (p. 506). By combining the earlier "relationship"-oriented suggestions with more direct behavioral enhancement approaches, the counselor may be able to minimize client resistance.

Finally, Patterson and Eisenberg (1983) encourage the counselor who may have to work with the reluctant client:

A counselor who undertakes working with reluctant clients should have the commitment to stick with the process and not become just another person who eventually gives up. Giving up is just one more rejection that further builds the client's view that authorities can't be trusted. (pp. 162–163)

Summary

Client characteristics, such as attractiveness, gender, race, or reluctance, affect counseling outcomes. The discussion of client characteristics in this chapter has been designed to sensitize counselors to the full array of potential influences the client may bring to the counseling encounter.

The major points of this chapter were as follows:

1. As might be expected, counselees differ from noncounselees, particularly if the former articulate personal-social concerns.
2. Counselors are more attracted to clients who are younger and evidence pleasing behaviors during counseling. Clients found more attractive by the counselor are less resistant, talk more during therapy, and are more spontaneous. It appears that either verbally or nonverbally the counselor communicates to the client that he or she finds the client attractive in some way.
3. All other things being equal, some clients may prefer a counselor of a particular race or sex. On the other hand, race or sex of counselor will not compensate for ineffective counseling skills or a poor therapeutic relationship. Until client choice of counselor, however, has been shown to be significantly related to outcome in counseling, it is reasonable to suggest that the client have some choice of therapist and treatment throughout the counseling process (Manthei, 1983). The basic goal in working with nonvoluntary clients is to make them voluntary participants. Several specific steps may be followed to accomplish this end.

References

Apostal, Robert A. "Comparison of Counselees and Noncounselees with Type of Problem Controlled." *Journal of Counseling Psychology* 15 (1968):407–410.

Bednar, R. L., and S. L. Weinberg. "Ingredients of Successful Treatment Programs for Underachievers." *Journal of Counseling Psychology* 17 (1970):1–7.

Beier, E. G. "Client-Centered Therapy and the Involuntary Client." *Journal of Consulting Psychology* 16 (1952):332–337.

Benjamin, Alfred. *The Helping Interview.* Boston: Houghton Mifflin, 1981.

Berdie, R. F., and J. Stein. "A Comparison of New University Students Who Do and Do Not Seek Counseling." *Journal of Counseling Psychology* 13 (1966):310–317.

Brammer, L. M. *The Helping Relationship: Process and Skills.* Englewood Cliffs, N.J.: Prentice-Hall, 1979.

Brooks, Linda. "Interactive Effects of Sex and Status on Self-Disclosure." *Journal of Counseling Psychology* 21 (1974):469–474.

Broverman, I. K., D. M. Broverman, F. E. Clarkson, P. O. Rosenkrantz, and S. R. Vogel. "Sex-Role Stereotypes and Clinical Judgments of Mental Health. *Journal of Consulting and Clinical Psychology* 34 (1970):1–7.

Byrne, D. *The Attraction Paradigm.* New York: Academic Press, 1971.

Campbell, D. P. *The Results of Counseling: Twenty-Five Years Later.* Philadelphia: Saunders, 1965.

Carlson, Nancy L. "Male Client–Female Therapist." *Personnel and Guidance Journal* 60 (1981):228–231.

Coleman, E. "Counseling Adolescent Males." *Personnel and Guidance Journal* 60 (1981):215–218.

Collison, Brooke B. "Counseling Adult Males." *Personnel and Guidance Journal* 60 (1981): 219–222.

Cooke, M. K., and D. J. Kiesler. "Prediction of College Students Who Later Require Personal Counseling." *Journal of Counseling Psychology* 14 (1967):346–349.

Corrigan, J. D., D. M. Dell, K. N. Lewis, and L. D.

Schmidt. "Counseling as a Social Influence Process: A Review." *Journal of Counseling Psychology* 27 (1980):395–441.

Davis, C. S. D., D. A. Cook, E. J. Heck, and R. L. Jennings. "Differential Client Attractiveness in a Counseling Analogue." *Journal of Counseling Psychology* 24 (1977):472–476.

Doleys, E. J. "Differences Between Clients and Non-Clients on the Mooney Problem Check List." *Journal of College Student Personnel* 6 (1964): 21–24.

Galassi, John P., and Merna D. Galassi. "Alienation in College Students: A Comparison of Counseling Seekers and Nonseekers." *Journal of Counseling Psychology* 20 (1973):44–49.

Gaudet, P. J., and W. Kulick. "Who Comes to a Vocational Guidance Center?" *Personnel and Guidance Journal* 33 (1954):211–214.

Gilbreath, Stuart. "Comparison of Responsive and Nonresponsive Underachievers to Counseling Service Aid." *Journal of Counseling Psychology* 18 (1971):81–84.

Goldberg, H. *The Hazards of Being Male.* New York: Nash, 1976.

Goldstein, A. P. *Structural Learning Therapy: Toward A Psychotherapy for the Poor.* New York: Academic Press, 1973.

———, **and N. R. Simonson.** "Social Psychological Approaches to Psychotherapy Research." In A. E. Bergin and S. L. Garfield, eds., *Handbook of Psychotherapy and Behavior Change.* New York: John Wiley, 1971.

Goodstein, L., J. Crites, A. Heilbrun, and P. Rempel. "The Use of the California Psychological Inventory in a University Counseling Service." *American Psychologist* 15 (1960):432.

Graff, R. W., and A. M. Horne. "Counseling Needs of Married Students." *Journal of College Student Personnel* 14 (1973):438–442.

Hardin, S. I., and B. J. Yanico. "Counselor Gender, Type of Problem, and Expectations About Counseling." *Journal of Counseling Psychology* 30 (1983):294–297.

Hare-Mustin, R. T. "An Appraisal of the Relationship Between Women and Psychotherapy." *American Psychologist* 38 (1983):593–599.

Heilbrun, Alfred B., Jr. "Interviewer Style, Client

Satisfaction and Premature Termination Following the Initial Counseling Contact." *Journal of Counseling Psychology* 21 (1974):346–350.

———. "Male and Female Personality Correlates of Early Termination in Counseling." *Journal of Counseling Psychology* 8 (1961):31–36.

Helms, Janet E. "Black Women." *The Counseling Psychologist* 8 (1979):40–41.

———. "Counselor Reactions to Female Clients: Generalizing from Analogue Research to a Counseling Setting." *Journal of Counseling Psychology* 25 (1978):193–199.

Hill, C. E., M. F. Tanney, and M. M. Leonard. "Counselor Reactions of Female Clients: Type of Problem, Age of Client, and Sex of Counselor." *Journal of Counseling Psychology* (1977):60–65.

Jennings, R. L., and C. S. Davis. "Attraction-Enhancing Client Behaviors: A Structured Learning Approach for Non-YAVIS, Jr." *Journal of Consulting and Clinical Psychology* 45 (1977):135–144.

Johnson, Deborah H. "Students' Sex Preferences and Sex Role Expectations for Counselors." *Journal of Counseling Psychology* 25 (1978):557–562.

Jourard, Sidney. *The Transparent Self.* Princeton, N.J.: D. Van Nostrand, 1971.

King, P. T., F. Newton, B. Osterlund, and B. Baber. "A Counseling Center Studies Itself." *Journal of College Student Personnel* 14 (1973): 338–344.

Larrabee, M. J. "Working with Reluctant Clients Through Affirmation Techniques." *Personnel and Guidance Journal* 61 (1982):105–109.

Lauver, P. J., M. A. Holiman, and S. W. Kazama. "Counseling as Battleground: Client as Enemy." *Personnel and Guidance Journal* 61 (1982):99–101.

Leonard, M. M., and A. M. Collins. "Woman as Footnote." *Counseling Psychologist* 8 (1979):6–7.

Lewis, K. N., C. S. Davis, R. L. Jennings, and B. J. Walker. "Attractive Versus Unattractive Clients: Mediating Influences and Counselors' Perceptions." *Journal of Counseling Psychology,* 28 (1981): 309–314.

Lunnenborg, Patricia W., and Marian H. Gerry. "Sex Differences in Changing Sex-Stereotyped Vocational Interests." *Journal of Counseling Psychology* 24 (1977):247–250.

Manthei, R. J. "Client Choice of Therapist or Therapy." *Personnel and Guidance Journal* 61 (1983):334–340.

Marlowe, Mike. "Boyhood Sex-Role Development: Implications for Counseling and School Practices." *Personnel and Guidance Journal* 60 (1981):210–214.

Marx, G. L. "A Comparison of the Effectiveness of Two Methods of Counseling with Academic Underachievers." Unpublished doctoral dissertation. University of Iowa, 1959.

Meadows, M. E., and M. C. Oelke. "Characteristics of Clients and Non-Clients." *Journal of College Student Personnel* 9 (1968):153–157.

Meinecke, Christina E. "Socialized to Die Younger? Hypermasculinity and Men's Health." *Personnel and Guidance Journal* 60 (1981):241–245.

Mendelsohn, G. A., and B. A. Kirk. "Personality Differences Between Students Who Do and Do Not Use a Counseling Facility." *Journal of Counseling Psychology* 9 (1962):341–346.

Minge, M. R., and T. F. Bowman. "Personality Differences Among Non-Clients and Vocational-Educational and Personal Counseling Clients." *Journal of Counseling Psychology* 14 (1967): 137–139.

Nutt, Roberta L. "Review and Preview of Attitudes and Values of Counselors of Women." *The Counseling Psychologist* 8 (1979):18–20.

Patterson, Lewis E., and Sheldon Eisenberg. *The Counseling Process.* Boston: Houghton Mifflin, 1983.

Pietrofesa, J. J., and N. K. Schlossberg. *Counselor Bias and the Female Occupational Role.* Detroit: Wayne State University, 1970. ERIC Documents, CG 006 056.

———, G. E. Leonard, and W. Van Hoose. *The Authentic Counselor.* Chicago: Rand McNally, 1978.

Redding, R. "Self-Referred Students and Other-Referred Students Using College Counseling Services." *Journal of Counseling Psychology* 18 (1971):22–25.

Riordan, R. J., K. B. Matheny, and C. W. Harris. "Helping Counselors Minimize Client Reluctance." *Counselor Education and Supervision* 18 (1978): 6–13.

Rossmann, J. E., and B. A. Kirk. "Comparison of Counseling Seekers and Non-Seekers." *Journal of Counseling Psychology* 17 (1970):184–188.

Scher, Murray. "On Counseling Men." *Personnel and Guidance Journal* 57 (1979):252–254.

———. "Men in Hiding: A Challenge for the Counselor." *Personnel and Guidance Journal* 60 (1981):199–202.

Schneidler, G. G., and R. F. Berdie. "Representativeness of College Students Who Receive Counseling Services." *Journal of Educational Psychology* 33 (1942):545–551.

Sharf, R. S., and J. B. Bishop. "Adjustment Differences Between Counseled and Noncounseled Students at a University Counseling Center." *Journal of Counseling Psychology* 20 (1973):509–512.

Simono, Ronald B. "Anxiety and Involvement in Counseling." *Journal of Counseling Psychology* 15 (1968):497–499.

Smaby, Marlowe, and Armas W. Tamminen. "Can We Help Belligerent Counselees?" *Personnel and Guidance Journal* 57 (1979):506–512.

Smith, Phyliss J. "Comparison of Counselees and Noncounselees with Reference to Holland's Theory." *Journal of Counseling Psychology* 24 (1977):244–246.

Stokes, Joseph, Ann Fuehrer, and Laurence Childs. "Gender Differences in Self-Disclosure to Various Target Persons." *Journal of Counseling Psychology* 27 (1980):192–198.

Thames, T. B., and C. E. Hill. "Are Special Skills Necessary for Counseling Women?" *The Counseling Psychologist* 8 (1979):17–18.

Thomas, H., and N. R. Stewart. "Counselor Response to Female Clients with Deviate and Conforming Career Goals." *Journal of Counseling Psychology* 18 (1971):352–357.

Toomer, Jery E. "Males in Psychotherapy." *Counseling Psychologist,* 7 (1978):22–25.

Williamson, E. G., and E. S. Bordin. "Evaluating Counseling by Means of a Control Group Experiment." *School and Society* 52 (1940):434–440.

Willis, T. A. "Perceptions of Clients by Professional Helpers." *Psychological Bulletin* 85 (1978):968–1000.

CHAPTER 4

Expectations and Goals of Counseling

Chapter Organizer

Aim of the Chapter
This chapter will explore the relationship of client expectations to goals during the counseling process. The discussion stresses mutuality and collaboration.

Chapter Preview
1. Client expectations influence specific goal establishment.
   a. Expectations can be either general or specific.
   b. College and high school students often expect counseling to help them specifically with school and career concerns.
   c. Subjects who have received prior help from counseling are more favorably predisposed to counseling.
2. Goals can be classified as immediate, mediate, or ultimate.
   a. The goals of counseling are self-exploration, self-understanding, and action.
   b. Action implies behavior change.
   c. Both client and counselor have a responsibility for movement toward goal achievement.
3. Through collaboration the client and counselor share responsibility for progress in counseling.

Relevant Questions
The following are several questions to keep in mind while reading this chapter:
1. How do client expectations influence goals?
2. What are all the implications of a "mutual" counseling relationship?

Introduction

In the previous two chapters we have discussed characteristics of counselors and clients. In this chapter we focus on those dimensions of counseling that concern both client and counselor: client expectations and counseling goals.

It is difficult for counseling to proceed unless client expectations are clarified and appropriate and workable goals are identified. The expectations clients have of counseling show their hopes and anticipations. These may be based on realistic perceptions of what counseling is all about and evolve into counseling goals, or they may not be realistic, in which case the counselor will have to, through initial structuring, clarify the process to the client. What eventually evolves are goals for counseling—in other words, the outcomes sought. In the final section we emphasize the importance of counselee-counselor collaboration throughout the therapy process. It is a process that emphasizes "mutuality." Neither the client nor counselor is more important than the other; they are, rather, equal, although contributions may differ in kind, to each other.

Client Expectations

Clients approach counseling with certain expectations. They expect to resolve a problem and they expect the counselor to behave in a helpful way. Shertzer and Stone (1980) suggest that expectations and goals differ in that "Expectancies are likely to stress remediation and repair; goal statements imply that counseling should be preventive and generative in nature" (p. 89). Client expectations may affect the direction and outcome of counseling. They also determine whether or not counseling will be continued after each session.

Problems Expected to Be Addressed

One must assume clients come to counseling seeking help—expecting problem resolution and/or anxiety reduction. If this is so, both action and insight approaches to counseling appear appropriate. Whether client expectations of the counseling outcome are general or more specific, they often differ from the goals the client eventually establishes. This is because the problem the client brings to counseling is frequently not the one that most needs to be addressed. Celotta and Telasi-Golubcow (1982) state, "Often a client's presenting problem can seem quite clear and simple to a student; yet it may in fact derive from a less clear and more complex problem. It is assumed here that the more complex (or higher level) problem must be addressed to facilitate change" (p. 74).

Client presenting problems can take many forms:

Select a career
Obtain occupational or educational information

Develop self-understanding
Receive better grades
Improve study habits
Plan a course of study
Select a college
Take a test
Discover interests or abilities
Improve peer relations
Discuss personal concerns
Obtain information about drugs or sex

Engelkes and Vandergoot (1982) did note that "In school settings, particularly college and secondary environments, the problems students see as appropriate for counseling are as expected. Their concerns are mainly with current academic pursuits and future career directions" (p. 15). Studies, however, have presented conflicting results in this regard. Gladstein (1969) noted that problems of high school students frequenting a university practicum center were diverse and multiple, not limited to only two major categorizations (educational and vocational). Van Riper (1971) reported junior high school students' expectations of counselors were primarily within the realm of educational planning and to some degree with other school problems. College students tend to indicate vocational-choice problems as most appropriate for college counseling centers, while adjustment to self and to others are considered least appropriate (Warman, 1960). Leviton (1977), studying high school students, found that they expected counseling to help them with academic planning, academic weaknesses, study skills, and career education.

In a comprehensive study of the content of dialogue in psychotherapy, Howard et al. (1969) studied the aspects of the patients' lives that they discussed most frequently. They reported that the typical content of dialogue focused primarily on the "outer," or interpersonal, sphere rather than the "inner," or intrapersonal, aspects of the clients' experience. The most frequent topics discussed were heterosexual relationships, occupational involvements, and hopes or fears for the future (p. 403). A five-dimensional thematic structure of dialogues revealed similarities in both patient-therapist samples as follows: parental family, conjugal family, fantasy, work and peers, and therapy and therapist. The presence of one theme did not preclude or indicate the presence of another theme. They were quite independent, and partially a function of the method of analysis.

Celotta and Telasi-Golubcow (1982) presented a problem taxonomy for classifying clients' problems. Their taxonomy has five levels:

Level 1   General Expectation Problems   These are perceptual in nature and are existing in what is perceived as an apparently threatening environment. Clients suffering from problems at this level experience difficulty in all interpersonal relationships, are difficult to treat, and are candidates for long-term therapy.

Level 2   General Cognition Problems Such problems are indicated through clients making "broad maladaptive statements about self or others." These problems are coded verbally and can be seen as "counseling" rather than "long-term" therapy problems.

Level 3   Specific Cognition Problems   These problems, while cognitive, deal with ideas, attitudes, or beliefs that affect the identified problems. Such cognitions have been culturally derived. These problems are more specific than those in Level 2 and as such are not as pervasive in their influence upon self-concept.

Level 4   Information Problems   These problems indicate lack of client information and can be dealt with in an educative fashion.

Level 5   Behavioral Problems   Behaviors are characterized by a "lack or excess of some type." Clients will benefit from practice of new behaviors. (pp. 74–75)

Trends in client problems can change over the years. Sharp and Marra (1971) found that over an eight-year period, the proportion of clients classified by problem-goal area shifted significantly. Problems of an emotional nature had increased fourfold, while educational problems declined similarly in a reverse fashion. It appeared that males were more likely to present vocational and educational problems, while females were more likely to present emotional problems. When client expectations are not met, clients leave counseling dissatisfied (Isard and Sherwood, 1964).

Expected Counselor Behavior   As mentioned in an earlier section, counselees generally expect to see a warm counselor who exhibits interest in the problems presented. There is a preference for a highly trained and expert counselor who displays confidence in his or her ability to help. Dreman and Dolev (1976), investigating the relationship between existing preferences and expectations, found that nonclients prefer a counselor who is significantly more active than they expected, particularly in the areas of symptom removal and behavioral change. Dreman (1977) found the same to be true of a client population. Subjects prefer counselors who can serve as agents of change.

Tinsley and Harris's (1976) findings on client expectations included an experienced, genuine, expert, and accepting counselor whom they could trust. Counselor directiveness and a beneficial outcome were expected but at a lower level. Implications of this study had more meaning. The clients seemed to believe that counseling is generally helpful, but were somewhat doubtful that counseling would be helpful to them. Tinsley and Harris concluded that while "client expectancies may be important determinants of where he or she turns for help, the possibility is raised that many potential clients never seek counseling because of their low expectancy that they will be helped" (p. 176). Sex differences in this study appeared: females expected the counselor to be accepting and nonjudgmental, whereas males expected a more directive, critical, and analytical counselor.

Cash et al. (1978) studied client help-seeking attitudes and perceptions of counselor behavior. They found that subjects who had previously received professional help for psychological problems were more favorably disposed toward counseling. This included greater recognition of need, stigma tolerance, interpersonal openness, and confidence in mental health practitioners. They reported that "Help-seeking attitudes were found to represent a significant positive influence on the counselors' perceived expertise, trustworthiness, regard, empathy, genuineness, and general helpfulness; on subjects' expected willingness to return for a second interview; and on their expectancies of improvement across a variety of personal problems" (p. 264). Client expectations can and do *change.* In Gladstein's (1969) study, fewer clients indicated after counseling that they had expected help in the vocational area. He went on to suggest that "the client may come to interviews with more than one expectation and that he will be generally satisfied if only part of his expectations are met. Thus, it seems reasonable to assume that rapport can be established without always meeting all of the client's expectation" (p. 480).

To go one step further, client personality may also determine expectations of counselor behavior. Byrne (1963), in a more general vein, established that such factors as similar attitudes, self-concepts, and socioeconomic status produce positive effects, while dissimilar attitudes produce negative effects. In an interesting study by Neufeldt et al. (1977), it was found that client levels of cognitive development did not influence client evaluations of counseling sessions. On the other hand, client cognitive characteristics are reflected in expectations and preferences (Neufeldt, 1978). In a study specifically related to counseling, Fernbach (1973) looked at authoritarianism and preferred counseling style. He found that authoritarian students preferred a directive therapist, while nonauthoritarian students preferred a nondirective therapist. This finding was consistent with Secord and Backman's (1964) summarizations that authoritarians prefer status-laden leadership, with strong authority and direction on the part of the leader. Authoritarians are actively hostile toward weak leaders. Nonauthoritarians prefer more democratic and nondirective leadership. Students with negative attitudes about self have psychological needs related to increasing authoritarianism and an external locus of control. Among males this negativeness is also associated with a decreasing need for approval and interpersonal trust (Fischer and Turner, 1970). Expectations of individuals who have not been in therapy, however, are not found to be related to counseling approaches. Sobel and O'Brien (1979) looked at expectations for counseling success in specific reference to analytic, behavioral, and Gestalt modalities. They concluded: "Apparently individuals who have not actually been in personal counseling, and who are not exposed to a particular counselor, do not always have general preconceived notions about the effectiveness of three popular approaches" (p. 464).

Goals of Counseling

Specific goals for counseling are unique to each client and involve, among other factors, the client's expectancies. Long-range goals and process goals, however, are common to all counseling. Goals may be seen as roads for the client and counselor to travel. While it is true that not all roads will take us somewhere, it is equally true that there are many roads to "Heaven." In a way, the counselor's behaviors are shaped by goal considerations; that is, the counselor utilizes techniques and procedures designed to facilitate

Table 4.1
A Model for
Facilitative Human
Relationships

Condition	Immediate (Process)	Mediate (Subgoals)	Ultimate
Empathic understanding	Intrapersonal exploration	Development of individual potentials:	Self-actualization, self-realization, self-enhance-ment, or fully functioning person:
Nonpossessive warmth			
Genuineness	Self-disclosure	Self-understanding	
Intensity and intimacy of contact	Self-exploration	High school graduation	Acceptance of self and others
Concreteness	Self-awareness	College education Employment Satisfaction in work	Empathy Deep interpersonal relationships
		Marriage	Democraticness Openness to experience Creativity Honesty Responsibility Geniuneness Responsible independence Consistency between self and self-ideal

Source: C. H. Patterson, "A Model for Counseling and Other Facilitative Human Relationships" in W. Van Hoose and J. J. Pietrofesa, *Counseling and Guidance in the Twentieth Century* (Boston, Houghton Mifflin, 1970), p. 185. Reprinted with permission.

is, the counselor utilizes techniques and procedures designed to facilitate their accomplishment, but counseling goals also reflect the counselor's philosophy of life.

Long-Range Goals

Long-range goals tend to be vague and perhaps unattainable. They do not really lend themselves to the development of researchable hypotheses on the efficacy of counseling. For these reasons such goals may be criticized. On the other hand, broad goals can provide a philosophical overtone to the counseling process, not only regarding the outcomes of counseling but also the relationship between helper and helpee. Long-range goals may be as follows:

1. To become self-actualizing.
2. To attain self-realization.
3. To become more fully functioning.

Seiler and Messina (1979) defined mental health counseling with apparent long-range goals. They state, "Professional mental health counseling is an interdisciplinary, multifaceted, holistic process of the (1) promotion of healthy life-styles, (2) identification of individual stressors and personal levels of functioning, and (3) preservation or restoration of mental health" (p. 6).

Byrne (1963) and Patterson (1970) classified the above as ultimate goals. Ultimate goals reflect a view of the individual and of life's meaning. They are abstract and philosophical. Basically, ultimate goals focus on client awareness that leads to the actualization of potential within an individually satisfying lifestyle.

Seiler and Messina, Byrne, and Patterson also discussed two other categories of goals—intermediate (mediate) and immediate goals. The former indicate client expectancy, while the latter are specific evidences of momentary change in counseling. (See Table 4.1.) Mediate goals can be subgoals in the service of an ultimate goal, whereas immediate goals focus on the counseling process itself.

Pate (1980) proposed that counseling goals must be based on a developmental, nonpathological orientation. Developmental tasks and goal categories, then, might well be related in such a fashion. Developmental tasks could be described at different levels of abstraction and articulated with goals. (See Figure 4.1.)

Process Goals

Goals common to the counseling process may be much more specific. *Client self-exploration* is an immediate process goal. Verbal exchange is basic to communication. For much growth to occur in counseling, the client must be willing to self-disclose and explore behavior and feelings. Simply to suggest self-exploration as a goal, however, is not sufficient. It cannot be an end goal for counseling. Just "talking about" a problem does not generally lead to more effective behavior. An individual may feel better after talking, per-

Figure 4.1
Developmental
Tasks and Goal
Categories

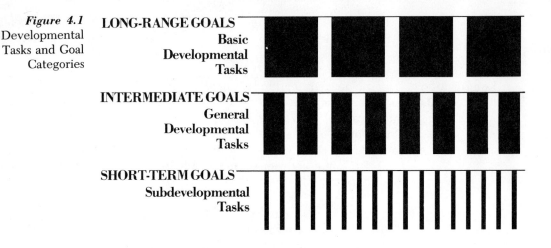

haps as a result of energy expenditure, but the next day anxieties about the same problem have returned. We have all seen people with a need to constantly talk about the same problem to anyone with whom they come into contact.

A second goal of counseling is *self-understanding,* or integrating in a meaningful pattern information about self and recognizing the need for behavior change. Self-understanding is not an adequate final goal. Again, we recognize that a person might understand quite well the "why" of behavior and also recognize the self-defeating nature of behavior, but yet do nothing to change. Again, we have seen people who constantly say "I eat too much. I need to go on a diet" and, yet, they never do. Goodyear and Bradley (1980) warn counselors, for example, to be wary of client contracts designed simply to explore a problem.

Although this is a legitimate contract, we believe it is important in such cases to point out to the client that he or she will probably not be any different as a result of attaining that understanding. We all, even as trained counselors, engage in magical thinking and delude ourselves into believing that once we understand a problem it will be solved. (p. 515)

The final goal for the client is *behavior change,* or living more effectively as a result of the counseling intervention. We define *behavior change* to include not only problem resolution, increased personal effectiveness, and improved decision-making skills, but also to encompass attitudinal changes. Krumboltz (1966) postulated three action-oriented goals: altering maladaptive behavior, learning the decision-making process, and preventing problems. The therapeutic process leads eventually to behavior change by the client. (See Figure 4.2.)

There are, then, three basic goals to counseling: self-exploration, self-understanding, and behavior change. There is no set time schedule for accomplishing each, but counselor behavior at each stage is designed to facilitate goal attainment. (See model in Table 4.2.) Hershenson (1982) emphasizes the relatedness of these goals when he states that counseling "must provide the client with mastery skills and intellectual and emotional understanding. To leave a client with

Table 4.2
An Overview of an Organic or Developmental Model of Helping and Interpersonal Relating

Phase	Helper's Goal	Client's Goal
Pre-helping pre-communication phase: Attending	Attending. To attend to the other, both physically and psychologically; to give himself entirely to "being with" the other; to work with the other.	
Stage 1: Responding/ self-exploration	Responding. To respond to the client and what he has to say with respect and empathy; to establish rapport, an effective collaborative working relationship with the client; to facilitate the client's self-exploration.	Self-exploration. To explore his experiences, behavior, and feelings relevant to the problematic in his life; to explore the ways in which he is living ineffectively.
Stage II: Integrative understanding/ dynamic self-understanding	Integrative understanding. The helper begins to piece together the data produced by the client in the self-exploration phase. He sees and helps the other identify behavioral themes or patterns. He helps the other see the "larger picture." He teaches the client the skill of going about this integrative process himself.	Dynamic self-understanding. Developing self-understanding that sees the need for change, for action; learning from the helper the skill of putting together the larger picture for himself; identifying resources, especially unused resources.
Stage III: Facilitating action/acting	Facilitating action. Collaborating with the client in working out specific action programs; helping the client to act on his new understanding of himself; exploring with the client a wide variety of means for engaging in constructive behavioral change; giving support and direction to action programs.	Acting. Living more effectively; learning the skills needed to live more effectively and handle the social-emotional dimensions of life; changing self-destructive and other-destructive patterns of living; developing new resources.

Note: The model has a prehelping phase and three stages.
Source: From *The Skilled Helper*, by G. Egan, p. 30. Copyright © 1975 by Wadsworth Publishing Company, Inc. Reprinted by permission of the publisher, Brooks/Cole Publishing Company, Monterey, California.

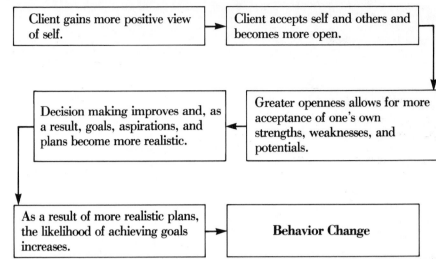

Figure 4.2
The Effects of the
Therapeutic
Process

Source: Adapted from J. J. Pietrofesa et al., *The Authentic Counselor,* 2nd ed. (Chicago: Rand McNally, 1978), p. 37.

only understanding is to leave him or her powerless to implement the insights gained through counseling, and to leave a client with only skills may be to create an automaton at best, or a potential monster at worst" (p. 408).

Defining Goals   Goal definition is crucial, for not only does it provide direction in counseling, but it also is used to measure counseling success. Generally, the most acceptable goal involves increased behavior effectiveness. A clearly stated goal communicates to the client that the purpose of counseling is serious and designed to facilitate behavioral changes in the clients' life. Paritzky and Magoon (1982), for example, suggest becoming sufficiently specific by "converting generalized goal statements into observable, measurable characteristics . . ." (p. 381).

Frey and Raming (1979) felt that few models adequately described the goals and methods of counseling; they suggested taxonomic research to develop a classification model. Their research, which organized and described "theoretical positions in counseling and psychotherapy by combining multivariate procedures with the time-honored method of rational classification," led to seven goal clusters.

Goal 1:   Transfer of therapeutic learning to outside situations. Change is made in the real world of the client. The client acquires adaptability and planning skills in problem areas.

Goal 2:   Awareness and acceptance of self in conflict. The client understands self and reorders thinking about self.

Goal 3:   Specific symptom removal. There is a focus on personal concerns and a resolution of psychological symptoms, confused objectives, or specific problems.

Goal 4:   Strengthened ego functioning. Client behavior becomes more congruent with inner ego states.

Goal 5:   Awareness of positive inner resources. The client develops greater feelings of adequacy, mastery, competency, creativity, and responsibility.

Goal 6:   Learning to respond to and control the environment. The client adapts to or changes conflictual situations in a self-satisfying manner.

Goal 7:   Awareness of negative thoughts and feelings. The client is better able to accept, integrate, and change distressing feelings, through reeducation and reordered thinking about negative thoughts and feelings. (pp. 31–32)

Frey and Raming (1979) then identified six processes of counseling related to these goals: (1) client acceptance, (2) active critical questioning, (3) recognition and interpretation of unconscious material, (4) manipulation of client anxiety, (5) reeducation about emotional conflicts, and (6) support of the client's autonomy (p. 32). (See later chapters for a full discussion of the counseling relationship and counselor skills.) Hershenson (1982) pointed out that of Frey and Raming's goals, four (1, 3, 4, and 6) relate to mastery, while three (2, 5, and 7) relate to understanding.

Client-Counselor Collaboration

Counseling involves collaboration between client and counselor; both should accept responsibility for what occurs during counseling. Some clients, and in certain instances some counselors, assume that since the counselor is highly trained and brings a great degree of expertise into counseling, the counselor should provide direction at all stages. We feel, contrary to this position, that it is important for the client to participate equally. The client, for example, should participate in establishing goals. The counselor may clarify and even suggest possible goals and courses of action, but the client and counselor should make final decisions jointly. There are a variety of reasons for this. Foremost is the belief that the individual is responsible for his or her own behavior. One widely accepted tenet of counseling is that the counselee "owns" behavior. Behavior change will not occur if the client does not assume responsibility for his or her actions. And change is further facilitated if the client is collaborating with someone who can model responsible decision-making behavior. As we will note in Chapters 5 and 6, certain theoretical positions espouse such particular goals as integration, behavior change, or self-actualization. Such goals tend to be quite general and allow for much individual variation. The client should define the more specific outcomes for counseling. The counselor subsequently facilitates and is comfortable with this process.

Counseling is meaningless without mutual collaboration between the client and counselor. This is not only true in the selection of goals, but it is just as valid at other times. Although the client generally selects the topics to be discussed, it is appropriate for the counselor to provide direction. In some instances, the counselor may have to be more active than in others. For example, in working with children, the counselor may have to assume more initiative in generating topics, but the child has the option to respond or not.

There is at least one major impediment to collaboration—negative self-images on the part of the client or the counselor. In many cases, clients see the counselor as being capable of healthier functioning than themselves and, furthermore, that counselors see themselves also as functioning more effectively than the client (Jorgensen and Hurst, 1972). Jorgensen and Hurst also found that clients assume that given the same problems, the therapist would find a more appropriate and healthier resolution (p. 261). Such assumptions would contribute to the notion that the client is unable to participate in mutual goal selection or decision making. Counselors and clients should avoid such a trap.

The client and counselor are, in reality, allies. They are equally responsible for their participation in counseling. The result should be the growth of the inner resources of the counselee, so that he or she is more likely to interact responsibly with others and is more able to function adequately without counseling.

Summary

Client expectations, the goals of counseling, and the place of values in counseling are of mutual concern to counselor and client. It is in these areas that counselor-client collaboration often begins during the therapy process. The degree of the success of collaboration during the early stages of counseling greatly influences the direction and success of collaborative efforts during the later stages. The major points of this chapter are as follows:

1. Client expectations, reflecting identified problem areas, may take many forms. Various studies of students in high school or college settings suggest that they expect counseling to help them particularly with academic and career concerns. Generally, individuals who had received prior therapeutic help were more favorably disposed toward counseling.

2. The three goals of counseling are (a) self-exploration, (b) self-understanding, and (c) behavioral change. Goals for counseling are defined as specifically as possible. Client expectations should be considered in the formulation of such goals.

3. The counselee and counselor mutually accept responsibility for the progress of coun-

seling. Goals are defined jointly. Both the client and counselor feel that they are equal, responsible, and mutually involved.

References

Byrne, Richard H. *The School Counselor.* Boston: Houghton Mifflin, 1963.

Cash, T. F., J. Kehr, and R. F. Salzbach. "Help-Seeking Attitudes and Perceptions of Counselor Behavior." *Journal of Counseling Psychology* 25 (1978):264–269.

Celotta, Beverly, and Hedwig Telasi-Golubcow. "A Problem Taxonomy for Classifying Clients' Problems." *Personnel and Guidance Journal* 61 (1982):73–76.

Dreman, S. B. "Expectations and Preferences of Clients for a University Student Counseling Service." *Journal of Counseling Psychology* 24 (1977):459–462.

———, **and A. Dolev.** "Expectations and Preferences of Nonclients for a University Student Counseling Service." *Journal of Counseling Psychology* 23 (1976):571–574.

Egan, Gerard. *The Skilled Helper.* Monterey, Calif.: Brooks/Cole, 1975.

Engelkes, James R., and David Vangergoot. *Introduction to Counseling.* Boston: Houghton Mifflin, 1982.

Fernbach, Robert. "Authoritarianism: A Selection Variable for Psychotherapy." *Journal of Counseling Psychology* 20 (1973):69–72.

Fischer, E. H., and J. L. Turner. "Orientations to Seeking Professional Help: Development and Research Utility of an Attitude Scale." *Journal of Consulting and Clinical Psychology* 35 (1970):79–90.

Frey, David H., and Henry E. Raming. "A Taxonomy of Counseling Goals and Methods." *Personnel and Guidance Journal* 58 (1979):26–33.

Gladstein, Gerald A. "Client Expectations, Counseling Experience and Satisfaction," *Journal of Counseling Psychology* 16 (1969):476–481.

Goodyear, Rodney K., and Fred O. Bradley. "The Helping Process as Contractual." *Personnel and Guidance Journal* 58 (1980):512–515.

Hershenson, David B. "A Formulation of Counseling Based on the Healthy Personality." *Personnel and Guidance Journal* 60 (1982):406–409.

Howard, Kenneth L., David E. Orlinsky, and James A. Hill. "Content of Dialogue in Psychotherapy." *Journal of Counseling Psychology* 16 (1969): 396–404.

Isard, E. S., and E. J. Sherwood. "Counselor Behavior and Counselee Expectations as Related to Satisfactions with Counseling Interview." *Personnel and Guidance Journal* 42 (1964):920–921.

Jorgensen, Gerald T., and James C. Hurst. "Empirical Investigation of Two Presuppositions in Counseling and Psychotherapy." *Journal of Counseling Psychology* 19 (1972):259–261.

Krumboltz, John D. "Behavioral Goals of Counseling." *Journal of Counseling Psychology* 13 (1966):153–159.

Leviton, Harvey S. "Consumer Feedback on a Secondary School Guidance Program." *Personnel and Guidance Journal* 55 (1977):242–244.

Neufeldt, S. A. "Client Cognitive Characteristics and Preference for Counseling Approaches." *Journal of Counseling Psychology* 25 (1978):184–187.

———, **J. M. Zimmer, and D. M. Mayton II.** "Client Cognitive Levels and Counseling Approaches." *Journal of Counseling Psychology* 24 (1977): 448–451.

Paritzky, Richard S., and Thomas M. Magoon. "Goal Attainment Scaling Models for Assessing Group Counseling." *Personnel and Guidance Journal* 60 (1982):381–384.

Pate, R. H., Jr. "The Counselor in a Psychological Society." *Personnel and Guidance Journal* 58 (1980):521–524.

Patterson, C. H. "A Model for Counseling and Other Facilitative Human Relationships." In W. Van Hoose and J. J. Pietrofesa, eds., *Counseling and Guidance in the Twentieth Century.* Boston: Houghton Mifflin, 1970.

Pietrofesa, J. J., G. E. Leonard, and W. H. Van Hoose. *The Authentic Counselor.* Chicago: Rand McNally, 1971, rev. ed., 1978.

Secord, P. F., and C. W. Backman. *Social Psychology.* New York: McGraw-Hill, 1964.

Seiler, Gary, and James J. Messina. "Toward Professional Identity: The Dimensions of Mental Health

Counseling in Perspective." *American Mental Health Counselors Association Journal* 1 (1979):3–8.

Sharp, W. Harry, and Herbert A. Marra. "Factors Related to Classification of Client Problem, Number of Counseling Sessions, and Trends of Client Problems." *Journal of Counseling Psychology* 18 (1971):117–122.

Shertzer, Bruce, and Shelley C. Stone. *Fundamentals of Counseling.* Boston: Houghton Mifflin, 1980.

Smith, David W. "Value Systems and the Therapeutic Interview." In H. J. Peters, *Counseling: Selected Readings.* Columbus, Ohio: Charles E. Merrill, 1962.

Sobel, Harry J., and Bernard A. O'Brien. "Expecta-tions for Counseling Success." *Journal of Counseling Psychology* 26 (1979):462–464.

Tinsley, Howard E. A., and Donna J. Harris. "Client Expectations for Counseling." *Journal of Counseling Psychology* 23 (1976):173–177.

Van Hoose, William H., and John J. Pietrofesa, eds. *Counseling and Guidance in the Twentieth Century.* Boston: Houghton Mifflin, 1970.

Van Riper, B. W. "Student Perception: The Counselor Is What He Does." *The School Counselor* 19 (1971):53–56.

Warman, R. E. "Differential Perceptions of Counseling Role." *Journal of Counseling Psychology* 7 (1960):269–274.

PART II

Theoretical Foundations

CHAPTER 5

Affective Theories of Counseling

Chapter Organizer

Aim of the Chapter
This chapter will provide brief descriptions of the major affective theoretical positions in counseling.

Chapter Preview
1. Therapy encompasses many theoretical approaches to counseling the individual. There are varying degrees of similarity among these theories.
2. Therapeutic effectiveness is a function of counselor and client personality and comfort rather than theoretical orientation.
3. Diagnosis is used initially to assess potential benefits of therapy for a client.
4. Facilitative therapists are effective, regardless of orientation.
5. Affective theories have as their focus individual feelings and attitudes, which have to be understood before behavior can be changed.
6. Most affective theoretical approaches to counseling are descendants of psychoanalysis, which was conceptualized by Sigmund Freud. Psychoanalysis presents a complete formulation of personality. Psychotherapy is based on the development of self-understanding which leads to the resolution of unconscious conflicts.
7. Alfred Adler's individual psychology, which developed directly from psychoanalysis, views the individual as a whole.

According to Adler, what is crucial is not the reality of life, but rather the meaning individuals give to it. One particular contribution of Adler was his recognition of the importance of birth order. The counseling process includes the establishment of a relationship, exploration of client goals and lifestyles, an interpretation of client "mistakes," and a reconstruction and re-education of client goals.

8. Transactional analysis stresses understanding the transactions between people and patterns of interaction that control individuals. Early childhood influences are seen as having a major impact upon adult development. Therapy is aimed at freeing the adult to enjoy fully his or her reasoning and to grow productively.
9. Carl Rogers' (Rogerian) therapy and client-centered therapy are synonymous. They are based on perceptual psychology, which maintains that the self elicits a perceptual field which in turn precipitates behavior. Individuals are conceptualized positively and motivated toward self-actualization. The role of the counselor is to provide the proper climate and atmosphere in counseling which would help that growth process. Essential conditions that the counselor provides to attain that end are positive regard, empathy, congruence, and concreteness.

10. Existential counseling reflects a philosophy or "mood" that embraces several philosophies. Individuality, freedom, responsibility, honesty, and commitment are the basic attributes to be considered within the theoretical framework. There are few specific counseling techniques associated with this approach to counseling.

11. Gestalt counseling views the individual as a sum of more than its parts. Awareness, which leads to maturation, is the essential goal of Gestalt counseling. The counseling itself attempts to unify the experience of the individual within the environment. It is an active, confrontative approach concerned with experience in the here-and-now.

Relevant Questions

The following are several questions to keep in mind while reading this chapter:

1. What is the role of the id, ego, and superego in the formation of pathological anxiety? Indicate how repression, suppression, and regression work to defend the individual. Compare the goals of psychoanalysis to those of client-centered psychotherapy.

2. Why does motherhood have so much prestige in individual psychology? What are the three basic "mistakes" that can be made with children? What is an inferiority complex and what is its antithesis? How is a first-born child different from a third-born child? Compare Adler's view of self-determinism to Freud's.

3. As viewed in transactional analysis, describe the process of selecting an unhealthy life position. What are those positions? Compare the functions of each of the ego states. How do they compare to the id, ego, and superego? Describe contamination and exclusion. What are the results of each?

4. What difficulties might exist for the client-centered counselor in trying to work with a client with distorted perceptions of reality? How can incongruencies in client perceptions be confronted within a client-centered framework?

5. What are the major philosophical contributions of the existentialists that might have meaning for all schools of counseling? How may they help counselors deal with clients from a general, rather than limiting, perspective?

6. What are the essential philosophical elements that underlie Gestalt counseling? What personal values, if they conflict in some ways with these elements, may give rise to maladaptive behavior?

7. What are the major differences among the affective theories presented? How might each be employed to greatest advantage?

8. What types of clients might benefit from a particular approach?

9. How is the client-counselor relationship more important to certain approaches than to others?

Introduction

Therapy is a term applied to a wide variety of therapeutic approaches. These approaches may be quite different. In Chapters 5 and 6, we present an overview of the most established and best-recognized theories. We are not concerned with determining which approach is "better." We believe strongly that therapeutic effectiveness is related to both counselor and client personality and comfort; in other words, different counseling approaches may be more effective with particular clients at certain stages of development and of the therapeutic process. Ewing (1977) states, "Some therapeutic systems are more helpful to particular presenting problems than are others" (p. 338). Essentially our belief is that no *one* therapy is best for all clients. To some degree, then, diagnosis is initially important in counseling in the assessment of the potential benefits of therapy for a client. In some cases the therapist may have to make referrals or bring the client to some point at which counseling can be helpful.

It is likely that "good" therapists are "good" regardless of theoretical approach; that is, there are characteristics of effective therapists that transcend theoretical constructs. The work by Combs and his associates (1969), cited more extensively in Chapter 2, supports this contention. Fiedler noted in two studies in 1950 that more highly trained therapists of different therapeutic orientations agreed more with each other conceptually about an ideal therapeutic relationship than they agreed with less well trained therapists of the same orientation. In addition, the therapeutic relationships established by "experts" of a particular orientation was more similar to relationships created by "experts" of different orientations than to those of "nonexperts" with the same theoretical orientation. An analysis of psychotherapy outcome studies by Smith and Glass (1977) did not support the idea that counseling success depended on theoretical orientation. They compared the effectiveness of the following ten orientations based on 400 controlled and statistically integrated evaluations: psychodynamic, Adlerian, eclectic, transactional analysis, rational-emotive, Gestalt, client-centered, systematic desensitization, implosion, and behavior modification. Few significant differences in effectiveness were found. On a more general level, "virtually no difference in effectiveness was observed between the class of all behavioral therapies . . . and the nonbehavioral therapies . . ." (p. 752). They reached a very interesting conclusion:

The results of research demonstrate the beneficial effects of counseling and psychotherapy. Despite volumes devoted to the theoretical differences among different schools of psychotherapy, the results of research demonstrate negligible differences in the effects produced by different therapy types. Unconditional judgments of superiority of one type or another of psychotherapy, and all that these claims imply about treatment and training policy, are unjustified (Smith and Glass, 1977, p. 760).

Various degrees of convergence among therapeutic approaches are observable. Krasner (1978) predicted that "In the future there will be a major convergence between the 'subjectivity' of the humanist and the behaviorist's shift away from apparent 'objectivity.' . . ." (p. 803). Perhaps we have seen this already happen with the introduction of the cognitive-behaviorism dialogue.

As we discuss counseling theories, it will be helpful for the reader to keep in mind the specific features of each theory. Tables 5.1 and 6.1 summarize each approach in terms of (1) major theorists, (2) philosophical view of the individual, (3) stated goals, (4) features of the therapeutic relationship, (5)

Table 5.1
Affective Theories of Counseling

Approach	Major Theorists	View of Individual	Goals
Psychoanalytic	Sigmund Freud; Karen Horney; John Rosen; Anna Freud; Harry Stack Sullivan; Edward Bordin; Franz Alexander; Otto Rank; Carl Jung; Erik Erikson.	Early childhood development crucial influence on adult personality; person influenced by unconscious; deterministic; reductionistic; instincts innate and biological.	Revelation of unconscious; resolution of repressed conflicts; personality reconstruction; reconstruction of past experiences; disclosure of memories.
Adlerian	Alfred Adler; Rudolf Dreikurs.	Motivated by social urges; conscious, not unconscious, is center of personality; people determine fate; feelings of inferiority overcome by seeking power; person is good.	Change lifestyle; development of social interest; self-determinism; increase awareness; discovery of mistakes; develop superiority and new life goals.
Transactional analysis	Eric Berne; Roy Grinka; T. Harris.	Potential for choice is present in each individual; antideterministic; can leave behind early programming; has Parent, Adult, and Child ego states.	Evaluation of appropriateness of decisions; autonomy; removal of game-playing behaviors; change in life scripts; spontaneity; to experience freedom of choice.
Client-centered	Carl Rogers; Angelo Boy; Gerald Pine; W. R. Coulson.	Individual has potential for "good"; rational person who is moving toward self-actualization; capacity to find own direction.	Self-exploration; increased openness to experience; greater ability to perceive realistically and, as a result, improved decision making. Greater acceptance of self and others.
Existential	Ludwig Binswanger; Henri Ellenberger; Rollo May; Sidney Jourard; Victor Frankl; Abraham Maslow; J. Bugental; C. Moustakas; A. Van Kaam.	Person is defined through action and freedom to choose; psychological health determined by grasp of meaning of life; only individual existence is relevant.	Acceptance of responsibility; achievement of potential; maximization of potential; freedom; authentic being; awareness of existence; establishment of will.
Gestalt	Fritz Perls; Ralph Hefferline; William Passons; Paul Goodman; J. Fagan; I. Shepherd.	Antideterministic; has capacity to assume responsibility to live integrated life; more than sum of parts; coordination of parts of person into a system.	Awareness; maturation; integration; responsibility; wholeness; authentic and vital living; completion of unfinished business; growing up.

Table 5.1 (Cont.)

Approach	Therapeutic Relationship	Therapist's Role	Therapeutic Techniques
Psychoanalytic	Remains "anonymous"; crystallizes during transference.	Interprets resistance, projection, transference; clarifier; confronter.	Interpretation; free association; dream analysis; analysis of resistance; questioning; use of projectives; confrontation; clarification.
Adlerian	Friendly relationship; equalitarian; warm; caring; empathic.	Diagnostician; dream analyst; interpreter.	Explanation; exploration of client goals; interpretation; reconstruction of goals; re-education.
Transactional analysis	Equalitarian; contractual arrangement.	Teacher; trainer; resource person; encourager; diagnostician; identifies alternatives.	Explains; analyzes; structural analysis of ego states; analysis of transactions; script analysis; game analysis; role-playing; focus on present.
Client-centered	Warmth, genuineness, empathy, and regard are crucial to process; I-thou relationship.	Provide appropriate climate; use of self as therapeutic instrument; establish freedom to grow.	Reflection; clarification; empathy; listening; reassurance.
Existential	Authenticity and encounter stressed so relationship seen as important; spiritual or even mystical.	Grasp client's being; establish an authentic encounter; attempt to understand.	Techniques not well-developed; paradoxical intention; de-reflection.
Gestalt	I-thou encounter.	Confrontation; frustrates client; helps client make interpretations; clarifies various awareness levels; focuses on what and how; active.	Confrontation; empty chair; reversals; verbal approaches to awareness; dream work.

the therapist's role, and (6) therapeutic techniques used. The text discussion expands on these ideas.

This chapter deals specifically with affectively oriented theories of counseling. This means that the theories are at least minimally concerned with and frequently attempt to understand and accept the client's feelings. All of these theories support the attempt to help the client develop some level of self-understanding. It is believed that insight will permit the client's feelings to change. When one feels differently, then it is believed that one will act differently. The theories in this chapter are all in some way descendants of psychoanalytic theory; therefore psychoanalysis is treated first. It is followed by discussions of Adlerian counseling, transactional analysis, client-centered counseling, existential counseling, and Gestalt counseling.

Psychoanalysis

Theoretical Beginnings

Psychoanalysis comes from two words: *Psyche* means "soul," and *analysis* implies a "taking apart." Its development is closely associated with the work of Sigmund Freud (1856–1939). Freud emphasized that "by isolating and examining the neglected and hidden aspects of our souls, we can acquaint ourselves with those aspects and understand the roles they play in our lives" (Bettelheim, 1983, p. 12). Psychoanalysis is a complete theory of personality generated concurrently with its therapeutic techniques. It is based on acquiring an understanding of oneself and one's unconscious conflicts and reworking or reconstructing their effects on the individual.

Freud's friend and colleague, Josef Breuer, stumbled on "the talking cure" in his work with Anna O. (Jones, 1959). Freud, who was originally trained as a physician and then specialized in neurology, took this simplistic concept, which Breuer called "catharsis," and through dedication, courage, and hard intellectual work developed it into a method of therapy that is intricately integrated with the theory of personality.

Fine (1979) divides Freud's work into four periods:

1. The exploration of neurosis, from inception of practice (1886) until the *Studies on Hysteria* (1895).
2. Self-analysis, 1895–1899.
3. Id psychology, in which the first system of psychoanalytic psychology was elaborated, roughly 1900–1914.
4. Finally, ego psychology, involving a considerable extension and elaboration of the earlier ideas, lasting from 1914 until 1939. (p. 20)

View of the Individual

Freud's theory of the individual is a deterministic one. Freud believed that this psychic determinism suggests that, in the mind, nothing happens by chance or at random. Therefore, all behavior has meaning if we can only have sufficient insight to identify and understand it. Behavior is determined by previous behavior and biological drives. By the age of five, the basic personality has been established.

Mental Processes Freud defined three constructs of the mind: the conscious, unconscious, and preconscious. Freud (1963a) indicated in "The Unconscious" (1915) that the concept of the "unconscious" won psychoanalysis the name of "depth psychology." The *conscious* is all that we are aware of in ourselves and our environment. The *unconscious* is the vaster area encompassing those events, wishes, desires, and impulses that have been repressed or censored from the conscious mind. These mental acts are not available to conscious awareness but nonetheless may, and very frequently do, affect our behavior. The *preconscious* is the censor that acts on the memories in the unconscious. If the memory passes scrutiny, it is allowed to pass into consciousness; if not, it is repressed into unconsciousness and must remain there. Memories in the unconscious are not yet conscious but, on association with a conscious thought, can be brought to consciousness without the resistance that accompanies an unconscious memory.

Structure of the Mind Freud divided the mind into three parts: id, ego, and superego. The *id* functions by "primary process." Its sole purpose is to obtain pleasure. As the source of all our drives, it is present at birth. It operates "on the pleasure principle, is animalistic, remains basic throughout life, and takes no precautions in expressing its purposes: the survival of the individual and successful reproduction" (Leak and Christopher, 1982, p. 316). Freud at first believed that the id contained the drives toward sexuality and self-preservation but later revised this to the dual drives of sexuality and aggression. The *sexual drive* is the erotic component of our mental activities; the *aggressive drive* is the purely destructive component. The two drives are always fused, but in differing degrees. All destructive, aggressive acts have some amount of unconscious sexual meaning to their actor and, therefore, some unconscious sexual gratification. Conversely all sexual behavior provides the release of some unconscious aggressive drive. All individuals have these drives and must learn to deal with their existence.

The *superego* is the base of our moral and social values. While we are not born with a superego, it emerges as a result of the introjection of the moralistic warnings and values of our parents and other adults. It is essentially our "conscience" and approves or disapproves of our behavior or wishes, critically observes the self, administers self-punishment, demands repentance for wrongdoing, and rewards the self with self-praise and self-love (Brenner, 1974). The superego functions largely unconsciously and would instill altruistic behavior in the individual, locking the person into rigid morality, if it were not monitored and influenced by a healthy ego (Leak and Christopher, 1982).

The *ego,* like the superego, is not present at birth. Both structures evolve out of the id as the infant develops. The id calls for gratification of all its drives without regard for moral or social appropriateness. Therefore, as the infant develops, the superego emerges to offset the drives of the id. The ego then becomes the "middleman" between the id and superego. The ego functions as a "secondary process" by observing the id to ensure that plea-sure is obtained in accordance with strict conditions. The instinctual drives of the id are continually attempting to force their way into the ego where they may gain access to our motor apparatus, thus achieving gratification. In cases which the ego evaluates as favorable (ego syntonic), the ego aids the id by becoming aware of the entry of the impulse, feeling the accompa-nying tension, and finally experiencing the relief when gratification is real-ized (A. Freud, 1966). The ego evaluates the instinctual drives with respect to "the demands of reality and, more than that, to conform to ethical and moral laws by which the superego seeks to control the behavior of the ego" (A. Freud, 1966, p. 7). Therefore, if the drive is viewed with displeasure (ego dystonic), it is subject to modification, criticism, and/or rejection by the ego. Anna Freud refers to this as a period of war. The impulses fight for entry into the ego, hoping to overthrow it by a "surprise attack." The ego counter-attacks and tries to invade the id's territory. The ego's purpose is to perma-nently disengage the unacceptable instinctual drives by employing the ap-propriate defense mechanisms, which will make secure its own boundaries. Consequently, "No longer do we see an undistorted id impulse but an id impulse modified by some defensive measure on the part of the ego" (A. Freud, 1966, pp. 7–8).

Defense Mechanisms   To analyze the functioning of the id, ego, and su-perego the therapist must understand the functioning of the defense mech-anisms. Brenner (1974) tells us that defense mechanisms are generally used in clusters, rarely singly or even in pairs. A sampling of the most common defense mechanisms and their descriptions follow.

Repression was the earliest resistance recognized by Freud and is the most common. It is employed by literally everyone. Repression is the ego's refusal to allow a forbidden id impulse or accompanying memories, emo-tions, desires, or wish-fulfilling fantasies to become conscious. It is the "for-getting" of a memory, but it is an unconscious forgetting. The person who has repressed memories is not aware that something is forgotten. The pro-cess of repressing is to separate completely from the ego the forbidden memory, wish, emotion, or fantasy and, thus, force it to become a part of the id. Repression needs to be differentiated from *suppression,* which is the conscious attempt to forget something. Suppression differs from repres-sion in that the ideation is conscious and uncomfortable and the individ-ual decides to forget it—or at least not to deal with it in the hope that it will be forgotten. Suppression is not normally considered a defense mechanism.

Reaction formation is the blocking of an impulse that the ego labels dan-gerous and whose presence causes anxiety. By strengthening and emphasiz-ing the opposite impulse, reaction formation keeps the forbidden impulse blocked out of awareness. This process also occurs unconsciously and is not limited to the blocking of socially unacceptable impulses. For example, hate could appear as a reaction formation against love if for some reason love was viewed as a threat. A client might then use it to guard against the growth of feelings of love toward the therapist in an analytic relationship. Generally, however, it occurs when, for example, a person renders unconscious the emergence of hateful feelings for his or her baby or parent and replaces it with love, worship, or idealization.

Isolation is the recollection of memories of the past without the accompanying feeling or emotion. It is said that the affect is isolated from the memory. The affect or the emotion was repressed, but the memory of the wish or incident remains conscious. In this way we bar from consciousness frightening or painful memories of emotion and thus reduce their threat. This explains how and why a person can discuss calmly, without reliving the pain, memories of being abused as a young child.

Undoing is the attempt to "undo" an act or impulse from the id that the ego considers dangerous, such as a hostile or sexual act. For example, a four-year-old boy hits his one-year-old sister and then kisses her to undo the harm that he thinks was caused by his unconscious wish or impulse.

Denial is in effect when certain unpleasant or unwanted aspects of the outside world's reality are blocked from one's consciousness or, at the very least, when the powerful consequences of their presence are minimized. Therefore, a person who wants to believe he is a bright, even gifted, student must deny the external reality of his poor school grades and inability to communicate effectively if he is to maintain that belief.

Projection is the act of not being aware of one's own wish or attitude and instead attributing it to some other person or external object. This defense mechanism is most common in childhood, when one views one's own attitude or impulse as unacceptable and then unconsciously tries to banish it by projecting it on another. "It is as though such persons said unconsciously, 'It's not *I* who have such a bad or dangerous wish, it's he' " (Brenner, 1974, p. 92).

Regression occurs when the ego is faced with severe conflicts with the id impulses; the ego may regress to a previous stage where a sense of equilibrium is maximized and anxiety is minimized. At other times the regression will go to a previous phase where an old conflict is renewed; in such a case, equilibrium is not found. The points to which a person regresses are called points of fixation. As we develop through the psychosexual stages, there are some points that have given us a high degree of satisfaction and others that provided us with great frustration. When the ego is threatened, we use the defense mechanism of regression to return to an earlier, more primitive stage to either re-experience the wonderful gratification or to unconsciously solve its frustrations. Therefore, the three-year-old child who wants to nurse at his mother's breast after his sister's birth is regressing to a pleasurable phase from a currently troublesome stage. Fixation is a developmental concept, whereas regression is a defense mechanism.

Sublimation is the unconscious taking of a forbidden impulse and, through secondary processing, turning it into a related yet socially acceptable activity that still gratifies the basic impulse. Brenner (1974) cites the example of a young child who wants to play with his feces but due to the forbidden nature of this activity instead makes mud pies and perhaps later becomes a sculptor. It is commonly believed that many of our aggressive drives are sublimated into acceptable sporting activities and competitive games and that sexual drives are sublimated into such activities as working and seeking power, influence, and money.

Turning against the self occurs when the ego feels threatened by the impulses of another. Feeling helpless or frightened to defend herself, the person may identify with the assaulting person against herself. *Identification* is used for purposes of defense and consists of merging with the identified object. The identity of the self is confused with the identity, wishes, behaviors, and impulses of another. Therefore, if one merges (identifies) with the threatening object, then one must turn against the self as the threatening object has. An example is a young child who is abused by a parent. The parent is the primary care giver and the object of love, the mirror of self and the provider of life. It is too dangerous to consider repudiation of this powerful figure, therefore the child identifies with the parent and disapproves of himself, punishes himself, and unconsciously begins to hate himself. The result of this is depression. It is less threatening at the time to hate oneself than it is to hate one's parent.

Rationalization is the process of organizing facts, attitudes, and beliefs into an explanation that conceals the true motivation for an individual's behavior and instead provides an explanation that is believed to be more acceptable both socially and personally. The individual fears disapproval by self or others and, in an attempt to deflect that disapproval, chooses to see the contributing facts differently. These facts are distorted and organized so as to support the individual's beliefs or behavior. These explanations are frequently good enough to fool others, but even when they are not, it is impossible to challenge their veracity successfully.

Stages of Development   Freud introduced the concept of infantile sexuality when he described the stages of sexual drive. The stages are not discrete, as they are often portrayed. As development occurs, one stage merges with the next to effect a smooth transition, hardly noticeable.

The *oral* stage occurs at birth and lasts about one and one-half years. The mouth is the center of gratification. The primary sexual organ is the mouth as it seeks to suck, bite, and mouth objects as its source of pleasure.

The *anal* stage follows for the next one and one-half years, and the anus becomes the central area of sexual tension and pleasure. The pleasure emanates from the elimination and retention of feces.

The *phallic* stage begins near the end of the third year of life. The genitals become the primary sexual organ. The penis becomes the principal organ of interest for children of both sexes. The female's primary organ of sexual gratification is the clitoris, which is seen as the analogue of the penis. Impulses of looking at others' organs and exhibiting one's own are normal for children in this stage.

During this stage the *Oedipal* wishes emerge. These are impulses to love and cherish the parent of the opposite sex and to see, to some extent, the parent of the same sex as a rival. The child has fantasies of removing and then replacing the same-sex parent in order to have the opposite-sex parent all to him or herself. The conflict that results from the Oedipal wishes range from the very subtle to the patently obvious, when the same-sex parent feels rejection and competition. Healthy resolution of the conflict occurs when the child gains a realistic perspective of the idealized opposite-sex parent, identifies with the same-sex parent, and establishes a comfortable love relationship with both parents. As the earlier childhood psychosexual stages are being organized at the onset of puberty into adulthood, the *genital phase* begins. It is at this point that one usually acquires the capacity for adult orgasm, which incorporates more of the body than just the penis or clitoris; in fact, the entire genitalia is involved, thus the term *genital phase* is used rather than *phallic stage.*

Neurosis   A neurotic conflict is an unconscious conflict between the id and ego. The id is seeking to discharge its impulse, and the ego is following the superego's command to ward off the discharge of the impulse and block its path to consciousness. The id never stops seeking discharge and the ego, due to the superego's demand, distorts these instructional drives so that they are hardly recognizable. Still the superego is not satisfied and causes the ego to feel guilt, which transforms any possible feelings of satisfaction into feelings of punishment. The ego is constantly expending its energy to keep the drives from gaining access to consciousness and the motor apparatus. This continuous release of energy makes the ego relatively deficient, and the neurotic conflict at last overwhelms the tired and overextended ego and breaks into consciousness and behavior (Greenson, 1967). Thus, neurosis can be described as the breakdown in the functioning of the ego in the face of the relentless id.

Goals   The goal of psychoanalysis is to make the unconscious accessible to consciousness by identifying and overcoming the resistances. While this is, of course, an impossible ideal, Freud stated in 1904 (in "Freud's Psychoanalytic Method") that the aim of treatment is always the realistic recovery of the patient such that it restores "his ability and capacity for enjoyment and an active life" (Freud, 1963b, p. 60). If the cure is not complete, one hopes for at least an improvement in the mental condition of the client as well as a reduction in the severity of the symptoms.

The Therapeutic Process   The task of therapy is to bring into consciousness the unconscious impulses of the id, ego, and superego that are causing the neurotic conflict. Analyzing the ego defenses, understanding the points of developmental fixation, and seeking out clues to the unconscious will guide the process. The therapist must establish a good working alliance with the patient that will promote trust, understanding, and belief in the theoretical stance of the therapist. It must also facilitate cooperation between the "patient's reasonable ego and the analyst's analyzing ego" (Greenson, 1967, p. 46). The patient produces material for the analysis through free association, transference reactions, and resistances.

Free Association   In *free association,* the id is requested to speak while the ego is asked to remain silent (A. Freud, 1966). This is accomplished by promising the id that its uttered impulses will not be hushed nor threatened with guilt. However, it is not promised that the id impulse can be gratified. "Free association has the priority over all other means of producing material in the analytic situation" (Greenson, 1967, p. 32). To have free associations, the patient is asked to relax with eyes closed and verbalize the first thoughts that enter his or her mind, no matter how trivial they may seem. These associations will be centered around either a dream, daydream, wish, thought, or behavior.

Transference Reactions   *Transference reactions* include the patient's "experiencing feelings, drives, attitudes, fantasies and defenses toward a person in the present which are inappropriate to that person and are a repetition, a displacement of reactions originating in regard to significant persons of early childhood" (Greenson, 1967, p. 33). Transferences can be either positive or negative, and patients will likely feel both during different stages of the therapy. *Positive transferences* are the different forms of sexual attraction including liking, loving, and respecting. *Negative transferences* are different forms of aggressiveness, including hate, anger, rage, dislike, or argumentativeness.

Resistances   *Resistances* are all the forces within the client that resist the analysis or that fight against making conscious the unconscious material. The resistances wish to maintain the status quo and are repetitions of all the defense mechanisms the client has used before. The resistances are employed to avoid painful affects, such as guilt, anxiety, and shame.

To succeed in the task, the analyst will use confrontation, classification, interpretation, and working through (Greenson, 1967).

Confrontation is the act of moving the client to face his or her avoidance. It is undertaken only when there is a reasonable expectation that the client will be able to recognize that which he or she is resisting. The good therapist is generally able to bring the client to this awareness without a confrontation and, of course, that is preferable.

Clarification occurs when the therapist brings the phenomenon under discussion into sharper focus. It may consist of clarifying details of material being resisted so that it makes more sense to the client. It will make the resistance more understandable and permit the third step, interpretation, to occur.

Interpretation is the act of making material that is unconscious or preconscious conscious. It is to make conscious the "meaning, source, history, mode or cause of a given psychic event" (Greenson, 1967, p. 39). Often more than a single interpretation is needed. Since the therapist does not want to heighten the client's resistance, the interpretations will likely be small ones, which eventually will be brought together into an integrated insight.

Working through is the process of helping an insight lead to change. It refers to continued work analyzing resistances that prevent an insight from leading to change. It also suggests the broadening and deepening of insights and analysis of resistances already started. In short, working through is the process of assimilating insights into a meaningful composite that can be useful to the client.

Summary and Evaluation

A rather abbreviated summary of psychoanalytic theory has been presented. It was principally Freud's ideas and creativity, mixed with his dedication and ability to persevere in the face of disapproval from his scientific contemporaries, that yielded this theory of personality and treatment of neurosis. Ninety years later, it is still a powerful force in psychology. Most other theories have evolved in some way from Freud's thinking. While the practice of pure psychoanalysis seems to have declined, ego psychology, psychoanalytic psychotherapy, Kohutian self psychology, and various neo-Freudian branches are still very popular.

Freud's thinking yielded a psychology that looked at the functioning of the mind (unconscious, preconscious, conscious); defined the structure of the mind to include the id, ego, and superego; and explained their conflict, which, when inadequately defended, causes neurosis. Further, Freud developed the concepts of infantile sexuality and stages of development. He was able to generate the first techniques for conducting analysis and psychotherapy. He gained access to the unconscious first through hypnosis and later through free association and dream interpretation. Freud's work provided an understanding of the dynamic of transference in the client-therapist relationship. The use of the transference relationship and its interpretation, as well as the interpretation of other unconscious material evolving out of free association and dream interpretation, promotes greater awareness of self by the client. This increased awareness calms the conflict between the id and the ego, thus helping the client to work through the neurosis and seek a happier and healthier life.

Criticism of psychoanalysis suggests that the theory is far too deterministic and too greatly reduces the individual's responsibility for his or her behavior. It seems to suggest that if one suffered shortcomings during childhood, then the resultant effects are beyond one's personal immediate responsibility. In addition, the deterministic view of the individual appears both pessimistic and animalistic in its outlook toward the human impulses. Critics often charge that insight alone does not cause people to change. Insight needs to be accompanied by attempts at behavior change. They charge that without attempts to change one's behavior, psychoanalysis becomes an exercise in intellectualization, yielding self-aware neurotics, but neurotics nonetheless. Finally, criticism is leveled at psychoanalysis for a lack of empirical validation. The only research used is the case study, which yields limited results.

Suggested Readings

Brenner, C.   *An Elementary Textbook of Psychoanalysis.* New York: Anchor Press, 1974.

Freud, A.   *The Ego and the Mechanisms of Defense.* New York: International Universities Press, 1966.

Greenson, R. R.   *The Technique and Practice of Psychoanalysis: Volume I.* New York: International Universities Press, 1953.

Jones, E.   *The Life and Work of Sigmund Freud: Volumes I–III.* New York: Basic Books, 1953.

Kohut, H.   *The Analysis of the Self: A Systematic Approach to the Psychoanalytic Treatment of Narcissistic Personality Disorders.* New York: International Universities Press, 1971.

Adlerian Counseling (Individual Psychology)

Theoretical Beginnings

Alfred Adler's individual psychology is an outgrowth of psychoanalysis. It considers individuals as a whole, thus one part of a person cannot be changed without changing the other parts. There are three interlocking questions that all people must solve and in doing so construct their life goal and style of life.

Alfred Adler (1870–1937), originally an ophthalmologist, then a neurologist, studied with Freud and later broke with him over differences about their views of neuroses, defenses, repression, unconscious impulses, and childhood sexuality. Adler reduced the sexual development of children to a minimum and saw aggression arising from "masculine protest," leaving little to psychoanalysis (Jones, 1955). Adler formulated his individual psychology and became interested in children; in 1922 he established the first child guidance clinic and introduced the concept of family therapy. His writing establishes him as a man who as early as 1927 recognized the inequality that exists between men and women (Adler, 1954).

View of the Individual

Adler believed that human beings live in a world of *meanings*. It is not the reality itself that is so important but, rather, the meaning we give to it. We give meanings to our experiences to make them consistent with our individual "meaning of life." Behavior, attitudes, postures, expressions, mannerisms, ambitions, hopes, goals, character traits are all consistent with the individual's meaning of life. "In all his actions there is an implicit reckoning up of the world and of himself; a verdict, 'I am like this and the universe is like that'; a meaning given to himself and a meaning given to life" (Adler, 1958, p. 4).

Basic Life Questions   Adler's view of persons centers around three main *ties,* or problems, which compose personal reality and therefore must be dealt with. The strong social base of Adler's theory is demonstrated by the social aspect of the ties. These three basic questions are always being asked and must continually be answered. As they are answered, they demonstrate the individual's meaning of life. The first tie is that we are living here on earth with only the resources available, under the restrictions and the opportunities this setting and these resources provide. We must develop in body and mind to sustain our lives and ensure the continuance of life as we know it. This is a problem that all people are challenged by and must seek to answer. In every age, a solution is found, but it is always necessary to strive for improvement. Solving the second problem helps one to find the answer to the first.

The second tie is that individuals belong to the human race and are therefore associated with other humans. Each individual has certain inherent weaknesses and limits that make it impossible to live in isolation. In isolation, we would perish. We need others and the services and products of others to exist. We need to associate with others, adapt to them, and be interested in them. Friendship, social feelings, and a sense of cooperation with others is the solution to this problem. Adler believes that learning to cooperate allowed human beings to develop the concept of division of labor. This concept has permitted us to use the services and skills of all people to increase our security; it has provided an opportunity for all to contribute to the continuance of society. Without division of labor, there would be no cooperation between people, and each person would have to "wrest" a living from the earth with no cooperation in the present and no benefits of cooperation from the past.

The third tie is that human beings are of two sexes. The future of our society depends on our approach to the other sex (not the opposite sex) and our ability to fulfill our sexual roles. The relationship between the two sexes is a problem that requires persons to develop an individual and a common life. Love and marriage problems are included in this third tie.

Adler views the *woman's role* as equal to a man's role in the division of labor and laments men's need to dominate women, seeing domination as destructive for both sexes in their quest for finding a meaning to life (Adler, 1954). Adler sees motherhood as taking the highest place in the division of labor, so high that its true value can never be correctly rewarded. The woman's role is equal to the man's, however, whether she "keeps house" or "works independently."

The three ties define three problems: "how to find an occupation which will enable us to survive under the limitations set by the nature of the earth; how to find a position among our fellows, so that we may cooperate and share the benefits of cooperation; how to accommodate ourselves to the fact that we live in two sexes and that the continuance and furtherance of mankind depends upon our love-life" (Adler, 1958, p. 7). These ties are grouped under three general headings: occupational, social, and sexual. A successful solution to one problem stimulates a successful solution to the next and so on. In fact, to be successful in solving one problem, an individual must be close to solving all three problems. Adler sees the three as parts of a larger single problem: that of preserving and furthering life in our environment.

Development of the Individual   Individual psychology places great emphasis on the woman's role as mother. Her role is to guide the infant's development so that the growing child will be able to respond correctly to the demands of social living. Mothers are the source of social feeling because their role as primary care giver and their prolonged contact with the child shapes the life of the child (Adler, 1963). Adler sees three dangerous areas that result in *mistakes* when children give them incorrect meanings. The first of these involves children "whose organs are imperfect or whose glandular secretions are abnormal" (Adler, 1958, p. 14). An imperfection in one's organs does not necessarily compel a mistaken style of life. Two children with the same malady may give it different meanings and therefore its effects would be quite different. One child might allow the organ inferiority to overcome him, while the other might permit it to stimulate her to develop unusual competencies. It is when people have had to struggle hard against difficulties of health and body that great contributions have emerged as well as a personal sense of the meaning of life. One cannot judge from the body how the mind will develop. Adler believes that children born with imperfect organs or glands are frequently not trained to deal with their imperfections and as a consequence fail to use this "burden" successfully.

The second mistake in the meaning given to life emanates from the pampered child. These children are trained to expect that their wishes must be fulfilled, to believe that they will be granted a position of prominence without working to achieve it, and to expect to receive from others without any giving in return. Pampered children are deprived by the loss of independence since they do not know how to solve problems except by expecting others to do it for them. They have no confidence in themselves. They can only make demands on others, often by appearing to be "loving" when they do not know love or cooperation as human beings. When their expectations are not fulfilled, they feel betrayed and hostile and make attempts at revenge. They feel wronged, as if others are against them. Their meaning of life is to obtain everything they want—including an inflated sense of their own importance.

The third situation that promotes mistakes involves neglected children. These children have never been taught the essence of love and cooperation. They will overrate their difficulties and consequently underrate their ability to solve them. They experience society as cold and distant and expect it to continue thus; therefore they do not learn that they can win affection and esteem by doing things that others find useful. These children feel unwanted and often hated. What is worse, they are unable to recognize those actions that would help them to overcome these feelings, to find love, cooperation, and trust. Cooperation is the best, if not the only, method to avoid the development of neuroses. Therefore, children need to be trained in it and encouraged to cooperate with other children of their age in all sorts of play and work. *Social interest* is the greatest value in the meaning of life.

Birth Order   Adler was the author of the concept of *birth order* in the family constellation as influencing one's style of life. The oldest child was raised as an only child for a specific period of time and during that time was probably spoiled and treated as the center of attention. When the second child appears, the first finds herself with a rival for her parents' love and attention. If, however, the child was adequately prepared for the arrival, adaptation is easier and the child has an opportunity to cooperate in performing tasks for the younger sibling, thus instilling in her a sense of social interest and responsibility. The youngest child has a greater number of human beings in his life from the start. Since he has an older sibling, he is well stimulated and often will work to catch up to or exceed the older sibling. The youngest will act as if he were always in a race, needing to hurry to seek competence and superiority. The first-born will feel competent and secure until the younger sibling threatens to pass her. In effect, each child is viewed differently by society, parents, and peers and therefore is treated somewhat differently. However, it is not just how they are treated, but how they *interpret* that treatment and their situation that affects them.

Primary Life Goal   Individual psychology views the human soul as striving toward a *life goal* that is dynamic and teleological in nature; "The psychic life of man is determined by his goal" (Adler, 1954, p. 24). That psychic life is the way the human spirit uses feelings, thinking, will, and dreams to adapt and respond to its environment. The goal of every human being is formed in the first five years of life and is a striving to be superior or God-like. One's lifestyle is the way one lives to attain one's goals. Therefore, Adler believes that a person must be viewed as whole: A person's lifestyle is determined by his life goals. These goals—unlike the id, ego, and superego—are not conflicting parts of a whole that develop neurotic symptoms when the conflict is not resolved. Any "symptoms," according to individual psychology, are precisely what is called for given the chosen goals. It is only necessary to better understand the goals to see the usefulness of the symptoms.

When a person believes that he made a realistic effort, and still is unable to attain superiority, he then will become discouraged. Being unable to stand the feelings of inferiority that invade him, he will try to behave *as if* he felt superior. He has not changed his goal of being superior to any difficulties that confront him. He has, however, changed his *attempt* to overcome the problem by struggling to solve it to *pretending* he has solved the problem. Still, the feelings of inferiority will accumulate and the resulting self-deception will increase his tension. While we all feel some feelings of inferiority, they usually serve to focus our energy and resources on solving the problem. Adler invented the concept *inferiority complex* to describe the case where our failure discourages us, where we are not properly equipped to solve a problem and instead become convinced that we are unable to master it (Adler, 1954). Therefore, both anger and tears can express the feeling of inferiority.

When a person feels inferior, she will react by seeking the compensating exaggerated feelings of superiority without working to solve the problem. She might use anger and threaten people or use tears or whining to manipulate them, but the result will always be empty since feelings of competence will always evade the individual. This is the neurotic individual who has limited her achievements by limiting her resources. She will keep at a distance the three ties that must be mastered and will work on only those issues she feels able to dominate. This typifies the pathological overstriving for power and dominance of the neurotic. When this occurs ordinary relationships with people will no longer be satisfactory. This exaggerated drive for power and dominance soon forces individuals "into an attitude of resistance against the ordinary tasks and duties of everyday life" (Adler, 1954, p. 70). They begin to attack the lives of others to defend their own. Soon they see themselves fighting the world, and the world fighting them. All of that person's symptoms are just the behaviors needed to attain the desired "feeling of superiority" even though that goal is elusive and attainment is fleeting. Adler refers to these people as discouraged and mistaken rather than sick. To understand them, one needs to understand the meaning of life they seek and the style of life they use to attain their life goals. Trying to alter the symptoms only is foolish and nonproductive.

Goals   Individual psychology is based on the concept of self-determinism. Adler views humans as free, able to make choices and do what they wish. He does not view them as sick or driven by unconscious drives and conflicts, which prevent them from making decisions and putting them into action. Therefore, the goal of therapy is not to remove the symptoms but to increase individuals' self-awareness sufficiently for them to recognize their basic mistakes. This recognition gives them the opportunity to correct their mistakes and change themselves. The focus is on the individual's goals, lifestyle, attitudes, and motivation. It attempts to permit the individual to "discover the mistake made in the whole style of life, in the way the mind has interpreted its experiences, in the meaning it has given to life, and in the actions with which it has answered the impressions received from the body and from the environment" (Adler, 1954, p. 47). While the meaning given to life, the goals pursued, the style of life used to pursue those goals, and the emotional disposition are ordinarily fixed after five years of life, they can be changed later if individuals free themselves from the basic mistakes that occurred in their childhood.

The Therapeutic Process

Essentially, individual psychology has four phases: (1) establishment of a warm, caring, empathic relationship between the client and counselor, (2) exploration of the client's goals, lifestyles, interpretations given to important experiences, and the meaning given to life, (3) interpretation of the client's "mistakes," and (4) reorientation, including re-education, which will permit reconstruction of the individual's goals, lifestyle, and meaning of life and thus enable the client to seek solutions to the three basic ties.

Adler recommended the use of several approaches to understanding the individual's goals and lifestyle. First is the use of the individual's *earliest childhood memory*. This memory will indicate both how long standing is the individual's lifestyle and the circumstances in which this approach to life was developed. It is, in essence, a metaphor for one's lifestyle and view of oneself; it is a starting point in the autobiography one has selected for oneself. Adler believed that one remembers the memories that are consistent with one's lifestyle and emotional disposition and forgets those that are inconsistent. As one changes, so too will the memories (Dreikurs, 1950).

Dreams are another diagnostic tool to be used to understand the client. Like Freud, Adler saw dreams as a window to understand the individual. Adler, however, saw dreams, be they daydreams or sleep dreams, as the "bridge from yesterday to tomorrow" (Adler, 1954, p. 94). Dreams help one to identify the direction in which a person is moving and the conflicts impeding movement. The dream intensifies emotion to illustrate the problem and provide a focus for the rehearsal that attempts to solve the problem. The dream helps the individual decide how to approach the problem, thus providing confidence. In short, it is an attempt at solving one of life's problems and as such indicates the individual's struggle for power and superiority and highlights that person's method of approaching and solving problems.

The third diagnostic approach is to seek to understand the effect on individuals of their position in the family constellation. As described previously, *birth order* plays an important role in the development of the child. Understanding of this phenomenon must be gained through clients' interpretations of their experience. Understanding is gleaned by the counselor, who uses it to help clients understand this influence on them and on their lifestyle.

The counselor will often encourage individuals to talk about their *childhood* to gain a better understanding of their lifestyle and the basic "mistakes" displayed in day-to-day behavior. Special attention is given to social interest and social interactions. The counselor will relate past and present behavior to show the continuity of a client's lifestyle, not to show causal influences.

Interpretation is used by Adlerians to illustrate the client's purpose for specific behaviors. The client is helped to see the continuity between basic "mistakes," lifestyle and the striving for superiority, or against inferiority, to enable her to reconsider and change her basic orientation to life. This *insight* is sought for the client so she can translate it into action. Adlerians stress the need for clients to take action to change not only their life goals but also their style of life. Since one's style of life is the behavior used to attain life's goals, Adlerians encourage and urge their clients to initiate behavioral changes in their life.

Summary and Evaluation

Adler's break with Freud gave rise to individual psychology. Concepts developed by Adler have widespread popularity today but are rarely credited to him. Among them are the "inferiority complex," the concept of birth order and its effects, treatment of couples rather than individuals in marriage counseling, treatment of families as a unit, treatment of children in child guidance clinics, the understanding of dreams as problem-solving rehearsals, and the emphasis on taking action to overcome one's basic "mistakes" and discouragement. Adler viewed the individual as a whole and maintained that no single aspect (symptom) could be changed without changing other interlocking aspects of a person's lifestyle. He believed that ridicule and punishment serve only to strengthen an individual's feeling of inferiority; therefore, he encouraged clients to change their basic life goals.

Criticism of the Adlerian approach comes from the psychoanalytic group. They dispute his differences with Freud, especially the minimal use he makes of the unconscious and the ego defenses. Adler's view of self-determinism—the use of a conscious self-understanding directed toward specified goals—is criticized for being simplistic and superficial. Individual psychology has little following today as a discrete therapeutic approach since Adler's contributions have been absorbed into the mainstream of many other more dominant theories.

Suggested Readings

Adler, A.   *Understanding Human Nature.* New York: Fawcett Premier, 1954.
———.   *What Life Should Mean to You.* New York: Capricorn Books, 1958.
———.   *The Problem Child.* New York: Capricorn Books, 1963.
Dreikurs, R.   *Fundamentals of Adlerian Psychology.* New York: Greenberg, 1950.
———.   *Psychodynamics, Psychotherapy, and Counseling.* The Alfred Adler Institute of Chicago, 1967.

Transactional Analysis

Theoretical Beginnings

Transactional analysis stresses understanding the transactions between people as a way to understand the different personalities that comprise each of us. Each of these personalities behaves in a distinct pattern and at various times is in control of the person. When one of the personalities (ego states) is in rigid control and is unwilling to relinquish that control at appropriate times, it is said to be pathological.

Eric Berne (1910–1970) had been trained in psychoanalysis and analyzed by Erik Erikson. As a psychiatrist in the army, however, he began to work increasingly with groups. Berne developed transactional analysis for the group setting.

Berne founded and edited the *Transactional Analysis Bulletin* in 1961, which in 1971 evolved into the *Transactional Analysis Journal* published by the International Transactional Analysis Association (ITAA) which was formed in 1964 in San Francisco.

Berne had published three books prior to publication of *Games People Play* in 1964. That book, however, propelled him into the limelight by becoming a surprise best seller. This popularity, at first, worried Berne, who feared that it would undermine the seriousness of his work. Rather than detracting from his work, it drew many professionals to read the book who then, having become interested in transactional analysis, took up further study.

View of the Individual

Berne believed that while the kind of person that we become is highly influenced by our parents during infancy and childhood, we are entirely free to alter and change ourselves at any time. A person actively chooses the role played in life and consequently the behavior for that role but has probably long since forgotten making the choice. Since the behavior and style of life were chosen initially, they can be reconsidered and changed, if so desired. People are seen as ultimately responsible for their behavior and their life decisions.

Social Intercourse Transactional analysis views motivation from the perspective of the person's basic needs. The basic needs are stimulus hunger, recognition hunger, and structure hunger. *Stimulus hunger* is a craving for and appreciation of stimuli that are provided by physical intimacy. Touching, feeling, fondling, embracing, and physical closeness, for example, gratify stimulus hunger. The physical strokes of stimulus hunger become sublimated into more subtle and less physical "strokes" and become the object craved in *recognition hunger.* Although one comes to seek symbols of recognition rather than physical contact, individuals never lose their craving for the physical strokes. Recognition hunger seeks any physical (nod) or verbal (greeting) evidence of recognition. Those who withhold exchanging recognition gestures are seen as being rude. A *stroke* is defined as any act that implies recognition of another's presence and as such becomes the basic unit of social action (Berne, 1964). An exchange of strokes between two people is called a *transaction.* A transaction is the basic unit of social intercourse.

"After stimulus hunger and recognition hunger comes structure hunger" (Berne, 1964, p. 16). This is the hunger to structure a person's waking hours and therefore escape boredom by maximizing the number of permissible strokes one can receive. The method used to structure the risk encountered in our waking hours is called *programming.* Five structures will be discussed here: rituals, pastimes, activities, games, and intimacy.

Rituals are the safest type of social interaction since they are prescribed forms of behavior that enable us to get through specific social situations. Examples are introductory behavior (Hello–Goodbye), greetings (How are you? Fine.), weddings (Congratulations, I'm happy for you. Thank you.) or funerals (My sympathies. Thank you.). Rituals ease immediate tension and act as ice breakers, but if the people do not know what to say or do next, the tension mounts. Frequently, rather than face this situation, they avoid it by substituting such behaviors as helping the hostess serve drinks or prepare food.

Pastimes are semiritualistic transactions whose purpose is to structure an interval of time. Rituals often precede and follow the pastime. Pastimes generally occur prior to the start of an activity, such as a meeting or a party, and form the basis for selecting friends since they are organized around such concepts as sex, age, marital status, and cultural or business interests. They minimize the risk—and therefore the excitement—by taking the form of social low-keyed, nonmeaningful talk.

Activities are goal-oriented tasks that deal with the material external reality. The task of the activity dictates the interaction between the people, and its successful completion generally brings the strokes.

Games are a continuing series of complementary transactions that progress to predictable outcomes. They are superficially believable transactions with a concealed motivation that "hook" one of the participants and gratify the other. They are characterized by having both an ulterior motive and a payoff. The game is basically dishonest and misleading and has a dramatic outcome. The payoff is a feeling, generally anger, guilt, or depression. Some are deadly serious games with high stakes, possibly suicide. There are numerous games described in *Games People Play* (1964), some of the most popular are "Kick Me," "Now I've Got You, You Son of a Bitch," and "I'm Only Trying to Help You." Games are taught to us by our parents and as such become family tools for relating to one's parents, grandparents, and children. People pick friends who play the same games. Games fall between pastimes and intimacy since pastimes become boring with repetition but intimacy exposes people too much. Games are a good compromise (Berne, 1964).

Intimacy is "a genuine interlocking of personalities" (Berne, 1961, p. 81). Intimacy requires individual awareness of previous programming of games as well as the spontaneity to liberate oneself from the rut of game playing and to choose to relate as a more honest, direct, and feeling person. It requires the attainment of autonomy from the teachings of the past, specifically the games that we were taught and that our parents were taught.

Life Positions   Anywhere from their first or second to their seventh year of life, people develop a mental attitude that influences all of their transactions. Over time it determines their destiny and frequently that of their children and their children's children. It follows, therefore, that their mental attitude was greatly influenced by their parents' and grandparents' mental attitude. This mental attitude manifests itself in a role, called *life position*, which the person plays. The life position is an attitude about both "I" and "you" being either "O.K." or "not O.K." The four basic life positions are:

1. *I am O.K.; you are O.K.*   This is the healthiest position to hold. Unfortunately, it is infrequently adopted. This position maintains basic acceptance of self and others and trusts their growth to be positive. It must be adopted early in life; it would be very difficult to adopt later because the individual's prior learning will bias the life position.

2. *I am O.K.; you are not O.K.*   This position is adopted by self-centered, arrogant people who believe that in this world they are right and others are wrong. No one else can be trusted. It is a paranoid position that distorts the person's objectivity about both the self and others. Less extreme forms of this position are "do gooders," who see themselves as above others but willing to lower themselves to help them.

3. *I am not O.K.; you are O.K.*   This is the most common life position, especially in those who seek counseling. It is a self-depreciating position that sees the self as inadequate and others as adequate. It is a depressive state, compelling people to be ingratiating and deferential to others to procure strokes. Suicide is popular with people in this position, who feel so bad about themselves in comparison to others that they seek to end their misery.

4. *I am not O.K.; you are not O.K.*   This is the position adopted by children who have been rejected by their parents and think that it was because there was something wrong with them (I am not O.K.). This feeling of personal hopelessness is generalized to everyone. They received no strokes from their parents and none from their contemporaries, therefore no one is O.K. Depression and despair are common manifestations of this position.

Ego States   Berne saw in his clinical work three distinct types of behavior, which he believed emanated from distinct ego states. Ego states are "state of mind and their related patterns of behavior as they occur in nature" (Berne, 1961, p. 11). They are the Parent, Adult, and Child.

The *Parent* comprises those feelings, attitudes, and behaviors that are usually attributed to a parental figure. It is an authoritative voice which is likely to elicit a childlike response from the listener. It is the ego state that resembles the person's parent during the period of his or her childhood. It is our parent's voice inside of us, which can be both prejudicial and nurturing (Berne, 1961). The *Prejudicial Parent* is restrictive, nonrational, and prohibitive. It uses words like *don't, never, disgusting,* and *wrong.* It functions primarily to recall past learnings from one's parents and does not make situational judgments in contemporary settings. The *Nurturing Parent* frequently shows sympathy and then nurturance for another. It is protective and soothing. "The *function* of the Parent is to conserve energy and diminish anxiety by making certain decisions 'automatic' and relatively unshakable" (Berne, 1961, p. 67). The Parent's influence is helpful and causes little if any conflict as long as the decisions it makes happen to be consistent with the current situation and the cultural values in force. Lastly, it also helps the individual effectively parent his or her own children.

The *Adult* ego state performs the functions of gathering, assimilating, and evaluating data about the current reality. It is an autonomous function which then determines feelings, attitudes, and behaviors based on the immediate scene. It is the force that stimulates us to seek pleasure or improve feelings about ourselves. It also helps us to make decisions based on our frustrations and disappointments. It is able to evaluate feelings and make decisions using them and externally gathered data. The Adult has an objective relationship to the person's environment; it is organized, intelligent and, through its reality-testing ability, able to adapt to changes (Berne, 1961). It is not a ruling ego state but serves to keep the Child and Parent contemporary and struggles to maintain a balance. Its involvement with the outside world makes the Adult necessary for survival.

The *Child* is the relic of one's childhood and is composed of three different forms: the Natural Child, the Adapted Child, and the Little Professor. The *Natural Child* is the part of us that is impulsive, highly feeling oriented, spontaneous, and happy. It enjoys life and new discoveries maximally. It is also capable of rebelliousness against the Parent. The *Adapted Child* is the part of the Child that has needed to adapt to the *Parental Influence* through compliance. It is a muted child. The *Little Professor* is the child's attempt to begin to use reason and logic as an adult. It is the spark that ignites evaluation, creativity, and reason.

The Child is the most valuable part of a person's personality (Berne, 1972). Release of the Child is usually frowned on by society; it brings out the Parent in others. Therefore, the Child seeks its expression in sporting events, playing with children, or at parties, especially if alcohol is served because the alcohol inhibits or *decommissions* the Parent.

Transactions   As stated previously, a transaction is an exchange of strokes. Transactions are communications from an ego state in one person to an ego state in another. The *transactional stimulus* is the first statement or behavior that acknowledges the presence of another and solicits the *transactional response,* which acknowledges the recognition. *Simple transactional analysis* involves diagnosing which ego state initiated the transactional stimulus in the first person and which ego state initiated the transactional response. When vectors (see Figure 5.1) are parallel, they are appropriate and follow the natural order of transactions. These are said to be *complementary.* They facilitate further transactions. They may emanate from the same ego states in both people (child ⇌ child) or may speak to a complementary ego state (parent ⇌ child).

In a crossed transaction, the vectors are not parallel and therefore cross. This violates natural human transactions and halts meaningful communication. For example, the stimulus from the Adult is the question, "What caused you to do that?" but, instead of eliciting an Adult response, it is re-

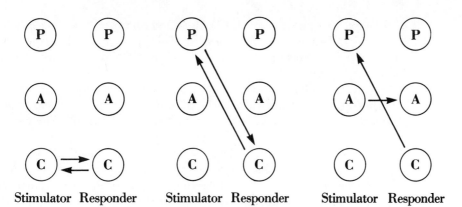

Figure 5.1 Complementary Transactions   **Figure 5.2** Crossed Transactions

sponded to by the Child, "Oh, I don't know, I do everything wrong in your eyes!" (See Figure 5.2.)

Ulterior transactions are those used in playing games. They have double messages and are delivered to two ego states simultaneously. The obvious message is the socially acceptable one. For example, the Adult says, "Let's get away from this city and go for a relaxing picnic to this quiet place I know." The responder's Adult says, "I need that, let's do." However, the stimulus is also covertly speaking from his Child saying, "Let's go to a private place and have sex." Her response, "I need that, let's do," is accepted as the response from her Child. If she did not hear the psychological "hook" and did not intend to respond to his Child message, difficulties will be encountered. (See Figure 5.3.)

The second form of ulterior transaction is one that is used in making a sales pitch. The attempt is to have the stimulator's Adult speak words to the responder's Adult but speak meaning to the responder's Child. The hope is to elicit a response from the Child rather than the Adult. For example, the stimulator's Adult says, "This is our very best product. It's used by those who know a great deal about such things, but it's probably too expensive for your use." The responder's Child says, "No, I'll take it." (See Figure 5.4.)

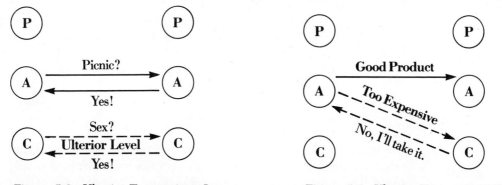

Figure 5.3 Ulterior Transactions: I   **Figure 5.4** Ulterior Transactions: II

Psychopathology   Berne (1961) identified two categories of pathology: structural and functional. *Structural pathology* refers to abnormalities in the psychic structure of the Parent, Adult, and Child. They are exclusion and contamination.

Exclusion is when one ego state predominates and, in doing so, excludes the others. In healthy individuals, shifts from one ego state to another occur appropriately. Boundaries of each ego state are sufficiently flexible to permit the shifting. When the boundaries are too flexible, shifting occurs at the appearance of very small stimuli. The person lacks a sense of stability and identity. When the boundaries are rigid, the amount of stimuli needed to prompt a shift becomes much greater. When the boundaries are so rigid that shifts are not possible, then one constant ego function takes over and excludes the others. The person who is under the control of this Child when others are functioning as Adults and the person who is unable to loosen up at parties because he has excluded his Child are illustrations of this.

Contamination occurs when one ego state intrudes into another. Frequently it is the Adult that is contaminated by the Child or Parent. The contamination inhibits the Adult in its data processing tasks by distorting its data—and thus its view of reality—with prejudices of either the Child or the Parent. The result is inappropriate behavior.

Functional pathology concerns the permeability of ego boundaries and the fluctuation (liability of cathexis) from one ego state to another. This is the state of flexible-to-rigid ego boundaries, which promotes too frequent and rapid transitions between ego states (identity crisis) or makes the shifting sluggish or nonexistent (exclusion).

Goals   Transactional analysis is not satisfied with helping clients to show improvement, it wishes to cure them. It wishes to turn "frogs" into "princes" and "princesses" (Berne, 1972). Berne (1966) enumerated four objectives in counseling that seek the goal of transforming the client into a prince or princess.

1. Help the client to identify and decontaminate any ego state that has been distorted.
2. Help the client to be able to use all ego states when appropriate. This means to either build effective ego boundaries or make rigid boundaries more flexible.
3. Help the client free the Adult to enable its full use to reason and to grow productively.
4. Help the client to evaluate and alter an inappropriate life position and adopt "I am O.K.; you are O.K."

Clients are asked to state their individual goals for counseling, and contracts are used liberally to identify these goals in specific and measurable terms. The contracts spell out the goal to be achieved, the roles of the client and counselor, and the means for achieving these goals.

The Therapeutic Process While transactional analysis was generated to work with people in groups, it is also effective in individual counseling. The client is taught the theory through readings, workshops, and instruction. Knowledge of the theory and language is a necessary prerequisite.

Stages of Counseling Berne identified five stages to the counseling.

1. *Structural Analysis.* This is the first step of counseling. It helps clients to identify their ego states and to recognize the operation of each state. Work will deal with development of boundaries, contamination, and stabilization so that the Adult can take its rightful place of maintaining control. Treatment may not need to go beyond this first step if the ego is relatively well developed and the Child and Parent are able to respond to the Adult and yet be distinct from it.

2. *Transactional Analysis.* The second step of counseling is to understand the transactions one makes with others. Crossed, complementary, and ulterior transactions are taught by analyzing the client's transactions and those of the group members, if counseling is being conducted in a group. This is a prerequisite for the third step.

3. *Game Analysis.* Engagements of pastimes and games are analyzed. The counselor must be able to help the client to determine the payoff gained from pastimes and games. Games are emphasized since they are dishonest transactions and yield no lasting or profitable gain. The objective is to enable the client to stop playing games and to take the appropriate risks to seek intimacy.

4. *Script Analysis. Scripts* are a series of games that are organized into a recurring theme, such as a series of games which make the subject a "victim" and consequently helpless. They are dictated by one's life position. Unless interrupted, scripts will last a lifetime and be passed on to one's children. A script analysis serves to identify one's script, to recognize its theme and its relationship to the chosen life position. This is a difficult step since it requires clients to see their mistakes. It can cause depression.

5. *Relationship Analysis.* This is the final step in counseling and is used sparingly and judiciously since clients may find it too intrusive. It is the analysis of the client's marital and peer relationships. It is often used as "homework" to help the client to distinguish and clarify ego states and their transactions.

Kinds of Counseling Responses Berne (1966) identified eight categories of therapeutic interventions in transactional analysis. They are the following:

1. *Interrogation.* This is questioning that is directed to the client's Adult and is pressed until the counselor gets an Adult response. It can be a very

confrontative technique and must be used carefully. It should not be overused or the client will end up giving a historical dialogue.

2. *Specification.* When the Adult of the counselor and the Adult of the client identify the location of the ego state that initiated a transaction, specification is said to have occurred. The counselor may need to reiterate and remind the client of this understanding to prevent her denial of it later and to enable her to use it in the future.

3. *Confrontation.* This is used to point out inconsistencies in the client's statements and behavior. It uses previously specified understandings to help the client who is unable to recognize the inconsistencies or who is trying to "cop out" and not accept responsibility.

4. *Explanation.* This is an Adult-to-Adult explanation of some aspect of transactional analysis. It is a teaching mechanism intended to help the client understand something that is not clear. It requires a listening Adult if it is to be productive.

5. *Illustration.* This is an anecdote that serves to illustrate a point. It may follow a confrontation and give a humorous touch to the transaction. Thus the humor appeals to the client's Child, while the point of the illustration appeals to the Adult.

6. *Confirmation.* When previous confrontations and illustrations help the client to remove a specific type of transaction, but that behavior recurs later, the counselor points this out to the client. This is a confirmation and should be used only when the client has an effective Adult that can successfully fight off the recriminations of the Parent or exploitation of the therapist by the Child.

7. *Interpretation.* This is the process of interpreting to the Child the reasons for his behavior using psychoanalytic procedures. It deals with the pathology of the Child. The counselor decodes the client's pathology, rectifies distortions, and helps him to be less reactive to it. A functional Adult is necessary for this process (Berne, 1966).

8. *Crystallization.* This is another Adult-to-Adult statement that crystallizes the client's awareness that, if she chooses, she may give up playing games. The Child and Parent need to be prepared since their cooperation with the Adult is mandatory. The client needs to make the final decision and as such cannot be hurried.

With crystallization, transactional analysis is completed. The use of interpretation is not essential for termination. Now the Adult should be firmly established as the executive. It will not always be the manifested ego state, but it will be able to reason and to decide which ego state will dominate at any particular time.

Summary and Evaluation   Transactional analysis was developed by Eric Berne for use primarily in group treatment. It posits three types of need: stimulus hunger, recognition hunger, and structure hunger. In each of these needs, people are seeking some sign of recognition, called strokes, and thus the hunger becomes the motivation to seek strokes. People develop life positions that emphasize their basic attitudes toward themselves and others. The healthy life position is "I am O.K.; you are O.K." People are composed of three ego states, namely the Parent, Adult, and Child. These ego states talk to ego states in other people. When that communication is crossed or indirect, problems arise and often elicit unhealthy strokes. Psychopathology occurs when boundaries between the ego states are either too flexible or too rigid. The counselor helps the client to clarify and keep distinct the three ego states while helping the Adult to function as the executive without being contaminated by the Child and Parent.

Berne is said to have contributed to the counseling field by developing a theory that gives the individual responsibility for his or her behavior. As a self-deterministic theory, it allows the individual to conceptualize himself and his interactions and alter them quickly. The concepts are readily understandable by the public and thus are widely read and used. Transactional analysis provides simple metaphors of behavior in the form of games, which are easily recognized and applied to oneself. Unlike the jargon of psychoanalysis, the language in transactional analysis is understandable and lends itself to use by people who are unsophisticated in psychology. Finally transactional analysis is goal directed and as such can be applied to specific client problems.

Those who criticize the theory believe that it is too simplistic and consequently too superficial. Some professionals have lost respect for it because of its mass popularity. Because of that popularity, the theory is often used by people who do not fully understand it and who use it to intellectualize about their problems and hide behind labels.

Suggested Readings   Berne, E. *Transactional Analysis in Psychotherapy.* New York: Ballantine Books, 1961.
———. *Games People Play.* New York: Grove Press, 1964.
———. *Principles of Group Treatment.* New York: Oxford University Press, 1966.
———. *What Do You Say After You Say Hello?* New York: Bantam, 1972.
Harris, T. A. *I'm OK—You're OK.* New York: Harper & Row, 1969.

Client-Centered Therapy

Theoretical Beginnings   The emphasis in client-centered therapy is on providing facilitative conditions that allow the client the freedom and safety necessary for growth.

Client-centered therapy and Carl Rogers (1902–   ) are almost synonymous. Since 1942, when his book *Counseling and Psychotherapy* was first published, client-centered therapy has been continuously developed as an approach for human growth and change. Rogers's writings are often said to reflect his early upbringing on a farm and the training he received at Union Theological Seminary before he transferred to Columbia. While in his earlier writings he focused on individual therapy, he has displayed great interest in group therapy during the past two decades. Rogers's great impact on therapeutic practice over the past thirty years very much reflects his prolific writing during those years and the attractiveness to clinicians and the lay public of his philosophical approach. While Rogers is often appreciated for his philosophical contributions, he has also made significant contributions to counseling research. He must be seen, then, not only as a practitioner but also as a scientist.

View of the Individual

Rogers's therapy can be divided into three concepts, even though each concept cannot be accurately assessed independent of the other two. The *organism* is composed of all that individuals are: their physical being, their thoughts, and their behavior. The "organism is at all times a total organized system in which alteration of any part may produce changes in any other part" (Rogers, 1951, p. 487). Individuals, then, react to the total *perceptual field*, which is their reality. Any event, in and of itself, is not crucial. What is important is the perception of the event, making reality individualistic and subjective.

Most client-centered therapists subscribe to a view of the individual based on phenomenological psychology, that is, that the self elicits the perceptual field and subsequent behavior. Some question can be raised, then, about the client's ability to deal with reality. The question becomes, "Is there an objective reality distinct from the individual's view of it." Hansen et al. (1977) state:

> While examining Rogers' position on the structure of personality, we should keep in mind his conception of reality. Reality is what is perceived as reality by the individual. It makes little difference what actually happens in an event; what is important is the individual's perception of the experience. In this view, the person chooses a response to the event based on his or her perception of it, not the actual event. Hence, we are not reactive beings, but we respond to situational events by an active thought process. We are not passive in the situation, but active agents. (p. 117)

As a person interacts with the environment in his or her perceptual field, the *self-concept* starts developing—that is, the "I" and "me" of the personality. Perception of experience is influenced by a need for positive regard, which Rogers (1959) states is a universal, pervasive, and persistent need in human beings. Since this need for positive regard can be satisfied only by others, the self-concept is a learned sense of self and is based on individuals' perception of the regard they have received from outside the self. Parents and other significant people impose conditions of worth that must be met before they give their children positive regard. These conditions become an integral part of the children's self-regard system. Conflict, then, arises when individuals must choose between the need for positive regard and an organism need that is not in accord with significant others' conditions of worth. In such a situation, individuals are likely to perceive organism needs as bad—that is, in opposition to their being a good person.

Any experience that is not consistent with the self-concept is seen as a threat because it would disturb the self-concept by being contrary to the conditions of worth that one has incorporated. As a consequence one limits one's "reality" and awareness by assimilating only those experiences that are consistent with prescribed conditions of worth. Anxiety or tension arises from the discrepancy that exists between the experiencing self and the conceptualization of self when an event is contrary to the self-concept. Disintegration of personality, conflict, and anxiety accompany each other. Mental health, or adjustment, occurs when one is able to incorporate without distortion the experiences of daily living and one's own reactions to those occurrences. The self-concept then becomes flexible, more accepting of what is happening, more in touch with reality.

The client-centered approach conceptualizes the individual as motivated in positive directions; that is, the potential for self-actualization is present in all people. Individuals are rational and have the ability, if resources are mobilized, to control their own destiny. If the proper environment is created, individuals will "flower and grow." Contrary to some other theorists, the client-centered counselor sees people as good or—at the very least—neutral.

Goals The basic goal for the client is to become more fully functioning. Some of the changes that can be expected with client-centered counseling are that clients become:

a. more realistic in their self-perceptions,
b. more confident and self-directing,
c. more positively valued by themselves,
d. less likely to repress aspects of their experiences,
e. more mature, socialized, and adaptive in their behavior,
f. less upset by stress and quicker to recover from it,
g. more like the healthy integrated well-functioning person in their personality structures. (Rogers, 1961, p. 375)

The counselor's goal is to recognize and confront the incongruency between the client's experiences and self-concept. The counselor should encourage clients to become open and to feel safe enough to drop all defenses. Rigidities relax and clients are able to deal more effectively with the ambiguities of their existence. (Living comfortably with ambiguity is a counselor-modeled characteristic that is also important during this process.) As the process develops, decisions are made and insights are generated that allow clients to learn to trust themselves more. The psychological set generated by clients feeling better about themselves enhances the accomplishment of the specific therapeutic goals established for each client.

In an interesting new look at an earlier book, Boy and Pine (1982) discuss two phases of a "refined" client-centered approach. They identify the first-phase objectives as follows:

1. Has achieved an emotional catharsis and is no longer overwhelmed by incapacitating feelings.
2. Is more open and honest in assessing the self and the attitudes and behaviors that constitute the self.
3. Shows a movement from emotionally-based communication to rationally-based communication.
4. Is motivated and willing to energize the self toward solving or resolving a problem. (p. 20)

Phase two is seen as the point when the needs of the client are paramount. During phase two, specific client-defined goals are approached with some degree of therapeutic flexibility.

The Therapeutic Process   The major thrust for the client-centered counselor is to create the proper relationship, climate, and conditions for enhancing the process of therapeutic growth. These elements per se will be sufficient to propel a client toward behavior change. Snyder (1982) reflects this idea in the following statement:

From a phenomenological perspective, the counselor or therapist does not attempt to collect data, but rather desires to establish in an explicit manner the connectedness that is central to the counselor or therapist and client who are meeting in the world. In knowing the client, the counselor or therapist desires to enhance his or her awareness of the relation between him or herself and the client and the influence each has on the other. (p. 366)

Client-centered counseling is an if-then proposition. If certain conditions are present, then the client will become more self-actualized, which is the inherent tendency of the organism—to develop all its capacities in ways that serve to maintain or enhance itself (Rogers, 1959, p. 196). This striving for self-actualization is the primary motivational force in the individual.

Rogers (1961) states the if-then propositions as follows:

If I [the counselor] can create a relationship characterized on my part:

by a genuineness and transparency, in which I am my real feelings;

by a warm acceptance of and prizing of the person as a separate individual;

by a sensitive ability to see his world and himself as he sees them;

Then the other individual in the relationship:

will experience and understand aspects of himself which previously he has repressed;

will find himself becoming better integrated, more able to function effectively;

will become more similar to the person he would like to be;

will become more self-directing and self-confident;

will become more of a person, more unique and more self-expressive;

will be more understanding, more acceptant of others;

will be able to cope with problems of life more adequately and more comfortably. (pp. 37–38)

The conditions necessary for growth, which clients should perceive in the therapeutic relationship, are unconditional positive regard, genuineness or congruence, and empathic understanding. Unconditional positive regard from the counselor is crucial to the helping relationship in view of the fact that clients' present feelings of worth are based on certain conditions. The counselor offers positive regard with no strings attached and no conditional clauses. This attitude, a caring acceptance of clients' individuality, is derived from the belief that clients will discover within themselves the necessary resources for their growth. The "counselor chooses to act consistently upon the hypothesis that the individual has a sufficient capacity to deal constructively with all those aspects of his life which can potentially come into conscious awareness" (Rogers, 1951, p. 24). Eventually clients come to the understanding that they are able to take charge of their own lives and that the counselor's belief in them is well founded.

Genuineness, or congruence, is the ability of counselors to be aware of their own inner experiences and to allow them to be apparent in the helping relationship. Verbal and nonverbal communication are in accord, making counselors transparent to clients as they interact. This transparency can help to reduce some of the risk of sharing themselves with others.

The conditions just described set the stage for the main event—empathic understanding. This is the crux of client-centered therapy and of the concept for which this approach was named. Counselors who immerse themselves in their clients' experience walk a mile in the other's shoes, so to speak. The counselors become part of their clients' world, seeing it through their eyes. Counselors' interventions reflect not only clients' explicit feelings but also those that are implicit and must be brought into the area of clients' awareness—especially those feelings that have not been verbalized because they are inconsistent with clients' self-concepts. Furthermore, clients should receive support, understanding, and acceptance of their newly emerging self-concept.

In summary, if the three therapeutic conditions are met, one would expect several things to occur in therapy. First, the client will explore feelings and attitudes at deeper levels. Consequently, new meanings and understandings previously not developed will be achieved. The freedom to explore felt by the client (because of the safety of the therapeutic environment) allows for the consideration of material that at other times, in other places, and with other people may have been too threatening. Further, acceptance by the counselor encourages greater prizing by clients of themselves. Clients develop more self-acceptance. For some clients, this may be one of the few times that they will feel cared for in ways that have "no strings attached." The openness and realness of the counselor will stimulate client growth; that is, the client will become more open and real. This realness and openness encourages the client to experience in the "here and now." There is more immediacy of experiencing, greater concreteness of expression, and less vagueness and "aloofness." The client will become more open to the environment, leading to greater flexibility and less rigidity in perceptions. The client-centered counselor would find these changes to be characteristic of the therapeutic process.

The important question for Rogers, then, is how to create the helping relationship. Technique is not the important issue in client-centered counseling; the primary cause of client change and growth is the therapeutic relationship itself. This relationship is not limited to professionals but can exist in other circumstances: "I have long had the strong conviction—some might say it was an obsession—that the therapeutic relationship is only a special instance of interpersonal relationships in general, and that the same lawfulness governs all such relationships" (Rogers, 1961, p. 39). Rogers has made a major contribution to counseling by bringing to the fore and enumerating those basic conditions necessary to the counseling process regardless of the technique utilized.

Transference and countertransference are seen as labels that deny the importance of the I-thou relationship between client and counselor. They are not therapeutic issues for the client-centered counselor as they might be for counselors of other schools.

Some early research studies by Rogers and Dymond (1954), Hogan (1948), and Raskin (1949) indicate that as a counseling relationship progresses, there is a decrease in the amount of client defensiveness, an increase in congruence between the self and experience, and a tendency for clients to see themselves as the locus of evaluation. Studies by Truax and Carkhuff (1967) and Carkhuff and Berenson (1967) show that, given unconditional positive regard, genuineness or congruence, and empathic understanding, clients will move into self-exploration, which will lead to positive changes. Not only are these conditions factors in client growth, but Truax (1963) and Truax and Carkhuff (1965) have found the levels of these conditions to be significant. These and other studies led to the development of scales to measure the requisite conditions (Truax, 1961, 1962a, 1962b; Carkhuff, 1967). This research was the basis for the elaboration of Rogerian concepts into what is known as the "Carkhuff Model," published in 1969 in *Helping and Human Relations: A Primer for Lay and Professional Helpers.* Robert Carkhuff divided the counseling process into two parts: the initial, or facilitating, stage and the action stage. The first stage is essentially Rogerian in that it establishes a working relationship based on empathy, respect, concreteness, and genuineness. The final, or action, stage requires the counselor to confront the client with discrepancies that have been noted, to get the client involved in what is going on in the counseling relationship at that point in time, and to help the client move toward action. This final stage, then, has extended the Rogerian concept.

Several recent studies reflect an interest in client cognitive characteristics and preference for a particular theoretical approach to therapy as well as in the behavior of the client-centered therapist during counseling. Neufeldt (1978) noted that subjects choosing an insight counselor had a significantly higher capacity for formal thought than subjects choosing the behavioral counselor. The behavioral counselor's statements were rated as more personal, pleasing, clear, and superficial on a semantic differential, and the behavioral counseling experience was seen as more positive and practical. The insight counseling experience was seen as relatively more complex.

Hill et al. (1979) compared the verbal responses of Rogers, Perls (Gestalt counseling), and Ellis as they counsel the same female client. They concluded that Rogers avoided evaluation, interpretation, probing questions, reassurance, criticism, praise, or description, while generally encouraging, reflecting, and restating. Meara et al. (1979), in an analysis of the same interviews, compared the stylistic complexity of each therapist. It was expected that Rogers would take a passive approach with brief, infrequent, and stylistically simple responses. In general, it was found that the client's interaction with Rogers was less complex than with Ellis but more complex than with Perls. Rogers, then, was more complex than expected. The client stated that she was most comfortable with Rogers, that he made her feel good about herself, but that she would have difficulty showing anger with him. The client thought Rogers would be good for a person who was just starting in counseling. She liked Rogers and he made her deal with her "feeling" self. This same client in another study by Meara (1981) was found to use more "doing" verbs with Rogers than with the other two counselors. There was then "consistency between Rogers' stated policies for the interview, notably, to understand the client's inner world. And so in the interview, he talks more often about what things are like for her—her states—and what she is feeling" (p. 117). It is suggested at least from these few studies that Rogers's behavior in therapy reflects his conceptual approach.

Summary and Evaluation

The client-centered approach reflects a sincere commitment to the self-actualization process. In many ways it is closely related to the existential approach to counseling, which will be discussed next in this chapter. Much emphasis is placed on the I-thou relationship of counselor and client—a relationship that, if founded on certain conditions, may well be sufficient to encourage client change. At the very least these conditions are prerequisite to the implementation of other therapeutic interventions.

The major contributions of client-centered therapy have been the identification of the necessary therapeutic characteristics of the counselor during the counseling process and development of a philosophy that conceptualizes the individual in a positive, growth-oriented context. It clearly places responsibility for growth with the client. The counseling relationship is seen as a facilitative one between counselor and client that conveys respect, warmth, and caring. A weakness, if we can call it that, is the degree to which it can be practiced by counselors. It takes a "special" person to be as fully accepting and as effective a listener as Carl Rogers is. Further, it may well be effective with high-initiative clients; clients who have little initiative may require a more active counselor.

A major difficulty with the client-centered approach, as suggested earlier, is with individuals whose perceptions are significantly different from the perceptions of others and who, because of those distortions, continuously engage in self-defeating behaviors that may become destructive of themselves or significant others. What responsibility does the counselor have in such instances to confront the client with such observations? According to some critics of client-centered therapy, the establishment of the therapeutic relationship will be insufficient to change inaccurate perceptions outside the therapy situation. In their view, responsive counselor behaviors could in certain circumstances reinforce those distorted perceptions. This clearly implies that counselors must recognize and confront the incongruency in the client between the experience and the self-concept.

Suggested Readings
Boy, A. V., and G. J. Pine. *Client-Centered Counseling: A Renewal*. Boston: Allyn and Bacon, 1982.
Hart, J., and T. Tomlinson. *New Directions in Client-Centered Therapy*. Boston: Houghton Mifflin, 1970.
Rogers, C. R. *Counseling and Psychotherapy*. Boston: Houghton Mifflin, 1942.
———. *Client-Centered Therapy*. Boston: Houghton Mifflin, 1951.
———. *On Becoming a Person*. Boston: Houghton Mifflin, 1961.

Existential Counseling

Theoretical Beginnings
Individual existence is the central concern in existential counseling. Existential counseling has a rich European philosophical heritage. The contributions of the European existentialists Heidegger, Kierkegaard, Sartre, and Jaspers are found in the therapeutic formulations of May, van Kaam, Frankl, Jourard, and Moustakas. *Existential psychotherapy* is the term applied to all the various conceptualizations of this approach. It seems to signify that there is some agreement among them, when in fact there is a great deal of diversity. As far back as 1964, Friedman recognized this in his statement that "Existentialism is not a philosophy but a mood embracing a number of disparate philosophies, the differences between which are more basic than the temper which unites them" (p. 104). That mood has become somewhat more explicit since 1964; that is, there has been an attempt to identify some potential specificity of therapeutic applications based on philosophical elements common to the various existential approaches.

Two individuals in particular have greatly influenced existential philosophy and therapy. The first was Søren Kierkegaard (1813–1855), born in Copenhagen, who proposed that an individual "scrutinize his or her own life before entering into the lives of others. In stressing the concepts of individuality, freedom, responsibility, honesty, and commitment, Kierkegaard offers a dynamic basis for beginning and maintaining the counseling relationship and a provocative stimulus to the furthering of counseling theory" (Dopson and Gade, 1981, p. 148). Influenced by the European existentialists, Rollo May provides the best insights of an American-born writer into existential thought. May was a counselor at Michigan State College (1934), now Michigan State University, before he entered Union Theological Seminary. He received a Ph.D. in psychology from Columbia University in 1949. His studies in psychiatry and psychology helped further the application and interpretation of existentialism to therapy.

View of the Individual   ***Being and Choosing***   Existence and being are key philosophical considerations. The notion of "being-in-the-world" evolves into a discussion of choice, freedom, and responsibility. Frankl (1967) has this to say about "being-in-the-world":

> analysis would reveal that there is no such thing as cognition outside the polar field of tension between object and subject. To understand the phrase . . . properly, one must recognize that being human means being engaged and entangled in a situation, and confronted with a world whose objectivity and reality is in no way detracted from by the subjectivity of that "being" who is in the world. (p. 138)

Further, though, is the concept of "transcendence"; for some this takes on religious overtones (God), but in broader perspective it refers to the search beyond human nature. While there may be some limitations from outside environmental influences or from the past, individuals are blessed with freedom and an ability to make choices at all levels of existence. Although choices are based on the past, present, and future, people can transcend any "limiting" influences. Making decisions necessitates accepting responsibility for the actions that follow. The great emphasis placed on choice-making is reflected in the statement by Frankl (1967) that "I prefer to live in a world in which man has the right to make choices, even if they are wrong choices, rather than a world in which no choice at all is left to him" (p. 13).

The importance of being-in-the-world is reflected in the following statement by van Kaam (1969):

> To be man is thus fundamentally and essentially to exist, and to exist means to-be-in-the-world. The subject which is man simply does not happen without being involved in the world; it presents itself only in relation to the world. The subject "I", the self that I am, cannot occur other than as the source of activity which is in some way oriented to the world as it appears. The self cannot be conceived, affirmed, experienced, or imagined without the world or some aspect of the world to which the self is directed or in which it is involved. Expressions such as I think, I do, I feel, I imagine, I anticipate, I dream, and I own all imply a being-in-the-world, always presuppose something which is more than the isolated self alone. (p. 21)

The being-in-the-world for each person is accompanied by "becoming" dimensions. People are always in the process of change or "becoming" and moving toward actualization of potential.

Individuals are not viewed simply as rational beings. In fact, Kierkegaard would object to any minimization of the role of emotions in order to emphasize the place of reason. He would conceive the person "in balance," with both "passion" and "intellect" shaping decisions and actions. Kierkegaard would not disavow order in the world. Reality is systematic and comprehensive. While not everything may be understood, life's meaning and self-awareness are discovered through reflection. The search for meaning is a lifelong one.

Existential Anxiety and Guilt   Existential anxiety arises from the contemplation of death or "nothingness." Other terms such as *nonbeing* or *nonexistence* are used, but a basic truth for all individuals is this confrontation with death; a truth that presents anxiety. Everyone has a choice to contemplate or ignore existential anxiety.

Existential guilt occurs when persons feel that they have not become what they might have become. Potential has not been achieved; actualization has been limited. Existential "neurosis" evolves from "existential anxiety and guilt." Neurosis emanates from the anxiety of a lonely, ambiguous, meaningless life that is manageable only through neurotic, self-defeating ways.

Goals   The goal for existential counseling is to help clients find purpose or meaning in life. To this end the client makes choices and assumes responsibility for his or her existence. Cunningham and Peters (1973) summarize the goals of existential therapies:

1. To make the client more aware of his existence.
2. To elucidate the client's uniqueness.
3. To foster freedom in the client.
4. To improve the client's encounters with others.
5. To foster responsibility on the part of the client.
6. To help the client establish his will to meaning. (p. 71)

The client "is," comes to sense his or her own uniqueness, and assumes responsibility for life's choices during the process of therapy.

The Therapeutic Process   There are few specific counseling "techniques" or "strategies" associated with existential counseling. The process is one of attempting to help clients "experience," to become more aware of self and the world around them. "Authenticity" or being real in-the-moment is an important consideration for both client and counselor, but again this is not a technique but an "experiencing."

Mutual Experience of Counselor and Client   The existential counselor is one who listens, understands, and through mutually experiencing the moment with the client, helps the client to a greater understanding of his or her life. The behavior of counselors can vary considerably during the counseling interview simply because client and counselor differ at any moment. There are, however, some identifiable philosophical characteristics common to existential counselors. There is an emphasis on

1. the person-to-person approach
2. mutuality in the counselor-client relationship
3. responsibility for both the client and counselor to assume
4. a growth orientation
5. dealing with client as a whole person
6. client choice and decisionmaking; the absence of which implies non-being
7. the counselor serving as a model in life-style toward the achievement of human potential
8. increasing client freedom in the search for meaning
9. reduction of client dependence
10. a desire for authentic being. (Buhler and Allen, 1972, pp. 90–91)

Within the freedom of the therapeutic environment, the client is able to "experience" subjectively and honestly and to move toward actualization of potential. Existential anxiety and guilt are legitimate concerns for the client and can be a starting point for fuller self-understanding. The emphasis is on removing the psychological boundaries that restrict one's personal freedom and growth.

The counselor tries to understand the client's unique world and see how the client experiences within it. But Beck (1963) suggests that "existential analysis involves more than empathy. It is a system calling for a reconstruction of and a 'living along with' the client which exceeds the bounds of merely trying to understand one's client" (pp. 105–106). Counseling becomes a "we" experience—that is, counselor and client mutually experience during the session. The counselor then is not only an observer but also a participant.

Causal relationships are not of particular concern to the existential counselor, and issues of transference, countertransference, and personality defense and distortion mechanisms are only important in an existential (in-the-moment experiencing) sense. In other words, the client's defense mechanisms are attended to by the counselor only as they affect the client's ability to experience, not as a categorization of the client's past or future behavior. Freedom, meaning, spirituality, and responsibility are far more basic issues. Frankl (1967a) says, "Approaching human beings merely in terms of techniques necessarily implies manipulating them. Approaching them merely in terms of dynamics implies reifying them, making human beings into mere things. And these human beings immediately feel and notice the manipulative quality . . ." (p. 139). Sartre (1953) puts it poignantly: "Nor is man to be *used* by means of his own manipulation of himself as a psychological machine to be adjusted." Concepts of adjustment and normality, therefore, would be viewed askance as therapeutic ends.

Confrontation of Basic Life Issues   The client is asked to confront the basic philosophical issues of living; issues which, if avoided, lead to an existential crisis or neurosis. Certain issues are fundamental to the human condition, among them, dependence versus independence, rational versus irrational, and freedom versus determinism. The resolution of these dilemmas helps establish purpose and meaning in life. Existential counseling then identifies and examines "critical inner realities." The crucial issues are despair, anxiety, guilt, death, and nothingness. These crises, while they may appear to be abstract, can be confronted in human experience.

The abstract nature of this venture is reflected in some ways by the aspect of "spirituality" in existentialism, which suggests that it is necessary to move beyond the psychological plane and on to a spiritual—not necessarily religious—plane. Techniques then will not be helpful; perhaps the counselor's best attribute may be a healthy "philosophy of life." On the other hand, Dopson and Gade (1981) are more explicit as to the potential ramifications of Kierkegaard's philosophy:

The ethical stage of dialectical thought is particularly useful to counseling practice and involves the use of vigorous self-confrontation to attack false self-images and create an emergent self-validating and self-reliant person. Kierkegaard's concepts are particularly useful in counseling to reduce client anxiety and establish commitment to the therapeutic change. (p. 152)

Logotherapy   Frankl's logotherapy is an example of the existentialists' emphasis on responsibility, meaning, and purpose within the context of the I-thou relationship. Individuals strive for purpose but when their "will to meaning" is frustrated, they develop a sense of "meaninglessness" in the "void." This existential "void" creates neurosis. It is obvious to Frankl that a counselor cannot "prescribe" meaning, but the counselor can help the client find purpose in life. Interestingly, logotherapy is an existential approach with two definable techniques: paradoxical intention and dereflection. The first, paradoxical intention, asks that the client "intend" that which he or she anticipates with fear. During counseling the client experiences whatever has been frightening. This technique may not only involve a reversal of attitude, but the use of it within a humorous context. It is thought that this process of distancing from the attitude reduces the neurosis. It may reflect the practical wisdom of "learning to laugh at oneself." Dereflection asks the client to disregard the difficulty or ignore the neurosis and concentrate or focus on something different. The new focus is away from self. This technique is used to de-emphasize excessive self-observation or self-attention.

Summary and Evaluation Since there are few techniques of existential counseling, there is a paucity of research directly associated with the approach. The client-centered research, as well as the great many studies available on the counseling relationship—on authenticity in particular—would have specific relevance for existential counseling. (See Chapters 8–10.)

We would view existential counseling or psychotherapy more appropriately as a philosophy of counseling rather than as a particular "method" of counseling. Basic philosophical issues involve the following:

1. Individuals are not to be "used," manipulated, or adjusted.
2. Freedom and responsibility are fundamental counseling concerns.
3. Living and the making of choices cannot be separated; we are our choices.
4. Being-in-the-world is existence. Individuals create themselves and one cannot go beyond "being."
5. The influences of environment as well as those of the past can be transcended.
6. Existential counseling is flexible and changes moment-to-moment. It is "being" with a client.

Counseling becomes an existential inquiry that helps individuals make choices for which they will assume responsibility. Existentialism may be best conceived, perhaps, as philosophy applied in a clinical setting.

The contributions of existential counseling clearly lie in the philosophical arena. Issues that deal with life's meaning and values are central to all therapeutic encounters. Notions on "authentic" being mesh nicely with concepts presented by other affectively oriented theories. Criticism of existential counseling might focus on (1) the diverse nature of its contributors, (2) the lack of specific, systematic therapeutic approaches, and (3) the insufficient research base of support.

Suggested Readings Frankl, V. E. *Psychotherapy and Existentialism: Selected Papers on Logotherapy.* New York: Simon & Schuster, 1967.
May, R. *Man's Search for Himself.* New York: New American Library, 1953.
———. *Existential Psychology.* New York: Random House, 1961.
Sartre, J. P. *Existential Psychoanalysis.* Chicago: Gateway, 1953.
van Kaam, A. *Existential Foundations of Psychology.* New York: Doubleday, 1969.

Gestalt Counseling

Theoretical Beginnings Gestalt counseling focuses on awareness of the whole person. The introduction of Gestalt psychology at the turn of the century laid the groundwork for Gestalt counseling approaches that are at present most clearly identified with Fritz Perls (1894–1970). Gestalt psychology was introduced in response to experimental psychology with its emphasis on component elements of existence, that is, on the parts rather than the whole. Complex human functioning was seen as nothing more than simple, stable personality elements joined in various combinations at different moments. The Gestalt view was that the whole is more than just the summation of its parts.

Gestalt psychology, initially proposed by Christian von Ehrenfels, was supported by the experimental work of Max Wertheimer, Kurt Koffka, and Wolfgang Kohler. A variety of the perceptual studies they generated continue to challenge the atomistic approaches to psychology. Wertheimer in particular played an important role in the future development of Gestalt psychology when he generated the "law of membership character": Elements of a given form or event are definable only in terms of their relationships within that event. Further, wholes are experienced even when a piece is missing or distorted. This led to another law of Gestalt psychology (Pragnanz), which states that a form (Gestalt) is perceived in a structured, orderly, closed, and even stable manner. The theory basically sees relations among parts as secondary; association is minimized, and the building of mosaics in perception is disregarded. Perception is not seen to depend on learning or experience. The individual's perceptual task is to see order and meaning contained in the overall structure of an event. Frederick (Fritz) Perls is the name most often associated with Gestalt therapy, which focuses on the awareness of experiences in the here-and-now.

View of the Individual   According to Passons (1975) and summarized here, Gestalt therapy is based on several assumptions:

1. Individuals are a totality consisting of interrelated parts (i.e., body, emotions, thoughts, sensations, and perceptions). None of these can be understood outside the context of the whole person. Individuals are also part of their environment and cannot be understood apart from it.
2. Individuals choose how they respond to external and internal stimuli; they are not reactors but actors. They are capable of making these choices, because they have the potential to be fully aware of all sensations, thoughts, emotions, and perceptions.
3. Individuals have the capacity to govern their own life effectively.
4. Individuals cannot experience the past or the future; they can only experience themselves in the present.
5. Individuals are basically neither good nor bad.

Some of these beliefs—a person is neither good nor evil, for example—are found in other approaches.

Personality Development   The motivating force of personality development in Gestalt therapy is self-actualization, which smacks of Carl Rogers. There is a difference, however, in that Rogers views self-actualization as a potentiality, a goal to strive for, whereas Gestaltists state, "Becoming is the process of being what one is and not a process of striving to become" (Kempler, 1973, p. 262). The term is defined, then, as present-centered, the emphasis on the here-and-now.

As children develop, one of their first discoveries is the world outside of themselves. They recognize that there is "a place where they stop and their environment begins," if only in terms of what is inside their body and what is outside. During the developmental process, they learn to distinguish between "me" and "them." Perls calls this the "ego boundary." The ego boundary is further differentiated by identification and alienation. Identification with a family or group results in a sense of cohesion and love within the ego boundary. Alienation, the opposite pole, brings with it a feeling of strangeness and conflict; it is the result of disowning that which is perceived as threatening. During the process of personality development, the self and the self-image are formed. The self is what one actually is; the self-image is what one should be according to expectations of others. The self prompts the individual to actualization, while the self-image attempts to hinder the process. Frustration is seen as a positive element in the development of the self: "Without frustrations there is no need, no reason, to mobilize your resources, to discover that you might be able to do something on your own" (Perls, 1969, p. 32). Without frustration, one is relying on others for support instead of being self-supporting. Maintaining a self-image that is not consistent with the self is a source of tension for an individual and can lead to personal and physical stress that can be harmful.

Perceptual Field   One of the major concepts of Gestalt psychology is the perceptual field, what an individual perceives and how it is limited. The word *gestalt* means "whole." The human being always strives to organize stimuli into wholes, since isolated parts of anything have no meaning. Closure, proximity, and similarity involve principles that illustrate this process. An individual will view a figure of broken lines and mentally construct from it the object it most closely resembles. Closure has implications for therapy in the sense of the need to "finish unfinished business." As for proximity, the distance between one stimulus and another influences how the stimuli are perceived; the closer the stimuli, the closer the relationship between them is perceived to be. If one is pleased by eating an ice cream cone, then pleasure and cones are related to each other in an individual's perception. And stimuli that are similar will be grouped together in one's perceptual field. One looks for similarity to create order out of the chaos of various stimuli that are constantly present in one's awareness. It is fundamental that stimuli have meaning only as they are organized in the mind and that the above principles are ways in which one organizes.

We do not respond to every stimulus in our perceptual field, and what we respond to is related to our various levels of awareness. For example, "As I sit here writing, I am vaguely aware of my surroundings, the chair I'm sitting on, the pen I'm holding, and the room I occupy. What I am most aware of right now is organizing my thoughts and getting them down on paper. As I tire, I'm becoming aware that my back is starting to ache from being in this position and a cup of coffee would taste good to me. Coffee would help alleviate my flagging energy, and just getting up and making it would relieve my back for a while. As I continue to write, the need for coffee is becoming more persistent, so nagging, in fact, that it is interfering with what I wish to write. That's enough—time for a coffee break." This illustration is an example of the figure-ground principle of Gestalt psychology. Initially the figure, or the more important object of awareness, was the thoughts and the writing of them. The ground, or background, was the environment, which included a kitchen where coffee was available. As awareness shifted to coffee, the Gestalt of the thoughts and writing closed, and a new one was formed. Coffee became the figure, and writing the ground. When a shift of emphasis occurs—when figure and ground change positions—the Gestalt is formed; what was once of primary importance is no longer so.

On the other hand, Yontef (1971) points out:

When a need is met, the Gestalt it organized becomes complete and it no longer exerts an influence—the organism is free to form new gestalten. When the gestalt formation and destruction are blocked or rigidified at any stage, when needs are not recognized and expressed, the flexible harmony and flow of the organism/environment field is disturbed. Unmet needs form incomplete gestalten that clamor for attention and, therefore, interfere with the formation of new gestalten. (p. 3)

At any given time, the perceptual field of the individual is organized with reference to her or his needs and the activities that will satisfy them (Coleman, 1960). The level of awareness, which is always changing, sets the limit for the perceptual field.

Insight learning is another important principle of the Gestalt view. Through the process of problem solving or seeking a solution to conflict, the perceptual field may be "restructured," relationships changed, and some new insights generated. A new solution may be found. This, in counseling, may be accompanied by an "incubation" period—a time when the client mulls over the problem and then at some point attacks the problem differently. While arriving at this new strategy may appear spontaneous, it is a process that occurred over some period of time.

The past is not completely ignored in counseling. Its importance is seen to be how it affects the individual in the present. For example, one issue might involve "unfinished" business from the past. The past may be re-enacted or brought back through fantasy experiences in order to "complete" closure. This is an important issue in light of the previously identified assumptions of Gestalt counseling—that if unfinished business is a central point of one's existence, it will impede personal growth. Individuals in fact can become "stuck" on unfinished business; this idea may be similar to Freud's notion of fixation.

Goals   The main objective of Gestalt counseling is the integration of the individual, a bringing together of all the parts that he or she has disowned, along with recognition that the individual is self-regulating. Perls (1948) states:

> The treatment is finished when the patient has achieved the basic requirements: a change in outlook, a technique of adequate self-expression and assimilation, and the ability to extend awareness to the verbal level. He has then reached that state of integration which facilitates its own development, and he can now be safely left to himself. (p. 585)

Increasing awareness is of paramount importance, and awareness alone is curative. With awareness, "the organism can work on the healthy Gestalt principle: that the most important unfinished situation will always emerge and can be dealt with" (Perls, 1969, p. 51). It can be seen, then, that integration is an ongoing process, which ceases only when one dies.

"Maturation" has also been noted as a primary goal. Perls sees this as the individual "growing up" and finally assuming responsibility for his or her life. At this point the individual does not lead his or her life according to the present expectations of others or through expectations instilled in the past. Old business is finally put away, and the person can more fully live in the "now."

Several other key principles have been identified as basic to the Gestalt view of the person. Naranjo (1970) listed nine such valuative elements:

1. Live now. Be concerned with the present rather than with the past or future.
2. Live here. Deal with what is present rather than with what is absent.
3. Stop imagining. Experience the real.
4. Stop unnecessary thinking. Rather, taste and see.
5. Express rather than manipulate, explain, justify, or judge.
6. Give in to unpleasantness and pain just as to pleasure. Do not restrict your awareness.
7. Accept no should or ought other than your own. Adore no graven image.
8. Take full responsibility for your actions, feelings, and thoughts.
9. Surrender to being as you are. (pp. 49–50)

The Therapeutic Process   Gestalt therapy is based on structured "unifying" of experience and on the dynamic unity of person and environment. It places considerable focus on the identification of emotions enmeshed in actual experience and action. Gestalt counseling is active, confrontative, and concerned with what is experienced in the "now." The past is a memory, the future is a fantasy, and they are important only as they are experienced in the present as such. Much of Gestalt counseling involves "retrieving" what has been disowned by the clients, by having them experience these "splits" as they exist. One split that is often seen is what Perls describes as "topdog" and "underdog," which can coexist in one personality: "The underdog is the Mickey Mouse. The topdog is the Super Mouse" (Perls, 1969, p. 18). The topdog is authoritarian and knows what is best, while the underdog is defensive and apologetic. Perls states, "Once we recognize the structure of our behavior, which in the case of self-improvement is the split between the topdog and the underdog, and if we understand how by listening, we can bring a reconciliation of these two fighting clowns, then we realize that we cannot deliberately bring about changes in ourselves or in others" (Perls, 1969, p. 20).

One way to bring about an awareness of this split is the two-chair method, which is used extensively in Gestalt counseling. A client sits in one chair and role plays topdog speaking to underdog. He or she then switches chairs and responds as underdog to topdog. This method is also used in the resolution of unfinished business, which is a Gestalt that hasn't had closure. In order for a client to be fully aware of what is happening now, it may be necessary to terminate some concerns from the past and redirect the client's energy to the present. As an example, a female client has mourned for a dead parent but has not verbalized the feelings that were left unsaid to that parent. She may then be invited to complete the Gestalt by placing her parent in the empty chair, sharing her feelings, and finishing her unfinished business.

Nonverbal behavior is important in Gestalt therapy as a contrast to what is said and as an emphasis on what is said. If a client says that she is comfortable but her hands are clenched, the counselor then confronts the incongruence. Or if she is sharing her feelings, the counselor may suggest the body position that would correspond to the verbalization. The counselor attempts to increase client awareness by having the client "experience" rather than intellectualize. Various forms of experiencing may be used. Gestalt counselors employ an assortment of powerful tools to this end. For example, there are some very specific verbal techniques associated with Gestalt counseling. The following list shows several of the more common techniques, along with the client behavior each attempts to address (Passons, 1975):

Client Concern or Deficit	*Gestalt Verbalization*
(1) Ambivalence toward situation	(1) Ask client to omit qualifiers, e.g., may or possibly.
(2) Not listening to self	(2) Ask: "Are you listening to what you are saying?"
(3) Lack of experiencing own behavior	(3) Ask questions of "How" and "What" rather than "Why."
(4) Distorted messages through question-asking	(4) Say: "Please change the question to a statement."
(5) Improper word usage	(5) Ask client to change passive voice to active voice.
	(5a) Say: "Change 'need' to 'want.'"

		(5b)	Say: "Change 'know' to 'imagine.'"
		(5c)	Say: "Change 'have to' to 'choose to.'"
		(5d)	Say: "Change 'can't' to 'won't.'"
		(5e)	Say: "Change 'but' to 'and.'"
(6)	Depersonalization of self	(6)	Say: "Change 'we' to 'I.'"
		(6a)	Say: "Change 'you' to 'I.'"
		(6b)	Say: "Change 'it' to 'I.'"
(7)	Unaware of affect	(7)	Say: "Stay with that feeling."
(8)	Has to explore behavior or feeling further	(8)	State: "Say again but exaggerate feeling" or "Say again."
(9)	Unaware of reactions of others or self	(9)	Ask client to say: "I'm aware that I ____."
		(9a)	Ask client to say: "I'm aware that you ____."
		(9b)	Ask: "Can you be aware of ____?"
		(9c)	Ask: "What do you experience?"
(10)	Unaware of *Now* experience or involvement	(10)	Ask: "What are you aware of now?" or ask counselee to complete: "Now I am aware ____."

Other Gestalt techniques are personalization and projection: *Personalization* means changing impersonal comments stated with "you" to more personal ones stated with "I." In the previous transcript, the statement ". . . if you make a mistake, everybody looks at you" becomes much more honest and direct when the "you's" are replaced with "I" and "me." *Projection* is the process by which clients associate with someone else that part of themselves that they are unwilling to own. The counselor has the clients role play that other person to see if the projection actually fits them. These are but a few of the many techniques of the Gestaltist. All the methods rely on client awareness and responsibility.

Gestalt counselors make little use of diagnostics; rather, they see each session as an I-thou encounter (see the discussion on existential counseling). While much emphasis is placed on the enhancement of awareness, the client is encouraged in counseling to try out and to "experiment" with new behaviors. It has been found to be particularly helpful behaviorally in "freeing" overly constrained people. Shepherd (1970) noted this: "In general,

Gestalt therapy is most effective with overly socialized, restrained, constricted individuals—often described as neurotic, phobic, perfectionistic, ineffective, depressed, etc.—whose functioning is limited or inconsistent, primarily due to their internal restrictions, and whose enjoyment of living is minimal" (p. 234).

A study by Sobel and O'Brien (1979) looked at expectations for counseling success among analytic, behavioral, and Gestalt approaches. Of the three approaches, Gestalt counseling was ranked first for expectancy of long-term cure by older females, young males, and young females, while older males ranked it second of the three. At least for a superficial encounter, subject expectations were positive toward Gestalt counseling.

The study by Meara et al. (1981), which looked at semantic communication by Perls, Rogers, and Ellis, summarized Perls's comments about his counseling session with the client, Gloria. Perls's purpose was to frustrate and manipulate the client into confronting herself, thus exposing her phony mask. Perls displayed a significantly higher use of action-experiential verbs than did either Rogers or Ellis. This is consistent with his intention to force the client to stay with the here-and-now. In Meara et al. (1979) the client in the filmed interview was reported as saying the session with Perls was most valuable for her and that he made her feel her fighting self. On the tracking and convergence of four measures of stylistic complexity for the client and Perls, there was evidence of concerted action. Finally, Hill et al. (1979) summarized their study of Perls's filmed interaction with the same client:

Gestalt therapy relies on two key processes in counseling: an awareness of the here-and-now experiencing and the resolution of polarities or discrepancies. The results reflect . . . his use of both nonverbal referents and confrontations to focus on . . . present experiencing and to address discrepancies in her behaviors. He also used direct guidance, interpretation, and information. His repertoire of responses was wider than the other two counselors (note: Rogers and Ellis), and he did not rely on any one type of response . . . a large number of responses were confrontations. (p. 202)

Summary and Evaluation

Gestalt counseling presents an interesting integration of Gestalt psychology and existential philosophy. Its basic proposition is that self-awareness is essential to the integration of the individual in a holistic fashion. Counseling is a confrontative, dynamic process that emphasizes the I-thou relationship in the here-and-now.

Gestalt concepts help to remind us of present-centeredness, and the totality of the individual as a focus during therapy. The therapist can be active and creative throughout the process of helping clients discover themselves. At times Gestalt counseling may be too gimmickry-ridden, with emphasis on technique rather than the client. With the stress placed on the growth of self-awareness, the potential also exists that the translation of awareness into behavior change may be forgotten.

Suggested Readings

Fagan, J., and Shepherd, I. eds.   *Gestalt Therapy Now.* New York: Harper Colophon, 1970.

Perls, F.   *Gestalt Therapy Verbatim.* Moab, Utah: Real People Press, 1969.

——.   *In and Out of the Garbage Pail.* Moab, Utah: Real People Press, 1969.

——, R. Hefferline, and P. Goodman.   *Gestalt Therapy: Excitement and Growth in Human Personality.* New York: Dell, 1951.

Polster, E., and M. Polster.   *Gestalt Therapy Integrated.* New York: Brunner/Mazel, 1973.

Summary

No one therapy is best for all clients, but an understanding of the various theoretical approaches to counseling enables the counselor to maximize personal therapeutic strengths. Research supports the belief that there are virtually no differences in effectiveness among therapies. This chapter reviewed various affective theoretical approaches to serve as a springboard for the reader's study of each theory in greater depth. The major points of each theory reviewed are as follows:

1. According to Freudian psychoanalytic theory, there are three mental constructs of the mind: the conscious, unconscious, and preconscious. The mind is composed of the id, ego, and superego. Individuals use numerous defense mechanisms to ward off unwanted anxiety. The primary personality is formed in the early developmental stages which progress from the oral to the phallic stage. The therapeutic process must deal with transference reactions and resistances with confrontation, clarification, and interpretation.

2. Adler's individual psychology posits that we live in a world filled with personal meanings which form our reality. There are three basic questions which each person must seek to answer. They are in the occupational, social, and sexual spheres. The role of women is held extremely high. Life goals are the product of the striving of the human soul. Birth order in the family constellation is important in the evolution of a child's personality.

3. Transactional analysis suggests that individuals have three basic needs: stimulus hunger, recognition hunger, and structure hunger. Games are complementary transactions that have predictable and therefore "safe" outcomes. By eleven years of age, each person develops a mental attitude that evolves into a life position. We are composed of three ego states: Parent, Adult, and Child. Pathology has two categories: structural and functional. There are five stages in the therapeutic process and eight therapeutic interventions.

4. Rogers' client-centered counseling emphasizes the importance of the counselor-client relationship in helping the client to change. Core conditions (empathy, genuineness, regard, and respect) are essential in providing a climate of safety necessary for client growth.

5. Existence and being are the key philosophical issues for the existential counselor. The client is viewed as "free" to choose, having the capacity to transcend past experiences.

6. Gestalt counseling emphasizes that the whole is more than the sum of its parts, and

subsequently attempts to see meaning within a total individual perspective.

Awareness in the here-and-now is a central focus.

References

Adler, A. *Understanding Human Nature.* New York: Fawcett Premier, 1954.

———. *What Life Should Mean to You.* New York: Capricorn Books, 1958.

———. *The Problem Child.* New York: Capricorn Books, 1963.

Beck, C. E. *Philosophical Foundations of Guidance.* Englewood Cliffs, N.J.: Prentice-Hall, 1963.

Berne, E. *Transactional Analysis in Psychotherapy.* New York: Ballantine Books, 1961.

———. *Games People Play.* New York: Grove Press, 1964.

———. *Principles of Group Treatment.* New York: Oxford University Press, 1966.

———. *What Do You Say After You Say Hello?* New York: Bantam, 1972.

Bettelheim, B. *Freud and Man's Soul.* New York: Alfred A. Knopf, 1983.

Boy, A. V., and G. J. Pine. *Client-Centered Counseling: A Renewal.* Boston: Allyn and Bacon, 1982.

Brenner, C. *An Elementary Textbook of Psychoanalysis.* New York: Anchor Press, 1974.

Buhler, C., and M. Allen. *Introduction to Humanistic Psychology.* Monterey, Calif.: Brooks/Cole, 1972.

Carkhuff, R. R. *Helping and Human Relations: A Primer for Lay and Professional Helpers, Volume 1, Selection and Training.* New York: Holt, Rinehart and Winston, 1969.

———, and B. G. Berenson. *Beyond Counseling and Therapy.* New York: Holt, Rinehart and Winston, 1967.

Coleman, J. C. *Personality Dynamics and Effective Behavior.* Chicago: Scott, Foresman and Company, 1960.

Combs, A., D. W. Soper, T. Gooding, J. A. Benton, Jr., J. F. Dickman, and R. H. Usher. *Florida Studies in the Helping Professions.* Gainesville: University of Florida, 1969.

Cunningham, L. M., and H. J. Peters. *Counseling Theories.* Columbus, Ohio: Charles E. Merrill, 1973.

Dopson, L., and E. Gade. "Kierkegaard's Philosophy: Implications for Counseling." *Personnel and Guidance Journal* 60 (1981): 148–152.

Dreikurs, R. *Fundamentals of Adlerian Psychology.* New York: Greenberg, 1950.

Ewing, D. "Twenty Approaches to Individual Change." *Personnel and Guidance Journal* 55 (1977):331–338.

Fiedler, F. E. "A Comparison of Therapeutic Relationships in Psychoanalytical, Nondirective, and Adlerian Therapy." *Journal of Consulting Psychology* 14 (1950a):436–445.

———. "The Concept of an Ideal Therapeutic Relationship." *Journal of Consulting Psychology* 14 (1950b):239–245.

Fine, R. *A History of Psychoanalysis.* New York: Columbia University Press, 1979.

Frankl, V. E. "Logotherapy and Existentialism." *Psychotherapy: Theory, Research and Practice* 4 (1967a):138–142.

———. *Psychotherapy and Existentialism: Selected Papers on Logotherapy.* New York: Simon & Schuster, 1967b.

Freud, A. *The Ego and the Mechanisms of Defense.* New York: International Universities Press, 1966.

Freud, S. *The History of the Psychoanalytic Movement and Other Papers.* New York: Collier Books, 1963a.

———. *Sigmund Freud: Therapy and Technique.* New York: Collier Books, 1963b.

Friedman, M. "Existential Psychotherapy and the Image of Man." *Journal of Humanistic Psychology* 4 (1964):104–117.

Greenson, R. R. *The Technique and Practice of Psychoanalysis: Volume 1.* New York: International University Press, 1967.

Hansen, J. C., R. R. Stevic, and R. W. Warner, Jr. *Counseling: Theory and Process.* Boston: Allyn and Bacon, 1977.

Hill, C. E., T. B. Thames, and D. K. Rardin. "Comparison of Rogers, Perls, and Ellis on the Hill Counselor Verbal Response Category System." *Journal of Counseling Psychology* 26 (1979):198–203.

Hogan, R. "The Development of a Measure of Client Defensiveness in the Counseling Relationship." Unpublished doctoral dissertation. University of Chicago, 1948.

Jones, E. *The Life and Work of Sigmund Freud: Volume 2.* New York: Basic Books, 1955.

Kempler, W. "Gestalt Therapy." In R. Corsini, ed., *Current Psychotherapies.* Itasca, Ill.: Peacock Publishers, 1973. Pp. 251–286.

Krasner, L. "The Future and the Past in the Behaviorism-Humanism Dialogue." *American Psychologist* 33 (1978):799–804.

Leak, G. K., and S. B. Christopher. "Freudian Psychoanalysis and Sociobiology." *American Psychologist* 37 (1982):313–322.

Meara, N. M., H. B. Pepinsky, J. W. Shannon, and W. A. Murray. "Semantic Communication and Expectations for Counseling Across Three Theoretical Orientations." *Journal of Counseling Psychology* 28 (1981):110–118.

———, J. W. Shannon, and H. B. Pepinsky. "Comparison of the Stylistic Complexity of the Language of Counselor and Client Across Three Theoretical Orientations." *Journal of Counseling Psychology* 26 (1979):181–189.

Naranjo, C. "Present-Centeredness: Technique, Prescription, and Ideal." In J. Fagan and I. L. Shepherd, eds., *Gestalt Therapy Now.* Palo Alto, Calif.: Science and Behavior Books, 1970.

Neufeldt, S. A. "Client Cognitive Characteristics and Preference for Counseling Approaches." *Journal of Counseling Psychology* 25 (1978):184–187.

Passons, William R. *Gestalt Approaches in Counseling.* New York: Holt, Rinehart and Winston, 1975.

Perls, F. "Theory and Technique of Personality Integration." *American Journal of Psychotherapy* 2 (1948):563ff.

———. *Gestalt Therapy Verbatim.* Moab, Utah: Real People Press, 1969.

Raskin, N. J. "An Analysis of Six Parallel Studies of the Therapeutic Process." *Journal of Consulting Psychology* 13 (1949):206–220.

Rogers, C.R. *Client-Centered Therapy.* Boston: Houghton Mifflin, 1951.

———. "A Theory of Therapy, Personality and Interpersonal Relationships, as Developed in the Client-Centered Framework." In S. Koch, ed., *Psychology: A Study of a Science, Volume 3, Formulation of the Person and the Social Context.* New York: McGraw-Hill, 1959. Pp. 184–256.

———. *On Becoming a Person.* (Paperback ed.) Boston: Houghton Mifflin, 1961.

Sartre, J. P. *Existential Psychoanalysis.* Chicago: Gateway, 1953.

———, and R. F. Dymond, eds. *Psychotherapy and Personality Change: Coordinated Studies in the Client-Centered Approach.* Chicago: University of Chicago Press, 1954.

Shepherd, I. L. "Limitations and Cautions in the Gestalt Approach." In J. Fagen and I. L. Shepherd, eds., *Gestalt Therapy Now.* Palo Alto, Calif.: Science and Behavior Books, 1970. Pp. 234–238.

Smith, M. L., and G. V. Glass. "Meta-Analysis of Psychotherapy Outcome Studies." *American Psychologist* 32 (1977):752–760.

Snyder, D. M. "Some Foundations of Counseling and Psychotherapy from a Phenomenological Perspective." *Personnel and Guidance Journal* 60 (1982):364–367.

Sobel, H. J., and B. A. O'Brien. "Expectations for Counseling Success." *Journal of Counseling Psychology* 26 (1979):462–464.

Truax, C. B. *A Scale for the Measurement of Accurate Empathy.* Discussion Paper No. 20. Wisconsin Psychiatric Institute, University of Wisconsin, 1961.

———. *A Tentative Scale for the Measurement of Unconditional Positive Regard.* Discussion Paper No. 26. Wisconsin Psychiatric Institute, University of Wisconsin, January 1962a.

———. *A Tentative Scale for the Measurement of Therapist Genuineness or Self-Congruence.* Discussion Paper No. 35. Wisconsin Psychiatric Institute, University of Wisconsin, May 1962b.

———. "Effective Ingredients in Psychotherapy: An Approach to Unravelling the Patient-Therapist Interaction." *Journal of Counseling Psychology* 10 (1963): 256–263.

———, and R. R. Carkhuff. "Personality Change in Hospitalized Mental Patients During Group Psychotherapy as a Function of the Use of Alternate Sessions and Vicarious Therapy Pretraining." *Journal of Clinical Psychology,* 21 (1965):327–329.

———, and R. R. Carkhuff. *Toward Effective*

Counseling and Psychotherapy: Training and Practices. Chicago: Aldine, 1967.

van Kaam, A.   *Existential Foundations of Psychology.* New York: Doubleday, Image Books, 1969.

Yontef, G. M.   *A Review of the Practice of Gestalt Therapy.* Los Angeles: Trident Shop, California State University, 1971.

CHAPTER 6

Cognitive and Behavioral Theories of Counseling

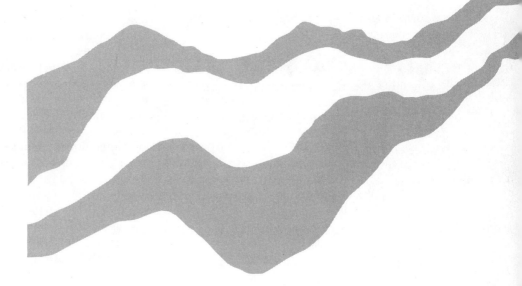

Chapter Organizer

Aim of the Chapter

This chapter will provide brief descriptions of the major cognitive-behavioral approaches to counseling.

Chapter Preview

1. Cognitive theories of counseling suggest that thinking precedes feelings, while the behavioral theories focus on specific behavior change and assume that feeling and attitude change will follow.
2. An essential consideration for this group of theories is cognitive and behavioral functioning and processes within a reality-based framework.
3. The trait-and-factor approach applies a mathematical model in the assessment of personality with the intention of enhancing client decision making. Assessment, diagnosis or analysis, and prognosis are essential elements of counseling within this framework.
4. Rational-emotive therapy is active-directive and described as being more time efficient than other therapies. Irrationality is viewed as the source of most emotional problems.
5. Behavioral counseling suggests that learning occurs in three paradigms: classical conditioning, operant conditioning, and imitative learning. Reinforcement is an event that occurs after an emitted response and

increases the probability of its occurring again in similar circumstances. To learn a new behavior, use is made of a continuous reinforcement schedule while an intermittent schedule is used to strengthen it against extinction. Shaping is the process of learning progressively more complex behaviors. Goals are always specified in behavioral counseling. There are five steps in the therapeutic process. Examples of behavioral techniques include: relaxation training, assertiveness training, and systematic desensitization.

6. Reality therapy contends that people have two basic needs which when unmet cause pain and an identity of failure. These needs are the need to love and be loved and the need to feel worthwhile to another and to oneself. The basic concept of reality therapy is responsibility.

Relevant Questions

The following are several questions to keep in mind while reading this chapter:

1. What are the differences between a cognitive and a behavioral approach to counseling?
2. What limitations do you foresee with certain clients for this group of theories?
3. What counseling process is followed by the trait-and-factor counselor? How do source and surface traits differ? What is the rela-

tionship between the two during the measurement phase?

4. What relationship exists, as seen by Albert Ellis, among thinking, feeling, and behaving? How does this ABC model of behavior suggest for the counselor a resolution to self-defeating thoughts, feelings, and behaviors?

5. Compare classical conditioning to operant conditioning. How are phobias learned? How can the counselor use the shaping mechanism in counseling? Compare the goals of behavioral counseling to those of reality therapy. If a counselor is trying to extinguish a given behavior and accidentally reinforces it once in the process, what effect will this have?

6. In what ways is reality therapy similar to rational-emotive therapy? How does reality therapy explain the process followed by those individuals who are "unhealthy"? What label is used to identify them? What are the three identities a person can achieve? Describe each of them.

Introduction

This chapter briefly describes the cognitively and behaviorally oriented theories of counseling. The discussion considers the trait-and-factor approach, rational-emotive therapy, behavioral counseling, and reality therapy (see Table 6.1). These theories assume that what the client thinks and does is the fundamental element on which counselors have to focus. Essentially, two basic propositions are posited: (1) thinking precedes feeling, and (2) doing can change feelings and attitudes about self and environment. These theories place less emphasis on the counseling relationship than do the affectively oriented theories, but this is not to suggest that the counselor is antagonistic. Generally, the counselor's role is conceptualized as active, even directive, and may at times resemble the role of a teacher. The process of organizing perceptions and behavior and the learning of such a process during counseling is a basic part of the counseling process.

Trait-and-Factor Theory

Theoretical Beginnings   The trait-and-factor approach applies mathematical considerations to personality measurement in order to assess the role of personality factors in individual behavior. The personality factors considered are similar to those addressed by "humanistic" theories; the difference is that trait-and-factor theory analyzes them quantitatively. It measures and correlates multiple personality variables and then groups them according to function. These functional groups are used to predict underlying patterns of personality. This accumulation of data and the counseling process that follows aim to help clients make the best decisions for themselves. For some writers, then, this is essentially considered as a decision-making model; for other writers this might be considered a cognitive model.

While E. G. Williamson (1900–1982) is the person most readily associated with trait-and-factor theory (or directive counseling), the approach is built

Table 6.1
Cognitive and Behavioral Theories of Counseling

Approach	Major Theorists	View of Individual	Goals
Trait-and-factor	E. G. Williamson; Carl Spearman; D. A. Paterson.	Stabilized at maturity; rational and irrational conflict in individual; individual is conglomeration of abilities, aptitudes, interests, and potentials.	Achievement of excellence; movement toward potential; striving to be rational; rational evaluation of choices; maximization of capabilities; catharsis; reeducation.
Rational-emotive	Albert Ellis.	Individuals are rational; but have potential for faulty thinking; reason controls emotion; forward-looking; meaning of human worth is experiential and personal; A-B-C theory of personality.	Eliminate self-defeating behavior; more tolerant philosophy of life; encourage critical thinking; reduction of irrationality.
Behavioral	B. F. Skinner; John Krumboltz; Hans Eysenck; Joseph Wolpe; Arnold A. Lazarus; Carl Thoreson; A. Bandura.	Individual behavior shaped by cultural learnings; person is neutral at birth with equal potential for good or bad; behavior is orderly.	Elimination of maladaptive behavior; behavior change; client-defined goals; new conditions created for learning.
Reality	William Glasser; G. L. Harrington.	Person can develop either a "success" or "failure" identity; motivation toward growth; people have needs to be loved and to love and to feel worthwhile.	Acquisition of realistic behavior; development of responsible behavior; planning for change; development of success identity.

on the earlier works of Francis Galton, Carl Spearman, and L. L. Thurstone. Williamson's purpose, first and foremost, was to help clients achieve excellence and reach their full potential through counseling.

View of the Individual   While the affective experience of the client is not ignored, rationality is considered to be the major asset of the individual. Subsequently, great importance is placed on the use of rational processes in planning and decision making. Williamson (1970) writes, "without in any way neglecting the affective richness of the full life of the human being . . . still I feel that man's capacity to strive to become rational is among his greatest—if not the greatest—assets and capabilities. This is the reason why counseling to me, in the one-to-one relationship at least, takes the form of helping the individual . . . to make a rational evaluation of optional choices with full awareness of alternatives" (p. 311). Irrationality is acknowledged to be part of the person.

Table 6.1 (Cont.)

Approach	Therapeutic Relationship	Therapist's Role	Therapeutic Techniques
Trait-and-factor	Rapport important.	Diagnosis; clarification; assessment; analysis; prognosis; psychometrics; synthesis; follow-up; eclectic choice of techniques.	Diagnostician; active; facilitates formulation of plans of action; teacher.
Rational-emotive	Relationship not essential, but rapport important.	Encourages; persuades; analyzes; active-directive teaching; homework assignments; prescribes.	Active; didactic; challenging; demonstrate problems are related to irrational beliefs; counterpropagandist; teacher; helps in re-evaluation of self-talk.
Behavioral	Good working relationship important, but not overemphasized; good relationship necessary but not sufficient.	Desensitization; deep muscle relaxation; assertiveness training; implosion, aversion therapy; operant conditioning; reinforcement.	Didactic; active, directive; functions as a teacher; reinforcer; role model.
Reality	Involved and warm; involved.	Confrontation; debate; advice; instruction; self-disclosure.	Encourages client to face reality; clarifier; model; stimulator; goal setter; teacher.

Although the irrational and rational processes are in conflict, the rational process can be helped to control the distortion that arises from irrationality.

Trait-and-factor theory views the individual as a conglomeration of abilities, aptitudes, interests, and potentials organized in unique fashion. This pattern of organization can be measured and identified once it has stabilized at maturity. Each person strives to maximize his or her capabilities within the limitations of the environment. Williamson's notions of "achievement of potential," "the pursuit of excellence," and "becoming" are quite consistent with humanist concepts of self-actualization. In fact, Williamson would consider himself without question to be a humanist.

Goals   One goal of trait-and-factor theory, or the "directive" approach to counseling, is "to increase rational behavior" (Ewing, 1977, p. 334). However, Williamson expressed the ultimate goals of counseling in a far broader fashion.

Williamson's emphasis is on helping the client achieve excellence. His book *Counseling Adolescents* (1950) noted several counseling services that in effect became goal statements:

1. Counseling is *guided learning toward self-understanding*.
2. Counseling is *reeducation or re-learning* which is needed or desired as means to life adjustment.
3. Counseling is *assisting the counselee in understanding and applying learnings to daily living*.
4. Counseling aids the client in *experiencing catharsis* of disruptive emotions.
5. Counseling helps with some form of *reeducation* after catharsis has occurred. (pp. 209–210)

All counseling objectives would clearly be identified in the service of the overall goals stated earlier: (1) striving for excellence and (2) development of human potential. Clients identify "life's goals" that would provide satisfaction. These "life's goals" may be mediated by environmental, personal, and social forces, which the client would consider in reaching a final decision. Specific counseling process goals of self-understanding, catharsis (self-exploration), and behavior change would be an integral part of this approach.

There has been a historical misunderstanding of this approach, perhaps because of the misnomer "directive counseling," that clients are told or ordered to do certain things. Williamson (1970) clarifies this and elaborates even more on counseling goals for the counselor:

Nor have I ever looked upon counseling, contrary to some misinterpretations and misperceptions, as a means of "directing" or assigning students into occupational choices or jobs. Rather I have looked upon counseling as one of many means open to help the individual . . . become aware of alternative choices as to style of living, both within and outside a vocation, and to evaluate alternatives in terms of consequences, rewards, and opportunities before making his choice. (p. 310)

The Therapeutic Process

A full six-step process can be identified:

1. Analysis—which helps the counselor understand the client through the data accumulation and its integration into a comprehensive record.
2. Synthesis—which orders and arranges the data to determine the client's strengths and weaknesses.
3. Diagnosis—which identifies the problem and its causes. The counselor's expertise and intuition are crucial during this stage.
4. Prognosis—which attempts to predict the client's chances of success or failure in moving to resolve a particular problem.
5. Resolution—which attempts to provide direct help for an identified problem.
6. Follow-up—which attempts to find the outcome of counseling as well as help the client deal with future problems. (Pietrofesa et al., 1980, p. 96)

Psychometrics Psychometrics and prediction are an integral part of the counseling process. The trait-and-factor practitioner feels that "source" traits elicit "surface" behaviors, which may appear in various combinations. Consequently, a great deal of emphasis is placed on identifying the various personality or functional capabilities of the client by means of tests, measurements, and other methods of data accumulation. A profile of individual traits is compiled to help in the assessment of the total personality. Personality assessment is conducted within a multidimensional perspective. The counselor looks for clusters of traits, with the hope that the information provided will allow the client to reach the best decision possible.

The clinician will diagnose, give a prognosis, and attempt to treat the client based on such assessment. While the assessment is conducted as objectively as possible, the counselor utilizes a relatively intuitive basis for some interpretations (for example, the use of the Rorschach or the Thematic Apperception Test). There is, then, an intermingling of the objective with the subjective, regardless of the claims by some clinicians of the "completeness" of their scientific inquiry.

Rational Decision Making The counselor may well be seen as a teacher who examines issues with clients in a rational way. Williamson considered counseling to be not only the pursuit of excellence, but a search for "truth" and an attempt to define values by the client. He suggested that counseling cannot be valueless—and neither can the role that the counselor plays in the counseling process. What the counselor stands for, however, is clearly stated—these are values that are representative of the pluralistic values found in a democratic society.

Specific counseling techniques may vary with client and problem, and, in fact, may utilize techniques associated with other counseling approaches. For example, the establishment of rapport might require skills used by nondirective counselors, while the decision-making stage might utilize rational-emotive skills. (See the following section.) The counselor may challenge, advise, reflect, clarify, diagnose, and even refer to other agencies at times. There is no restriction of counselor behaviors except as they might diverge from philosophical tenets or from the generalized or specific client goals.

We have mentioned the close relationship among behavioral and cognitive theories and trait-and-factor counseling. Ivey and Simek-Downing (1980) suggested the following decision-making model as applied to "effective" trait-and-factor approaches:

1. During the *problem definition phase* of the interview, explore openly and frankly with the client several alternative definitions of the problem . . . With the client, order priorities and start solving the problems one by one.
2. During the *work phase*, take one of the problems from the list and move through it in detail, exploring *both the individual and her or his environment.* . . . At times during this phase, techniques of other theories (psychodynamic, behavioral, rational-emotive) may prove useful to clarify and elucidate points.
3. During the *decision for action phase,* generate creatively with the client the

full range of possible alternative actions. . . . Then prioritize those alternatives and contract for action in the environment. (p. 292)

It is clear that, with some modification, trait-and-factor concepts will continue to be implemented in cognitive-behavioral counseling techniques.

Summary and Evaluation

While some confusion has existed regarding trait-and-factor counseling and the term *directive counseling* which had been ascribed to it, the trait-and-factor approach can be viewed as a problem-solving process. As such, the decision-making process may be facilitated by many of the techniques long associated with trait-and-factor practitioners. A process of analysis, synthesis, diagnosis, prognosis, resolution, and follow-up, if systematically pursued and enhanced with other counseling skills can be quite effective in helping clients define and reach their goals.

The trait-and-factor approach appears to be most effective in educational and career settings where the potential for job fit and school choice exists. Its strength lies in its vigorousness and use of objective data, in contrast to subjective considerations by the therapist. Diagnostic concepts associated with this approach have been incorporated in distinct ways in many therapeutic models. Most criticisms of the trait-and-factor approach center on its lack of attention to the client's affective domain, the degree of control the counselor exerts on client decision making, and an overemphasis on "objective" data, which may not be as objective as the therapist would have the client believe.

Suggested Readings

Froelich, C.P., and J. G. Darley. *Studying Students.* Chicago: Science Research Associates, 1952.

Parsons, F. *Choosing a Vocation.* Boston: Houghton Mifflin, 1909.

Williamson, E. G. *How to Counsel Students: A Manual of Techniques for Clinical Counselors.* New York: McGraw-Hill, 1939.

————. *Counseling Adolescents.* New York: McGraw-Hill, 1950.

————, and J. D. Foley. *Counseling and Discipline.* New York: McGraw-Hill, 1949.

Rational-Emotive Therapy

Theoretical Beginnings

Rational-emotive therapy, or RET, is active-directive and didactic. It is based in philosophic thought, and its supporters believe that it is more time efficient than other theories. Albert Ellis (1913–   ) is credited with the development of this counseling approach. Ellis, who was first a marriage counselor and then an orthodox psychoanalyst, broke with the classical approach to adopt neo-Freudianism. Disappointed with the minimal changes observed in clients, he became interested in learning theory, which led to the development of RET (Frey and Raming, 1979). Ellis (1980) identifies several influences that helped him to conceptualize his theory; they are a predilection for efficiency, a predilection for philosophy, a predilection for working, a predilection for teaching, and a predilection for skepticism, empiricism, and science. RET is generally felt to be appropriate for clients who can be reached verbally; this might exclude certain categories of autistic children, schizophrenics, or brain-damaged adults.

View of the Individual   The RET approach is based on the concept that human beings are different from other animals: They have values, they are able to think, and they develop cognitive structures. RET consciously and actively attempts to change values and thinking and the associations that are made between these aspects of the individual. Ellis, then, believes that the human is both a rational and irrational animal; irrationality is the source of emotional problems, such as guilt, anxiety, anger, and depression. Emotions are difficult to separate from thinking because "it appears to be almost impossible to sustain an emotional outburst without bolstering it by repeated ideas" (Ellis, 1967, p. 49). These repeated ideas are what Ellis calls self-talk, internalized sentences based on an individual's belief system.

The relationship among values and behaving suggested by Ellis differs from the models suggested by other therapists. Thinking, feeling, and behaving are seen as occurring simultaneously. Ellis (1974) states, "When they emote, they *also* think and act. When they act, they *also* think and emote. When they think, they *also* emote and act" (p. 313). Basically, people will feel the way they think. Strong beliefs cause emotional reactions and, if the beliefs can be changed, the emotional responses can be changed. If done consistently, emotional predispositions can permanently be altered in accord with philosophical tenets. Changes in thought, values, and philosophy then alter emotional affects and subsequent behavior. People can reindoctrinate themselves with different beliefs, can change their values, and, as a result, can behave quite differently.

Individuals are predisposed through heredity and environment to respond to a negative event with both rational and irrational thinking. They may want or desire certain things and, when they are unable to get them, condemn themselves and others. Rational thoughts might include "This is unpleasant" or "I don't like this." What then follows, Ellis would note, are the irrational sentences: "This is awful," "I can't stand it," or "I am worthless because this has happened." These irrational thoughts lead to the emotional upset and disturbance. Ellis (1967) postulated that "emotional disturbance, therefore, essentially consists of mistaken, illogical, unvalidatable sentences or meanings which the disturbed individual dogmatically and unchallengingly believes, and upon which he therefore emotes or acts to his own defeat" (p. 82). Ellis has devised an ABC model for behavior: A is the *activating* event, B is the *belief* system, and C is the emotional *consequence*. Unlike $S \rightarrow R$ where the stimulus is the cause of the response, A is not the cause of C, rather B (the self-talk) is the cause. Feelings are excited by the perception of a particular event and what is thought about it. Ellis (1967) states "that every human being who gets disturbed really is telling himself a chain of false sentences—since that is the way humans seem almost invariably to think in words, phrases, and sentences. And it is these sentences which really are what constitute his neuroses" (p. 28). For example, two individuals visit a flower garden (A). One individual experiences joy and a sense of awe at being surrounded with such beauty (C). The other individual experiences anxiety and depression (C) because she tells herself that her garden will never be as nice as this one and that she's a failure (B). The first individual has not subjected herself to any irrational ideas pertaining to her self-worth. Rather, she has told herself that she is in pleasant surroundings (B). A simplistic example, to be sure; however, the second individual has engaged in at least one illogical idea; that is, it is awful when things are not the way one wishes them to be. The challenge to the individual is to understand and change the self-defeating belief system in order to get the emotional consequence to change.

Neurosis is seen to result from irrational thinking and behaving—a natural state that afflicts everyone to some degree. Further, psychopathology is seen as learned and aggravated by the imposition of irrational beliefs from significant others which become self-imposed. People are victims of fallacious, culturally imposed thoughts that continuously affect behavior. These are maintained through autosuggestion and repetition by the individual.

Irrational beliefs are grounded in magical thinking—that is, needing rather than wanting, awfulizing, and "musterbating." The last may take the following forms: (1) "I must be perfect so that others will approve of me," (2) "Others must treat me fairly," and (3) "Situations *must* be the way that I want them." It is "awful" and "terrible" if these "musts" do not eventuate, and life becomes intolerable.

Ellis (1967) has identified eleven irrational ideas "which would seem inevitably to lead to widespread neurosis" (p. 61). Following is a brief explanation of each:

1. *"It is absolutely essential for an individual to be loved or approved of by every significant person in his or her environment."* The idea is irrational because it is impossible to be loved and approved of by everyone and still be self-directed. It's the adage "You can't please everyone, so you might as well please yourself."

2. *"It is necessary that each individual be completely competent, adequate, and achieving in all areas if the individual is to be worthwhile."* The pressure to be totally competent is tremendous, and the goal is doomed to failure. An individual who ascribes to this idea views any activity in terms of competition rather than enjoyment.

3. *"Some people are bad, wicked, or villainous, and these people should be blamed and punished."* Everyone makes mistakes, and blame and punishment are ineffective in behavior change. One is not worthless because one errs; the "crime" is in being human.

4. *"It is terrible and catastrophic when things are not the way an individual wants them to be."* When life is not going our way, it is unpleasant but hardly a catastrophe. "Catastrophisizing" doesn't change a thing and only causes us to feel worse. If we could view situations as merely bothersome, then we could either change the situation or accept it. Agonizing over situations is painful and solves nothing.

5. *"Unhappiness is a function of events outside the control of the individual."* Unless one is physically abused or deprived, people and events do little harm to individuals. It is a person's perceptions of experiences that do psychological damage and perceptions are, indeed, under the control of an individual.

6. *"If something may be dangerous or harmful, an individual should constantly be concerned and think about it."* This is an irrational idea since thinking about a dangerous situation doesn't change it, may lead to its occurrence, and can even make it worse than it actually is. Rationally, one should attempt to evaluate an event objectively and, if possible, alleviate or eliminate the fearful elements.

7. *"It is easier to run away from difficulties and self-responsibility than it is to face them."* Running away from a problem never solves it. The situation remains and eventually must be dealt with if it is to be resolved.

8. *"Individuals need to be dependent on others and have someone stronger than themselves to lean on."* Being dependent on others always puts one in a subordinate position and is not conducive to self-growth.

9. *"Past events in an individual's life determine present behavior and cannot be changed."* What has happened in the past is real and, as such, cannot be changed. However, an individual's past need not determine her or his future behavior. One does have the ability to effect any changes in present and future behavior.

10. *"An individual should be very concerned and upset by other individuals' problems."* If dealing with another person's problems places an overwhelming burden on an individual, that individual compounds the problem and thus is less able to help the person whose problem it actually is.

11. *"There is always a correct and precise answer to every problem, and it is catastrophic if it is not found."* Searching for the perfect solution is a frustrating and futile activity. Believing that there must be a correct solution to a human situation inevitably results in continuing dissatisfaction, since a precise answer does not exist. (Ellis, 1973a, pp. 152–153)

Ellis maintains that these illogical ideas are taught by parents, are reinforced by society, and are the primary causes of emotional disturbance. Counselors help clients to recognize that they should not rate themselves in any way and that they can always accept themselves. This, if understood, will eliminate many of these eleven irrational thoughts.

Goals

The major client goal of RET, as stated by Ellis (1973), is the "minimization of the client's central self-defeating outlook and his acquiring a more realistic, tolerant philosophy of life" (p. 184). Clients are able to relax and be less hard on themselves and others. Verbalizations and values that lead to disturbances are discarded. The major goal for all effective counselors "whether or not they realize what they are doing, [is to] teach or induce their patients to reperceive or rethink their life events and philosophies and thereby change their unrealistic and illogical thought, emotion, and behavior" (Ellis, 1962, pp. 36–37). Ellis and Harper (1961) state, "With this kind of highly active-directive, unpampering approach, I often find that I can push negativistic and inert people into self-healing action when a passive, nondirective technique would merely encourage them to continue their defeatist and defeating tendencies forever" (p. 168). Finally, clients become more independent of others' evaluations and look to themselves for positive reinforcement of behavior.

The Therapeutic Process

The main purposes of RET counseling are (1) to demonstrate to the client that self-talk is the source of the disturbance, and (2) to reevaluate this self-talk in order to eliminate it and subsequent illogical ideas. RET is viewed by Ellis as a comprehensive system, so that emotive-evocative approaches are used to confront individuals with their feelings, in order to get clients to acknowledge those feelings. The basic work of the RET counselor is shaped by Ellis's statement that "If . . . people essentially become emotionally disturbed because they unthinkingly accept certain illogical premises or irrational ideas, then there is good reason to believe that they can be somehow persuaded or taught to think more logically and rationally and thereby to undermine their own disturbances" (1962, p. 191). Ellis "cures" unreason with reason (Ewing, 1977). Homework and assignments may be used to desensitize the client to irrational beliefs and related feelings.

In the initial interview, the responsibilities of counselor and client are defined. The counselor explains the process as a learning experience through which the client will examine his or her manner of thinking and behaving. The client is responsible for practicing any learning acquired during the counseling sessions. Practicing means homework.

The counselor proceeds to establish a working relationship with the client by utilizing attending skills, by assisting the client in verbalizing personal concerns, and by deciding on appropriate behavior modification. The counselor-client relationship, however, is not seen as the crucial ingredient in the therapeutic process. Counselor acceptance would be viewed as "needing the approval of someone else" and would become a self-defeating end. The need for "counselor approval" is seen as irrational, that is, the client can do without it. Counselees can be shown that they can accept themselves whether or not anyone else in the entire world accepts them. Ellis would believe that regard is truly unconditional if the necessity for acceptance by the therapist is not a string attached to the counseling process. As Johnson (1980) points out: "In working with clients, Ellis would very strongly and vigorously attack (he uses the term attack frequently) the illogical belief systems of clients and try to force them to see that their beliefs were illogical. He would spend little time in building rapport with clients and would not be concerned that his vigorous approach could alienate clients" (p. 49). Johnson does state, however, that some RET counselors spend more time than Ellis in building rapport.

Some illogical ideas will likely be attendant upon the client's problems. The counselor confronts these immediately with Ellis's ABC method of analysis; using the ABC method to analyze illogical ideas will be the client's homework. Confrontation is a major ingredient in RET, since this school of counseling does not believe that the simple expression of feelings and a nurturing relationship will get to the root of a client's irrational thinking. Counselors take an active role in the early sessions by consistently challenging the client's internalized beliefs, which maintain the client's self-defeating thinking and behaving. Client resistance may be encountered at this point, and several sessions may be devoted to working through this resistance.

RET counselors do not ignore the expression of feelings; rather, they evoke and confront them in the client. Emotions are dealt with in concrete fashion. Exercises may even be used in groups to help participants get in touch with their feelings. This, then, helps to identify the clients' ABC process and to change their basic philosophy of life.

As mentioned earlier, homework is assigned to the client. Material may have to be read or films viewed. A major portion of homework is the application of the ABC method of analysis to situations that induce negative emotional responses (for example, anxiety, guilt, and depression). The client is taught to challenge, contradict, and rethink those internalized beliefs, with their accompanying "shoulds" and "musts," that control the negative emotional state. The client is encouraged to formulate, and subsequently examine for feasibility, alternate ways of thinking and acting. New behavior proceeding from new thinking is put to the test outside the counseling sessions, and the results are then reported to the counselor. This is, in effect, "in vivo" desensitization. Ellis would suggest that behavior changes effect emotional changes. All changes—emotional, cognitive, behavioral—are interactive, and RET is a concerted effort to change the irrational and self-defeating thoughts of the individual. While the assignments may be conceived and directed by the therapist, care is taken to help the client become self-directive. This is done, even though the counselor may be authoritative, by teaching the client the scientific, logical, empirical method that is used. The therapist throughout assumes the role of a "teacher more than that of an intensely, relating partner" (Ellis, 1974, p. 231). The client is taught to be independent and to act and work without concert of a therapist or peer group. If this is not achieved, therapy would not be considered to have been effective. As therapy progresses, counselor direction decreases while client self-direction increases. This would not be dissimilar to a teaching approach with any subject matter, and, in fact, the client is seen as a learner.

If the client has successfully accomplished what she or he has set out to do, the counselor offers positive reinforcement. Even if the results of the experiment were less than expected, if beliefs (B) concerning the activating event (A) are no longer irrational, the emotional response (C) will be disappointing rather than catastrophic. If the new behavior has failed in that the emotional response (C) was highly negative, the client will be confronted with the illogical thinking most emphatically and the process will begin again. It is important to note that clients are not initially exposed to highly threatening situations, since this may elicit an avoidance response, which will temporarily remove anxiety but will also encourage more of the original irrational thinking. The counselor will help the client get to point D where the counselor will dispute and teach the client how to dispute the various rational and irrational hypotheses the client holds about the self in the world. At D clients are asked to look at "Why they can't stand something?" or "Why is an occurrence awful or terrible?" Ellis (1974) states that this is the quickest way in therapy to help people change self-defeating emotional responses. At point E the client realizes a new effect and might say "It's too bad if he rejects me! I don't have to reject myself! I cannot please everybody." A restatement occurs rationally and there is acceptance of things the way they are without the emotion-causing negative cognition. The client at this point loses C. C becomes just another behavioral effect (E); in other words, there may be feelings of unhappiness or sorrow, but the client would stop deflating or depreciating the self. The client has been helped to "rethink" the irrational. Counselor interpretation has helped in the rethinking process. The rethinking allows the client to mobilize personal resources to tackle and change the problem.

Goldfried and Goldfried (1980) describe four general steps in rational restructuring: (1) helping clients recognize that cognitions mediate emotional arousal, (2) helping clients recognize the irrationality of certain beliefs, (3) helping clients understand that unrealistic cognitions mediate their own maladaptive emotions, and (4) helping clients to change their unrealistic cognitions (pp. 103–107). More specifically, Ellis (1973) presents some of the techniques used by the RET counselor:

1. Identifies basic irrational ideas underlying disturbed behavior
2. Challenges and confronts client to validate these ideas
3. Attempts to demonstrate the illogical nature of the thinking
4. Logically analyzes the thoughts to minimize the irrational beliefs
5. Demonstrates the inoperativeness of the beliefs and how they lead to emotional and behavioral disturbances

6. Uses absurdity and humor to confront the irrationality of the client's thoughts
7. Explains how the irrational thoughts can be replaced with rational ones that are more empirically grounded
8. Teaches the application of the scientific method to thinking so that the client will be able to apply it to present or future ideas.

The RET counselor simply helps the client to mobilize for action, having faith in the client to do so rapidly once shown how. The alternative is lengthy insight therapy to sort out values and feelings. The effect of RET is thought to generalize to all aspects of the client's life. The same principles applied to one specific problem area in counseling can be applied to another problem area by the client. The counselor in some instances may initially have to show how this is done, but once the technique is learned, the client will be able to make such transfers without assistance.

Mahoney and Arnkoff (1978) write, "Although RET has become a more and more popular therapy over the last decades, this popularity can hardly be attributed to the strength of its empirical support. Until very recently there were only a handful of controlled experimental evaluations of RET and these offered only modest support for its clinical efficacy" (p. 705). Many studies, however, support the major hypothesis of RET: that B (belief systems), rather than A (activating event), is the cause of C (emotional consequence). Among these are Frank (1968), Folkins (1970), Davitz (1969), and Geis (1966). Other studies have shown that emotional disturbances are significantly correlated with the irrational ideas listed by Ellis. Two of these are Tosi and Carlson (1970) and Velten (1968). The idea that homework assignments are a valid tool for behavior change has been supported by Ritter (1968), Davison (1965), and others. Smith et al. (1979) found that rational-behavior therapy achieved significant treatment gains with offenders in a work release setting.

A number of recent studies looked at the behavior of the RET counselor during counseling. Hill et al. (1979) analyzed transcripts of filmed counseling sessions by Carl Rogers, Fritz Perls, and Albert Ellis. Of the three Ellis was the most active, using mostly information, direct guidance, minimal encouragers, interpretations, closed questions, and restatements. They concluded that Ellis challenged irrational cognitions, replacing them with new rational thinking. His style was mainly information giving, interpreting, guiding, and offering minimal encouragers. Meara et al. (1979) conducted a stylistic investigation of client-counselor language and the stylistic complexity of the interviews by Rogers, Perls, and Ellis. It was anticipated that Ellis would assume the role of an active explainer, and that his responses would be frequent, detailed, elaborate, and complex. This was supported. Ellis's language was most complex of the three therapists, while the client conversely was most complex with Ellis. The client had a hard time trying to keep up with Ellis and noted that he appealed to her thinking, not feeling self. Meara et al. (1981) in a later study of the Rogers, Perls, and Ellis dialogue with the female client did note that Ellis used action verb types frequently, but there were no significant differences from the other two therapists.

Summary and Evaluation

The RET approach is an active-directive therapy, in which the client is a learner and the counselor is a teacher. The counselor actively attacks the client's irrational assumptions to achieve valuative and behavioral changes. It has only been recently that RET has received the attention it deserves; some of this attention has developed because of an interest in cognitive behaviorism—a surprising new interface between behaviorists and cognitive psychologists. Much of cognitive behaviorism operates from tenets similar to those employed by RET. Take, for example, several cognitive-behavioral tasks listed by Blocher (1980):

Arrive at a mutually defined and accepted identification of the client's problem or concern that includes an awareness of the emotional components, that is, where or why the client hurts.

Develop a mutually agreed upon statement of goals or desired outcomes to which both counselor and client are explicitly committed.

Restructure the client's cognitions by developing a problem-solving or decision-making framework, an appropriate set of causal attributions regarding the dynamics of the problem, and an appropriate set of self-statements about the severity and probable outcome of the situation.

Specify carefully the needed changes in client behavior and provide modeling practice and reinforcement of these "target" behaviors.

Provide for the transfer and maintenance of the target behavior in the "real world" of the client's environment before terminating contact. (pp. 336–337)

It appears that RET, whether it retains its traditional form or is integrated into a broader cognitive-behavioral model, will continue to be a dynamic force in therapeutic practice.

Of existing counseling theories, Albert Ellis in RET has best been able to conceptualize the thinking process and the role it plays in client cognitive development. A major point, however, made by critics of RET is that they are not ready to accept the formulations posited in RET about the relationship between thinking and feeling. Such criticism centers on skepticism that "internal dialogue alone triggers emotions and more consideration has to be given to other influences. In the future development of RET, especially with the emergence of other cognitive approaches, terms such as *rational* and *adaptive* will have to be defined more clearly. On the other hand, RET strategies are particularly helpful in restructuring client thinking and belief systems during counseling; RET is one treatment of choice in working with the depressed client. While it may be difficult to test some of the hypotheses made by RET supporters (for example that thoughts generate feelings), the research evidence for RET's effectiveness is impressive at this time.

Suggested Readings

Beck, A. T. *Cognitive Therapy and the Emotional Disorders.* New York: International Universities Press, 1976.

Ellis, A. *Reason and Emotion in Psychotherapy.* New York: Lyle Stuart, 1962.

————. *Humanistic Psychotherapy: The Rational-Emotive Approach.* New York: Julian Press, 1973.

————, and R. Grieger. *Handbook of Rational-Emotive Therapy.* New York: Springer, 1977.

————, and R. A. Harper. *A New Guide to Rational Living.* Rev. ed. Hollywood: Wilshire Books, 1975.

Behavioral Counseling

Theoretical Beginnings

Behavioral counseling involves the application of experimentally derived and established principles of learning to weaken or eliminate maladaptive behavior and to build or strengthen replacement behaviors that are adaptive. The foundation for behavioral counseling is learning theory, developed by numerous philosophers, clinical psychologists, experimental psychologists, and researchers. Unlike most of the other theories of counseling and psychotherapy reviewed in this text, there is no one thinker who discovered and developed this theoretical approach.

Gray (1932) is credited as the first to use the term *behavior modification* (Farkus, 1980), when he promoted its use in the educational setting. *Behavior therapy* was introduced by Skinner and Lindsley (1954) in their report "Studies in Behavior Therapy, Status Reports II and III," which reported on their work with psychotic patients. The terms *behavior therapy* and *behavior therapist* were first published in a professional journal by Lazarus (1958) when he argued for adding more "objective, laboratory-derived therapeutic tools to more orthodox psychotherapeutic techniques" (Lazarus, 1971, p. 2). In 1959, Eysenck also used the term *behavior therapy* and in rapid succession published two journal articles (1959, 1963) and two books (1960, 1964), which quickly introduced and explained the theory to fellow professionals.

The field of behavioral counseling (or therapy) began with animal research, from which evolved learning theory. The early 1950s saw the initiation of testing the theory on people. During the middle and late 1950s techniques of behavior change were emphasized (Farkas, 1980). More recently, the field is being stretched by Meichenbaum (1974) and Beck (1976) into cognitive-behavior modification, which is discussed in this chapter.

View of the Individual

In general, very little attention has been given to a theory of personality in the behavioral counseling model. Attention has focused mainly on how people learn and can change unhelpful and troublesome learnings. Most behaviorists adhere to the tabula rasa, or blank-slate, theory of John Locke:

People are born into this world neither intrinsically good nor bad; they are neutral. As they interact with their environment, which includes significant others, their experiences and resultant behavior are recorded on the slate—initially in chalk, if you will, which can easily be erased. If the behavior is consistently reinforced, the chalk is traced over in paint, still not indelible, but much harder to remove from the slate. The question, then, is "How does any behavior come to be written on the tablet in the first place?"

Learning Behavior   Behaviorists believe that behaviors are learned through three paradigms: classical conditioning, operant conditioning, and imitative learning.

1. *Classical Conditioning*   A number of things in our environment elicit a human response spontaneously. Therefore the response is not learned. Examples include a puff of air on the eye, which elicits a blink; a loud noise, fear; food, salivation. Because the reaction is natural to all of us at birth, the stimulus is called an *unconditioned stimulus*. This kind of stimulus does not need to have a response conditioned to it; the response follows naturally and is called the *unconditioned response*. A *neutral stimulus* is one that does not elicit a specific subject response repetitively. Watson and Rayner (1920) found that, when a neutral stimulus (white rat) was presented simultaneously with the unconditioned stimulus (loud noise), the unconditioned response (fear) became the conditioned response for the neutral stimulus. Now, since the white rat (neutral stimulus) elicited a response (fear) and would do so repeatedly, the white rat is called the conditioned stimulus and the fear is the conditioned response. A previously neutral stimulus that has been paired with an unconditioned stimulus in eliciting the unconditioned response is called a *conditioned stimulus*. The response that has been learned is called a *conditioned response*. Pavlov (1927) and his dogs are an example of learning through classical conditioning. The presence of food (unconditioned stimulus) caused the dog to salivate (unconditioned response). This type of behavior is an innate characteristic, which enables an organism to maintain itself. When the ringing of a bell (conditioned stimulus) is added to the appearance of food, the dog learns to salivate at the sound of the bell (conditioned response).

It is obvious at this point that the conditioned stimulus and its conditioned response will continue their cause-and-effect relationship forever if nothing interferes with it. Phobias and sexual perversions are examples of learning by classical conditioning. For example, if Jessie gets into an elevator (neutral stimulus) and it gets stuck between floors, which is a trauma (unconditioned stimulus), fear (unconditioned response) will be elicited. The elevator then becomes the conditioned stimulus and the fear is the conditioned response. Jessie will avoid all elevators in the future, often climbing many floors by stairs if needed. In sexual situations, stimulation (unconditioned stimulus) elicits an orgasm (unconditioned response). If the person plays with the other's hair or an object such as shoes (neutral stimulus) during the orgasmic phase, then the object will become the conditioned stimulus and the orgasm, the conditioned response. Thus learning has occurred.

2. *Operant Conditioning*   B. F. Skinner (1938) is credited with defining the laws of operant conditioning. This approach suggests that behavior (stimulus) occurs spontaneously or at random and some event follows the behavior that is experienced as giving pleasure (reinforcement). This reinforcement increases the chance that the stimulus will reoccur in the future. Thus a dog comes when she is called and is rewarded with a piece of food. The likelihood of her coming the next time she is called has been increased. If no reinforcement is ever given (including petting or any kind of attention), the probability of her coming the next time will not change.

3. *Imitative Learning*   Imitative learning is also known as modeling, social learning, and observational learning. In many cases, learning occurs when no apparent reinforcement is forthcoming. Bandura's (1969) work has refined this theory of learning. In imitative learning, a person sees another's behavior, which "teaches" him what to copy. If the model is rewarded for the behavior, the lesson is strengthened. If the behavior is performed by the observer and is reinforced, the learning is strengthened. This is a very popular method of learning and as such is very important. Commercials and styles of clothing worn as well as behaviors adopted from admired athletes are vivid examples of the potency of imitative learning. This explains why the saying "Do as I say and not as I do" has no effect. If people want their children to behave honestly and responsibly, then they must model it for them and preferably reward the children when they behave accordingly.

Factors in Learning Behavior

Reinforcement   Reinforcements are by definition those events that, when they follow behavior, increase its probability of recurring. There are two general types of reinforcement: positive and negative.

Positive reinforcement is the presentation of a pleasurable event following some behavior. It increases the likelihood that the behavior will be repeated. Any form of recognition may be reinforcing; examples are presentations of a gift, money, or food. Positive reinforcers are determined by the recipient. Therefore, what might be a reinforcer for one person might be poison for the next. Additionally, what constitutes punishment for Jane (being scolded by the teacher) might be reinforcing for Bill, who experiences it as attention and recognition. Careful attention must be given to the individual's values and the valence given to possible reinforcements.

Negative reinforcement is "the operation of removing an aversive stimulus contingent upon a response" (Michael and Myerson, 1962, p. 384). Since negative reinforcement is a form of reinforcement, it must by definition increase the probability of recurrence for the targeted behavior. For example, people agree to shun Billy until he begins to speak without yelling. The behavior of shunning Billy is aversive and the act of removing it on evidence of his emitting the target behavior (speaking in a moderate voice) is an example of negative reinforcement.

Punishment   Punishment must be differentiated from negative reinforcement since they are often confused. Punishment is the application of an aversive response after the display of a disapproved behavior. Punishment is by definition the application of an aversive event that will *decrease* the likelihood of the target behavior's recurrence. Therefore, if a child does something a parent wants and that parent hugs him, which makes the child feel embarrassed and uncomfortable enough to persuade him not to repeat the act, it must be said that the hug was punishment.

Schedules of Reinforcement   The frequency and timing of the application of providing a reinforcement is called a *schedule of reinforcement.* The best schedule of reinforcement to initially condition a response is called *continuous reinforcement.* It is the application of the reinforcement after each successful presentation of the target behavior. For example, to condition your dog to come when it is called, present the dog a morsel to eat immediately after she has obeyed the command. Do this for 20 to 30 times or until it is obvious she will obey. While this schedule is best to condition a new behavior, it shows the least resistance to being extinguished. That is, if the reinforcement is delivered each time (like a candy machine) and then ceases to provide the reinforcement for some reason, the act that has been conditioned will soon cease (extinction). With the candy machine, about two or three trials without receiving the reward will warrant an "Out of Order" sign.

Intermittent schedules are very resistant to extinction. They do not provide the reinforcement every time but instead, intermittently. A *ratio schedule* provides a reinforcement after a predetermined number of correct responses. Therefore, every fifth correct response would be reinforced. A better method is to use an average of every fifth response, such as the third, eighth, tenth, seventeenth, twenty-fifth, and so on. An *interval schedule* has to do with the lapse of time since the last correct reinforced response. The reward is delivered on the first correct response after the lapse of the predetermined period of time.

These intermittent responses are much more resistant to extinction since the subject does not know exactly when the next reinforcement will be administered. An intermittent reward schedule is not as effective as continuous reinforcement to initially condition a behavior, but the learning lasts longer. Gambling is a perfect example of intermittent reinforcement and the gambling addiction speaks of the strength of both imitative learning and intermittent reinforcement.

Extinction   Behavior that has been conditioned will occur for as long as it elicits intermittent reinforcement. The cessation of *all* reinforcement will result in the behavior disappearing. This disappearance is termed extinction. Emphasis must be given to the concept of withdrawing all reinforcement consistently. Take as an example withdrawing attention from a child when he is whining; if after several days, during which the whining has decreased, the parent slips and responds to the whining, the result has been to create an intermittent reinforcement schedule. Thus the very behavior that was targeted for extinction has instead been made more resistant to extinction and more persistent.

Generalization   Generalization is the principle that permits us to transfer learning from one situation to another when there is some similarity in the situations. This helps us economize our time since we do not need to go through a complete learning process for each new situation we encounter. Thus people, who have learned that being assertive yields positive benefits in one situation, will be able to apply this learning in similar situations. However, these situations are in some way different and therefore people need to recognize this difference and develop the ability to discriminate.

Discrimination   This is a person's ability to discriminate between two or more similar stimuli that give different responses to the conditioned stimulus. For example, if one stimulus reinforces the behavior while the other extinguishes it, the act of responding appropriately to this is called discrimination. An appropriate response is to increase one's response rate to the reinforcing stimulus and decrease the response rate to the extinguishing stimulus.

Shaping   The learning of complex behaviors starts with learning simple behaviors and then using the laws of discrimination, extinction, generalization, and, of course, reinforcement to learn successively more complex behaviors until the target behavior is learned. In short, a rather crude approximation of a complex target behavior is emitted and then reinforced. After this behavior is learned, then a closer approximation of the behavior will be reinforced while all others will be extinguished. The subject will need to discriminate this to seek out another closer approximation, which in turn will be reinforced while the old approximation will be extinguished. Shaping occurs naturally when parents give their child attention when she makes her first approximation of a word such as "m, m, m, m." But after a lapse of time this becomes less exciting and therefore yields less intense reinforcement for the child. This pushes the child to utter the closer approximation of "ma, ma, ma." Then the child will learn other single words and begin to put together two, three, and four words and finally make a sentence and then several sentences. All of these closer approximations are reinforced while the previous approximations are no longer reinforced and therefore extinguished. Examples of shaping programs can be found under "Sample Counseling Programs" in Chapter 13 of this text.

Personality Development   It can be seen that the basis for the structure of a person's personality are the behaviors she learns. If behavior is reinforced by a potent reinforcer, then it will be learned. Since Mother is the provider of nourishment, the infant generalizes to pleasing her and then generalizes to pleasing Father. Their giving of love, attention, and recognition are potent reinforcers. The effect of those reinforcers is of utmost importance especially during infancy and later during childhood. The child will further generalize behaviors that please Mother and Father by behaving in the approved way even when they are not present because of her knowledge of their approval. As the child grows, her environment has an increasingly powerful effect on her. Her personality develops as she is acted on by environmental reinforcers. Some reinforcers act on behavior that is maladaptive or inappropriate. As normal, adaptive behaviors are learned, so too are maladaptive ones. All behaviors that are evidenced are in some way reinforced and therefore experienced as pleasurable. Behavior that is maladaptive either brings the person into conflict with society or fails to bring pleasure to the person (that is, brings anxiety). Therefore the counselor must be adept at understanding reinforcement and must be able to identify those forces that maintain behaviors that the client seeks to extinguish.

Goals   To reiterate, the goals of behavioral counseling will vary with each client. However, these goals are specific for the client and are enumerated during the history-taking. Krumboltz (1966) has said that counseling goals should be stated differently for each individual client; should be compatible with, though not necessarily identical to, the values of the counselor; and should be observable. The necessity for the goals to be compatible with counselor values is significant, because once the decision is made to accept a client, the responsibility for the outcome is the counselor's. The counseling is conducted in the framework of client awareness and desire to achieve the goals he or she has set. Essentially, the goal of counseling is to extinguish the client's identified maladaptive behavior and to introduce or strengthen adaptive behavior that can serve as a replacement and enable her to live a productive, happy life.

The Therapeutic Process   A warm, empathic relationship is essential before any work can be undertaken. The counselor must establish a good working relationship to determine the client's problems and gain his cooperation (Krumboltz, 1966).

Steps in the Therapeutic Process   The behaviorist takes much time with the client to define specific concerns and to outline specific techniques. Blackham and Silberman (1971) have suggested four steps, which are paraphrased here, to facilitate this procedure.

1. *Problem Definition*   It is necessary to determine all the circumstances surrounding the inappropriate behavior. What are the client's strengths, weaknesses, and limitations? Essentially, the counselor needs to ascertain when the problem occurs, what precedes and what follows it, and what about the behavior is reinforcing to the client.

2. *Ascertainment of Developmental and Social History* The client's history is valuable insofar as it may delineate many problem areas as well as indicate physical reasons for certain behavior. The counselor specifically seeks information about the client's development, the changes that occurred, and how he adapted to these changes. The client's sense of control over his life and his problems needs to be assessed. The client's ability to relate to others and to his environment is also assessed. Finally the counselor seeks to understand the client's culture, value structure, and behavioral norms from both a historical and current perspective.

3. *Specification of Counseling Goals* The goals for an individual client will depend on the specific problem. Both the counselor and client come to an agreement on what actually is the problem. It is the counselor's responsibility, at this point, to decide if the goal is within his or her realm of expertise and in accord with ethical considerations. Goal setting depends on the data collected in steps 1 and 2. Goals need to be specified in terms that are behavioral and observable to ensure (a) the application of the appropriate techniques, and (b) agreement as to when they have been attained. The specification of goals is described in depth in Chapter 12 of this text.

4. *Selection of Methods to Be Utilized* While the techniques used in the counseling process will vary, they must be compatible with the client's goals. Krumboltz (1965) states, "Counseling consists of whatever ethical activities a counselor undertakes in an effort to help the client engage in those types of behavior which will lead to a resolution of the client's problems."

   In addition to the above four steps outlined by Blackham and Silberman is this fifth step.

5. *Evaluation and Termination* The client's progress toward the specified goals will be evaluated at regular intervals. If the evaluation yields negative results, the goals and/or the techniques need further assessment and possible alteration. If the evaluation is positive and the goals have been attained, then the client is ready to either determine new goals to work toward or to terminate counseling.

Techniques of Behavioral Counseling As step 4 above outlined, there are several techniques of behavior counseling. A few of the more common behavior techniques are relaxation training, systematic desensitization, and assertiveness training.

Relaxation Training Training in relaxation is appropriate for anyone who is tense or anxious. It was introduced as deep muscle relaxation by Jacobson (1938) and popularized by Wolpe (1969) as an important step in systematic desensitization. Training can be conducted by the counselor in her or his office or as homework using relaxation tapes (Lazarus, 1971). Essentially, the client is taught to flex muscle groups to a straining point and focus on the feeling produced, recognizing it as tension. The client is then told to relax those muscles by "letting go of the tension" gradually and notice the resultant feelings of relaxation, calmness, and warmness. The muscle groups might start with the right then left fist and arm, the right then left foot and leg, the buttocks, the abdomen, the back, the head (including the area around the eyes and jaw), the neck, and then the shoulders.

If a person is generally anxious, training in relaxation will help her to recognize signs of the anxiety, realize that she can control those feelings and become more relaxed, and teach her the process of relaxing. The theory states that a person cannot feel two incompatible feelings simultaneously. Since tension or anxiety are incompatible with relaxation, they cannot be experienced at the same time; therefore, one of the feelings (hopefully the tension) will need to diminish while the other increases. This concept is the operational principle, called *counterconditioning,* in systematic desensitization.

Systematic Desensitization   This technique is used when anxiety is the product of either thoughts about or exposure to a specific, identifiable event. It is a step-by-step method used to replace the anxiety associated with the event or thoughts about the event by the incompatible feeling state of relaxation. Therefore, the client "unlearns" to associate the event with anxiety and "learns" to associate relaxation with it.

Wolpe (1969) suggests three steps to the procedure:

1. Training in deep muscle relaxation;
2. The construction of anxiety hierarchies;
3. Counterposing relaxation and anxiety-evoking stimuli from the hierarchies. (Wolpe, 1969, p. 100)

For a description of the procedure used, the reader is encouraged to read Wolpe (1969) or Lazarus (1971).

Assertiveness Training   Assertiveness is the appropriate expression of a person's feelings other than anxiety. People who are assertive are able to express their opinions, desires, wishes, disappointments, regrets, and feelings, such as being hurt, sad, happy, or angry. Assertive people usually feel good about themselves and frequently achieve their wishes. "Assertive training, generally speaking, is required for patients who in interpersonal contexts have unadaptive anxiety responses that prevent them from saying or doing what is reasonable and right" (Wolpe, 1969, p. 61). The training consists of counterconditioning the anxiety that inhibits being assertive and operant conditioning the act of being assertive. It is wise to use a shaping strategy in the training to ensure that the client will start with easy situations and progress to more difficult ones. Again, every effort is made to ensure gradual success and to continue to build on all previous successes. A failure stops progress. Finally, clients must learn that they can conduct the test for assertiveness at any time. The test asks the question, "Did my behavior in the given situation improve, decrease, or have no effect on my self-esteem?" If the answer is "improve" or "have no effect on" the self-esteem, then the person was appropriately assertive. If it decreased self-esteem then that individual was not appropriately assertive. Too frequently, people evaluate their assertiveness based on its effect on others and, as a consequence, find that they need to express themselves with extra force, often becoming aggressive, insulting, and hostile, thus "bullying" people into being compliant. Remember, assertiveness is learning to express one's honest feelings in an appropriate manner; it should make the client feel good about herself or himself, not manipulate others.

Summary and Evaluation

Behavioral counseling is based on learning theory. Behaviorists believe that personality is the composite of what the person has learned in the process of interacting with the environment. The three modes of learning are classical conditioning, operant conditioning, and imitative learning. There are a few innate influences on our feelings and behavior, and they are not amenable to change. Therefore, behavioral counseling focuses on that which is available to our control. The counselor who conducts behavioral counseling will be a warm, empathic person and will establish a strong working relationship with the client and take a detailed behavioral history. Counselor and client together will identify problem areas, specify specific behavioral goals to be achieved, select the appropriate techniques to achieve those goals, and, finally, evaluate progress during and at the conclusion of counseling.

Behavioral counseling has fostered the application of behavioral goals to counseling. These goals permit the counselor and client to identify specific limits to their counseling, specify the criteria for termination, permit the use of contracts, and incorporate a built-in method for measuring results. In addition, behavioral counseling has contributed counseling techniques that are easily defined, taught, and used. Criticism is directed at the cold and distant manner in which some behavioral counselors conduct their sessions. The method finds the relationship between the counselor and the client to be unimportant to the therapeutic outcome, and as a result, client treatment often seems impersonal. Finally behavioral counseling makes no attempt to treat that which is not overt and quantifiable; it ignores the realm of feelings and conflicts that defy definition.

Suggested Readings

Bandura, A. *Principles of Behavior Modification.* New York: Holt, Rinehart and Winston, 1969.

Krumboltz, J., and C. E. Thoresen, eds. *Counseling Methods.* New York: Holt, Rinehart and Winston, 1976.

Lazarus, A. A. *Behavior Therapy and Beyond.* New York: McGraw-Hill, 1971.

Mahoney, M. F., and C. E. Thoresen. *Self-Control: Power to the Person.* Monterey, Calif.: Brooks/Cole, 1974.

Wolpe, J. *The Practice of Behavior Therapy.* New York: Pergamon, 1969.

Reality Therapy

Theoretical Beginnings

Reality therapy holds that people have two basic needs. Behavior that helps the individual to meet these needs is seen as responsible, behavior that does not is irresponsible. People have the ability to choose to develop identities that are oriented to success or failure by how they choose to satisfy their needs.

William Glasser, born in 1925 and originally trained in psychoanalysis, grew increasingly disenchanted with its lack of effectiveness during his work at the Veterans Administration Neuro-psychiatric Hospital in West Los Angeles and at the Ventura School, an institution for the treatment of older adolescent girls in California. Glasser wrote *Mental Health or Mental Illness?* (1960). In it he began to formulate the theory that he would label reality therapy in 1964. He solidified his ideas at the Ventura School and expressed the theory in the book *Reality Therapy: A New Approach to Psychiatry* (1965), which today remains the authoritative work on the theory. Also, as a result of his work at Ventura School, Glasser began to apply reality therapy to the school setting. He sees two developmental crisis points in the life of children. One of these is the age range of 5 to 10, which is when children, who now attend school, often experience failure and its accompanying feelings for the first time. Secondly, children also learn how it feels not to be cared about by important people (teachers and staff) in their lives. Glasser wrote *Schools Without Failure* (1969), which emphasizes learning without failing, discipline without punishment, and self-responsibility. Today, the idea of *Schools Without Failure* has increased in popularity, both in public and private schools, as well as in institutions like the Ventura School. His most recent work, *Stations of the Mind* (Glasser, 1981), lends support to his theory by explaining how the brain works in a manner that permits the brain to be used in both personal and professional living. As founder and president of the Institute of Reality Therapy, Glasser and his colleagues published its first journal, *Journal of Reality Therapy*, in September 1981.

View of the Individual

Reality therapy stipulates that people have two basic needs, which if unfulfilled cause pain. They are: *"The need to love and be loved and the need to feel that we are worthwhile to ourselves and to others"* (Glasser, 1965, p. 10). The need to feel love and be loved includes all forms of affection from friendship to parental love. Every person needs to feel love throughout life. It is necessary both to love someone and to feel loved. When we are unable to fulfill our need for love, we suffer from anxiety, self-blame, depression and anger and possibly withdraw from society. Glasser believes that death results if a person experiences a complete deficit of love early in life. Later in life, a total deficit of love might stimulate sufficient depression to cause suicide or psychosis.

The need to feel worthwhile to ourselves and to others is as important as loving and feeling loved. The needs are intertwined and seemingly interdependent. A person who feels worthwhile to himself and to others is able to love others and in turn to be loved. The person who feels loved by others is most likely able to feel worthwhile to others and to herself and consequently able to love.

The act of loving does not connote total approval of the person's behavior. Children, as well as adults, are able to recognize the difference between right and wrong. When the child receives approval for behavior known to be wrong, she harbors confusion, which inhibits the development of feeling worthwhile. When the child senses the approval for what is known to be wrong, he has taken the first step toward becoming a spoiled child. Children will behave in a manner designed to get their parents to set behavioral limits and establish appropriate expectations. It is these expectations that give children a chance to seek approval and gain self-respect.

Glasser believes that for a person to feel worthwhile, he must have some kind of a yardstick with which to measure himself. Yardsticks are standards of behavior, such as morals, rules, values, or other estimates of right and wrong. These standards are given to us as children by our parents. They indicate when and how we have failed ourselves, as well as when we have been successful. The failure to meet appropriate standards leads to anxiety, guilt, or self-disapproval and stimulates us to work to overcome it. If as young children we fail to learn to fulfill our needs, we will suffer, and this suffering will push us to relieve the pain in ways that will only cause more pain, which will accumulate for our whole life. If, however, we are taught to satisfy our needs, the more we accomplish this the happier our life will be. Since life changes, we need some flexibility to permit us to learn new ways to satisfy our needs. Therefore, when people are suffering psychological problems, it can be assumed that they lack the proper involvement with someone and, therefore, are unable to satisfy their needs (Glasser, 1965).

People who are able to satisfy their needs develop a *success identity.* These people exhibit two traits (Glasser and Zunin, 1973). The first trait is the awareness that someone in the world loves them and that they love at least one other person. The second trait is the knowledge that most of the time they are worthwhile persons and that at least one other person also thinks them to be worthwhile. The success identity develops in stages (Wubbolding, 1981). First is the *Do It Person* stage where the person begins to "do it," which means to initiate on the desire to improve, no matter how minimal is this beginning.

The second stage of development of the success identity is the *Positive Symptom Person.* In this stage the individual: (1) *acts constructively,* that is, acts assertively to express herself and contribute to her enhancement while she acts altruistically for the welfare of others; (2) *feels positive,* which entails using the good feelings of happiness, joy, trust, and self-acceptance to control the continuance of positive growth; (3) *thinks rationally* rather than thinking irrationally (psychotically), thus the person seeks to approach problems and issues reasonably, thoroughly, and maturely; (4) *centers on healthy activities* by following a responsible diet and getting appropriate exercise that satisfies her physical needs.

The third and final stage in the success identity is the *Fulfilled Person* who feels free, is having fun, feels love for and loved by others, and feels competent and has a sense of self-worth.

Just as there are stages in the success identity, there are three stages in the *failure identity* (Wubbolding, 1981). The first stage is the *Give Up Person* who begins to give up being responsible for making his behavior meet the standards of expectation. The second stage in the failure identity is the *Symptom Person* who after giving up being responsible begins to act out his frustration and maladaptive attempts to satisfy his needs, becoming emotionally upset, possibly psychotic, or exhibiting a psychosomatic disease. The final stage is the *Negatively Addicted Person* who, due to his compounding failures, allows himself to become addicted to food, drugs, or gambling. The negatively addicted person is lonely, self-critical, irrational, unhappy, irresponsible and maintains rigid, ineffective behaviors that seek only temporary relief (Glasser, 1972). The positively addicted person, on the other hand, feels involved, self-accepting, rational, happy, and responsible and maintains flexible, effective behaviors.

Reality therapy's basic concept is individual *responsibility.* Being responsible is being able to fulfill one's needs in a manner that does not deprive others of the opportunity to fulfill their needs. Responsible persons are able to initiate appropriate behaviors that both fulfill their needs and meet their standards, thus helping them to feel worthwhile. The ability to be responsible is learned and therefore can be taught. The responsibility for teaching responsibility lies with the parents. Those who have not learned to be responsible or who have lost that ability are described as *irresponsible.* These are the people others call mentally ill, neurotic, or psychotic. The use of these terms, according to reality therapy, excuses the individual from being responsible by implying that irresponsibility is caused by events, internal or external, over which the person has no control. Reality therapy believes that responsibility is taught through exposure to love and discipline and that everyone is capable of learning it. The earlier one learns it, the better will be that person's quality of life. Glasser believes that children want to be responsible, but they need parents to demonstrate a model of responsibility to learn it. Irresponsible parents will rear irresponsible children. It is the parents' responsibility to fulfill their children's needs of loving, being loved, and feeling worthwhile which facilitates the children's ability to do the same with other adults and children. For example, a mother will show her love and responsibility by giving her children both discipline and love. If she permits her children to behave irresponsibly by ignoring or excusing their actions, she is showing impaired love. Self-respect is taught through discipline, and closeness to others is taught through love (Glasser, 1965). The parent must communicate that she or he loves the child enough to demand that the child behave in an appropriate manner, according to established values, rules, and standards.

While reality therapy does not adhere to a developmental model, it does identify two periods of development as critical. The first crucial period is between the ages of 2 and 5 (Glasser, 1975). This is a critical time because it is the onset of verbal responses from the child. Here children learn to be social, to verbalize their ideas, and to develop their intellectual curiosity and thinking skills. All of these skills are necessary to enable children to fulfill their needs. Children need love, consideration, a sense of importance from and involvement with their parents. They need to be able to express their views, to have them elicited and listened to. Children need to learn to be on their own with their friends and learn how to handle life's problems and crises. They should not be protected from the social "facts of life" with their friends unless the consequence of some action may be dangerous.

The second period of importance is the span between 5 and 10 years of age. This is important because the child leaves the home to attend school and, hopefully, to gain an education. Schooling is an important process to teach the child the skills and knowledge necessary to achieve status and success. Unfortunately, it is also a place where children are taught the concept of failure. Children spend so many of their waking hours at school memorizing, seeking right answers, and emphasizing grades rather than learning skills of thinking, reasoning, and seeking goals that will clarify the direction of their lives (Glasser, 1975). In *Schools Without Failure,* Glasser (1969) addresses this problem in detail and shows how the application of reality therapy to public education can eliminate the problems of teaching children how to fail and how to develop a failure identity.

Finally, those people who fail to learn how to fulfill their needs and consequently develop a failure identity create for themselves pain and discomfort. They deal with their pain in two general ways (Glasser and Zunin, 1973). They either deny reality or ignore it. The denial of reality necessitates the fabrication of a fantasy to replace the reality. This fantasy changes reality so as to protect the person from the pain of failure, replacing that pain with delusions of success.

Those who ignore the reality are seen by others to be "out of touch" with the real world, but these people do not need to use fantasy or delusions to change reality. They simply ignore it.

Goals Reality therapy was developed to deal with people who found it easier to seek pleasure by denying or ignoring the reality of the world around them than dealing with it. Therefore, the generic aim of the therapy is to "lead all patients toward reality, toward grappling successfully with the tangible and intangible aspects of the real world" (Glasser, 1965, p. 6). To accomplish this, reality therapy attempts to teach children in a rather short but intense time frame what it takes normal, healthy people years to learn about fulfilling their needs. Clients need to learn how to be involved with people by first learning to be involved with the counselor and then generalizing this involvement to others. Clients learn to set standards of behavior and to evaluate themselves by these standards. In this way, clients are taught self-responsibility and self-respect.

The Therapeutic Process

The counselor who uses reality therapy will be a real person to the client. She will model for the client responsibility, self-respect, and self-love. She will exhibit the ability and desire to extend herself and her feelings to another person, the client. The counselor will engage in conversation about anything that will stimulate the client's thinking and expression of his values, interests, hopes, and opinions to lay the foundation for a successful interchange. The counselor will most likely use: *confrontations* about the client's behavior; *humor* when it is appropriate to laugh at aspects of one's life; *conversation* about apparently nontherapeutic subjects such as literature, sports, sex, and politics; *goal setting* to help establish a direction to life; *pointing out* the unrealistic aspects of irresponsible behavior; *advice* regarding how to fulfill a need; *debate* to better understand how the counselor maintains her sense of responsibility as well as to allow the client to test himself and his convictions against those of a respected person (Glasser, 1965); *instruction* to help the client relearn his values and methods to meet his needs; and *self-disclosure* by discussing her own experiences, values, opinions, and difficulties.

Glasser (1965) indicated that reality therapy is composed of three separate but intertwined procedures. First is involvement. This is the process of the counselor becoming involved with the client, intellectually as well as emotionally. It is accepting and understanding the client as he is and establishing a working relationship that will facilitate the counseling process. Second, the counselor must communicate to the client both rejection of maladaptive behavior and acceptance of him as a person. The attempt is to strike a delicate balance of communicating rejection of the behavior but not of the person. Third, the counselor must instruct the client to find better ways to fulfill his needs. This can occur only after the client has admitted that his behavior is irresponsible and wrong. This last procedure also presupposes that the counselor has the knowledge and the skill to help the client in the necessary way.

Essentially, Glasser identifies eight steps to reality therapy (Glasser and Zunin, 1973; Evans, 1982). He cautions that, while the steps are "simple and clear-cut" to define, they are not simple concepts for the counselor to effect in practice (Evans, 1982).

Step 1: Involvement   The counselor must first make friends with the client. The counselor needs to be a warm, empathic person who communicates caring for the client. The counselor may need to self-disclose to show her values and a willingness to have them challenged. The counselor will need to become involved with the client within limits that will avoid entanglement. Glasser believes this may be the most difficult step of therapy and indicates that it takes creativity and personal attributes that cannot be taught (Evans,

1982), but it is vastly important. If the counselor fails to establish the working relationship stipulated in this step, movement to additional steps of therapy is impossible.

Step 2: Focus on present behavior   While feelings and behavior are interrelated, the primary emphasis in reality therapy is on behavior. Feelings are discussed, but only in relation to the client's behavior. Glasser sees behavior as comprising three things: "How do you feel? What do you think? What do you do?" (Evans, 1982, p. 461). Physical behavior is emphasized because it is the most amenable to the client's control. When behavior changes, feelings and thinking that are associated with it will also change.

Step 3: Focus on the present   Steps 2 and 3 emphasize the present rather than the past. While the past may be discussed, the counselor will be careful to avoid blame and any reinforcement of the failure identity. The past will be discussed only as it (a) reinforces character-building experiences of the past and is related to the present, (b) identifies constructive alternatives that the client might have chosen, or (c) indicates why the client's choice of behavior did not lead him into more difficulty (Glasser and Zunin, 1973). Reality therapy believes that only present behavior can be changed; discussing the role that the client's past plays in the present only excuses the client's immediate sense of responsibility.

Step 4: Self-evaluation   Reality therapy places responsibility on the clients to evaluate their behavior as responsible or irresponsible according to established standards. Unless they make an evaluation that the behavior is irresponsible and is not helping them to fulfill their needs, there will be no motivation to change. Irresponsible behavior is that which contributes to their identity as a failure. It is the clients' responsibility to evaluate their behavior, not the counselor's. The counselor needs to provide the impetus and guidance to let them evaluate their happiness and see how their behavior contributes to it. The counselor does not tell the client what decisions to make to become happy but does confront them so that they can evaluate them realistically.

Step 5: Make a plan   Formulation of a plan to help the client to change behavior may now proceed. Responsible alternatives are identified, and steps needed to achieve the behavior are spelled out. This plan may take the form of a written contract; it should be periodically evaluated and altered if needed.

Step 6: Commitment   This step determines whether the plan will be successful. The client is asked to make a commitment to carry out the plan. Early in therapy, the client may make a commitment to do it for the therapist. This solidifies the social aspect of the therapy while moving the client closer (as therapy progresses) to making a personal commitment to carry out the plan for himself when he is ready.

Step 7: Accept no excuses   The counselor needs to make it clear that there are no excuses if the client does not carry out the plan. The counselor does not humiliate or blame the client, instead she seeks a new commitment from him to fulfill the plan. The client gains strength when he understands that these responsibilities for which he made a commitment are still his and that no one will excuse him from fulfilling them.

Step 8: Eliminate punishment   Punishment is seen as blaming and humiliating the client, thus reinforcing his failure identity. Punishment is usually administered by someone who feels hurt by the failure and wishes to inflict his pain upon the culprit's already accumulated pain (Evans, 1982). Also, punishment has the effect of relieving the major part of the motivation to renew the commitment to fulfill the responsibility. Rather than punishment, Glasser suggests that people should suffer either the "natural" consequences, if there are any, or "reasonable" consequences of their behavior that have been agreed on previously (Evans, 1982). The reasonable consequences are better if they are in some way related to the task to be performed and if their effect is of reasonable duration and intensity. Remember, the aim is not to make the client feel worse for failing, but to reinforce the notion of responsibility for oneself while trying to preserve the commitment to carry out the plan.

Summary and Evaluation

Reality therapy is predicated on the notion that behavior either helps or hinders the fulfillment of a person's basic needs. These needs are to love and feel loved by others and to feel worthwhile to oneself and others. Behavior that fulfills these needs is responsible, that which does not is irresponsible. Irresponsible behavior leads people to develop a failure identity, which perpetuates further failures. It is the counselor's job to reverse the process and help the client to develop a success identity, which failed to develop at crucial periods in the client's life. The counselor can accomplish this by following an eight-step approach that emphasizes the client's present behavior and the evaluation of that behavior in terms of existing standards, both social and personal. Clients are helped to make plans and establish a commitment to change their behavior in order to become more responsible. Once a commitment is made, there are no excuses for noncompliance, only reasonable, previously agreed upon consequences. The emphasis is on helping clients to see their irresponsible behavior as inhibiting their happiness and successfulness and then helping them find a way to change.

Reality therapy has contributed a relatively simple theory stressing self-determinism and self-responsibility. It is positive in that it provides people the opportunity to change their behavior. Basically a short-term form of therapy, its concepts are very useful in child rearing and for use with people in correctional facilities. Those who criticize the theory indicate that it is very simplistic and has few theoretical constructs. It discounts two very important concepts: the impact of the unconscious and the effect of the individual's development. The final criticism is that reality therapy is value laden, providing an opportunity for counselor abuse.

Suggested Readings   Glasser, W. *Mental Health or Mental Illness?* New York: Harper & Row, 1960.
————. *Reality Therapy: A New Approach to Psychiatry.* New York: Harper & Row, 1965.
————. *Schools Without Failure.* New York: Harper & Row, 1969.
————. *Identity Society.* New York: Harper & Row, 1972.
————. *Stations of the Mind.* New York: Harper & Row, 1981.

Summary

This chapter summarized the basic cognitive and behavioral approaches to therapy, while the preceding chapter discussed the affective theories. There are many obvious areas of agreement and disagreement among the theories. We feel that counselors should keep their focus on client growth and leave to theoreticians the debate over which theory is most effective. Each therapeutic approach may have something to offer a client, and the effectiveness of an approach depends on both client and counselor characteristics. With this in mind we move in the next chapter toward an integrated approach to counseling.

Cognitive and behavioral theories assume that the basic focus of counseling should be on what the client thinks and does. The essential propositions of these approaches are that thinking precedes feeling, and doing changes feelings and attitudes about self. Although the counselor-client relationship is not ignored, the counselor's role is conceptualized as more active-directive and even didactic. The counselee is viewed as a learner who may be given "homework" assignments in order to practice newly acquired learnings and behaviors. This chapter reviewed various cognitive-behavioral theoretical approaches to serve as a springboard for the reader to review each theory in greater depth. The major points of each theory reviewed are as follows:

1. The trait-and-factor approach applies mathematical considerations to measurement in counseling. It attempts to measure individual traits to aid the client in reaching decisions. Rational elements of the individual are seen as moderating irrational forces. The client is seen as a conglomeration of abilities, aptitudes, interests, and potentials. A six-step therapeutic process of analysis, synthesis, diagnosis, prognosis, resolution, and follow-up is designed to measure these traits and help the client make appropriate personal, educational, and career choices.

2. Rational-emotive therapy, developed by Albert Ellis, is an active-directive approach designed to change self-defeating thoughts and behaviors of individuals. Ellis believes individuals to be both rational and irrational, but irrationality is the source of most emotional problems. Self-talk, repeated internalized sentences, gives rise to the negative feelings individuals experience. An ABC model for behavior is posited, i.e., *A* is the activating event, *B* is the belief system, and *C* is the emotional conse-

quence. It is the belief about an event, not the event itself, that is seen as causing the emotion. The counselor's role is to help clients re-think their life-events and philosophies.

3. Behavioral counseling attempts to apply experimentally derived and established principles of learning to change maladaptive behaviors. Behaviorists believe that behavior is acquired through classical conditioning, operant conditioning, and imitative learning. The goals of behavioral counseling vary with each client and are enumerated during a history-taking phase. The therapeutic process is a matter of problem definition, taking a developmental and so-

cial history, specification of counseling goals, selection of counseling methods, evaluation, and termination.

4. Reality therapy, developed by William Glasser, sees people as acting to satisfy their needs: they develop identities to achieve that end. Feelings of being loved and worthwhile are essential in living. People may develop either a failure or success identity. The basic concept of reality therapy is individual responsibility in initiating appropriate behaviors to satisfy these needs. Self-respect is attained through discipline and love. Counseling is seen as a process of involvement, communication, and instruction.

References

Bandura, A. *Principles of Behavior Modification.* New York: Holt, Rinehart and Winston, 1969.

Beck, A. T. *Cognitive Therapy and the Emotional Disorders.* New York: International Universities Press, 1976.

Beck, C. E. *Philosophical Foundations of Guidance.* Englewood Cliffs, N.J.: Prentice-Hall, 1963.

Blackham, G. J., and A. Silberman. *Modification of Child Behavior.* Belmont, Calif.: Wadsworth, 1971.

Blocher, D. H. "Some Implications of Recent Research in Social and Developmental Psychology for Counseling Practice." *Personnel and Guidance Journal* 58 (1980):334–336.

Davison, G. C. "Relative Contributions of Differential Relaxation and Graded Exposure to in Vivo Desensitization of a Neurotic Fear." *Proceedings of the 72nd Annual Convention of the American Psychological Association* (1965):209–210.

Davitz, J. *The Language of Emotions.* New York: Academic Press, 1969.

Ellis, A. *Reason and Emotion in Psychotherapy.* New York: Lyle Stuart, 1962.

———. "Rational-Emotive Psychotherapy." In D. Arbuckle, ed., *Counseling and Psychotherapy.* New York: McGraw-Hill, 1967.

———. "Rational-Emotive Therapy." In R. Corsini, ed., *Current Psychotherapies.* Itasca, Ill.: F. E. Peacock, 1973.

———. "Rational-Emotive Theory: Albert Ellis." In A. Burton, ed., *Operational Theories of Personality.* New York: Brunner/Mazel, 1974.

———. "Rational-Emotive Therapy." In J. J. Pietrofesa et al., *Guidance: An Introduction.* Chicago: Rand McNally, 1980.

———, and R. A. Harper. *A Guide to Rational Living.* Englewood Cliffs, N.J.: Prentice-Hall, 1961.

Evans, D. "What Are You Doing? An Interview with William Glasser." *Personnel and Guidance Journal* 60 (1982):460–464.

Ewing, D. "Twenty Approaches to Individual Change." *Personnel and Guidance Journal* 55 (1977):331–338.

Eysenck, H. J. "Learning Theory and Behaviour Therapy." *Journal of Mental Science* 105 (1959):61–75.

———, ed. *Behaviour Therapy and the Neuroses.* New York: Pergamon, 1960.

———. "Behaviour Therapy, Extinction, and Relapse in Neurosis." *British Journal of Psychiatry* 109 (1963):12–18.

———, ed. *Experiments in Behaviour Therapy.* New York: Pergamon, 1964.

Farkus, G. M. "An Ontological Analysis of Behavior Therapy." *American Psychologist* 35 (1980):364–374.

Folkins, C. H. "Temporal Factors and the Cognitive Mediators of Stress Reaction." *Journal of Personality and Social Psychology* 14 (1970):173–174.

Frank, J. D. "The Influence of Patients' and Therapists' Expectations on the Outcome of Psychotherapy." *British Journal of Medical Psychology* 41 (1968):349–356.

Frey, D. H., and H. E. Raming. "A Taxonomy of Counseling Goals and Methods." *Personnel and Guidance Journal* 58 (1979):26–33.

Geis, H. J. "Guilt Feelings and Inferiority Feelings: An Experimental Comparison." *Dissertation Abstracts* 13 (1966):8515.

Glasser, W. *Mental Health or Mental Illness?* New York: Harper & Row, 1960.

———. *Reality Therapy: A New Approach to Psychiatry.* New York: Harper & Row, 1965.

———. *Schools Without Failure.* New York: Harper & Row, 1969.

———. *Identity Society.* New York: Harper & Row, 1972.

———. *Stations of the Mind.* New York: Harper & Row, 1981.

———, **and L. M. Zunin.** "Reality Therapy." In R. Corsini, ed., *Current Psychotherapies.* Itasca, Ill.: F. E. Peacock, 1973.

Goldfried, M. R., and A. P. Goldfried. "Cognitive Change Methods." In F. H. Kanfer and A. P. Goldstein, eds., *Helping People Change.* New York: Pergamon, 1980.

Gray, J. S. "A Biological View of Behavior Modification." *Journal of Educational Psychology* 23 (1932):611–620.

Hill, C. E., T. B. Thames, and D. K. Rardin. "Comparison of Rogers, Perls, and Ellis on the Hill Counselor Verbal Response Category System." *Journal of Counseling Psychology* 26 (1979):198–203.

Ivey, A. E., and L. Simek-Downing. *Counseling and Psychotherapy: Skills, Theories, and Practice.* Englewood Cliffs, N.J.: Prentice-Hall, 1980.

Jacobson, E. *Progressive Relaxation.* Chicago: University of Chicago Press, 1938.

Johnson, N. "Must the Rational Emotive Therapist Be Like Albert Ellis." *Personnel and Guidance Journal* 59 (1980):49–51.

Krumboltz, J. D. "Behavioral Counseling: Rationale and Research." *Personnel and Guidance Journal* 44 (1965):383–387.

———. "Behavioral Goals of Counseling." *Journal of Counseling Psychology* 13 (1966):153–159.

Lazarus, A. A. "New Methods in Psychotherapy: A Case Study." *South African Medical Journal* 32 (1958):660–664.

———. *Behavior Therapy and Beyond.* New York: McGraw-Hill, 1971.

Mahoney, M. J., and D. B. Arnkoff. "Cognitive and Self-Control Therapies." In S. L. Garfield and A. E. Bergin, eds., *Handbook of Psychotherapy and Behavior Change.* New York: Wiley, 1978.

Meara, N. M., H. B. Pepinsky, J. W. Shannon, and W. A. Murray. "Semantic Communication and Expectations for Counseling Across Three Theoretical Orientations." *Journal of Counseling Psychology* 28 (1981):110–118.

———, **J. W. Shannon, and H. B. Pepinsky.** "Comparison of the Stylistic Complexity of the Language of Counselor and Client Across Three Theoretical Orientations." *Journal of Counseling Psychology* 26 (1979):181–189.

Meichenbaum, D. *Cognitive-Behavior Modification.* Morristown, N.J.: General Learning Press, 1974.

Michael, J., and L. Meyerson. "A Behavioral Approach to Counseling and Guidance." *Harvard Educational Review* 32 (1962):382–402.

Pavlov, I. P. *Conditioned Reflexes.* Oxford: Oxford University Press, 1927.

Pietrofesa, J. J., B. Bernstein, J. Minor, and S. Stanford. *Guidance: An Introduction.* Chicago: Rand McNally, 1980.

Ritter, B. "The Group Desensitization of Children's Snake Phobias Using Vicarious and Contact Desensitization Procedures." *Behavior Research and Therapy* 8 (1968):127–132.

Skinner, B. F. *The Behavior of Organisms.* New York: Appleton-Century-Crofts, 1938.

———, **and O. R. Lindsley.** *Studies in Behavior Therapy, Status Reports II and III.* Office of Naval Research Contracts, 1954.

Smith, R. R., W. O. Jenkins, C. M. Petko, and R. W. Warner, Jr. "An Experimental Application and Evaluation of Rational Behavior Therapy in a Work Release Setting." *Journal of Counseling Psychology* 26 (1979):519–526.

Tosi, D. J., and W. A. Carlson. "Client Dogmatism and Perceived Counselor Attitudes." *Personnel and Guidance Journal* 48 (1970):657–660.

Velten, C. A. "A Laboratory Task For Induction of Mood States." *Behavior Research and Therapy* 6 (1968):473–482.

Watson, J. B., and R. Rayner. "Conditioned Emotional Reaction." *Journal of Experimental Psychology* 3 (1920):1–14.

Williamson, E. G. *Counseling Adolescents.* New York: McGraw-Hill, 1950.

——. "A Concept of Counseling." In W. Van Hoose and J. J. Pietrofesa, eds., *Counseling and Guidance in the Twentieth Century.* Boston: Houghton Mifflin, 1970.

Wolpe, J. *The Practice of Behavior Therapy.* New York: Pergamon, 1969.

Wubbolding, R. E. "Balancing the Chart: 'Do It Person' and 'Positive Symptom Person'." *Journal of Reality Therapy* 1 (1981):4–7.

CHAPTER 7

The Content of Counseling: An Eclectic Model

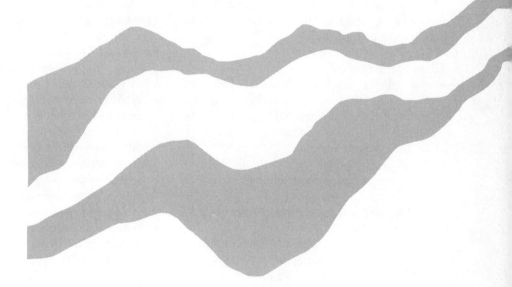

Chapter Organizer

Aim of the Chapter

This chapter will present an eclectic model of counseling as the basis for understanding the "content of counseling."

Chapter Preview

1. An eclectic counseling model offers the benefit of allowing the practitioner to use the best of each approach, to accommodate personal strengths and preferences, and to adjust to client variability.
2. Perceptual psychology and the concept of self provide for a comprehensive view of counseling content.
   a. The self is a composite of various percepts.
   b. The ability to satisfy one's needs helps to determine self-concept.
   c. The self-concept is born of human interaction.

3. The perceptual model can incorporate both insight and behavioral approaches to achieve behavior change in the client.

Relevant Questions

The following are several questions to keep in mind while reading this chapter:

1. What are the strengths and weaknesses of an eclectic approach to counseling theory?
2. Define *self-esteem*. How does self-esteem differ from self-concept? What is the difference between a global self-concept and self-percepts?
3. How does the self-concept maintain itself in the face of inconsistencies?
4. Why would success experiences be more important in the development of a positive self-concept than failure experiences?

Introduction

The earlier chapters in this section described the various theoretical approaches to counseling. These descriptions were not meant to be comprehensive views of these schools of thought but rather introductions to further study. We now present an eclectic model that takes into consideration the "content" of various counseling approaches, allowing counselors to implement those approaches that meet their needs.

An Eclectic Approach to the Content of Counseling

While this book is most fundamentally concerned with the process of counseling—the way the counseling interaction occurs and the helping skills most useful in facilitating counselee growth—counselors need to recognize that there is content to counseling. The content of counseling is the material that the counselee may discuss during a session. An encompassing, unifying, and eclectic model of content and a theoretical model for counseling were proposed by Pietrofesa et al. (1971) in *The Authentic Counselor.* While grounded primarily in perceptual psychology and the self-system, it also incorporates contributions from the variety of theoretical systems reviewed earlier. This chapter presents a counseling framework that utilizes ideas from each of the theories in an attempt to help counselors implement a personalized, client-based counseling approach. Within the broader concept of a self model we will discuss need satisfaction, perceptual field, and developmental concerns of the client. Barrett and Harren (1979) suggested that a "self" model could be the unifying factor of a variety of theories of therapy.

This theoretical emphasis on the self has been paralleled by a correspondingly widespread phenomenon by researchers and practitioners alike. In fact today it is apparent that the influence of the self as a theoretical construct has become a factor unifying behavioral, psychoanalytic, neo-Freudian ego-psychology, humanistic-existential, and transpersonal approaches. In short, the construct of self and the experience of self-conception may be the core theoretical variables in evolving models of personality theory and psychotherapy practice. Indeed, we believe that the construct of self is the catalytic agent in the development of comprehensive personality models and that this construct is essential for unifying and refining our conceptualizations of human functioning. (p. 35)

Dimond et al. (1978) develop the importance of what they term "prescriptive eclecticism" in individualizing counseling and psychotherapy.

To achieve an individualized treatment plan, psychotherapists must be able to draw upon a vast array of theory and technique and not be bound by any single approach to psychotherapy. . . . What is necessary for the practice of prescriptive eclecticism is a framework that permits flexibility in the process of individualizing treatment yet does not lose the benefits of information from theory and research in psychotherapy. (pp. 239–240)

Self-Concept   The self-concept reflects who the person is. It not only includes feelings (self-esteem) toward the self and others, but also the moral structure, attitudes, ideas, and values that propel one to action or, on the other hand, inaction. The self-concept includes feelings about self—both physical self and psychological self—in relation to the environment. It is a system that plays a crucial role in determining responses to experience and even selects what experiences will be engaged in.

The self-image has many parts with both a structure and a function. The self-structure contains numerous traits, some more important than others. Overall feeling about the self provides a degree of cognitive and conative unity to the various subsystems.

Self-concept refers to that particular cluster of ideas and attitudes we have about our awareness at any given moment in time. Or, another way of looking at it is to view our self-concept as the organized cognitive structure derived from experiences of our own self. Thus, out of our awareness of ourselves grows the ideas (concepts) of the kind of person we see ourselves as being. Self-concept, then, is the cognitive aspect of the self.

Self-esteem, on the other hand, is the affective dimension of the self. Not only do we have certain ideas about who we are, but we have certain feelings about who we are. Self-esteem, then, refers quite literally to the extent to which we admire or value the self. (Hamachek, 1980, p. 83)

The self-concept can be considered a hypothetical construct that includes three major dimensions. The first dimension is the self as seen by the self. This may be reflected in such statements as the following:

"I am kind."
"I am warm and friendly."
"I am aggressive."
"I am strong."
"I am seductive."
"I am inadequate."

Obviously, such feeling and beliefs have great impact on what the individual does. The underachiever in school or the person who makes an inadequate vocational choice sees the self as less than adequate and behaves in like fashion. Minorities, for example, with positive self-concepts have a greater chance to succeed than minorities with negative self-concepts (Comas-Diaz et al., 1982, p. 306).

A second dimension of the self-concept is the self as seen by others, or

"This is how I think others see me." Statements such as the following reflect this:

"You see me as friendly."
"You see me as confident."
"You see me as attractive."
"My peer group thinks I am tough."

Self-concept tends to form early with the experiences of the small child with "valued others." Social learning occurs through the modeling of others, while introjection is the process whereby others are seen as a significant force in one's life. Self-attribution also occurs; that is, the observation of one's own behavior leads to the formation of generalizations about the self. Environment plays a role, but it must be remembered that environment is partly of the person's own making.

By their actions, people play a role in creating the social milieu and other circumstances that arise in their daily transactions. Thus, from the social learning perspective, psychological functioning involves a continuous reciprocal interaction between behavioral, cognitive, and environmental influences. (Bandura, 1978, p. 345)

Generally, there is a relationship between past experience and so-called objective reality. In other words, when people in the environment respond to a young girl as if she were competent, she will believe that others view her as competent. At some time the evaluation of others is assimilated into the self-structure. This may not, however, be true at any specific point in time. Furthermore, emotional insecurities and anxieties may cloud such perceptions, even to the extent that they are completely out of touch with the real beliefs of others. People will use various defenses to cling to earlier structured beliefs about the self. Accuracy of self-perception is also undoubtedly related to the accuracy of the perceptions of significant others. If parents have distorted perceptions of their child, the child's personal adjustment will reflect this.

The third dimension of the self-concept is the ideal self. This dimension refers to "the type of person I would like to become." Aspirations, goals, and even dreams are reflected through the ideal self.

"I want to become a teacher."
"I would like to be a better parent."
"I want to have lots of money."

The ideal self is important in establishing life's directions. Obviously, goals that are too far distant or never accomplished create disappointment and disillusionment and breed an unhealthy self-concept. Healthy goals are reachable goals and are flexible. *Extremely* rigid timelines for accomplishment are generally unhealthy. (See Figure 7.1.)

Within the healthy person, there should be a good deal of compatibility among the three dimensions of the self. In other words, self-consistency is basic to competency in human functioning. The healthy, "more mature" person has a more "stable" self-concept (Heath, 1980, p. 395). If discrepancy exists among the components, anxiety is created. Parts of the self must be consciously hidden, distorted, or disguised from either self or others. The reduction of the discrepancies among the various parts of the self-concept has historically been a focus in counseling. This idea is reflected in the Johari window. (See Figure 7.2.) Counseling, group or individual, affects the hidden self.

The Johari window points out that there are certain things known and not known about the self and also things that are known or unknown by others. Certain principles might be cited in relation to Figure 7.2.

1. Areas are generally not of the same size.
2. Area I involves behavior and motivation known to self and others. It grows as counseling progresses.
3. Area II reflects behavior and motivation known to self but hidden from others. In a new group or at the beginning of counseling, this area is large.
4. Area III is a blind area, representing behavior and motivation not known to the self but recognized by others. In counseling this may be material reflected by the counselor, which may be met with resistance from the client.
5. Area IV represents behavior and motivation known neither to self nor others.
6. The major purpose of interaction is to increase area I. (See Figure 7.3.)
7. Area IV is not likely to change in typical relationships.
8. If change occurs in one of the quadrants, another area must also change.
9. It takes energy to hide things; this is why interpersonal functions improve as I gets larger.
10. If a threat is present, area I will not increase. Generally, forced awareness is undesirable.

As suggested earlier, area I is small at the beginning of a relationship but increases as the relationship becomes closer and warmer.

The counseling relationship endeavors to enlarge the free area and reduce the blind and hidden areas. As the client engages in self-disclosure, the hidden area is reduced and as the counselor responds, reflects, personalizes, and initiates, the client's blind area is reduced. Self-awareness is increased through this process, which allows for further self-disclosure.

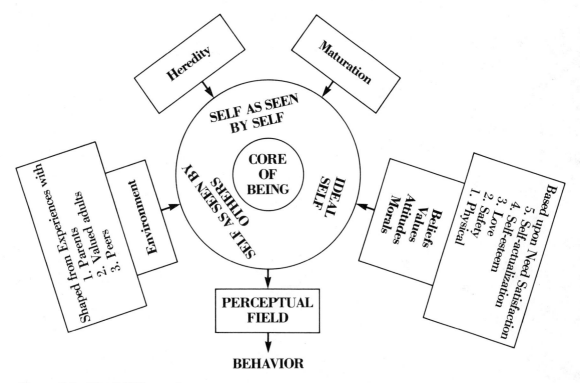

Figure 7.1 The Self-Concept

Source: Adapted from J. J. Pietrofesa et al., *The Authentic Counselor,* 2nd ed. (Chicago: Rand McNally, 1978), p. 22.

Healthy people deal directly with anxiety caused by threat, and threat becomes a short-lived experience. Less healthy people do not cope directly with the threat, perhaps because of less self-insight and greater defensiveness, and the threat persists. Healthy behavior is replaced with either misperceptions, distortion, or denial.

One's self-concept tends to reinforce itself through selective perception. A person selects from an experience that which reinforces the self-concept already developed and rejects whatever might be contrary to present feelings or beliefs. Selective perception and defensive, or distortive, mechanisms are used to reinforce and protect present self-image and maintain self-consistency. Children who see themselves as smart behave in that fashion, select those occurrences that substantiate that belief, and discard or distort any encounters that contradict that belief (Pietrofesa et al., 1971, p. 24). Watson and Lindgren (1979) state that "we are ever ready to defend our

Figure 7.2
A Model of
Awareness in
Interpersonal or
Intergroup
Relations (Johari
Window)

Known to Others	I. Area of Free Activity	III. Blind Area—Blind to self, seen by others
Not Known to Others	II. Avoided or Hidden Area—Self hidden from others	IV. Area of Unknown Activity

Source: From *Of Human Interaction* by Joseph Luft by permission of Mayfield Publishing Company. Copyright © 1969 by the National Press.

Figure 7.3
Change in
Relationship Affects
Self

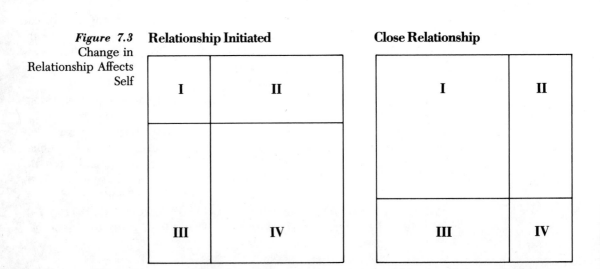

Relationship Initiated

Close Relationship

evaluation of our self. We become aggressive or show other defensive maneuvers when something threatens our self-evaluation" (p. 334). Surprisingly the self-evaluation that is defended may or may not be positive; it is consistency that is sought. For example, Gage and Berliner (1979) note that "students who have acquired poor self-concepts in some areas seem to reject their own success experiences. . . . Presumably they do so because those experiences are not congruent with their self-concepts" (p. 188).

Heredity and maturation indirectly influence self-concept development. What we have inherited determines to some extent how others see and behave toward us. As a result, it affects how we feel about ourselves. An inherited handicap does not cause negative feelings, but rather the negative attitudes come from the disgust, dismay, or embarrassment displayed by others. Maturation—the gradual unfolding of physical potentialities—also affects others' behavior toward us.

One's self-concept primarily develops from interaction with parents, valued adults, and peers. Human interaction is more likely to have an impact on self-concept than is an encounter without human meaning: A grade of B means little unless someone says, "That's terrific" or "That's the same as failing." The child is born without a view of self, and it is generally within the context of the family that a self-concept starts to form. The early years, then, are crucial, and one cannot deny the importance of the natural or surrogate parents. Valued adults—grandparents, aunts, uncles, teachers, or counselors—also have an important role to play in fostering a healthy self-concept. It should be emphasized that adults need to be valued by the child, or their impact on self-development will be minimal. The teacher who is unimportant to the child will not generally affect self-concept. Also, the peer group can have great impact on self-development. This appears to be particularly true during the adolescent years when, in fact, peer influence often outweighs parental influence. While this may be a valid generalization, it is now thought that adolescents who have "clarified their values and set their own standards are not likely to be overly affected by pubertal changes or the peer approval or disapproval brought about by them" (Dacey, 1982, p. 99).

While much of the self-concept is developed in the early years of childhood, we must realize that it can be changed throughout the life span. Self-concept is more difficult to change as one gets older, but it can be accomplished through social interaction. This is an important consideration; the counselor can never assume that the client is a "hopeless case."

Impressive as the evidence may seem for early determination of personality and for its stability over time, there are also reasons for believing that one's self-concept can change. The findings do not suggest that the self is completely formed during early childhood. Also, even though a general personality trend may be established quite early, the manner in which it is expressed may continue to be quite susceptible to change. My own personal experience as a psychotherapist is quite consistent with a large body of clinical literature that strongly indicates that youth and adults can change both their behaviors and feelings about themselves at any point in time. (Hamachek, 1980, p. 85)

Frequent success and reward will help to form a positive self-concept, which will encourage individuals to enter into further growth-enhancing situations. Bandura (1977) identifies the notion of "self-efficacy," that is, a conviction that one can successfully accomplish a desired outcome. This helps to determine the amount of effort expended and the degree of persistence displayed when obstacles are encountered.

Need Satisfaction   The capability individuals have to satisfy personal needs helps to determine the way they view themselves. If needs that arise are met routinely, a fairly positive self-image develops. If needs are not satisfied, frustration and hostility, as well as a negative self-concept, may result. Conversely, self-concept affects need expression. The healthy person expresses a love need that takes into consideration the well-being of the love object, while an unhealthy individual may express love in a sadistic-masochistic manner. Kirkpatrick (1979) states, "A need exists when a desire to attain or acquire something motivates a person to act or feel in certain ways. The satisfaction or lack of satisfaction of needs determines if people grow or stagnate" (p. 386).

Needs can be categorized into two broad areas—physical and psychological. Obviously, basic physical needs have to be met minimally for the human being to survive.

Maslow (1954) presented a hierarchy of need levels, which we have condensed as follows:

1. Physical needs
2. Safety needs
3. Love needs
4. Esteem needs
5. Self-actualization needs

Perhaps the most important contribution of the Maslow schema is not just the identification of certain categories, but rather that these needs are conceived in hierarchical form. Higher-level needs concern the individual only after lower-level needs have been satisfied. When individuals, then, have satisfied lower-level needs, they "will feel motivated to satisfy higher growth (or being) needs . . . not because of a deficit but because of a desire to gratify the higher needs (Biehler and Snowman, 1982, p. 374). Generally, if lower-level need satisfaction is withdrawn, the person regresses to satisfy the more basic need. For example, many American youth leaving for the Vietnam War were most likely concerned with self-esteem needs. In combat, many regressed to satisfaction of physical safety needs. Individuals functioning at different need levels do not easily understand each other's behavior. Furthermore, an individual functioning at a higher-need level may not understand or accept his or her own lower-need-level behavior. The graduate student, whose psychological safety is threatened in a class, may cheat to pass the course, and later, when the threat is removed, feel quite guilty and anxious about the behavior. At this point, defensive reactions may be utilized to reduce such anxiety.

Jourard (1963) categorizes individual needs this way:

1. *Survival needs* are concerned with self-preservation and safety. Psychological, as well as physical safety, are involved. If the person feels threatened psychologically, anxiety arises, perception narrows, and behavior may become inappropriate.
2. *Physical needs* encompass the desire for food, drink, relief from pain, sleep, shelter, and waste elimination. Such needs are usually routinely satisfied. If they are not, however, they can dominate behavior.
3. *Love and sex needs* reflect the necessity to be loved, and consequently, the ability to love others. Sex and love may be intertwined but not necessarily, for the former may be strictly physiological.
4. *Status, success, and self-esteem needs* include achievement motivation designed to create feelings of adequacy, usefulness, and confidence.
5. *Physical and mental health needs* develop a sense of well-being. If needs are not met, physical or psychological illness occurs.
6. *Freedom needs* accentuate the desire to make choices for oneself.
7. *Challenge needs* are designed to stimulate growth and avoid boredom and feelings of emptiness.
8. *Cognitive clarity needs* help to resolve incompatible beliefs.
9. *Varied experience needs* seek personal stimulation and movement toward a more full-functioning life (pp. 33–39).

Perceptual Field and Behavior

Our self-concept determines our perceptual field, the way we view the external world. Therefore, the way we behave in the world is a consequence of how we perceive it. We organize our perceptual field in a fluid manner according to our own individual needs. Each of us behaves according to what we see, not to any particular set of objective facts. This is not to suggest a one-to-one relationship between behavior and perception. For example, if we perceive the environment as hostile, we can either strike out at it or withdraw into a corner. Snyder (1982), in summary, states:

From a historical phenomenological context, though, perspective is seen as the development of what is perceived, of what the world is. Perspective becomes of vital importance in understanding the world about us. It is the basis with which each of us enters into the world. To find truth then is to understand the perspectival experience of the individual. (p. 365)

There is some mutuality in the relationship between self-concept and behavior. The image one has of the self helps to determine the behavior in which one engages, and correspondingly, the behavior's perceived effectiveness helps to establish or change a self-image. If one has a "poor" self-concept, the behavior that emanates from it is seen as self-defeating, destructive, or worthless. Behavior may change and become more efficient. This will have little effect on improving self-concept unless the perceptions and defenses surrounding the behavior also change. If the preceding is accomplished, then the behavior will have to be maintained for a period of time before the self-concept becomes more positive. As an illustration, it will be noted that short-term behavioral changes do not have much impact on self-image. Individuals who have "low" or "poor" self-concepts will initially reject success experiences because of their inconsistency with the prevailing image. On the other hand behavioral changes leading to success, if they are maintained, will change the attitudes toward the self in a more positive direction.

Another attribute of the self, then, is that it tends to perpetuate itself. People like consistency and order. Contrary events and perceptions to the self-image create anxiety. Individuals, then, resort to a variety of mechanisms that are distortive or defensive. They range from simple defense mechanisms to psychoses and suicide. A simple continuum might be conceived as follows:

Healthy Behavior	Defense Mechanism	Neurotic Behavior	Personality Disorders: Drug Addiction or Alcoholism	Psychotic Behavior	Suicide

Generally, the distortion of reality that occurs at each level is greater than at the previous level, but every reaction is a response to anxiety within the self. If self-concept is to change, the mechanisms that protect and maintain the concept must be understood. The counselor needs to understand what the client is telling himself or herself, for this is the emotion-arousing stimulus. A client can be helped to eliminate negative statements about the self and to think more positively. If this positive thinking is maintained for a period of time, the self-concept will become more positive. It is important to stress that changes "in self-concept will follow changes in behavior only if the latter accord with reality" (Gage and Berliner, 1979, p. 188).

Developmental Concerns

We have tried to point out that self-concept, need satisfaction, environmental influences (family, peers, etc.), perceptual field, and behavior form the content of the counseling session. Whatever the content—a client's relationship with her mother or an inability to achieve a desired goal—it should be viewed from a developmental perspective. While crisis situations are often presented to the counselor, developmental concerns are a major focus of the counselor's work. Havighurst (1948) presented a series of developmental tasks in a sociopsychological framework. Developmental tasks are events that occur at particular points in an individual's life; their successful completion stimulates that individual to additional growth and increases the chance of success with later tasks. Developmental tasks incorporate the skills, attitudes, and knowledge that people need to master as they grow and mature. The tasks reflect cultural demands and mastery, as one level prepares the individual to master future tasks. Havighurst (1948) does suggest that failure to master a task results in greater maladjustment, social disapproval, and increased difficulty in mastering later tasks.

Erikson (1968) also viewed psychosocial development sequentially. The eight stages describe the polarities, but the outcome is generally a balance between the two extremes. Individuals proceed along predetermined steps according to their readiness, with each step related to the others. Healthy functioning depends on appropriate development and sequence (Erikson, 1968, pp. 91–141). Tables 7.1 and 7.2 summarize stages of development, psychosexual stages, related elements of the social order, significant relations, and psychosocial modalities. While tasks and stages can be seen as consistent over time, counselors will have to remember that decisions and experiences "will be different from those of the preceding age. Future clients will be living in a different world—a different social environment" (Havighurst, 1980, p. 328).

In an excellent analysis of the work of Havighurst, Erikson, and others, Zaccaria (1965) identified fifteen common elements of these various developmental approaches:

1. Individual growth and development are continuous.
2. Individual growth can be divided into periods or life stages for descriptive purposes.
3. Individuals in each life stage can be characterized by certain general characteristics.
4. Most individuals in a given culture pass through similar developmental stages.
5. The society makes certain demands upon individuals.
6. These demands are relatively uniform for all members of the society.
7. The demands differ from stage to stage as the individual goes through the developmental process.
8. Developmental crises occur when the individual perceives the demand to alter her or his present behavior and master new learnings.
9. In meeting and mastering developmental crises, the individual moves from one developmental stage of maturity to another developmental stage of maturity.
10. The task appears in its purest form at one stage.
11. Preparation for meeting the developmental crises or developmental tasks occurs in the life stage prior to the stage in which it must be mastered.
12. The developmental task or crisis may arise again during a later phase in somewhat different form.

Table 7.1
Stages of Development

Oral sensory	Trust vs. mistrust							
Muscular-anal		Autonomy vs. shame, doubt						
Locomotor-genital			Initiative vs. guilt					
Latency				Industry vs. inferiority				
Puberty and adolescence					Identity vs. role diffusion			
Young adulthood						Intimacy vs isolation		
Adulthood							Generativity vs. stagnation	
Maturity								Integrity vs. disgust, despair

Source: Reprinted from *Childhood and Society,* 2nd Edition, Revised, by Erik H. Erikson, by permission of W. W. Norton & Company, Inc. Copyright 1950, © 1963 by W. W. Norton & Company, Inc.

13. The crisis or task must be mastered before the individual can successfully move on to a subsequent developmental stage.
14. Meeting the crisis successfully by learning the required task leads to societal approval, happiness, and success with later crises and their correlative tasks.
15. Failing in meeting a task or crisis leads to disapproval by society. (p. 373)

With mental health statistics continuing to indicate increased numbers of mental health problems, counseling must emphasize preventive rather than curative components. A developmental focus helps to achieve this. The importance of Maslow's, Erikson's, and Havighurst's works for counselors is that they are "(a) empirically based, (b) developmentally oriented, and (c) derived from the study of healthy, rather than pathological, personality patterns" (Hershenson, 1982, p. 407).

Table 7.2

Psychosocial Crises and Related Elements

	A *Psychosocial Crises*	B *Radius of Significant Relations*	C *Related Elements of Social Order*	D *Psychosocial Modalities*	E *Psychosexual Stages*
I	Trust vs. Mistrust	Maternal Person	Cosmic Order	To get To give in return	Oral-Respiratory Sensory- Kinesthetic (Incorporative Modes)
II	Autonomy vs. Shame, Doubt	Parental Persons	"Law and Order"	To hold (on) To let (go)	Anal-Urethral, Muscular (Retentive- Eliminative)
III	Initiative vs. Guilt	Basic Family	Ideal Prototypes	To make (= going after) To "make like" (= playing)	Infantile-Genital, Locomotor (Intrusive, Inclusive)
IV	Industry vs. Inferiority	"Neighborhood," School	Technological Elements	To make things (-completing) To make things together	"Latency"
V	Identity and Repudiation vs. Identity Diffusion	Peer Groups and Outgroups: Models of Leadership	Ideological Perspectives	To be oneself (or not to be) To share being oneself	Puberty
VI	Intimacy and Solidarity vs. Isolation	Partners in friendship, sex, competition, cooperation	Patterns of Cooperation and Competition	To lose and find oneself in another	Genitality
VII	Generativity vs. Self-Absorption	Divided labor and shared household	Currents of Education and Tradition	To make be To take care of	
VIII	Integrity vs. Despair	"Mankind" "My Kind"	Wisdom	To be, through having been To face not being	

Source: From Erik Erikson. "Identity and the Life Cycle." *Pyschological Issues* 1 (1959):166. Reprinted by permission.

Implications for Counseling

The preceding model describes the content of counseling and presents an eclectic, theoretical framework for the counselor. Pietrofesa et al. (1971) describe the rationale for such a model as follows:

One reason for presenting this elemental model is that it provides much in the way of allowing the counselor to focus upon growth of the counselee in a variety of fashions. the counselor can focus upon the needs of the individual or the self-concept or any of its percepts. The counselor can focus upon peer or parental influences of past determinants of behavior. (p. 31)

Boyd (1970) stresses the importance of self-concept in counseling. She found that the counselee's self-concept will determine the method of establishing rapport, the means of motivating the counselee, and the counseling techniques utilized. Boyd goes on to say, "To bring about change the counselor has to have an understanding of the counselee's self-concept" (p. 307).

The following illustrative dialogues make this point.

Counselor: Any particular thing you'd like to talk about?

Counselee: I don't know. [laugh] I think that I would really like to talk about what happened after last week's session—how I felt. I just really felt guilty about talking to someone else I didn't even know about my mother. I don't know why I felt that way. I had to call my house for a reason and my mother answered the phone. I was *really* short with her. I think it opened up some wounds. Maybe it has something to do with my busy life. I'm really busy, and that could have something to do with it. I'm sure it was not all last week's session. But, I know that I felt very fatigued after I talked with you and really *drained*.

The client is talking about her relationship with significant others—both her mother and the counselor. As the counseling continues, the topic changes to feelings about self and the impact the client's mother had on such attitudes.

Counselee: I've gone through a lot of things with her. She has a really fantastic complexion, and so does my father. So my face breaks out, and she would complain, "What's wrong with your face?" Then, I went to a dermatologist for *years* and she kept saying, "He's not doing any good. Quit taking those pills he's giving you and quit the sunlamp treatments." She'd always talk about my face and I was getting tired of it. I used to blow up about this, too.

Counselor: You're resentful, because you were doing everything you could to please your mother, and, yet, she was never satisfied.

Counselee: Right, right. The face thing bugged me, but it would hurt me. I was never good enough or pretty enough. She'd tell me, "You make yourself look ugly. I don't like the way you cut your hair." She thinks that long, flowing hair and milky white complexion is what I'm supposed to look like. That's the way she was when she was younger. I know it's not going to happen. I'm satisfied with the way I look. There's nothing I can do to change it. This is the way I feel, and I think she's starting to accept this. She hasn't really got on me about my face, because she knows how upset it makes me. What difference is it the way someone looks?

Counselor: Your mother just can't accept you the way you are, and somehow this makes you feel guilty. You really would like to change if you could.

Counselee: Yes, I think that's part of it. That's partly correct. I felt subconsciously maybe that if your mother tells you, maybe she's right. Why don't I look this way or how does she want me to look?

It is apparent in the preceding dialogue that the client is concerned with love and esteem needs in the relationship with her mother. At this point in the session the client and counselor would explore need satisfaction as well as self-concept. In an excellent article Kirkpatrick (1979) provides a model that gives a structure for applying Maslow's hierarchy of needs in counseling. He believes that "the counseling relationship can be described in terms of two variables measured simultaneously: Who is satisfying the client's needs? At what level in the hierarchy?" (p. 388). Kirkpatrick, concluding his article, notes that the use of Maslow's concepts helps to provide the "systematic eclecticism" necessary for deciding which counseling techniques are most appropriate with any given client.

In the preceding sequence, the client presents some basic self-doubts and a negative self-image particularly in her views of the physical self. The following counseling content revolves around perceptual field and behavior.

Counselor: So, in a way, you feel an obligation to get that degree because you know people are going to look more favorably upon you.

Counselee: You've got to have an education to get the job, but then there's times too when you're going to be overqualified and you can't get the job you're looking for. But then, why don't some of these places just open up more on-the-job-training? I mean look at the want ads. All the time: 'experienced preferred' or 'experience necessary'—all others, don't apply. There's a thousand jobs in the paper, and there might be 999 people out of work. Somebody has got to be matched up there. It just doesn't seem right. I mean, maybe that's what we are supposed to do to keep our economy balanced. You know, keep a thousand jobs vacant: then the more money you spend on the ad looking for somebody to work and the more money a person looking for a job pays to an employment agency to find them a job. It just seems that there should be a better system of matching people and jobs up. But, like I say, I definitely do want to get back in school, but I just need some direction. Actually what I need is for someone to tell me where I can go out and get all this free money that everyone talks about. You know, go and get this money to pay for an education, and you don't have to pay it back for 20 years. It should have easy monthly terms and all this good stuff. Oh well!

Counselor: You're feeling confused and would really like someone to tell you what to do. You would like to be able to get a loan.

Figure 7.4
Change in the
Self-Concept

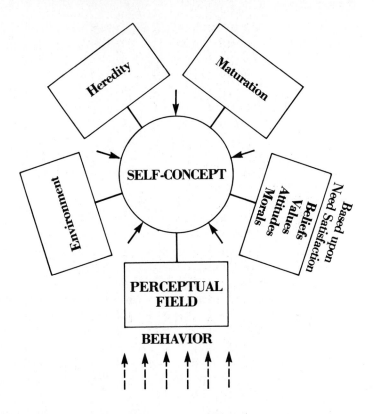

---►Insight counseling attempts to change self-concept, perceptual field, and so forth, in order to help the client develop greater self-understanding and behave more effectively.

- - -►Behavioral counseling attempts to change behavior, and as the individual becomes more effective in the environment, self-concept should change in a more positive way.

Counselee: Oh definitely. Yeah. The more money I could get, the more classes I could take. Then again, I don't want to get so far over my head to where I'm committed to take four or five classes at a time. I want to start getting back into the swing and taking just one class for the first couple of semesters and, after that, maybe build up to two, because the biggest problem I'm going to have is to retrain myself just to open the books. I love to read, but I like to read what I want to read. If somebody tells me, you have to read 27 pages from this chapter by next week, I'll put it off. I'll maybe skim through it the night before it's due; I'll read 26 pages or I might read 2 or 6 pages and say the hell with the rest of it.

Counselor: You feel disappointed in yourself because you can't organize more effectively.

At this point the counselor could start to move toward a behavioral plan of action.

The model provides a framework for using a variety of counseling approaches. For the sake of discussion, we can classify counseling approaches as either insight or behavioral. Too often, much time is wasted debating the benefits of one approach over the other. In actuality, both insight and behavioral counseling techniques are concerned with eliminating self-defeating behaviors and making client behavior more effective. Then, there are other methods that have the individual look at self-concept and its surrounding elements. Whatever the techniques, the client gains greater insight into behavior, and behavior changes accordingly. On the other hand, the counselor could use a behavioral approach to help the individual behave more effectively. (See Figure 7.4.) The counselor can help the client to change, then, in a variety of ways.

Summary

Counseling involves both process and content. Content dimensions include any topic the client might discuss—self-concept, personality needs, developmental concerns, perceptual field, or self-defeating behaviors, to name a few. The model presented accounts for much of what might be labeled counseling content and also allows for the integration of insight and behavioral techniques to achieve behavior change in the client. The model presents a theoretical framework that, it is hoped, enhances an eclectic, but systematic approach to individualized therapy.

References

Bandura, A. *Social-Learning Theory.* Englewood Cliffs, N.J.: Prentice-Hall, 1977.

Barrett, Thomas C., and Vincent A. Harren. "Perspectives on Self-Theory: A Comment on Loevinger and Kegan." *Counseling Psychologist* 8 (1979):34–38.

Biehler, R. F., and J. Snowman. *Psychology Applied to Teaching.* Boston: Houghton Mifflin, 1982.

Boyd, A. J. "Self-Concept and Its Implication for Counselors." New Orleans: APGA Abstracts, 1970.

Comas-Diaz, L., A. L. Arroyo, and J. C. Carlos. "Enriching Self-Concept Through a Puerto Rican Cultural Awareness Program." *Personnel and Guidance Journal* 60 (1982):306–308.

Dacey, John S. *Adolescents Today.* Glenview, Ill.: Scott, Foresman, 1982.

Dimond, R. E., R. A. Havens, and Arthur C. Jones. "A Conceptual Framework for the Practice of Prescriptive Eclecticism in Psychotherapy." *American Psychologist* 33 (1978):239–248.

Erikson, Erik. *Childhood and Society.* New York: W. W. Norton, 1950.

————. "Identity and the Life Cycle." *Psychological Issues* 1 (1959):166.

————. *Identity, Youth, and Crisis.* New York: W. W. Norton, 1968.

Gage, N. L., and D. C. Berliner. *Educational Psychology.* Chicago: Rand McNally, 1979.

Hamachek, Don E. "Psychology and Development of the Adolescent Self." In J. F. Adams, ed., *Understanding Adolescence.* Boston: Allyn and Bacon, 1980.

Havighurst, Robert J. *Developmental Tasks and Education.* New York: David McKay, 1948.

————. *Human Development and Education.* New York: David McKay, 1953.

————. "Social and Developmental Psychology: Trends Influencing the Future of Counseling." *Personnel and Guidance Journal* 58 (1980):328–333.

Heath, D. H. "Wanted: A Comprehensive Model of Healthy Development." *Personnel and Guidance Journal* 58 (1980):391–399.

Hershenson, David B. "A Formulation of Counseling Based on the Healthy Personality." *Personnel and Guidance Journal* 60 (1982):406–409.

Jourard, Sidney M. *Personal Adjustment.* New York: Macmillan, 1963.

Kirkpatrick, J. Stephen. "A Maslovian Counseling Model." *Personnel and Guidance Journal,* 57 (1979):386–391.

Luft, J. *Of Human Interaction.* Palo Alto, Calif.: National Press, 1969.

Maslow, A. H. *Motivation and Personality.* New York: Harper & Row, 1954.

Mouly, George J. *Psychology for Effective Teaching.* New York: Holt, Rinehart and Winston, 1973.

Pietrofesa, John J., George E. Leonard, and William H. Van Hoose. *The Authentic Counselor.* Chicago: Rand McNally, 1971.

Snyder, Douglas M. "Some Foundations of Counseling and Psychotherapy from a Phenomenological Perspective." *Personnel and Guidance Journal* 60 (1982):364–367.

Watson, Robert I., and Henry C. Lindgren. *Psychology of the Child and the Adolescent.* New York: Macmillan, 1979.

Zaccaria, J. S. "Developmental Tasks: Implications for the Goals of Guidance." *Personnel and Guidance Journal* 44 (1965):372–375.

PART III

The Counseling Relationship

CHAPTER 8

Regard and Respect

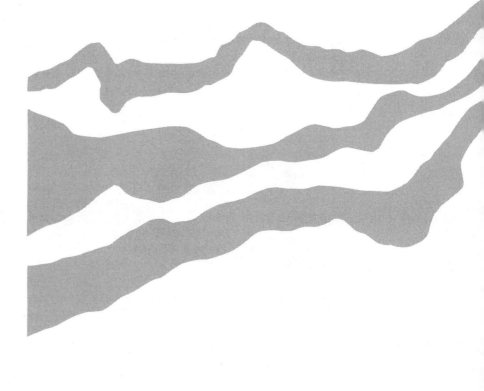

Chapter Organizer

Aim of the Chapter

This chapter will provide a brief overview of the counseling relationship and describe the counselor's implementation of regard and respect.

Chapter Preview

1. The counseling relationship is significantly influenced by the counselor's regard for the client and the counselor's expression of respect, authenticity, and empathy.
2. *Rapport* is a term often used to describe all of the dimensions of the counseling relationship.
3. Regard is an attitude the counselor holds toward the client; whereas respect represents behavior that conveys that attitude.
4. Warmth is a primary component of regard.
5. The concept of unconditional positive regard has been questioned.
6. Acceptance allows for freedom of client self-expression.
7. Respect includes warmth, readiness, listening, and recognizing the possible need for referral.
8. Research substantiates the importance of regard and respect in counseling.
9. The counselor must give evidence of self-regard and self-respect.
10. Client regard and respect for counselors influence counseling outcomes.

Relevant Questions

Following are several questions to keep in mind while reading this chapter:

1. What are the three major therapeutic ingredients in an effective helping relationship?
2. What are your working definitions of *regard* and *respect?*
3. How can positive regard be demonstrated in an unconditional way?
4. How does counselor self-regard enter into the communication of respect for others?
5. Can counselor training programs enhance students' ability to demonstrate respect? How?

Introduction

This section is designed to be an intense look at the therapeutic ingredients of the counseling relationship, namely, regard and respect, authenticity, and empathy. The extensive treatment of these areas reflects our firm belief that these therapeutic ingredients are necessary and, for highly initiating clients, sufficient conditions that support efforts to grow. The absence of these conditions will impede client understanding and growth. These basic and fundamental elements of the counseling relationship are important regardless of the counseling approach or techniques used by the counselor. The three chapters that make up Part III examine each of these elements in turn.

Several terms may be used to describe the basic characteristics of regard, authenticity, and empathy. For example, regard may be linked to acceptance, respect, trust, warmth, and interest. Authenticity may be related to honesty, self-disclosure, congruence, genuineness, and realism. Empathy may be characterized by such terms as sensitivity, understanding, perceiving, reflecting, and communicating. Truax and Carkhuff (1967b) summarizes the interrelatedness of these conditions as follows:

> To be facilitative toward another human being requires that we be deeply sensitive to his moment-to-moment experience, grasping both the core meaning and significance and the content of his experiences and feelings. Such deep empathic understanding requires first that we have at least a degree of warmth and respect for the other person. Thus, empathic understanding can scarcely exist without a prior or concomitant feeling of nonpossessive warmth. In turn, neither the empathy nor the warmth could be constructively meaningful in any human encounter unless it were "real." Unless the counselor or therapist is "genuine" in relating to the client, his warmth and empathy may even have a potentially threatening meaning. To be understood deeply by a potential enemy or by an unpredictable "phony" can be deeply threatening rather than facilitative. (p. 32)

It is important to note that these three basic conditions of the counseling relationship build on one another sequentially. Authenticity is expressed most effectively after the demonstration of respect. Empathy is expressed most effectively after respect and authenticity have been exhibited. Only after these components have been established can counselors most effectively demonstrate their counseling skills.

The counseling process conducted within this relationship may vary according to the methodology of the counselor and to the counseling setting. However, we want to stress that client gains can occur as a result of the effectiveness of the counseling relationship itself. Counselor regard and respect, authenticity, and empathy can, by themselves or in combination, help individuals to gain self-understanding, to improve their decision-making skills, and to change their behavior.

Components of the Counseling Relationship

In general, a good counseling relationship is similar to any good interpersonal relationship. Yet, this relationship doesn't "just happen." An effective counselor should understand the various aspects of the counseling (helping) relationship and know how to implement them through action. Gazda (1973) provides a concise outline of the most commonly accepted components of this relationship in Figure 8.1.

Let us take this opportunity review some general characteristics of the counseling relationship. According to Boy and Pine (1982), a counseling relationship can be described as face-to-face, person-to-person, human, reciprocal, empathic, client-centered, liberating, and confidential; such a relationship includes commitment, mutual respect, effective communication, and genuine acceptance.

Egan (1982) indicates that

a good working relationship contributes to getting the work of helping done. Therefore, helpers establish different kinds of relationships with different clients. For example, although all these relationships need to be based on respect, not all will involve the same degree of warmth. Some clients are helped by a closer, more intimate relationship; others are helped by one that is more matter-of-fact. (p. 35)

Carl Rogers (1961) places a great deal of emphasis on the counseling relationship. He believes a counselor should review the following considerations before establishing this helping relationship:

1. Can I *be* in some way that will be perceived by the other person as dependable or consistent in some deep sense?
2. Can I be expressive enough as a person that what I am will be communicated unambiguously?
3. Can I let myself experience positive attitudes toward this person—attitudes of warmth, caring, liking, interest, and respect?
4. Can I be strong enough as a person to be separate from the other? Can I be a sturdy respector of my own needs as well as his?
5. Am I secure enough within myself to permit him his separateness?
6. Can I let myself enter fully into the world of his feelings and personal meanings and see these as he does?
7. Can I be acceptant of each facet of this other person which he presents to me?
8. Can I act with sufficient sensitivity in the relationship that my behaviors will not be perceived as a threat?
9. Can I free him from the threat of external evaluation?

Figure 8.1
Outline of the Key
Concepts of a
"Helping"
(Problem-Solving)
Relationship

PROCEDURAL GOALS: Self-Exploration ➤ Better Self-Understanding ➤	**More Appropriate Action** or Direction
FACILITATIVE DIMENSIONS ◄─► (Suspend Acting on Evaluations)	**INITIATIVE DIMENSIONS** (Conditional-Judgmental)
1st Empathy (Depth–understanding) ◄─►	**7th Confrontation** (Pointing out discrepancies)
2nd Respect (Belief in)	**8th Immediacy** (Telling it like it is between helper and helpee)
3rd Warmth (Caring–love) ◄─►	
Base- or Rapport-building **Phase** (Helper's tenderness emphasized, helper "earns the right" to risk conditionality)	**Risk-taking Phase** (Helper's toughness or self- confidence and knowledge emphasized)

◄─►

4th Concreteness
(Ability to be specific)

5th Genuineness
(Honesty–realness)

6th Self-disclosure
(Ability to convey
appropriately "I've been
there too.")

Note: Each of the eight dimensions involves the act of perceiving (becoming aware of)
and the act of responding (acting on awareness).
Source: From Gazda, George, *Human Relations Development: A Manual for Educators.*
Boston: Allyn and Bacon, 1973, p. 24.

10. Can I meet this other individual as a person who is in the process of *becoming,*
    or will I be bound by his past and by my past? (pp. 50–55)

Delaney and Eisenberg (1972) expand on these considerations. They
focus on the client's perceptions as part of the criteria for establishing a facilitative relationship. Their criteria follow:

1. Did I understand what the client was saying?
2. Did the client realize I understood him?

3. Did I see the world of the client through the client's eyes?
4. Did the client realize that I perceived with him?
5. Was I warm, compassionate, and interested in the client; and did I demonstrate this by my demeanor?
6. Did the client perceive my desire to be warm and interested in him?
7. What emotions am I feeling toward my client and how are these emotions influencing my actions toward him?
8. Are there certain things I am reluctant to say to my client? If so, what implications does that inhibition have for our relationship?
9. On what important issues do the values, beliefs, and opinions of my client differ from mine? Are those differences influencing my ability to accept him?
10. Was that person in the counseling session really me? Was I genuine and honest as a person?
11. Was the client aware that I was genuine and honest with him?
12. Did I behave in a professional manner, offering my services and my help where it was appropriate?
13. Did the client perceive me as a professional person capable of and desirous of helping him?
14. In brief, did I establish a facilitative relationship with the client as demonstrated by my behavior and perceived by the client?
15. Did I meet the goal of this relationship: helping the client to talk about those personally relevant things which the client felt were necessary for me to understand him. (pp. 59–60)

The counseling relationship between a professionally trained, competent counselor and an individual seeking help is effective to the degree that the counselor can help that individual. To establish the best therapeutic relationship possible for helping the client, the counselor takes specific actions to set the stage for client growth.

Therapists and counselors have long recognized that a warm, caring attitude fosters an effective therapeutic relationship. The term *rapport* has often been used to describe this attitude and its effect on the total relationship.

Establishing rapport may be a long-term process, requiring patience and understanding. Nevertheless, the sooner it's established, the better. We recognize, as do Pietrofesa et al. (1978), that "counseling rapport is a dynamic, changing entity and as such varies from session to session even with the same counselee" (p. 55). We believe, however, that the assurance of confidentiality and the counselor's demonstration of respect, authenticity, and empathy can establish and maintain a state of rapport.

Rapport, as defined so far, is rather intangible and almost mystical—something that just does or does not happen. Thus, it is difficult to measure. Many researchers and practitioners have worked at further defining and evaluating aspects of the counseling relationship, including rapport. For example, Shertzer and Stone (1980) have described rapport as an initial condition that influences the counseling process. They consider rapport to be "a quality, a mutual understanding, a respect, and a sustained interest that should be communicated from the first through the last contact" (p. 261).

The Concepts of Regard and Respect

We see regard, on the part of a counselor, as the most fundamental concept in the counseling relationship, for it is upon regard that one builds respect.

Regard is the *attitude* that the counselor holds toward the client and the counseling relationship. How one regards another affects one's perceptions of that person, whether in a counseling setting or not. Counselors must be cognizant of their attitude toward others. In placing themselves in a position to work with another individual, counselors must regard that individual as being worthy in her or his own right and worthy to be involved in the counseling relationship. If they do not hold this fundamental regard for others, they should not be working as counselors.

The second dimension, respect, is more than attitude. The counselor's *respect* is the *behavior* he or she engages in toward the client. Through both verbal and nonverbal communication, counselors can express respect for their clients.

To consider a simple illustration of regard and respect, let us assume that Andy Howard, an agency counselor, has agreed to meet with Chuck Louis, a substance-abuse client. Chuck requested the appointment. First, Andy—as counselor—regards Chuck as a worthwhile person who deserves his time and involvement in a counseling setting. Second, Andy—as counselor—respects Chuck by keeping the appointment on time and by allowing him to voice his concerns as he sees them. Based on his initial attitude of *regard,* Andy then demonstrates *respect* for Chuck—the client—through his actions.

Although these concepts seem simple, often counselors tend to move quickly to use their counseling skills without establishing a base for counseling.

The Nature of Regard In this section, we shall expand on the meaning of regard and discuss the elements of unconditional positive regard, acceptance, caring, and interest. As we have mentioned, *regard* is an attitude held by the counselor toward the client. Various attitudes can be held, and they range from unconditional positive regard, as espoused by Rogers (1961), to minimum regard, as propounded by certain counselors of the behaviorist field.

In behavioral counseling literature, much less attention is given to the notion of regard for the client's dignity than to the notion that action is necessary to solve the concerns of the client. Directive, or counselor-centered, counseling sessions can be beneficial, and behavioral counselors do regard their clients as worthwhile. However, the client-centered counselor, unlike the directive counselor, assumes that the client has the potential to solve his or her own concerns without being directed by the counselor.

The concept of positive regard seems a keystone of most approaches to the counseling relationship. As Belkin (1980) indicates, "Positive regard is an attitude, a health-engendering attitude that inevitably makes the client feel more secure, more worthwhile as a person, more willing to grow and prosper" (p. 69).

Unconditional Positive Regard   Carl Rogers formulated the concept of "unconditional positive regard" in his early work. This acceptance of the client has had a tremendous influence on the theory and practice of counseling. In describing unconditional positive regard, Rogers (1967) states:

> It means that there are no *conditions* of acceptance, no feelings of "I like you only *if* you are thus and so." It means a "prizing" of the person, as Dewey has used that term. It is at the opposite pole from a selective evaluating attitude—"You are bad in these ways, good in those." It involves as much feeling of acceptance for the client's expression of negative, "bad," painful, fearful, defensive, abnormal feelings as for his expression of "good," positive, mature, confident, social feelings, as much acceptance of ways in which he is inconsistent as of ways in which he is consistent. (p. 76)

There has been much debate over the use of *unconditional* to describe positive regard. Belkin (1980) suggests that the elimination of *unconditional* from the phrase strengthens the concept and makes it less open to controversy. He states, "Rogers himself had been much criticized for the use of the absolute term *unconditional,* since it is probably impossible not to be influenced by certain conditions in our dealings with others—particularly such an important *other* as the client" (p. 69). Belkin also believes, however, that positive regard involves a genuine and sincere acceptance for the client as he or she is.

Brammer (1979) elaborates on the term unconditional:

> The literature on helping shows that the term "unconditional" appears to be controversial. It means that literally no conditions or judgments will hamper the helpee's expression of feelings or ideas. I consider unconditionality relative to stages in the process of helping. In the first contacts it is important to convey through acceptance and warmth the attitude that "I neither approve nor disapprove of what you are saying. I want you to express yourself freely, and I will respect your right to feel as you please and to act as you feel within the limits of our mutual welfare. I want you to become your most real and effective self. Furthermore, I want to be with you because you are a person." Later in the helping process, when the relationship is well established, the helper begins to experience a variety of feelings toward the helpee. Then the regard becomes more conditional. Helpers express more of their own approving and disapproving attitudes, thus tending to reinforce or diminish certain behaviors in helpees. The helper's spontaneous and authentic behaviors become more apparent as the trust level

deepens and the helpee is more open to honest feedback from the helper (pp. 40–41)

The term *nonpossessive warmth* has also been used to describe unconditional positive regard. For example, Truax and Carkhuff (1967b) use the phrases "nonpossessive warmth" and "unconditional positive regard" interchangeably. They state that "The dimension of *nonpossessive warmth* or unconditional positive regard, ranges from a high level where the therapist warmly accepts the patient's experience as part of that person, without imposing conditions; to a low level where the therapist evaluates a patient or his feelings, expresses dislike or disapproval, or expresses warmth in a selective and evaluative way . . ." and that "Nonpossessive warmth for the client means accepting him as a separate person and, thus, a willingness to share equally his joys and aspirations or his depressions and failures. It involves valuing the patient as a person, separate from any evaluation of his behavior or thoughts" (p. 58).

In sum, we believe that positive regard for the client is necessary. However, we recognize that not all counselors can honestly give unconditional positive regard, and in some instances this might even be inappropriate.

Acceptance   Acceptance is a key component of the counselor's positive regard for the client. Much support has been given to this contention. Boy and Pine (1982) indicate:

Acceptance means that there are no reservations, conditions, evaluations, and judgments of the client's feelings, but rather a total positive regard for the client as a person of value. The client is valued and accepted as a person regardless of the negative feelings expressed. Genuine acceptance is unaffected by any differences in the client. It is not acceptance up to this or that point and no further, but acceptance even though the client possesses values, attitudes, and feelings different from those of the counselor. (p. 136)

Schofield (1967) indicates that "acceptance of the patient is a complex of therapist attitudes that includes respect for the patient, as an individual, positive regard for his personality and his potential, warmth, kindness, and continuing willingness to help no matter what the symptoms or defects of the patient. Most crucially, this attitude of acceptance requires that the therapist relate to his patient in a nonjudgmental, noncritical, nonpunitive way" (p. 143).

Lewis (1970) views acceptance as an attitude through which "the counselor attempts to communicate to the client that he values him as a person and that the client can feel free to express himself as fully as possible" (p. 73). He stresses that the attitude of acceptance on the part of the counselor should allow clients to express their feelings freely no matter how hostile or outrageous. He describes the most extreme possible application of this rule "in the story of the mental patient who informed his therapist,

'I am God,' to which the therapist replied, 'All right, I'll let you be God' "
(p. 92).

Pietrofesa et al. (1978) discuss the question "Does acceptance of the client
mean counselor's approval of undesirable behaviors?"

The counselor accepts the counselee as a worthwhile individual—a person with
respect and dignity who has the right to make choices for him/herself. This, then,
is not to say that acceptance implies approval of specific behaviors. In fact, the authentic counselor may very well in effect say, "I do not necessarily approve of your
behavior, but I grant you the right to make decisions for yourself—decisions for
which you must accept the responsibility." (p. 55.)

Inherent in this dimension of acceptance are assumptions or attitudes on
the part of the counselor. These would include viewing the client as one
who has infinite worth and dignity, the ability and right to make personal
decisions, and the responsibility for living his or her own life.

Through acceptance, the counselor makes the counseling session a place
where clients can explore their inner world. We believe that acceptance
places a positive tone on the psychological climate of the counseling session.
Defensive attitudes are less likely to be shown by clients, and clients are
more likely to be involved in the counseling process when the counselor
really accepts them.

In sum, acceptance is an expression of the positive regard the counselor
holds for clients; it allows them to feel free and secure. As clients experience
the acceptance of the counselor, trust and belief in the willingness of the
counselor to help are established. They can then be involved in the relationship in a meaningful way. Thus, acceptance is an essential component of
the counselor's regard for the client, which is basic to the total counseling
process.

Caring   Caring is another way of expressing the attitude of regard for another, but it goes beyond respect, warmth, and acceptance. Caring seems
to involve the counselor in a very sensitive and personal manner. Often confused with love, caring is an extremely personal outreaching. It can lead
counselors to an emotional involvement that interferes with their helping.
Recognizing this possible danger, counselors must realize, nonetheless, that
caring can help their clients feel worthwhile and can help establish the kind
of relationship necessary to deal with real concerns. Aspy (1972) states:

When we value another person and relate to them in such a way that we demonstrate the convictions that they deserve all the things characteristic of a "good life,"
we have positive regard for that person. This kind of caring, since it is based on
a deep conviction, is not a *technique* for building "good" relationships. It is not
something we *use*. It is something we *are*, or it does not exist. (p. 85)

Deep caring on the part of the counselor for the client can be considered
to be either filial love or agape. To distinguish them, Wrenn (1973) defines

filial love as "an expected love, a love within a structured relationship. The counselor is often seen by others as exhibiting this kind of love within a school setting. He is *expected* to care, it is part of his duty, and in turn he at least hopes for some response of appreciation from the students" (p. 279). On the other hand, agape is "a love for those to whom one does not have any structured responsibility. It is a concern for a person as a person, with *no expectation* of a return from the other individual" (p. 279). Brammer and Shostrom (1960) describe agape as "a type of love in which a person seeks to assist other people to grow, contributes unequivocally to the welfare of the love object, and allows the loving person to be used for the self-enhancement of the loved" (p. 156). Whatever the differences between filial love and agape, it is important to note that both show a deep and personal caring for the welfare and growth of the client. We believe that a professionally trained counselor can exhibit love and caring and, further, that he or she might well expect this approach to lead to client self-exploration and behavior change.

Another, less intense aspect of caring is interest. Simply being interested in the client can be most beneficial in counseling. On this point, Rogers (1951) relates the following anecdote: "One student successfully completed therapy with a second counselor some months after a single interview with a first counselor. When the contacts were finished, he was asked why it had seemed possible to work through his problems with the second counselor, but had broken off with the first counselor after one interview. He thought for a moment and replied, 'You did about the same things he did, but you seemed really interested in me' " (p. 69).

We believe the counselor demonstrates his or her regard for the client by showing interest in that individual both as a person and as someone who has the potential to grow. In Blocher's (1966) view, a counselor helps accept a client by showing interest and concern. He feels clients are turned off when counselors show disinterest, boredom, and a lack of caring. In other words, interest and concern are essential ingredients of caring. However, as Wrenn (1973) points out, "[T]o care is not a professional garment to be donned in one's office—it is so very apparent there as a garment" (p. 280). Competent counselors are accepting, concerned, and caring individuals. They feel a positive regard for all people, not just their clients, and exhibit this regard in a counseling relationship by being respectful.

In sum, the definition of *regard* for clients varies with the attitude of the counselor. Some counselors regard clients as having the potential within themselves to do or achieve anything. Other counselors regard the clients as individuals who need their professional expertise to live effectively. All counselors, regardless of the degree of regard they hold for their clients, must genuinely regard them in a positive way, as unique individuals who *deserve* attention and understanding, if only because they have come to them expecting aid. Based on this positive regard, counselors can then express respect to their clients.

The Nature of Respect   We believe the counselor's behavior toward the client demonstrates the counselor's respect for the client. Egan (1982) supports our view. He states, "If it [respect] is to make a difference, it cannot remain an attitude, just a way of viewing human beings. Respect makes a difference only when it becomes a value—that is, an attitude expressed behaviorally" (p. 121). The counselor's belief in the worth and potential of the client seems to be a precondition for this behavior. Gazda (1973) states, "If the helper can value and believe in the helpee and can *communicate* [our italics] this to him, the helpee also begins to value himself, to gain confidence in his ability to overcome his particular deficits, and thus to risk involvement with the helper and the process of helping and problem solving" (p. 56). Thus, the attitude (positive regard) and its translation to action (respect) are necessarily linked.

Levels of Respect   Carkhuff (1969a) ranked the levels of respect that can be expressed by counselors as follows:

Level 1. The verbal and behavioral expressions of the helper communicate a clear lack of respect (or negative regard) for the helpee.

Level 2. The helper responds to the helpee in such a way as to communicate little respect for the feelings, experiences, and potentials of the helpee.

Level 3. The helper communicates the minimal acknowledgment of regard for the helpee's position and concern for the helpee's feelings, experiences, and potentials.

Level 4. The helper clearly communicates a very deep respect and concern for the helpee.

Level 5. The helper communicates the very deepest respect for the helpee's worth as a person and his potentials as a free individual. (pp. 178–179)

At the highest level, Carkhuff believes the helper does everything he or she can to enable the helpee to act most constructively and emerge most fully.

In this section, we shall expand on the meaning of respect and discuss its various aspects, such as warmth, readiness, listening, and possible referral.

We agree with Egan (1982) that counselors translate their attitude into respectful behavior when they do the following:

attend and listen actively to clients

suspend critical judgment

communicate accurate empathic understanding

express reasonable warmth or friendliness

help clients identify and cultivate their own resources

provide encouragement and support and

help clients get the work of each stage of the helping process done. (p. 132)

Aspects of Respect It is apparent that respect can be shown in a variety of ways. One frequently mentioned approach is the counselor's expression of warmth. Carkhuff (1969a) describes warmth as "one of several possible vehicles for communicating respect" (p. 180).

Gazda (1973) identifies warmth as one of the facilitative conditions essential for setting up a helping relationship. He believes this distinction emphasizes the importance of warmth in the process of helping. Gazda (1973) defines *warmth* as "the physical expression of empathy (understanding) and respect (caring). It is generally communicated through a wide variety of non-verbal media such as gestures, posture, tone of voice, touch, or facial expression" (p. 87). He cautions the counselor to remember that any one form of nonverbal communication carries different meanings in different cultures.

Respect involves the counselor's readiness to work with the client. The counselor must mentally and physically prepare to meet the client. The counselor should put other business aside and reserve the counseling time for counseling. This readiness and preparation is expected of professional counselors.

Professional conduct on the part of the counselor can effectively express respect for the client. As counselors meet their clients on time, provide appropriate and relaxing surroundings, maintain confidentiality in the counseling relationship, and remain ethical in their behaviors, they express respect for the client.

Listening to the client and accepting his or her statements is an important expression of respect. By listening effectively, the counselor not only shows interest and concern, but also gathers data to better understand the client and his or her primary concern. Listening, as a counseling skill, is discussed in more detail in Chapters 11 and 12.

Respect for the client is also shown when the counselor recognizes that he or she is not the appropriate counselor for that client or for that client's concern. Counselors should feel no guilt or shame if they meet a client whom for some reason they cannot accept or respect. Not all counselors can relate effectively to all clients. However, the counselor has the responsibility to inform the client of this and to refer the client to other counselors or resources.

Research on Regard and Respect For many reasons, research on regard and respect has been difficult to carry out. The very concepts have been hard to define and are often defined differently by different researchers. Many of their components, such as warmth, acceptance, and caring, tend to overlap. Even though the basic concept of respect has been distinguished from genuineness and empathy, these three dimensions of the counseling relationship influence one another and are, at times, exhibited in various combinations.

Early reports on counselor characteristics, ingredients in the counseling relationship, and counseling effectiveness tended to be based on opinion rather than objective evidence. One step toward objectivity was made when Berger (1952) developed a 28-item scale for measuring the acceptance of others while conducting research on respect. A person who scored high on this measure did not dominate, reject, or infringe on the rights of others but did try to set up a satisfactory relationship and serve others. Rogers's (1957) tentative definitions of *empathy, warmth,* and *genuineness* provided further guidelines to aid researchers in their investigations of the counseling relationship and its component parts.

Truax and Carkhuff (1967b) indicate that research in the area of therapeutic ingredients of the counseling relationship has been based on the client-centered orientation of Carl Rogers. Regard and respect, often researched as nonpossessive warmth, are basic components of the client-centered counseling style. Yet, counselors from many philosophical orientations can exhibit respect, genuineness, and empathy. As a case in point, a study by Fischer et al. (1975) found no differences between the orientations of humanistic, psychodynamic, or behavioristic therapists in terms of empathy, warmth, or genuineness offered in the therapeutic relationship.

Halikides (1958) investigated the relationship between positive personality change and the counselor variables of empathic understanding, unconditional positive regard, genuineness, and reflection of affective expression. A high degree of unconditional positive regard was significantly associated with the "most successful" cases. Barrett-Lennard (1959) devised a Relationship Inventory to ascertain client perceptions of the counselor and the counseling relationship. This inventory measured empathic understanding, level of regard, unconditionality of regard, genuineness, and willingness to be known. Level of regard and unconditonality of regard were associated with successful therapy.

In the 1960s many research efforts were begun by investigators such as Truax, Berenson, and Carkhuff. Space does not permit a full listing of their studies. Particularly helpful, however, are *Toward Effective Counseling and Psychotherapy: Training and Practice,* by Truax and Carkhuff (1967b); *Sources of Gain in Counseling and Psychotherapy,* by Berenson and Carkhuff (1967); *Beyond Counseling and Therapy,* by Carkhuff and Berenson (1967); and *Helping and Human Relations* (Volume II), by Carkhuff (1969).

In part, regard and respect are based on counselor attitudes and perceptions. Rokeach (1960) investigated open-mindedness, or "low dogmatism," to determine if it was effective in the counseling relationship. Studies by Russo et al. (1964), Allen (1967) and Mezzano (1969) have indicated that open-mindedness, or full acceptance of the client, is directly related to effective counseling relationships and counseling outcomes. Other research on counselors' attitudes carried on by Combs and Soper (1963) at the University of Florida found that effective counselors had a positive attitude of acceptance toward clients. They suggested that effective counselors were oriented toward people rather than things and saw people (clients) as able, dependable, and friendly rather than unable, undependable, and unfriendly. Donnan et al. (1969) studied prospective college freshmen's perceptions of counselors. They found that counselors who were outgoing, warm-hearted, and easygoing were perceived as offering a higher degree of unconditional positive regard to their clients.

Research efforts in the 1970s followed the pattern set in the 1960s. The effects of dogmatism and open-mindedness on the part of the counselor were investigated by Tosi (1970), who found that client ratings of the counseling relationship became increasingly higher as the counselor became more open-minded and accepting. Foulds (1971) indicated that more open-minded and less dogmatic counselors were more self-actualized and more able to effectively communicate the facilitative conditions, including warmth, to their clients. Wright (1975) found that dogmatism during counseling was an unstable characteristic of counselors. He also noted it significant that low-dogmatic counselors expressed unconditional regard more than high-dogmatic counselors.

In a study related to the training of counselors, Truax and Lister (1970) pointed out that counselor's knowledge and training had less effect on the outcomes of counseling than did their attitude and feelings. The importance of a positive attitude was also noted by Jackson and Thompson (1971), who found that effective counselors were more positive in their attitudes toward self, toward most clients, and toward counseling.

Counselor warmth toward the client was investigated by Johnson (1971), and his findings indicated that warmth of interaction is directly related to positive attitudes of the counselor. He found that warmth was "significantly related to being liked and trusted, to being perceived as similar both as a person and in beliefs and values, to being perceived as accepting of the subject and of his position, and to being perceived as an understanding person" (p. 214).

Zarski et al. (1977) found that the counselor's level of social interest was positively correlated with the client's satisfaction with the counseling relationship. This indicates that, in clients' eyes, interest in people and society is an important counselor attribute. We see interest as one aspect of the attitude of regard.

Robiner and Storandt (1983) investigated the influence of chronological age of clients and counselors on the facilitative attitude of regard. They found that age does not exert a significant influence on the client's perception of the counselor's demonstration of regard.

Having shown how essential regard and respect are to a counseling relationship, let us now see how they can be demonstrated by the counselor. Most recently, the emphasis in counseling research seems to focus on such counseling skills as attending, listening, and responding rather than on the counseling relationship itself and its facilitative core conditions. Goldman (1977) and Barclay (1980) both indicate that more and more of the research in counseling will be done in field studies and in observation of hard data, rather than on the basis of insight and understanding as suggested in the earlier work of Rogers.

Fuqua and Gade (1982) state, "In the past decade or so we have witnessed in counselor education a strong interest in determining and isolating discrete skills in the counseling process" (p. 282). However, the following generalizations may be drawn from research in the area of the counseling relationship and regard and respect:

Researchers have made significant progress beyond their previously held subjective views on counselor attributes and the counseling relationship through: (1) the formulation of research instruments and methodologies, (2) the increased amount of research being conducted in this area, and (3) research with larger populations both within and outside of clinic settings. Prominent in this trend toward more objective research have been Rogers, Truax, Carkhuff, Berenson, Gazda, their colleagues, and their doctoral students.

Research in the dimensions of the counseling relationship has been geared to the Rogerian, client-centered approaches. However, several studies have indicated that counselors of various theoretical orientations recognize the value of and exhibit the therapeutic conditions of regard and respect, as well as empathy and genuineness.

In general, the research findings have indicated that counselors and therapists are more successful in aiding client growth, self-exploration, and change when they are accepting of themselves and others, open-minded, and self-actualized and when they can demonstrate respect, warmth, and acceptance. Currently research seems to place more emphasis on training helpers in learning facilitative core conditions, such as regard and respect for the client, through such counseling behaviors as attending, listening, and responding.

Regard and Respect in the Counseling Relationship

Having reviewed various aspects of these terms, we shall now look at regard and respect in the counseling relationship from three different perspectives: (1) as the counselor regards and respects self, (2) as the counselor regards and respects self in relation to the client, and (3) as the client regards and respects the counselor. We will then discuss how the counselor can best demonstrate regard and respect for the client.

Counselor Self-Regard and Self-Respect   It is important for counselors to recognize the influence of their values, beliefs, and attitudes on their regard for themselves. For counselors to aid others effectively, they must be in tune with themselves.

Counselors perceive and behave on the basis of their knowledge of self, understanding of self, acceptance of self, and respect for self. Before understanding, acceptance, and respect comes knowledge. Appell (1963) states:

The most significant resource a counselor brings to a helping relationship is himself. It is difficult to understand how a counselor unaware of his own emotional needs, of his expectations of himself as well as others, of his rights and privileges in relationships, can be sensitive enough to such factors in his counselee. More than that, it would seem that he needs to experience himself as a person of worth and of individuality before he can afford another such privilege. Indeed, in a most profound sense, the greater his congruence, the freer he can be in assisting others to actualize themselves. (p. 148)

Carkhuff (1969a) concurs, stating that "to the degree that the helping person is himself open to a wide range of experiences in himself, to that degree can he be open to a wide range of experiences in another person, and, in turn, enable the other person to become open to a wide range of experiences in himself. The degree to which the helper understands and accepts himself is related to the degree to which he understands and accepts others" (p. 35). Benjamin (1981) expresses it this way: "I believe the more we know about ourselves, the better we can understand, evaluate, and control our behavior and the better we can understand and appreciate the behavior of others. . . . [O]riented to ourselves, we may become comfortable with ourselves and thus be able to help others become comfortable with themselves and with us" (p. 6). It is important for counselors to look at their past experiences, environment, and behaviors. It is their perceptions about themselves, not others' perceptions of them, that influence their behavior.

Tyler (1969) states that attitudes of counselors "are not the products of a year's cultivation or of specific educational experiences like counselor training programs. They grow from the responses a person makes to all the experiences of his life" (p. 33). Nevertheless, she believes that counselors relate to and work with individuals, not humankind, and that the important attitude is toward individuals, not humankind.

However, other researchers believe that counselors' basic view toward humanity is most influential in their work with individuals. Arbuckle (1975) states:

The counselor, then, should be one whose values are marked by a strong faith in people, a belief that people *can* grow and develop, that they can stand tall and have pride in self. To become this sort of person, the counselor must be a knowledgeable person, but far more important, this knowledge must have helped him move along the road to wisdom, which includes compassion and love and understanding, ingredients that are often missing from knowledge. (p. 395)

Combs et al. (1971) also believe that counselors' perceptions of others and themselves indeed influence their behavior in the counseling relationship. In their research, these authors distinguish good helpers from poor ones on the basis of their attitudes toward people. In his research into attitudes toward others, Rokeach (1960) found that dogmatism influences people's acceptance of others. He was able to distinguish between open and closed persons based on their belief-disbelief systems. In a related study, Wright (1975) discovered that counselors who were closed or highly dogmatic in their belief system viewed individuals as helpless, inadequate, and unable to handle life situations, and tended to treat clients in a critical and nonaccepting manner.

From our perceptual backgrounds, we believe that counselors' views toward humankind in general influence their attitudes toward themselves and, in turn, affect their perceptions and regard for their client and their behavior as counselors.

Benjamin (1981) states that when counselors know, and are comfortable with, themselves, they become at ease in working with others—their own self does not get in the way of understanding, and relating to, clients. Likewise, Gurman (1972) found "that therapists relatively free of psychological disturbance, yet willing to acknowledge emotional discomfort when it is present, are better able to respond facilitatively to their patients" (p. 169).

Finally, counselors' self-confidence seems directly related to positive perceptions of the counselors by their clients. Counselors, who know, accept, and respect themselves, will be self-confident and able to enter into a counseling relationship with a positive attitude that benefits the client greatly. We shall now see how counselors' self-respect can enhance the counseling relationship.

Counselor Regard and Respect for Self in Relation to the Client

When counselors have positive self-regard, they can respect themselves in their relationships with others and maintain an ethical approach in the counseling relationship. Following the ethical standards of the American Association for Counseling and Development (Appendix A), counselors promote the welfare of the client, keep information in confidence, inform the client of the conditions under which counseling is given, and terminate the relationship if they feel a personal limitation or lack of competence. Ethically, counselors do not use the client to fulfill their own needs. If counselors are respectful of themselves as well as of their clients, there is no need for them to attempt to hasten "progress" from session to session or during a specific session. Rogers (1951) and Wrenn (1973) agree that counselors should allow clients to proceed at their own pace—should not push them into an area or commitment that they are not able to handle or that would be right only from the counselors' point of view.

Wrenn (1973) adds that "respect for self means also that you do not let clients impose on you. You are concerned for them, but they cannot abuse your time or self-respect" (p. 284). In effect, counselors provide services that meet the client's needs but not to the exclusion of their own.

Counselors who respect themselves can be authentic and at ease in their counseling relationship with others. In being sensitive to their own needs they can be sensitive and empathic to the client's. The counselors' approach and behavior need to be genuine. Counselors must be themselves and at times be self-disclosing. Clients can see through a counselor front or phoniness. If the counselor doesn't truly respect the client, counseling effectiveness is seriously impaired. Chapter 9 discusses inauthenticity further.

Although counselors should be aware of their beliefs and values, they must never impose them on the client. Sprinthall (1971) points out that to hold a value-neutral position is impossible and states, "Since values are conceptualized as major determinants of human behavior, the value question cannot be ignored" (p. 52). If counselors have really made an attempt to know themselves, they will have reviewed their attitudes and beliefs regarding clients of another race, sex, age, religion, social class, and culture. Although counselors often profess their openness toward, and acceptance of, all clients, they need to ask themselves honestly if indeed they can relate well to clients from different backgrounds, including the opposite sex.

In a 1982 study, Sladen reported that "findings suggested that a client's preference for a counselor of similar race or socioeconomic background rather than one of dissimilar background may not rest solely on actual differences in empathic skills between the counselors but instead may also be based on the client's biased estimate of differences" (p. 564). Counselors need to recognize this possible bias on the part of clients as well as on their own. In addition, as Moore and Strickler (1980) point out, counselors need to recognize continuing sexism in counseling.

Regardless of the counselor-client variables involved, counselors need to assess their attitudes toward potential clients: If these attitudes seem likely to interfere with their acceptance of a particular client, counselors should not enter into a working relationship with that individual. If, during the course of the counseling relationship, they find that their beliefs drastically conflict with the client's and inhibit their ability to help the client, they should terminate their involvement, allowing the client to establish a counseling relationship with someone else. Many reality or rational-emotive counselors would disagree with our viewpoint, believing that it might be proper for counselors to determine what is best for their clients based on the counselors' attitudes and beliefs. However, our stance is that counselors aid their clients, as the clients act on their *own* insights and beliefs and take responsibility for their actions. Having examined counselor attitudes to clients and counseling, let us now turn to clients' perceptions of their counselors.

Client Regard and Respect for the Counselor

Client perceptions of the counselor are extremely crucial in establishing an effective counseling relationship. If clients hold their counselors in positive regard and respect them, they have made a first step toward establishing an effective relationship. As Benjamin (1981) states, "Trust in the interviewer by the interviewee and the conviction that the interviewer respects him are, of course, only part of the goal of a helping interview, whether it be between teacher and pupil, supervisor and worker, doctor and patient, or rehabilitation worker and client; but without these, little that is really positive will be accomplished" (p. 5).

When the client assumes that he or she can believe in the counselor, trust is established. Blocher (1980) and Stensrud and Stensrud (1981) both indicate that client perceptions of the counselor's trustworthiness are important in the counseling process. We believe that when the client believes in and trusts the counselor, the client shares more and gets more involved in the counseling relationship.

According to Delaney and Eisenberg (1972), "[O]nly when the client becomes aware of the counselor-related characteristics will he feel free and comfortable to say the things he wants to say and at the rate and in the manner he wants to say them" (p. 51). They indicate that client perceptions of the counselor are based on client awareness that the counselor—

knows how I feel.

has respect for me, is kind, and accepts me for what I am, is not harsh or threatening.

is not a phony, or putting on a facade, but is the person he or she presents to me.

is a person capable of helping me with my problems.

Boy and Pine (1978) support the notion that counselors who establish therapeutic credibility are able to work effectively with their clients. When clients see counselors as capable and credible, they feel confidence in the counselor and in their relationship.

In sum, it appears that clients have positive regard for counselors whom they see as self-confident, empathic, accepting, genuine, honest, open, trustworthy, confidential, and professionally competent. This positive perception may encourage clients to participate more fully in the counseling relationship, as they sense a secure and trusting environment for self-exploration and growth.

Counselor Demonstration of Regard and Respect

Demonstrating Regard   Regard is the counselor's basic attitude toward the client and the counseling relationship. This attitude cannot be faked, because it must be perceived as sincere and honest by the client for the counseling relationship to be effective. In this discussion, we assume that a counselor truly accepts the client as being worthwhile and accepts the counseling relationship as an effective way of helping that client.

Benjamin (1981) states that "acceptance means treating the interviewee as an equal and regarding his thoughts and feelings with sincere respect. It does not mean agreeing; it does not mean thinking or feeling the way he does; it does not mean valuing what he values. It is, rather, the attitude that the interviewee has as much right to his ideas, feelings, and values as I have to mine and that I want to do my utmost to understand his life space in terms of his ideas, feelings, and values rather than in terms of my own" (p. 41).

Egan (1982) describes the counselor's "orientation toward" the client (regard) to include attitudes that are translated into behaviors (respect). His attitudes of orientation toward the client include:

1. Being "for the Client." The counselor's manner indicates that he or she is "for" the client simply because the client is human.

2. Willingness to Work with the Client. Respectful helpers are available to their clients.
3. Regard for the Client as Unique. Respect is translated into a regard for clients' individuality.
4. Regard for the Client's Self-Determination. The helper's basic attitude is that clients have the resources to help them live more effectively. (pp. 121–122)

To allow clients to be human—to be themselves—counselors must accept their clients as they present themselves at any given moment. Clients often challenge this acceptance to see if they can really trust the counselor. Thus, acceptance must be shown consistently, during every session of the counseling relationship.

We offer the following as ways to gain client acceptance:

Warmth and respect can be communicated or not communicated by the therapist in a variety of ways: by sitting silently for a full session with a client who is weeping, struggling, and experiencing a deep "aloneness"; by genuine laughter as the patient recounts an incident in his life; by being willing to accept the patient's choosing *not* to share an experience; by agreeing to extend the therapeutic session for two hours or more when that is possible and appropriate; by the apologizing for unintentionally hurting the client by act, gesture, or word; and, by being open enough to voice his own feelings when he has been hurt or angered by the client. (Truax and Carkhuff, 1967a, p. 314) A school counselor may find a client whipping out a cigarette, and the counselor's acceptance of this can be indicated by passing an ashtray to him. Obvious and studied verbal insolence is another means by which the counselor may be tested, and the counselor's capacity to accept such behavior is a good measure of his professional competence and personal security. (Arbuckle, 1975, p. 207)

In addition to physical indications of acceptance, verbal responses can convey to clients an acceptance of their statements and voiced concerns. Two examples follow:

Client: I'd like to talk to you again, but I don't know if I can make these appointments every Tuesday at this time.
Counselor: I'll look at our schedule to arrange a time that would be better for you, so we can continue to meet.

Client: You don't know what it's like to be made fun of and ridiculed behind your back.
Counselor: It may not be easy for you to discuss this, but if you want to talk about it, I'll listen and work with you.

A point to be made here is that in accepting clients' mannerisms and statements, counselors do not have to agree that these are correct. They are accepted as legitimate at this point in time. This acceptance allows clients to explore themselves and their concerns by expanding on previously accepted statements and reviewing previously accepted behaviors.

Demonstrating Respect In addition to showing acceptance and positive regard for their clients, counselors' actions of respect express belief in their clients' worth. Respect is shown when counselors are sincerely interested in their clients and use their professional training and skills to the best of their ability. Counselors are willing to give their time to their clients and to become involved and committed to aiding them. In working with their clients, they follow the ethical guidelines of their profession.

Providing privacy and adequate, relaxing surroundings conveys respect for the client. Counselors also should make a point of meeting their clients on time and notifying them if they cannot make the scheduled appointment. While in the counseling session, there should be no interruptions, such as phone calls or messages delivered by secretaries.

Sensitivity to, and respect for, the client is shown when counselors attempt to understand the client's feelings, experiences, and behaviors by using the basic counseling skills of attending, listening, and responding. Attending to a client encompasses both physical and psychological aspects. Brammer and Shostrom (1982) list four physical indications of acceptance and respect—eye contact, facial expression and nodding by the counselor, friendly tone of voice and even inflection, and close physical distance and inclined posture. Carkhuff (1973) indicates that effective counselors attend to a client by maintaining eye contact, facing the client, inclining their bodies toward the client, and being physically close to the client. One must be careful, however, as some clients are bothered psychologically by this closeness and focused attention. The counselor then needs to respect the psychological distance that seems appropriate for that client.

By psychologically attending to the client, the counselor indicates a willingness to be "in tune" with the client. Facial expression, especially eye contact, should show acceptance and suspended critical judgments. (Other aspects of attending will be discussed in further detail in Chapter 11.) Brammer (1979) lists four guidelines for effective attending behavior:

1. Establish *contact* through looking at helpee, when they talk.
2. Maintain a *natural relaxed posture* that indicates your interest.
3. Use *natural gestures* that communicate your intended messages.
4. Use *verbal statements* that relate to statements without interruptions, questions, or new topics (p. 71)

Gazda (1973) provides a slightly different set of guidelines for demonstrating respect:

1. Initially, the helper is most effective in responding with respect when he can be non-evaluative with the helpee. In addition, the helper should encourage the helpee to express himself fully.
2. Initially, the helper should respond in a modulated tone of voice until a basis is built for warm expression. With some helpees initial expression of warmth would be inappropriate.

3. Respect is perhaps best communicated when the helper gives the helpee his undivided attention and demonstrates that he is committed to understanding the helpee.
4. The helper should provide conditions that will allow the helpee to reveal himself to the helper so that the helper can develop positive regard for the helpee. Since there is no initial basis on which the helper can like the helpee, the helper must create conditions so that respect can happen.
5. With the development of a facilitative base the helper can respond with respect when he is genuine and spontaneous. He demonstrates helpee respect when he shares his full range of feelings with the helpee. (pp. 56–57)

While these guidelines can be useful, counselors must also listen carefully, so that their responses indicate to clients that they either understand or are attempting to understand their clients' feelings and meaning as well as the content expressed. (Listening and responding skills will be reviewed in Chapters 11 and 12.)

Counselors demonstrate respect by not pushing the client into areas of discussion for which he or she is not ready. However, they may support positive action or statements that the client shares. Egan (1982) indicates that reinforcement demonstrates respect, stating:

Helpers show respect when they reinforce all constructive action on the part of the client—for instance, when clients work at self-exploration or when they take even tentative steps in the direction of constructive behavioral change. Respect is also shown by refusing to reinforce the client's self-destructive behavior. (p. 126)

It is important for counselors to guard against imposing their values and attitudes on clients through selective reinforcement. Counselors in touch with themselves are aware of their verbal responses and physical mannerisms, as they convey positive regard, acceptance, and respect to their clients.

Implications for Counselor Training in Regard and Respect

Positive regard toward clients is an attitude that can be cultivated. Training can help counselors learn to communicate regard and respect effectively. When counselor trainees take an in-depth look at themselves, their client populations, and their behaviors in interpersonal helping relationships, they gain a deeper perspective for understanding and accepting clients.

Without the ability to respect and accept clients, trainees will find it very difficult to be genuine or empathic in a counseling relationship. Thus, counselor training programs should provide the opportunity for trainees to understand the attitude of regard and the expression of respect and to evaluate their abilities in demonstrating these skills so key to the counseling relationship. Arbuckle (1975) states that "understanding and acceptance of one's fellows cannot be taken for granted, and it should be the central core of any program of counselor education" (p. 388). In this section we will look at supervision, counselor study of self, counselor sensitivity to others, and counselor understanding of, and experience in using, techniques to express respect.

Carkhuff (1969b) indicated that supervisors' behaviors seem to be a critical variable in effective counselor training. We believe that trainees tend to move in the direction of their supervisors' behaviors in establishing interpersonal relationships. These behaviors may be less effective than many supervisors believe. Thus, before a counselor training program is established and implemented, the supervisors must evaluate themselves and their methods of facilitating counseling relationships. Supervisors should be able to model *effective* behaviors that demonstrate regard for and respect of clients.

Counselors in training need to look at themselves also, so they can understand and accept themselves as worthy of respect. Tyler (1969) states: "Training for counseling is not just a matter of developing a few new skills. It requires setting one's psychological house in order, so that one knows who he is and where he is going" (p. 37). Combs et al. (1971) agree on this point, stating, "Because beliefs about themselves are so very important, training programs for professional helpers increasingly deal with the *person* of the helper" (p. 14). We believe that counselors need to develop a sensitivity to their own values and to understand how these values can either help or hinder their interaction with clients.

Changes in self-concept and in acceptance of self and others often occur in the course of counselor training programs. Gazda (1973) states that "an obvious first step in improving one's perceptual skills is to achieve a more comprehensive understanding of oneself. This can be accomplished to some degree by introspection (observing and analyzing one's own behavior) and by participating in a counseling or training group experience where this is the main point of emphasis. In such groups, one may enter into relationships with others where feedback is given and received" (p. 40). We recommend participation in growth group experiences, not only to sensitize trainees to themselves but to others as well.

Alternative ways of becoming sensitive to others are reading literature pertinent to various groups and living with members of other cultures. Such sensitivity allows trainees to better express positive regard for others. Ivey and Leppaluoto (1975) state:

The provision of professional services to persons of culturally diverse backgrounds by persons not competent in understanding and providing professional services to such groups shall be considered unethical. . . . It shall be equally unethical to deny such persons professional services because the present staff is inadequately prepared. . . . It shall be the obligation of all service agencies to employ competent persons or to provide continuing education for the present staff to meet the service needs of the culturally diverse populations it serves. (p. 749)

The understanding of self and others aids counselors in respecting and accepting others. Counselors must learn how to apply this understanding effectively. As the research findings of Kaul and Schmidt (1971) indicate, the training program should include direct attention to the manner of communication in counseling, as well as to the content discussed in that communication.

Truax and Carkhuff (1967a) state:

The evidence that therapists do not always practice what they preach implies that the therapist in training could perhaps profit from less theoretical and intellectual training and more specific training of how to make operational the effective ingredients in psychotherapy. Specifically, measuring instruments used in current research could be directly applied to training programs. Thus tape recordings of psychotherapy rated very high in the known elements of effective psychotherapy could be selected to provide concrete examples for beginning therapists, and such scales could also be used to evaluate the trainee's own early therapy behavior to give him immediate and concrete informational feedback telling him how well he is learning to operate with his concepts. (p. 382)

The process of demonstrating respect, warmth, and acceptance can be taught to trainees. Physical expression of respect for the client can occur in the attending, listening, and responding behaviors of the counselor. Ivey (1971), Carkhuff (1973), and Brammer (1979) stress the importance of posture and eye contact in showing regard for the client. These authors provide detailed exercises that can be used by counselor trainers. Their practical benefits include direct feedback in a systematic process. Role-playing or actual counseling sessions with clients, which are video-taped and/or audio-taped, can be analyzed according to a variety of rating scales. Means for self-evaluation should be provided *throughout* the entire program of counselor training so that effective trainees can be encouraged to continue their training and ineffective trainees, to look at other career possibilities.

Summary

In this chapter, we discussed the counseling relationship and the concepts regard and respect. These concepts were defined, and their importance in the total counseling relationship was discussed. Rapport, unconditional positive regard, acceptance, caring, and warmth were also examined.

We reviewed regard and respect in the counseling relationship from both the counselor's and client's points of view. Examples of counselor expression of regard and respect were provided and related research was discussed. Finally, we suggested directions for counselor training, based on the material presented in the chapter.

The major points of this chapter were as follows:

1. Three essential elements of the counseling relationship are counselors' positive regard for the client, authenticity on the part of counselors, and empathic understanding by counselors.
2. Counselor regard and respect are basic to the counseling relationship.
3. Regard is the attitude counselors hold toward the client and the counseling relationship.
4. Counselors must regard the client as worthwhile.
5. Regard involves a caring for the client that is not possessive.
6. There is some movement to eliminate *unconditional* as a term applied to positive regard.
7. Respect is the behavior counselors demonstrate toward the client in the counseling relationship.
8. Respect involves a philosophy that is reflected in the way we treat others.
9. Researchers and practitioners have continually worked at defining and evaluating aspects of the counseling relationship.
10. The counseling relationship is significantly influenced by counselor self-regard and self-respect in relation to the client and by the client's regard and respect for the counselor.
11. Counselors demonstrate respect through both verbal and nonverbal behaviors.
12. Research and training indicate that counselors can learn to demonstrate positive regard and respect for their clients.

References

Allen, T. W. "Effectiveness of Counselor Trainees as a Function of Psychological Openness." *Journal of Counseling Psychology* 14 (1967):35–40

Appell, Morey L. "Self-Understanding for the Guidance Counselor." *Personnel and Guidance Journal* 42 (1963):143–148.

Arbuckle, Dugald S. *Counseling and Psychotherapy: An Existential-Humanistic View.* 3d ed. Boston: Allyn and Bacon, 1975.

Aspy, David. *Toward a Technology for Humanizing Education.* Champaign, Ill.: Research Press Company, 1972.

Barclay, James. "The Revolution in Counseling. Some Editorial Comments." *Personnel and Guidance Journal* 58 (1980):457.

Barrett-Lennard, G. T. "Dimensions of the Client's Experience of His Therapist Associated with Personality Change." Unpublished doctoral dissertation. University of Chicago, 1959.

Belkin, Gary. *An Introduction to Counseling.* Dubuque, Iowa: Wm. C. Brown, 1980.

Benjamin, Alfred. *The Helping Interview.* 3rd ed. Boston: Houghton Mifflin, 1981.

Berger, E. M. "The Relation Between Expressed Acceptance of Self and Expressed Acceptance of Others." *Journal of Abnormal and Social Psychology* 47 (1952):778–782.

Blocher, Donald H. *Developmental Counseling.* New York: The Ronald Press, 1966, 2d ed., 1974.

———. "Some Implications of Recent Research in Social and Developmental Psychology for Counseling Practice." *Personnel and Guidance Journal* 58 (1980):334–336.

Boy, Angelo, and Gerald Pine. "Effective Counseling: Some Proportional Relationships." *Counselor Education and Supervision* 18 (1978):137–143.

———. *Client-Centered Counseling: A Renewal.* Boston: Allyn and Bacon, 1982.

Brammer, Lawrence M. *The Helping Relationship.* Englewood Cliffs, N.J.: Prentice-Hall, 1979.

———, **and Everett Shostrom.** *Therapeutic Psychology.* Englewood Cliffs, N.J.: Prentice-Hall, 2nd ed., 1960, 4th ed., 1982.

Carkhuff, Robert R. *Helping and Human Relations.* Vol. I. New York: Holt, Rinehart and Winston, 1969a.

———. "Critical Variables in Effective Counselor Training." *Journal of Counseling Psychology* 16 (1969b):238–245.

———. *The Art of Helping, An Introduction to Life Skills.* Amherst, Mass.: Human Resource Development Press, 1973.

Combs, Arthur, Donald Avila, and William Purkey. *Helping Relationships: Basic Concepts for the Helping Professions.* Boston: Allyn and Bacon, 1971.

————, and D. W. Soper. "The Perceptual Organization of Effective Counselors." *Journal of Counseling Psychology* 10 (1963):222–226.

Delaney, Daniel, and Sheldon Eisenberg. *The Counseling Process.* Chicago: Rand McNally, 1972.

Donnan, H. D., Grady Harlan, and S. A. Thompson. "Counselor Personality and Level of Functioning as Perceived by Counselees." *Journal of Counseling Psychology* 16 (1969):482–485.

Egan, Gerard. *The Skilled Helper.* Monterey, Calif.: Brooks/Cole, 1982.

Fischer, F., G. J. Paveza, N. S. Kickertz, L. J. Hubbard, and S. B. Grayston. "The Relationship Between Theoretical Orientation and Therapists' Empathy, Warmth and Genuineness." *Journal of Counseling Psychology* 22 (1975):399–403.

Foulds, M. L. "Dogmatism and Ability to Communicate Facilitative Conditions During Counseling." *Counselor Education and Supervision* 11 (1971):110–114.

Fuqua, Dale, and Eldon Gade. "A Critical Reexamination of the Practice Component in Counselor Training." *Counselor Education and Supervision* 21 (1982):282–294.

Gazda, George. *Human Relations Development: A Manual for Educators.* Boston: Allyn and Bacon, 1973.

Goldman, Leo. "Toward More Meaningful Research." *Personnel and Guidance Journal* 55 (1977):363–368.

Gurman, Alan S. "Therapists' Mood Patterns and Therapeutic Facilitativeness." *Journal of Counseling Psychology* 19 (1972):169–170.

Halikides, G. "An Experimental Study of Four Conditions Necessary for Therapeutic Change." Unpublished doctoral dissertation. University of Chicago, 1958.

Ivey, Allen. *Microcounseling: Innovations in Interviewing Training.* Springfield, Ill.: C. C Thomas, 1971.

————, and Jean Leppaluoto. "Changes Ahead! Implications of the Vail Conference." *Personnel and Guidance Journal* 53 (1975):747–752.

Jackson, M., and C. L. Thompson. "Effective Counselor: Characteristics and Attitudes." *Journal of Counseling Psychology* 18 (1971):249–254.

Johnson, David W. "Effects of Warmth of Interaction, Accuracy of Understanding, and the Proposal of Compromises on Listener's Behavior." *Journal of Counseling Psychology* 18 (1971):207–216.

Kaul, Theodore, and Lyle Schmidt. "Dimensions of Interviewer Trustworthiness." *Journal of Counseling Psychology* 18 (1971):542–548.

Lewis, Edwin C. *The Psychology of Counseling.* New York: Holt, Rinehart and Winston, 1970.

Mezzano, J. "A Note on Dogmatism and Counselor Effectiveness." *Counselor Education and Supervision* 9 (1969):64–65.

Moore, Helen, and Catherine Strickler. "The Counseling Profession's Response to Sex-Biased Counseling: An Update." *Personnel and Guidance Journal* 59 (1980):84–87.

Pietrofesa, John, George Leonard, and William Van Hoose. *The Authentic Counselor.* Chicago: Rand McNally, 1978.

Robiner, William, and Martha Storandt. "Client Perceptions of the Therapeutic Relationship as a Function of Client and Counselor Age." *Journal of Counseling Psychology* 30 (1983):96–99.

Rogers, Carl R. *Client-Centered Therapy.* Boston: Houghton Mifflin, 1951.

————. "Training Individuals to Engage in the Therapeutic Process." In C. R. Strother, ed., *Psychology and Mental Health.* Washington, D.C.: American Psychological Association, 1957.

————. *On Becoming a Person.* Boston: Houghton Mifflin, 1961.

————. "The Conditions of Change from a Client-Centered Viewpoint." In Bernard Berenson and Robert Carkhuff, eds., *Sources of Gain in Counseling and Psychotherapy.* New York: Holt, Rinehart and Winston, 1967.

Rokeach, Milton, and John Regan. "The Role of Values in the Counseling Situation." *Personnel and Guidance Journal* 58 (1980):576–582.

Russo, J. R., J. W. Kelz, and G. R. Hudon. "Are Good Counselors Open-Minded?" *Counselor Education and Supervision* 3 (1964):74–77.

Schofield, William. "Some General Factors in Counseling and Therapy." In Bernard Berenson and Robert Carkhuff, eds., *Sources of Gain in Counseling and Psychotherapy.* New York: Holt, Rinehart and Winston, 1967.

Shertzer, Bruce, and Shelley Stone. *Fundamentals of Counseling.* Boston: Houghton Mifflin, 1980.

Sladen, Bernard. "Effects of Race and Socioeconomic Status on the Perception of Process Variables in Counseling." *Journal of Counseling Psychology* 29 (1982):560–566.

Sprinthall, Norman A. *Guidance for Human Growth.* New York: Van-Nostrand Reinhold, 1971.

Stensrud, Robert, and Kay Stensrud. "Counseling May Be Hazardous to Your Health: How We Teach People to Feel Powerless." *Personnel and Guidance Journal* 59 (1981):300–304.

Tosi, Donald. "Dogmatism Within the Counselor-Client Dyad." *Journal of Counseling Psychology* 17 (1970):284–288.

Truax, C. B., and Robert Carkhuff. "New Directions in Clinical Research." In Bernard Berenson and Robert Carkhuff, eds., *Sources of Gain in Counseling and Psychotherapy.* New York: Holt, Rinehart and Winston, 1967a.

———. *Toward Effective Counseling and Psycho-therapy: Training and Practice.* Chicago: Aldine Publishing, 1967.

Truax, C. B., and J. L. Lister. "Effectiveness of Counselors and Counselor Aides." *Journal of Counseling Psychology* 17 (1970):331–334.

Tyler, Leona E. *The Work of the Counselor.* New York: Appleton-Century-Crofts, 1969.

Wrenn, C. Gilbert. *The World of the Contemporary Counselor.* Boston: Houghton Mifflin, 1973.

Wright, Wilbert. "Counselor Dogmatism, Willingness to Disclose, and Clients' Empathy Ratings." *Journal of Counseling Psychology* 22 (1975):390–394.

Zarski, John, Thomas Sweeney, and Robert Barcikowski. "Counseling Effectiveness as a Function of Counselor Social Interest." *Journal of Counseling Psychology* 24 (1977):1–5.

CHAPTER 9

Authenticity

Chapter Organizer

Aim of the Chapter
This chapter will explain why counselor authenticity is so important.

Chapter Preview
1. Depersonalization and nonbeing pervades our present culture.
   a. Suppression of the basic core of self consumes energy.
   b. Various mechanisms are used to escape anxiety.
2. Congruence, genuineness, and authenticity are interchangeable terms.
3. Research substantiates the importance of authenticity in counseling.
4. The counselor's being serves as a model for the client.
5. Counseling technique is less important than counselor goodwill.
6. The counselor may engage in facilitative self-disclosure.
   a. Genuineness does not excuse destructiveness.
   b. Counseling is for the client not for the counselor.

Relevant Questions
Following are several questions to keep in mind while reading the chapter:
1. Does counseling involve "putting on a front"?
2. How does self-disclosure differ from authenticity?
3. How does one determine if self-disclosure is appropriate? What guidelines might be used?
4. What types of childhood socialization teach that being authentic is unwise? Give examples.

Introduction

At long last, counseling professionals are recognizing the importance of authenticity to the progress of any helping relationship. Textbooks today must explore in depth the issue of authenticity and such related concerns as genuineness, congruence, openness, spontaneity, honesty, and self-disclosure. Only when those who hope to practice counseling appreciate the centrality of these issues can they apply the theories and techniques they have learned for the greatest benefit of the client.

This chapter examines the components of authentic behavior in counseling and reviews pertinent research. Training programs have yet to incorporate research findings into their criteria for counselor selection, but with increased investigation of this topic, such changes should be forthcoming. The last section of this chapter examines logical extensions of research findings on authentic behavior to training programs for counselors.

The American way of life reflects the "sickness" of maintaining facades and withholding ourselves from relationships with others. In fact, depersonalization has progressed to the point where we are attracted to substitute weekend groups—"substitute" in the sense that they replace more meaningful contact in our personal lives with superficial activities.

Depersonalization is also reflected in certain aspects of women's liberation. For some, involvement in the movement means assuming less than healthy attributes of male behavior, such as treating other people as objects and having little concern for them. Suddenly, men have become sex objects, and while it may be said that turnabout is fair play, it is still an extremely unhealthy lifestyle.

Martin Heidegger, the author of *Existence and Being* (1949) and *Being and Time* (1927), may well be considered the father of "authenticity." Heidegger concerns himself with authentic versus inauthentic existence. He emphasizes the "self-being" that can be achieved only through acts of freedom and responsibility. An individual is not merely a substance or a cognitive machine. The individual is a "center for responsibility" and becomes truly human only by accepting that responsibility.

It is unlikely that someone would ever be either totally authentic or totally inauthentic. Instead it is a question of degree. Carkhuff (1969) writes, "Man's search in helping and in life is a search for authenticity, both intrapersonal and interpersonal" (p. 208). Jourard (1971), on the other hand, notes the prevalence of unhealthy human dynamics: "I believe, and I am not alone in this belief, that man is sick—not just neurotic and psychotic people, but so-called 'normal' man, too—because he hides his real self in his transactions with others" (p. 138). This, then, may be the modern American illness—perpetual deceit of other people. Why must we hide ourselves from others? Why can't we be authentic? Of what are we frightened? Rejection? Disdain? Being left without any defenses? Why do we treat others in kind?

Depersonalization of self and others has become a way of life. We want to remain aloof and uninvolved. We learn to perform in this manner through the socialization process (which eventually becomes internalized) perpetrated by parents, teachers, and other well-meaning adults. We come to recognize the rather bizarre fact that we cannot be honest with others—that we must deny who, or what, we really are. We don't trust others enough to respond to them honestly, and we raise our children to follow such beliefs. This lack of honesty creates a way of life that fosters sickness. Abraham Maslow (1962, p. 181) points out the inevitable consequences: "If this essential core (inner nature) of the person is frustrated, denied, or suppressed, sickness results, sometimes in obvious forms, sometimes in subtle and devious forms, sometimes later."

Self-alienation and the lack of authenticity constitute a way of life so commonly accepted that no one is aware of it. It may be difficult to recognize such pervasive "unopenness," or lack of transparency, but simply ask yourself, "Do I have a close friend in whom I could confide completely?" When we ask ourselves this question, we start to realize the shallowness of our interpersonal relations. Popular "help" columns continually warn young marrieds not to be completely honest with each other and not to disclose all of their past history, for fear such information could be used against them. It may well be that if you have one real friend in a lifetime, a friend you can be completely honest with, you are a fortunate person indeed.

In the face of rampant inauthenticity, we turn to artificial devices to reduce or escape anxiety—alcohol, drugs, and narcotics, to name a few. These, of course, enhance perceptual distortions that arise from defense mechanisms, antisocial behavior, neuroses, and psychoses. Indulgence in such crutches is, moreover, symptomatic of the fundamental cause of the anxiety: Lack of authentic behavior is the primary contributing factor to free floating anxiety. Jourard (1964) states, "If becoming known by another person is threatening, then the very presence of another person can serve as a stimulus to evoke anxiety . . ." (p. 26). The solution, then, is not to continue to distort what is real, not to persist in the denial of experience, but to be able to be open in one's encounters with others.

Being open means stripping away masks. It means being honest. Hurley and Hurley (1969) suggest that "humans often relate to each other so completely in terms of roles that it has become increasingly difficult to separate the 'real self' from the role-player, both in the more intimate within-in-the-family roles as well as in the more external type-of-employment roles" (p. 271). The healthy individual, on the other hand, is able and willing to control self-disclosure on the basis of situational appropriateness (Derlaga and Grzelak, 1979). Research strongly suggests a strong correlation between neuroticism and low-intimacy levels of self-disclosure (Cunningham and Strassberg, 1981).

"Man, perhaps alone of all living forms, is capable of being one thing and seeming from his actions and talk, to be something else" (Jourard, 1971, p. 4). If we accept the notion that such self-deception is unhealthy, then we can see that much of the counseling function has to do with the establishment of authenticity in the counselee. At the same time, it would be nonsense to suggest that the counselor could help the client achieve authenticity without personally being authentic. That would be a case of the blind leading the blind. We would do well, however, to remember the cautionary statement of Truax and Carkhuff (1967): "Although the therapist's genuineness seems basic to his interpersonal skills, genuineness alone and of itself is not maximally therapeutic; rather the absence of genuineness is antitherapeutic" (p. 330). The counselor must be real and, thereby, express goodwill toward the client. To do otherwise would be to inhibit and taint with collusion the entire counseling process. It is as if the client were saying:

You can know me truly only if I let you, only if I want you to know me. Your misunderstanding of me is only partly your fault. If I want you to know me, I shall find a means of communicating myself to you. If you want me to reveal myself, just demonstrate your goodwill—your will to employ your powers for my good, and not for my destruction (Jourard, 1964, p. 5).

The development within the counselee of resistance to an inauthentic counseling relationship is certainly understandable. Clients simply become tired of reacting to another inauthentic person. They have experienced unrealness in the "outside" world and do not want to relate to another unreal, although educated, person (Dreyfus, 1967, p. 577). Clients are quite able to recognize a phony or role-playing counselor. They reject dishonesty in this supposedly close and meaningful relationship. If the counselor is not authentic, clients will not "invest" themselves in the process. They will withhold and not reveal, just as they do in their relationships with other nonsignificant beings.

Key Concepts in the Nature of Authentic Behavior

Before moving on to an analysis of authenticity, it is necessary to define the terms we shall be using.

Authenticity involves being "genuine" or "real." It indicates an openness in dealing with others and behavior that truly reflects the core of one's being. Authentic individuals accept their experiences and the world as it is. Authentic behavior is a being in the world as one is. It reflects a commitment to life and being. Authenticity involves establishing life's goals and assuming responsibility for attaining them in a world that allows for real, rather than role-playing, behavior.

Genuineness is the quality that may best be described as "being at one with one's self." Genuineness is synonymous with realness, honesty, or authenticity. The genuine counselor employs no facades. Defenses are lowered, and he or she is open to, and integrated into, the human experience.

Congruence refers specifically to the "transparency" of the therapist in the relationship (Truax and Carkhuff, 1965, p. 4). Self-congruence encompasses, not only the element of self-awareness, but also the presentation to the patient of a real person in the encounter (Truax, 1963, p. 259). Congruence comprises a cohesiveness among one's values, attitudes, and beliefs—it represents psychological health and well-being.

Self-disclosure can be considered to be synonymous with self-revelation. Disclosing personal ideas, values, feelings, and experiences, the counselor is perceived as a unique individual. McCarthy (1982) and McCarthy and Betz (1978) distinguish between "self-disclosure" and "self-involving" statements. They define the former as statements referring "to the past history or personal experiences of the counselor"; the latter are "direct present expressions of the counselor's feelings about or reactions to the statements and/or behaviors of the client" (p. 538). For the purposes of this chapter, self-disclosure refers to both types of statements. The writers do suggest, however, that counselor self-disclosure involving personal, past history has only limited use.

Spontaneity, which proceeds from a natural feeling, disposition, or particular mood without constraint, is an act freely done or a thought freely uttered in accordance with one's native impulses. Guided by the facilitative nature of the helping relationship, it is reflective of the "here-and-now" or "immediacy" element in counseling.

The terms *congruence, genuineness,* and *authenticity* may be used interchangeably for the purposes of this book. Obviously, *openness* and *honesty* are intricately meshed in these concepts. Self-disclosure and spontaneity are general indications that an individual is congruent, genuine, or authentic.

Authenticity in the Counseling Relationship

Dynamics of the Authentic Counseling Relationship

The authentic relationship involves human interaction that helps a person function more fully. Comprehension of one's being in the world builds a clearer perception of personal values and helps one to attain one's goals. Life becomes real and is no longer a matter of maintaining phony or superficial relationships with others—relationships based on the idea that "you recognize what I am not, and I'll recognize what you are not, and we can go on deceiving each other for as long as we would like." This superficiality is exemplified in a discussion with a schizophrenic who is describing how he felt before and during his psychosis.

People weren't real and in fact neither was I. I could step back and actually watch myself performing in a play or a movie. Yes, that's it exactly. I was an actor performing on a stage and I was sitting there watching me say lines that I had been taught, but that I really did not feel or mean. I was kind where I did not want to be. I was being the phony that all through my life others had taught me to be. I wasn't real. It was a dream, I wasn't real.

At least this person recognized the lack of authenticity in his relationship with others; many people go through life without ever doing so. Kazan (1967) makes the interesting point, in his novel *The Arrangement,* that if one becomes too authentic, one will be committed to an institution (pp. 419–420).

Counselors must avoid perpetuating this "sickness," this lack of authenticity too often found in human interaction. If counselors expect to have healthy clients, then they must reflect healthy attributes. Counselors must be able to interact as complete beings with the counselees.

Authentic interaction underlies the entire counseling relationship. Counselors are not teachers or preachers; they have no particular mandate to impose on others. They are exempt from the need to withhold themselves from others. Counselees can easily sense inauthentic counselors through nonverbal behaviors, tonal quality, or verbal inconsistencies. The authentic counseling relationship is of utmost importance, for it demonstrates to counselees that they are independent human beings who are responsible for their own behavior—that they must develop meaning in their own lives. Lack of genuineness subtracts from this responsibility. Belkin (1981) writes:

To appreciate fully the idea of genuineness, we must be sensitive to the many roles we are expected to play during the course of our daily lives. A role is a social mask—a persona—which we wear in the presence of others in order to define and reinforce a situation by establishing clear limits as to the participation of each character. When the counselor wears a mask, he is saying in effect to the client, "I am the counselor and you are the client—don't you forget it." The client, acquiescing to the situation, agrees to recognize the role of the counselor and to respond to the counselor as he plays that role. (p. 160)

Ivey and Simek-Downing (1980) state:

The counselor who is genuine and authentic presents no mixed messages. Verbal and nonverbal behavior are integrated. The counselor is truly himself or herself. The congruent, intentional counselor does not present information in a defensive or evasive manner, avoids being "professional" and planned, does not avoid expressing relevant personal thoughts and feelings in an interview and makes an effort to be open and honest with the client. (p. 103)

Counselor Transparency   The authenticity of counselors cannot be superficial; it must be basic to the core of their being. Counselors are not "salespeople" portraying a front of friendliness in order to sell their goods. Adults over thirty sometimes think that, by dressing or speaking like youth, they are saying, "Look, you can trust me." Trust is much more basic than simple physical displays. Rogers (1962) thought that *transparency* was a good term to describe a nonsuperficial realness. He wanted the counselee to see clear through him, and, when the counselee could do this, he felt a meaningful encounter would take place. The genuine helper does not hide behind a professional role. Helping others is part of a lifestyle—it is not a role or a mask to be used for the moment (Egan, 1975, p. 90).

Therapist transparency serves a number of vital functions within the counseling relationship. Perhaps the most significant function is that counselees can imitate the model counselors provide. Jourard (1971) substantiates this, stating that if the counselor "spontaneously and honestly conveys his thoughts and reactions, I believe he is not only communicating his concern, but he is in effect both eliciting and reinforcing kindred uncontrived behavior. . . ." (p. 142). In essence, then, clients see spontaneous, real, healthy individuals and, in the process of identification, move in that direction themselves. This may be a tedious process, for upon first contact clients may withdraw, fearful of the anxiety that being real provokes. But if counselors continue to be authentic and if their transparency displays their goodwill, withdrawn counselees will eventually disclose themselves so that their counselors can help. In this regard, Jourard (1971) does say that "evidently it is only the therapist's goodwill which needs to be predictable, not his specific responses to a patient's disclosure" (p. 140).

Therapist transparency encourages transparency in clients by reducing the ambiguity in therapy and thus allaying any anxieties and fears about the therapeutic encounter. Counselors model self-disclosure and, in the process, convey the appropriateness of discussing personal concerns in this close relationship. By being open and transparent, both counselors and counselees have a relatively higher degree of self-communication, which will certainly be a major factor in facilitating communication between two individuals. If either one is unaware of personal feelings or confused about the relationship, the counselor will be handicapped in the communication of goodwill. For Yates and Schmidt (1959), this implies that the counselor must work for "the acceptance and understanding of himself and the client for what they are and for what they must be at any given moment. Then the counselor and client have less need to defend themselves and confuse the existing relationship through being something which they are not, or in other words, sharing an 'unreal relationship' " (p. 154).

When counselors withhold their "real self," they must expend energy in order to maintain the deception. This has to cause a certain tenseness and exhaustion within the counselor. Counselor spontaneity and openness can prevent this unnecessary expenditure of energy. Jourard (1971) writes, "When I become strictly technical and hence impersonal with my patients, I have learned it is usually because I have become anxious. When I am lucky enough to recognize my anxiety, I will sometimes say, 'you are making me anxious.' If I am angry, I let this be known" (p. 147). Counselors do this spontaneously, but at the same time they must be sensitive to their counselees. Nonetheless, counselors gain no advantage by withholding their feelings or displaying something they do not feel. Rogers (1958) states, "Certainly the aim is not for the therapist to express or talk about his own feelings, but primarily that he should not be deceiving the client as to himself. At times he may need to talk about some of his own feelings (either to the client, or to a colleague or superior) if they are standing in the way . . ." (pp. 133–134). It takes, as Arbuckle (1967) recognizes, maturity to be authentic and to be able to express feelings:

I would think, however, that this is indicative of a high level of therapist free-dom—to be able to honestly experience feelings toward the client, and certainly reporting such feelings to the client is indicative of a high level of congruence.

But he goes on to say:

There would be a difference of opinion on just what feelings should be reported to the client, but the therapist who must close himself to personal feelings which he might have toward the client has not yet reached a very high level of either Being or Becoming! (p. 111)

Counselor Attitudes Versus Counselor Techniques   Counselor tech-nique is of less importance than what counselors are as individuals—human beings of goodwill who are concerned with fostering growth within their clients. We discussed the importance of "self as instrument" in Chap-ter 2. Counselors' attitudes are far more basic and crucial in the counseling relationship than are their specific behaviors. Who counselors truly are will be reflected in the relationship with their clients. Rogers (1951) writes that "the [counselor] who tries to use a 'method' is doomed to be unsuccessful unless this method is genuinely in line with his own attitudes" (p. 11). On the other hand, to state that counselors must drop all technique is equally ridiculous. Counselors need to develop a personal counseling style that paves the way for authentic encounters.

The counseling relationship stresses a genuine human encounter, not the implementation of a specific technique. The importance of various schools of psychology can, as a result, be deemphasized. Fiedler (1950) in his classic study suggested that therapists generally agree on the most effective type of therapeutic relationship and that theoretical differences are the result of poor communication between therapists of different schools (pp. 239–245). Counselors can learn a variety of gestures—nods of the head or the grunt like *uh-huh*—thought to foster growth, but counselees tend to recognize them for what they are—simply a bag of tricks. Counselors' re-flection of feelings and content appears to be useful, but it must be accompa-nied by a wider variety of authentic counselor reactions.

I find myself sometimes giving advice, lecturing, laughing, becoming angry, inter-preting, telling my fantasies, asking questions—in short, doing whatever occurs to me during the therapeutic session in response to the other person. This change could mean either that I am growing as a person and as a therapist or else that, through lack of close supervision, I am losing in 'discipline'. (Jourard, 1971, p. 146)

I observe as I do during the whole period of therapy what genuine reactions his behavior causes in me. It might well be the same adverse reaction which he often experiences from others, without being aware that he causes these reactions him-self, at least partially. From sharing my personal reaction with him we can see more clearly the variety of reactions his behavior may bring about in others. My reaction and my willingness to reveal my reactions opens him up to a greater willingness to evaluate and communicate his own feelings. (Colm, 1965, p. 139)

However, Combs et al. (1969) state that an emphasis on method may be characteristic of the non-growth facilitator. They state:

We suspect a major problem of poor helpers is the fact that their methods are unauthentic, that is, they tend to be put on, contrived. As such, they can only be utilized so long as the helper keeps his mind on them. That, of course, is likely to be disastrous on two counts. In the first place it separates him from his client or student, and the message conveyed is likely to be that he is not 'with it,' is not really interested, or is a phony. Second, it is almost never possible to maintain attention to the 'right' method for very long. As a consequence the poor helper relapses frequently to what he believes or his previous experience has taught him, and so the method he is trying to use fails because of the tenuous, interrupted character of his use of it. (p. 76)

Counselor Self-Disclosure   Being genuine or authentic does not, under any circumstances, allow counselors complete freedom of expression, either verbally or behaviorally. Situational variables—for example, the nature of material, timing, stage of counseling, and client sensitivity, awareness, and expectation—influence the amount and degree of disclosure by the counselor. During the early stages of counseling, for example, the focus is on the client as well as on the communication of empathy. At this stage, the emphasis is on understanding, not on behavior change. Self-disclosure by counselors is not important during this responsive stage. Furthermore, counselors do not offer every thought or feeling that comes into consciousness, but only those that will facilitate growth in the client. Carkhuff (1969) notes that "the key to the self-disclosure dimension is the word 'appropriate.' It is most appropriate for a helpee functioning at a high level and least appropriate with a helpee functioning at a low level" (p. 187). Perhaps the greatest difficulty in existential counseling is recognizing when the counselee is ready to experience what may well be the shock of an authentic encounter. The primary reason for the existence of the counseling relationship is so the client can grow, more effectively understand herself or himself, and can satisfy personal needs.

Counselor self-disclosures are inappropriate if they take the client's attention away from his or her own personal problems. Remember, facilitative self-disclosure is curvilinear. Too much or too little decreases client self-disclosure and makes the counselor less attractive. Counselors who are genuine must be constructive agents, not destructive ones. They must not impede counselee growth in order to satisfy their own needs. An overemphasis on being genuine can be an excuse for destructiveness or inexperience. Too great a reliance on confrontation becomes aggression rather than authenticity. The counselor must exercise good judgment as to the appropriateness of the degree of openness provided at any particular time. When therapists combine aggressiveness with openness, therapeutic casualties occur. Counselors must remain "relevantly authentic"; they must be aware of and sensitive to the client's ability to grapple with revelations of his or her being and experience.

Research on the Authentic Counseling Relationship

Research—especially that of the last decade—has substantiated the central role of authenticity in successful counseling. This section examines in depth the counselor attributes that are necessary for an authentic relationship to be possible and summarizes the research that has led to these conclusions.

Early research studies on counselor congruence came from the client-centered group. Rogers (1962) observed that the therapists who were most successful in dealing with unmotivated, poorly educated, resistant, chronically hospitalized individuals were, first of all, real; they reacted in a genuine way as persons and exhibited their genuineness in their human relationships. Truax (1963) found a significant tendency for therapists in improved cases to be rated higher in self-congruence during the therapeutic sessions than therapists in nonimproved cases (p. 259). There was a significant relationship from moment to moment throughout therapy between transparency (or self-congruence) of the therapist and transparency (or self-disclosure) for the patient (Truax and Carkhuff, 1965, p. 8).

Halikides (1958) found that counselors' genuineness was significantly associated with case outcome at .001 level of significance. Staudenmeier (1967) reported that one of the three most effective behavior classifications for less experienced counselors was "counselor communicates honestly"; in addition, counselees found counselors' behavior least effective when it failed to communicate honesty, understanding, and availability (p. 116). Demos (1964), despite the fact that the relationship between congruence and comfort was not found to be significant, did find that the most successful counselors received better ratings on these scales than did the least successful counselors (p. 283). Subjects tend to disclose themselves more deeply to persons offering the highest levels of genuineness, empathy, and warmth. This leads to a more open, full relationship in and out of psychotherapy (Shapiro et al., 1969, pp. 290–294). This conclusion was supported by Hountras and Anderson (1969), who found a significant relationship between genuineness (also respect and empathy) and self-exploration in all problem categories for clients of both sexes (pp. 45–48).

Truax (1968) hypothesized that patients receiving high levels of reinforcement through accurate empathy, nonpossessive warmth, and genuineness would show greater self-exploration and therapeutic improvement than patients receiving low or negative reinforcement. His findings affirmed the hypothesis. Reacting to a number of their own studies, Truax and Carkhuff (1967), wrote that "research seems consistently to find empathy, warmth, and genuineness characteristic of human encounters that change people for the better" (p. 141). They go on to say, "These findings might mean that we should aim at being what we are in our human encounters—that we would openly be the feelings and attitudes that we are experiencing" (p. 142).

It is not only counselors whose inauthenticity can affect the functioning of others. A lack of authenticity, or genuineness, in parents plays a role in retarded development of children. A variety of studies focus on the ambivalence of feelings communicated by the parent to the child. Mark (1953) found that mothers of schizophrenic children displayed attitudes of both excessive warmth and objective aloofness (pp. 485–489). Eisenberg and Kanner (1956) concluded that the typical autistic family does not provide warmth or a flexible, growth-promoting emotional atmosphere (pp. 556–566). Truax and Carkhuff (1967) summarized that "the parent's inauthenticity and lack of genuineness were suggested by their frequent references to 'observing' their children, as though they were clinical subjects" (p. 119).

Since 1970 several studies have looked at the authenticity and genuineness variable in human relationships, in counseling, and in the counselor. Donnan et al. (1969) studied the relationship between personality factors and counselor functioning as judged by counselees. They tried to determine if counselor personality was associated with perceived congruence. They noted that the counselor who was most venturesome, uninhibited, and spontaneous was perceived to be most trustworthy, while the most sensitive counselor was viewed as most congruent. Fischer et al. (1975) divided clinical practitioners into three major theoretical orientations—psychodynamic, behavioristic, and humanistic. They analyzed interviews to determine clinicians' degree of genuineness. There were no significant differences among therapists of any of the three theoretical orientations.

Altmann (1973) studied the relationship between counseling conditions and client continuation of therapy. While empathy was rated significant, genuineness was not. He did state, however, that "stayers" were provided with higher levels of genuineness than "leavers." Bednar and Weinberg (1970), evaluating the effectiveness of treatment programs for underachieving college students, found that high levels of therapeutic conditions (including genuineness) were associated with improved academic performance. Vitalo (1970) concluded that a high level of functioning on empathy, positive regard, and genuineness is a prerequisite for even the effective implementation of systematic conditioning and extinction procedures. He felt that this supported the notion that "at the center of all fruitful interpersonal learning experiences is a primary core of facilitative interpersonal dimensions presently including empathy, personal regard, and genuineness" (p. 143).

Hayden (1975) investigated the relationship between the verbal behavior of experienced therapists and their effectiveness. He found that the more effective the experienced therapist, the higher the levels of offered empathy, positive regard, and genuineness and the more likely the therapist was to use "inner focus" and confrontation of client experience (p. 384). Tosi (1970) found that client ratings were progressively higher for less dogmatic counselors—counselors who displayed more openness.

A number of studies have specifically examined self-disclosure and interpersonal dynamics. Client self-disclosure appears to increase most significantly when the client perceives the counselor as self-disclosing and as facilitative (Halpern, 1977, pp. 41–47).

In a study by Spiritas and Holmes (1971), female subjects were exposed to a revealing model, to a nonrevealing model, or to no model before being interviewed. The subjects gave longer and more revealing responses after being exposed to a revealing model than they did after being exposed to a nonrevealing model. They also talked longer to female interviewers than to male interviewers but revealed the same amount of information regardless of sex. Thase and Page (1977) found in both laboratory and nonlaboratory settings that individuals exposed to a high-disclosing model were significantly more willing to engage in self-disclosure than those exposed to a low-disclosing model.

Casciani (1978) investigated the effect of a model's race and sex on the content and length of client self-disclosure. He found that the subject's depth of disclosure, speech duration, and number of self-references were not related to the model's race or length of disclosure. Subjects did disclose at greater depths and for longer durations after observing models of the same sex. Interestingly, he also noted that individuals who were more selective (had stronger biases) about such personal characteristics of counselors tended to be more reserved about revealing personal information. The results of this study are clearly related to the counselor's potential influence on client behavior through self-disclosure.

Counselor self-disclosure does more than increase client self-disclosure. Johnson and Noonan (1972) wished to learn how acceptance and reciprocation of self-disclosures (on the part of the counselor) affect the development of trust. Their results indicate that a person's response to another's self-disclosure is essential in the development of trust.

These results implied that a counselor will build a high level of trust with his client to the extent that he responds with acceptance to the client's self-disclosures, and reciprocates the client's self-disclosures with equally revealing disclosures about himself. Such actions not only will increase the client's trust in the counselor, but also will increase his liking for the counselor. (p. 415)

May and Thompson (1973) and Nilsson et al. (1979) found that perceptions of counselor self-disclosure, mental health, and helpfulness were all positively correlated. Dies (1973) also evaluated the impact of therapist self-disclosure on clients. The results demonstrated that self-revealing therapists were judged as more friendly, disclosing, trusting, intimate, helpful, and facilitating but also as less relaxed, strong, stable, and sensitive.

Research has also shown that the type of counselor self-disclosure affects client response. Counselor self-disclosure (or statements about self in this case) can be either positive or negative. Positive self-disclosure involves statements that center on personal strengths or positive experiences of the counselor; negative self-disclosures are counselor statements that reveal personal weaknesses or mistakes. Hoffman-Graff (1977) found that negatively disclosing interviewers were viewed as significantly more warm, empathic, and credible than their positively disclosing counterparts. Hoffman and Spencer (1977) concluded that subjects react differentially to positive and negative self-disclosure. They note that the benefits of each type of disclosure depend on the nature of client change.

In situations in which clients are unaware of the severity of their problems, positive self-disclosure might have a powerful impact. In situations in which clients are overemphasizing the severity of their problems, negative self-disclosure might change their perceptions with a resultant change in their behavior. (p. 389)

Our concept of self-disclosure is more in keeping with the concept of sharing here-and-now feelings than it is with the notion of sharing interpersonal conflicts and concerns. Jourard and Jaffe (1970) found that self-disclosure begat self-disclosure. They felt that their "most striking" finding was that subjects disclosed themselves on a variety of personal topics. The duration of the experimenter's disclosures affected the duration of the subjects' utterances. This also provided support for those who contend that a verbal pattern is established in counseling (see Chapter 11). Giannandrea and Murphy (1973) found that an intermediate number of interviewer self-disclosures resulted in significantly more students returning for a second interview than did few or many self-disclosures. They concluded that a moderate number of self-disclosures effectively increases counselor attractiveness. Mann and Murphy (1975) also noted that an intermediate number of disclosures resulted in significantly more subject disclosures and led subjects to describe the interviewer as significantly more empathetic, warm, and congruent. Timing of interviewer disclosures had no effect. These findings lent support to the idea that too much or too little self-disclosure or genuineness is not facilitative. Murphy and Strong (1972) reported that interviewer self-disclosure increased the interviewee's perceptions of the interviewers' willingness to be known as persons and increased the students' feelings of warmth, friendliness, and being understood. McCarthy (1979) found that counselors were rated more expert, attractive, and trustworthy when they disclosed feelings about or reactions to the client during therapy, rather than when they responded with their own experiences from the past. Counselors who responded more with the here-and-now encouraged greater client self-referents.

Client self-disclosure was the focal point of several researchers. Heibrun (1973) conducted two studies on the history of self-disclosure in females. He found that the late-adolescent girls who were more likely to defect from therapy had a self-rated history of greater self-disclosure than girls who continued. A second study showed that terminators were higher self-disclosers to males, whereas continuers were higher self-disclosers to females. He interpreted this pattern to indicate that dependent females gravitate more to fathers as targets of self-disclosure and seek out directions and solutions.

In such situations, nondirective approaches frustrate the client into termination.

Many researchers have examined differences in client self-disclosure by sex. Females are generally more willing to disclose than males (Annis and Perry, 1977; DeForest and Stone, 1980). Gitter and Black (1976) found differences in the amount of self-revealing information according to content, target person (person being talked to), and sex of subject. The amount of information revealed was a function of being a low, medium, or high revealer. More intimate items were less readily disclosed than superficial ones (p. 331). Females revealed more intimate information than did males. High revealers not only disclosed more information than did low revealers, but they were also more sincere.

Going one step further, Highlen and Gillis (1978) found that females expressed more feelings than males and that, in addition, they vented more positive than negative feelings to same-sex individuals than to opposite-sex friends. Subjects had greater anxiety in negative affect situations. The optimal situation for affective self-disclosure involved females disclosing positive feelings to a same-sex best friend. Males, on the other hand, appear to be more willing than females to disclose to strangers and casual acquaintances, but some researchers interpret this as an avoidance of emotional intimacy with close friends (Stokes et al., 1980). Highlen and Johnston (1979) noted that in significant interactions affective self-disclosure is situation specific. They concluded that intimacy level is a crucial consideration that influences affective self-disclosure and anxiety in dyadic interactions. They found that individuals rely more on tone of voice than words to convey feelings. These findings have significant implications for the development of listening skills in counselors.

The client's sex is a given, but there are ways for counselors to increase self-disclosure for men and women. Doster and Slaymaker (1972) found that individuals who were more averse to uncertainty or novelty tended to look at an interview as a potentially low-disclosure involvement experience. High-anxiety subjects anticipated more superficial communication and greater personal discomfort than did low-anxiety subjects. Public aspects of the self generated greater self-disclosure by the client—that is, they were willing to discuss the obvious. Doster (1975) again noted that low-defensive, low-anxious subjects were most successful in overall participation in experimental interviews. It is important to note, though, that individuals did reveal more if they received training in self-disclosure. Video and audio pretraining procedures have significantly increased the number of self-disclosures (Stone and Stebbins, 1975). Stone and Gotlib (1975) found that both instructional and modeling procedures can be used to significantly increase self-disclosures. In the same vein, high self-actualizing people initially displayed a significantly higher rate of affective self-disclosures compared to moderate or low self-actualizing individuals (Hekmat and Theiss, 1971). High self-actualizers did not respond as well to social reinforcement of affective self-disclosures as did the low and moderate self-actualizers. The former group, it was speculated, responded more to the therapist as a model than as a dispenser of reinforcement.

A number of the preceding studies concerned the impact of situational variables on self-disclosure. The focus of studies by Chelune (1977), Neimeyer and Banikiotes (1981), and Neimeyer et al. (1979) looked at the variability in self-disclosure across targets—that is, self-disclosure flexibility. They suggested that disclosure flexibility is related to social perceptiveness. They found that highly flexible disclosers showed greater affective empathy and more accurate perceptions of appropriate, facilitative responses than did less flexible disclosers. It might well follow that individuals who were "low in their flexibility would be inattentive to the subtle cues mediating disclosure's appropriateness and therefore exhibit approximately the same amount of disclosure, regardless of the target or situational context. Conversely, those high in flexibility would reflect an awareness of the subtle cues mediating disclosure's appropriateness and therefore modulate their disclosures accordingly" (p. 546).

Implications for Counselor Training in Authenticity

It is obvious that the ideas presented in this chapter hold several implications for counselor education. Educators must assume certain responsibilities. As a first step, they must place less emphasis on the orientation with which the student emerges. The basic attitude must be genuine. If the counselor's genuine attitudes "lead him in the direction of some other orientation, well and good" (Rogers, 1951, p. 432). Eclecticism should be stressed, and each counselor encouraged to develop a personal, "authentic" style of counseling. Trainees should be helped to incorporate good interpersonal skills so that they become natural responses and do not appear to be contrived.

This chapter has placed a good deal of emphasis on the humanness of counselors and their ability to relate well and to be spontaneous and honest with others. Can we accomplish this training in graduate school? Most likely the foundations for humanness are laid much earlier. If this is true, appropriate selection of counselors becomes much more important. In addition greater degrees of self-awareness must be developed, as Dreyfus (1967) recognizes.

Since research seems to suggest that no one technique is more effective than any other, it seems ludicrous to teach technique. One can teach theory, but not humanness. Emphasis in training programs should be on increasing self-awareness, sensitivity, and spontaneity. Helping would-be therapists to be more human with freedom to respond should be the goal. (p. 577)

Graduate students can be brought to function at higher levels of facilitativeness with greater self-acceptance. Carkhuff and Truax (1965) compared graduate students, experienced therapists, and lay personnel. The only significant difference was between the genuineness of the experienced and lay groups. This suggested that, with experience, the therapists themselves come to be more freely, easily, and deeply involved in the therapeutic encounter. Thus, specific didactic and experiential training of school counselors can bring about therapeutic personality change within them (Carkhuff and Berenson, 1967, p. 293).

Additional studies have focused on changing counselor behavior in the direction of greater openness. We contend that counselors are more open and genuine when they possess a high degree of positive attitudes and values toward themselves and others (Selfridge and Vander Kolk, 1976). Such positive attitudes result in more fully functioning lifestyles, and such counselors are received more positively by clients. Training procedures can deal with the personal dimensions that effect genuineness and self-disclosure in counselors. Lin (1973) found that the degree of perceived counselor genuineness and congruence was linearly related to level of counselor self-confidence. Gurman (1972) found a relationship between therapeutic facilitativeness and therapists' mood patterns. He observed a significant relationship between therapists' hedonic (positive feelings) level and the level of genuineness and self-disclosure. He concluded that therapists who are relatively free of emotional conflict but who are also willing to acknowledge internal discomfort are better able to respond nondefensively. Fry (1973) predicted that training for helping skills, when paired with desensitization, would improve ratings of the trainees' helping functions. Fry found that once the helper is desensitized to personal feelings of anxiety, the helper moves more spontaneously and fosters higher levels of genuineness. Finally, Delaney et al. (1969) tested the hypothesis that students in practicum would exhibit an increase in genuineness. Mean scores of therapist-offered conditions, including genuineness, increased with progressive stages of supervised practice. It was also found that empathy, warmth, and genuineness correlated highly with each other.

Truax and Carkhuff (1967), in an enlightening discussion, present their approach to genuineness-training. Their program involves a number of components to include the following:

1. The active "shaping" of counselor-trainees' responses designed to make them more authentic and more reflective of their own person.
2. The use of spontaneous discussions throughout the counselor-trainees' training course. Emphasis is placed upon the rating and discussion of samples at the counselor-trainees' counseling experiences.
3. The use of role-playing for counselor-trainees to encourage self-exploration.
4. The presentation of a genuine being in the person of the counselor-supervisor who acts as a model for the counselor-trainees.
5. The provision of therapy experiences for the counselor-trainees. (pp. 332–335)

Highlen and Voight (1978) concluded that multiphase training strategies are more effective than "one-shot, short-term interventions in the development of affective self-disclosure."

Finally, a study by Pierce and Schauble (1970) examined the behavior of counseling interns for growth in the "facilitative dimensions of empathy, regard, genuineness, and concreteness." They found that interns whose supervisors were themselves functioning at high levels in all four of these dimensions changed significantly and positively. Interns whose supervisors functioned at low levels did not change; indeed they declined slightly. Pierce and Schauble concluded:

> Thus, in terms of therapeutic functioning, it may be concluded that while graduate training may help the counselor-trainee to improve his therapeutic skills; in fact, this is not always the case. Indeed, graduate training may even act as a negative influence on the prospective therapist's interpersonal behavior. The present study makes evident that the individual supervisor has a great deal of impact, for better or for worse, on trainee behavior. (p. 215)

Summary

Counseling, to be most effective, must be based on authentic human relationships. Everyday human interaction tends to be devoid of authenticity and is a transaction that involves mutual self-deception. As Jourard (1971) states: "In a society which pits man against man, as in a poker game, people do keep a poker face; they wear a mask and let no one know what they are up to. In a society where man is for man, then the psychological iron curtain is dropped" (p. 6).

The philosophical founding stone of counseling necessarily includes the idea of "one person being for another person." Barriers have to be pushed aside in order to grow in self-realization. On genuineness, Rogers (1962) has written, "I have sometimes wondered if this is the only quality which matters in a counseling relationship" (p. 156). Other qualities—such as interest and empathy—are important, but they must be genuine in order to make a difference. Counselor technique is much less important than counselor personality, since expert technique cannot conceal counselor inadequacies, insensitivity, and lack of care. Counselees can quickly see through any counselor facade. It is unrealistic to think that counselors can be genuine or authentic in all of life's dealings, but they must be real in the counseling relationship, or personal growth will not be fostered in the counselee.

You show me, through your personal example, that I don't have to wait until I am stronger or more perfect to start living, for you share not only your warmth and intensity but your own pain. Because you appear to be so strong and wise, it would be easy for me to isolate you on a pedestal and make your example an unattainable ideal. You put yourself within reach when you share your own struggle without bogging me down. If you can be who you are while you struggle and suffer, then I too can transcend my own despair. (Webster, 1974, pp. 288–289)

The major points of this chapter were as follows:

1. Self-being is accomplished through acts of freedom that reflect authenticity. An inauthentic lifestyle is unhealthy.
2. Counseling helps clients deal with their existence. Counselors provide models of authentic behavior.
3. Counselor genuineness has a positive effect on counseling outcome.
4. Authentic counselors are open in their deal-

ings with people, reflecting a commitment to life. Spontaneity and self-disclosure are indications of genuineness. Counselor self-disclosure increases client self-disclosure through the modeling process.

5. Counselors should be comfortable with themselves. Concealing a part of the self from others consumes much energy.

6. Counselor technique is of much less importance than the personal quality of authenticity in the helper.

References

Altmann, H. A. "Effects of Empathy, Warmth, and Genuineness in the Initial Counseling Interview." *Counselor Education and Supervision* 12 (1973):225–229.

Annis, L. V., and D. F. Perry. "Self-Disclosure Modeling in Same-Sex and Mixed-Sex Unsupervised Groups." *Journal of Counseling Psychology* 24 (1977):370–372.

Arbuckle, Dugald S. *Counseling and Psychotherapy: An Overview.* New York: McGraw-Hill, 1967.

Bednar, Richard L., and Steve L. Weinberg. "Ingredients of Successful Treatment Programs for Underachievers." *Journal of Counseling Psychology* 17 (1970):1–7.

Belkin, G. S. *Practical Counseling in the Schools.* Dubuque, Iowa: Wm. C. Brown, 1981.

Carkhuff, Robert R. *Helping and Human Relations: A Primer for Lay and Professional Helpers: Selection and Training.* New York: Holt, Rinehart and Winston, 1969.

————, **and B. G. Berenson.** *Beyond Counseling and Therapy.* New York: Holt, Rinehart and Winston, 1967.

————, **and Charles B. Truax.** "Training in Counseling and Psychotherapy: An Evaluation of an Integrated Didactic and Experiential Approach." *Journal of Consulting Psychology* 29 (1965):333–336.

Casciani, J. M. "Influence of Model's Race and Sex on Interviewees' Self-Disclosure." *Journal of Counseling Psychology* 25 (1978):43–440.

Chelune, G. "Disclosure Flexibility and Social-Situational Perceptions." *Journal of Consulting and Clinical Psychology* 45 (1977):1139–1143.

Colm, H. "The Therapeutic Encounter." *Review of Existential Psychology and Psychiatry* 5 (1965):137–159.

Combs, A. W., et al. *Florida Studies in the Helping Professions.* Monograph No. 37. Gainesville: University of Florida Press, 1969.

Cunningham, J. A., and D. S. Strassberg. "Neuroticism and Disclosure Reciprocity." *Journal of Counseling Psychology* 28 (1981):455–458.

DeForest, C., and G. L. Stone. "Effects of Sex and Intimacy Level on Self-Disclosure." *Journal of Counseling Psychology* 27 (1980):93–96.

Delaney, D. J., T. J. Long, M. J. Masucci, and H. A. Moses. "Skill Acquisition and Perception Change of Counselor Candidates During Practicum." *Counselor Education and Supervision* 8 (1969):273–282.

Demos, George D. "Application of Certain Principles of Client-Centered Therapy." *Journal of Counseling Psychology* 11 (1964):280–284.

Derlaga, V. J., and J. Grzelak. "Appropriateness of Self-Disclosure." In Chelune, G. J., *et al.*, eds., *Self-Disclosure.* San Francisco: Jossey-Bass, 1979.

Dies, Robert R. "Group Therapist Self-Disclosure: An Evaluation by Clients." *Journal of Counseling Psychology* 20 (1973):344–348.

Donnan, H. H., G. E. Harlan, and S. A. Thompson. "Counselor Personality and Level of Functioning." *Journal of Counseling Psychology* 16 (1969):482–485.

Doster, Joseph A. "Individual Differences Affecting Interviewee Expectations and Perceptions of Self-Disclosure." *Journal of Counseling Psychology* 22 (1975):192–198.

————, **and Judith Slaymaker.** "Need Approval, Uncertainty, Anxiety, and Expectancies of Interview Behavior." *Journal of Counseling Psychology* 19 (1972):522–528.

Dreyfus, Edward A. "Humanness: A Therapeutic Variable." *Personnel and Guidance Journal* 45 (1967):573–578.

Egan, G. *The Skilled Helper.* Monterey, Calif.: Brooks/Cole, 1975.

Eisenberg, L., and L. Kanner. "Early Infantile Autism: 1943–1955." *American Journal of Ortho-Psychiatry* 26 (1956):556–566.

Fiedler, Fred E. "The Concept of an Ideal Therapeutic Relationship." *Journal of Consulting Psychology* 14 (1950):239–245.

Fischer, J., G. Paveza, N. Kickertz, L. Hubbard, and S. Grayston. "The Relationship Between Theoretical Orientation and Therapists' Empathy, Warmth, and Genuineness." *Journal of Counseling Psychology* 22 (1975):399–403.

Fry, P. S. "Effects of Desensitization Treatment on Core-Condition Training." *Journal of Counseling Psychology* 20 (1973):214–219.

Gazda, George M. *Human Relations Development.* Boston: Allyn and Bacon, 1973.

Giannandrea, Vincenzo, and Kevin C. Murphy. "Similarity Self-Disclosure and Return for a Second Interview." *Journal of Counseling Psychology* 20 (1973):545–548.

Gitter, A. George, and Harvey Black. "Is Self-Disclosure Self-Revealing?" *Journal of Counseling Psychology* 23 (1976):327–332.

Gurman, Alan S. "Therapists' Mood Patterns and Therapeutic Facilitativeness." *Journal of Counseling Psychology* 19 (1972):169–170.

Halikides, G. "An Experimental Study of Four Conditions Necessary for Therapeutic Change." Unpublished doctoral dissertation. University of Chicago, 1958.

Halpern, T. P. "Degree of Client Disclosure as a Function of Past Disclosure, Counselor Disclosure, and Counselor Facilitativeness." *Journal of Counseling Psychology* 24 (1977):41–47.

Hayden, Brian. "Verbal and Therapeutic Styles of Experienced Therapists Who Differ in Peer-Rated Therapist Effectiveness." *Journal of Counseling Psychology* 22 (1975):384–389.

Heibrun, Alfred B. "History of Self-Disclosure in Females and Early Defection from Psychotherapy." *Journal of Counseling Psychology* 20 (1973):250–257.

Heidegger, M. H. *Sein und Zeit—Being and Time.* Halle: Max Neimeyer, Verlag, 1927.

———. *Existence and Being.* Chicago: Gateway, 1949.

Hekmat, Hamil, and Michael Theiss. "Self-Actualization and Modification of Affective Self-Disclosures During a Social Conditioning Interview." *Journal of Counseling Psychology* 18 (1971):101–105.

Highlen, P. S., and S. F. Gills. "Effects of Situational Factors, Sex, and Attitude on Affective Self-Disclosure and Anxiety." *Journal of Counseling Psychology* 25 (1978):270–276.

———, **and B. Johnston.** "Effects of Situational Variables on Affective Self-Disclosure with Acquaintances." *Journal of Counseling Psychology* 26 (1979):255–258.

———, **and N. L. Voight.** "Effects of Social Modeling, Cognitive Structuring, and Self-Management Strategies on Affective Self-Disclosure." *Journal of Counseling Psychology* 25 (1978):21–27.

Hoffman, M. A., and G. P. Spencer. "Effect of Interviewer Self-Disclosure and Interviewer-Subject Sex Pairing on Perceived and Actual Subject Behavior." *Journal of Counseling Psychology* 24 (1977):383–390.

Hoffman-Graff, M. A. "Interviewer Use of Positive and Negative Self-Disclosure and Interviewer-Subject Sex Pairing." *Journal of Counseling Psychology* 24 (1977):184–190.

Hountras, Peter T., and Dervyn L. Anderson. "Counselor Conditions for Self-Exploration of College Students." *Personnel and Guidance Journal* 48 (1969):45–48.

Hurley, John R., and Shirley J. Hurley. "Toward Authenticity in Measuring Self-Disclosure." *Journal of Counseling Psychology* 16 (1969):271–274.

Ivey, A. E., and B. Simek-Downing. *Counseling and Psychotherapy: Skills, Theories, and Practice.* Englewood Cliffs, N.J.: Prentice-Hall, 1980.

Johnson, David W., and M. Patricia Noonan. "Effects of Acceptance and Reciprocation of Self-Disclosures on the Development of Trust." *Journal of Counseling Psychology* 19 (1972):411–416.

Jourard, Sidney M. *The Transparent Self.* Princeton, N.J.: D. Van Nostrand, 1964, rev. ed., 1971.

———, **and Peggy E. Jaffe.** "Influence of an Interviewer's Disclosure on the Self-Disclosing Behavior of Interviewees." *Journal of Counseling Psychology* 17 (1970):252–257.

Kazan, Elia. *The Arrangement.* New York: Stein and Day, 1967.

Lin, Tien-Teh. "Counseling Relationship as a Function of Counselor's Self-Confidence." *Journal of Counseling Psychology* 20 (1973):293–297.

McCarthy, P. R. "Differential Effects of Self-Disclosing Versus Self-Involving Counselor Statements Across Counselor-Client Gender Pairings." *Journal of Counseling Psychology* 26 (1979):538–541.

———. "Differential Effects of Counselor Self-Referent Responses and Counselor Status." *Journal of Counseling Psychology* 29 (1982): 125–131.

———, and N. E. Betz. "Differential Effects of Self-Disclosing Versus Self-Involving Counselor Statements." *Journal of Counseling Psychology* 25 (1978):251–256.

Mann, Brenda, and Kevin C. Murphy. "Timing of Self-Disclosure, Reciprocity of Self-Disclosure, and Reactions to an Initial Interview." *Journal of Counseling Psychology* 22 (1975):304–308.

Mark, J. C. "The Attitudes of the Mothers of Male Schizophrenics Toward Child Behavior." *Journal of Abnormal and Social Psychology* 48 (1953): 485–489.

Maslow, Abraham H. *Toward a Psychology of Being.* Princeton, N.J.: D. Van Nostrand, 1962.

May, O. Phillip, and Charles L. Thompson. "Perceived Levels of Self-Disclosure, Mental Health and Helpfulness of Group Leaders." *Journal of Counseling Psychology* 20 (1973):349–352.

Murphy, Kevin C., and Stanley R. Strong. "Some Effects of Similarity Self-Disclosures." *Journal of Counseling Psychology* 19 (1972):121–124.

Neimeyer, G. J., and P. G. Banikiotes. "Self-Disclosure Flexibility, Empathy, and Perceptions of Adjustment and Attraction." *Journal of Counseling Psychology* 28 (1981):272–275.

Neimeyer, G. J., P. G. Banikiotes, and P. C. Winum. "Self-Disclosure Flexibility and Counseling-Relevant Perceptions." *Journal of Counseling Psychology* 26 (1979):546–548.

Nilsson, D. E., D. S. Strassberg, and J. Bannon. "Perceptions of Counselor Self-Disclosure: An Analogue Study." *Journal of Counseling Psychology* 26 (1979):399–404.

Pierce, R. M., and P. G. Schauble. "Graduate Training of Facilitative Counselors: The Effects of Individual Supervision." *Journal of Counseling Psychology* 17 (1970):210–215.

Rogers, Carl R. *Client-Centered Therapy.* Boston: Houghton Mifflin, 1951.

———. "The Characteristics of a Helping Relationship." *Personnel and Guidance Journal* 37 (1958):6–16. In James F. Adams, *Counseling and Guidance: A Summary View.* New York: Macmillan, 1965. Pp. 141–153.

———. "The Interpersonal Relationship: The Core of Guidance." *Harvard Educational Review* 32 (1962):416–429. In James F. Adams, *Counseling and Guidance: A Summary View.* New York: Macmillan, 1965. Pp. 153–164.

Selfridge, Fred F., and Charles Vander Kolk. "Correlates of Counselor Self-Actualization and Client-Perceived Facilitativeness." *Counselor Education and Supervision* 15 (1976):189–194.

Shapiro, J. G., H. Krauss, and C. B. Truax. "Therapeutic Conditions and Disclosure Beyond the Therapeutic Encounter." *Journal of Counseling Psychology* 16 (1969):290–294.

Spiritas, Alexis A., and David S. Holmes. "Effects of Models on Interview Responses." *Journal of Counseling Psychology* 18 (1971):217–220.

Staudenmeier, James J. "Student Perceptions of Counselor Behavior Contributing to a Helping Relationship." *The School Counselor* 15 (1967):113–117.

Stokes, J., A. Fuehres, and L. Childs. "Gender Differences in Self-Disclosure to Various Target Persons." *Journal of Counseling Psychology* 27 (1980):192–198.

Stone, Gerald L., and Ian Gotlib. "Effects of Instructions and Modeling on Self-Disclosure." *Journal of Counseling Psychology* 22 (1975):288–293.

Stone, Gerald L., and Larry W. Stebbins. "Effect of Differential Pretraining on Client Self-Disclosure." *Journal of Counseling Psychology* 22 (1975):17–20.

Thase, M., and R. A. Page. "Modeling of Self-Disclosure in Laboratory and NonLaboratory Interview Settings." *Journal of Counseling Psychology* 24 (1977): 35–40.

Tosi, Donald J. "Dogmatism Within the Counselor-Client Dyad." *Journal of Counseling Psychology* 17 (1970):284–288.

Truax, Charles B. "Effective Ingredients in Psychotherapy: An Approach to Unraveling the Patient-Therapist Interaction." *Journal of Counseling Psychology* 10 (1963):256–263.

———. "Therapist Interpersonal Reinforcement of Client Self-Exploration and Therapeutic Outcome in Group Psychotherapy." *Journal of Counseling Psychology* 15 (1968):225–231.

———, and Robert R. Carkhuff. "Client and Therapist Transparency in the Psychotherapeutic Encounter." *Journal of Counseling Psychology* 10 (1965):256–263.

———, and Robert R. Carkhuff. *Toward Effective Counseling and Psychotherapy.* Chicago: Aldine, 1967.

Vitalo, Raphael L. "Effects of Facilitative Interpersonal Functioning in a Conditioning Paradigm." *Journal of Counseling Psychology* 17 (1970): 141–144.

Webster, Cindy Lee. "Effective Counseling: A Client's View. *Personnel and Guidance Journal* 52 (1974):288–289.

Yates, J. W., and Lyle D. Schmidt. "The Counselor's Self-Concept." *Vocational Guidance Quarterly* 7 (1959):151–154.

CHAPTER 10

Empathy

Chapter Organizer

Aim of the Chapter

This chapter will introduce the reader to empathy—its development, ingredients, and effects on counseling. Relevant research will be cited to substantiate the effects that empathy can have on the outcome of counseling.

Chapter Preview

1. Empathy is the ability to understand the roles, feelings, and experiences of others.
2. Historical development of the concept is closely associated with Rogers's development:
   a. nondirective period, 1940–1950
   b. reflective period, 1950–1957
   c. experiential period, 1957–present
3. Empathizing is vicariously experiencing another's world; whereas sympathizing is identifying with and sharing another's feelings and attitudes. Projecting is attributing one's own feelings, perceptions, or attitudes to another.
4. To respond empathically, it is helpful for counselors to sense
   a. how they might feel in a similar situation (self-judgment)
   b. how others they know might feel (normative judgment)
   c. how this particular person feels in this specific situation (differential relationship)
5. To be effective, counselors need to be psychologically mature—aware of and comfortable with their own feelings, thoughts, and experiences. This awareness and comfort will provide relative immunity to threat within the counseling relationship.
6. The empathic relationship provides clients with a warm, trusting atmosphere in which they will be understood. These qualities promote their self-exploration and self-understanding, which lead to greater self-acceptance.

Relevant Questions

The following are several questions to keep in mind while reading this chapter:

1. What is my personal definition of *empathy* and how does it vary from the text's or Rogers's?
2. In what ways is empathy applicable to the counseling theories covered in Chapters 5 and 6?
3. What areas of my personal life lack the understanding and integration I would like and consequently inhibit my empathic responses?
4. In a counseling relationship, how might I react to a warm, empathic counselor? Would I profit or suffer? What would be the development of our relationship?
5. What outcomes might I expect for clients

involved in an empathic counseling relationship?

6. In what fields other than counseling is the

application of empathy useful and/or important?

Introduction

Empathy is the ability of individuals to listen to and understand the thoughts, feelings, beliefs, and experiences of others. It is an essential ingredient of effective counseling. Communication of empathy transmits the counselors' willingness and ability to help clients without judging, lecturing, or unnecessarily stimulating their anxieties. In the presence of empathic counselors, clients feel freer to expose themselves within the counseling relationship and, consequently, become more familiar with and accepting of themselves. Such awareness and self-acceptance are preconditions for change, and empathy is the most effective means of promoting them.

The Concept of Empathy

Historical Antecedents

Broadly defined, *empathy* is the ability to understand the roles, feelings, and attitudes of others. The process of understanding others is not unique to counseling. The eminent social philosopher George Herbert Mead (1934) postulates that the child's ability to understand and "role-take" the attitudes of others in specific social situations is the genesis of one's concept of self. The self can take on attitudes of others and adapt them for the self. Thus, beginning with role-taking in its simplest form and progressing to taking, adapting, and adopting more complex attitudes of others (who become "generalized others"), we form ourselves into whole entities, fully human.

While Mead does not use the term *empathy,* the ability to understand others and adopt their attitudes clearly depends on empathic capability. Mead's concept of role-taking closely resembles Jourard's (1971) belief that to know another person, one must be relaxed and almost merge with the other, thus inviting and promoting disclosure of the other person's inner being.

Carl Rogers was introduced to the idea of listening for feelings by a Rankian-trained social worker, who saw the client-therapist relationship as being curative in its own right. As Rogers's counseling developed, he placed more stress on the empathic content of the therapist's response. These responses were to be offered in a free, permissive, and nonauthoritarian atmosphere, where clients would feel at ease in discussing, at their own pace, those subjects and feelings they felt to be important. The therapeutic attitude helped clients gain a gradual insight into themselves and their situations. Hart (1970) referred to this early phase of Rogerian philosophy as the nondirective period (1940–1950), which evolved into the reflective period (1950–1957). This second period was characterized by reflection of the affective portion of the clients' message, continuation of the absence of threat in the therapeutic relationship, and mirroring of the clients' phenomenological world. The emphasis was on helping clients to develop a sense of congruence between their self-concept and the world as they experienced it. Rogers's (1957) article "The Necessary and Sufficient Conditions of Therapeutic Personality Change" launched what Hart (1970) called the experiential period (1957–present). In this bold and definitive article, Rogers postulated that the presence of the six following conditions were not only necessary but sufficient for constructive personality change to occur:

1. Two persons are in psychological contact.
2. The first, whom we shall term the client, is in a state of incongruence, being vulnerable or anxious.
3. The second person, whom we shall term the therapist, is congruent or integrated in the relationship.
4. The therapist experiences unconditional positive regard for the client.
5. The therapist experiences an empathic understanding of the client's internal frame of reference and endeavors to communicate this experience to the client.
6. The communication to the client of the therapist's empathic understanding and unconditional positive regard is to a minimal degree achieved. (Rogers, 1957, p. 96)

The experiential period is marked by a shift from specific techniques (involving feeling) to the establishment of a philosophy or attitude that manifests itself in a variety of counselor behaviors. The shift is from what counselors do to how they do it—from technique to genuineness. Counselors must respond with personal meaning that reflects the underlying attitude incorporated in the six conditions (Rogers et al., 1967).

Empathy can be communicated in a trusting and permissive relationship through the medium of therapist genuineness (see Chapter 9). The goal is to accomplish three objectives:

1. to refer directly and help the individual refer directly to his present experiencing,
2. to allow him to feel this present experiencing more intensely, to grapple with it, face it, tolerate it, work it through, and
3. to help him put its implicit meaning into concepts which accurately state it. (Gendlin, 1961, p. 245)

The act of sharing an experience with someone is a process that eludes definition. It is a sensing, an often intuitive communication between two people, that goes beyond the normal reflective response of counselors. It is a relationship marked by a singleness of purpose and intensity such that both the counselor and the client share even physiological responses

(Robinson, Herman, and Kaplan, 1982). The relationship is inversely related to their maintaining emotional separation (Corcoran, 1982). Its very existence can create a natural "high" in the client for being so deeply understood, cared for, and accepted by another person. This then becomes the foundation for therapy as well as for the establishment of other relationships.

Empathy Defined

Empathy has been defined in a variety of ways by a variety of authors. During his reflective period, Rogers (1951) defined it as

> the counselor's function to assume, in so far as he is able, the internal frame of reference of the client, to perceive the world as the client sees it, to perceive the client himself as he is seen by himself, to lay aside all perceptions from the external frame of reference while doing so and to communicate something of this empathic understanding to the client. (p. 29)

Rogers altered his definition slightly for his 1957 article "The Necessary and Sufficient Conditions of Therapeutic Personality Change," writing that "to sense the client's private world as if it were your own, but without ever losing the 'as if' quality—that is empathy . . ." (p. 99).

Regarding the process of empathizing, Barrett-Lennard (1962) placed great stress on sensing the meaning behind the spoken message:

> Qualitatively it is an active process of desiring to know the full present and changing awareness of another person, of reaching out to receive his communication and meaning, and of translating his words and signs into experienced meaning that matches at least those aspects of his awareness that are most important to him at the moment. It is an experiencing of the consciousness 'behind' another's outward communication, but with continuous awareness that this is originating and proceeding in the other. (p. 3)

The definition of *empathy*, as it is used in this text, centers around the process of the relationship. The process of being empathic occurs in a sensitive and intimate relationship in which one person becomes increasingly more aware of the other's private perceptions of his or her world, feelings presently experienced, feelings presently "blocked" or denied to awareness, and the meanings he or she ascribes to these perceptions and feelings. To be empathic, one must free oneself to see, understand, and experience life through another's inner being and to sense the continual changes taking place therein. It means being aware of and sensitive to another's perceptions, feelings, experiences, and personal meanings and then communicating that awareness in such a way that the other person can recognize its accuracy and "own" it. It enables one to view another with a freshness and strength that will generate new meanings and insights, which, once considered in this trusting and intimate environment, will take the awareness, understanding, and experiencing (the relationship itself) to new depths.

Sympathy, Projection, and the Empathic Response

Empathy—vicariously experiencing the feelings, perceptions, and world of another—is quite different from projection and sympathy, especially within the framework of the counseling experience. Mead (1934) writes, "Sympathy comes . . . in the arousing in one's self of the attitude of the individual whom one is assisting, the taking the attitude of the other when one is assisting the other" (p. 299). *Sympathy* means that one person identifies with and shares the feelings of another, as do counselors who hear a client express his or her feelings about an experience then imitate and "own" those same feelings: They put themselves in the place of the client. Mead goes on to state:

to identify yourself sympathetically with him, by taking his attitude toward, and his role in, the given social situation, and by thus responding to that situation implicitly as he does or is about to do explicitly; in essentially the same way you take his attitude toward yourself . . . , and are thus made self-conscious. (p. 300)

Of course, there is a pitfall with sympathy. When clients express pain related to a particular experience and counselors identify with them, the counselors will feel the clients' pain. Like their clients, they may well be overwhelmed and stymied by such feelings. In such a case, counselors can become focused on their own feelings and unable to be sensitive to the changing perceptions and feelings in their clients. Thus, their ability to be empathic—to free themselves to see, understand, and experience life through another's inner being—is severely depleted. It is essential at this point that counselors initiate a process to understand their feelings and the source of those feelings. A counselor may wish to do this with his or her counselor, a supervisor, or a trusted colleague. The purpose of this self-inspection is to work through one's own feelings and to separate one's experience and feelings from those of the client. This will then allow the counselor to experience the client's frame of reference without identifying personally with it.

Projection, too, can impede the development of an empathic relationship. *Projection* can be defined as "the act of attributing to another one's own feelings, perceptions, or thoughts." In projecting, counselors listen to their clients' messages and interpret the underlying feelings or meanings to conform to their own. No conscious thought is given to the process when the counselors unconsciously assume, given a specific situation, "I feel A and B, therefore the client feels A and B." Once counselors project to their client, the empathic relationship is suspended—the length of that suspension depends on the tenaciousness of the counselor-held projection. Counselors who find themselves projecting to their clients should seek counseling to increase their awareness of self, to "own" their feelings, and recognize the distinction between themselves and their clients. If this self-exploration and understanding does not occur and the projection continues, the counselors will become destructive to their clients and to themselves.

If sympathy and projection can be mistaken for empathy, one might ask,

"What is the basis for making an empathic response?" Shantz (1975) discusses three types of judgments, each of which can form the basis of an empathic response. The first, self-judgment, is being aware of how one would feel in the situation (or felt in a similar one) and assuming the other would feel the same way. In this case it seems that the more similar the two people are, the more likely they will be to make an accurate empathic response. Carkhuff (1971) states the premise that helpers from the same community as the client will be more effective than helpers from outside. Therefore, black people will be more effective with blacks, poor people with poor people, and people of one ethnic group with others of the same group. The process of this type of empathizing is one of simple generalization from oneself to the client's specific dilemma as illustrated here:

Client: So after I called and he said that the apartment was available, I went over immediately after work. Then he sees that I am black and he knows I have two children and he says that he is sorry but he just rented the apartment. Man, I know he's lying, but what can I do?

(The counselor, having been treated in a similar fashion, is aware of having felt angry, helpless, and discounted as a person. She senses these same feelings in the client.)

Counselor: You feel really angry with him because he discounts you as a person and denies you something because you are black and a mother, but yet you feel helpless to do anything about it.

Some skeptics suggest that an empathic response is a projection. A self-judgment can indeed be a projection. However, we do not believe that just because the source of awareness of a feeling is the counselor's inner feeling, it is necessarily projection. In the dialogue with the black mother, the counselor was aware of her own feelings and consciously checked out their appropriateness to the client's words. Finding them to "fit," the counselor stated them to ascertain their accuracy. This is not projection, notably because the counselor makes the conscious effort and acknowledges that the judgment might be in error. However, it cannot be emphasized enough that counselors who are not constantly testing their assumptions and understandings may well be guilty of projecting.

A normative judgment is the second basis for generating an empathic response (Shantz, 1975). The foundation for such a judgment is the awareness of how "most" people or a "typical" person would feel if they were in that situation or were presenting that nonverbal gesture. As with self-judgment, empathic response here involves generalization—but it is not based on the counselors' personal emotional experiences. This response is based on what the counselor believes most people would do or feel in the same circumstance:

Client: So after I found out I was pregnant I told my boyfriend and he . . . well . . . he said go get an abortion. So before I realized what I was doing, I was at the clinic filling out the forms and . . . it was done. After, I was numb . . . I didn't know what had happened or what. And then it hit me . . . what it was that I had done and I just cried and cried. I couldn't stop because when I did, I would just think about it again.

(The counselor considers what the client has said and states to himself that most people he knows would feel sad at losing this life that was a part of them, angry at themselves for blindly submitting, and responsible for eliminating a life.)

Counselor: You are experiencing a great deal of sadness at losing your baby, and I sense your feelings of responsibility for having gone through with it.

In this case—being male and childless—the counselor had no similar experiences but could abstract from his awareness of what he knew others had felt, and seeing that it fit, he responded accordingly.

The final type—what Shantz calls "differential judgment"—calls for counselors to assess what their clients feel in a specific situation. It is accomplished by considering both normative data and nonverbal factors, placing more emphasis on the latter. Differential judgment involves attending to such nonverbal behaviors as facial expression, body position, muscle tone, breathing tempo, and voice tone in the client and looking for their conflict or congruence with the verbal message (Satir, 1972). Since every behavior expresses current feelings, counselors can enhance their empathy by recognizing and responding to the meanings of their clients' behaviors.

To make this kind of a judgment, counselors must listen closely to what their clients are saying and how they are saying it. Knowing the "what" and "how" of the clients' message will add significantly to understanding what they are saying about a particular situation. The following excerpt illustrates this concept:

Client: Then after everyone at the party had voted and we were called together to hear the result . . . it was . . . uh . . . announced that my husband and I were voted the couple with the best marriage. (The client is speaking quietly and deliberately, not smiling, with moist eyes, and shallow breathing. She seems to be struggling to keep from crying.) Imagine that, all of our best friends think ours is the wonderful union they wish they had.

(Seeing no cues to indicate happiness over receiving such an honor, the counselor focused on the controlled pause and the sad, moist eyes and responded.)

Counselor: And instead of helping you feel proud and pleased, I sense in your voice and eyes sadness and a desire to cry.

Because the counselor was attentive to and placed more weight on non-verbal cues, she could recognize and respond to the feelings in the client at that particular moment. She was not misled by what she or most people would feel in that situation. At the same time, being aware of how differently she might have felt permitted her to experience a contrast, which highlighted the client's apparent sadness.

Developing the Empathic Relationship

Counselor Adjustment   Counselors must be able to experience a wide range of emotions and perceptions to offer high levels of empathy and, thus, create the deepest empathic relationship. To do so, counselors must be "together" themselves. Rogers (1975) states that the better integrated counselors are within themselves, the deeper the level of empathy they can offer.

Counselors need to be at ease with themselves and confident of their ability to relate to others. Lin's (1973) study supports the strong relationship between the level of counselor self-confidence and the degree of empathy that was offered. Gurman's (1972) study suggests that happy counselors are more facilitative and that those who express satisfaction with their own lives are better able to understand their clients without distortion. Peebles (1980) found that the longer the counselors continued in their personal therapy, the higher the level of empathy and genuineness they offered their clients. Meanwhile, Selfridge and VanderKolk (1976) found the "freshness" of the personal functioning (self-actualization) of school counselors to be highly related to their ability to accurately perceive and effectively communicate empathy. Bergin and Jasper (1969) point out that therapist disturbance and anxiety interferes with their ability to provide high levels of empathy to their clients. And another study, by Bergin and Solomon (1970), ascertains that depression and anxiety in counselors is negatively and significantly correlated with levels of empathy offered.

Apparently, increased experience enhances therapists' ability to provide high levels of empathy (Mullen and Abeles, 1971). Hayden (1975) and Barrett-Lennard (1962) have found that experienced counselors offer the highest levels of empathy to their clients and communicate that empathy more specifically to them and that their clients show the greatest amount of change.

Lutwak and Hennessy (1982) analyzed the level of empathy demonstrated in a counseling session by persons enrolled in a thirteen-session training program. They found that level of empathy is determined by the counselor's personality characteristics. Four hierarchical stages of conceptual development represent the counselor-trainees' conceptual levels. Stage 1 is concrete and tied to cultural standards and rules; stage 2 is typified by functioning with a high degree of resistance to authority; stage 3 is characterized by relationships based on mutuality, not authority, and is therefore more abstract and complex; and stage 4 functioning is more abstract with people having an open relationship with their environment. Trainees in stages 1 and 2 had significantly lower (destructive) empathy ratings than did those in stages 3 and 4. The authors believe that the ability to perceive the "as if" quality of empathy is too complex for lower-functioning persons to master even in highly structured training programs (p. 259).

If counselors are to offer a free and safe atmosphere and to listen for the surface and hidden meanings in their clients' message, they need to be able to concentrate a considerable amount of energy, in both physical and psychological attention, on the speaker. They cannot be distracted by their inner concerns, feelings of defensiveness, or lack of integration. The process of being empathic and experiencing such an intimate relationship makes it necessary for counselors at various times to disclose personal feelings or thoughts; recognize and respond to anger, love, or ambivalence directed at them; and understand and respond to depression, sadness, happiness, or feelings of suicide, among many other unpredictable feelings, thoughts, and experiences. These responses may need to be made to clients of both sexes who find their counselors physically and/or psychologically attractive or unattractive or to clients whom the counselors find attractive or unattractive. Thus, it is imperative that counselors are psychologically mature, open to and comfortable with their feelings and experiences, and relatively immune to threat (Hogan, 1975). They must also be flexible, and tolerant and accepting of others vastly different from themselves. Hogan (1975) has found the following descriptions to be characteristic (or uncharacteristic) of an empathic person:

Characteristic
1. Is socially perceptive of a wide range of interpersonal cues.
2. Seems to be aware of the impression he makes on others.

Uncharacteristic
1. Does not vary roles: relates to everyone in the same way.
2. Judges self and others in conventional terms like 'popularity,' 'the correct thing to do,' social pressures, etc. (p. 15)

Counselors need to be sensitive not only to their clients' feelings and awareness but also to their own if they are to maximize their sensitivity, their perceptions of others' experiences, and the accuracy of their empathic responses, which represent their level of understanding. Without understanding, there can be no basis for helping another person. This fact applies to all theoretical constructs for helping people: The understanding component of empathy is common to all theories.

Fiedler (1950) concluded from two research studies that therapists of different schools of psychotherapy, including psychoanalytic, nondirective, eclectic and Adlerian, agree that the ideal therapeutic relationship is warm, accepting, and understanding. Another study (Fischer et al., 1975) asked practicing therapists to categorize themselves as belonging to one of three orientations: psychodynamic, behavioristic, or humanistic. Ratings of empathy were then tabulated from recordings of each therapist's interview with a pseudoclient. While the humanistic school was consistently rated highest, no significant differences were found in either warmth, genuineness, or empathy across the three orientations. Furthermore, the writings of psychoanalytic, eclectic, and client-centered orientations all stress the importance of the counselors understanding sensitively and accurately the inner experiences of the clients (Rogers et al., 1967; Havens, 1978). If counselors cannot understand clients and their concerns two things will occur: First, the clients will be quick to recognize this low empathy and not return; and second, the counselors will respond to irrelevant data, possibly give poor direction, but, most importantly, communicate the lack of caring and understanding that has previously pervaded the clients' life. Thus, instead of helping to solve a problem, counselors who lack understanding become a part of the problem.

Mutual Communication

As has been previously posited, empathy is the understanding of another person that develops out of a relationship between two people. However, understanding alone is not sufficient. In the therapeutic relationship, counselors must communicate their understanding to their clients if the clients are to gain a wider and deeper perspective of themselves.

Let us now look at how a counselor and client might embark on this endeavor. The client's talking about his thoughts, feelings, experiences, and self-appraisal communicates to the counselor the data about who the client is and what problems he is experiencing. The counselor attempts to understand what is said and sometimes what is not said. She compares it to what the client has said previously and reflects that understanding to them in an enlightening, caring way. Hearing this statement, the client senses the caring and the accuracy of the counselor's understanding. This affects him in two ways. First it adds to his understanding about himself, which prompts more talking and exploring. Second, it provides the client with, very possibly, the first opportunity he has had to be himself in the presence of a nonthreatening, caring other to whom he may ascribe credentials, authority, and competence, which is undeserved but, at that moment, useful and productive to the client. Now the client has started his "journey into himself" in which the counselor will act as the guide. The client will become more able to assess himself, identify his strengths and deficits, and slowly make strides toward change. The key has been the empathic quality of the relationship.

Not every therapeutic relationship is characterized by the kind of sharing we have just described. Some counselors are too impatient. They are, as a consequence, insensitive to the clients' need to pace themselves in their journey. Clients, too, are impatient to deliver themselves from the pain they are experiencing and so entice the counselor to feel guilty that he or she is not "solving" the problem. The danger is that the counselor will be seduced by his or her guilt feelings, override the empathic relationship, and resort to those behaviors intended to deliver the other from the dilemma as soon as possible. This collusion between the client and counselor shifts the responsibility for the exploration in this "journey" and its attendant understandings from the client to the counselor. The guide becomes the director.

Exactly what happens when counselors take over the driver's seat? Counselors listen patiently for a period of time, begin to understand the confusion or conflict, then, becoming aware of what action they would take, suggest the same to their clients. In short, counselors find themselves giving advice to their anxious, confused clients who, not having the same insights, see no basis for the suggestions. The result is to further confuse clients, because they will begin to focus on the counselors' words rather than their own confusion. The stage is now set for the counselors to "take over." The emphasis has changed from the clients exploring and their counselors understanding and responding to one where counselors explore and their clients try to understand and respond accordingly.

What is necessary for growth is the development of an "attitude" of mutual exploring and understanding, as reflected in the empathic relationship. Counselors, being outside the dilemma but "inside" the understandings and meanings, often have clearer and quicker perceptions than their clients. Counselors must remain conscious of this and endeavor to stay with the clients' pace. This ability to stay with clients is aided by communication of the empathic response. The responses are more than the simple reflection of feeling—they are "calls through the darkness, 'Am I with you?' " (Rogers, 1951, p. 113). At times, these responses will penetrate the clients' half-understandings or confused feelings and, in fact, provide some direction or insight that gently ushers the clients' awareness forward. Interpretations, too, may be given; to be useful, however, they must be the verbalization of the clients' experiencing. While the clients cannot yet verbalize the insight, the foundation for future understanding has been set and identified in the clients' experiencing. If the foundation has not been established, the interpretation, instead of being facilitative, will provoke defensiveness (Hart, 1970) and will be less likely to facilitate change (Claiborn, et al., 1981).

Not only must counselors be leery of progressing too fast but also of moving too slowly. Often counselors will be satisfied simply to track their clients and, in effect, retard exploration. At these times the counseling session seems to be circling, going nowhere. The clients are exploring themselves at a faster pace and a deeper level than their counselors can understand. The counselors are, in fact, frustrating the client's work. Soon the client will become disillusioned with the process or, if fortunate, with the counselor. He or she will terminate either by faking progress or failing to arrive at future appointments. An observant and sensitive counselor will "hear" the client's disappointment and anger and seek supervisory help to better understand the client.

Counselors need to be sensitive to the flow of feelings within themselves that sense how their clients receive the empathic responses. It is possible for clients to acknowledge the response, without disagreeing and still indicate to their counselors that the meaning is not fully realized. It is this subtle sensing that requires fully integrated counselors who possess a continual genuine attitude of shared experiencing. Cameron (1963) describes this attitude with sensitivity and perceptiveness, saying:

> [T]he good therapist, like the good gardener, waits until he recognizes something which is struggling to emerge, and then makes it easier for it to emerge. He never tries to drag anything up from the unconscious or deep preconscious into awareness. (p. 769)

Counselors must always be confirming their accuracy and the adequacy of the pace of counseling, since it is their responsibility to understand their clients, to be aware of any schism, and to take corrective measures.

Experiencing Versus Evaluating

To develop true empathy, counselors need to rid themselves of the evaluative attitude. We have been discussing empathy as a relationship of experiencing that permits two people to grow in mutual understanding and awareness. This can be accomplished only when counselors successfully enter the world of their clients. As they attempt to do this, counselors may find themselves thinking some of the following:

1. I can feel the immensity of your pain and grief.
2. When we discuss those feelings, your mind goes blank and leaves you feeling empty and confused.
3. It sounds as if you are saying that you think of yourself as being happy and that yet there are moments you feel unfulfilled.
4. I can sense your intense pain when you feel rejected and unloved. It feels similar to your experiences as a child with your parents—overwhelming.

Such thoughts reflect the counselors' involvement in their clients' world. On the other hand, the evaluative perspective, illustrated by the thoughts below, reflects a separation from the clients' world.

1. Boy, that was certainly the wrong thing to do!
2. She is certainly hostile but yet in a very passive way; I would diagnose her as passive-aggressive.
3. Well, now I wonder what he will do: Is he going to see that you cannot say those kinds of things to people in authority?
4. I hope I am giving her the right responses.

The two sets of thoughts represent the empathic counselor trying to get inside and look out, on the one hand, and the evaluator being outside trying to look in, on the other. The empathic counselor is obviously much more an integral part of the exploring in the relationship. The evaluator might as well be watching a television program as listening to his or her client.

The importance of being an exploring, empathic counselor is to model and reinforce those same behaviors in their clients. If counselors offer high levels of empathy, it is likely that their clients will explore themselves at higher levels. If counselors model evaluative, calculating, and intellectualizing behaviors, so too will their clients. An inappropriate amount of time and energy will then be spent seeking solutions without adequate understanding or client readiness to move forward.

Expected Outcomes   The reader may now see the empathic relationship as quite attractive but still hold reservations regarding its effectiveness. The position embraced in this text suggests that all people, especially those in a state of incongruence, are seeking relationships that offer warmth, trust, and understanding. It is within these relationships that clients can best find room to search themselves and reevaluate—possibly to reorganize, reorder, or replace aspects of what they find. This chapter emphasizes the empathic relationship as the basis of helping and suggests that, while counselors need to have a wide knowledge and understanding of counseling theory and research, significant client gains can be realized simply by establishing an empathic relationship.

Clients often come to counselors in a state of sadness, confusion, and ambiguity. They are aware something is troubling them and a few may even know the specific nature of their problem, but rarely do they know what to do about it. Some fear the discovery process, since it might uncover feelings that would further complicate their attitudes toward themselves. Furthermore, clients bring to the session the same fear of rejection and need of acceptance that they feel outside. They will employ with counselors those "skills" that they have found effective at manipulating others' perceptions of them. However, in the kind of counseling we recommend, clients are repeatedly greeted with their counselors' attempts to understand and experience them, not with conventional responses that judge, evaluate, or reject. Initially, clients may be confused by and skeptical of these new responses, but as they experience genuineness, warmth, and understanding, clients will become encouraged and more spontaneous in their exploration of feelings.

Jourard (1971) calls this "the experience of being permitted to 'be'—to be himself; . . . It is the experience of feeling free to be and to disclose himself in the presence of another human person whose goodwill is assured, but whose responses are unpredictable" (p. 139).

Empathic responses place value on clients as human beings worth caring for. Clients may experience this as a feeling of being respected or prized. The prizing is of clients as a whole, including those parts of themselves they like and those they dislike. If people whom clients respect place value on them, they can begin to value and gain confidence in themselves. This confidence will encourage them to explore deeper feelings and thinking. Counselors' empathic responses help their clients to experience themselves more deeply—at first through the eyes of their counselors but soon through their own.

The ability and desire to experience oneself does increase within an empathic relationship. Jourard (1971) suggests the client will become "sensitized to the nuances of his own feelings (and those of the therapist) as they ebb and flow in the relationship. The patient becomes more transparent to himself!" (p. 37). The state of being transparent to oneself implies a total self-awareness. The client will experience more feelings and more awareness of his or her situation and values, which will be of use in planning for the future.

Research on the Empathic Relationship

Topic Change   A variety of consequences of the empathic relationship that have a research basis are noted in this section. Empathic responses have a pronounced effect on clients' change of topics during the sessions. Grater and Claxton (1976), using doctoral interns in a counseling practicum, found that clients changed the focus from themselves to someone else after a counselor response that reflected a low degree of empathy. In randomly selected segments of counseling interviews, 22 of the 27 incidents of topic change were preceded by responses where the level of empathy was lower than the counselor's average level for the interview. In 8 of the incidents, the level of empathy, as rated on Carkhuff's scales (1969a), was one full level or more lower than the average level. Holder's (1968) findings add emphasis to those of Grater and Claxton. Holder compared the initial interviews of counselors functioning high in empathy with those functioning low. Those functioning high received an overall rating above a level 3.0 on the Carkhuff (1969a) scale. The results indicate that the high-empathic relationships had an average of 2 topics discussed. Sessions with the counselors emitting low empathy, on the other hand, had a mean of 3.33 topics. The difference in the number of topics discussed was significant at .05 level. Thus, research shows that low-empathic responses affect clients' exploration by causing the shift of topics, often from internal (me) emphasis to external (she, he, they) emphasis. If depth of exploration and understanding is to occur, clients need to be encouraged to explore single topics more thoroughly and to keep the focus on themselves. (See Chapter 12.)

Length of Interview   When counselors communicate a high degree of understanding to their clients, clients are willing to continue the conversation for a longer period of time. Holder found few topic changes for the high-empathic relationship. That same research also found that, due to the fewer topic changes, significantly more time was spent discussing each topic than in the low-empathy interviews.

Carothers and Inslee (1974) investigated the level of empathy offered by volunteer telephone services and its effect on the length of the call. The results demonstrated that as the level of understanding increased, so did the length of the interaction between the volunteer and the caller. The average length of a call for the low-functioning volunteers (level 1.0–1.49) was 9 minutes, whereas 27 minutes was the mean for those functioning high (level 2.5 and above on the Carkhuff [1969a] scale).

Altmann (1973) assigned seven doctoral-level counselors to nineteen college students who had indicated a desire to meet with a counselor weekly for ten weeks. Eight clients discontinued after the initial interview, while the remaining eleven fulfilled their contract. Ratings of the beginning, middle, and end of the initial interview indicated that nine of the eleven clients who stayed received empathy above the median level, based on all nineteen interviews: The eight who terminated received empathy below the median. In addition, Altmann found the empathy offered to the "levers" decreased significantly from the start to the finish of the interview, while there was a significant increase for those who stayed. It appears from this research that the length of the interaction within a session and the client's willingness to continue the relationship to further sessions may be greatly influenced by the level of empathy offered to the client. Low understanding has the effect of shortening, if not terminating, the counseling relationship.

Level of Self-Exploration The ability to explore oneself is a precondition to self-understanding. If counselors are unable to establish the conditions to facilitate client exploration at deep levels, client self-awareness and self-understanding will suffer. Cannon and Pierce (1968) found that the level of client self-exploration was a function of the level of conditions (empathy, warmth, and genuineness) offered by the counselor. Holder et al. (1967) ascertained that low-functioning clients were significantly influenced by the levels of empathy, genuineness, and warmth offered by their counselors. The high-functioning clients continued to explore themselves independent of the level of conditions offered. The low-functioning clients explored themselves at relatively high levels when their counselors' offerings were high and at relatively low levels when the conditions were experimentally lowered.

Truax (1968) placed thirty state hospital patients into four groups, which met twice weekly for twelve weeks. The purpose was to ascertain what effect the levels of empathy, warmth, and genuineness offered by a counselor would have on client self-exploration. The results showed that those clients who received the differential reinforcement of high levels of empathy, warmth, and genuineness showed greater self-exploration and therapeutic improvement than those patients who did not.

In another study of schizophrenic patients, Rogers et al. (1967) state:

The deeper the level of the therapist's understanding and genuineness in his relationship with his patient, the more his patient was likely to exhibit a deeper level of self-experiencing and self-exploration at every point of therapy—initially, throughout therapy, and at termination. (p. 83)

The research we have described illuminates the facilitative effects of high levels of warmth, genuineness, and empathy. It is postulated here that if high levels of empathy are offered to clients, warmth and genuineness must accompany them. Empathy without warmth and genuineness will not be experienced as understanding by clients. It will not, therefore, foster self-exploration, and may even retard it.

Outcome Measures of Change   Many researchers have found that accurate empathy is related to successful outcome measures of counseling. Truax (1963) used blind-empathy ratings of counseling sessions with schizophrenic clients and compared them to change in personality and behavior. Psychological test changes and diagnosis-of-personality-change indicated the change in personality, while the amount of time spent in the hospital measured the change in behavior. The correlation between the empathy levels and outcome was .77, which is significant (P < .01). The other outcome measure was a pretherapy/post therapy evaluation of the degree of change in the functioning of the personality, as rated by two psychologists using the Rorschach projective test and the Minnesota Multiphasic Personality Inventory (MMPI). The correlation between these evaluations and the level of counselor empathy was .48 (P < .05). Those counselors rated high with respect to empathy, among other qualities, tended to improve the psychological functioning of their schizophrenic clients, while those with less empathy impaired the functioning of their clients. This finding is corroborated by Rogers et al. (1967) who found that the schizophrenic clients who received the highest level of accurate empathy in their therapeutic relationships, showed the most reduction of schizophrenic pathology, as measured on the subscale for schizophrenic tendencies of the MMPI. On the other hand, evidence was found that those clients who received low empathy in their therapeutic relationships showed a slight increase in their schizophrenic pathologies. Even those clients who received no psychotherapy did better than the low-empathy group. Thus, it should be emphasized again that counseling can be constructive or destructive and that the level of accurate empathy offered by the counselor seems to be a significant determining factor here.

In a study of twenty-one therapists and forty-two clients at the Counseling Center of the University of Chicago, Barrett-Lennard (1962) evaluated the counselors in five areas: (a) level of regard for the client, (b) degree to which regard is unconditional, (c) empathic understanding, (d) congruence, and (e) willingness to be known. The ratings were made following the fifth interview and at predetermined points thereafter. Indices of change included the Taylor Manifest Anxiety (MA), the D Scale of the MMPI, Q adjustment, and others. The results after five interviews showed that each relationship factor, except the last (willingness to be known), would predict the index of change. The group of clients who received high empathy as measured by both the counselor and client showed the greatest change. The group with a high-empathy rating from the client and low rating from the counselor showed the second greatest degree of change. The group with high counselor rating and low client rating showed the third most change, while the least amount of change was shown by the group that received a low rating from both the counselor and the client. Thus, it can be deduced that the group who received the highest level of empathy as rated by the clients, not the counselors, will show the greatest amount of healthy change. This conclusion is supported by a similar finding by Rogers et al. (1967). They found that, in predicting the outcome of the counseling, the assessment of the therapeutic relationship (empathy) by the counselor is "less satisfactory and presumably less valid than the assessment by the patient or by an unbiased judge" (p. 78). It becomes abundantly clear that empathy must be communicated to clients to be effective and that clients are the ultimate judge of its accuracy and use in their therapeutic exploration.

Mullen and Abeles (1971) selected the tapes of clients of thirty-six counselors at a university counseling center. These clients had seen only one counselor and had been pre- and post-tested using the scores of the clinical scales of the MMPI. A five-minute segment of each session was rated according to warmth and empathy. The mean number of sessions was eleven. The results showed that in every incident (n=5) where the level of empathy was low in the three stages of counseling—early, middle, and late—the outcome was unsuccessful. There was a significant relationship between high-empathy levels and successful outcomes.

Educational Settings   Two studies by Stoffer (1970) and Aspy (1969) suggest that helpers who function high in empathy have a greater impact on the learning of their students than those who don't. Aspy taped the interaction of six teachers with their sixth-grade reading group in March and again in May. Using high- and low-I.Q. grouping for each teacher, the average amount of gain by the students with the three high-functioning teachers was significantly greater (P < .05) than those with the three low-functioning teachers. The gain was demonstrated on four of the five subtests of the Stanford Achievement Test, including test-word meaning, paragraph meaning, word study, and language. No difference was found in the spelling subtest.

Stoffer (1970) identified students in grades 1–6 who: (1) were experiencing behavioral problems, (2) were one grade or more retarded in placement or achievement, (3) had an I.Q. of 80 or above, and (4) were receiving failing grades. Thirty-five adult female volunteers met with the thirty-five children for 30–60 minutes twice weekly for a mean number of eleven weeks. The volunteers were instructed to establish good relationships with their children but were not told how to do it. Recordings were made of an early and a late interview. High ratings of accurate empathy in the late interviews were significantly related to gains in achievement, as measured by teachers' grades, wide-range achievement tests, and the Gray Oral Reading Test. The study showed that volunteers who are warm and understanding will have a therapeutic effect on children, whereas those who are not warm and understanding may have a deleterious effect.

Thus, it is seen that high levels of empathy, warmth, and genuineness enhance the ability of helpees to remain focused on themselves for longer periods of time, heighten self-exploration, lengthen the therapeutic relationship, and in general improve the opportunity for a successful, healthy outcome. In addition, when helpers in the schools offer high degrees of these conditions, the cognitive growth of youngsters benefits significantly.

Implications for Counselor Training in Empathy

When we look around, we quickly recognize that some people seem to be more understanding and empathic in both their attitudes and behaviors than others. This attitude is learned early in life and is strengthened as children learn congruent behaviors throughout their development. Some people have refined both the attitude and the behavior of empathy more than others. However, since the foundation has been built in our childhood role-taking, the potential remains, to be nurtured and developed. A more sophisticated and sensitive empathic attitude and skill can be learned at any age.

Empathy and Intelligence Researchers have found that the ability to learn empathic skills has little, if any, relationship to one's intelligence. Bergin and Solomon (1970), in a study of eighteen postinternship students in clinical and counseling psychology, found that students' grades and Graduate Record Exam scores were unrelated to their ability to be empathic. In a second study, with a separate and larger group of psychology students, Bergin and Jasper (1969) again found no relationship between the students' empathic ratings, Graduate Record Exam scores, and grade-point averages. Hurst and Shatkin (1974) found that linear combinations of grade-point average, quality of undergraduate college, major area of study, recommendations, and work experience were unrelated to ratings of empathy, respect, and genuineness for students in counselor training.

Finally, Gantt et al. (1980) trained forty-seven junior college students in communication skills, including empathy, in a ten-week introductory mental health course. Students were pretested, post-tested, and tested after a nine-month follow-up period. Results again demonstrated ability to improve empathic sensitivity in paraprofessionals significantly in a short training program. The students' empathic sensitivity was not only maintained over the nine-month follow-up period; it was significantly increased. In a final finding, the authors found no statistical relationship between verbal SAT scores and empathic sensitivity before or after training. It is therefore clear that the usual indicators of academic excellence are not valid indicators of empathic ability.

**Empathy and
Modeling**

How then is empathy learned? Empathy is modeled by empathic people and then practiced—just as foul shooting is practiced by the professional basketball player—repeatedly and continuously. In a study by Perry (1975), sixty-eight clergymen were exposed to one of six training groups. The independent variables were: (1) receiving instructions or (2) not receiving instructions about the nature of empathy and being exposed to a (3) high-empathy model, (4) low-empathy model, or (5) no model. The results show that those exposed to the high-empathy model offered significantly higher empathy to their clients than either the low-empathy model group or the no-model group. It was also found that receiving didactic information about empathy and being instructed to be empathic had no effect. High-empathy model subjects increased their empathic output at trial 1 (after seeing four modeling displays) and leveled off at trial 2 (after viewing eight modeling displays). The no-model subjects made no significant changes, while the low-model group's empathy decreased at trial 1 and decreased still more at trial 2. Finally, when instructions about empathy were pitted against the various models, it was found that the instructions had no effect.

Dalton, Sundblad, and Hylbert (1973) produced a video tape that included an introduction to and discussion about empathy (advanced organizer), a high-empathy model, and a series of built-in silences after a client's statement for a subject's covert practice. The 187 undergraduates who were majoring in rehabilitation education were randomly assigned to the three treatment groups. The results showed that the students exposed to the video tape displayed a higher level of empathy than did either the treatment control, which read about counseling behavior, or the proper control group. In a second study by Dalton and Sundblad (1976), 90 residence-hall assistants were randomly assigned to one of three treatment groups. The experimental group (T_1) viewed the ninety-minute tape mentioned previously, then underwent five systematic training sessions lasting two hours each. The second treatment group (T_2) viewed only the advanced organizer, which included the criterion measure, and then underwent the same systematic training. The third group (T_3) also viewed the advanced organizer and then completed the usual training program for resident assistants. Results of the study again demonstrated the excellence of modeling over didactic information. The group that viewed the tape with the model and covert practice was significantly higher in empathic responses (level 2.14) than was either of the other groups (levels 1.28 and 1.16), which viewed only the advanced organizer. It was also found that systematic training resulted in significantly higher empathy than did modeling alone. It should be mentioned that the systematic training in empathy permitted the empathic level of T_2 to approximately equal the level of T_1 (level 2.4). However, the systematic training model, which will be discussed in Chapter 12, utilizes the modeling phenomenon to a great extent. Therefore, by the completion of the treatment, both groups T_1 and T_2 had been subjected to extensive modeling in the training.

Using a treatment procedure similar to the one used in the two preceding studies, Hector et al. (1981) attempted to teach counselor trainees to respond to anger and depression by randomly dividing fifty graduate counseling students into four treatment conditions and a control. The experimental group (T_1) viewed a video tape, which included an introduction that emphasized the importance of responding to the negative feelings of the client, and two role-played interviews, which focused on feelings of loneliness and anxiety. A pause, built in before each counselor response, permitted the trainees to practice a response both covertly and then verbally. The second treatment group (T_2) viewed the same video tape as T_1 except that the counselor responses were deleted, thereby eliminating the modeling. The third group (T_3) saw a video tape of a lecture on the importance of responding to negative client feelings and one role-play model of a counselor responding consistently to the clients' anxious feelings. There was no provision for trainee practice. Finally T_4 watched a video tape of a role-played presentation of a counseling trainee in a supervision session that dealt with the trainee's inconsistent responding to the client's anxiety. The supervisor's comments were received with insight and understanding by the trainee. Results again indicated that trainees in T_1, who had seen a model and had been able to practice verbally, responded more consistently than any of the other four treatment groups. "These results seem to imply that verbal practice plus modeling is better than either verbal practice or modeling alone" (p. 56).

Berenson (1971) randomly selected forty-eight senior-level elementary education students and assigned them to a treatment group and three control groups. The experimental group (Ex) received twenty-five hours of training in the discrimination and communication of empathy, positive regard, genuineness, concreteness, immediacy, significant other references, and confrontation. The training control group (Ct) received didactic training in the above dimensions but no practice or use of rating scales. Of the remaining control groups, one was notified of its involvement in an experiment (Ch) and another had no knowledge of the experiment (Cp). Results yielded no significant difference after treatment for the three control groups, whereas the empathic level of the experimental group was significantly higher (level 2.66). In addition, the supervisors rated these student teachers in the experimental group as significantly higher in total competency, general teaching competency, classroom management, understanding of teaching, and understanding of children. Again, there was no significant difference among the controls as rated by their supervisors. In short, the experimental group accepted and encouraged the feelings and ideas of their pupils better than the controls, and they did so over an extended period of time.

Finally, Pierce and Schauble (1970) investigated the effects of supervisors on their supervisees. The variables evaluated were empathy, positive regard, genuineness, and concreteness. The twelve supervisors, Ph.D faculty, were rated as high- or low-functioning in the core conditions,. Those rated high achieved mean ratings above a level 3.2 in all of the conditions, while those rated low received mean ratings hovering near the 2.0 level in all of the conditions. The supervisees were advanced counseling students who had completed 80 percent of their doctoral work. The results indicated that the supervisees of the high supervisor group improved significantly on all of the conditions. As a consequence, they were functioning significantly higher than the supervisees of the low supervisor group. Subjects in the low supervisor group showed no significant differences from their supervisors at the start of the study and achieved no significant improvement.

It is painfully clear that didactic training has no effect on a person's ability to be empathic. However, exposure to a taped or live model who exhibits high-empathic skills can have a significant and positive effect. Exposure to a low-empathic model, on the other hand, can have a detrimental effect. This is as true for the trainee in the training process as it is for the counselee in the counseling process. Finally, a systematic training program of forty hours (Truax and Lister, 1971) or twenty hours (Berenson, Carkhuff, and Myrus, 1966) can effectively raise the empathic level of the trainees.

Knowledge about the acquisition of empathic understanding and communication skills has been applied to a variety of fields. Because of widespread dissatisfaction with physicians' ability to communicate effectively with their patients, Poole et al. (1979) designed a training program in interpersonal communication to address that problem. Brown and Elmore (1982) designed and implemented a course in communication skills for all dental students at their school. Empathy training is being taught to couples in marriage counseling (Beottcher, 1977; Wells and Figurel, 1979) as well as to divorcees (Avery and Thiessen, 1982), and to adolescents (Haynes and Avery, 1979) to aid them to increase their satisfaction and involvement in relationships now and in the future. Because we are all involved in relationships, anyone can benefit from the acquisition of empathic skills.

To reiterate, empathic effectiveness can be best fostered when the student understands the concept of empathy, views an excellent model, and undergoes systematic training. Once proficiency is gained, trainees must continuously practice and use empathy to integrate it into their attitude and personality. In short, it must become authentic.

Summary

This chapter introduced the reader to the concept of empathy. Its development has been traced from Rogers's nondirective period to today's emphasis on the spontaneous and warm sharing of the client's world.

The following implications can be generated from this chapter:

1. Empathy occurs in a sensitive and intimate relationship, where one person becomes increasingly more aware of the other's private, inner world of perceptions, feelings, and experiences.
2. Counselors can use themselves and their experiences to generate impressions that are

useful as a guide to understanding their clients and their clients' unique situations.

3. Counselors must be careful to recognize the distinction between themselves and their feelings and those of their clients.

4. Counselors need to be continually involved in their own process of growth and self-understanding, which enables them to be more effective.

5. The use of empathy promotes a warm and trusting counseling atmosphere, which facilitates the therapeutic outcomes of self-exploration, greater client self-acceptance, self-prizing, and self-awareness.

References

Altmann, H. A. "Effects of Empathy, Warmth, and Genuineness in the Initial Counseling Interview." *Counselor Education and Supervision* 13 (1973): 225–228.

Aspy, D. "The Effect of Teacher-Offered Conditions of Empathy, Positive Regard and Congruence upon Student Achievement." *Florida Journal of Educational Research* 11 (1969):39–48.

Avery, A. W., and J. D. Thiessen. "Communication Skills Training for Divorcees." *Journal of Counseling Psychology* 29 (1982):203–205.

Barrett-Lennard, G. T. "Dimensions of Therapist Response as Causal Factors in Therapeutic Change." *Psychological Monographs* 76, 43 (1962):(Whole No. 562).

Bergin, A. E., and L. G. Jasper. "Correlates of Empathy in Psychotherapy: A Replication. *Journal of Abnormal Psychology* 74 (1969):477–489.

———, and S. Solomon. "Personality and Performance Correlates of Empathic Understanding in Psychotherapy." In J. T. Hart and T. M. Tomlinson, eds., *New Directions in Client-Centered Therapy.* Boston: Houghton Mifflin, 1970. Pp. 233–236.

Berenson, B. G., R. R. Carkhuff, and P. Myrus. "The Interpersonal Functioning and Training of College Students." *Journal of Counseling Psychology* 13 (1966):441–446.

Berenson, D. H. "The Effects of Systematic Human Relations Training upon Classroom Performance of Elementary School Student Teachers." *Journal of Research and Development in Education* 4 (1971):70–85.

Boettcher, R. R. "Interspousal Empathy, Marital Satisfaction, and Marriage Counseling." *Journal of Social Service Research* 1 (1977):105–113.

Brown, J. C., and R. T. Elmore. "Interpersonal Skills Training for Dental Students." *Psychological Reports* 50 (1982):390.

Cameron, N. *Personality Development and Psychotherapy: A Dynamic Approach.* Boston: Houghton Mifflin, 1963.

Cannon, J. R., and R. M. Pierce. "Order Effects in the Experimental Manipulation of Therapeutic Conditions." *Journal of Clinical Psychology* 24 (1968):242–244.

Carkhuff, R. R. *Helping and Human Relations: A Primer for Lay and Professional Helpers.* Vol. I: *Selection and Training.* New York: Holt, Rinehart and Winston, 1969(a).

———. *Helping and Human Relations: A Primer for Lay and Professional Helpers.* Vol. II: *Practice and Research.* New York: Holt, Rinehart and Winston, 1969(b).

———. *The Development of Human Resources.* New York: Holt, Rinehart and Winston, 1971.

Carothers, J. E., and L. J. Inslee. "Level of Empathic Understanding Offered by Volunteer Telephone Services." *Journal of Counseling Psychology* 21 (1974):274–276.

Claiborn, C. D., S. R. Ward, and S. R. Strong. "Effects of Congruence Between Counselor Interpretations and Client Beliefs." *Journal of Counseling Psychology* 28 (1981):101–109

Corcoran, K. J. "An Exploratory Investigation into Self-Other Differentiation: Empirical Evidence for a Monistic Perspective on Empathy." *Psychotherapy: Theory, Research and Practice,* 19 (1982):63–68.

Dalton, R. F., Jr., and L. M. Sundblad. "Using Principles of Social Learning in Training for Communication of Empathy." *Journal of Counseling Psychology* 23 (1976):454–457.

———, Jr., L. M. Sundblad, and K. W. Hylbert. "An Application of Principles of Social Learning to Training in Communication of Empathy." *Journal of Counseling Psychology* 20 (1973):378–383.

Fiedler, F. E. "The Concept of the Ideal Therapeutic Relationship." *Journal of Consulting Psychology* 14 (1950):239–245.

Fischer, J., G. J. Paveza, N. S. Kickertz, L. J. Hubbard, and S. B. Grayston. "The Relationship Between Theoretical Orientation and Therapists' Empathy, Warmth, and Genuineness." *Journal of Counseling Psychology* 22 (1975):399–403.

Gantt, S., D. Billingsley, and J. A. Giordino. "Paraprofessional Skill: Maintenance of Empathic Sensitivity after Training." *Journal of Counseling Psychology* 27 (1980):374–379.

Gendlin, E. T. "Experiencing: A Variable in the Process of Therapeutic Change." *American Journal of Psychotherapy* 15 (1961):233–245.

Grater, H., and D. Claxton. "Counselor's Empathy Level and Client Topic Changes." *Journal of Counseling Psychology* 23 (1976):407–408.

Gurman, A. S. "Therapist's Mood Patterns and Therapeutic Facilitativeness." *Journal of Counseling Psychology* 19 (1972):169–170.

Haase, R. F., and D. T. Tepper, Jr. "Nonverbal Components of Empathic Communication." *Journal of Counseling Psychology* 19 (1972):417–24.

Hart, J. T. "The Development of Client-Centered Therapy." In J. T. Hart and T. M. Tomlinson, eds., *New Directions in Client-Centered Therapy.* Boston: Houghton Mifflin, 1970.

Havens, L. "Explorations in the Uses of Language in Psychotherapy: Simple Empathic Statements." *Psychiatry* 41 (1978):336–345.

Hayden, B. "Verbal and Therapeutic Styles of Experienced Therapists Who Differ in Peer-Rated Therapist Effectiveness." *Journal of Counseling Psychology* 22 (1975):384–389.

Haynes, L. A., and A. W. Avery. "Training Adolescents in Self-Disclosure and Empathy Skills." *Journal of Counseling Psychology* 26 (1979):526–530.

Hector, M. A., K. L. Davis, E. A. Denton, T. W. Hayes, C. Patton-Crowder, and W. K. Hinkle. "Helping Counselor Trainees Learn to Respond Consistently to Anger and Depression." *Journal of Counseling Psychology* 28 (1981):53–58.

Hogan, R. "Empathy! A Conceptual and Psychometric Analysis." *The Counseling Psychologist* 5 (1975):14–18.

Holder, T. "Length of Encounter as a Therapist Variable." *Journal of Clinical Psychology* 24 (1968):249–250.

———, R. R. Carkhuff, and B. G. Berenson. "The Differential Effects of the Manipulation of Thera-

peutic Conditions upon High and Low Functioning Clients." *Journal of Counseling Psychology* 14 (1967):63–66.

Hurst, M. W., and S. D. Shatkin. "Relationship Between Standardized Admissions Variables and Certain Interpersonal Skills." *Counselor Education and Supervision* 14 (1974):22–31.

Jourard, S. M. *The Transparent Self.* New York: D. Van Nostrand, 1971.

Lin, T. "Counseling Relationship as a Function of a Counselor's Confidence." *Journal of Counseling Psychology* 20 (1973):293–297.

Lutwak, N., and J. J., Hennessy. "Conceptual Systems Functioning as a Mediating Factor in the Development of Counseling Skills." *Journal of Counseling Psychology,* 29 (1982):256–260.

Mead, G. H. *Mind, Self and Society: From the Standpoint of a Social Behaviorist.* Chicago: University of Chicago Press, 1934.

Mullen, J., and N. Abeles. "Relationship of Liking, Empathy and Therapist's Experience to Outcome of Therapy." *Journal of Counseling Psychology* 18 (1971):39–43.

Peebles, M. J. "Personal Therapy and Ability to Display Empathy, Warmth and Genuineness in Psychotherapy." *Psychotherapy: Theory, Research and Practice* 17 (1980):258–262.

Perry, M. A. "Modeling and Instructions in Training for Counselor Empathy." *Journal of Counseling Psychology* 22 (1975):173–179.

Pierce, R. M., and P. G. Schauble. "Graduate Training of Facilitative Counselors: The Effects of Individual Supervision." *Journal of Counseling Psychology* 17 (1970):210–215.

Poole, A., B. Desmond, and R. W. Sanson-Fisher. "Understanding the Patient: A Neglected Aspect of Medical Education." *Social Science and Medicine* 13 (1979):37–43.

Robinson, J. W., A. Herman, and B. J. Kaplan. "Autonomic Responses Correlate with Counselor-Client Empathy." *Journal of Counseling Psychology* 29 (1982):195–198.

Rogers, C. R. *Client-Centered Therapy.* Boston: Houghton Mifflin, 1951.

———. "The Necessary and Sufficient Conditions of Therapeutic Personality Change." *Journal of Consulting Psychology* 21 (1957):95–103.

———. "Empathic: An Unappreciated Way of Being." *Counseling Psychologist* 5 (1975):2–10.

———, E. T. Gendlin, D. J. Kiesler, and C. B. Truax,

eds. *The Therapeutic Relationship and Its Impact: A Study of Psychotherapy with Schizophrenics.* Madison: University of Wisconsin Press, 1967.

————, and B. Stevens. *Person to Person: The Problems of Being Human.* Lafayette, Calif.: Real People Press, 1967.

Satir, V. *People Making.* Palo Alto, Calif.: Science and Behavior Books, 1972.

Selfridge, F. F., and C. VanderKolk. "Correlates of Counselor Self-Actualization and Client-Perceived Facilitativeness." *Counselor Education and Supervision* 16 (1976):180–194.

Shantz, C. V. "Empathy in Relation to Social Cognitive Development." *The Counseling Psychologist* 5 (1975):18–21.

Stoffer, D. L. "Investigation of Positive Behavioral Change as a Function of Genuineness, Non Possessive Warmth, and Empathic Understanding." *The Journal of Educational Research* 63 (1970):225–228.

Truax, C. B. "Effective Ingredients in Psychotherapy: An Approach to Unraveling the Patient-Therapist Interaction." *Journal of Counseling Psychology* 10 (1963):256–263.

————. "Therapist Interpersonal Reinforcement of Client Self-Exploration and Therapeutic Outcome in Group Psychotherapy." *Journal of Counseling Psychology* 15 (1968):225–231.

————, and J. L. Lister. "Effects of Short-Term Training upon Accurate Empathy and Non-possessive Warmth." *Counselor Education and Supervision* 10 (1971):120–125.

Wells, R. A., and J. A. Figurel. "Techniques of Structural Communication Training." *The Family Coordinator* 28 (1979):273–281.

PART IV

The Counseling Process

CHAPTER 11

Counseling Techniques: I

Chapter Organizer

Aim of the Chapter

This chapter will acquaint the reader with the techniques of initiating, structuring, and terminating counseling.

Chapter Preview

1. The extent of counselor preparation depends on counselor mind set.
2. The initial interview is crucial, since it is a primary determinant of whether or not the client will return.
   a. Simple rules of courtesy are followed while completing the preliminary forms.
   b. The major purpose of the first session is to establish rapport.
   c. Structure involves a definition of the nature, limits, and goals of counseling.
   d. Client behavior is affected by perceived counselor expertness.
3. Attending behavior communicates that the counselor is focusing solely on the client.
   a. Eye contact is the most basic ingredient of good attending.
   b. Attending skills can be practiced and improved.
4. Client behavior is a rich source of information for the counselor.
5. A verbal pattern may be established during counseling.
   a. Client verbal behavior can be modified.
   b. A verbal pattern, once established, is difficult to change.
6. Counselor questioning is not in itself productive.
   a. Counseling is not an interrogation.
   b. Good questions are open ended.
7. Periods of silence should be productive.
8. Transference in counseling should be resolved and not encouraged.
9. Either the client or counselor may terminate counseling contacts.
   a. Time-limited counseling has a positive effect on client growth.
   b. Counseling should end on a positive note.

Relevant Questions

The following are several questions to keep in mind while reading this chapter:

1. How can the counselor establish rapport during the initial counseling session?
2. What common courtesies may the counselor display?
3. How might a counseling session be structured?
4. How might the counselor terminate a session?

Introduction

Counseling with its many theoretical underpinnings has a number of specific attributes, which can be implemented in fairly simple fashion. This chapter is concerned with those specifics that should be considered early in the counseling process. They include attending, listening, and observation skills. The initial session of counseling attempts to place into perspective what counseling is all about. This will be discussed in the following sections. We will also discuss the development of structure, how to cope with transference, and basic elements to consider when terminating counseling.

Initiating Counseling

Preparation The extent of preparation for the initial counseling session really depends on the counselor and the counselor's perception of his or her own role. Obviously, the time available for preparation is an important influence, since without time, no preparation will take place regardless of the counselor's intentions.

First, the counselor's own psychological set should be considered. The counselor needs to be able to look at records and background material without drawing inferences and jumping to conclusions. The counselor who cannot do this should go into the initial session without extensive preparation. Otherwise the counselor might find that he or she is directing the interview into areas that are not of major concern to the client.

Counselor A, reviewing a client's folder, finds that he has been referred by his parents for excessive truancy. Jimmy has been absent thirty-five times over a three-month period. The following dialogue occurs after introductions have taken place and some structure has been established.

Counselor: Really nice day outside, isn't it?
Client: Yeah, it would be nice to get out in the snow.
Counselor: Anything in particular you would like to talk about?
Client: Well, I've been having some difficulty with my girl. Her parents are planning to move, and I'm trying to talk her into staying here. She has an aunt, but her mother is really giving us a hard time.
Counselor: It sounds like you are having a rough time there. But, Jimmy, one of the things I've noticed is you've been absent from school quite a bit, and your mother is worried. What is going on?

The counselor in this instance came in with a set: Absenteeism was the major concern. In this case, it went so far as to prevent the counselor from even listening very well. The fact that the client may have already introduced some relevant material was disregarded. The next brief dialogue is an example of more subtle influence in a similar situation of a young lady experiencing academic difficulty in school.

Counselor: Jane, what would you like to talk about?
Client: I really don't know. I, uh . . .
Counselor: How are things going at school?

While it might appear that the counselor is just trying to get the client started, the subtle influence of providing direction can be seen in the statement. Why didn't the counselor ask how things were with her family, church, or friends? As it turned out, the girl's major concerns focused on her father's recent death, but this did not reveal itself until the third session. The first two sessions were spent dealing with ways she could improve her school work.

A second aspect of preparation is the counselor's definition of his or her role. If the counselor is primarily concerned with information dissemination, test interpretation, or job placement, preparation for an interview would be fairly extensive. If the major concern centers on counseling, the counselor then has to decide how much preparation is best without creating negative bias toward the client.

Intake Procedures

If preliminary forms need to be completed, it is best accomplished with a secretary. The first contact with the counselor should always be very personal. We might mention that the friendliness of the secretary—his or her ability to make the client comfortable initially—is an important factor. The secretary should introduce the client to the counselor by name. Upon meeting the client, the counselor should be friendly and hospitable. Simple rules of courtesy should be followed. Shaking hands, being on time, greeting the client by name, and smiling are appropriate. We might underscore the importance of being on time for counseling sessions. We need only recall our own feelings of unimportance, aggravation, and anger when we have been kept waiting at a doctor's or a dentist's office.

In many cases, it is the small courtesies that are important, but these should be spontaneous and not contrived. In some cases, the client must walk with the counselor from the reception room to an office. In other cases, the client and counselor may simply begin with some "social conversation." In either case, small talk may help the client feel at ease. The conversation may be about the weather, sports, or an interest of the client. The counselor should avoid social conversation that might contribute to negative feelings. Tyler (1969) points out, for example, that mentioning a relative, although commonly done during greetings, might produce resentments about comparisons, rather than any pleasant feelings. Nonetheless, it is next to impossible to establish any rules about potential safe areas for social conversation. General questions are probably the best way to get the client to begin:

What would you like to talk about today?
Where would you like to begin?
You are free to discuss whatever you would like.
What brings you to our center?

Bordin (1968) points out, "A directive lead seems to be a demand for a client to talk about a very specific topic in restricted terms as contrasted with a nondirective lead which is a more general invitation to communicate, sometimes including a relatively unrestricted designation of a topic" (p. 156).

Establishing Rapport

Perhaps the major purpose of the first counseling session is the establishment of rapport. This is critical in many instances in determining whether or not the client will continue. Establishing rapport initially is a complex task, and while the counselor will have to develop rapport at the beginning of each following session, it is never quite as difficult as during the initial session. This is the first time the client and counselor have met, and so there will be a testing-out period by the client. The counselor will have to be concrete, and this will call for adaptation to the client's verbal expression. Errors by the counselor may not be as easily forgiven as they might may be later during the counseling process. Finally, it is during this session that the client will initially decide whether or not to return.

Effective attending and observing skills, as discussed later in this chapter, are essential prehelping skills, which will contribute to the development of rapport. Reflection of feelings and meanings, as discussed in the next chapter, also help to accomplish this end. Questions should be kept to a minimum. Excessive questioning gives the client the impression that counseling is interrogation and establishes a communication pattern that will be difficult to change in future counseling sessions (if there are any).

Clients may initially test acceptance by their counselor. They might challenge the counselor or present superficial concerns. They might present "safe" topics in order to be fully accepted—accepted without evaluation or condemnation. The counselor should be prepared to suspend judgment and withhold diagnosis.

Establishing Structure

After an initial greeting and casual conversation with the client, the counselor will want to establish structure. Structuring involves the counselor's definition of the nature, limits, and goals of the general counseling process and the particular relationship at hand. Structure provides the client with a framework or orientation for therapy, with a counseling road map, thus reducing the ambiguity of the relationship (Brammer and Shostrum, 1977, p. 192). Some clients will require more structure than others (Stein and Stone, 1978). Generally such structure involves the communication of what counseling is and what can be expected from it. The confidential nature of counseling should be mentioned. Additional housekeeping explanations, which involve both time and physical limits, are outlined.

The counselor will want to define for clients (1) the nature of counseling, (2) the counselor's role and responsibilities, (3) the client's role and responsibilities, and (4) the goals of counseling. Basically, such structure serves to clarify the expectations of clients and also to reduce any fears present. Confused individuals are likely to approach the first interview feeling a minimum of responsibility for self and a maximum of fear, insecurity, and defensiveness. Continued miscues (for example, failing to clarify the nature of counseling) on the part of counselor in structuring the relationship seem to cause the clients to depend on the counselor, to feel rejected and hostile if the counselor refuses to solve their problems, and finally to flee the interview in defensiveness and fear and not keep subsequent appointments (Curran, 1944, p. 189). Clients might not understand what counseling is and, consequently, be very hesitant about entering counseling and even somewhat defensive. They might express such feelings in a number of ways:

"I really don't know what to say."
"Where would you like me to begin?"
"I really don't want to be here, but my wife insists I need help?"
"A friend told me I needed a shrink, so I thought I'd come in to see you."

The counselor might plan an informal explanation. This should not be done in a canned or mechanistic way. The explanation should be short and simple; it should not increase the client's anxiety level. Shertzer and Stone (1980) write:

The definitional process is important. Conveying the essence of the relationship without engaging in a miniature lecture is most essential. When the situation calls for structuring, counselors would do well to remember that there is no substitute for simplicity, modesty, and sensitivity in their definition. (p. 273)

The following is one short illustration:

Perhaps, I might first tell you a little of what counseling is. Counseling hopefully will enable you to understand yourself better. Please feel free to talk about anything you would like to. Everything you say is, of course, confidential. I'll try to help you clarify your feelings and behavior and as we go along even help you decide on a plan of action. We do have fifty minutes together. Do you have any questions? [Pause] No? Well, in that case, why don't you tell me something about yourself?

The explanation could well be longer and include additional points. For example, Ingham and Love (1954) suggest the following inclusions:

1. It is appropriate to know oneself better.
2. It is better to develop understanding than to blame.
3. Emotions are real and important.
4. There is total freedom of expression.
5. The past can help one to understand the present.
6. Change is an important consideration that emanates from greater self-understanding.

It is important to avoid a lengthy diatribe. The client might simply stop listening or, even more catastrophic, assume that the counselor will continue to do all the talking. The preferred approach, then, might be to give a quick overview, as suggested earlier, and later clarify structure, whenever necessary.

Structuring, however, is not a process that takes place only during the initial interview. As counseling progresses, the counselor may see a need to repeat or to restructure the relationship. During the structuring process, the client is also free to express . . . feelings and attitudes regarding the relationship. (Pietrofesa et al., 1978, pp. 65–66)

The client may have questions about the counseling process not only during the initial interview but throughout the counseling contact. We would hope that the counselor would answer such questions at any time and recognize the need to clarify the structure further.

Establishing structure also calls for the recognition of limits, such as time, space, and physical limitations. Bixler (1949) presented several general principles.

1. Limits are minimal and consonant with the security of the client and therapist.
2. Limits should be applied nonpunitively.
3. Limits should be well defined in regard to such things as action, time, and number of appointments.
4. Limits should be structured *at the proper time.* (pp. 1–11)

Time limits are important because most counselors have appointments on a continuous basis or have other duties to perform. An explanation of the time available to accomplish desired ends should be made during the first session. In some cases, it can stimulate a client to present the "real" reason for counseling and may minimize avoidance behavior (socializing, for example). Such limits also prevent possible feelings of resentment by both client and counselor. Without proper structure, clients might feel they are not getting enough time. And counselors might become resentful of clients who continue past the allotted time, since it either reduces time available for the next client or eliminates the counselor's time for self.

It is usually best to bring the session to an end by saying something similar to, "Well, I see our time is up." Time limits are adhered to unless unsettling emotional development is presented. Even in this case, it is best to suggest that a topic can be talked about during the next time together. As mentioned earlier, some clients might try to prolong sessions by asking questions that require detailed answers or to engage the counselor in social conversation. It is best to suggest that "perhaps, we can talk about this the next time."

The length of counseling sessions may vary from 20 to 50 minutes. Less than 20 minutes does not allow enough time to develop a relationship that will be meaningful.

The length of the entire process may also be broached. If, for example, the client is interested in vocational counseling, which would not require an extensive period of time, the counselor might say, "We'll need about ten sessions together." On the other hand, if a much longer period of time is required, the client should also be informed of this possibility. *Some real ethical issues arise when counselors continue to see clients for extensive periods in order to maintain a caseload and a certain level of income.*

Some physical limits may be necessary with children. Certain materials may be "toyed" with while others may not. In play therapy, certain objects may be attacked, but there are obvious limits to physically abusing the therapist. Windows may not be broken or furniture destroyed.

The structuring of the confidential nature of counseling is also an important consideration. In most cases, it can be quickly noted, "What we say is strictly confidential. It is just between you and me." In instances where parents bring children for counseling, the child may want to know what will be reported to the parents. It is our belief that any material discussed with the parent should be agreed to (by the child) before it is discussed with the parents. Such discussions are usually conducted with the child present. Obviously, the parents should be informed of this prior to counseling. This may not be a major issue today, since there is increased recognition that the family is a unit and needs to be counseled together. It will also be less of an issue in the future with increased recognition of the rights of a minor.

Practicum students, however, must face the fact that supervisors and colleagues may observe sessions or review counseling tapes. Clients should be informed of this in writing before the initial session, and, furthermore, the counseling center should get a signed release. The counselor, however, might say in the initial interview the following:

As you know we are being taped, and at times observed by my supervisor. This is done to see how well I am doing as a counselor. [Pause] Did you have any questions?

It is crucial that the counselor be comfortable about being observed; otherwise, the counselor's anxiety will be communicated to the client. In cases where we have noted a client's becoming disturbed over observation or taping, the counselor was anxious and gave an inadequate explanation. While lack of structuring can create anxiety in the client, structuring performed in an inadequate fashion also creates anxiety.

Here are several opening statements by counselors-in-training:

I would like you to realize our session is being taped. This taping is to assist me with my counseling practice and is shared only with my supervisor. However, I don't want you to be concerned about this, because whatever we talk about today will be completely confidential. In the 45 minutes we have, I'd like you to feel free to discuss anything that concerns you. Perhaps we can start with you telling me why you have come here.

Today we have 45 minutes together. This meeting, as are all the other meetings, is being tape-recorded. It is used to help you by allowing me to review this session. Everything that we talk about, however, will be kept in the strictest of confidence. The time we have together will be used in any way you want it to be used. Where would you like to begin?

I'm Mrs. ———. You are probably not familiar with our counseling procedures here. From your application you know our session is being taped. What is said is still private and confidential between us. We have 45 minutes, and we'll use it in whatever way will benefit you.

John, we have 45 minutes in which you may share some of your concerns. As you know our sessions will be taped, although whatever is said in here will remain between us. The tapes are heard only by my supervisor and me in order to improve my counseling skills. You may use this time to freely talk about what concerns you. So . . . what would you like to talk about?

It is important to recognize that structure also provides the counselor with reassurance—a certain security exists in knowing that the framework has been clarified for the client. Such limitations then have a definite value for the counselor.

In the first place, they allow the counselor to be more comfortable and to function more effectively. They provide a framework within which the counselor can be free and natural in dealing with the client. When the relationship is poorly defined, there is always the possibility that the counselee may make too heavy demands on the counselor. The result is that the counselor remains subtly defensive, on guard lest his desire to help should ensnare him. (Rogers, 1942, p. 108)

One last caution might be made: Counselors should not structure so often that the client comes to see counseling as an extremely limited and rigid process. Actually, structuring is intended to imply just the opposite—that there is freedom in counseling. Robinson (1950) points out that the counselor's compulsion to structure frequently is a symptom of inadequacy rather than a strength of technique.

Terminating the Initial Interview   The basic goals of the initial interview are to establish structure, develop rapport, and begin client exploration. It is also important to terminate in a facilitative manner. The counselor's ability to terminate might determine whether or not the client will return. The counselor will probably want to note several minutes before the session's end, "Well, we have about five minutes left." It is best also to have the secretary knock on the door or use a wristwatch alarm to indicate this fact. This procedure frees the counselor from continually watching the clock. The interview can then continue, but at the same time move to less intense material. It is unwise to conclude a session on a highly emotional issue. In some cases, the client might purposely introduce a new issue in order to prevent the termination of the session. The counselor might best respond to such an attempt with "That is obviously something you feel a need to consider. Perhaps we can take it up next week." A variety of statements may be used to close the session:

"Well, I see our time is up. I look forward to seeing you next week."
"There are a number of interesting points then to take up during our next appointment."
"I'll be happy to see you again next week. Let me walk you to the secretary's desk and help to arrange the appointment for next week."

We feel it is appropriate to stay with the client until the next appointment is made. Again, it is a reflection of friendliness toward the client. A successful first session can bring a warm glow to the counselor, for as Tyler (1969) points out:

The initial interview is the hardest part of our task—the part that demands from us the most intensive concentration. Each person constitutes for us a new adventure in understanding. Each is destined to broaden our own lives in directions as yet uncharted. Each initial interview renews our appreciation of the challenge and the fascination of the counseling task. (p. 63)

The following examples of closing dialogues of initial sessions illustrate the preceding points:

(1)

Counselee: Like maybe the family could set aside a special time on Friday to talk about various things? One of the startling things I've often found about teenagers: Always, invariably they would say that their parents don't understand them, or that one thing they would change at home if they could, was "I wish mother would listen to me."

Counselor: How does that make you feel about your own daughter?

Counselee: Now I make more time to be with her, and I set up a certain time that I'm with her—my wife and daughter. Very little television is watched. Now we spend time with her on her homework or talking to her. Then I block out a time that I spend just with my wife. There's not time for television when all that's done. But I feel very strongly that she needs that interaction.

Counselor: [Knock—indicates five minutes left.] You are really proud because you've given a special time to your daughter, so that perhaps your daughter won't have that to say about you when she moves into that age.

Counselee: Right. I think, recently I read something about kids preferring television to their fathers. It's not hard to believe, you know, but I think it's tragic. And it comes from that being-so-busy: I gotta go to work, and what-have-you. I think one of the only real complaints I would have about my parents was my father didn't have much time. I know he loved us dearly and we're quite close now, but he always worked two jobs. I recall writing an essay why your father is the best father in the world and I made it all up. I wrote how I wanted him to be and I won the contest. The first-place prize was five dollars and two tickets to the Varsity Theater, with you and your dad. You know, I was all excited about it, but he didn't have time for us to go to the thing.

Counselor: You felt disappointed because your father didn't share your joy, and now you're using this past experience to provide a different experience with your daughter.

Counselee: Right, and because I just like it. It's just so much fun for me. I wish I had eight kids, you know.

Counselor: You're even having fun doing it.

Counselee: Yeh, kids are really funny, man.

Counselor: That knock meant we had five minutes left. Do you want to come back and talk a little more about your family?

Counselee: That time went by fast. Was that forty-five minutes?

Counselor: Yes.

Counselee: It was fast. I would like to continue.

Counselor: Let's go out and make another appointment with the secretary.

(2)

Counselee: A good day for me at work is being able to get around and talk to people, and even when I'm talking to them I'm not really that relaxed. I feel inferior around a number of people.

Counselor: You feel uncomfortable because of the job situation—your lack of education.

Counselee: Yes, my education is it. My education is what's really stopping me from being able to hold a conversation, a good conversation, and feeling comfortable.

Counselor: OK, now at the same time, though, don't most of the people at the shop have the same educational background?

Counselee: There's a wide variety of people there. Different nationalities and different ages, too. It's really a mixed up thing. Some people I can talk to and other people I can't. I don't feel I'm able to talk with enough people there. The people that I find things in common with me, I can talk to pretty easily. But with the people that I don't have anything in common with, it's really uncomfortable. I find it hard to strike up a conversation with them, to say something comfortable. Lots of times I say things but afterwards I say, "Well why did I say that? You know, that really seemed stupid."

Counselor: OK, you feel embarrassed because you can't communicate with the people you don't have something directly in common with.

Counselee: Yep, it's really hard to communicate with them. . . .

Counselor: We have five minutes left. If you want to come back next week, we can talk a little bit more about it.

Counselee: OK. There's hope for me, huh? Do you think this is going to be something easy, or is it, ah, going to be a long hard thing?

Counselor: It's difficult to say, you know.

Counselee: We have to talk some more and everything.

Counselor: Yes. I want to get to know you a little better. Why don't we go set up an appointment for next week, and we can talk further.

Counselee: OK.

Client and Counselor Responses to the Initial Interview

Clients obviously respond differently to the initial interview. Some of the differences are related to perceptions of counselor style and client expectation for the counselor. Ziemelis (1974), utilizing a 2×3 factorial design, studied the effects of client preference and expectancy on the initial counseling interview process. He reported that matching clients with more-or-less preferred counselors had only minimal (but reliable) effects on client-and-counselor evaluation of the process and outcome. However, such matching did strongly affect the quality of *in vivo* interview behavior, as judged by observers. Furthermore, the results indicated that it is more important to prevent clients from establishing negative expectations about their counselors than to arouse positive expectations. Krause (1968) concluded from his study that immediate and extensive focusing on, and clarification of, the clients' problems enhances their motivation for treatment more than clarification of expectations for treatment.

Counselor-client assignments also must consider the counselors' impression of the client. Brown (1970) tried to determine whether the counselors' first impressions were related to outcomes. He studied first-impression variables, which included intensity of client concern, physical attractiveness, client ease of expression, assessment of client potential for change, and the counselors' liking for themselves. The results of the research did suggest that the first impressions of counselors and how effectively they live their own lives are related to selected outcomes and should be considered in making counseling assignments. A highly significant correlation was obtained between personal liking and potential for change. This suggests that counselors like clients they perceive to have the potential for change and are most satisfied with the progress of those same clients (p. 557).

Other writers have looked at the initial interview along related dimensions. Borreson (1965) noted that counselors do develop systematic biases in diagnostic classification. Eells and Guppy (1963) found that preferences develop among counselors for particular types of problems. Counselors have also been found to be unequally effective with all clients (Weigel et al., 1967). Taplin (1968) reported that experienced counselors display more confidence in their impressions of clients than their inexperienced counterparts. Impressions and outcome may well be influenced by the perceptions counselors have of their own role; for example, counselors who prefer to deal with personal-social problems may not respond well to clients present-ing a vocational-educational concern (Danskin, 1957).

Tessler (1975) attempted to find out what determined clients' reactions to initial interviews. He noted that relationship-centered satisfaction was "affected by value similarity and the formality of the counselor's demea-nor." Problem-centered satisfaction, on the other hand, was affected by "be-liefs concerning the extensiveness of the counselor's professional experi-ence" (p. 190).

Attending to the Client Nonverbally

Nonverbal behavior plays an important role in counseling. Visual cues affect the client's perception of the counselor (Strong et al., 1971). Goldstein and Sies (1974) suggest

[I]n addition to verbal communication, there exists another complex medium of human communication that includes bodily appearance and personal behavior; personal dress, carriage, bodily movement, physical gestures, facial expressions, and general expressions of emotions. This is to say that there are, in effect, special-ized forms of body communication present in each society whose communication significance has been institutionalized and, therefore, will be readily recognized and interpreted. (p. 126)

Counselor attending behavior is essentially nonverbal communication. It reflects the counselor's complete attention on client nonverbal and verbal behaviors. Attending behavior can help to communicate respect and atten-tiveness to the counselee and to establish the necessary ingredients for a helping relationship. Such behavior makes the counselor more effective in both observing and responding skills. While attending behaviors set the stage for later helping skills, it is essential that the counselor continue to use them at all counseling stages. They express to the client the level of accep-tance, approval, agreement, rejection, or indifference of the counselor (Hackney et al., 1970, p. 343). Attending behaviors simply reflect good inter-personal skills basic in any human encounter. They are not exclusive to counseling. On the other hand, they can be taken for granted or performed in a perfunctory or sloppy manner. Observing a couple dating or becoming acquainted, one is struck by the excellent attending and apparent caring. The same couple, perhaps five years after marriage, might well reflect little in the way of good attending behavior. One partner might be reading a newspaper or listening to a television program while the other is speaking. Often in marriage counseling we hear, "We never talk [meaningfully] any-more." Poor attending is not conducive to effective human communication, and has no place in a helping relationship.

Attending behaviors accomplish several purposes:

1. *Communication of Individual Attention* Attending behaviors commu-nicate nonverbally "I am listening to you and only you." They can act as a reinforcement for the clients to continue to speak.

2. *Communication of Respect* Counselors, by attending, communicate respect for the client, as if to say, "What you say is so important, I will attend to you."

3. *Modeling of Effective Behavior* Counselors can act as models for their clients. Through their modeling behavior, counselors are afforded the opportunity to demonstrate effective interpersonal skills for clients. After several sessions, counselors will often report how clients have altered their own attending behaviors. With the modeling concept, counselees learn to utilize attending behaviors outside the counseling framework.

4. *Improvement of Counselor Discrimination* Good attending behaviors can actually help counselors focus on the client. It helps to maintain alertness and to provide for more effective discrimination.

The Counseling Environment

The counseling environment should be comfortable (but not too relaxing) and attractive. There should be a minimum of distractions. Interruptions for telephone calls or "door messages" should be eliminated. Nothing can be as aggravating to a client as a phone call, after which the counselor says the equivalent of "Now what were you saying?"

The counselor-client interaction should be free from such barriers as a desk. Too often a desk reflects a superior-inferior dimension, which has no place in a counseling relationship. White (1953) found that the simple rearrangement of a desk, which was reported as a barrier to communication, could produce a change in doctor-patient communication. By removing the desk on alternate days, he noted that 55 percent of the patients were at ease when the desk was not present, while only 11 percent were at ease with the desk. Perception of the desk as a barrier may well depend on the degree of anxiety in the client. Widgery and Stackpole (1972) reported that highly anxious interviewees perceived credibility to be higher with no desk present. An inverse relationship was found for the low-anxiety group. Since most clients reflect higher levels of anxiety, these findings may be quite important.

Even soothing background music has been found to be helpful in counseling sessions—it promotes more effective interaction than either stimulating music or no music (Mezzano and Prueter, 1974). While the writers would find music during counseling to be distracting, such music might well be provided in a waiting room.

Counselor-Client Interaction

Counselor-client interaction includes physical attending, which communicates involvement, attention, caring, and openness. Studies of affiliative behavior indicate that smiling, head nodding, gesturing, eye contact, and body lean are important nonverbal indicators (Mehrabian, 1970). Minimally then, effective attending behavior involves:

Good Eye Contact The counselor looks the client in the eye. This is not an unwavering stare, which is rather distressing to a recipient. In a helping relationship, eye contact can be maintained for rather lengthy periods of time. Many of us become uncomfortable when someone does not look us in the eye—it can represent a sign of distrust. On the other hand, some clients have been taught that avoiding another person's eyes is a sign of respect. The counselor should be aware of such cultural influences, but it should not affect the counselor's behavior. A study by Ivey et al. (1968) found eye contact to be the most basic ingredient of attending.

Leaning Forward   This posture indicates complete involvement, an "I am ready to work" attitude. Such a position might actually help the counselor listen more effectively.

Open Body Posture   The counselor should avoid crossing arms or legs. Body language experts tell us crossed arms indicate a withholding of self to some degree.

Facing the Client Squarely   Such a position maximizes counselor involvement. Carkhuff (1977) states, "One way of posturing ourselves to attend to the helpee is to face her fully. Whether standing or sitting, we may turn to the helpee and face her squarely—our left shoulder to her right shoulder and vice versa. . . . See how differently we feel about the helpee when we posture ourselves in this manner from how we feel when we posture ourselves for our own purposes" (p. 34).

Friendly and/or Appropriate Facial Expression   Initially, the counselor's facial expression should be friendly; later it should reflect appropriate emotional affect. A smile is likely to be well-received by a new client.

Suspended Value Judgments   Expressions of shock, dismay, or disgust have little place in the counseling setting. The counselor may offer personal values for consideration in later stages of counseling, but they are never imposed.

Absence of Counselor Distractions   The counselor should be aware of and minimize any personally distracting physical mannerisms (for example, hair twirling). A major advantage of video-taping counselors-in-training is that it allows counselors to quickly note any distracting mannerisms they may not be aware of (see Figures 11.1 and 11.2).

In summary, the optimal attending position includes eye contact, facing the helpee squarely, leaning forward, assuming an appropriate facial expression, and nodding one's head (see Figure 11.2). No barriers should be present, but a desk or table might be off to the side. The counselor does not maintain a rigid position, but is relaxed. It might be most effective to initiate counseling with a less intense attending position (not leaning fully forward), since some clients react defensively to the optimal attending position. Once the client begins to discuss meaningful material, the counselor may, however, move to the maximally effective position. The effective counselor will also learn to relate attending position to emotional intensity. For example, if after a light moment, the counselor wants to indicate "Let's get back to

Figure 11.1 Minimally Effective
Attending Position

Figure 11.2 Maximally Effective
Attending Position

work," he might lean fully forward. We might conclude by noting that the absence of nonverbal corroboration severely limits the extent to which a message is judged as empathic and warm (Haase and Tepper, 1972, p. 423).

Research on Counselor Attending Behavior

Physical Distance   A number of studies have examined the effect of "proxemics," or the physical distance between counselor and client. Proxemic preference largely reflects cultural bias and can influence the reception of verbal communication. Hall (1959) related personal distance with purpose of the communication act (p. 209). (See Table 11.1.) Most individuals prefer to sit opposite each other when the distance is equal to or less

Table 11.1
Relationship of Space and Communication in the American Culture

Distance	*Communication Act and Purpose*
1. Very close (3 in. to 6 in.)	Soft whisper; top secret
2. Close (8 in. to 12 in.)	Audible whisper; very confidential
3. Near (12 in. to 20 in.)	Indoors, soft voice; outdoors, full voice; confidential
4. Neutral (20 in. to 36 in.)	Soft voice, low volume; personal subject matter
5. Neutral (4½ ft. to 5 ft.)	Full voice; information of nonpersonal matter
6. Public distance (5½ ft. to 8 ft.)	Full voice with slight overloudness; public information for others to hear
7. Across the room (8 ft. to 20 ft.)	Loud voice; talking to a group
8. Stretching the limits of distance	20 ft. to 24 ft. indoors; up to 100 ft. outdoors; hailing distance, departures

Source: Chart from THE SILENT LANGUAGE by Edward T. Hall. Copyright © 1959 by Edward T. Hall. Reprinted by permission of Doubleday & Company, Inc.

than a side-by-side position (Sommer, 1959). Haase and DiMattia (1970) found that the most preferred illustrated seating position among counselors, administrators, and clients was one that depicted individuals interacting over the corner of a desk (see Figure 11.3).

On the other hand, Broekmann and Moller (1973) found that individuals may prefer a more formal seating position under unfamiliar circumstances, whereas a more informal position is preferred under more familiar circumstances. Lott and Sommer (1967) observed that people sat further from higher- and lower-status individuals than from peers.

Interaction distance, then, can play an important role. Haase (1970) found students preferred distances of 30, 39, and 50 inches. Greater distances were perceived to be significantly less preferable.

Greene (1977) found that physical proximity strengthened adherence to a counselor's recommendations when accepting feedback was offered and lowered compliance when neutral feedback was expressed. Dinges and Oetting (1972) looked at the relationship between distance and anxiety. Females at all distances responded with greater anxiety than males. Nearer distances of 30 inches and greater distances of 88 inches received the highest-anxiety ratings, while intermediate distances received significantly

Figure 11.3
Optimal
Client-Counselor
Attending Positions

lower-anxiety ratings. Individuals who are submissive, dependent, and display socially correct behavior, self-control, and consideration of others prefer greater distances between chairs (Broekmann and Moller, 1973). Dominant, self-assured, and independent-minded persons who show less social correctness, self-control, and consideration prefer middle and nearer distances. Graves and Robinson (1976) looked at proxemic behavior as it relates to inconsistent verbal and nonverbal messages. Inconsistent messages were associated with greater interpersonal distances, especially when the nonverbal messages were negative and the verbal messages were positive. Such inconsistent messages, the researchers felt, were interpreted as deceiving and dishonest.

Physical touch appears to have some impact on client evaluations of counseling. Aguilera (1967) found touching between staff and psychiatric patients increased approach behaviors. In addition, Pattison (1973) reported increased self-disclosure in females touched by counselors when compared with controls. Alagna et al. (1979) reported that clients who were touched evaluated counseling more positively than no-touch controls. Stronger effects occurred when the clients were touched by opposite-sex counselors. While these studies report the positive effects of touching in counseling, counselor-client touch might raise other issues, such as transference, that would have to be dealt with in counseling.

Facial Expression and Nodding   Facial expression and head nodding play a role in the counseling dialogue. Smiling, for instance, can communicate "I enjoy meeting you." Head nodding is appropriate, as long as it is not used to manipulate the counselee. Counselor nonverbal behaviors are potent reinforcers. In fact, research has shown that client nonverbal behaviors can reinforce counselor behaviors (Lee et al., 1979). Tepper and Haase (1978) found that (1) nonverbal cues accounted for significantly greater message variance than did the verbal message, and (2) vocal intonation and facial expression proved to be significant contributors to final judgments of facilitative conditions. They found it notable that the facial expression cue played such a dominant role in the communication of empathy, respect, and genuineness. Hill et al. (1981) stressed that counselor nonverbal-verbal congruence was significantly related to counseling outcome, while nonverbal abilities and behaviors alone were not. Seay and Altekruse (1979) also found that nonverbal behaviors were related to facilitative counseling conditions, but the relationship was complex and was modified by the verbal style of the counselor.

Hackney (1974) hypothesized that (1) expressionless stimulus would produce low levels of self-expression of feelings, (2) a smile would produce significantly higher levels of self-expressed feelings, and (3) the combination of a smile and a nod would produce optimum levels of expressed feeling. The hypotheses were supported for females receiving a female presenter. Female subjects, though, were more uncertain when confronted with nonverbal behavior from a male. The writer concluded that "female subjects may be more responsive to another female who gives nonverbal feedback, particularly when that feedback contains an affect display such as a smile" (p. 177). D'Augelli (1974) found a low but significant relationship between nonverbal behaviors in helpers and how others viewed their helping. Smiling and nodding were most consistently related to performance. Smiling helpers were viewed as warm, while nodding indicated empathic understanding. The researcher noted that the small correlations suggested that nonverbal attending was but one of many cues to which helpees respond (p. 363).

A study by Hill and Gormally (1977) asserted that time of introduction of nodding and smiling by the counselor could be important. They found that these two nonverbal counselor behaviors did not affect discussion of feelings when the counselors engaged in these behaviors after some time had passed in counseling. They concluded, "Because the later introduction of nodding and smiling did not significantly increase the production of affective self-referents, it may be critical to establish these behaviors in the initial period of the interview" (p. 97).

A comprehensive study of nonverbal behavior was completed by La-Crosse (1975). He defined affiliative nonverbal manner as including smiles, positive head nods, gesticulations (movement of hands not in contact with other body parts), 80 percent eye contact, direct shoulder orientation (0 percent angle), and a 20 percent forward body lean. Unaffiliative nonverbal behavior included 40 percent eye contact, 20 percent reclining angle, 30 percent shoulder angle away, and none of the other categories. Results indicated that counselors in the affiliative role were perceived to be significantly more attractive and persuasive than their unaffiliative counterparts. Active counselors were also viewed as more attractive. Siegel (1980) found that counselor attending behavior even affected client perceived expertness ratings. They concluded that counselors who choose not to display appropriate nonverbal behaviors hinder their own counseling efforts.

Body Position and Movement   While studying the effects of nonverbal counselor behavior, Smith-Hanen (1977) controlled for movement, four arm positions, and six leg positions. She found counselor movement had no significant effect on the judged levels of warmth and empathy, but arm and leg positions did. The arms-crossed position was rated as coldest and least empathic. Leg positions had more complex distinctions. The position in which one leg is crossed over the other with the ankle of the crossed leg resting on the knee of the opposite leg was judged coldest and least empathic; the position in which legs are crossed at the knees was not rated as cold or empathic.

Genther and Moughan (1977) looked at the responses of introverts and extroverts to helper nonverbal behavior, in this case leaning forward compared to sitting upright. All individuals rated the forward attending posture as more attentive. Extroverts viewed the listener in the upright position as even more threatening than did the introverts. In no case was the listener in the forward attending posture rated more negatively than the listener sitting upright. Fretz et al. (1979) examined the effects of eye contact, direct body orientation, and forward lean on client evaluations. Subjects rated male and female counselors who provided high levels of these nonverbal behaviors as more attractive and facilitative.

Cash et al. (1975) found a physically attractive counselor was perceived more favorably in such areas as intelligence, friendliness, assertiveness, trustworthiness, competence, warmth, and likeability than the opposite. Cash (1974) noted more self-disclosure occurred with attractive strangers than unattractive ones. Goldstein (1971) had concluded earlier that attraction to the counselor by the client attenuates client covert resistance and increases commitment to therapy. Counselor "physical attractiveness alone may be sufficient to cue client judgments of competence and likeability" (Cash et al., 1975, p. 277). Finally, Strong et al. (1971) found that counselors with greater frequencies of nonverbal movements received higher ratings in perceived attractiveness than counselors who evidenced low frequencies of movements.

Expertness can to some degree mask "unattractiveness" or poor attending. Strong and Dixon (1971), concluding their study, wrote, "Obviously, if one must be an unattractive, discourteous fellow, one had better be an expert" (p. 570). In their research, Strong and Dixon described the unattractive role as follows: "His face was expressionless; he did not smile; he occasionally covered his face with his hands and rubbed his eyes to indicate boredom. He often turned to the side rather than directly toward the subject and occasionally looked at material on his desk and made notes on it" (p. 563). Poor attending? Indeed. One subject stated, "I felt like getting up and walking out so as not to waste my time or his" (pp. 569–570). Two others commented, "I should have busted him in the nose just for the hell of it" (p. 570).

Observing Nonverbal Behavior

Communication occurs on both verbal and nonverbal levels. The latter may not be as easily understood as the former, but it is observable and measurable. Nonverbal behavior can have a more important meaning than what is conveyed by words. Since the totality of nonverbal cues at any moment can be highly complex, it is important that a single behavior not be taken out of context.

Communication is continually taking place with or without words. While many people believe that this is a recent revelation of the body language researchers, Freud (1959) commented in 1905, "He that has eyes to see and ears to hear may convince himself that no mortal can keep a secret. If his lips are silent, he chatters with his finger-tips; betrayal oozes out of him at every pore" (p. 94).

Types of Nonverbal Behavior   Both nonverbal (kinesis) and paralinguistic behaviors, which are defined below, convey important messages in any relationship. They are an important part of a total message.

Paralanguage is some kind of articulation of the vocal apparatus, or significant lack of it, i.e., hesitation between segments of vocal articulation. This includes all noises and sounds which are extra-speech sounds, such as hissing, shushing, whistling, and imitation sounds, as well as a large variety of speech modification, such as quality of voice (sepulchral, whiney, giggling), extra high-pitched utterance, or hesitation and speed in talking. . . . *Kinesis* is articulation of the body or movements resulting from muscular and skeletal shift. This includes all actions, physical or physiological, automatic reflexes, posture, facial expressions, gestures, and other body movements. (Key, 1975, pp. 128–129)

Nonverbal behavior can emphasize an emotional quality or, on the other hand, negate the verbalized emotional message. It can confirm or deny what has been said. We often tend to forget this. We need only observe the interaction between a puppy and its owner to recognize the importance of paralinguistic and nonverbal behaviors.

Cultural background influences nonverbal and paralinguistic behavior. In America, with its diverse ethnic communities, such messages between people of different upbringing can easily be misinterpreted. Certain individuals might have been taught to suppress hand or facial expression, while others may not show emotional response. We generally find that Arabs tend to stand closer, while Orientals tend to touch more and speak louder. Tactile relationships in America are minimized, perhaps due to their sexual overtones and our puritan heritage.

Identification of nonverbal behavior and the ascription of meaning to such behavior ranges from idiosyncratic to highly systematized interpretations. Feldman (1959) and Sielski (1979) considered certain meanings to be attached to the following mannerisms:

Erect head: feelings of esteem, pride, confidence, courage.
Bowed head: humility, resignation, shame, submission.
Touching nose: anxiety, stage fright, doubt, puzzlement.
Rapid eye-blinking: mechanism of displacement.
Artificial cough: criticism, doubt, surprise, anxiety.
Whistling or humming: genuine or faked self-confidence.
Fixing neckties: emphasizing masculinity.
Pressing head with hands: despair, helplessness.
Placing head between two palms: feeling sad or exhausted, thinking.
Placing index finger along the nose: suspicion.

Closing nostrils with fingers: contempt.
Closing ears with hands: unwillingness to listen.
Putting arms akimbo: firmness.
Crossing arms over chest: "straightjacket," defensiveness, rejection.
Outstretched arms: call attention, surprise, alarm, blessing.
Forming ring with fingers: unity, perfection.
Rubbing thumb and middle finger: search for solution.
Finger or knuckle cracking: hostility, aggressiveness, frustration.
Playing with ring or handbag: release of tensions or decision making.
Embarrassed hands: suppression of bad habits.
Hands at sides: openness.
Chin stroking: evaluation
Clenched hands with thumbs rubbing against each other: reassurance.
Hands outstretched, palms up: helplessness, resignation.
Lip biting: nervousness.
Finger drumming or foot tapping: boredom, waning interest.

Nonverbal behavior is generally related to either the verbal communication or the emotional experience of the speaker. Sielski (1979) states that a certain gesture does not have the same meaning "all the time. Body language, just as spoken language, can be accurately understood only in the context of the entire behavior pattern of a person" (p. 240).

Nonverbal behavior tends to increase with the emotional involvement of the individual. Kagan et al. (1965) have reported their extensive research on gestures—arm and hand movements and postural movements. They found that there were variations of awareness in clients.

1. *Awareness* Client is aware of behavior and means to use it.
2. *Potential Awareness* Client knows of behavior if attention is called to it.
3. *Lack of Awareness* Client is unaware of behavior and is oblivious of the action even if attention is called to it.

They found that, while overt gestures might last only a short period of time, the emotional state that produced them is of greater length. Furthermore, they identified six types of nonverbal behaviors:

1. *Emphasis* Brief gestures designed to stress a point. Generally, the client is unaware of them due to the short duration of time over which they extend.
2. *Facilitation* Gestures that attempt to clarify and help the speaker with word-release.
3. *Portrayal* Such gestures are designed to give examples or illustrations of such comments as "The fish was this big."
4. *Revelation-Unaware* Unconscious gestures that arise from intense feelings.

5. *Revelation-Aware* Gestures that the client acknowledges as habitual, rather than associated with any particular tension.
6. *Affect Demonstration* Behaviors deliberately designed to show feelings. They can be deceptive, or they can be a sincere display to help the counselor understand.

Nonverbal behavior has also been studied in counselors. While smiling, head nodding, and other nonverbal communicative gestures in isolation rarely constitute a large portion of conversation, Matarazzo and Wiens (1972) did report that head nodding and saying "mm-hmmm" did increase the duration of utterances in speakers. They also found that if interviewers increased the duration of their own utterances, a corresponding increase occurred in the duration of speaking of the interviewee. The increase in duration of speaking by the interviewer was interpreted as increased interest in the session (p. 94). Packwood (1974) reported that counselor loudness was a characteristic ingredient of persuasion. Costanzo et al. (1969) reported on voice quality profile and perceived emotion and found that peak-pitch voices were judged as portraying grief, peak-loudness voices as anger or contempt, and peak-tempo voices as indifference.

Kennedy and Zimmer (1968) looked at the reinforcing value of expressions such as "mm-hmm," "Good," "I see," and a paraphrase. They concluded that "the paraphrase and the neutrally toned 'mm-hmm' utterance were shown to be effective reinforcers . . . while the use of 'mm-hmm' with affirming head nod and smile and the 'I see' verbalization were clearly ineffective in promoting operant production" (p. 361). They concluded: "The assumption that specific utterances, such as 'mm-hmm,' 'Good,' 'I see,' etc., are equally effective and therefore can be casually incorporated into more general statements of reinforcement does not appear tenable" (p. 361).

In summary, it is important to recognize the importance of nonverbal behaviors by both counselees and counselors to their relationship. Such behavior should be noted in context and responded to. Both paralinguistic and nonverbal client behaviors provide rich resources to respond to. At the same time, counselors should be aware of their own nonverbal behavior and respond to it accordingly.

Observation   Observation is important to counselors. Client behavior is a rich source of information. Individuals have been taught to disguise verbal messages, but generally not their behavior. Physical messages are difficult to hide, because they are involuntary reactions of the autonomic nervous system. Facial expression alone accounts for 55 percent of a message (Mehrabian, 1968). Observation of behavior, then, provides a wealth of material to which counselors may respond and is a skill that can facilitate client awareness and congruence. It also allows for immediate feedback on the progress of counseling. Galvin and Ivey (1981), while noting the importance of attending behavior, implicitly suggest the crucial nature of observation by the counselor. They write, "More skilled professionals may demonstrate effective attending skills but may find it useful to concentrate on points where eye contact is broken, a noticeable body shift occurs. . . . In this way, the counselor can search for a pattern of breaks in the interview that may point to more significant data" (p. 537). This observation could relate to the client or to the counselor's own behavior.

There are certain difficulties in the use of observation. The two most important ones are counselor bias, or distortion, and poor insight. Observation is selective, and too often counselors respond only to behaviors that support what they believe. They tend to disregard evidence contrary to their beliefs. Excellent examples of this can be found in marital discord. A spouse may see a great number of "negatives" in the partner, and through selective observation and distortion, build up over the years a number of examples for each general negative. There is total disregard for any behavior to the contrary. It is sometimes quite an eye opener for a husband or a wife to hear a different opinion of the spouse by a friend or an acquaintance.

Many of us are also handicapped by being raised in a culture that emphasizes response to verbal cues and disregard for nonverbal ones. As a result, the insights provided by observation are questionable. They may become too global or they may simply be misinterpretations. It takes much practice to develop the degree of skill necessary to use observation effectively.

Using Behavioral Cues to Make Observations

Effective observation involves two steps. First, the observation of specific behavioral cues by the counselor and, second, the drawing of an inference based on the specific behaviors. Observations can be rated for effectiveness on a continuum according to how conducive they are to client growth. (See Figure 11.4.)

Low-level observations should be generally avoided, for they contribute

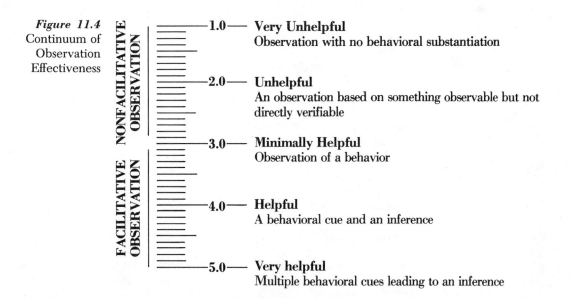

Figure 11.4 Continuum of Observation Effectiveness

NONFACILITATIVE OBSERVATION

1.0 — **Very Unhelpful**
Observation with no behavioral substantiation

2.0 — **Unhelpful**
An observation based on something observable but not directly verifiable

3.0 — **Minimally Helpful**
Observation of a behavior

FACILITATIVE OBSERVATION

4.0 — **Helpful**
A behavioral cue and an inference

5.0 — **Very helpful**
Multiple behavioral cues leading to an inference

little to the counseling session. At their worst they can be quite destructive. Clients confronted with such poor observations might leave counseling because of their dismay with the counselor. Observations with no behavioral substantiation are overgeneralizations or whims of the counselor. They have no justification in basis of fact. Counselors at times justify such observations by saying, "My third sense just told me." Following is an illustration of the use of a very poor observation. It occurred within the first 10 minutes of an initial interview. The 16-year-old client did not return for counseling, even though her referral form indicated she needed a great deal of help.

Client: I've settled back in at school, though, for the past two weeks. The teachers are trying to be helpful. In fact, one of the teachers brought me here to the center for counseling today, because I do not have any transportation. My parents have let up a bit, too. I guess they were quite upset to think that their little girl might actually run away from home. I'm going to try a little harder to get along. [She smiles.]
Counselor: I notice a great deal of fear in your eyes.
Client: Fear? No, not really.
Counselor: Well, they're beautiful eyes anyway.

The observation of fear had no substantiation in either a verbal or behavioral context. When the observation was rejected by the client, the counselor attempted to rescue himself by commenting on the attractiveness of the client's eyes. Undoubtedly the response, which changed the subject of conversation, completely detracted from the progress of the session.

More effective observations are based on specific behavioral cues, which can lead to more abstract observations involving the client's immediate feelings. The observation of specific behaviors, such as finger- and foot-tapping, rapid speech, and frequent looking at a wristwatch, can lead to an inference of the client being impatient or needing to be elsewhere. Such an inference can then be "checked out" with the client, possibly encouraging the client's expression of a concern that is impeding client-counselor interaction. The counselor can respond to a variety of client behaviors:

Facial Expression

Client: That last statement made me think about when I was a kid. My parents would make me go along with them to visit my grandparents.
Counselor: Are you aware that you are smiling?
Client: Yeah. I would have a pretty good time once I got there. My grandfather and I would play cards for hours on end and the meals that we would have were great.

Mannerisms

Client: Jim really resented it when I would say no. He periodically would blow off some steam about a wife's duty and that kind of thing. He even kept count of the number of times we had slept together over a six-month period. It shocked me—you know, how infrequently we did have intercourse.

Counselor: Jane, I've noticed that for the past few minutes you haven't looked at me. You have been looking at the floor. Your face has turned red also.

Client: I am really embarrassed talking about this. I really didn't know if I was going to be able to talk about our sex life, but in the first few years of marriage, you could say the lack of it created more fights than anything else.

Energy Level

Client: [Has entered the room, sat down in his chair in a rather slumped fashion.]

Counselor: You really look like you're dragging.

Client: Oh, man, you better believe it. School days are getting to be too much. I've been going since 5:30 this morning until now. I just want to lay down and die.

Noncongruent Behavior

Client: This guy I knew a few years back at the plant—when I was on the line—well, I got word he's had this massive heart attack. He is really laid up. He's the guy I told you about a couple of weeks ago. The one I would go drinking with and get into so much trouble with. It is kind of sad.

Counselor: On the one hand you say it is sad, but on the other you are smiling.

Client: Oh, I'm smiling because the guy turned out to be a bastard. He really kind of deserves everything he gets. What I meant by "sad" is that that was a few years back now, and I get kind of down thinking about how time is flying by. I'm going to be 39 in a couple of months. My kids are getting ready for college. The whole thing scares me.

Counselor: You're really frightened because you are getting older, and you don't know what is in store for you.

In each of the previous illustrations, the counselor used her skills of observation to add to the client's awareness of what is going on inside, rather than writing them down and filing them away, only for her use. Observations can make a definite contribution, since significant revelations might not surface in the client's awareness without them.

In summary, it is important for the counselor to observe and understand nonverbal cues emitted by the client. While most people learn to disguise verbal messages, they are not as able to hide physical signals. Counselor sensitivity to nonverbal cues plays an important role in communication during the helping process. Physical messages should be responded to and understood not only by the counselor but also by the counselee. Emotional data can be quite clearly communicated in a nonverbal fashion. An interesting illustration from a family interaction is described by Wiener et al. (1972):

When the mother leans forward she is flirting with the therapist, when the father taps his foot he is signaling to grandmother and daughter to limit the mother's flirtatiousness; when the grandmother and the daughter cross their legs toward each other they are telling the mother to stop flirting; when the mother leans back she is saying that she understands their message. (p. 198)

We are not necessarily suggesting that counselors interpret nonverbal behavior but rather that they respond to or point out nonverbal behavior in order to facilitate client self-awareness:

Client: I really don't have much to say today. [tapping foot]
Counselor: Do you know that you are tapping your foot?
Client: No. I guess I'm feeling some impatience. [pause] Even more so—some confusion. I don't know what to do. Everything is going sour.

In this instance, a simple "Are you aware?" response moved the client "off center." Observational skills, then, do not have to be mystical to be effective. Counselors can respond to a variety of nonverbal cues in the counselee.

1. *Posture* reflects involvement, interest, and underlying attitudes.
2. *Mannerisms* can reflect feeling behind a statement (or even reactions to counselor verbalizations). Banging a fist on one's knee makes a statement stronger than it might otherwise seem.
3. *Physical energy levels* might well indicate involvement, enjoyment, or depression.
4. *Incongruent behavior* should be quickly responded to by counselors. If a client is discussing a "down" problem and is smiling, the contradictory messages provide a source of data to which the counselor should respond.

At the very least, counselor observations are responses to behavioral data. Effective observations are based on specific client behaviors, which lead to a counselor inference to be checked out with the client. Observations that are totally subjective should be avoided. Not only are effective observations invaluable to counselor verbal responses, but the same guidelines should be followed when observations are to be written up for forwarding to other helpers.

Interacting with the Client Verbally

Listening   If we had to pinpoint a crucial helping skill, it would have to be the ability to listen. Listening is the foundation stone upon which all higher-level helping responses are built. It conveys to clients that they are valued by the counselor. Attending and observing are considered prehelping skills. Listening is the next skill the counselor will use, and in doing so, further respond to clients.

Listening is very hard work. It is difficult to listen for several very important reasons. First, good listening involves focusing on a person other than ourselves. Good listeners are able to forget themselves. They can leave behind their fears, anxieties, angers, and personal involvements irrelevant to the relationship and completely focus on the client. This is not easy to do, since, to ourselves, we are the most important persons in the world. For example, counselors who are anxious about being observed will stop listening and concentrate on making a good response. Then, when they do make a response, it may well appear inappropriate in light of unheard material.

The second barrier to good listening is the speech-thinking rate differential. People speak at about 150–250 words per minute, while people think at three times that speed. Listeners tune the speaker out at certain points, assuming "Well, I've heard this before" or "I know where this is going. I'll come back later." Of course, tuning out backfires on the counselors if the client is "sneaking in" crucial material while their mind is wandering. Ineffective listening often takes on a "tune-in, tune-out, tune-in" pattern. We become selective rather than total listeners.

Listening at deeper levels is even more complicated. Counselors need to be able to get beyond the superficial material, and listen to what may not be specifically stated. In other words, counselors must be constantly "reading between the lines" and responding to what they see there, not just to the superficial content of the client's message. Clients may not be able to verbalize many pertinent feelings, and it is extremely important that counselors listen with "the third ear."

Carkhuff and Pierce (1977) suggest several ways to improve listening skills. First, listen for the important things being said about the self. There should be a reason for listening. This is often not as easy as one might think, since the most important elements need to be inferred in many cases. They are not always directly stated. Sometimes it is what the speaker leaves out, or does not say, that is most important.

Effective attending makes the counselor an active listener. He not only hears the words and the sentences but hears the ways the words and the sentences are being modified by nonverbal and paralinguistic cues. What is the helper listening for? Feelings and content. He wants to know about the experience and behavior of the client and the feelings that suffuse them. His ability to listen underlies his ability to understand the client from the client's frame of reference. Good listening supplies him with the building blocks of accurate empathy. (Egan, 1975, pp. 69–70)

Following is a dialogue with a young lady who harbors a good deal of resentment toward her mother. It should provide an example of listening to what is implied rather than specifically stated:

Client: And say I supposed I do love her because of the fact that I make an effort, you know, on her birthday and Mother's Day, and things like that—get her something. If I didn't get her something—a lot of times I didn't want to—this is the way I felt—but I would because she was my mother. For *sure,* I know I don't like her, but the loving part I don't know.

Counselor: You apparently feel obligated to love her.

Client: Yes, I think that's what . . . It's more obligation I think than love, but I really don't know what that means. If you have to question it, I don't think there's too much of it there. This is the way I feel. If you have to ask yourself, "Do I love this person?" then I don't know how much was really there to begin with. It isn't something you can turn on and turn off. All of a sudden I'm supposed to love my mother? You know, I don't know.

Counselor: It seems that, the way I understand it, that you feel obliged to follow some sort of a program. You have programmed yourself to say, I am my mother's daughter, and therefore I must love my mother, and I must do things that will please her, or things that I view will please her—and you feel inside perhaps some resentment that you're putting this on yourself.

Second, the counselor should suspend judgment, particularly during the initial stage of counseling. Being judgmental interferes with listening. The counselor should allow "the helpee's message to sink in without trying to make decisions about it" (Carkhuff and Pierce, 1977, p. 52). Avoid leaping to conclusions about the helpee. They simply lead us to a biased interpretation of what follows.

Third, in order to focus completely on the client, try to "resist outside distractions." Always minimize such distractions, but if they do occur, it is important to continue to listen intensively.

Fourth, wait to respond. While Carkhuff and Pierce (1977) suggest a 30-second wait before responding, a 10-to-15-second pause after the client has finished is probably sufficient. The short pause allows the listener to formulate the most accurate and concise response. Such pauses also increase client initiative.

Fifth, recall content as you listen. Content recall makes for more effective listening and should be practiced often. While simple content reflection is not a very helpful response, it does at least indicate to the client that the counselor has been attentive (see Chapter 12).

Sixth, and most important, "look for themes" while listening. Intellectualizations, stories, or statistics, while not major themes, do provide the context within which important generalizations of behavior may be found. For example, a client may describe a class in which he was afraid to answer a question, then an argument during which he should have "spoken his mind." Such incidents might well suggest that "When confronted by an authority figure, you seem to withdraw." Such insights lend themselves to program development and behavior change.

Verbal Patterning and Communication Responses

While we have discussed the importance of nonverbal behavior, it is implicit in our position that verbal behavior and patterning is essential to communication. Semanticists study verbal meanings. While obviously unable to provide a basis for completely understanding interpersonal communication, the study of verbal interaction can provide a great many insights. Meara et al. (1979), in their analysis of three approaches to therapy and general expectations about counselor and client stylistic complexity, indicate that it should be possible to investigate many phenomena of counseling by analyzing the structural properties of language.

The nature of speech has been studied for a great number of years. Perhaps, the most extensive research in the anatomy of the interview, as it relates to counseling and therapy, was begun by Matarazzo and Wiens in 1954. They reported on their research in *The Interview* in 1972. They point out that the study of speech has focused upon either what speakers say or how they say it. The former approach, *content analysis,* looks not only at such variables as grammatical usage, but also at the themes being conveyed. While the research of Matarazzo and Wiens is highly technical, it may well be worthwhile to review some of the specific findings that affect counseling dynamics more directly.

Generally, interrupting the counselee has been viewed as negative counselor behavior. Matarazzo and Wiens suggest that this might not always be so. They concluded a section on the interruption variable:

Whereas in our society interrupting behavior often has a negative implication, our research has revealed a positive element. Time after time after time we have observed the highest degree of spirited animation and rapport between our interviewer and his applicant when the former began the interruption segment of the interview. . . . That is, at the present we are conceiving of interruption behavior as possibly constituting another example to the interviewee that the interviewer is interested in him or otherwise fully involved with him. Sensing this the interviewee engages in kind (steps up his own tempo of interaction, resulting in an increase in his own rate of interruption of the interviewer). (pp. 116–117)

Basically, interruption behavior by clients can be modified through counselor behavior. If counselors care to decrease their clients' interruption behavior, the counselors can simply reduce their interruption of the clients. In actuality what Matarazzo and Wiens report is that each of the three speech variables—duration of utterance, reaction time latency (duration of silence from one speaker to next), and interruptions—"can be increased or decreased by a change in kind from the conversational partner" (p. 113). Reaction time latency seems to affect interviewee initiative. They noted that if the interviewer increases reaction time latency from 5 to 15 seconds, the percentage of interviewee initiative increases from 25 percent to 65 percent of the time (p. 45).

Matarazzo and Wiens also studied interviewer style of speaking and its influence on duration of utterance in the interviewee. They compared interviewers who were essentially neutral to interviewers who used interpretive statements. Under conditions of interpretation, there was a "dramatic and statistically significant" drop of 25 percent in the interviewee's mean duration of utterance (p. 131). Interpretive statements certainly produced a high degree of withdrawal and noninvolvement on the part of the interviewees.

One general observation that we have made and that is supported by the Matarazzo and Wiens study is that verbal patterning does establish itself during the period of time the counseling is conducted. For example, we suggest that if a question-and-answer pattern is followed initially, the counselee will continually look for questions to respond to and will provide little initiative or future direction. A set has been established. Further, if the counselor attempts to change this set, the client will resist. What might well develop in establishing a communication style is that the counselee assumes a subrole depending on the interaction and role assumed by the counselor. Seals and Troth (1969) attempted to analyze counselee subrole behavior during a period in the interview in which the verbal behavior of the client was consistent. Judges studied verbatim transcripts of fifty different counselees, and a taxonomy was developed. Ten categories of subroles were established.

Information-giving
Exploration
Passivity
Disconcertation
Information-gathering
Conversational
Defense reaction
Conclusion
Adaptation
Support-seeking

Counselees were found to spend more time playing the exploration subrole than any other respective subrole. It would appear to us that certain subrole behavior could be established—encouraged or discouraged—early in an interview. Along with the establishment of a particular subrole would come specific verbal behaviors that would be difficult to change in the context of the relationship. Troth et al. (1971) supports the applicability of a subrole-counseling-interaction approach as a research tool for studying the counseling interaction.

Clients certainly bring a language pattern with them to counseling. Changes during therapy in a language pattern might well indicate increased client well-being. Goldstein and Sies (1974) suggest that the schizophrenic presents a particular linguistic pattern to the therapist:

[T]he schizophrenic's language should become most disorganized when the topic under discussion is one of personal significance, and less disorganized when the topic has neutral value. (p. 93)

They continue:

In addition to avoiding meaningful communication, the schizophrenic frequently avoids initiating communication and interpersonal interaction with others. Schizophrenic avoidance or passivity can also be observed in their linguistic behavior . . . schizophrenics prefer the impersonal construction in which an idea or concept is preceded by *there are*, i.e., "There are men who. . . ." (pp. 93–94)

Grummon (1950) found that during successful treatment the use of negatives decreased in psychotic individuals. Further, he noted that better adjustment was associated with longer clauses, an increased use of subordinate clauses, and a shift from past-time references to present and future time. Other changes in client language patterns during successful therapy include shifts from self-depreciation and ambivalence toward self to self-approval (Raimy, 1948; Todd and Ewing, 1961), from less nonself-talk to more self-talk (Braaten, 1961), and an increase in feeling words (Berg, 1958). Cope (1969) found a correlation between verbal fluency and psychological health.

In a metalanguage analysis of counselor and client verb usage in counseling, Bieber et al. (1977) found that counselor and client appeared to be "tracking" each other in the use of verb types. Initial verb usage identified the client as the agent of some action, while later verb usage identified the client with an inner state of feeling, sensing, or knowing. The phenomena suggested that counselor and client are involved in "concerted activity." Bieber et al. suggested further research into linguistic structure and the counseling process.

It is not enough to look at the flow of the speech pattern and verbal behavior from counselor to client. The impact of the client's verbal behavior on the counselor also needs to be understood. While Matarazzo and Wiens contend that interviewers influence the verbal behavior of the interviewee in a variety of ways, including manipulation of response latencies, there is also support for the contention that the interviewee can influence the interviewer (Lauver et al., 1971). The speech behaviors of both participants in counseling are interdependent and are contingent on each other. The study of Lauver et al. (1971) indicated that a client "was able to unobtrusively effect change in the speech and silence behavior of counselors" (p. 26). They went on to suggest that, while Matarazzo and Wiens consider reinforcement and modeling as possible means to modify client speech characteristics, their study more easily supported "reinforcement than modeling as the mechanism of change" (p. 29). They did not suggest, however, that modeling should be ruled out as a modifier. They wrote, "Modeling may account most economically for client-counselor concordance, but reinforcement seems a more potent explanation" (pp. 29–30).

Modeling behavior can affect communication. One study was designed to look at the influence of peer modeling behavior on the avoidance of communication in counseling sessions (Smith and Lewis, 1974). Avoidance of communication was considered to be superficial talk, hostile remarks, preoccupation with "side" issues, or intellectualizations. Smith and Lewis found that the observation of a peer model, participating in counseling on video tape, was effective in reducing avoidance behaviors.

Counselor verbal styles affect therapist effectiveness, since they influence client behavior. Even at the simplest level (say, amount of counselor talk), it was found that counselors with low amounts of talking are evaluated most favorably on a liking dimension, while counselors with high amounts of talking are evaluated most strongly on a domineering dimension (Kleinke and Tully, 1979).

Counselor verbal behavior, while not the only variable, is an important determinant of such important factors as counseling climate, client participation, and interview pace. Training counselors in verbal interaction analysis can have an influence, then, on client behavior.

Use of Questions in Counseling

Questions, by themselves, are generally of no real therapeutic value in counseling. They are unlikely to be perceived as anything but the gathering of information (Elliott, 1979). This does not mean that questions are not asked by the counselor. The important point to be made is that it is the responses to the answers of the questions that can become helpful. Counselors often ask too many questions. This results in an interview that is counselor-directed and disjointed. Such sessions resemble police interrogation. How old are you? How many brothers and sisters do you have? Do you like school? How long have you lived in Detroit? Do you like the Jones School better than the Smith School? Hill and Gormally (1977) note that "questions contain demand characteristics for answering" and that too often questions do not typically elicit feelings from clients (p. 97).

Too frequent question-asking often is engaged in by insecure counselors who (1) do not know how else to respond, (2) want to fill in information gaps, or (3) want to protect themselves from making an inaccurate reflection. Often the result is that clients assume their counselors are gathering information in order to solve detailed problems later or that the counselors are dumb or insensitive for not knowing the answer that has already been supplied—albeit subtly. Shertzer and Stone (1980) state, "The overuse of questions in personal counseling runs the risk of causing the counselees to conceptualize the situation as an inquisition in which they need only sit back and direct their thinking along the lines indicated by the questions" (p. 274).

There is a difference between poor questions and good questions. Poor questions are content-oriented rather than feeling-oriented. They can be answered simply and provide clients with little growth in insight. Poor questions (Do you go to school? How old are you?) are closed-ended and require only short answers. Good questions help clients to gain insight or stimulate them to think further. Questions are justified if they get clients "started" or suggest more fruitful topics for discussion. Questions may be scaled from 1 to 5 for rating purposes:

1.0   Distracting. Irrelevant. Detracts from counseling.
2.0   Related to content of subject under discussion.
2.5   Related to feeling ("How does that make you feel?")
3.0   Asks about feeling and meaning.
3.5   Directs attention to a deficiency of the counselee.
4.0   Asks about client's goals.
5.0   Action- or behavior-change oriented. Helps client to look at alternatives.

Galvin and Ivey (1981) distinguish between closed and open questions.

Closed question: Leads to short answers on the part of the client. Often begins with "is," "do," "are," or a similar stem.

Open question: Allows more client talk time. Typically begins with "what," "how," "why," or "could." Special note: The sentence stem is a useful clue as to whether or not a question is open or closed, but the actual content of the question may override the stem. The major issue is whether or not the question encourages more client talk. (p. 539)

Ehrlich et al. (1979) identified six counselor verbal responses: affect, content, influencing, advice, open question, and closed question. They found that open questions elicited the longest client responses and the second highest percentage of present tense verbs. Conversely, closed questions were generally ranked lowest on various dependent measures. The counselor who used closed questions was rated very low on the attractiveness, expertness, and trustworthiness dimensions. Professional counselors are more likely to use open questions, while untrained counselors are more likely to resort to direct guidance (Howell and Highlen, 1981).

While counselors often recognize the importance of not asking frequent questions in later stages of counseling, they tend to ask many questions during the first session. This may reflect the desire to "get to know" the client and a certain amount of nervousness. This is done with the good intention of stopping the questions once "the client feels at ease." Counselors need to recognize, though, that the initial session establishes a particular verbal pattern that is difficult to break—a pattern that also reflects the status of each person in the relationship. If the pattern that gets established is question-answer, a superior-inferior relationship is implied. Such a pattern may be very resistant to change later. Practicum students often emerge from a first counseling contact to be told by their supervisors that they have asked too many questions. They return the next week to find that the client does not respond without being asked a question.

Silence   Silence in the interview can have any number of provocations. Myers and Myers (1973) suggest several types of silences. We have tried to adapt them to specific representations in counseling.

1. Silence reflects anger, frustration, and tension. It is a withholding of the expression of these feelings. This occurs quite frequently in counseling when the client does not want to be there.
2. Silence can indicate intense listening to an interesting story.
3. Silence also indicates listening to something that is boring. Clients may become bored by lack of movement and, as a result, withdraw into silence.
4. Silence occurs when one cannot think of something to say.
5. Silence occurs when thinking about something said. Perhaps this is the type of silence that most often occurs—the counselor has responded and the client is silent while thinking about the response.
6. Silence can represent a lack of understanding of what was said.
7. Silence can indicate meditation or contemplation.
8. Silence can also mean "Enough said. The topic has been exhausted."
9. Silence can occur between close friends or lovers. It can suggest a certain warmth or comfort at being near the counselor.
10. Grief can be portrayed by silence. For example, the client may become silent after talking about the death of someone close. Other painful feelings that surface can also cause the client to resort to silence.
11. Silence can also be a nonverbal challenge. It is as if the client is saying, "Go ahead and see if you can help me. I dare you." It can also be an attempt to wait out the counselor.

Obviously, silence means many things. Silence is also a technique to be used by the counselor, although it is difficult to know when to use it. Silence, however, can be quite therapeutic (in 5, 7, and 9 above, this is particularly true). Silence too often carries only a negative connotation. Because our culture has taught us to be uncomfortable with silence, counselors often avoid any possibility of silence in an interview. We remember one counselor who, after an interview, said, "I couldn't stand those interminable silences." His supervisor asked him to go through the tape with a stopwatch and time the length of each silent period. The counselor was quite embarrassed to report that the longest silence was eight seconds.

Silence has several beneficial values. Brammer and Shostrom (1968) point out that (1) silence makes the client talk, (2) some introversive people may find that they can be quiet and still be liked, (3) silence allows the client to think and gain insights, and (4) silence slows the pace of the session (pp. 214–215).

Generally, the counselor should allow the client to break a period of silence, particularly if it has been introduced by the client. Obvious sensitivity is called for. If the counselor can see that the client is embarrassed or uncomfortable, the counselor may want to break the silence. This should not develop into a contest. The counselor may want to try such statements as "That seems to puzzle you" or "It's pretty hard to respond to that."

The counselor has to become comfortable with periods of silence. A certain amount of time should be allowed to pass for the client to respond. This should be true of the first interview as well as of later sessions. If the impression is created in the initial session that the counselor will "rescue" the client from any silence, a pattern will become established that will be hard to change later. Once the client becomes comfortable and recognizes a certain amount of responsibility for either continuing or discontinuing the silence, quiet periods may provide some of the values cited earlier.

Tindall and Robinson (1947) classified pauses by counselors providing educational skills into three types. The first was the deliberate pause designed to achieve some emphasis. The second type was the organizational pause designed to effect transition. The third type was natural termination used to close counseling. Howell and Highlen (1981) examined the effects of counselors' experience on their verbal responses. They found that both untrained and professional counselors employed silence as an initial response. Their reliance on silence, however, most likely occurred for different reasons. Untrained counselors seemed confused about what to say, whereas professional counselors may have employed silence to process the clients' statements.

Silence, like talking, does not necessarily lead to insight. However, silence, within the proper context and with appropriate counselor interventions, can have beneficial results, such as fostering insight or responsibility in the client. The latter benefit, ironically, can lead to feelings quite opposite from the nature of silence itself—such as responsibility for interview progress, which can cause them to talk more. Too often the more frequent the counselor's leads, the less clients talk (Carnes and Robinson, 1948).

Transference

Transference can be a major consideration in the early stages of counseling. Transference and countertransference are discussed a great deal in psychoanalytical literature but are infrequently touched on in counseling books. Yet, both occur quite frequently in counseling relationships. Transference involves clients feeling and acting toward the counselor as they did to other individuals in the past (mother or father, for example). Brammer and Shostrom (1968) point out that "in a broad sense, the term refers to any feelings expressed or felt by the client toward the therapist, whether a rational reaction to the personality of the therapist or the unconscious projection of earlier attitudes and stereotypes" (pp. 232–233). We believe, however, that transference should not refer to all of the client's feelings toward the counselor, but only to feelings that arise from past interpersonal experiences with significant personages. A certain degree of irrationality is present.

[I]n the analytical situation the patient not only talks about his present and past troubles, but also shows emotional reactions to the analyst. These reactions are frequently irrational in character. A patient may forget entirely his purpose in coming to analysis and may find nothing important except being bored or appreciated by the analyst. He may develop altogether disproportionate fears about jeopardizing his relationship to the analyst. He may transform the situation, which in actuality is one in which the analyst helps the patient to straighten out his problems, into one of passionate struggle for the upper hand . . . he may react with violent anger. A patient may, contrary to his own interest, secretly pursue the purpose of defeating the analyst's endeavors. (Hendrick, 1958, p. 193)

Transferences can be either positive or negative. The former are friendly, while the latter are unfriendly. Colby (1951) distinguishes between transference improvement and aggravation:

A "transference improvement" consists of rapid amelioration of the patient's neurosis due to the particular nature and intensity of his transference onto the therapist. For example, a patient who equates neurosis with punishment for sins may give it up to win the approval awarded by a loving protector in the person of the re-edited parent, the therapist. A "transference aggravation" refers to an increase in the neurosis brought on by the type of transference made by the patient. For instance, if the patient anticipates physical contact with the therapist, the frustration of this desire may heighten her presenting symptoms. (pp. 107–108)

The therapist may become a rival, an "ideal" role model, a source of authority, or a parent. Pietrofesa et al. (1978) point to several signs that indicate transference:

1. The counselee displays likes or dislikes out of proportion to the situation.
2. The counselee may show too much interest in the counselor or overemphasize a counselor trait. He/she may display over-concern for the counselor's welfare.
3. The counselee may not be able to focus upon any concern. He/she may continually misunderstand what the counselor is saying.
4. The counselee may engage in attention-seeking behaviors, e.g., continual tardiness or illness. (p. 98)

Transferences are generally a combination of the above rather than representative of a single category. They are basic to analysis, since they give evidence of prior neurotic relationships. They then develop into major focal points in therapy.

Psychotherapists traditionally make use of transference in two ways:

First, by evaluating what transference role the patient is forming, the therapist gains understanding of what is being relived and re-experienced rather than being remembered. Secondly, the therapist may confront the patient with a transference to show him something he is unaware of or to overcome a resistance. (Colby, 1951, p. 113)

We do feel strongly that the counselor response should facilitate the client's ability to understand and cope with the feelings of transference. If a transference forms, it does in fact reveal many unresolved conflicts, fears, and biases.

Particular types of counseling relationships are more conducive to transference. The relationship in which counselors are authoritarian and appear to be experts is directive and may precipitate more transference feelings than a more equalitarian relationship. Generally, for a transference to continue over a period of time, counselors must also assume the role—play the mother or father figure. If counselors discourage transference feelings, they are not likely to arise in a close relationship. This is particularly true when counselors engage in self-disclosure. The more clients know their counselors, recognize the counselors' feelings, and perceive them as unique individuals, the less likely transference will develop. The more aloof and distant counselors are, the more the opposite is true.

We suggest several steps in dealing with transference feelings:

1. *Consider the client a person of worth and dignity.* The counselor must truly display positive regard.
2. *Engage in self-disclosure:* If the client truly perceives the counselor's uniqueness, the client is not likely to see the counselor as someone from the past.
3. *It is important to recognize transference feelings when they appear and not to encourage them.* It is sometimes difficult for counselors not to be flattered by the additional attention they receive from positive transference feelings. But if they encourage them, the transference will continue and will eventually foster negative feelings.
4. *Accept, clarify, reflect, and interpret the feelings of transference.* The counselor helps the client recognize and take responsibility for the transference (Pietrofesa et al., 1978, p. 98). Counselor responses can help the client see the irrationality of the displaced perceptions.
5. *Ignore positive transferences (and they will likely dissipate),* but respond to negative ones.

Countertransference refers to unconscious feelings brought out in the counselor as a result of the feelings of transference displayed by the client.

The counselor may want to please, become jealous, or "fall in love." Excessive concern over success with a client can also give evidence of feelings of countertransference. These feelings need to be resolved, for "counseling is for the client not the therapist."

Terminating Counseling

Termination considerations involve (1) bringing an interview to a close, and (2) ending a series of contacts with a client.

Terminating a Counseling Session

We have discussed some aspects of termination in the previous sections on structure and initiating an interview. It was suggested that a reference to time limits could make it easier to conclude a counseling session. Time limits should be clearly established during the initial interview.

There are various other devices the counselor can utilize to conclude a session. Summary statements can be useful. The general feeling tone and direction of the interview can be synthesized. Or the client could well be asked to summarize the day's session. The phrase "Perhaps, you could summarize for me how you feel about today's session" can be used. Summaries help to clear up any possible misunderstandings that have developed. One brief note, however, about the use of summary statements to begin a counseling session is in order. We generally feel that it is unwise to summarize a previous session at the beginning of an interview. This is essentially counselor direction and may well take the client far afield from a more pressing concern.

Nonverbal gestures can be used, such as looking at a watch or simply standing up. If the client is engaged in decision making or problem solving, action-oriented strategies or alternatives might well be suggested (see Chapter 13).

Terminating a Series of Counseling Sessions

The decision to terminate a counseling contact can be made by the client or, in some cases, the counselor. Toward the end of counseling, client responses become quite positive. Clients begin to give verbal cues that they are considering termination with such statements as, "I feel I've come a long way." The client may well hesitate to actually suggest discontinuation, since there is probably some discomfort at ending a very close relationship. The counselor, then, may suggest ending the relationship. The counselor can help the client at this point with the suggestion "You should feel free to return if at any time you would like some additional help."

Counselors should be supportive at this stage of counseling and should communicate faith in the client's ability to make it alone. Statements such as "Yes, you really have come a long way" are quite acceptable. Counselors may also express feelings toward the client at that time—such as some sadness because of the ending of the contact, but great pleasure at the positive change in the client. If the counselors feel that termination is not in the best interest of the client, they should say so. A statement such as "I would think it best, Jim, for you to continue in counseling a while longer to see if you can work on _____" is one possibility. Finally, counselors ought to initiate termination when they believe that the goals set for counseling have been achieved.

Time-limited counseling will generally enhance the therapeutic process. There are some indications that if clients recognize that there is only a certain amount of time available, they may be more open to the helping process. Shlien (1957) noted that time-limited therapy is as good as a longer-therapy process. Munro and Bach (1975) asked the question "What effect would limiting the time in counseling have on a client's improvement, both as self-perceived and as perceived indirectly through objective measures?" They found that time-limited counseling affected client progress much more positively than did undetermined-time counseling.

Counseling should end on a positive note, and the counselor should try to reinforce the client's new behaviors. The following dialogue illustrates this:

Counselor: You said that, although there wasn't too much you could do to change other people, there were some behaviors that you have learned that would help you. You said that you were going to continue these behaviors. There were other new behaviors, which you were going to try but the situation hasn't come up.

Client: It seems as if I've come a long way, then.

Counselor: It does seem like that.

Client: It's amazing.

Counselor: You feel pleased with what has happened in the counseling sessions, because you have stopped telling yourself some things that made you less effective as a person.

Client: Right!

Counselor: You have chosen a few small behaviors to work on and could see the process from exploring and practicing new behaviors. You are pleased with the change. Now you can apply the same process to other situations and other things you tell yourself. . . .

Client: . . . and follow through. That's what I never did before. It just never came across.

Counselor: It was just getting to the action stage.

Client: Right. When it came to following through . . . well, it just didn't happen, at least not consistently.

Counselor: You feel better with yourself, because you are beginning to follow through more consistently.

Client: So much better.

Counselor: Is there anything else you'd like to talk about?

Client: I can't think of anything.

Counselor: Well, if you ever would like to see me again, please call. I've really enjoyed being with you.

Summary

This chapter discussed initial considerations in the development of the counseling relationship. Attending, listening, observing and basic communication skills need to be placed in proper perspective by the counselor. Once this is accomplished, decision-making, problem-solving, and program-development skills can be incorporated into counseling. Brammer (1977) writes, "A helper must be taught specific skills to match helping attitudes" (p. 305). This chapter addressed several of these basic counselor skills.

The major points of this chapter were as follows:

1. Counselors need to be able to look at background material without drawing inferences. With every client, counselors have to decide how much preparation is best without "prejudicing" themselves toward a particular mind set.

2. Simple rules of courtesy should pertain to counseling, just as they might in everyday social situations.

3. Establishing rapport is more complex during the initial interview than at any other time in counseling.

4. Attending and observation aid in the development of rapport in counseling.

5. Establishing structure involves defining the nature of counseling, counselor-client roles and responsibilities, and the goals of counseling. Limits are generally minimal, but may relate to time and facilities.

6. It is unethical for the counselor to see clients for extensive periods of time just to maintain a caseload and a certain level of income. Determination of when to cease counseling can be initiated by either counselor or client.

References

Aguilera, D. C. "Relationships Between Physical Contact and Verbal Interaction in Nurses and Patients." *Journal of Psychiatric Nursing* 5 (1967): 5–21.

Alagna, F. J., S. J. Whitcher, J. D. Fisher, and E. A. Wicas. "Evaluative Reaction to Interpersonal Touch in a Counseling Interview." *Journal of Counseling Psychology* 26 (1979):465–472.

Berg, I. A. "Word Choice in the Interview and Personal Adjustment." *Journal of Counseling Psychology* 5 (1958):130–135.

Bieber, Michael R., Michael J. Patton, and Addie J. Fuhriman. "A Metalanguage Analysis of Counselor and Client Verb Usage in Counseling." *Journal of Counseling Psychology* 24 (1977):264–271.

Bixler, R. H. "Limits Are Therapy." *Journal of Consulting Psychology* 13 (1949):1–11.

Bordin, Edward S. *Psychological Counseling.* 2d ed. New York: Appleton-Century-Crofts, 1968.

Borreson, A. M. "Counselor Influence on Diagnostic Classification of Client Problems." *Journal of Counseling Psychology* 12 (1965):252–258.

Braaten, L. J. "The Movement from Non-Self to Self in Client-Centered Psychotherapy." *Journal of Counseling Psychology* 8 (1961):20–24.

Brammer, Lawrence M. "Who Can Be a Helper?" *Personnel and Guidance Journal* 55 (1977):303–308.

—— and Everett L. Shostrum. *Therapeutic Psychology.* Englewood Cliffs, N.J.: Prentice-Hall, 1968, rev. ed., 1977.

Broekmann, Neil C., and Andre T. Moller. "Preferred Seating Position and Distance in Various Situations." *Journal of Counseling Psychology* 20 (1973):504–508.

Brown, Robert D. "Experienced and Inexperienced Counselors' First Impressions of Clients and Case Outcomes: Are First Impressions Lasting?" *Journal of Counseling Psychology* 17 (1970):550–558.

Carkhuff, Robert R. *The Art of Helping.* Rev. ed. Amherst, Mass.: Human Resource Development Press, 1977.

———— and R. M. Pierce. *Trainer's Guide: The Art of Helping.* Rev. ed. Amherst, Mass.: Human Resource Development Press, 1977.

Carnes, Earl F., and Francis P. Robinson. "The Role of Client Talk in the Counseling Interview." *Educational and Psychological Measurement* 8 (1948):635–644.

Cash, T. F. "Self-Disclosure in the Acquaintance Process: Effects of Sex, Physical Attractiveness, and Approval Motivation." Unpublished doctoral dissertation. George Peabody College, 1974.

————, Phyllis J. Begley, David A. McCown, and Beverly C. Weise. "When Counselors Are Heard But Not Seen: Initial Impact of Physical Attractiveness." *Journal of Counseling Psychology* 22 (1975):273–279.

Colby, Kenneth Mark. *A Primer for Psychotherapists.* New York: The Ronald Press, 1951.

Cope, Corrine S. "Linguistic Structure and Personality Development." *Journal of Counseling Psychology Monograph,* Part 2, 16 (1969) 19 pages.

Costanzo, Frances S., Norman N. Markel, and Philip R. Costanzo. "Voice Quality Profile and Perceived Emotion." *Journal of Counseling Psychology* 16 (1969):267–270.

Curran, C. A. "Structuring the Counseling Relationship." *Journal of Abnormal and Social Psychology* 39 (1944):189–216.

Danskin, D. G. "A Role-ing Counselor Gathers No Moss." *Journal of Counseling Psychology* 4 (1957):41–43.

D'Augelli, Anthony R. "Nonverbal Behavior of Helpers in Initial Helping Interactions." *Journal of Counseling Psychology* 21 (1974):360–363.

Dinges, Norman G., and Eugene R. Oetting. "Interaction Distance Anxiety in the Counseling Dyad." *Journal of Counseling Psychology* 19 (1972):146–149.

Eells, K., and W. Guppy. "Counselor's Valuations of and Preferences for Different Types of Counseling Problems." *Journal of Counseling Psychology* 10 (1963):146–155.

Egan, Gerard. *The Skilled Helper.* Monterey Calif.: Brooks/Cole, 1975.

Ehrlich, Robert D., Anthony R. D'Augelli, and Steven J. Danish. "Comparative Effectiveness of Six Counselor Verbal Responses." *Journal of Counseling Psychology* 26 (1979):390–398.

Elliott, Robert. "How Clients Perceive Helper Behaviors." *Journal of Counseling Psychology* 26 (1979):285–294.

Feldman, Sandor S. *Mannerisms of Speech and Gesture in Everyday Life.* New York: International Universities Press, 1959.

Fretz, Bruce R., Roger Corn, Janet M. Tuemmler, and William Bellet. "Counselor Nonverbal Behaviors and Client Evaluations." *Journal of Counseling Psychology* 26 (1979):304–311.

Freud, S. "Fragment of an Analysis of a Case of Hysteria" (1905). In *Collected Papers.* Vol. 3. New York: Basic Books, 1959.

Galvin, Maryanne, and Allen E. Ivey. "Researching One's Own Interviewing Style: Does Your Theory of Choice Match Your Actual Practice?" *Personnel and Guidance Journal* 59 (1981):536–542.

Genther, Robert W., and James Moughan. "Introverts' and Extroverts' Responses to Nonverbal Attending Behavior." *Journal of Counseling Psychology* 24 (1977):144–146.

Goldstein, A. P. *Psychotherapeutic Attraction.* New York: Pergamon, 1971.

Goldstein, Susan B., and Luther F. Sies. *The Communication Contract.* Springfield, Ill.: Charles C Thomas, 1974.

Graves, James R., and John D. Robinson. "Proxemic Behavior as a Function of Inconsistent Verbal and Nonverbal Messages." *Journal of Counseling Psychology* 23 (1976):333–338.

Greene, Les R. "Effects of Verbal Evaluative Feedback and Interpersonal Distance on Behavioral Compliance." *Journal of Counseling Psychology* 24 (1977):10–14.

Grummon, D. L. "An Investigation into the Use of Grammatical and Psycho-Grammatical Categories of Language for the Study of Personality and Psychotherapy." Unpublished doctoral dissertation. University of Chicago, 1950.

Haase, Richard F. "The Relationship of Sex and

Instructional Set to the Regulation of Interpersonal Interaction Distance in a Counseling Analogue." *Journal of Counseling Psychology* 17 (1970):233–236.

——— **and Dominic J. DiMattia.** "Proxemic Behavior: Counselor, Administrator, and Client Preference for Seating Arrangement in Dyadic Interaction." *Journal of Counseling Psychology* 17 (1970):319–325.

——— **and Donald T. Tepper, Jr.** "Nonverbal Components of Empathic Communication." *Journal of Counseling Psychology* 19 (1972):417–424.

Hackney, Harold. "Facial Gestures and Subject Expression of Feelings." *Journal of Counseling Psychology* 21 (1974):173–178.

———, **A. E. Ivey, and E. R. Oetting.** "Attending, Island, and Hiatus Behavior." *Journal of Counseling Behavior* 17 (1970):342–346.

Hall, E. T. *The Silent Language.* New York: Doubleday, 1959.

Hendrick, Ives. *Facts and Theories of Psychoanalysis.* New York: Knopf, 1958.

Hill, C. E., et al. "Nonverbal Communication and Counseling Outcome." *Journal of Counseling Psychology* 28 (1981):203–212.

——— **and James Gormally.** "Effects of Reflection, Restatement, Probe, and Nonverbal Behaviors on Client Affect." *Journal of Counseling Psychology* 24 (1977):92–97.

Howell, Jane M., and Pamela S. Highlen. "Effects of Client Affective Self-Disclosure and Counselor Experience on Counselor Verbal Behavior and Perceptions." *Journal of Counseling Psychology* 28 (1981):386–398.

Ingham, H. V., and R. Lemore Love. *The Process of Psychotherapy.* New York: McGraw-Hill, 1954.

Ivey, Allen E., Cheryl J. Normington, C. Dean Miller, Weston H. Morrill, and Richard F. Hasse. "Microcounseling and Attending Behavior: An Approach to Prepracticum Counselor Training." Part 2, *Journal of Counseling Psychology* 15 (1968):1–12.

Kagan, Norman, David R. Krathwohl, and William W. Farquahr. *IPR-Inter-Personal Process Recall. Stimulated Recall by Videotape.* Educational Research Series No. 24. East Lansing: Michigan State University, 1965.

Kennedy, John J., and Jules M. Zimmer. "Reinforcing Value of Five Stimulus Conditions in a Quasi-Counseling Situation." *Journal of Counseling Psychology* 15 (1968):357–362.

Key, Mary Ritchie. *Paralanguage and Kinesics.* Metuchen, N.J.: Scarecrow Press, 1975.

Kleinke, Chris L., and Tracy Beach Tully. "Influence of Talking Level on Perceptions of Counselors." *Journal of Counseling Psychology* 26 (1979):23–29.

Krause, Merton S. "Clarification at Intake and Motivation for Treatment." *Journal of Counseling Psychology* 15 (1968):576–577.

LaCrosse, Michael B. "Nonverbal Behavior and Perceived Counselor Attractiveness and Persuasiveness." *Journal of Counseling Psychology* 22 (1975):563–566.

Lauver, Philip J., Jan D. Kelley, and Thomas C. Froehle. "Client Reaction Time and Counselor Verbal Behavior in an Interview Setting." *Journal of Counseling Psychology* 18 (1971):26–30.

Lee, Dong Yul, E. T. Hallberg, J. H. Hassard, and R. F. Haase. "Client Verbal and Nonverbal Reinforcement of Counselor Behavior: Its Impact on Interviewing Behavior and Postinterview Evaluation." *Journal of Counseling Psychology* 26 (1979):204–209.

Lott, D., and R. Sommer. "Seating Arrangements and Status." *Journal of Personality and Social Psychology* 7 (1967):90–95.

Matarazzo, Joseph D., and Arthur Wiens. *The Interview.* Chicago: Aldine Publishing, 1972.

Meara, N. M., J. W. Shannon, and H. B. Pepinsky. "Comparison of the Stylistic Complexity of the Language of Counselor and Client Across Three Theoretical Orientations." *Journal of Counseling Psychology* 26 (1979):181–189.

Mehrabian, A. "Communication Without Words." *Psychology Today* 2 (1968):52–55.

———. "Some Determinants of Affiliation and Conformity." *Psychological Reports* 27 (1970):19–29.

Mezzano, Joseph, and Bruce Prueter. "Background Music and Counseling Interaction." *Journal of Counseling Psychology* 21 (1974):84–86.

Munro, J. N., and T. R. Bach. "Effect of Time-Limited Counseling on Client Change." *Journal of Counseling Psychology* 22 (1975):395–398.

Myers, G., and M. T. Myers. *The Dynamics of Human Communication.* New York: McGraw-Hill, 1973.

Packwood, William T. "Loudness as a Variable in Persuasion." *Journal of Counseling Psychology* 21 (1974):1–2.

Pattison, J. E. "Effects of Touch on Self-Exploration and the Therapeutic Relationship." *Journal of Consulting and Clinical Psychology* 40 (1973):170–175.

Pietrofesa, John J., George E. Leonard, and William Van Hoose. *The Authentic Counselor.* Rev. ed. Chicago: Rand McNally, 1978.

Raimy, V. C. "Self-Reference in Counseling Interviews." *Journal of Consulting Psychology* 12 (1948):153–163.

Robinson, F. P. *Principles and Procedures in Student Counseling.* New York: Harper, 1950.

Rogers, Carl R. *Counseling and Psychotherapy.* Boston: Houghton Mifflin, 1942.

Seals, James M., and William A. Troth. "Identification of Counselee Subroles: An Exploratory Approach." *Journal of Counseling Psychology* 16 (1969):495–498.

Seay, Thomas A., and Michal K. Altekruse. "Verbal and Nonverbal Behavior in Judgments of Facilitative Conditions." *Journal of Counseling Psychology* 26 (1979):108–119.

Shertzer, Bruce, and Shelley C. Stone. *Fundamentals of Counseling.* Rev. ed. Boston: Houghton Mifflin, 1980.

Shlien, John M. "Time-Limited Psychotherapy: An Experimental Investigation of Practical Values and Theoretical Implications." *Journal of Counseling Psychology* 4 (1957):318–322.

Siegel, Jeffrey C. "Effects of Objective Evidence of Expertness, Nonverbal Behavior and Subject Sex on Client-Perceived Expertness." *Journal of Counseling Psychology* 27 (1980):117–121.

Sielski, Lester M. "Understanding Body Language." *Personnel and Guidance Journal* 57 (1979):238–242.

Smith, Joyce A., and William A. Lewis. "Effect of Videotaped Models on the Communications of College Students in Counseling." *Journal of Counseling Psychology* 21 (1974):78–80.

Smith-Hanen, Sandra S. "Effects of Nonverbal Behaviors on Judged Levels of Counselor Warmth and Empathy." *Journal of Counseling Psychology* 24 (1977):87–91.

Sommer, R. "Studies in Personal Space." *Sociometry* 22 (1959):247–260.

Stein, Marsha Lomis, and Gerald L. Stone. "Effects of Conceptual Level and Structure on Initial Interview Behavior." *Journal of Counseling Psychology* 25 (1978):96–102.

Strong, Stanley R., and David N. Dixon. "Expertness, Attractiveness, and Influence in Counseling." *Journal of Counseling Psychology* 18 (1971):562–570.

———, Ronald G. Taylor, Joseph C. Bratton, and Rodney G. Loper. "Nonverbal Behavior and Perceived Counselor Characteristics." *Journal of Counseling Psychology* 18 (1971):554–561.

Taplin, J. R. "Impression of the Client as a Function of Perception Mode and Clinicians Experience." *Journal of Counseling Psychology* 15 (1968):211–214.

Tepper, Donald T., Jr., and Richard F. Haase. "Verbal and Nonverbal Communication of Facilitative Conditions." *Journal of Counseling Psychology* 25 (1978):35–44.

Tessler, Richard C. "Clients' Reactions to Initial Interviews: Determinants of Relationship-Centered and Problem-Centered Satisfaction." *Journal of Counseling Psychology* 22 (1975):187–191.

Tindall, R. H., and Francis P. Robinson. "The Use of Silence as a Technique in Counseling." *Journal of Clinical Psychology* 3 (1947):136–141.

Todd, W. B., and T. N. Ewing. "Changes in Self-Reference During Counseling." *Journal of Counseling Psychology* 8 (1961):112–115.

Troth, William A., Gwendolyn Lee Hall, and James M. Seals. "Counselor-Counselee Interaction." *Journal of Counseling Psychology* 18 (1971):77–80.

Tyler, L. *The Work of the Counselor.* New York: Appleton-Century-Crofts, 1969.

Weigel, R. G., D. M. Cochneour, and R. L. Russell. "Relationship of Type of Student Problem and Perceived Outcomes of Counseling." *Journal of College Student Personnel* 8 (1967):26–31.

White, A. "The Patient Sits Down." *Psychosomatic Medicine* 15 (1953):256–257.

Widgery, Robin, and Cecil Stackpole. "Desk Position, Interviewee Anxiety, and Interviewer Credibility: An Example of Cognitive Balance in a Dyad." *Journal of Counseling Psychology* 19 (1972):173–177.

Wiener, Morton, Shannon Devoe, Stuart Rubinow, and Jesse Geller. "Nonverbal Behavior and Nonverbal Communication." *Psychological Review* 79 (1972):185–213.

Ziemelis, Andris. "Effects of Client Preference and Expectancy upon the Initial Interview." *Journal of Counseling Psychology* 21 (1974):23–30.

CHAPTER 12

Counseling Techniques: II

Chapter Organizer

Aim of the Chapter

This chapter will provide additional insight into the components of empathy—namely, content, nonverbal behaviors, and feelings. Emphasis will be placed on acquiring the skill to respond empathically to others. Finally, other counseling concepts such as diagnosis, interpretation, clarification, immediacy, and confrontation will be discussed.

Chapter Preview

1. Empathic responses focus on three primary areas: content, nonverbal behavior, and feelings.
   a. Responding to the content portion of clients' messages informs them that the counselor understands the literal part of the communication.
   b. Noting the clients' nonverbal behaviors will provide a rich source of information about their immediate feelings.
   c. Attending to the clients' feelings, implied or explicitly stated, will enable the counselor to develop a deeper understanding of clients and their situations.
2. Accurate empathy considers content, nonverbal behaviors, and feelings and weaves them together to form a concise response, in the "You feel _____ because _____" pattern.
3. Counselors model optimal pacing in order to facilitate in-depth exploration by the client.

4. "Red threading," or the identification of recurring themes in counseling, is the key to the metaphor of the client's basic conflict.
5. Personalization is the process of empathically aiding clients to talk about themselves instead of others.
6. Diagnosis is an interpersonal process whose purpose is to understand the clients and their worlds well enough to help them to change. Diagnosis does not involve the use of labels to sort people into convenient categories that aid the counselor and harm the client.
7. The use of counseling goals clarifies the counseling relationship and the direction in which it should grow. Their omission fosters disorganization and rambling conversation.
8. Interpretations are counselor insights shared with the clients to enhance their self-awareness. They need to be made in an empathic atmosphere, which takes the clients' readiness into account.
9. A clarification is an interpretation that helps the client assimilate new awarenesses into a deeper understanding.
10. Counselors need to be aware of and sensitive to what occurs in the counseling relationship between themselves and the client. This awareness, called *immediacy*, provides important data for counseling.

11. A *confrontation* is a counselor statement that combines immediacy, empathy, and interpretation for the purpose of helping clients to crystallize their inconsistencies of expression and behavior.

Relevant Questions

The following are several questions to keep in mind while reading this chapter:

1. What is the most important component of empathy—what clients say or how they say it?

2. How does personalization differ from an empathic response, and when is it best employed?

3. What is the relationship between diagnosis and the establishment of counseling goals?

4. How does an interpretative response differ from clarification? What is the therapeutic value of each?

5. How can counselors employ sensitivity to themselves for the therapeutic gain of the client?

Introduction

The preceding chapter presented several concepts, among them the initiation of counseling, attending behavior, counselor observations, and nonverbal communication. These fundamentally important concepts are prerequisites for the material presented in this chapter. While much of counseling is an art—the art of "sensing" another's inner feelings and motivations—the means used to communicate these insights rely on specific skills. These skills include counselors' attending behavior, observing and understanding clients' nonverbal behavior, and finally responding empathically to promote clients' self-awareness. These empathic responses give rise to interpretation, clarification, immediacy, and confrontation. These techniques use empathy as their base but—due to their deeper probing—evoke higher anxiety levels in clients. Thus, it is advantageous for counselors and clients to agree on the definition of the problem and the goal to be achieved. This will focus the counseling by defining the areas that will receive the primary concentration of attention and energy. In short, no concept presented in this chapter exists in isolation. Each dovetails with all the other counseling concepts.

Responding Empathically

Responding to Content

Conversation in counseling has very little in common with conversation in social situations. In the counseling setting, the emphasis is on the client's exploration and the communication of that exploration to the counselor, who in turn seeks to understand. The counselor, then, communicates her or his understanding to the client in order to promote further exploration. Social conversation in contrast does not emphasize understanding others. Too often, the purpose of social communication is to verbalize the speaker's point of view. Arguments are a case in point: When the conversation begins, the communication is calm, deliberate, and carefully worded. Progressively, however, the pace quickens, loudness heightens, and interruptions increase. While this does not constitute communication, it does satisfy individual needs for venting opinions. Neither participant is able to demonstrate an understanding of the other's perspective. This pattern of conversation does not advance understanding, nor does it alter the opinions of those involved. There is no room in counseling for cajoling, persuading, or arguing. Here, exploring, thinking, feeling, and understanding are emphasized. Growth and change are the helpee's responsibility. The helper's task is to create a positive climate and environment and to provide understanding and the skills that are necessary to allow the client to assume his or her responsibility.

Once counselors have appropriately initiated counseling (see Chapter 11), and have invited their clients to share their purpose for seeking the appointment, the content of the counseling session will be evidenced. As clients begin to disclose information, the process will benefit if (1) they can sense the counselors' understanding, (2) they can "hear" what the counselors think they said, and (3) the counselors can feel assured that the clients agree with their understanding. These objectives can be partially accomplished when counselors respond to the content of the clients' message.

The counselor must listen carefully to the client's statement, seek out its essence, and restate it. The counselor should aim for a concise response that communicates understanding and uses enough synonyms to avoid being repetitive and boring. Inexperienced, and even experienced, counselors have difficulty reflecting content in a concrete fashion—a fashion that does not shift the focus from the client to the counselor. Remember, in responding to the content, the counselor is trying to (1) communicate understanding, (2) provide the client with an opportunity to hear what she or he has said, (3) focus on the client's message in such a way as to encourage further self-exploration, and (4) communicate respect and caring for what the client considers to be important. If the counselor's responses are as long as or longer than the client's statement, they will shift the focus to the counselor, slow down exploration, and communicate that the counselor was unable to discriminate the meaningful from the less meaningful material. It is true, however, that a concise synopsis of the client's content will facilitate further content communication:

Client: I'm not sure that I should try to visit Shelly. She and I had a falling out not too long ago.
Counselor: You had an argument with her recently?
Client: Well, I wrote to her and she didn't answer.
Counselor: So it is still unresolved.
Client: I also wrote to Maureen, and she said that Shelly was in one of her moods of not communicating with anyone, even her mother. But I don't know.
Counselor: Sounds like you are as cut off from Shelly as her mother is.
Client: Yes, but . . . I did talk to her on the phone when I got back and she sounded friendly . . . but I still feel uneasy about seeing her, or I don't know that she'd really want to see me because we broke apart.

Counselor: Even though she sounded okay, you still are not convinced she wants to see you.

Client: Yeah, I dated a fellow that she had been going with, but . . . I thought she was all through with him . . . but she got mad at me and I felt bad about it.

Counselor: She had stopped seeing him, so you thought it was okay to date him but you were mistaken.

Client: Well, I didn't then and don't even now think the guy was that important to me. But, more than that, I'm sorry I hurt Shelly and lost her as a friend.

Counselor: So giving up the fellow is less the issue than losing Shelly's friendship.

Client: I knew it had happened to her before. She even told me earlier that a former girlfriend had dated someone she was going with and how it had upset and disturbed her. I should have known better.

Counselor: And because you knew about it happening before, you should have been able to keep this from happening.

Client: It's even worse than that. She had become distrustful of girlfriends because of the early experience. I thought I had helped her to overcome this, but now I wonder whether I have.

Counselor: So instead of helping her, you think you might have hurt her even more.

Client: Yeah . . .

When the counselor responds with a content reflection, the client is encouraged to continue disclosing more content. Content responses do not encourage the disclosure of feelings and, in fact, do little to move the client to in-depth exploration. In the above illustration, the client talked almost exclusively of her girlfriend's dilemma and little about her own situation. While content responses would lose their effectiveness if used continuously, they can be effective in conjunction with other types of responses.

Responding to the Nonverbal

Each of us sends a continuous message to others even when we are not talking. As mentioned in Chapter 11, the nonverbal cues emitted by a client are a rich source of information. Since it is the one aspect of communication that seems to be under less conscious control, it can usually be trusted to be a valid indicator of the client's state. Counselors who learn to be sensitive to the nonverbal message and master the skill of effectively responding to it have added a powerful and useful tool to their repertoire. Their clients see them as more empathic (Seay and Altekruse, 1979; Tepper and Haase, 1978; Hill et al., 1981), more expert (Claiborn, 1979; Siegel, 1980) and more attractive and trustworthy (Claiborn, 1979).

Responses to physical cues include (1) questions or statements intended to increase the client's awareness, (2) content reflections, or (3) statements reflecting the "experiencing" of the counselor. A few comments below illustrate alternative responses:

Client: [Silent and shifting nervously in her chair. She is facing the counselor but her eyes scan anxiously about.]

Counselor (1):   I sense your discomfort at being here. Could you describe to me what you are feeling?

Counselor (2):   It must be difficult for you to decide what you are going to do here with me.

Counselor (3):   You look terribly uneasy to me, and I can feel some of those same feelings in me as I sit here with you.

The first response is a reflection of the feelings she read. The purpose is to communicate the counselor's awareness of the client's feelings, to show acceptance of those feelings, and ask the client to focus on and describe them. The second response deals with the content that the counselor speculates is the motivation for the nonverbal behavior. The effect of this content response is to encourage the client to talk about alternative ways of behaving with the counselor. The third response shares both the counselor's reading of the client's feelings and the personal disclosure that she, too, has some of those same feelings. This may help the client to feel accepted and understood by the counselor, since they have something in common.

It is suggested that responses to nonverbal cues contain references to the specific behavior observed and the counselor's speculation of its meaning. Observations can be made on posture, facial qualities, tone of voice, physical appearance, clothing, jewelry, hand gestures, shallow or rapid breathing, and many other behavioral traits. Observations that are couched in words and tone of voice that communicate their speculative nature generally do not create a defensive attitude in the client.

Client: [Head down with speech slow and low] You know, it doesn't bother me that Dad thinks I cannot do anything right, but I do wish he could say some nice things to my brother.

Counselor: Bill, you say that your father's disapproval does not sadden you, but you look and sound sad, with your head down and your voice is so low I can barely hear it.

Client: Yeah, I guess I am just kidding myself . . . it has really hurt me and I don't want my brother to have to feel the same thing.

This response gently pointed out the contrast between what the client said (content) and how he said it. The effect was to help renew his awareness of his feelings and to clarify his concern for his brother. Responding to the nonverbal communication encouraged the client to become aware of himself and to reflect on that awareness. This awareness might lead the client to disclose more feelings to the counselor or generate new exploration and understanding.

Responding to Feeling

The third aspect of a client's message are implicitly or explicitly stated feelings. While feelings are difficult to understand, they are the most productive entry into a client's world; they are the key to empathic responses for several reasons. First, responding to feelings promotes discussion of here-and-now issues (immediacy). Second, discussing a client's immediate feelings tends to diminish intellectualizations and resistance. Third, responding to feelings encourages clients to become increasingly aware of their feelings, label them, and develop tolerance to them. When clients are unable to put their feelings into words, they are often unaware of their affective responses even in situations that seem obvious to others (Krystal, 1979). Inability to verbally express feelings often leads clients to (1) express feelings somatically (as psychosomatic complaints) without awareness (Krystal, 1979) and (2) remain unaware of the message communicated by the feeling and, therefore, unable to make productive use of the feeling. Feelings have an expressive and a cognitive component. The expressive component is the physiological sensation. It is the upset stomach, the headache, the diarrhea, or the lower back pain. Here the body is sending a physiological message to the brain indicating that something needs special attention. Without this physiological message, life expectancy would be very short since the individual would not recognize the pain of a heart attack, a brain concussion, or a ruptured appendix, and therefore would not seek medical help. All emotions are experienced physiologically.

The cognitive component is the meaning of and the story behind the feeling. For example, the meaning of fear and anxiety is the belief that something terrible is about to happen. The story behind the fear concerns impending danger from an external source; for anxiety, there is a sense of internal danger. Further exploration is needed before the counselor can fully describe the story of the client's impending danger, possibly to bring it into the client's conscious awareness. It is crucial, however, to see feelings as signals and to help the client understand the story behind them. Responding empathically to feelings promotes client's awareness and acceptance of their feelings and an understanding of their usefulness as meaningful messages.

Client: You know, I really get down at this time of the year; Christmas is a time we used to get together with the whole family, but now all the kids are gone and living their own lives . . . and Bill . . . well it seems that I'm the only one who really misses getting together.

Counselor: I sense your feelings of loneliness and sadness.

Client: [Nodding her head yes] It is sad . . . I really miss my children and especially at this time of year . . . but I know they cannot get here, but

. . . that doesn't take away my missing them and wishing they were here.
. . . Sometimes it is so great, I just want to cry . . . and Bill thinks that
is just stupid!

Counselor: Your feelings of loneliness and sadness are heightened by Bill's
reaction to you.

Client: Yeah, it is as if I'm all alone—with no one near me and that . . .
actually that is what I feel all of the time, but it just seems to get worse
now.

Responding to feelings reinforced the client's awareness. Labeling feelings motivated her to use those feelings as a key to unlock that part of herself that has been less accessible. Feeling responses encouraged feeling disclosures—the best indicators of the immediate state of the client.

The reader is encouraged to review Chapter 10 and the work of Shantz (1975). We reviewed her presentation of the three judgments one can make to approximate a speaker's feelings. They include self-judgments, in which counselors ask what they have felt or might feel in a similar circumstance, and normative judgments, which ask what people they know might have felt if they had experienced what the client described. Finally, counselors may ask the above questions and attempt to read the nonverbal cues, which can often lead to a differential judgment. Counselors would do well to review this cognitive structure as they listen to clients.

In addition to asking these questions, counselors should listen for feelings or phrases that imply feelings. The authors have found it helpful to label these feelings and "nonverbally" repeat them. This labeling and repeating seems to impress the feelings into the counselor's memory and permit continued concentration on the conversation. When the client has concluded, those feelings that were repeated subvocally are available for recall. In addition, subvocal repetition enhances the counselors' ability to consider feelings and to be open to more cues.

It is suggested that counselors commit to memory seven broad categories of feelings: *happy, sad, strong, weak, angry, confused,* and *afraid.* Each of these categories contain a multitude of feeling words. Counselors will find it helpful to incorporate into their working vocabulary words describing feelings at three levels of intensity: high, medium, and weak. Table 12.1 provides examples from the authors' vocabulary; one should keep in mind that these terms might not adequately describe the reader's or a client's intensity

Table 12.1
Feeling Words

Intensity of Feelings	Categories of Feelings						
	Happy	*Sad*	*Strong*	*Weak*	*Angry*	*Confused*	*Afraid*
High	ecstatic	despair	confident	spent	furious	torn	horrified
Medium	excited	disgusted	alive	drained	annoyed	baffled	shaken
Weak	pleased	crummy	able	weary	irritated	ambivalent	anxious

levels. Feeling words and counselor responses must be geared to the client's vocabulary and manner of expression as well as the client's level of awareness and exploration.

Since one can hear and think much faster than one can talk, more is taking place in counselors' minds than listening. Listening and thinking is a very demanding activity. The following is a portion of the second counseling session with a 19-year-old woman. The counselor's thoughts are stated at the right, with the content of the interview at left.

Transcript of Session	*Counselor Thoughts*
Client (1): I guess I've always lived in someone else's shadow. New interests were more or less forced upon me. Their hobbies were my hobbies. That type of thing. I don't even know what my hobbies are [heavy laughter] . . . and that to me is really sad.	*Feels insignificant, helpless* *Easily led and influenced* *Does not know herself, deeply saddened and I wonder if embarrassed about admitting it*
Counselor (1): You feel separated from yourself and sad about it.	
Client (2): Yeah . . . Their ideas and so forth . . . and now, oh boy, I really feel lost.	*Sense a feeling of being overwhelmed about being lost, confused about who she is*
Counselor (2): You seem confused about who Judy is. . . .	
Client (3): I've wondered about that. It didn't really . . . what I felt and what I thought really didn't seem to matter to the most important people in my life . . . and maybe that's the part that really hurts. Whenever I tried to exert myself, I always got—phew—squashed down.	*Wondered . . . uncertain* *Again, feelings of insignificance, like a nonperson* *Tries to stand up and feels stepped on again*
Counselor (3): You felt squashed and hurt by people closest to you.	
Client (4): Basically that's it. . . . Yeah. That's really one of the	*Aware she lives a facade for others, but it was too much*

major causes of the breakup of the marriage. I couldn't fake it any longer.

Beginning to care about self?

Counselor (4): You felt independent enough to stop it. . . . Your feelings about yourself demanded some action, huh?

Client (5): Yeah, I was into a lot of hurt, anxiety, anger, frustration, mainly frustration.

Hurt, anxious, angry, and frustrated, which is helplessness and anger about feeling helpless

Counselor (5): I sense your feelings of helplessness and anger about it.

Client (6): Yeah, and all I could do was to suppress them. What else could I do? I remember one time I thought, "This is it . . . I'm going to make a decision." The first time with a job application, and it was something I thought I really could enjoy doing. Well, I did exert myself and I did express my opinion and I think that was the last time I ever voiced my opinion. [Laughs] I ended up picking my teeth up off the floor is what it amounted to. It was a really ugly scene. [Smiling]

Fearful about owning the feelings?

Feels tentatively strong and resolved

Feels direction in life

Voice tells of a disappointment, new anger and feels squashed again, but is smiling and laughing

Counselor (6): I'm confused, you're telling me that you felt squashed and disappointed again as you laugh and smile.

Client (7): I think I'm doing it out of . . . sometimes when I laugh or I smile it's to hide what I really feel.

Covering up real feelings . . . maybe afraid of them

Counselor (7): What is it you are feeling?

Client (8): Hurt and anger . . . same feelings. But I'd rather sit here and laugh about it than sit

Hurt and angry again . . . hold down the sadness and pretend happiness

here and cry. But probably it would have been much healthier for me to cry.

Counselor (8): The tears are there because the sadness is there, and you are used to pretending to be something you are not, as you are pretending now.

It is obvious that many avenues of thought and feeling emerge in a counseling session. Counselors need to maintain an overall focus on the direction of the session to decide how and to what they will respond. In the above illustration, the counselor understood the client's sense of alienation from herself and the resultant feelings of being squashed, hurt, and angry. The counselor believed that her best route to understanding the client was to understand the client's feelings. If this was the preferred route for her, she might have concluded—and justifiably so—that the preferred road for the client would be to become acquainted with her alienated self.

Obviously, the focus of the counseling session would have been drastically different had the counselor responded to the client's hobbies at Client (1) instead of the alienation and sadness. Responding to the content would have encouraged a content response; getting the client to express the alienated feelings again would have been difficult. At Client (3) the counselor might have asked who she was trying to influence with her thinking and why. This, too, would have altered the focus of the session. It illustrates, however, the temptation to seek information, even if it is unlikely to further the counseling task but will only be a "filler"—and possibly a destructive one at that. Finally, Counselor (3) demonstrated that one can respond to feelings by asking a timely question. The question called for a description of *what* the client was feeling at that moment (immediacy). This response caused the client to focus on the here-and-now, on the very feelings that she has been avoiding. One would hope that this communicated to the client that the counselor was (1) accepting of her and her negative feelings, (2) not afraid of those feelings, and (3) interested in who she really was, not the facade. Had the counselor responded to content, the client might have read the communication as: (1) My feelings are secondary to "why" they are; (2) my feelings scare her because I don't know what to do with them; she wants me to talk about the more intellectual "why"; or (3) she thinks that this is hard work and wants to deal with something easier.

Of course, communication is based on more than a brief exchange, and when clients repeat themselves, the communication becomes more substantial and meaningful. Effective counselors need to be aware of not only what the client is communicating to them but what they are communicating to the client. This phenomenon is called "immediacy."

Ideally, the mode of responding to feelings varies during the course of

the counseling session. Carkhuff et al. (1980) suggests the format "You feel
_____." We believe that this is an excellent phrase to use in training,
since it places emphasis on the feeling to the exclusion of any accompanying
explanation. Because feelings are often difficult to "hear" and respond to,
we recommend that early in training students respond only to feelings, until
they are able to "hear" feelings and develop a good working vocabulary of
feeling words (see Table 12.1). We suggest that students practice responding
to feelings with each other in training as well as with their friends, spouses,
teachers, and others. It is important to notice how a casual feeling response,
when not overdone, can alter the course of any conversation.

Once students have mastered listening for feelings and developed an adequate affective vocabulary, they are ready to seek more variety in the response format. Some alternatives are (1) "That must make you extremely
happy," (2) "I can sense your grief," (3) "You have found within yourself
a new sense of confidence and strength." All of the above examples respond
to the clients' feelings and help them to crystallize, clarify, and "own" the
feelings as their own. Thus, counselors can respond continually to feelings
without sounding like a computer. Counselors need to be cognizant of the
congruence between the tone of their voice and the affect communicated
by their words. Counselors who are "techniquing" it will respond to the clients' sadness or desperation with a cold voice. There is nothing more chill-
ing than the monotonic response, "You . . . feel . . . sad." Responses that
sound as if an unpracticed actor is reading them will not promote an intimate and trusting relationship. Involvement and understanding need to be
communicated with words, tone of the voice, and other nonverbal behaviors. Counselors who have developed an extensive, easily accessible feel-
ing-word vocabulary will have little fear of being stumped for a response.
Energy and attention that was previously focused on the counselor's fear
can now be focused on the client.

Finally, a word of caution is in order about the response "You feel that
_____." When counselors use the word *that* or when the word *think*
can be substituted for *feel* without injuring the meaning of the sentence,
they are responding to content, *not* feelings. "You feel that you would like
to get started now" is really saying "You think that you would like to get
started now." A more appropriate feeling response might be "You are feeling impatient." Counselors must think carefully before responding. Clients
will wait, especially when patience has been modeled by the counselor.

Structuring the Empathic Response

Responding
with Accurate
Empathy
Previously, we have discussed responding to the content of a client's message—that is, its literal meaning. This communicates that the counselor is
listening to the client. Secondly, we have emphasized responding to the client's expressed or implied feelings. This communicates deeper sensitivity
and understanding on the part of the counselor. Now, we need to integrate
the two into a single response to express accurate empathic understanding.

Carkhuff et al. (1980) suggests the format, "You feel _____ because _____." This format emphasizes feelings in the context of what the client has stated (content). The content explains and complements the feelings, while the feelings elaborate the content. Feelings and content fit together like clasped hands; they are interwoven to provide more meaning. Counselors bring the content and feeling together in order to help the client clarify their relationship to each other.

Again, it is recommended that, as counselors listen to their clients, they enhance their recall by nonverbally repeating the stated or implied feelings. Once the content is available for quick recollection, the counselor determines what feeling(s) are dominant and formulates a concise response to bring the content and feelings together. It is important to remember that the focus should be on the clients and what they say, not on the counselors' responses. Therefore, we must emphasize the necessity for accurate but short counselor responses. This may be one of the most difficult tasks to learn. We are accustomed to using far more words than necessary. We will even repeat our messages if the listener is not quick to respond. In counseling, however, quite the opposite is necessary. Carefully considered, short, concrete statements delivered in appropriate affective tones are optimal. If the counselor response has the effect of losing the client, silence would have been preferable. At least then the focus of the conversation would have remained with the client. Counselor responses need to (1) communicate understanding to the client, (2) serve as a method for the counselors to confirm their understanding, (3) help the client to see the relationship between his feelings and what the feelings are about, (4) communicate the counselors' acceptance of the client as a person, (5) serve as an effective and gentle push for the client to continue exploration, and finally (6) give the client an opportunity to label and own her feelings and problems and to seek a solution.

The following transcript of a counseling session between a 23-year-old male client and his female counselor illustrates meaningful responses:

Client (1): Ah . . . well, I didn't get that job. You know, the one I thought I might get. Remember I said I had taken a few interviews, and, ah, so there was a job that I interviewed for and passed the test. But I didn't get it. I'm a little discouraged, and, ah, that's just the way it goes. So now everything's really open again.

Counselor (1): Um . . . You're discouraged, because you were hoping they'd accept you and they didn't.

Client (2): Well there was, yeah, there was a little hope, I wanted at least to be able to say no. Which I thought I might do, you know, as I found out a little bit more about the job. So . . . I guess I've been thinking today, you know, I guess I'd really like to, to get that degree out of the way. One way or the other, you know, even if that would mean taking some courses that I don't like, but at the same time, just getting the degree, getting that particular aspect of things out of the way.

Counselor (2): You feel more determined to go back to school and get the degree.

Client (3): Ah, yeah. I mean determination is . . . well, I'd just like to do it and have that out of the way, and then just wait and see what happens in the meantime. Cause I just don't have the direction right now. I just don't have, you know it's really hard to . . . I'd like some goals, but I can't get my . . . focus on anything in particular, so that's about the only really tangible thing I have. I don't really have anything I can really reach for. Um, my wife and I talked about pursuing something within the church where I could get paid for it. Ah . . . that's something that all I can do is keep my eyes and ears open. I don't really have, ah, you know, a real place to, to look right now. And I guess, you know, I'm still pretty up in the air.

Counselor (3): There's a lot of uncertainty still—about job possibilities. One tangible focus you see is to go back to school.

Client (4): Yeah, that's right there . . . you know, if I was taking at least one class and just, you know, doing it, I think it would bring a little, sort of . . . at least there would be an area that was a little established . . . calm down.

Counselor (4): You are uptight right now, because it seems you're not doing anything.

Client (5): Well, yeah, I, that's been really aggravated by the fact that I'm really in a sense not doing—well, I can't say not doing anything—but with the financial pressure . . . dollars and cents is a real pressure. And, ah, my wife and I, ah, we can cope with it most of the time, but it has to get brought up, you know. It gets brought up when, ah, well you know, money . . . you know, when something's wanted and it can't be afforded. And then it gets to, well, you know: well, I need a job and I need a good paying job and . . . and this type of thing.

Counselor (5): You're feeling pressured because of your finances.

Client (6): Yes. [Pause] It's not a constant thing. It's just something that, you know, between me and my wife has to get talked about once in a while. You just can't keep it, you can't not talk about it, cause all it does is sort of, you don't want to lose lines of communication. I would say I need some dollars and cents.

Counselor (6): I'm confused because I hear you stressing a need for earning money and at the same time a decision to return to school. I'm confused about how you see those both . . .

To this point, the counselor has attempted to reestablish the trusting relationship that existed in the previous session, which may have lessened over time. Her responses are intended to communicate accurate empathic understanding, integrating both feeling and content. At Counselor (6), the counselor discloses in a confrontive manner to stimulate clarification.

Client (7): How it's going to take place? I don't know really. Um . . . It's just you know, yeah it's something I'm going to have to try and reckon with. Cause, um, logically I don't even see how I can even get into school this winter, right now, you know, because of money. And, ah, I don't know.

Counselor (7):   So you want to return to school because it would give you more of a feeling of accomplishment, that you were moving somehow. But yet you're uncertain that you can afford it.

Client (8):   Yes, I think so—in that, in that one particular area. You know, I told you my basic situation the fact that, you know, I did attend a university. I have a lot of hours, but I don't have a degree. And, ah . . . I don't know, maybe just personal satisfaction, just to get a degree and get it out of the way . . . have it . . . you know, it's not pride, it's just to do something, do something in one area in my life.

Counselor (8):   You feel an urgency to move somehow, to improve your life.

Client (9):   Yes, I think so. Cause I, ah, I suppose we talked about this in the last two sessions, and I mentioned to my wife today: I can cope with really working at anything. And, ah, I guess there's something that, you know, there's something within me that just feels that there is something in the future. Something a little more, maybe prestigious . . . ah, a little more settled, a place where I'm really in my niche and at the same time earning a living. And, ah, but I think, you know I think that has to be . . . reached for, I think it has to be worked for at this point in time.

Counselor (9):   You feel restless because you haven't found your niche. . . . And you want to move toward finding it.

Client (10):   Yes.

Counselor (10):   But at the same time a more immediate pressure is financial.

Client (11):   Yes, it's, it's maybe not as bad as, ah . . . with some people. Cause I don't seem to be a, you know, I . . . I don't seem to stay under pressure that long. I mean, I can experience it and know that it's real. But, ah, I don't know, I really have a, just a real attitude of optimism. I mean it was always going to get better . . . tomorrow, tomorrow, tomorrow, tomorrow. And, ah, I don't get buckled too often.

Counselor (11):   So you're feeling pressured to find a job, and you are hopeful that something will turn up.

At (10), the counselor might well have been silent to encourage the client to continue considering his previous reference to restlessness and wanting to go beyond this, rather than moving so quickly to the concrete issue of financial pressure. The counselor's impatience precluded dealing with the possibility of the client's feeling like a failure as a provider for his family and himself.

Client (12):   Yes. I feel basically right where I was when I first started talking with you. Except for that one avenue, you know, that one avenue of thinking in terms of Christian work. And the only light that I seem to have gotten in that direction since I talked with you is the fact that I think I'll have to move towards some denominational lines. I think I'll have to, ah, I mean that's the way I see it now. Ah, be a Methodist or be a Presbyterian or something like that, and just see what kind of things are open. And, ah, so that's the only thing, and I just sort of thought about it.

Counselor (12): You feel blocked from working for the church, unless you become a member of a specific denomination.

Client (13): Um, yes, I think so, in a lot of ways. I think there's opportunities among probably some of the large denominational churches. I mean opportunities that are there right now and could be pursued and taken a look at.

Counselor (13): So, in order to reach toward this future goal that you have a sense of, one decision that you feel confident about is to choose a specific denomination to become a part of.

Client (14): Um, yes. I just ah, I just stumbled on that in the last couple of days. My wife and I are looking for a church, a fellowship of some sort. We've, ah, had a lot, we're much more comfortable with home Bible studies and such things. But, ah, I just came in touch with a, with a larger church. And, ah, that's where I grew up. And I can see that there's a need, there's a need in there, for people who care. And, ah, so, if that could be arranged and that would be comfortable with my family, that might be an opportunity to just . . . try and, you know, try and contribute to their particular church, and at the same time keep my eyes and ears open for a, you know, for some kind of work maybe.

Counselor (14): So you see some possibility there, but there's still a lot of if's about it.

Client (15): Oh, yeah, a lot of if's. I've always been kind of a dreamer. You know, kind of a visionary person. And, yet, haven't, ah, haven't yet singled out anything to bring that about. And I don't, ah, you know . . . I'd like to in my lifetime pull one of these visions out of my head and really move towards it.

Counselor (15): You feel frustrated, because the visions don't become reality.

Client (16): Yes, I suppose.

Counselor (16): And you'd like to learn how to make at least one of those visions happen.

Client (17): Um hum. I have a lot of head knowledge for success, but I've never done it . . . you know. I've, I've seen, you know, I've seen success in my life, to the degree that, ah, good things have happened around me. But, um, success by the definition of attaining a goal, I've never had that kind of success.

Counselor (17): And so you're dissatisfied with yourself, because you haven't attained a goal that you set for yourself.

The counselor at (16) is beginning to focus the client on what he would like to make happen in his life. At counselor (17) the client is helped to own a personal feeling ("dissatisfied with yourself") and the responsibility for the content (what the client has been unable to accomplish).

Client (18):   Yeah, I haven't set very many.
Counselor (18):   So before you can attain a goal, you have to set a goal.
Client (19):   Right.
Counselor (19):   A specific goal.
Client (20):   [Pause] Yeah, so generally I guess that's it. [Pause]
Counselor (20):   And so . . . what I hear you saying, John, is you still want to work on making vague dreams into a specific goal that you can move toward. . . . But at the same time, you haven't felt ready to set a goal.
Client (21):   Yes, if I'm hearing you right, ah, it's I'd like to, ah, I'd like to get a hold of a goal and move toward it. At the same time, what I begin, what I do right now, I'd like to have it in . . . harmony, you know, with this goal, I'd like to have everything starting to work together.
Counselor (21):   When will you know that it's time to concretize that goal?
Client (22):   Well, I don't know. Ah, "concretize"—what do you mean exactly?
Counselor (22):   Ah, make concrete, specific.
Client (23):   That's, I, that's hard to say, you know. I don't know if I'm kind of copping out or, ah, maybe I just don't know how to go about it.
Counselor (23):   You're confused, not really sure if you're fooling yourself but yet sense you don't know what to do next. Maybe if we can begin to list some alternatives and evaluate them one at a time, together we can get a better "fix" on the choices and find out if you are ready to concretize them.
Client (24):   Okay . . . ah, that sounds good.

The counselor has confronted the client on his lack of specific goals and has given him an opportunity to move toward making them specific. Counselor (23) presents a specific goal for the immediate future—that of clarifying choices about the selection of future goals. The first step is mentioned—listing alternatives and then evaluating them. This definitive direction taken by the counselor entices the client to do something about his dilemma of feeling confused and listless.

Inaccuracy   There will be instances when the counselor simply misunderstands the client. The confusion emanates from the counselor; the counselor is responsible for overcoming it. The confusion might come from the counselor's misreading the feelings or misconstruing the content. In this event, the client will either point out the error and correct it or be inadvertently shifted to a less productive target.

Client (1):   I don't know why, but when I feel that I am being lied to, I get so angry I almost explode. I could kill the person lying to me. My husband does that to me, and I have to leave the room so I won't attack him.

Counselor (1):   And you don't know why he continues to do that, and that perplexes you.

Client (2):   Yeah, I don't know why he does it . . . Why does he do it? Tell me. I've asked him not to, and . . . oh, well, it never does any good . . . he'll not change.

Counselor (2):   And because you don't see any chance for him to change, you just get so angry that you feel rage!

Client (3):   No, that is not where the rage is—but that does make me know that there is no chance for our relationship to improve. I don't know why it makes me so damn angry.

This dialogue contains two responses that, owing to their inaccuracy, slow the pace of the client's exploration. In Client (1), the woman expresses confusion, anger to the point of explosion, and possibly fear about not being able to control her impulses. The counselor responds inaccurately to both feelings and content. The counselor has responded to the least important aspect of her statement and then adds, without previous knowledge, that she does not know why her husband lies. The client's response at (2) may, because of the "yeah," mislead the counselor into believing that he is on the right track. The counselor has helped the client ignore her feelings of confusion, anger, and fear. He sidetracked her to figure out "why" her husband behaves as he does. At Client (3), the client informs the counselor that he is incorrect, and then she reverts to the original issue of feeling confused about her inordinate anger.

Frequently, clients will be able to tell the counselor that some misunderstanding has occurred, but the result is to divert and delay the process of exploration and understanding. In the example here, the counselor needed to listen more carefully to the theme of the session and harness his impatience to understand the rage.

Pacing   Pacing is of utmost importance in counseling. If the counselor talks quickly, interrupts the client, and leaves no silences between statements, it is likely that the client will follow that model. The result will be a fast paced, even frantic, counseling session. It is doubtful that deep self-exploration can occur under these conditions. The counselor should instead model a counseling pace that not only permits, but encourages, deep consideration of the thoughts and feelings expressed. This slower pace will allow counselors more time to think and ready their responses. It may be necessary to confront the talkative client about a pace that makes it difficult for the counselor to reply and to think and process what has taken place. A simple response such as the following would suffice:

"John, I am aware that you talk rapidly for long periods, during which you express a number of feelings and thoughts. By the time that you pause, I'm feeling so overwhelmed that I have difficulty formulating a response; and before I can, you are off again. Let's try to slow things down a bit and give both of us more time to think. I'll help you to do this as we progress."

It appears that John is overwhelming the counselor just as he overwhelms himself. The counselor who allows the rapid pace to continue perpetuates John's problem. It's possible that John's intention (conscious or unconscious) is to keep the counselor off balance by his rambling style and fast pace. A counselor who is off balance, trying desperately to catch up, will not probe sensitive areas. Whatever the reason for such behavior, the helpful counselor will take charge of the session and establish those procedures that promote effective counseling. Optimally, there will be several seconds of silence between statements and responses. Both participants need to learn to recognize and patiently wait for one another to think and prepare their responses. Certainly, the counselor will model this behavior and encourage the client to adopt it.

Pacing also refers to counselors' decisions about when it is appropriate to make a specific response. Exploration is a process that often takes time. The amount of time will vary with the client. As they select their responses, counselors must be sensitive to each client's pace of exploration. Frequently, counselors will "hear" feelings and issues many minutes, or even a session or two, before their clients discover them. Counselors have two alternatives: (1) help clients discover their feelings themselves or (2) communicate to clients what they have heard. If the second alternative is selected, counselors will wish to consider the intensity of the communication to be used: Will they hint at their awareness or emphasize it? The answer can be found in the counselor's careful assessment of her overall understanding of the client, including his readiness for this insight, the strength of the relationship, and the influence the insight may have on his exploration and understanding. Going too fast may cause clients confusion and frustration and possibly undue threat. Care must be taken to progress at a pace suitable to the client, not the counselor. It is the client who needs to understand herself and integrate new understanding into her perception of herself and the world. The focus needs to be upon *helping,* not forcing, the client to explore, understand, and increase her self-awareness. The true meanings of insights are not the insights themselves, but what use is made of them—a use that is helped by their gradual evolution. There are no magical insights that "cure." Counseling is the discovery of many insights, one at a time, in due order and in due time.

The pace of counseling can also be too slow. The client seems to be expressing similar feelings about the same situation. The session becomes repetitious, almost boring. If this climate continues, chances are that the client will become restless, feel impatient, and choose not to return. Here, the counselor may find himself or herself responding only to superficial feelings and, consequently, giving the client no hint of direction. The counselor might ask: "What am I doing to maintain this pattern of stagnation?" Alternative behaviors include asking the client questions to seek further elaboration, responding to the deeper (often hidden) feelings, identifying what it is that client is avoiding, or summarizing what is understood in order to provide a fresh view. Most often, the counselor will find success by responding to the underlying feelings stimulating the feelings that are being expressed. There are always deeper feelings for the counselor sensitive enough to find them.

Counselors often respond to surface feelings expecting that to be effective. When it is not, they blame the theory, saying that responding to feelings does not work. Rarer are the counselors who wonder if they have responded fully enough. While it can be discouraging and there may be a risk, counselors need to ask what deeper feelings have prompted these feelings of inertia to surface. The clients are aided greatly in their quest for understanding when they become aware of the underlying feelings that prompt their behavior.

While it is preferable that counselors understand what their clients are trying to communicate, they cannot always do so. Clients are often confused about their feelings and thoughts, and this results in confused (and confusing) expressions. Since counselors are gaining their understanding from the clients' frame of reference, they can also become confused at this point. Too often, however, inexperienced counselors refuse themselves permission to be confused and pretend to be "with the client." The disservice of this act is obvious: The clients are led to believe that they are making sense, and blissfully continue in their confusion. These counselors have unknowingly allowed a potent intervention to slip away by this self-protective act. Counselors will benefit both themselves and their clients when they respond in a genuine fashion: "I'm confused. Could you say that again?" The result will help the clients clarify and better understand themselves and increase the trust level of the relationship.

Themes   Clients present a variety of different feelings, thoughts, and beliefs in any single statement. It becomes the counselors' responsibility to decide which of these feelings, thoughts, or beliefs is most deserving of a response. This decision can best be made by counselors who have identified the basic theme their clients are expressing. Once that is established, the counselors respond to those feelings and that content that, in their judgment, will best promote exploration and understanding. Obviously, counselors would not respond to feelings and content that would slow or sidetrack the clients' progress. Therefore, it is of paramount importance for counselors to identify the theme of the counseling session.

There may be several themes expressed simultaneously. First, there may be a general theme involving the clients' feelings of disliking themselves. Second, another theme may emerge regarding the clients' need to have others like, love, or admire them and when other people do not, the effect it has on them. Finally, as a manifestation of the previous theme, the behavior exhibited to elicit others' approval might be the topic (theme) currently under discussion. The themes are interrelated and influence each other immensely. Let us take one example. The most basic theme is the client's sense of not liking herself. It is manifested in numerous ways. Among these are the overt feelings of self-depreciation, self-blame, and depression as well as behaviors that allow others to discount the client's sense of feeling important. Second, there is the disappointment in others for not meeting her expectations. For example, a person might do something in his own best interest, which is, inadvertently, not in the client's best interest. This is experienced by the client as rejection and a lack of caring and results in a deep sense of pain, disillusionment, and disappointment. This sense of disappointment is easily evoked and causes others to be continually cautious, protective, and eventually irritated with the client. Finally, there is a sense of the client's not knowing herself, which is often the product of fearing to discover something that might be unlikeable. This client is likely to seek protection by allowing others to form her opinions, instruct her in her activities, and compliment her efforts. When other people find themselves constantly having to protect the client, they become so tired of sacrificing and giving to her that they transmit messages of disapproval. These messages push the client even harder to seek approval. In addition, people who invest themselves in protecting others in all likelihood do not like themselves either, since they are unwilling to stop protecting the other and risk a loss of affection.

Themes that are important tend to be repeated throughout the session(s). They appear and reappear as might a red thread that is woven in a cloth. The process of identifying the reappearing theme is called "red threading." The red thread may appear in various forms and in different contexts. Consider the client who begins the session complaining about the teacher who caught her cheating, and progresses to talk of her difficulty relating to her father, and ends by complaining about how you confront her with inconsistencies in her statements. The red thread is this client's difficulty relating to authority figures in her world, originally her father. This general theme can be explored and better understood by discussing any of the more specific themes. The "red thread" concept is the key to the metaphor of the client's basic conflict. Even clients may not be aware of its presence. Thus, counselors can advance their clients' understanding of themselves by helping them identify those themes. The identification of those themes helps clients understand the underlying conflicts and early experiences that have influenced them to experience themselves as they do. When those conflicts are labeled, understood, and differentiated, clients have more control over them and the feelings engendered by them. Therefore, one of the goals of counseling is to listen for common themes in order to help clients understand and gain better control over these conflicting parts of the total self.

This stage of counseling can occur only after counselors have achieved a sufficient understanding of their clients. Trust, warmth, good attending, and accurate empathy must precede, be concurrent with, and follow this process of helping the client identify and use themes effectively.

Personalization   Personalization is the process of helping clients to talk about themselves. It is helping clients to own their situations and accept the responsibility for improving them. If they are going to change their thoughts, feelings, or beliefs, they must first identify them as being theirs. They must "own" them. Human beings all experience a variety of feelings, some of which are more enjoyable than others. However, all of them (enjoyable and painful) are a part of the total self. If clients are to alter, modify, or change any of them, they must be aware of them. If they decline to be aware of part of their feelings, they are alienated from that part of themselves (Perls, 1969), and they lose control over what they are not aware of. What they lose control of, they are powerless to alter.

"Owning" feelings means accepting them, feeling them, and realizing that, indeed, these particular feelings do exist. It does not mean approving of them or feeling satisfied with their current status. For example, a client feels raging jealousy when his wife behaves in a friendly manner toward other men. Those feelings are his to own. That is, he created them; his wife did not. His wife's behavior was merely the catalyst that permitted him to get in touch with those feelings already within him (of not liking himself). A behavior does not create specific feelings. If a man kisses a strange woman in an elevator, she is likely to be startled and angered. If this same man kisses his mother, she is likely to feel loved and cherished. If, finally, he kisses his girlfriend, she may feel sexually aroused. The responsibility for all three different responses cannot be assumed by the act of kissing. The responsibility for the resultant feelings must reside with the women. The responsibility for the behavior (the catalyst) rests with the man. If any one of the women wishes to change her response to the stimulus (kiss), she must first "own" those feelings as hers and admit that she and only she has control over them.

People consciously and unconsciously avoid responsibility for their feelings and situations. Passons (1975) identifies many ways in which this is done: When talking, a client refers to himself or herself using the pronoun "you," the collective "we," or the impersonal "it." The counselor can help bring about personal responsibility in the client by encouraging him or her to use the pronoun "I." Making "I" statements promotes talking only for oneself and owning the feelings, beliefs, or thoughts stated.

Client (1):   "It's just not fair." Change to: "I think that it is unfair."
Client (2):   "You work hard, only to be disappointed. You just can't win."
     Change to: "I work hard, only to be disappointed. I just can't win."
Client (3):   "We always get put down. We might as well not try anymore."
     Change to: "I always get put down. I might as well not try anymore."

Passons (1975) suggests helping clients change questions into statements. Behind every question, there is a statement. If a statement can be identified and owned, clients' self-awareness will increase.

Client (1):   It's a pretty difficult path that I need to follow to change to be the way I want. Do you think you can help me?

Counselor (1):   You asked me a question, but I sense you are really expressing some personal sentiment.

Client (2):   No, I . . . I just wanted to know if you think that you can . . . [Pause] I guess . . . well, I guess that I was wondering if you can help me.

Counselor (2):   You feel uncertain that I am capable enough to help you go the direction you have chosen.

Client (3):   Yeah, I guess that is it. . . . But I think I know the answer . . . I guess I am really saying that it is going to be hard and I know it.

Counselor (3):   You are aware that the path will be painful and long, and you want to be reassured that I'll be able to help you over those rough spots.

Client (4):   Yeah, and I know you will be. Thanks.

Asking a client to own the statement behind the question, or to personalize a pronoun, may not yield such clean-cut results as illustrated here, but the potential remains needing only to be exercised.

Carkhuff et al. (1980) has extended his response format to "You feel _____ because you _____" to encourage clients to own their experiences. This is the first step to a response that helps clients to extend themselves into present awareness.

The second step is to personalize the problem. This helps clients put the problem into a personal perspective, identifying what it is that the clients cannot do that has created their dilemma. The format "You feel _____ because you cannot _____" is used for this response (Carkhuff et al., 1980). It is important for counselors to phrase their responses in the present tense, since they are working to help the client increase awareness of the here-and-now.

Awareness can be experienced only in the present (Perls, 1969). Therefore, effective counselors will couch responses in language that aids clients to experience their dilemma in the "now" and to take immediate ownership for the accompanying feelings and responsibility for the solution.

Once the problem has been personalized, counselors may wish to reevaluate the words used to describe the client's feelings. Are they as personal as the problem? Generally, personalized feelings reflect how clients feel about *themselves* knowing that they cannot accomplish this specific task.

The following is a short transcript designed to implement the concepts discussed. We encourage the readers to cover the counselor responses and practice responding.

Client (1):   I . . . I just can't lose any weight. . . . It never seems to want to come off, and when I do lose some weight it just comes right back on. It is just no use.

Counselor (1):   It must be discouraging for you to regain the weight after losing it.

Client (2): Yeah, it is discouraging. It has happened so often that I really don't even want to try anymore. You know . . . it wouldn't be so bad if I could keep it off—then I know I would be able to lose all this fat gradually, but I don't think I can try it again. Because I couldn't face gaining it again.

Counselor (2): The anticipation of feeling that discouragement again is strong and frightens you to the point of wanting to avoid it.

Client (3): Sure, and that is not the answer either, because I am so unhappy being fat. I am always sick, my legs ache, and I get tired so fast. Men don't ask me out, and I may never get married.

Counselor (3): Sounds like you are torn between risking the threat of another disappointment and risking the sadness that accompanies your being overweight.

Client (4): Yeah. Not a very good place to be . . . but I just can't get moving. Lately I try not to eat, but yet I do. I'm always hungry, and the food is there, and before I know it, I'm eating and can't stop. And after, I feel so bad but . . . well it happens again. Why, yesterday I finished off a half gallon of ice cream and seven cupcakes before I stopped.

Counselor (4): So while you're discouraged with yourself for overeating; you just cannot control those impulses.

Client (5): Yeah, I've never known what it's like to eat a little and be filled, and it probably never will happen to me. I get out there and eat and eat until everything is gone. . . . Then later regret it, but it's too late. And after all, what difference does it make? Look at me, and tell me another pound makes a difference.

Counselor (5): I still hear that conflict you're in. You want to lose weight, but it is hard work and, in the end, will it make any difference? You already feel so badly about yourself, you feel ambivalent about stopping.

Client (6): Well, wouldn't you? I . . . it is hard work . . . and it takes so long, and I am so hungry that I have to go eat, and do. Can't stop it . . . but really I do want to lose weight.

Counselor (6): I'm aware that I hear you expressing anger at me and wonder where that is coming from.

Client (7): I am feeling angry. There you are so thin . . . and here I am, fat. Wouldn't you be angry?

Counselor (7): What I hear you saying is that you would expect me to be angry just like you are.

Client (8): Yeah, I would.

Counselor (8): But I'm wondering what the anger is about.

Client (9): I don't know . . . at least I'm not sure if . . . but I know that I'm not really angry at you. Guess I'm angry at myself for not caring about myself more. Why can't I stop eating and lose weight? Others do . . . I've got to or else I'll be like this—with no man—forever.

Counselor (9): Yeah . . . You're feeling angry and disappointed with yourself, because you can't control your impulse to eat. You feel so badly about yourself that you give up that control, so it controls you.

Client (10): I guess, sure . . . it does control me. [Pause] Or at least I allow it to.

The reader will notice the depersonalized language expressed in Client (1). However, the counselor chooses to respond in such a way as to encourage the client to own the feeling in his more personalized "discouraging to you." The counselor continually brings the feelings home to the client, as at (2) with "frighten" and at (3) with "torn." The Counselor (4) response uses a personalized feeling and problem. The response at Counselor (6) reacts to the angry tone of voice in "Well, wouldn't you?" However, the counselor is attempting here to help the client own the feeling and identify its target. The counselor needs to retain his lack of defensiveness (remain open) and his fear of hurting his client's feelings. This allows the client to identify the dislike of herself and the anger at herself for giving up control to her impulses. The process of personalization requires time to evolve. Simplistic phrases used to fill in the blanks in the format "You feel _____ because you cannot _____" are usually insufficient and often mention feelings already obvious to the client. A very firm base of understanding must be built before the counselor can refer to the client's deficiencies. Attending, observing, responding to nonverbal communication, the content, and the feeling are also prerequisite to such identification.

Diagnosis Labeling clients' deficits in concrete terminology can be referred to as "making a diagnosis"—long a controversial issue in counseling. The concept of diagnosis has its roots in medicine. Medical consultants listen to patients describe symptoms, physically examine them, and diagnose the ailment, which determines the medicine to be prescribed. This, the medical model, involves a physician, a patient, a diagnosis, and a treatment. As counseling evolved from the medical practice of psychiatry, it necessarily involved the concept of diagnosis. The culmination of the work in diagnosis is displayed in the 222 specific mental disorders listed in *Diagnostic and Statistical Manual of Mental Disorders* (1980), which is published under the auspices of the American Psychiatric Association.

Diagnosis, as represented in that work, has been widely criticized on the basis of validity (Tyler, 1969), reliability, helpfulness in counseling (Hurst et al., 1969; Rogers, 1951), and the application of labels to people. Too often these labels have overshadowed people and have become a dominant force in their lives. Rogers (1951) has argued, that "in client-centered therapy . . . psychological diagnosis as usually understood is unnecessary for psychotherapy, and may actually be a detriment to the therapeutic process" (p. 220). He based his objections of diagnosis on its superficial and palliative characteristics as well as the God-like role in which it placed the counselor. Essentially Rogers believed that if behavior is to change, then a change in perception must be experienced from inside the client. "Intellectual knowledge cannot substitute for this" (Rogers, 1951, p. 222).

The point should be made that diagnosis in counseling does not determine the mode of treatment as much as it does in medicine. Many counselors rely on diagnosis because it promotes them as competent, knowledgeable professionals. Thus, it is often used to emphasize the difference between the client (unknowing) and the counselor (knowing). Finally, it can be misused by ineffective counselors and clients alike as a rationale for the client's irrational behavior.

Certain aspects of diagnosis are nevertheless helpful to counselors. Diagnosis is an interpersonal process whose sole purpose is to understand the client and his or her concerns well enough to guide the direction of counseling, and, in this sense, diagnosis helps the client to change. From the first moment of introduction, counselors are engaged in making several assessments. In forming a working understanding of the client, they attempt to answer several questions:

1. Does the client require or desire counseling?
2. If so, am I capable of providing what is needed, or should I make a referral?
3. Are my skills, theoretical approach, setting, and time limitations beneficial for the client and the problem?
4. What are the client's priorities?
5. What is the client's manifest problem(s) and what is its severity?
6. What is the most basic theme the client is expressing?

It is necessary that counselors form some basic assessment to make effective decisions about what types of clients and/or problems to accept and what counseling methods to employ.

Counselors direct their effort toward understanding the client throughout the counseling process. In doing this, they generate what Tyler (1969) calls a "working image" and Osipow and Walsh (1970) refer to as a "working hypothesis." These models of understanding emerge from the counselors' "growing perception as to the cause of [their] client's problems, what [they] must experience in order to change, and how [they] can use [themselves] in this relationship to help the client to make the necessary changes" (Kell and Mueller, 1966, p. 16). The understanding and identification of the deeper themes that emerge and the identification and description of the client's deficits can be called "diagnosis." Counselors diagnose the client's areas of concern, bringing them into awareness and integrating them into the client's perception of the self. Thus, *descriptive diagnosis* can be seen as an aid for the client's use. In the traditional medical model, diagnosis is only for the therapist's convenience and use.

We believe that counselors need to be able to understand current feelings, the history that gave rise to those feelings, and how these feelings are likely to be manifested in the client's life inside and outside of the counseling relationship. Understanding the client's perception of the original conflict permits the counselor to be more sensitive to covert feelings and provides an improved sense of the direction in which counseling should move.

For example, if the client experienced childhood feelings of being unloved by his parents, it is easier to understand his adult experiences of feeling unloved by others and by self and his desperate striving to seek affection. The counselor can begin to sense the client's internal pain and predict his feeling of rejection when she does not respond to his seductive inducements to give approval. Without this predictive ability, which evolves from a working hypothesis, subtle feelings might pass unnoticed. In short, the primary function of diagnosis, as described here, is to enable helpers to understand the client, speculate about future behavior, and establish the constructs and goals for the counseling process.

Setting Goals for Counseling

Once the counselor has established a good working understanding of the client and has been able to help the client identify and "own" her or his problem (deficit), it is time to establish the direction that the counseling will take. "Goals, or purposes, are the energizing fabric of daily living (Rule, 1982, p. 195). That "energizing fabric" can be established by the counselor and client determining the goals to be pursued.

Setting Goals with Clients

The setting of a goal models for the client the counselor's behavior of seeking direction in the counseling sphere. The direction provides criteria, which become a yardstick for measuring success. The clients can measure their growing ability to exert control over their life. The more specific the goals, the better understood they will be and the easier to ascertain their accomplishment (Rule, 1982).

Neil (1975) warns that the transition step between confusion and specification of the goal can be "the most difficult and crucial step in the entire helping process" (p. 139). The step preceding the identification of the goal, is labeling the specific problem (Carkhuff, et al, 1980). The goal is simply the flip side of the problem, stated in positive language. Carkhuff et al. (1980) suggest the use of the format "You feel _____ because you cannot _____ and you want to _____" to ensure the inclusion of (a) personalized feeling, (b) the client deficit, and (c) a general statement of the client's goal.

In the transcript of the session with the overweight client (partly repeated below, along with the dialogue that follows), the response at Counselor (9) identifies the helpee deficit:

Client (9):   I don't know . . . at least I'm not sure if . . . but I know that I'm not really angry at you. Guess I'm angry at myself for not caring about myself more. Why can't I stop eating and lose weight? Others do . . . I've got to or else I'll be like this—with no man—forever.

Counselor (9):   Yeah . . . You're feeling angry and disappointed with yourself, because you can't control your impulse to eat. You feel so badly about yourself that you give up that control, so it controls you.

Client (10):   I guess, sure . . . it does control me. [Pause] Or at least I allow it to.

Counselor (10):   You look and sound extremely drained and sad when you say that.

Client (11):   I guess I am sad. I feel like crying, but I am almost too worn out . . . pooped out. And I don't know what to do. What I've tried has not worked . . . [slightly sobbing] . . . and I don't know what to do, but yet I don't want to do nothing. I want to get started and lose some weight. If I could just get started!

Counselor (11):   While you're sad and discouraged with yourself about failing in your past attempts to lose weight, you want to do something constructive by getting started on a new diet.

Client (12):   Yeah . . . that's it. If I could just get started, I would feel a lot better about myself.

Counselor (12):   You feel hopeful that if you can just get started maybe things would turn out differently. Let's discuss what kinds of things we could do that would help you to lose ten pounds in five weeks. Okay?

Client (13):   Okay, that's not so much, I can lose that easily, especially when the water comes off in the first two weeks. Maybe we should make it three or four pounds a week.

Counselor (13):   Well, we could, but my preference is to start out low and then, when you get a good grasp of what is reasonable to expect of yourself after five weeks, we can renegotiate.

Client (14):   Okay . . . maybe we should talk about what I need to do.

After responding with the client's deficit at Counselor (9), the counselor continued to respond at an interchangeable level. Here, the counselor needs to develop a sensitive pace by reading the client's reaction to his responses and responding appropriately to that feedback. When he is persuaded that the client and he are progressing together and that the client is ready, the counselor suggests a general goal of getting started on a new diet in Counselor (11). When the client reacts positively, Counselor (12) suggests a specific goal—ten pounds in five weeks, which the client sees as attainable and agreeable.

We see the counselor's gentle progression from interchangeable responses that facilitate exploration and understanding to a labeling of the client's problem (deficit) and suggestion of a general goal to ameliorate that deficit. Upon acceptance of the general goal, the counselor makes it easier for the client to take action by suggesting a goal that is defined in behavioral terms and that clearly specifies when the client has attained the goal. Goals that are too broad in their definition are experienced as barriers to both the process and the outcome of counseling (Rule, 1982). In addition, Rule suggests that specific, future-oriented goals give clients a sense of freedom that releases them from the shackles of "past, uncontrollable drives" (p. 197). To further the client's progress to this freedom, the counselor and the client together need to develop the steps of the diet program (this undertaking is discussed in the next chapter as "Developing Counseling Programs").

Hackney (1973) suggests two general classifications of goals used in counseling: process goals and outcome goals. Process goals are counselor-oriented and relate to the therapeutic process of counseling. Typical goals in an initial interview might include establishing a warm and accepting climate, responding to the client's feelings, ascertaining the precipitating problem, and developing an accurate, empathic understanding of the client. Counselors will increase their effectiveness if they review these process goals prior to each counseling session. For client A, it may be preferable to slow the pace of counseling and identify the "red thread," while for client B the process goals might include recognizing and, in a nondefensive and accepting manner, respond to client anger that is directed at the counselor. Several process goals will be common to all clients, and several will be applicable only to specific clients.

Outcome goals will vary from client to client and depend on the result desired by the client and agreed to by the counselor. Identifying outcome goals with the client eases the counselor's task of selecting process goals. The outcome goals will influence the process goals, and the implementation of the process goals will affect the outcome.

Hill (1975) has created the Counseling Outcome Inventory (COI), which helps client and counselor to establish goals and to translate those goals into specific language. In addition, the COI provides a baseline against which to measure progress.

The following steps are recommended:

1. Clients are requested to list 15 characteristics, qualities, or descriptions that they feel are important. These might be qualities they proudly possess or respect in others and desire for themselves. The counselor's clarifications, suggestions, and questions are a necessary aid at this stage.
2. Counselors and clients specify at least one behavioral description of each of the 15 descriptions. For example, if one description is to be the correct weight for one's height and body build, the behavioral description might be to lose 25 pounds.
3. Clients then rank the 15 items, and the top 10 items are selected for use. The item that is the most important is given the rank of 10, while the least important receives the value of 1.
4. Clients are requested to evaluate themselves regarding their level of satisfaction ($+3$) or level of dissatisfaction (-3) for each item, using the values of $+3$, $+2$, $+1$, 0, -1, -2, and -3.
5. For each item, the rank value determined in step 3 is multiplied by the self-evaluation score in step 4 to obtain a weighted score. The sum of all 10 weighted scores provides a baseline score, which can be used for later comparisons.
6. It is suggested that counselors and clients agree on the items to be selected for immediate work. Consideration should be given to those goals

that have a greater likelihood for successful accomplishment to positively reinforce the clients' efforts.

As an example, let us consider Kay, a 35-year-old woman currently enrolled in graduate school. She is a bright, attractive mother of two young children and is struggling with the roles of being a parent, student, and an independent, self-fulfilled person. The roles involve unique sets of responsibilities and often entail differing aspirations. Exploration and understanding has culminated in the COI shown in Table 12.2.

The score of +23 illustrates the positive view that Kay has of herself but also shows her desire for improvement. Individual scores that are lower than her expectations of herself will guide her future counseling direction.

Criteria for Generating Counseling Goals

The following suggestions will enhance a counselor's creation and use of counseling goals:

1. Initially, goals will be vague and subjective; but, with progress in counseling, benefit will be derived if the terminal behavior is specified in concrete terms, as illustrated in Watson and Tharp (1977) and Goodyear and Bradley (1980).
2. To be effective, the client and counselor need to agree on goals and express commitment to work for their attainment. Understanding and agreement must also be shared on the methods used to achieve success.
3. The goals may be renegotiated, if client or counselor request that it be done.
4. The goals that will promote change will be those that call for a reasonable and workable goal exhibiting a high probability for successful attainment.
5. Goals that call for a decrease in one type of behavior will be enhanced

Table 12.2
A Typical Counseling Outcome Inventory

Rank	Characteristic	Behavioral Description	Rating	Value
10	Feel adequate	Seek and accept job demanding intelligence	+1	+10
9	Be assertive	State her feelings	+1	+ 9
8	Follow through	Start dissertation and complete in nine months	0	0
7	Good parent	Be consistent, don't back down	0	0
6	Be accepting	Accept, not judge, others	+1	+ 6
5	Be patient	Respond firmly, but kindly, to kids	+1	+ 5
4	Be organized	Establish and maintain a schedule	−1	− 4
3	Think fast on feet	Relax anxious feelings, freeing responses	0	0
2	Trim figure	Lose eight pounds	−2	− 4
1	Be athletic	Improve eye-hand coordination (racketball)	+1	+ 1
			Total	+23

by corresponding goals that solicit an increase in an inconsistent behavior. For example, a goal calling for a decrease in negative self-statements would best be accompanied by a goal eliciting an increase in positive self-statements.

6. The degree to which goals are accomplished can best be assessed when those goals are stated as measurable, observable terms (Krumboltz, 1966).

Goals emerge from assessment of the client's problem (diagnosis). Efficiency in counseling is increased when both the counselor and client agree on both the diagnosis and goals. Hurst et al. (1969) conducted a study using the Missouri Diagnostic Classification Plan (MDCP) with 156 university students who received counseling at a university counseling center. Both the clients and the counselor were asked to give primary and secondary diagnoses of the client's problem after termination. Primary diagnosis described the content of the problem, including these areas: vocational, emotional, and educational. The secondary diagnosis described the underlying causal factors of the content problem, including: (1) lack of information about self, (2) lack of information about the environment, (3) conflict with self, (4) conflict with significant others, and (5) lack of skills. Results, with one exception, yielded a significant relationship between client-counselor agreement on the diagnoses and beneficial outcomes of counseling. The study suggested that disagreement on diagnoses would most likely lead to different goals for the counselor and client and, therefore, result in conflict and ineffectiveness. Covert diagnosis, therefore, increases potential for conflict and inefficiency.

Goal setting, if done properly, can increase the commitment of both the counselor and the client to the counseling process. Specifying the working diagnosis and the counseling goal decreases verbal rambling and helps to give counselor-client interaction a meaningful direction. Goals provide a much-needed method for measuring the progress of counseling and indicating when termination is appropriate. Goals can combine the best of the humanist and behaviorist schools. It is possible to establish goals in the affective domain (for example, increase feelings of self-confidence as measured by increased assertive statements and positive self-comments). In short, goals help to clarify the road ahead and reduce the fears and ambiguity about getting there.

Using Rating Scales

Carkhuff (1969) has generated a scale to rate empathy by revising an earlier scale (Carkhuff and Berenson, 1967). The revised scale establishes five levels of empathy, ranging from Level 1, which detracts "significantly from the verbal and behavioral expressions of the helpee(s) in that they communicate significantly less of the helpee's feelings and experiences than the helpee has communicated himself" (Carkhuff, 1969, p. 174) to Level 5, which adds "significantly to the feeling and meaning of the expressions of the helpee(s) in such a way as to accurately express feeling levels above what the helpee himself was able to express" (Carkhuff, 1969, p. 175). Level 3.0 is the midpoint, typified by a response that is interchangeable with the helpee's and interweaves similar feeling and content into accurate empathy. More specifically, the ratings suggested by Carkhuff et al. (1980) are the following:

Level 1.0: Nonattending to the client
Level 1.5: Attending to the client
Level 2.0: Reflection of accurate content
Level 2.5: Reflection of accurate feeling (You feel _____.)
Level 3.0: Reflection of accurate feeling and content (You feel _____ because _____.)
Level 3.5: Reflection of accurate personalized meaning (You feel _____ because you _____.)
Level 4.0: Reflection of accurate personalized feeling, the client's deficit, and goal (You feel _____ because you cannot _____ and you want to _____.)

The reader will notice that the reflection of feeling is rated 0.5 points higher than the reflection of content. This occurs because understanding of and responding to feelings presents a higher level of understanding of the client's world and is often more difficult to communicate accurately.

Below are some client statements followed by several sample responses. The responses are rated using the empathy scale. It is suggested that the readers cover the responses and generate their own. Then they might read each of the alternative responses, rate them as Level 1.0, 2.0, 2.5, or 3.0, and compare them to their own.

Client (A): You know, every time I seem to meet anyone very neat . . . ah . . . I get all excited about them and really like them immediately . . . really well . . . do things for them . . . and all. Then after a bit of time I feel myself back away, see things I don't like, and I put distance between us almost without realizing it, except I do and so do they.

2.0 Counselor (1): You tend to really like people at first and then later find that you overreacted.

3.0 Counselor (2): You feel confused about your seemingly inconsistent behavior of approaching people and then backing off.

2.5 Counselor (3): That seems to upset you.

1.0 Counselor (4): Maybe they are doing something different that you don't see at first.

Client (B): I have a teacher who seems to pick on me all of the time. You know, she has never been married . . . and . . . well . . . I'm attractive, have a boyfriend, am popular, and other things, and I think she is jealous of me. But, boy, she picks on me, criticizes me in front of my class. . . . Last week I got so upset I cried.

1.0   Counselor (1):   I doubt that she is jealous, but maybe she thinks you are not serious enough.

2.5   Counselor (2):   It's really embarrassing and hurts you a lot.

3.0   Counselor (3):   It is distressing to have a teacher have such a strong and negative reaction to you.

2.0   Counselor (4):   She picks on you and yells at you in front of your classmates?

Client (C):   I'll tell you . . . if it happens one more time, I think I am going to punch him out. He does not have the right to tell me what to do . . . but he keeps trying. And it is getting to me. . . . He is just a pushy jerk . . . and I don't like to be pushed. Who does he think he is?

2.0   Counselor (1):   It sounds like he tries to push everyone around. Possibly he would stop if you ignored him.

3.0   Counselor (2):   It really brings out your anger when he hassles you.

1.0   Counselor (3):   Maybe he is just trying to be helpful, and you are not recognizing it.

2.5   Counselor (4):   You sound really furious, ready to hit him.

Advice is rated as a level 2.0 if it communicates to the client accurate understanding of the content. The rating of 2.0 does not reflect the rater's agreement with the advice.

Using Interpretation

Interpretation is a counselor statement that seeks to help clients become aware of unrealized concepts, feelings, aspects of their behavior, or causal conditions. Interpretation occurs only in the later stages of counseling, after counselors have gained a firm and deep understanding of the clients. It is mandatory that clients respect and trust their counselors' thoughts, insights, and motivations if interpretations are to be effective. This is a stage of counseling that must not be entered blissfully, with little thought, and yet it is a stage that can greatly benefit and develop the clients' self-awareness. Interpretations increase the personal involvement of counselors and subject them to a new and exciting risk with their clients. For these reasons, interpretations are one of the most controversial of counseling techniques (Troemel-Ploetz, 1980).

Interpretations help clients to progress in their awareness by providing them with a fresh view of the patterns, motivations, and consequences of their behavior. Consequences include the ways that particular behaviors interfere with the clients' self-interest (Austin, 1958). Interpretations are most effective when counselors can gently and Socratically help their clients develop a fresh view of themselves. However, there will be occasions when counselors will wish to state the interpretation more directly. Counselors are advised to keep the level of interpretation clear enough to allow their clients an opportunity to assimilate and own it. If the interpretation is too deep, clients can become overwhelmed, confused, and somewhat fearful and take defensive steps, such as denial, to escape (Helner and Jessell, 1974). Research has shown that effective interpretations are those that are almost in the client's awareness and are congruent with the client's belief (Claiborn, et al., 1981).

Learning takes place only when one is ready for it. Readiness occurs when one has mastered the previous step, not before. Interpretations lead to learning about oneself, but they need to be taken in steps. Therefore, the awareness of deep material is accomplished, not by deep interpretations, but by a series of shallower ones dealing with "nearly aware" material that is in concert with the client's perception and beliefs (Claiborn et al., 1981). The success of an interpretation cannot be correctly inferred by the clients' reply; it must be evaluated on the basis of the use clients make of it. Acceptance, or agreement, is different from owning and using the interpretation as a steppingstone to new exploration and understanding. Verbal acceptance does not automatically mean understanding. For example, verbal acceptance could be a cover for confusion rather than a sign of client comprehension.

To help make a problem more controllable, the counselor must carefully consider the timing, accuracy, delivery, and type of interpretation. If the clients' goals are to gain control over their destiny, researchers have found that the type of interpretation is an important variable. Beck and Strong (1982) found that for depressed clients, interpretations having a positive connotation were more effective than those with a negative connotation. A positively connotated interpretation is: "Being alone shows a great tolerance for solitude and basic self-satisfaction." The negatively connotated interpretation is: "Being alone indicates avoidance and rejection of others" (p. 553). The positively connotated condition allowed clients to integrate the interpretation and use it effectively to control their mood, whereas the negatively connotated condition encouraged the clients to worry about the re-emergence of the symptom. The research by Claiborn et al. (1981) illustrates that interpretations which are more congruent with the clients' beliefs are more facilitative of change than are highly discrepant interpretations. Research by Strong et al. (1979) concluded that interpretations which identify causal factors that clients can control are significantly better at motivating the client to make necessary changes than are interpretations which emphasize underlying conflicts that are not directly controllable. Finally, Averswald (1974) found that interpretations elicited a higher proportion of client self-reference affective responses than did counselor restatements, while Dowd and Boroto (1982) found that counselor interpretations near the end of a session enhance clients' motivation to see that counselor. All of this suggests that if the interpretation is reasonably accurate, is nearly congruent with the client's beliefs, deals with controllable factors, has a positive connotation, and is delivered by a caring, sensitive, and empathic counselor, it will be of maximum use to the client.

There are several types of interpretations. We have already discussed interpretation of the deficit (diagnosis); we will now discuss clarification, immediacy, and confrontation.

Clarification   Clarification interpretations are attempts to help the client crystallize awareness of beliefs, "thoughts and feelings around a particular subject, to focus his attention on something requiring further investigation and interpretation, to sort out a theme from apparently diversified material, or to summarize the understanding thus far" (Colby, 1951, p. 83). The intent is to clarify the nature of the client's problem in order to permit, if not promote, its assimilation into understanding. It can be beneficial for the counselor to point out the implications and innuendos of the client's thoughts and feelings as they are verbalized. It will help the client to separate reality from fantasy, to make new appraisals of expectations, and to recognize repetitious themes that emerge within each session or from session to session (Austin, 1958).

Immediacy   Immediacy involves the counselors' sensitivity to the immediate situation and understanding of the dynamics of what is occurring here and now with the clients. The interpretation of immediacy is the communication of this awareness to the clients. Such communication combines the counselors' sensitivity to the "now" with their ability to confront and self-disclose. Interpretations of immediacy are designed to facilitate the clients' awareness of their indirect communication of their present feelings and behavior (Turock, 1980). The counseling relationship is a microcosm of the clients' outside world; their behaviors in counseling represent their strategies for coping. Counselors who can sense the interplay and dynamics between themselves and their clients have a generous store of material and information. By presenting their "sensings" and understandings in a gradual and helpful manner, counselors can increase the clients' self-awareness and understanding. As with other types of interpretation, a formidable understanding of the clients must precede interpretations of this type.

Carkhuff (1969) suggests four guidelines to help counselors focus on the key question, "What is the helpee really trying to tell me that he cannot tell me directly?" (p. 211). They include:

1. Concentrate upon your experiencing in the immediate moment.
2. Disregard for the moment the content of the client's statements.

3. During moments of frustration and lack of direction, momentarily become an observer and ask "What is the helpee doing to slow us down?"
4. Periodically become an observer and sense the immediate situation by asking "What is going on right now?" (p. 211)

The interpretation of immediacy provides a means for counselors to respond effectively to dependency, manipulation, transference, trust, resistance, and countless other interpersonal issues.

Client (1):   So when my husband lies to you . . . he just has to know what it does to you . . . that I just explode with anger, so much so that I lose control. He just has to realize that!

Counselor (1):   Mary, could you say that again and this time take responsibility for your feelings . . . by using "I" statements?

Client (2):   What for? Why should I stop to nit pick? . . . You don't understand me, you didn't last week. I leave here and feel nothing gets accomplished. You never understand me.

Counselor (2):   I hear your anger directed at me when you say that I don't understand you. I sense in myself a feeling of being manipulated and intimidated when I confront you and ask you to own your feelings.

Client (3):   I do own them! I know that it is me that gets angry, so why do I have to say it? Damn! I just feel like getting up and walking out of here!

Counselor (3):   Your anger is so strong and, yet, I sense frustration—frustration with me.

Client (4):   [Turns away] Yes, I can't stand it when you sit there and remain so calm when I am over here blowing up. You always understand and say "Mary, I understand," when I'm going out of my mind!

Counselor (4):   So your anger is with me. . . . How can I remain in control while you're losing control?

Client (5):   Sure! But this means nothing to you. . . . We're talking about my life, not yours. You can just go home and forget it, but I can't.

Counselor (5):   You feel unimportant to me . . . not sure if you mean anything to me.

Client (6):   Yeah . . . Do I? You are so cool and collected, nothing I say gets you riled up.

Counselor (6):   I wonder if you feel this way with anyone else?

Client (7):   [Pause] Yeah, my husband is just the same way, well not just the same way. When I yell at him he yells back.

Counselor (7):   So when you hook him, it makes you feel that he cares at least enough to yell back, but since I don't react in the same way, you are not sure if I'm involved with you or care about you.

Client (8):   [Pauses for almost a minute; her face loses its intensity; closes eyes and takes a deep breath as she begins to speak] I . . . guess you're right. [Smiles] I do . . . and it works, but I didn't realize what it was that I did or why. I guess he does care, but I know you do too.

This example illustrates the building effect that an interpretation can have. In this case, the counselor responded in Counselor (2) to the anger and then disclosed the feeling of manipulation he was experiencing. This disclosure focused the discussion on the relationship in the present. The counselor fortunately was confident in his approach and understood the client's ploy. Having this understanding enabled him to respond to the underlying feelings rather than becoming defensive and responding to the superficial feelings and content—as the client's husband apparently does. If the counselor had become defensive, and claimed he cared about the client in Counselor (5), he too would have been "hooked" into protecting her and he would thus perpetuate the client's defenses and the maladaptive way in which she assures herself of being loved. Now she will need to confront the discrepancy in her husband's and the counselor's reactions and her role in eliciting them. The risk for the counselor can be high, but the rewards are worth it.

Confrontation　Confrontation is an active combination of immediacy, empathy, and interpretation. It is a statement by counselors that is designed to help the clients crystallize the inconsistencies of their expressions and their behavior. This crystallization will help them to strive for consistency in their life, thus reducing unwanted conflict, confusion, and anxiety.

Confronting someone normally connotes venting anger and aggressive behavior. Such actions have the effect of belittling, blaming, and embarrassing the receiver. Effects such as these are harmful and destructive, not only in social situations, but also in the counseling context. A confrontation in the counseling context is an assertive action, not an aggressive one. That is, it calls for counselors to take some risks, to avoid venting their own feelings, and to help their clients bring into awareness their discrepancies. In this sense, a confrontation is the counselors' demonstration of immediacy. The counselors must have a developed understanding of their clients to perceive discrepancies, inconsistencies in word and deed, distortions, defenses, and evasions. The relationships must contain the bond that will weather the precipitation of the crisis that results from the confrontation. Counselors declare their willingness to risk immediacy and their commitment to help work through the crisis when they confront their clients. Without this commitment, confrontation lacks therapeutic potential and can be quite harmful to both the client and the counselor. In a confrontation, the counselors model for the clients an active role that uses insight and understanding effectively to remove ambiguity and inconsistency and, thus, seeks deeper understanding of self and feelings. Unlike interpretations that explain problems and conflicts, confrontation helps the clients to see and experience them (Berenson and Mitchell, 1974).

Krumboltz and Thoresen (1969) indicate that it is beneficial for clients to view themselves from a different vantage point on two occasions: (1) when clients are not aware that their behavior is "inadequate" and believe that their problems are caused by factors over which they have no control, and (2) when clients have never permitted themselves to be aware of the consequences of their behavior.

Carkhuff (1969) has classified confrontations into three broad categories:

1. Confrontation of a discrepancy between the helpee's expression of what he wishes to be and how he actually experiences himself (his ideal versus his real self);
2. Confrontation of a discrepancy between the helpee's verbal expression of his awareness of himself (insight) and his observable or reported behavior;
3. Confrontation of a discrepancy between how the helper reportedly experiences the helpee and the helpee's expression of his own experience of himself. (p. 191)

Berenson and Mitchell (1974) identify five major types of confrontation: experiential, didactic, strength, weakness, and encouragement to action. An experiential confrontation defines the discrepancy between (a) how the counselor and client experience the counseling relationship, (b) the client's statement about self and her or his experience of self, or (c) the counselor's and client's subjective experience of the client. A didactic confrontation is the counselor's clarification of the client's "misinformation or lack of information about relatively objective aspects of his world or the therapeutic relationship" (p. 14). Objective data might include test results, interpretations of other's behavior, or predictions of possible consequences of chosen behavior. A strength confrontation is experiential in that it focuses on the counselor's or the client's experiencing resources or characteristics that are beneficial to the client. A confrontation of weakness points out the client's pathology, shortcomings, and weaknesses. Finally the encouragement-to-action confrontation refers to the counselor's "pressing the helpee to act on his world in some reasonable, appropriate, and constructive manner; and discouraging a passive stance toward life" (Berenson and Mitchell, 1974, p. 15).

Confrontations are classified as interpretations, since they generally evolve from the counselors' frame of reference and are owned by the counselors as their experience of their clients. As previously mentioned, interpretations are best provided in progressive steps that lead to deeper interpretations and understanding. So it is with confrontations. Effective confrontations need to minimize the likelihood of clients retreating and invoking defensive reactions. Therefore, counselors should begin with mild confrontations rather than risking the possibility of a debate and losing the qualities of an empathic, caring relationship. As with interpretations, a single confrontation will not permanently alter the clients' view of themselves or their behavior pattern (Ruble and Slivka, 1975). A series of confrontations, consistent in nature and delivered when the clients demonstrate readiness, possesses greater therapeutic potential and will lead to a greater degree of client self-exploration.

Summary

The best route to understanding clients is the establishment of a warm and trusting relationship. Counselors can achieve this by listening and responding to both the content and feeling portions of the clients' message. When the counselors can assimilate the feelings, content, and nonverbal portions of the clients' message, they can not only sense, but also communicate the deeper level of understanding that is vague even to the clients themselves. Additional implications are noted below.

1. Feelings generally fall within one of seven broad categories: happy, sad, strong, weak, angry, confused, and afraid.
2. Feelings are key to counselors' deeper understanding of clients, as well as to clients' self-understanding.
3. Accurate empathy combines the clients' content and feelings into one statement that communicates a clear and complete understanding to the clients. Such form as "You feel _____ because _____" may be used.
4. Counselors are advised to identify the general theme of the counseling session. Responding to the theme permits the clients to better understand the commonality of their concerns.
5. Personalization is the process of helping clients to talk about themselves and "own" the responsibility for improving their situation.
6. While diagnosis can be misused, it can also be used to guide counselors in assessing their clients and creating a "working

image." This image can lead counselors to identifying the deeper themes and deficits of their clients.
7. Goal setting provides direction for the counseling as well as a criterion to measure success.
8. Interpretation is a counselor statement that shares with clients concepts, feelings, behavior, or causal conditions that were not previously realized. An interpretation is used only in the later stages of counseling, after a thorough foundation of understanding has been established.
9. Clarification interpretations are responses to help clients clarify the nature of their problem and promote its assimilation into understanding.
10. Immediacy implies that counselors are aware of the immediate dynamics occurring between them and their clients and communicate this awareness to the clients.
11. A confrontation is a blend of immediacy, empathy, and interpretation; it aims to help clients become aware of and clarify their inconsistent expressions and behavior.
12. The dynamics noted in this chapter build on each other. Empathy provides the basis for all the other concepts. Personalization, diagnosis, goal setting, and interpretations build on the empathic foundation. While they increase the anxiety level of the counseling session, they also promote deeper understanding. Counselors must exercise care, intelligence, and sensitivity in their employment.

References

American Psychiatric Association. *Diagnostic and Statistical Manual of Mental Disorders.* 3rd ed. Washington, D.C.: APA, 1980.

Austin, L. N. "Dynamics and Treatment of the Client with Anxiety Hysteria." In H. J. Parad, ed., *Ego Psychology and Dynamic Casework.* New York: Family Service Association of America, 1958. Pp. 137–158.

Averswald, M. C. "Differential Reinforcing Power of Restatement and Interpretation on Client Production of Affect." *Journal of Counseling Psychology* 21 (1974):9–14.

Beck, J. T. and S. R. Strong. "Stimulating Therapeutic Change with Interpretations: A Comparison of Positive and Negative Connotation." *Journal of Counseling Psychology* 29 (1982):551–559.

Berenson, B. G., and K. M. Mitchell. *Confrontation: For Better or Worse!* Amherst, Mass.: Human Resource Development Press, 1974.

Carkhuff, R. R. *Helping and Human Relations: A Primer For Lay and Professional Helpers. Vol. I. Selection and Training.* New York: Holt, Rinehart and Winston, 1969.

———, **and B. G. Berenson.** *Beyond Counseling and Therapy.* New York: Holt, Rinehart and Winston, 1967.

———, **R. M. Pierce, and J. R. Cannon.** *The Art of Helping. Vol. IV.* Amherst, Mass.: Human Resource Development Press, 1980.

Claiborn, C. D. "Counselor Verbal Intervention, Nonverbal Behavior, and Social Power." *Journal of Counseling Psychology* 26 (1979):378–383.

———, **S. R. Ward, and S. Strong.** "Effects of Congruence Between Counselor Interpretations and Client Beliefs." *Journal of Counseling Psychology* 28 (1981):101–109.

Colby, K. M. *A Primer for Psychotherapists.* New York: The Ronald Press, 1951.

Dowd, E. T., and D. R. Boroto. "Differential Effects of Counselor Self-Disclosure, Self-Involving Statements, and Interpretation." *Journal of Counseling Psychology* 29 (1982):8–13.

Goodyear, R. K., and F. O. Bradley. "The Helping Process as Contractual." *Personnel and Guidance Journal* 58 (1980):512–515.

Hackney, H. "Goal-Setting: Maximizing the Reinforcing Effects of Progress." *The School Counselor* 20 (1973):176–181.

Helner, P. A., and J. C. Jessell. "Effects of Interpretation as a Counseling Technique." *Journal of Counseling Psychology* 21 (1974):475–481.

Hill, C. E. "A Process Approach for Establishing Counseling Goals and Outcomes." *Personnel and Guidance Journal* 53 (1975):571–576.

———, **L. Siegelman, B. R. Gronsky, F. Sturniolo, and B. R. Fretz.** "Nonverbal Communication and Counseling Outcome." *Journal of Counseling Psychology* 28 (1981):203–212.

Hurst, J. C., R. G. Weigel, R. Thatcher, and A. J. Nyman. "Counselor-Client Diagnostic Agreement and Perceived Outcomes of Counseling." *Journal of Counseling Psychology* 16 (1969):421–426.

Kell, B. L., and W. J. Mueller. *Impact and Change.* New York: Appleton-Century-Crofts, 1966.

Krumboltz, J. D. "Behavioral Goals for Counseling." *Journal of Counseling Psychology* 13 (1966):153–159.

———, **and C. E. Thoresen, eds.** *Behavioral Counseling: Cases and Techniques.* New York: Holt, Rinehart and Winston, 1969.

Krystal, H. "Alexithymia and Psychotherapy." *American Journal of Psychotherapy* 33 (1979):17–31.

Neil, T. C. "Turning Muddy Problems into Clear Solutions." *Personnel and Guidance Journal* 54 (1975):139–142.

Osipow, S. H., and W. B. Walsh. *Strategies in Counseling for Behavior Change.* New York: Appleton-Century-Crofts, 1970.

Passons, W. R. *Gestalt Approaches in Counseling.* New York: Holt, Rinehart and Winston, 1975.

Perls, F. S. *Gestalt Therapy Verbatim.* Lafayette, Calif.: Real People Press, 1969.

Rogers, C. R. *Client-Centered Therapy.* Boston: Houghton Mifflin, 1951.

Ruble, R. A., and S. Slivka. "To Confront or Not to Confront: Is That the Question." *The School Counselor* 23 (1975):11–15.

Rule, W. R. "Pursuing the Horizon: Striving for Elusive Goals." *Personnel and Guidance Journal* 61 (1982):195–197.

Seay, T. A., and M. K. Altekruse. "Verbal and

Nonverbal Behavior in Judgments of Facilative Conditions." *Journal of Counseling Psychology* 26 (1979):109–119.

Shantz, C. V.   "Empathy in Relation to Social Cognitive Development." *The Counseling Psychologist* 5 (1975):18–21.

Siegel, J. C.   "Effects of Objective Evidence of Expertness, Nonverbal Behavior, and Subject Sex on Client-Perceived Expertness." *Journal of Counseling Psychology* 27 (1980):117–121.

Strong, S. R., C. A. Wamback, F. G. Lopez, and R. K. Cooper.   "Motivational and Equipping Functions of Interpretation in Counseling." *Journal of Counseling Psychology* 26 (1979):98–107.

Tepper, D. T., Jr., and R. F. Haase.   "Verbal and Nonverbal Communication of Facilative Conditions." *Journal of Counseling Psychology* 25 (1978):35–44.

Troemel-Ploetz, S.   " 'I'd Come to You for Therapy': Interpretation, Redefinition and Paradox in Rogerian Therapy." *Psychotherapy: Theory, Research and Practice* 17 (1980):246–257.

Turock, A.   "Immediacy in Counseling: Recognizing Clients' Unspoken Messages." *Personnel and Guidance Journal* 59 (1980):168–172.

Tyler, L. E.   *The Work of the Counselor.* New York: Appleton-Century-Crofts, 1969.

Watson, D., and R. Tharp.   *Self-Directed Behavior.* Belmont, Calif.: Wadsworth, 1977.

CHAPTER 13

Planning for Change

Chapter Organizer

Aim of the Chapter

This chapter will introduce the student to sources of information, their use in decision making, and the process of planning counseling programs.

Chapter Preview

1. Information that can be used in counseling is generally of three types:
   a. information about the client's world
   b. information about the client provided by others
   c. information about the client provided through tests
2. Clients' problems are often reflected in their inability to make decisions in their life. This inability is frequently caused by inadequate decision-making skills.
3. The behavioral technique of shaping is used to establish counseling programs. Shaping is the process of reinforcing behavior that successively approximates the terminal behavior that has been identified as the goal.

Relevant Questions

The following are questions to keep in mind while reading the chapter:

1. What kinds of information would be useful to the client and how can they best be made available?
2. In selecting inventories and tests, what important issues must the counselor keep in mind?
3. How do people make decisions? What are the major requirements needed for skillful decision making?
4. What is a counseling program, and how is such a program to be used by the counselor?

Introduction

Counseling is effective when it promotes healthy change in clients. The change may appear in the clients' feelings toward themselves, in an increase in their self-confidence, or in a sense of self-awareness and understanding that permits an inner glow of peace to permeate their presence. Such emotional changes will be reflected in client behaviors, such as smiling, laughing, making positive self-statements, and decreasing negative self-statements and frowns.

Many such changes will occur as clients are encouraged to explore themselves in a safe, warm, and trusting environment. When this exploration results in a new awareness of self, changes in behavior will naturally follow. Behavior, which grows out of feelings, will need to change to be consistent with new feelings. Conversely, when outward behavior is altered and receives appropriate and positive reinforcement, feelings about oneself will frequently change to become consistent with the behavior.

The counseling approach advocated by this text blends the two principles stated above. The previous chapters have thoroughly introduced the readers to an empathic exploration of the self leading to a new awareness and understanding, which may result in new feelings and behavior. This chapter will introduce the role of information, tests, and decision-making strategies in the counseling process and describe how, in combination with counseling programs, they can promote healthy and desired client change.

Sources of Information in Counseling

Information used in counseling includes three types: (a) information about the client's world, (b) information about the client provided by others, and (c) information about the client provided by the client through tests.

Information About the Client's World

Information about the client's world includes information stored in printed, computerized, and audio-visual packages (Pietrofesa and Splete, 1976). Examples of printed information include higher-education data, such as entrance requirements, financial charges, and curriculi *(Profiles of American Colleges; American Junior Colleges;* and *Technical Education Yearbook);* job opportunities and descriptions *(Occupational Outlook Handbook* and *Dictionary of Occupational Titles);* sex information sources; community referral agencies; and drug information.

Computerized information has had a major impact on career guidance and is described in *Computer-Based Vocational Guidance Systems* (1969). Examples include the *Information System for Vocational Decisions* (ISVD) (Tiedeman, 1979) and the *Michigan Occupational Information System* (MOIS), which is currently in use in Michigan.

Audio-visual information is available on audio and/or video cassettes, tapes, records, film, microfilm, and microfiche.

These three kinds of information are increasing geometrically. Counselors will find it difficult to keep a grasp on current available sources. Hudson and Danish (1980) believe that counselors need to focus their attention on helping individuals acquire information through *"mass teaching* rather than *clinical model* of delivery" (p. 165). They state that the greatest barrier to acquiring information is the lack of familarity with potential sources. Therefore, the counselor's efforts are economized by providing skill training in information acquisition. They suggest a four-step process for collecting information: (1) identify personal information needs through inspection of personal goals, (2) identify potential sources of information based on personal needs, (3) record and categorize the various sources of information and the type of information provided in a useful catalogue for current and future use, and (4) continually update the catalogue of information resources. While counselors do not need to know the data available, they are more useful to their clients if they know the available sources and are able to evaluate certain information according to its accuracy and bias-free presentation, relative current validity, and availability to the client (Tyler, 1969).

Goldman (1967) identifies a dilemma that plagues counselors who attempt to integrate information about their clients' world into the counseling process. How do they utilize information without shifting the focus of counseling from the "internal to the external frame of reference, by shifting from feelings—values—goals to facts, and by evoking from the counselor persuasiveness and defensiveness, rather than acceptance, clarification, and interpretation" (p. 45)? The dilemma can best be alleviated if counselors carefully consider the following:

1. The use of information is not an end in itself but simply a tool for the counselors' and the clients' use within the counseling process. Information should not be considered valid and reliable just because it appears in an enduring form such as print.

2. Information is most helpful when the need for it grows out of the counseling process, when it relates to and promotes progress toward one of the clients' stated goals.

3. The value of information (like interpretation and insight) is enhanced when clients demonstrate commitment and interest by providing the needed information themselves. Counselors help by assisting their clients in their task, not by supplanting them.

4. Counselors do not provide their clients with unwanted and unrequested information, and the clients assume the responsibility for deciding which information is useful. As with interpretation (see Chapter 12), clients will use what they are ready to hear, not what their counselors are ready to tell.

5. Information that has been collected is best used when it is integrated into the normal counseling process. Information should be discussed in relation

to the clients' goals and is best presented through counselor responses that seek to explore and understand the clients' evolving thoughts, beliefs, feelings, and values.

In summary, information about the clients' world is best used when it is integrated into the counseling process, is assimilated into the clients' cognitive structure, and awakes feelings and thoughts that enlarge the clients' knowledge and awareness of themselves.

Information About the Client Provided by Others

This class of information includes cumulative records, biographies, anecdotal records, questionnaires, and personal statements. These represent statements of the clients' achievements (grades in courses) or someone else's personal reflections about the client.

Most clients will be able to provide any information that will be meaningful in counseling. In addition, when the information evolves from the natural counseling process, counselors are better able to explore and understand the thoughts and feelings their clients attach to the data. Too often, cumulative records are incomplete and inaccurate; others' reflections about clients are biased, prejudiced, and misleading; and self-statements and questionnaires are impersonal and sketchy. It is our view that any information worth having is information provided by the clients. Since counseling seeks to help clients alter their feelings and behavior, it follows that the counseling needs to deal with the clients' current thoughts and feelings about themselves, not the feelings of their teachers or previous counselors about them. Counselors need to understand their clients from an internal frame of reference, not from an external one offered by others. The counselor who begins to confront clients about how others see them, places herself or himself outside the client's frame of reference in an advisory relationship; this is the antithesis of the counseling relationship advocated in this text.

Information Provided by the Client Through Tests

We have already discussed the relevancy and validity of using the client's frame of reference as the primary source of information about the client. Tests are a convenient and efficient means of identifying, and possibly labeling, a sample of the client's behavior or attitudes, which might not be otherwise available. The use of tests in counseling has been the subject of controversy for years (Goldman, 1972; Goldman, 1982; Shertzer and Linden, 1982). Goldman (1982) states his belief that tests as used by counselors have made much difference in the lives of the people they serve" (p. 70). Others, such as Wesman (1972) and Prediger (1980), believe that counselors will increasingly need tests in the future and will be able to use them more effectively. Glaser (1980) reviews those recent developments and research in test construction and use that he believes to be outstanding. Although his overall view is optimistic, Glaser identifies areas of concern and those that need additional research if tests are to continue improving. Writers on both sides of the question caution the counselor to thoroughly understand tests, their purposes, selection criteria, and potential use with clients.

Purposes of Tests   Generally, tests may be viewed as a method of ascertaining new information or confirming previously held notions about the client. More specifically, tests can be used for three general purposes:

1. *To provide information to counselors to promote wiser decisions regarding their clients* (Algozzine et al., 1982). Tests included in this category are generally diagnostic. Some examples are self-report inventories, standardized personality tests, projective techniques, achievement tests, and aptitude tests used for selection and placement. Generally, counselors have little opportunity and are inadequately trained to employ diagnostic-type tests effectively, but they may find some of the personality inventories and problem checklists useful as aides in screening, referring, and understanding clients. Counselors have an obligation to be well informed about tests and to exercise care in the selection, administration, and interpretation of any test used.

2. *To provide the clients with information that will increase the wisdom of their choices* (Miller, 1982; Biggs and Keller, 1982). Tests can give clients a firmer understanding of their vocational and educational interests, abilities, traits, and achievements. While the interest inventory yields little new information to clients, it does collect and present that information in an organized and understandable fashion, increasing the impact and meaning of clients' self-knowledge. Aptitude tests can provide a reality-testing situation, giving clients an indication of their ability at the present time. When clients can compare their test results with those of an appropriate norm group, they may gain a better understanding of their strengths and weaknesses. Clients need this kind of information to test hypotheses about personal, social, and educational plans (Biggs and Keller, 1982).

3. *To provide clients with new understanding and awareness, which will facilitate continued self-exploration and self-evaluation* (Biggs and Keller, 1982). Tests may yield new information, which, through effective interpretation will stimulate new client thinking and exploration. The reader is urged to review the research data on the effectiveness of counselor interpretations provided in "Using Interpretations" in Chapter 12. In any event, interpretations, including test interpretations, should identify causal elements that the client can control, be positively rather than negatively connotated, and be mildly discrepant to nondiscrepant with the client's belief. The most valuable interpretations enhance the client's self-understanding while they excite his or her motivation and readiness to continue self-exploration.

Selection of Tests   Appropriate tests must be carefully selected so that they measure what the client and counselor think is being measured (validity), measure it accurately (reliability), and present the results to the client in a useful and meaningful manner (norms).

Validity is the single most important test attribute (Anastasi, 1982). Validity basically demonstrates satisfaction that "the test actually measures what it purports to measure" (Anastasi, 1982, p. 27). Anastasi identifies three types of validity: content, criterion-related, and construct. Content validity generally involves a detailed and systematic analysis of the test content to make sure that it covers a representative sample of the skill or behavior being evaluated. Achievement tests must have high content validity to be useful. Criterion-related validity describes the degree to which the test can predict client performance in a specific practical situation. The test "is checked against a *criterion,* i.e., a direct and independent measure of that which the test is designed to predict" (Anastasi, 1982, p. 137). Aptitude and ability tests need adequate criterion-related validity coefficients. Finally, construct validity "is the extent to which the test may be said to measure the theoretical construct or trait" (Anastasi, 1982, p. 144), such as intelligence, femininity, or anxiety.

Reliability refers to the consistency of the scores earned by the same person when retested; it is closely tied to the test's validity (Anastasi, 1982). A test that does not measure its identified trait with consistency is useless since it cannot be believed. However, a test with high reliability may be measuring consistently some trait other than the one intended. Therefore, counselors must choose a test that measures with reliability a trait that proves to be valid.

Norms reflect the nature of the group that is compared with the client; such comparison enhances the meaning of the client's test score. Thus if a client correctly completes 12 of 45 math problems and the normal high school junior correctly completes 12 problems, then the client is functioning (in mathematics) at the level of a high school junior. If the test is to be relevant, norms need to approximate client characteristics in a meaningful manner. Norms have been criticized by minority and disadvantaged groups as doing them a disservice by discriminating against them and having a deleterious effect on their future opportunities (Goldman, 1972). Careful review of the "norming" group is mandatory to ensure that they provide valid information rather than perpetuate discriminating and destructive beliefs.

Counselors are cautioned not to select tests that do not have adequate research to support their validity, reliability, and norm groups. Frequently, this criterion will limit counselors to a few well-chosen and intimately known tests that meet the needs of their working population. The tests that have such research may be older tests, since a great deal of time is required to compile ample research. Information about available tests is contained in *The Eighth Mental Measurement Yearbook* edited by Buros (1978). Several writers (Patterson and Watkins, 1982; Biggs and Keller, 1982) present a case for involving clients in the selection of tests. We concur with this recommendation. This text has promoted the idea that counseling is a cooperative relationship between two people who are intimately involved in exploration, understanding, and growth. The counseling tasks, thus far investigated, have been shared by the counselor and the client. We see no reason to shift the responsibility to the counselor at this time. If counseling is to benefit clients and help them to accept responsibility for making decisions in their life, the decisions regarding testing can easily be integrated into the counseling relationship. The need for a test will evolve from the counseling as problem areas are defined. Clients can then make use of the counselors' familiarity with and repertoire of tests to select the most appropriate instrument. Strong (1968, 1970) stated that the likelihood of test results being discredited by clients is inversely proportional to the level of their involvement in the selection process. So the clients' involvement in ascertaining a problem area, considering tests as a source of information, and selecting the specific instruments to be used will improve clients' use and ownership of the results.

Interpretation of Tests   Test interpretation, too, can benefit from its integration into the cooperative counseling process. Too often, counselors "give" interpretations and clients "get" them. Interpretations need to address the basic questions that first suggested taking a test. Addressing those concerns helps clients to attribute personal meaning to the results, which thus become useful for further exploration. Since the test results yield new information, chances are that awareness and feelings will be expressed. Effective counselors will elicit and be sensitive to the clients' feelings and thoughts about those results. Responding to thoughts and feelings can elicit more of the same, thus continuing the exploration-understanding cycle; in this sense, we can partially discount Goldman's belief that for "the most part, standardized tests seem to close rather than open counseling interactions" (1982, p. 71).

Counselors should study test results before attempting to interpret them. Results must be organized in a coherent pattern. The counselors themselves must understand the results, see groupings, and be aware of similarities and discrepancies. In their presentation, counselors must respect—and delineate—the limits of the test score, the limits of the amount of behavior or trait measured, and the nature and the appropriateness of the norm group (Miller, 1982). Descriptors such as very high, high, above average, below average, low, and very low are preferred because they avoid unwarranted specificity. In short, the interpretation—if it is to be effective—should take into consideration the limitations and strengths of the test. It is necessary to remember that test results communicate only a portion of the information about a client's present behavior. The results should receive no more credibility from counselors or clients than any other piece of information, including client self-statements (statements written by clients about themselves).

Miller (1982) suggests a five-step test interpretation process that counselors can use with clients, parents, teachers, and others in individual or group modes. The steps are outlined below.

Step 1: Understanding the Clients' Frame of Reference   It is suggested that the counselor begin the interpretation by exploring how clients felt on the day of the test as well as how they perceived and experienced the test. This step draws from clients the physical and attitudinal factors that may have influenced the test results. It communicates the counselor's concern for clients as individuals and the manner in which their personal feelings and attitudes can effect the test results.

Step 2: Setting the Stage   The counselor reviews with clients (preferably by asking them) the purpose for taking the test and sets the stage for understanding the interpretation of the results by reviewing with clients the psychometric concepts to be used. These include norms, stanines, percentiles, percentile ranks, percentile bands, and subtest scores. Clients should be encouraged to use visual aids, such as plotting scores on the profile sheets, in order to become familiar with scoring concepts.

Step 3: Re-examination of Test and Presentation of Scores   The test scores will be more meaningful if clients are reminded which type of questions represent which subtest or test scores. The counselor is encouraged to explore with the clients what the scores mean to them. The clients' understanding of and feelings about the results, rather than the test scores themselves, should be emphasized.

Step 4: Integration of Test Results with Other Available Information   The counselor may now emphasize the concept of a test's measuring only a portion of a person's behavior, attitudes, or traits. This can be accomplished by collecting other pertinent information about the clients from available records, the clients themselves, or the counselor and integrating that information into meaningful profiles or themes. Exploration of the test results and the clients' self-knowledge, past accomplishments, internal feelings, and future plans provides a helpful perspective for self-understanding.

Step 5: Planning for the Future   The final step is to help clients put their newly developed self-knowledge to productive use. Their plans for future schooling, training, occupational choice, and the like need to be re-examined in the light of their new self-knowledge. The counselor can thus help clients to improve their self-understanding and to use appropriate reasoning in planning their future.

Improving the Client's Decision-Making Skills

Clients often come to counseling because they are unable to make decisions in their life. Frequently a specific decision provokes the crisis that brings them to the counselor, but the crisis often reflects a general inability to make decisions. Counseling to improve decision-making skills has had numerous applications, including counseling with children (Russell and Thoresen, 1976), with high school students (Birk, 1976; Yabroff, 1969), with college students (Alvord and Gallacher, 1976; Rubinton, 1980) and with career, educational, and vocational problems (Magoon, 1969; Ferguson, 1976).

Decisions are important because they can open new avenues to clients while closing others. Thus, their lives are shaped by the decisions they have already made and their future is molded by the decisions they will make. The process goes on endlessly.

Steps in the decision-making process are often patterned after the Evans and Cody (1969) format:

1. Consideration of alternative course of action
2. Consideration of consequences of alternatives
3. Consideration of past experiences appropriate to the problem
4. Consideration of desirability of the consequences accruing from alternative decisions
5. Selection of a decision based on the considerations listed previously (p. 427)

Krumboltz (1966) suggests eight steps, which emphasize the generalization of the decision-making process to the client's life:

1. Generating a list of all possible courses of action
2. Gathering relevant information about each feasible alternative course of action
3. Estimating the probability of success in each alternative on the basis of the experience of others and projections of current trends
4. Considering the personal values which may be enhanced or diminished under each course of action
5. Deliberating and weighing the facts, probable outcomes and values for each alternative
6. Eliminating from consideration the least favorable courses of action
7. Formulating a tentative plan of action subject to new developments and opportunities
8. Generalizing the decision-making process to future problems (p. 156)

Whereas Evans and Cody consider past experiences and the desirability of alternative outcomes, Krumboltz elaborates on the process by asking the participants to consider their personal values, which influence the attractiveness of an alternative.

Gelatt et al. (1973) have stated that the three major requirements for skillful decision making are

a. Examination and recognition of personal *values.*
b. Knowledge and use of adequate, relevant *information.*
c. Knowledge and use of an effective *strategy* for converting this information into action. (p. 3)

Values can be identified and clarified in the counseling process that precedes the making of a decision. Values-clarification exercises—such as those offered by Simon, Howe, and Kirschenbaum (1972)—can be implemented in group-guidance, group-counseling, or individual-counseling settings.

Gelatt et al. (1973) divide the second major requirement, information, into four parts:

1. Possible alternative actions
2. Possible outcomes (consequences of various actions)
3. Probability of outcomes (relationship between actions and outcomes)
4. Desirability of outcomes (personal preferences) (p. 6)

They suggest that increasing the number alternatives from which to choose allows one to make a better choice. The amount and quality of information gathered and considered likewise affect the quality of the decision. Therefore, those cautions mentioned in the section of this chapter dealing with information apply to the implementation of the decision-making process. Decisions reflect the quality of the information gathered and the thoroughness with which it is considered.

The decision-making strategy involves calculating the risks associated with each alternative and taking responsibility for selecting the alternative that best promotes the client's desires (Gelatt et al., 1973).

Gelatt (1962) designed the decision-making model shown in Figure 13.1. It shows what Gelatt called "the cyclical nature of decisions" (p. 241). There are two types of decisions—terminal and investigatory. Investigatory decisions necessitate a cycle, which involves gathering more information and recycling the process until a terminal decision can be made. However, even a terminal decision may result in recycling, since it will yield new data and may modify the desired result. The following sequence of Gelatt's model may be used in the counseling process:

1. A purpose for making a decision becomes evident. An objective is identified.
2. Data that relate to the decision are collected.
3. Possible alternative actions are identified.
4. Possible outcomes for all the alternatives listed in step 3 are determined.
5. The probability of the outcomes identified in step 4 are predicted.
6. The desirability of the outcomes is estimated.
7. Estimates arrived at in step 6 are evaluated and a choice is made.
8. The decision is determined to be either terminal or investigatory. Recycling is considered; implementation depends on evaluation of the decision.

Decisions, like counseling, demand the active involvement of the clients. Most of the information used in the process is generated by them. Most importantly, for the decision to be useful and have a high probability of success, clients must be involved in the process. Gunnison et al. (1982) use Gelatt's decision-making model to illustrate the developmental nature of counseling by illuminating the private thoughts, feelings, and perceptions of the client and counselor in the counseling process.

Figure 13.1
Sequential Decision
Making

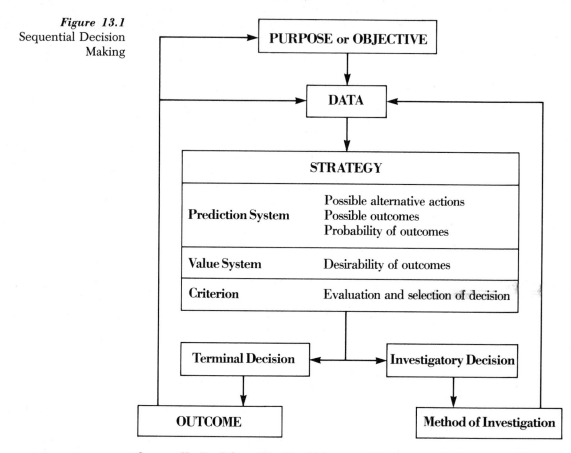

Source: H. B. Gelatt, "Decision-Making: A Conceptual Frame of Reference for Counseling," *Journal of Counseling Psychology* 9 (1962):242. Copyright 1962 by the American Psychological Association. Adapted by permission of the publisher and author.

If clients are unable to make decisions, this problem will surface during counseling. One of the first tasks of counselors is to help their clients identify the difficulty in making decisions and explore for understanding. If the exploration suggests a deficiency in decision-making skills, the task becomes one of teaching the skill in the course of making a particular decision. If the blockage cannot be remedied by skill building, then further exploration for understanding is necessary.

If skill building in making decisions is necessary, several modes of counseling can be implemented. Two such modes are Mitchell's (1973) catalytic counseling and Heppner's (1978) application of D'Zurilla and Goldfried's (1971) decision-making model to counseling. However, we recommend the problem-solving matrix suggested by Carkhuff (1973) in *The Art of Problem-Solving*. The principles of the model are listed here:

Step 1 Define a goal, identify aspects of the problem that are amenable to decision making. Using specific terms, describe the goal as deficits of the clients' behavior.

Step 2 Develop alternatives that are possible and meaningful. The alternative courses of action do not need to be exclusive and in fact may overlap.

Step 3 Generate the clients' list of personal values that are affected by the decision. State the values in terms that connote attraction. Rank order the clients' values 1–N (N = number of values). Now assign them weighted scores (1–10), with the first-ranked item receiving the largest weighted score (10) and the last-ranked value receiving the lowest weighted score (1). Assign appropriate weighted scores to the remaining values. One may use a weighted score twice or not at all (see example on page 356).

Step 4 Rate each alternative course according to each value. If a course contradicts a value, assign a negative valence (−). If a course is in accordance with a value, assign a positive valence (+). The valences (+ +), (+), (+ −), (−), and (− −) complete the continuum.

Step 5 Multiply the weighted score of each value by the contradiction or accordance rating arrived at in step 4. Thus, a weighted score of +8 multiplied by (− −) would yield a − 16, and a weighted score of +6 multiplied by (+ −) would equal 0.

Step 6 Sum the positive and negative values for each alternative course of action.

Step 7 The course of action that receives two-thirds of the total possible points is the preferred alternative.

Step 8 Inspection of the alternative courses of action may allow one to combine positive portions of two or more alternatives to create a best alternative.

Step 9 Implement the decision.

The decision-making matrix will resemble the one illustrated in Figure 13.2.

For example, let us consider the dilemma of Peg, a 28-year-old, unmarried pregnant woman. The counselor uses the skills to explore and understand to help her identify six alternative courses of action:

a. Have the baby, not marry the father, and live alone.
b. Have the baby, not marry the father, and live with her parents.
c. Have the baby, and marry the father.
d. Have an abortion, not marry the prospective father, and live alone.

Figure 13.2
Problem-Solving Matrix

Values Rank Order	Weighted Score	Alternative Courses of Action				
		A	B	C	D	E
1	( )					
2	( )					
3	( )					
4	( )					
5	( )					
6	( )					

e. Have an abortion, not marry the prospective father, and live with her parents.
f. Have the abortion, and marry the prospective father.

Further counseling helps to identify Peg's values as:

1. Wanting to have children.
2. Wanting a happy home for the child and herself, which means a home with a minimum of tension.
3. Marriage should be predicated on love, but she does not love the prospective father.
4. Abortion is wrong.
5. Having no job, she has financial needs.
6. She wishes to avoid the stigma of an illegitimate child.

The matrix takes the shape illustrated in Figure 13.3.

Since the ideal score would result in a $(++)$ in every box in one column, the resultant products would yield: $+20$, $+18$, $+16$, $+16$, $+12$, $+2$. Their sum equals 84, and 57/84 equals approximately 68 percent, which exceeds the 66 percent recommended for the preferred alternative. In this case, Peg decided to have the baby and live with her parents, thus keeping her options open for a future marriage.

Consideration in making decisions must be careful and thorough. When the decision that results from the problem-solving matrix does not "feel right," chances are the clients' values are incomplete or weighted incorrectly. It is suggested that counselors use the problem-solving matrix several times in their own life before utilizing it with their clients. Finally, counselors are cautioned about employing any decision-making process before they—and the client—have arrived at a firm understanding of the client. Decisions that are based on inadequate self-understanding can be destructive.

Developing Counseling Programs

The early stages of counseling involve gentle exploration of clients' worlds to gain an understanding of them, their thoughts, values, feelings, and behavior. Counselors will use reflection, clarification, confrontation, interpretation of immediacy, and "red threading" to aid the process. As has been mentioned, warm, empathic relationships are a necessary prerequisite to helping. In many cases, the empathic relationship alone will stimulate the clients to view themselves differently, resulting in healthier feelings and behavior. There are also instances when counselors may wish to implement a counseling plan that communicates the succession of therapeutic tasks that need to occur. This plan is referred to as a counseling program; its establishment is called program development.

Figure 13.3
Problem-Solving Matrix for Peg

Values Rank	Weighted Score	Alternatives					
		A	B	C	D	E	F
1. Children	(10)	++(+20)	++(+20)	++(+20)	--(-20)	--(-20)	--(-20)
2. Happy home	(9)	++(+18)	+(+9)	+(+9)	+-(0)	--(-18)	--(-18)
3. Marriage	(8)	+(+8)	+(+8)	--(-16)	++(+16)	++(+16)	--(-16)
4. Abortion	(8)	++(+16)	++(+16)	++(+16)	--(-16)	--(-16)	--(-16)
5. Finances	(6)	-(-6)	+(+6)	++(+12)	+(+6)	++(+12)	++(+12)
6. Stigma	(1)	-(-1)	--(-2)	+(+1)	++(+2)	++(+2)	++(+2)
Totals		(+55)	(+57)	(+42)	(-12)	(-24)	(-56)

Steps in Establishing a Counseling Program

Shaping is the process of reinforcing behavior that successively approximates the terminal behavior identified as the goal. It can be compared to the slow and methodical process of the artist who carefully transforms a block of clay into a beautiful sculpture. Each day, the clay approaches the final product, giving the artist a feeling of pleasure and pride that stimulates him to continue. Like the molding of a sculpture, behavioral shaping takes time and patience for both the counselor and the client.

The first task for the counselor is to identify the goal, or the terminal behavior. The goal must be clearly defined in behavioral terms through the cooperative effort of counselor and client. The reader is referred to Chapter 12 for detailed treatment of counseling goals. The terminal behavior of "losing 40 pounds" or "uttering more positive than negative self-statements" would be appropriate and amenable to the shaping strategy.

The second step is to define the clients' initial behavior (starting point). Since counseling begins with clients as they are and takes them where they want to go, so too, must the behavioral program. A thorough understanding of the client must be achieved before defining the initial behavior and planning the steps to be followed. It is important to start with a task that is easily accomplished by the clients—it can never be too easy.

The third step is to establish a chain of behavioral tasks that will gradually link the initial behavior with the terminal behavior. Each step of the chain adds a small component of new behavior to the client's repertoire, which helps that behavior to more closely approximate the terminal behavior. This new approximation then establishes a foundation for the next step in the program. The gap between the steps can never be too small. Unfortunately, it is frequently too large to ensure the client's mastery of it. Remember, if clients are unable to accomplish any one step, progress on the program stops.

The fourth step is to select potent reinforcers for those behaviors the clients desire to increase. Reinforcers need to be selected by the clients, since only they can determine the reinforcing effect. Reinforcements such as tokens, making positive self-statements, feeling proud, hearing praise from important others, paying oneself money, or treating oneself to a special event are some of the many positive reinforcements that can be employed.

Step five consists of making the reinforcements *contingent* on the desired behavior. Only after the client has successfully accomplished a task or demonstrated a behavior should the reinforcer be provided. It is the contingency that makes the reinforcer potent in establishing a desired behavior. Behavior is influenced more by the anticipated consequences of desired actions than by the immediate reinforcement itself (Bandura, 1976). Initially the reinforcement needs to be administered each time the new behavior occurs to strengthen the bond between the behavior and the reinforcer. After the link has been established, reinforce on a variable schedule (Walker and Shea, 1976). In a variable schedule, the rewards occur unpredictably. It is suggested that a variable-ratio schedule be used, since it produces higher levels of responsiveness (Bandura, 1976). The variable-ratio schedule will reinforce on the average of, for example, every tenth response. Therefore, reinforcement might occur on the fifth response, the ninth response, and the sixteenth response, which averages to every tenth response. "Behavior that has been reinforced on a thin variable-ratio schedule is exceedingly hard to extinguish because one's efforts are sustained by the belief that the actions will eventually prove successful and it takes a long time to realize that the rewards are no longer forthcoming" (Bandura, 1976, p. 22). Since counseling attempts to encourage clients to accept responsibility for their own behavior, self-reinforcement by the clients will reinforce this notion of independence. Bandura (1976) states that the highest level of autonomy is achieved by self-regulation.

Step six consists of identifying and reinforcing behaviors that are incompatible with the unhealthy behaviors the clients desire to extinguish. Inconsistent behaviors cannot coexist. Therefore, if the clients can identify and strengthen a behavior that is the opposite of or inconsistent with a behavior they wish to eliminate, their task will be much easier. The incompatible behavior may block the occurrence of the undesired behavior. For example, the man who has a tendency to eat a large and fattening lunch might substitute the eating of fresh fruit for lunch while taking a walk as incompatible behavior.

Step seven alerts counselors to evaluate the program and to be ready to change their strategy if they become aware of problems (Schaefer and Martin, 1975). The most common problem is having too large a learning task for the client to master in a single step. This will stop the program, slow progress (create a plateau), and/or the decrease clients' motivation (Watson and Tharp, 1972). Counselors should evaluate the tasks and consider the possibility of dividing a step into two or more tasks.

While counselors can use the Counseling Outcome Inventory (COI) discussed in Chapter 12 to identify the different client goals, the shaping process can best be used to identify intermediate goals, which act as building blocks for achieving the overall goal for counseling. Figure 13.4 illustrates the authors' design for programs to be used in counseling.

Sample Counseling Programs   The step-by-step procedure used in Figure 13.4 can be employed by counselors to outline the general direction and intermediate goals of counseling, as well as to provide a methodology for successively approximating a more specific terminal behavior. For example, consider Mary who came to counseling complaining of her weight of 301 pounds. Through the development of the warm, empathic relationship, several other dynamics came into focus. Mary, who had once been active in her church group, had terminated that relationship and was now spending most of her spare time watching television alone or with her parents, with whom she lived. Her self-concept was one of loneliness and self-doubt. She seemed tense when in the company of others, rarely speaking so as not to be noticed. Mary had little awareness

Figure 13.4
Outline for
Designing a
Counseling
Program

1. Identify goal	a. Behavioral terms b. Amenable to alteration
2. Define initial behavior	a. Qaulify client's status
3. Chain of tasks	a. Behavioral tasks b. Link step 2 with step 1 c. Keep gap small
4. Select needs	a. Selected by client b. Readily available
5. Arrange contingencies	a. Initially reinforce every correct response b. Later use variable schedule c. Shift to self-reinforcement
6. Identify incompatible behaviors	a. Reward those inconsistent
7. Evaluate program	a. Alert for plateaus or stoppage

of her feelings, was unable to feel happiness and pride or even sadness. She recognized only fear and negative feelings toward herself. Mary had graduated from high school with low grades and possessed insufficient skills to get a job. While she had a limited vocabulary and found it difficult to express herself (especially in writing), Mary did exhibit about average intelligence through her ability to abstract and grasp concepts. Her weight and negative self-concept had limited her ability to make friends. Her counselor visualized the following overview of the counseling program:

1. Training to be aware of and label feelings in the here-and-now.
2. Design diet to lose 100 pounds in 50 weeks.
3. Training and practicing to make more positive self-statements than negative ones.
4. Rejoin the church-group fellowship.
5. Learn and apply deep muscle relaxation.
6. Construct and implement an exercise program.
7. Attend secretarial school for three months to learn skills in English, math, typing, presentation of self, interviewing, and shorthand.
8. Acquire assertiveness training.
9. Apply for jobs.
10. Make at least two new friends.
11. Move out of parent's house.

The final goal is achieved at step 11 and represents the economic and emotional independence that the client seeks. The counselor and client now can construct a counseling program that will enable the client to successfully approximate and attain each of the stated intermediate goals. The counseling programs for steps 2 (diet), 5 (relaxation), 6 (exercise program), and 9 (apply for jobs) are reproduced below.

Counseling Program for Losing 100 Pounds in 50 Weeks

a. Receive consent of personal physician and achieve agreement for diet. Start with diet of 1500 calories per day.
b. Get baseline weight on a reliable scale.
c. Elicit and receive cooperative efforts of parents, specifically not to eat between meals in client's presence. It was decided not to request the parents to act as positive reinforcers, since their participation could not be predicted.
d. Remove all ready-to-eat food from the house.
e. Stock the refrigerator with carrots, celery, and other "munchables" low in calories.
f. Prepare Coverant Control Program (Horan et al., 1975).
   1. Identify highly rewarding images of being 100 pounds lighter—"coverant," pictures of the desired self after weight-reduction, such as seeing herself trying on a smaller size dress.
   2. Write images on 2½"-×-3" cards, which can be easily carried and read.
   3. Instruct client to read one of the images (coverants) each time she puts anything in her mouth to ingest (drink of water, lunch, coke, etc.) and to imagine the situation and positive feelings that accompany the image for 12–20 seconds.
   4. Train client in the office to imagine the highly rewarding thoughts and to feel the pleasure associated with the thoughts.
g. Implement coverant control program for 8 weeks and evaluate.
h. Drink glass of water at 10:30 A.M. and 3:00 P.M. each day (general snack time is 11:00 A.M. and 3:30 P.M.).
i. Weigh self each week and chart to show weight loss.
j. Reward self with $5.00, placed in jar on dresser each week that a loss of 2 pounds is recorded. Punish self by removing $5.00 for each week 2 pounds have not been lost. Money is to be spent every 3 months (possibly $60.00) on highly rewarding purchase or event (does not include eating).
k. After 8 weeks, implement diet of 1,000 calories per day and rewrite program.

Counseling Program for Learning and Applying Deep Muscle Relaxation in 8 Weeks

a. Introduce client to deep muscle relaxation (Lazarus, 1971). (See Appendix C.) Practice in the office to ensure understanding of the procedure.
b. Establish regular daily schedule for practicing relaxation.
c. Introduce client to series of relaxation cassette tapes by A. Lazarus (1971, p. 275). Client practices with "Relaxation I" tape each day for 10 days.
d. Client and counselor discuss procedures and situations for applying relaxation in daily living (counselor reinforcement and self-reinforcement).

 e. Client receives "Relaxation II" tape and practices relaxation each day for 10 days.

 f. Client and counselor discuss new relaxation techniques and new situations for application (counselor reinforcement and self-reinforcement).

 g. Client receives "Relaxation III" tape and practices daily for 10 days.

 h. Client and counselor discuss full relaxation program and identify problems of application, if any. Counselor seeks to have client reward self by finding new applications of the relaxation techniques. Application may be for social interactions (Pendleton et al., 1976), tension headaches (Epstein et al., 1976), or general anxiety (Chang-Liang and Denney, 1976) and may be used with children (Koeppen, 1974) or adults (Wolpe, 1969).

Counseling Program to Implement Exercise Program of Walking Briskly for 30 Minutes Within 15 Weeks

 a. Consult with physician regarding exercise program.

 b. Instruct client in proper clothing and footwear.

 c. Establish exercise schedule at same time every day (possibly as substitute for afternoon snack).

 d. Walk slowly for 10 minutes each day for 1 week.

 e. Walk slowly for 15 minutes each day for 1 week.

 f. Walk slowly for 20 minutes each day for 1 week.

 g. Walk slowly for 25 minutes each day for 1 week.

 h. Walk slowly for 30 minutes each day for 1 week.

 i. Recycle to step d and continue through step h, walking at moderate speed.

 j. Recycle to step d and continue through step h, walking at brisk pace.

 k. Continue to walk each day for 30 minutes at brisk pace throughout 50 weeks.

Counseling Program to Procure a Job Within 4 Weeks of Graduating from Secretarial School

 a. Identify sources that advertise job openings.

 b. Collect data regarding openings in the week before graduation.

 c. Decide which openings client is qualified for, and desires to apply for, before graduation.

 d. Rough out a résumé and application letter by graduation date.

 e. Final type résumé and letter in sufficient numbers by first day after graduation.

 f. Mail résumés with application letters by second day after graduation.

 g. Role play job interviews with counselor.

 h. Role play job interviews with a counselor unknown to client.

 i. Call potential employers who did not respond to application letters; ask if they have received the letters and are interested in an interview.

j. Rank order replies to application by twentieth day.

k. Interview lowest-ranked opening first for practice interviewing.

l. Interview remaining possibilities by twenty-fifth day.

m. Receive offers and use the problem-solving matrix discussed on pages 355–356 to select most attractive offer.

The above counseling programs have been carefully constructed to be applicable for Mary and may not be suitable for another client. Counseling programs are more effective when they (1) reflect the client's readiness to move to an action orientation, (2) are constructed cooperatively with the client, (3) start with the client's present development, (4) progress in small, understandable steps toward a well-defined goal, and (5) have occasional opportunity for evaluation. The counseling program can be only as good as the understanding that the counselor and client have of the problem being eradicated and goal being sought.

Summary

In summary, this chapter has attempted to define the role of information and testing in the counseling process. The empathic relationship is the foundation for implementing client action through the mechanism of decision making and the development of a counseling program. The goal of counseling is to help clients make some positive change in their life, and counselors can increase their effectiveness by wisely using information, tests, and decision-making programs and by constructing counseling programs that guide and reinforce productive and desired growth.

In addition, the following points have been emphasized:

1. Information can be valuable in counseling, but counselors should be cautious:
   a. Printed information is not necessarily valid.
   b. Information may be used in counseling, but its desirability and application should grow out of the counseling process—that is, clients should first express a need for the data and the ability to use it effectively.
2. Tests provide an outside source of new information or confirm previously known information, which can help clients to improve their decisions and promote their continued growth.
3. Ability to make decisions depends on the clients' readiness, their aspirations, their perceptions of the decision-making process, and their ability to use this process constructively.
4. Counseling programs are plans that gently shape the behavior of clients so that it progressively approximates the desired goal.
   a. Steps must begin with an initial (present) behavior and terminate at a specified goal.
   b. Steps need to gradually link the initial behavior to the terminal behavior. Care must be taken to ensure that the gap between the steps is small, which will promote their accomplishment.
   c. Use of reinforcement enhances attainment of specified goals.
   d. Care must be taken to include clients in all aspects of developing and using the counseling program. This will increase the clients' commitment to the program and encourage successful completion.

References

Algozzine, B., J. E. Ysseldyke, and C. Hill. "Psychoeducational Decision Making as a Function of the Amount of Information Reviewed." *Psychology in the Schools* 19 (1982):328–334.

Alvord, R. W., and D. Gallacher. "Tele-Tip: Information and Advice on Demand." In J. D. Krumboltz and C. E. Thoresen, *Counseling Methods.* New York: Holt, Rinehart and Winston, 1976. Pp. 389–397.

Anastasi, A. *Psychological Testing.* New York: MacMillan, 1982.

Bandura, A. "Social Learning Theory." In J. T. Spence, R. C. Carson, and J. W. Thibaut, eds., *Behavioral Approaches to Therapy.* Morristown, N.J.: General Learning Press, 1976. Pp. 1–46.

Biggs, D. A., and K. E. Keller. "A Cognitive Approach to Using Tests in Counseling." *Personnel and Guidance Journal* 60 (1982):528–531.

Birk, J. "Experienced-based Career Exploration." In J. D. Krumboltz and C. E. Thoresen, *Counseling Methods.* New York: Holt, Rinehart and Winston, 1976. Pp. 384–389.

Buros, O. K., ed. *The Eighth Mental Measurements Yearbook.* Highland Park, N.J.: Gryphon Press, 1978.

Carkhuff, R. R. *The Art of Problem-Solving: A Guide for Developing Problem-Solving Skills for Parents, Teachers, Counselors and Administrators.* Amherst, Mass.: Human Resource Development Press, 1973.

Chang-Liang, R., and D. R. Denney. "Applied Relaxation as Training in Self-Control." *Journal of Counseling Psychology* 23 (1976):183–189.

Computer-Based Vocational Guidance Systems. Washington, D.C.: Government Printing Office, 1969.

D'Zurilla, T. J., and M. R. Goldfried. "Problem Sharing and Behavior Modification." *Journal of Abnormal Psychology* 78 (1971):473–499.

Epstein, L. H., J. S. Webster, and G. G. Abel. "Self-Managed Relaxation in the Treatment of Tension Headaches." In J. D. Krumboltz and C. E. Thoresen, *Counseling Methods.* New York: Holt, Rinehart and Winston, 1976. Pp. 344–349.

Evans, J. R., and J. J. Cody. "Transfer of Decision-Making Skills Learned in a Counseling-Like Setting to Similar and Dissimilar Situations." *Journal of Counseling Psychology* 16 (1969):427–432.

Ferguson, J. "Career Guidance in the Community College." In J. D. Krumboltz and C. E. Thoresen, *Counseling Methods.* New York: Holt, Rinehart and Winston, 1976. Pp. 397–405.

Gelatt, H. B. "Decision-Making: A Conceptual Frame of Reference for Counseling." *Journal of Counseling Psychology* 9 (1962):240–245.

————, B. Varenhorst, R. Carey, and G. Miller. *Decisions and Outcomes (A Leader's Guide).* New York: College Entrance Examination Board, 1973.

Glaser, R. "The Future of Testing: A Research Agenda for Cognitive Psychology and Psychometrics." *American Psychologist* 36 (1981):923–936.

Goldman, L. "Information and Counseling: A Dilemma." *The Personnel and Guidance Journal* 46 (1967):42–46.

————. "Tests and Counseling: The Marriage That Failed." *Measurement and Evaluation in Guidance* 4 (1972):213–220.

————. "Assessment in Counseling: A Better Way." *Measurement and Evaluation in Guidance* 15 (1982):70–73.

Heppner, P. P. "A Review of the Problem-Solving Literature and Its Relationship to the Counseling Process." *Journal of Counseling Psychology* 25 (1978):366–375.

Horan, J. J., S. B. Baker, A. M. Hoffman, and R. E. Shute. "Weight Loss Through Variations in the Coverant Control Program." *Journal of Counseling and Clinical Psychology* 43 (1975):68–72.

Hudson, J., and S. J. Danish. "The Acquisition of Information: An Important Life Skill." *Personnel and Guidance Journal* 59 (1980):164–167.

Koeppen, A. S. "Relaxation Training for Children." *Elementary School Guidance and Counseling* 19 (1974):14–21.

Krumboltz, J. D. "Behavioral Goals for Counseling." *Journal of Counseling Psychology* 13 (1966):153–159.

Lazarus, A. A. *Behavioral Therapy and Beyond.* New York: McGraw-Hill, 1971.

Magoon, T. M. "Developing Skills for Solving Educational and Vocational Problems." In J. D. Krumboltz and C. E. Thoresen, eds., *Behavioral Counseling: Cases and Techniques.* New York: Holt, Rinehart and Winston, 1969. Pp. 343–396.

Miller, G. M. "Deriving Meaning from Standardized Tests: Interpreting Test Results to Clients." *Measurement and Evaluation in Guidance* 15 (1982):87–94.

Mitchell, J. S. "Decisions by Catalytic Counseling." *The School Counselor* 20 (1973):197–201.

Patterson, C. H., and C. E. Watkins, Jr. "Some Essentials of a Client-Centered Approach to Assessment." *Measurement and Evaluation in Guidance* 15 (1982):103–106.

Pendleton, L. R., J. L. Shelton, and S. E. Wilson. "Social Interaction Training Using Systematic Homework." *Personnel and Guidance Journal* 54 (1976):484–487.

Pietrofesa, J. J., and H. H. Splete. *Career Development: Theory and Research.* New York: Grune & Stratton, 1976.

Prediger, D. J. "The Marriage Between Tests and Career Counseling: An Intimate Report." *Vocational Guidance Quarterly* 28 (1980):297–305.

Rubinton, N. "Instruction in Career Decision-Making and Decision-Making Styles." *Journal of Counseling Psychology* 27 (1980):581–588.

Russell, M. J., and C. E. Thoresen. "Teaching Decision-Making Skills to Children." In J. D. Krumboltz and C. E. Thoresen, *Counseling Methods.* New York: Holt, Rinehart and Winston, 1976. Pp. 377–384.

Schaefer, H. H., and P. L. Martin. *Behavioral Therapy.* New York: McGraw-Hill, 1975.

Shertzer, B., and J. D. Linden. "Persistent Issues in Counselor Assessment and Appraisal." *Measurement and Evaluation in Guidance* 15 (1982):9–14.

Simon, S., L. Howe, and H. Kirschenbaum. *Values Clarification.* New York: Hart Publishing, 1972.

Strong, S. R. "Counseling: An Interpersonal Influence Process." *Journal of Counseling Psychology* 15 (1968):215–224.

———. "Causal Attribution in Counseling and Psychotherapy." *Journal of Counseling Psychology* 17 (1970):388–399.

Tiedeman, D. V. *Career Development: Designing Our Career Machines.* Cranston, R.I.: Carroll Press, 1979.

Tyler, L. E. The Work of the Counselor. New York: Appleton-Century-Crofts, 1969.

Walker, J.E., and T. M. Shea. *Behavior Modification: A Practical Approach for Educators.* Saint Louis: C. V. Mosby, 1976.

Watson, D. L., and R. G. Tharp. *Self-Directed Behavior: Self-Modification for Personal Adjustment.* Monterey, Calif.: Brooks/Cole, 1972.

Wesman, A. G. "Testing and Counseling: Fact and Fancy." *Measurement and Evaluation in Guidance* 5 (1972):397–402.

Wolpe, J. *The Practice of Behavior Therapy.* New York: Pergamon, 1969.

Yabroff, W. "Learning Decision-Making." In J. D. Krumboltz and C. E. Thoresen, eds., *Behavioral Counseling: Cases and Techniques.* New York: Holt, Rinehart and Winston, 1969. Pp. 329–343.

CHAPTER 14

Group, Couple, and Family Counseling

Chapter Organizer

Aim of the Chapter

This chapter will introduce counseling with groups. These groups may be composed of individuals who have never met before or a couple or a family who have lived together for a long period of time. The core counseling skills emphasized up to this point apply to group counseling, but in order to apply them correctly, counselors need specific knowledge about the specialized dynamics that characterize the population they are working with. First we will consider counseling a group created by the counselor specifically for that purpose. Second we will attempt to understand the unique structure of couples and families, not only to enhance our work with the family, but to understand the forces that *always* influence individual family members.

Chapter Preview

1. Group counseling can benefit clients and counselors, but it calls for special skills and knowledge on the part of the counselor.
   a. Groups are collections of people who share a common interest, goal, belief, purpose, or behavior.
   b. Common helping groups are guidance groups, counseling groups, T-groups, encounter groups, marathon groups, and task groups.
   c. Therapeutic forces in a group include cohesion, client expectations, group norms, self-disclosure, feedback, acceptance and validation, universalization, and reality testing.
   d. The prime advantage to group counseling is the opportunity it affords clients to receive validation and acceptance from peers in a real-life situation. The most important and most frequently encountered disadvantage of group counseling is the counselor's inability to work with a client on a given issue in the same depth as is possible in individual counseling.
   e. The counselor must establish groups with care. Issues needing particular consideration are the selection of members, the size of the group with which the counselor feels comfortable, the duration of counseling, and the leadership style.
   f. Counseling groups move through the stages of exploration, personalization, action, and termination.
2. Couple and family counseling differ from group counseling. The counselor must understand and apply all the skills that are used in individual and group counseling as well as those that build on systems theory.
   a. Families are a special type of a group that operates as a system. Systems have the properties of wholeness, structure, boundaries, and homeostasis.

b. Triangles constitute a framework for understanding how systems function.

c. The family life cycle includes six stages through which families pass as they develop.

d. The counselor needs to think carefully and formulate a plan of action during the first session if he or she is to understand the problem and encourage the family to return.

e. Counselors should follow a three-step process to help families to change.

Relevant Questions

The following are several questions to keep in mind while reading the chapter:

1. Compare group guidance and group counseling in terms of the objectives, purpose, and techniques used by the counselor.

2. Compare group counseling to family counseling. In what ways are they similar and how do they differ?

3. Explain what is meant by therapeutic forces in a group. Describe how three of the therapeutic forces affect the clients.

4. What is an enmeshed family? How does an engaged system differ from a disengaged system?

5. What are the stages of the family life cycle? For each stage indicate two stimuli that might impel a family to seek counseling.

6. There are three things a family counselor can do to help a family to change. Explain each of the steps and give at least one example of each.

Introduction

Group work is an effective means of teaching a number of skills to a variety of people as well as an effective means of helping people change. Research has demonstrated that groups are effective in teaching social skills to elementary school students (La Greca and Santogrossi, 1980); increasing teacher self-esteem and interpersonal communication skills (Robinson and Wilson, 1980); lessening depression (Hodgson, 1981) and test anxiety (Altmaier and Woodward, 1981) among college students; increasing self-confidence and life-skill knowledge and lowering dogmatism of police officers (Arthur et al., 1980); lowering the frequency of serious rule infractions of convicted felons (Leak, 1980); and increasing marital satisfaction and individual self-concepts through a marital enrichment program (Fenell et al., 1981).

In addition, group models have been recommended for the following purposes: adjustment groups for single parents (Simone, 1981); family enrichment (Hillman and Evenson, 1981); transitions for the divorced and separated (Prescott and Morris, 1979); management of stress and anxiety (Archer and Reisor, 1982); dealing with sexuality issues of the elderly (Capuzzi and Gossman, 1982) and the female college student (Snow, 1981); or as a method of intervention with suicidal clients (Hipple, 1982).

Obviously group work has extensive applications. In one of those applications, group counseling, the counselor's presence and contributions are as important as they are in individual counseling. Many of the same skills and attitudes are needed; they include attending, empathy, personalization, warmth, caring, authenticity, regard, and respect. However, the counselor uses these skills with six to eight clients in a vastly different manner than in individual counseling.

Groups and Group Counseling

Individuals and Groups   Groups are collections of people who share a common interest, goal, belief, purpose, or behavior. People are social animals who seek to satisfy their social needs through group membership. Families, religious groups, political groups, work-related groups, and exercise groups are a few common groups in contemporary society. To some extent, the type of person each of us has become is determined both by groups we have belonged to in the past and by current group memberships that help to define our present and future identities. This is not to suggest that the influence is simply directed from the group to the individual. Individual group members contribute to the identity of the group, and that identity, in turn, influences each group member. In short, all groups are systems that are influenced by their individual members and then influence those members in turn. (The discussion of marriage and family counseling provides a more detailed understanding of systems.)

Group characteristics are determined by the input received from its members. Those members collectively determine allowable group tolerances for acceptable behavior and expressed beliefs or attitudes. Since different groups have different compositions, they have slightly to dramatically different norms. The individual will influence the establishment of those norms and then be influenced by them. Those influences permit that individual to behave quite differently in different groups. In the social group, one woman may be humorous and outgoing; in the work group, serious and quiet; and in the athletic group, aggressive and dominating. Different groups permit various aspects of ourselves to emerge; sometimes these aspects are acceptable to the larger social group (society) and sometimes they are not. In short, we influence all of the groups to which we belong, but we are also susceptible to their influence. It is this influence on the individual exerted by the group that counselors need to understand and harness for productive group work.

Common Helping Groups   *Guidance Groups*   Typically used in the schools, group guidance is becoming increasingly relevant to other institutions and other age groups. Group guidance provides developmentally relevant information to groups so that the participants can apply it meaningfully to themselves and their lives. The content is most often personal, social, vocational, or educational. Counselors must first establish a need for the information for a given population. Second, they must select the most effective method of presenting the information and integrate it with a method that will enable members to personalize and utilize the information most productively. If the program does not help members to apply the information to themselves and use it productively, it is merely information giving, not group guidance. The guidance portion involves group members in discussing and sharing ideas, lessons, personal relevance, and application to eliminate or diminish developmental problems. It is, therefore, preventive in nature (Gazda, 1978).

Applications of group guidance might include the following: (1) using puppets to act out the resolution of disagreements between friends for elementary school children, (2) introducing the effects of smoking to middle school students, (3) showing a film or using values-clarification exercises to discuss the criteria for selecting a boyfriend or girlfriend for high school students, (4) forming a panel to discuss the effects of divorce on children with adults who are in the process of divorce or separation, and (5) bringing in a guest speaker to discuss issues of personal safety with the aged. Group leaders are limited only by their imagination and the available resources; instructional modes and topics for group guidance presentation are virtually limitless.

Group Counseling   While group guidance is designed to prevent developmental problems, group counseling serves both preventive and remedial purposes. Group counseling is defined as contact between a counselor and a group of clients, each of whom is in a state of discomfort, wishes to ease that discomfort, and is willing to do that in the social setting of a group. The members are essentially normal individuals who are suffering discomfort from a normal developmental issue and are not in need of more intensive individual counseling or therapy. The process relies on verbal sharing of personal feelings, thoughts, and concerns to achieve a better self-understanding and self-acceptance, and, if desired, to effect realistic behavioral and attitudinal changes.

Information giving, if there is any, is minimal in group counseling, since the focus is on the experiences of the members. Group members commonly respond to each other's experiences, thus fulfilling the "client" role of self-exploration, self-understanding, and self-acceptance and the "helper" role by reaching out to make meaningful contact with peers, inviting their self-disclosures and developing a personal openness and acceptance of their uniqueness as human beings. The group setting permits individuals to grow by role-taking the behaviors of both helper and helpee.

T-groups   T-groups are essentially training groups for skills in human relations "in which individuals are taught to observe the nature of their interactions with others and of the group process" (Rogers, 1970, p. 3). From these observations, the members of the T-group can understand how they function in groups, their impact on others, and how they can relate better to difficult interpersonal situations. T-groups were primarily targeted to the industrial field to help train managers and administrators in human relationship skills. Thus the National Training Laboratory (NTL) was established in 1947 (Rogers, 1970) and served as the model for T-groups throughout the nation. T-groups are not viewed as therapy or counseling groups; they are growth oriented rather than remedial. They deal with the here-and-now, not with a member's past behavior. Emphasis is placed on ascertaining the effect of individual behavior on the efficiency of the group process. Rogers (1970) reports that participants in the T-group often underwent intense and personal experiences that changed the levels of trusting and caring in their personal relationships.

Encounter Groups   Encounter groups were established and achieved popularity in response to a sense of personal and social alienation that people experienced in the 1960s and the effectiveness of T-groups in changing individuals' social skills and counteracting feelings of alienation. Encounter groups are a part of the larger movement by individuals to seek personal growth, to make connections with other people, and to rediscover and use the affective part of themselves. These people wanted to fulfill their human potential by emphasizing their human feelings and awareness.

Encounter groups were intended for normal individuals who felt no personal discomfort other than that resulting from the desire for psychic growth. Many encounter groups held formal interviews and used assessment procedures to screen out individuals with personal problems who needed remedial counseling or therapy. At first encounter groups were conducted by professionally trained facilitators, but as their popularity grew, less qualified leaders emerged who used questionable techniques and included no provisions for follow-up of participants after termination of the group. Encounter groups might meet on a scheduled basis, such as two hours per week for ten weeks, or for a weekend marathon.

Marathon Groups   These groups are conducted for an extended period of time, most often a weekend. They can be therapy groups, T-groups, or encounter groups. Essentially, the members come together to eat, sleep, and encounter one another in a sequestered atmosphere. The work of the group continues throughout the time they are together; as the time progresses, the participants and their normal defenses wear down, permitting the participants to divest themselves of their "outside" roles and facades. This divestiture promotes a more honest and less guarded encounter of others and of themselves. Obviously, the dropping of defenses is a potentially dangerous occurrence that increases a person's feeling of exposure and vulnerability. If an individual's vulnerability is exploited by another, serious psychological damage can result. It is, therefore, imperative to have a leader well trained in counseling and in the management of marathon groups.

Task Groups   Groups that focus on completing a specific task are referred to as task groups. Their duration is defined by the time it takes to complete the task, which is frequently determined by a deadline. Its membership may be voluntary (fund raising for a charity) or assigned (developing criteria for pay increases). Leadership may (1) be assigned to someone in the group by some authority figure outside the group, (2) be assigned through election by group members, or (3) be assumed by an emerging leader in the group. The sense of importance of group membership is determined by the importance of the task rather than by changes occurring within the individual or within the group. The purpose of the group process is to facilitate the completion of the task.

Therapeutic Forces in the Group Counseling Process

Forces are always at work in a group. It is imperative that the group counselor be cognizant of all the forces: those that facilitate the counseling process and those that retard it. Awareness of therapeutic forces permits the counselor to make appropriate interventions to enhance their development. This section will discuss eight therapeutic forces: cohesion, client expectations, group norms, self-disclosure, feedback, acceptance and validation, universalization, and reality testing.

Cohesion   The sense of belonging to a group, the feeling of emotional bonding to the group members and commitment to the group function, is defined as group cohesion. This commitment to the group function is such that members feel committed to each other and to each other's work. Cohesion entails tolerance for differences and for frustration, thus ensuring group stability. Without cohesion, group members can become easily discouraged and frustrated; they are likely to quit the group prematurely. To enhance cohesiveness in the early stages of the group, the leader needs to foster empathic understanding between members, authentic behavior, personal regard, and respect for each other. This can be accomplished by the counselor's enticing other members to respond to the speaker by asking such questions as:

"If you had just said what Bill said, how do you think you would feel?"
"How does it make you feel when you hear Bill say what he just said?"
"Who thinks they understand what Bill said? Tell him, starting with 'You feel _____ because _____.' "

Client Expectations   Clients' ability to benefit from the group experience is greatly enhanced when they know what to expect from the experience—what is expected of them and what they can expect from the counselor and from each other. The establishment of similar treatment expectations by group members will enhance the development of cohesion, will be therapeutic, and will decrease the likelihood of members dropping out (Stockton et al., 1981).

Member expectations can best be assessed and encouraged to develop along common avenues if counselors carefully screen the clients for group membership, state expectations as they set structure, and continually monitor the group to maintain the focus of members' expectations.

Group members should be able to cooperate with each other, able to verbalize their concerns, not in need of more intensive individual counseling or therapy, and willing to participate in group counseling. During the screening, the client needs to be informed of the following:

1. How a group experience is preferable to other forms of counseling for this specific client.
2. The expectation that members will share with others their thoughts, feelings, and experiences.
3. The expectation that clients will respond to the self-disclosure of other group members.
4. How the group counselor will behave in the group.
5. How a group is composed of individual members and how each one influences the development of the group and what it will become.
6. The frequency of group meetings, the duration of each session, and expectations about attendance.

Finally, it is helpful if the counselor helps each client to establish and then share with the group the personal goals (outcome expectations) that will guide his or her work in the group. Outcome expectations improve client gains in group counseling (Peteroy, 1979). During the screening interview, the counselor might ask the prospective group member to think about a goal, which will be discussed with the group during the first session. This discussion might lead to a request for specific help or behavior from the group members. An example is Judy's sharing her goal of "wanting to learn how to accept another's point of view without getting angry and overly assertive." She requested that, when anyone in the group thought she was getting angry or overly assertive, that person should say to her, "Judy, I sense you are getting angry and therefore not understanding the other person's point of view." This statement would make her aware of her behavior at that moment, and she could take measures to alter it while it was occurring.

Group Norms   Norms are the understandings and rules, both implicit and explicit, that govern the functioning of the group. Group functioning includes such areas as how members will behave to each other (critically or empathically), what can be discussed (topics) and how it will be discussed (third person or first person), assignment of member roles (positions of power and influence), and use of specific reinforcements and punishments to regulate member behavior.

It can be seen that the therapeutic usefulness of a group will be largely determined by the group norms. Therefore, the counselor needs to be acutely aware of this therapeutic force, especially in the early stages of group counseling. The counselor can influence group norms in two ways. First, the counselor uses the screening session to set the framework for establishing norms of self-disclosure, responding empathically to others, member ability to influence group development, and expectations about attendance. Second, Gazda (1978) suggests that the counselor's modeling of empathic responses "showing warmth and respect to all members and supporting shy members" (p. 41) can influence the establishment of group norms.

If the group norms established are at variance with individual norms, the individual may fail to develop a sense of belonging to the group, commitment to the group, desire to risk self-disclosure, and the ability to share empathic understanding with other group members. These failures will promote individual dropouts and, if widespread, the demise of the group.

Self-disclosure Client self-disclosure is the most basic goal of counseling. Without self-disclosure there can be no self-exploration, self-understanding, or movement to change. Further, in a group setting, self-disclosure builds trust in oneself and in the group (Harris, 1980). Therefore, when a member makes few verbal self-disclosures, there is a tendency to drop out (Stockton et al., 1981), which disrupts the development of trust and cohesion in the group.

As discussed in Chapter 12, we believe that all behavior—verbal and nonverbal—is meaningful and is somehow directed toward the individual's immediate personal goals. Therefore, the client need not speak in order to say something. We are self-disclosing at all times. However, verbal self-disclosure seems to involve more anxiety and risk than does nonverbal disclosure. Clients who choose to remain relatively quiet may be protecting themselves from this anxiety and threat (Harris, 1980). As stated in "Responding to the Nonverbal" (Chapter 12), the counselor is encouraged to help group members to verbalize their nonverbal self-disclosures. Such assistance will require counselors to have "wide vision," permitting them to scan all group members for nonverbal reactions to one member's statements. When a reaction is noted and the timing seems right to the counselor, the client may be enticed to verbalize the nonverbal response. This invitation is necessary for the more frightened, withdrawn, or shy client. Other members may not need any further invitation than the modeling of the group norm of self-disclosure.

It is also evident that self-disclosure encourages and elicits more self-disclosure. In the early stages of group development, it may be prudent for the counselor to model a moderate amount of self-disclosure (Morran, 1982). The reader is encouraged to review the section "Research on the Authentic Counseling Relationship" (Chapter 9) for a more detailed treatment of the choice of material, frequency and timing of counselor self-disclosure, and its effect on client self-disclosure.

Feedback The verbalization of other people's perceptions and reactions to our behavior is termed feedback. Giving feedback is one of the most powerful forces in group work—and one of the most abused. It is powerful because it encourages clients to experience another's perception of them and possibly to incorporate that perception into their self-concept. It can be abused if feedback is used as license to humiliate, criticize, ridicule, or injure another. Honesty is not the sole criterion of the appropriateness of feedback. Other more important criteria include the following:

1. Feedback should be beneficial to the receiver, not serve the needs of the giver. To that end, the feedback should be provided in a way that invites the receiver to hear it without becoming defensive.
2. Feedback is more effective when it is based on behavior that is describable. The farther removed feedback is from describable behavior, the less understandable and useful it will be to the receiver.
3. In the early stages of group development, positive feedback "is more readily accepted and leads to more change than negative" (Stockton and Morran, 1980, p. 10). In their review of the research literature regarding feedback, Stockton et al. (1981) state that "there is little or no evidence to indicate that positive feedback remains superior to negative as the group progresses to later stages. Nonetheless negative feedback early in the experience should be given with due caution, both to prevent premature termination and to promote safety for learning" (p. 10).
4. Feedback is most productive when it immediately follows the stimulus behavior. The receiver can recall the stimulus behavior with greater ease and there is less opportunity to deny or distort it (Stockton and Morran, 1980).
5. Feedback is more effective when it is confirmed and thus validated by others. Therefore, the receiver should be given an opportunity to solicit reactions from other group members regarding the original feedback.
6. Feedback is of greater benefit when the receiver is open and less defensive. Generally it is more productive to provide positive feedback to closed or defensive people before giving any negative feedback (Stockton and Morran, 1981). When individuals request feedback, it is received more openly and is thus more beneficial.
7. Feedback is more credible when the receiver trusts the giver and perceives his or her motive to be helpful.

There is reason to believe that feedback adhering to these seven guidelines will facilitate deeper interpersonal communication and group cohesion (Rose and Bednar, 1980). It will facilitate group development if the counselor models appropriate feedback, solicits positive feedback from group members, and instills the seven guidelines into the group norms early in the life of the group. As the group progresses, negative feedback, preferably following positive feedback, may be solicited in a caring and warm manner.

Acceptance and Validation   The issue of acceptance has been covered in depth in Chapter 8. It is important to reiterate here that the group setting provides many more opportunities for acceptance than individual counseling.

We believe that the most significant therapeutic force in counseling is the feeling that other people who are important in our lives understand us. When others care enough to try to understand us, our ideas, our behaviors, and our motivations without making judgments about our being "good" or "bad," we feel a sense of acceptance. This sense of acceptance validates the uniqueness of our sense of self. It validates our existence. When acceptance does not occur, we are not validated as unique human beings. Instead, we feel ignored, misunderstood, misperceived—in short, nonexistent. When our sense of our own existence is jeopardized, we may feel confusion, anxiety, depression, and self-blame because of the perceived disparity. This sequence of events frequently motivates people to seek counseling in order to "find themselves" or "discover who they are." Therefore, through the process of understanding, acceptance, and respect of who they are, people can validate their worth and existence as human beings. Then they are able to decide how, when, and in what way they wish to change.

Universalization   The process of hearing others struggle with concerns similar to our own helps us to universalize these issues. We are unique as individuals, but we have similar problems, worries, self-doubts, conflicts, and feelings. When we discover that others in the group share many of our concerns, it lessens our fears, anxieties, and feelings of alienation. Through universalization, the individual may rejoin humanity and find hope.

The counselor can facilitate universalization by asking if others have ever felt or behaved similarly. In addition, the counselor might watch the group for nonverbal reactions that suggest identification and then ask individuals to share what they were thinking or feeling. Universalization promotes group cohesion through the sharing of common problems or feelings.

Reality Testing   The group is a microcosm of the client's world in many ways. It is composed of the client's peers who have feelings, reactions, and behaviors similar to those of people outside the group. When group norms of caring, acceptance, and validation are established, the atmosphere of relative personal safety prevails. This safety will permit the client to explore who he is, find out how others perceive him and react to him, and see how that affects him. The group setting also supports experimentation in his attempts to initiate changes in himself. He may try to alter the way he perceives and reacts to others, the roles he takes for himself (victim, dominator, protector, and so forth), or the behaviors that prevent others from feeling close to him. In the group, he can experiment with changes as he feels comfortable and can request accurate feedback from group members. He is able to do more than talk about himself and his attempts to change; he can try out change in the sessions and can get immediate and honest reinforcement or suggestions for improvement. Thus, the group setting provides an opportunity to continually test one's reality.

Advantages and Disadvantages of Group Counseling

Counselors need to consider very carefully the mode of counseling that they will recommend to the client. It is unethical to place a client in a group because the counselor wants to fill a vacancy, giving little or no consideration to the client's needs, ability to use a group productively, ability to mesh with the other group members, or the appropriateness of the client's concerns—in terms of type or severity—to the group. Some of the advantages and disadvantages of group counseling are apparent; some are not. We have listed some of the more common and apparent advantages and disadvantages.

Advantages

1. Use of a group permits clients to use a "real life" setting to experiment with behavior change during the sessions, not just to talk about it.
2. Members receive acceptance and validation not only from the counselor but also from their peers.
3. Sharing personal concerns allows each member to realize that his or her concerns are not "abnormal."
4. Groups allow the counselor economy of time; in other words, counselors can see more clients than is possible in individual counseling.
5. Groups provide the individual with immediate and honest peer reinforcement.
6. Group members, especially youngsters, are often more amenable to the suggestions and interventions of their peers, rather than those of adults or other authority figures. Members' magnified sense of commonality of problems, life events, and life situation gives these peer interventions more credence.
7. Members are able to develop more egalitarian self-concepts by being able both to give and receive support, understanding, help, and acceptance.
8. Group counseling provides an opportunity to work *in vivo* on personal relationships (Cohn, 1977).

Disadvantages

1. Many clients' personalities do not lend themselves to a group setting. A quiet, shy client may be ignored, while a dominating client may either dominate the sessions or derail the process—rendering therapeutic use of the group ineffective.
2. Group work often precludes in-depth concentration on a client issue when it evolves. Work is often diluted, as is the counselor's contact with individual clients (Shertzer and Stone, 1980).

3. Many counselors feel uncomfortable working in a group setting because of their personal style, inadequate training, or both.
4. Because of the high value given to peer reaction, some clients may be afraid to jeopardize group acceptance by expressing their thoughts and feelings.
5. Cliques can develop that exclude some members and consequently cause divisiveness in the group. This will deter the development of group cohesion, a sense of trust, and the usefulness of the group.

Issues in the Group Counseling Process

Selection of Members   The selection of members needs thoughtful consideration. Of utmost concern must be a reasonable belief that the members will be able to work together. It is important for individuals to be able to identify with other group members on some issue, such as similarity of age, sex, identified problem, educational and/or socioeconomic level (Gazda, 1978).

Many counselors like to group clients who share similar problems. While the problems need not be exactly the same, groupings that focus on relationship problems, shyness, divorce-related concerns, or unemployment will give clients ready identification and the ability to profit vicariously from another group member's work in the group. Too much similarity might decrease member participation if boredom or redundancy occur.

The sex of the group members is an important issue. Gazda (1978) prefers "heterogeneously composed groups over homogeneously composed groups for counseling" (p. 54). We agree except in very few cases. The first exception is when the problems and/or goals are either sexually sensitive (teenage pregnancy) or sex-role based. The second exception is, as Gazda (1978) suggests, the homogeneous grouping of preadolescents. Gazda respects the children's natural developmental desires to seek same-sex groups.

Due to rapid and differing rates of development in youngsters, adolescents, and young adults, we believe that similarity in ages will help to consolidate a group. Issues being discussed by an adolescent (feeling attractive to the opposite sex) may be alien if not embarrassing to a preadolescent. This feeling of alienation will disrupt the cohesion of the group, possibly causing a member to drop out. Age differences seem far less important with adults.

Finally, care must be given to clients' educational and socioeconomic levels to ensure they will not be a barrier to the formation and development of the group. The counselor can help people of diverse economic and education backgrounds to relate to each other on the basis of more personal and human data. While differences may hinder early group work, they can be very fertile material for personal growth.

Group Size   The size of the group depends on such features as the purpose of the group, members' ages, problems to be shared, and personal style and preference of the counselor.

As the size of the group increases, each member has less time to be in the spotlight and may feel less involved with the group and the counselor.

Therefore we recommend six to eight members for counseling groups; the size of task groups depends on the complexity of their specific task. In general, six to eight members are enough to allow for the periodic absence of one or two members without destroying the counseling group. It is of sufficient size to permit member interactions while at the same time providing time for all members to participate if they wish.

Duration   Groups that meet in a school setting are limited by the time structure of the school. Again, the duration of a session is influenced by the age of the members and the purpose of the meeting. Unless the members are too young to sit and concentrate, groups generally last for 1½ hours. Shorter time periods preclude full member participation and may result in client frustration.

Groups can be long-term or short-term. This will depend on the members' concerns and availability as well as the counselor's personal desire. The group may be initiated with a time limit (twelve sessions) or may run until the group members decide to dissolve the group in favor of another mode of counseling or no counseling. A time limit often helps clients to overcome resistances and accomplish more in less time. If needed, time limits can be negotiated with a group at the appropriate time.

Co-leaders   The use of co-leaders can be beneficial in many ways. It is a less threatening way for an inexperienced counselor to enter practice as a group counselor. Not only does the inexperienced counselor see a live model, but he or she receives immediate and potentially useful feedback after each session. In addition, the use of a co-leader permits one counselor to "work" while the other monitors the group and involves others when it is appropriate to do so. Dinkmeyer and Muro (1979) suggest that co-leading will be most successful when

1. Both leaders possess a similar philosophical and operational style.
2. Both are of similar experience and competence.
3. The relationship between the leaders serves as a model for affective human interaction.
4. Both are aware of splitting and member loyalty ties to one or the other and can help the group deal with this.
5. Both agree on counseling goals and the process by which they are to be achieved, so that power struggles are avoided. (p. 250)

It is often suggested that co-leaders be of opposite sexes to provide diverse role models and a wider range of identification. While this may be preferable, it is not necessary. Finally, we suggest that co-leaders sit opposite each other in the group. If a client tends to speak to the leader, this seating arrangement widens their view of the group. It also permits one leader to talk while the other unobtrusively observes. Obviously, care needs to be taken in determining if a group will have co-leaders, who they will be, how they will work, and even where they will sit.

Stages in the Group Counseling Process

Each group assembled for counseling is unique in its membership and in the content discussed. Groups do, however, seem to pass through similar stages of growth. Each stage has characteristics that identify the type of issues and interpersonal dynamics present. The goal of the counselor is to keep the process moving. Due to the uniqueness of each stage, the counselors need to be continually aware of interpersonal dynamics and group processes and utilize the skills appropriate to those issues. The enemy of the group counselor is stagnation of group process.

There is general agreement that groups move through four stages (Cohn, 1977; Gazda, 1978; Dinkmeyer and Muro, 1979). The time spent in any one stage varies, and the progression through the stages is ragged and often confusing. In other words, a group may enter one stage, only to regress to the previous stage, and then re-enter the advanced stage again. Movement need not be orderly, although at times it is. Group development is complicated by the interacting forces within the group; not all members develop in the same way at the same time, and the progress of the group reflects that. The following discussion explores the group stages of exploration, personalization, action, and termination and outlines the counselor skills needed for each.

Exploration Stage   The first stage of the group may be termed the stage of exploration. This stage is characterized by caution, anxiety, and apprehension as members attempt to be known favorably to each other, identify the limits of the group, establish some group norms, establish roles of power and influence, and define personal and group goals. Sharing is generally social and superficial in this stage. In fact, the members will resist disclosure of important or threatening personal material until cohesion and trust are present. There is a tendency in this stage for members to avoid here-and-now topics in preference to talking about the past. This limits self-disclosure to a safe level, thus controlling risk and feelings of vulnerability.

Counselors need to employ a number of skills during this early stage. Among the most important are attending (see pages 270–277) and demonstrating regard and respect (see Chapter 8). Empathic skills are of utmost importance. The counselor should strive for Level 3 (interchangeable) responses in the early phase of the group. As in individual counseling, the counselor must be able to sense when the group is ready for higher levels of empathy to maximize productiveness and minimize feelings of exposure and vulnerability (see Chapter 12).

Counselor use of questions (see Chapter 11) can facilitate self-disclosure. In addition, observing and responding to nonverbal messages of members invites participation, which builds trust and cohesion. In short, the counselor will need to use the skills discussed throughout this text in order to help clients self-disclose, develop personal goals, feel safe in the group environment, and relate empathically to each other. When these characteristics are present, the group can successfully progress to the next stage: personalization.

Personalization Stage   The second stage of group counseling occurs as the group develops a sense of trust and cohesion. Trust develops as individual members gradually disclose immediate feelings and concerns to the group and then find the group responding in an accepting, empathic, and validating manner. Some groups will pass through a more conflict-oriented and confrontative stage before establishing group norms of empathy, warmth, and support (Rogers, 1970). Dinkmeyer and Muro (1979) believe that this is a natural human response of resistance to the establishment of group norms. The key concepts to be developed in this stage are trust, here-and-now self-disclosures, a personalized understanding of oneself, and an empathic understanding and response pattern to others in the group.

To facilitate personalized understanding, counselors will need to provide higher levels of empathy when conditions permit. They should help the group to focus on the use of "I" statements, speaking in the here-and-now (immediacy), understanding oneself, and understanding personal reactions to others' self-disclosures and to the group process. Counselors' use of personalization (see Chapter 12) will help clients to gain deeper understanding and acceptance of themselves and increasingly understand and accept others.

Action Stage   As understanding of self increases, so too will acceptance. As members accept who they are and understand, at least to some extent, what conditions, beliefs, or fears encouraged their development and inhibit their changing, they will gradually develop a greater feeling of control over their lives. When people feel more in control of their lives, they begin to seek ways to alter the aspects of themselves that they accept (that is, do not deny) but wish to change. Here the counselor needs to utilize the action-oriented skills discussed in Chapter 13.

Counselor use of higher levels of immediacy, confrontation, and program development will benefit group members at this stage. Clients may wish to begin their programs in the group or as homework between sessions in order to receive the social rewards that make the group so potent. The key concept of this stage is taking personal responsibility for oneself and changing aspects that are incongruent with one's ideal self-concept.

Termination Stage   The termination stage prepares clients for the end of group counseling. As work on individual goals begins to culminate, the original goals of the group will lose their usefulness. Nevertheless, group members will have developed a group identity and closeness that resist disbanding. Here the leader takes a less active role than in earlier stages. Members begin to review the group's and individuals' progress; they may make plans to see each other after termination. It is beneficial if the counselor helps the group to say goodbye and to progress through the appropriate stages of grieving. The counselor's return to interchangeable empathy and less confrontative and action-oriented skills prepares members for termination. At this time the counselor can respond to individual members' needs and desires for further counseling, either individual or group.

It can be seen that group counseling has a variety of applications. Many therapeutic forces are unique to groups. The counselor's task is to create a conducive atmosphere to promote the effectiveness of the therapeutic forces. While many of the attitudes and techniques that the counselor utilizes are by definition the same as those used in individual counseling, the manner in which they are applied and the stages through which the counseling progresses are influenced by the presence of several clients. The following section on couple and family counseling provides us with a look at yet another special application of counseling with a group.

Couple and Family Counseling

Counseling with a couple or a family involves theory, knowledge, and interventions different from but useful for individual counseling. Systems theory is the primary theoretical approach for understanding the functioning of couples and larger families.

The Family as a System   Systems theory for families has a number of properties that differ from the linear cause-and-effect (stimulus-response) thinking utilized in one-to-one counseling. These properties are wholeness, structure, boundaries, and homeostasis.

Wholeness   A system is comprised of a number of single elements. When these elements are functioning together as a system, they yield a product which is greater than the sum of its parts—this is wholeness (Bratcher, 1982). While this statement underscores the potency of systems, it also suggests that no element can act independently. Any action by one element (A) prompts the reaction of other elements (B, C, and D) and influences the direction of that reaction. When B reacts, A, C, and D must adjust, which again causes all the elements to react, and a new chain of new adjusting reactions is set in motion. Let us take one example. Father comes home to find Billy's bicycle and skateboard in the driveway. This prevents him from parking his car, and he enters the house scolding Billy vociferously. This frightens little Suzy, who promptly seeks the safety of her room, which arouses her mother's protectiveness; Mother, in turn, urges Father to voice his concerns more rationally. Father responds to Mother's urging by denying his unreasonableness and scolds her for sticking up for the kids. This, he feels, is what causes their lack of discipline. This criticism, in turn, causes Mother to be defensive, Billy to feel guilty and protective of her, and Suzy to sneak out of the house.

Systems theory stipulates that there is no linear causality. Behavior between two people always has some effect on a third person who witnesses it or has knowledge of it. The effect on the third person, will affect other people as well as the original person (people). This concept is referred to as circular or multidirectional causality. Change in any one part of a system will affect all other parts in some fashion.

Structure   A system is composed of *subsystems*. Subsystems are elements of systems that share some commonality and are as a result somewhat interdependent. Examples of family subsystems are parents, children, males, and females, to name a few. Subsystems may have many qualities in common; a few such qualities are goals, functions, behavior, sex, roles, values, and attitudes. Any common element can serve as the basis for forming a subsystem. In addition, any system may be a subsystem of a larger system. For example, an individual is a system of organs functioning to maintain his or her life. That same individual is a subsystem of a family, which is a subsystem of a neighborhood, which is a subsystem of a city, which is a subsystem of a state, and on, and on, and on.

Individuals generally belong to many systems and subsystems. For example, Mother is a member of the family subsystem of the community, which is a subsystem of the nation. In addition, she is a member of the PTA, an exercise club, and a local church, and she is also an executive in a company. These systems exist in proximity to the other systems. They influence each other in proportion to the physical and psychological distance between them; the closer they are, the more force they exert. For example, the family subsystem is physically and psychologically closer and more important to Mother than is the PTA or the exercise club; therefore, it exerts more influence upon her life and her decisions.

To think in terms of systems, one must first dispense with linear cause-and-effect thinking and begin to think in terms of multidirectional causation. One must watch the interaction between two people and ask oneself how this interaction affects a third person. *Triangles* are the framework for understanding how a system functions (Bowen, 1978). Murray Bowen developed the triangular concept to explain what happens to the unstable two-person system when it comes under stress. When stress develops, one member of the system, usually the more uncomfortable of the two, will "triangulate" with a third person to reduce the tension between the original dyad by shifting his or her attention to this other person. During a state of calm, the triangle contains two who are close and comfortable and one who is outside. The preferred position is one of the inside two. If the outsider becomes uncomfortable, he may try to form a twosome with one of the insiders and thus alter the forces of the triangle by becoming an insider and forcing one of the original insiders to become the outsider. Bowen suggests that, under stress, it is preferable to be the outsider and allow the insiders to fight. To do this, the outsider will need to resist being triangulated by the more uncomfortable insider. The forces of the triangle are constantly changing as members try to achieve closeness or to escape stress (Bowen, 1978). Each move by any one member of the triangle forces the others to make a compensating move. When one member of the triangle is able to step back from the action and limit her emotional involvement in the triangle, she will be able to act more independently and thus to "differentiate" herself from the system. Bowen (1978) calls this *"differentiation of self"* (p. 479). Let us return to our example of Mother, Father, Billy, and Suzy. Figure 14.1 shows various configurations of their family system. We find four triangles (in Figure a). When there is no stress, Mother and Father are the insiders with each child being an outsider of their respective triangles (Figure b). If stress occurs between Mother and Father, Mother will triangulate with Suzy, causing Billy and Father to be the outsiders of their respective triangles with Mother (Figure c). Father and Billy may triangulate to compensate for Mother's quest for closeness with Suzy (Figure d). After the stress between Mother and Father dissipates, the forces of the triangles again change to their more "fixed" pattern.

Boundaries Systems are defined by boundaries. Boundaries separate one system (or subsystem) from other systems by restricting exchange across them of such things as membership, information, ideas, physical distance, values, and influence. Boundaries bind together those things that give a system identity. This protects the system from losing its identity and merging with the larger system. Therefore, boundaries are family rules that govern

Figure 14.1 Family Model Triangulation

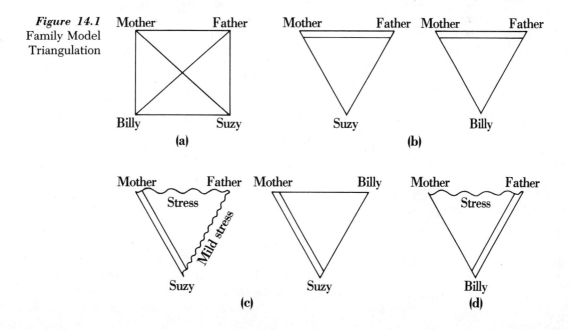

who or what will influence the system (family) or subsystem (individuals), when this influence may happen, and to what extent it will be permitted. The rules may have existed in the family for generations or be recent acquisitions, may be adopted from an outside system (religion) or internal frame of reference, may be in the member's awareness or beneath it, may be taboo or open to discussion, and may deal with the internal functioning of its members, covering such things as how to feel, think, and act (roles) in specific situations.

Systems with somewhat permeable boundaries are more easily influenced by their environment; in addition, they have more influence on their environment. These are called open systems. Systems whose boundaries are not permeable tend toward rigidity of ideas, beliefs, and rules and are called closed systems. Open systems possess flexibility to adapt to both environmental (a changing economy or societal norms, for example) and internal changes (say, maturation of children), whereas closed systems find it more difficult to adapt.

When boundaries between individuals within a family system are permeable to the point of being blurred, the system is said to be *enmeshed* (Minuchin and Fishman, 1981). Typical enmeshed families tend to have no closed doors in the home, no secrets, little individuality, and a strong sense of "togetherness." These families sacrifice the individuality of the person for the sake of the family.

At the opposite end of the continuum are *disengaged* families (Minuchin, 1974). These are families where an individual's boundaries are rigid; the sense of belonging to the system is sacrificed for the individuality of the members. Characteristics of this extreme include a sense of aloneness, little knowledge or caring about others in the system, little sense of commonality, and overly independent attitudes and behavior.

Enmeshment and disengagement lie at opposite ends of the continuum. The outcome of the family's style of boundary making determines whether or not pathology is present. If the family is able to adapt when it is appropriate to do so and does not go into crisis or injure its members, then it is healthy. If it is unable to adapt to the environment or to the growth of its members, then a variety of symptoms will give evidence of its pathology.

Homeostasis   The primary purpose of systems is to maintain themselves. Systems develop a pattern of operating that becomes comfortable because it is familiar and therefore has somewhat predictable consequences. When this balance is threatened, the system will invoke homeostatic mechanisms to bring it back in balance. This balance, called homeostasis, refers to a level of tension within certain limits that is tolerable to the family. When the tension becomes too high (or too low), some force within the family system will maneuver to counteract the stress and bring the system back within the homeostatic limits. This is analogous to the thermostatic control of a heating system. When the temperature dips four degrees below the setting, the theromostat triggers the furnace to warm the house. When the heat matches the setting on the thermostat, the furnace shuts off. Let's look at how this works in a family situation. Mother and Father are having marital tension which is felt by the son, who acts out both at school and home, which diverts Mother's and Father's attention from their conflicts to the son's behavior. The parents' collaboration on their common problem decreases their marital tension and increases their commonality. Furthermore, the son then controls the level of tension by monitoring his behavior. Homeostasis has been maintained. If the son's maneuver does not yield this result, then he is likely to intensify his acting out. The parents may then become so alarmed that they will seek outside, "expert" help and bring the son in to see a counselor to be "cured." The counselor's task is to understand the systemic dynamics and to recognize that the underlying problem in need of treatment is the marital relationship, not the son.

The Family Life Cycle   The counselor who intends to work with couples and families needs to understand family development over time, their conflicts, points of crisis, and the tasks they need to accomplish before facing the next developmental period. This understanding enhances the counselor's ability to make a family diagnosis. The following discussion outlines the family life cycle, the primary attitudinal task of each stage, and the second-order tasks of each stage as developed by Carter and McGoldrick (1980). The second-order tasks need to be mastered if the family is to maximize its development as a family. While divorces and remarriages alter this life cycle, it is beyond the scope of this book to explore those issues. Students are referred to Carter and McGoldrick's (1980b) book for further study.

Stage 1—Between Families: The Unattached Young Adult   This stage of the family life cycle centers on the young adult who is attempting to establish himself as an independent, self-sufficient individual. Previously this was a male-only life stage, but that has changed to include large numbers of women who are now able to leave their families of origin to establish their lives and careers independently. It is a very important stage because individuals need to establish their identity (Berman and Lief, 1975) and themselves as individual persons before bonding with another person to become a couple. Those who fail to establish their individual identity are frequently unable to bond appropriately with another for fear of merging and losing their sense of self. Their bonding is characterized by either a protective distance, often appearing as anger, or by overly close bonding (merging) which is especially sensitive and vulnerable to any nuance suggesting the partner's displeasure in the relationship.

The primary attitudinal task of this stage is to "accept the parent-offspring separation" (Carter and McGoldrick, 1980, p. 17). Some of the second-order tasks (Carter and McGoldrick, 1980) are to develop intimacy in relationships, establish self as differentiated from family of origin, and make a career choice and take steps to succeed in it.

Stage 2—The Joining of Families Through Marriage: The Newly Married Couple   This stage of development occurs when two young people give up their independent lives as *individuals* and join with the one they love to become a *couple*. In order to form a couple, the individual must further differentiate from the family of origin (Barcai, 1981) and incorporate the spouse's family into the new extended family. Becoming a couple requires two individuals to sacrifice some independence and freedom in order to establish a trusting and enduring identity as a couple. At first, the couple will need to learn that allegiance to the couple must outweigh allegiance to the family of origin. If this is not learned, then the spouses will triangulate with their respective families of origin during crises and appropriate communication and negotiation between the couple will not be learned. This stage has grown longer since the early 1960s, when couples began to delay the onset of parenthood (Wilkie, 1981).

Carter and McGoldrick (1980) indicate the primary attitudinal task is to make a commitment to the new system, while the behavioral tasks include formation of a new marital system and realignment of relationships with extended family and friends to include the spouse.

Stage 3—The Family with Young Children   This stage begins with the birth of the first child and ends when that child reaches adolescence. Generally there will be more than one young child in the family at the same time. This brings on a new responsibility for the couple. They must have established a "basic trust" in each other in the previous stage and formed a bond as loving adults whose identity includes being a couple (Barcai, 1981). This is a prerequisite since the "couple role sustains the parent/executive role. . . . If there is no healthy couple system functioning concurrently with the parental system, there will be pathology regardless of verbalized intent to the contrary" (Barcai, 1981, p. 355).

The new parents must now cope with an addition to the family that will disrupt their previously ordered and relatively simple life (Miller and Sollie, 1980). The stresses brought on by the new routine, sleepless nights, attention given to the baby that was previously given to the husband, the overwhelming sense of responsibility, and limited involvement outside of the home for the mother combine to make this stage the most popular stage for divorces (Beal, 1980).

Carter and McGoldrick (1980) suggest the attitudinal task is to accept new members into the system, while the behavioral tasks are to adjust the couple system to make room for a child, to take on parental roles in addition to roles as a spouse, and to adjust relationships with the extended family to encourage grandparenting and relative roles.

Stage 4—The Family with Adolescents   This stage challenges the flexibility and adaptability of the family more than any other. Barcai (1981) notes that during adolescence (notably age 14–15) abstract reasoning emerges. Barcai maintains that this reasoning stimulates the questioning that facilitates the adolescents' quest for identity. The continual struggle with their role in the family and their relationship with parents and peers calls for flexibility on the part of the family. The adolescent is "half in and half out of the family framework" (Barcai, 1981, p. 357). Herein lies the danger. The family must show some resistance to his leaving, but not so much as to force him to rebel. They must simultaneously permit the adolescent to leave while not looking as if he is not wanted. The family and the adolescent walk a narrow line together.

During this stage the family must adopt an attitude favoring increased flexibility of family boundaries so as to allow for the child's independence (Carter and McGoldrick, 1980). Further, Carter and McGoldrick suggest that the tasks include altering the parent-child relationship to permit the adolescent to move in and out of the system, refocusing the couple's attention on midlife marital and career issues, and beginning to prepare for growing old.

Stage 5—Launching Children and Moving On   This stage incorporates two phases. The first phase starts with the departure of the first child and ends when the last child leaves. The second phase begins when the couple is once again together as a couple and concludes at retirement. The focus of this stage is on "losing" one's children and preparing to "lose" one's work. To compensate for these losses, the couple pulls together and in many ways needs to renegotiate stage 2 tasks. Further compensations are the adoption of the families of their sons- and daughters-in-law and the development of their role as grandparents. At the end of this stage, unfortunately, instead of the freedom they dreamed about when the children were gone, middle-aged people are often saddled with the care and financial support of elderly parents (Shamas, 1980).

The primary attitude necessary is to accept a number of exits out of and entrances into the family system (Carter and McGoldrick, 1980). The tasks Carter and McGoldrick (1980) offer are re-establishing the marital system as a dyad; developing adult relationships with grown children, their spouses, and their parents; opening the family system to include in-laws and grandchildren; and beginning to deal with the decreasing physical abilities and eventual death of parents.

Stage 6—The Family in Later Life   This stage begins with retirement, which itself may cause stress due to changing economic resources and changing roles and sources of identification. Zube (1982) finds evidence to indicate colliding paths for older men and women. Older men, it appears, replace their aggressiveness with coping. Increased family activity, intimacy, and a sense of contentment occur in older men; older women, on the other hand, exhibit aggressiveness in their attempts to grow and extend their experience. Also, as people age there is a tendency toward androgenous roles and that may be a source of stress if the partner does not wish to share a role with which he or she is comfortable.

As the couple pulls together, communication is of utmost importance, especially as their roles slowly change. Without good communication, confusion can set in and lead to anger and a distancing of the relationship.

Finally, one of the most difficult losses one can endure is the death of a spouse in older age since it also means the loss of the couple identity (Boss, 1980). The death of a spouse and of one's friends forces the older person to focus on preparing for his or her own eventual death. This preparation is accomplished in part through reminiscing about one's life to one's children, grandchildren, and anyone else who cares enough to listen.

Carter and McGoldrick (1980) indicate the need for developing an attitude of accepting the shift in generational roles while working on the tasks of continued functioning as an individual or a couple as one physically declines, dealing with the loss of a spouse and friends while preparing for one's own death, and altering one's role to take advantage of the wisdom gained by living a long life.

The Process of Systems Counseling

Whether one is counseling a couple or a family, the basic process is the same. Once the clients enter the counseling room, there will be a clash between their agenda and the counselor's. The clients' agenda is based on linear thinking, which places blame on someone for causing the "problem"; the counselor's agenda is multidirectional and recognizes all of the family members as participants in the problem. It is not recommended that the counselor confront that difference directly, certainly not in the first several sessions. It is best to take some time to "help" the clients to think as you do about systems in a nonthreatening way.

If the counselor has seen one member of the system individually, we recommend that, before the couple or family is seen together, the other individuals also be seen individually. This is done (1) to get to know each person individually and (2) to avoid, as much as is possible, a feeling that the counselor is in a coalition with the person who was the original client. This is especially important if a client is bringing in a spouse to be seen as a couple. No longer is one individual the client—the individual's relationship is now the client. Individual sessions are not necessary if the first session is the first counselor-client contact.

Resistance to Change in the Family System   It is important to remember that clients' symptoms need to be viewed and understood as an attempt by the client(s) to either solve a crisis or reduce its intensity. In systems theory, one will recognize that the maintenance of a symptom has the cooperation, if not the encouragement, of others within the system and of influential adjacent systems. That is, the system, because of the mechanism of homeostasis, has a vested interest, however perverse it may seem, in maintaining the symptom in its existing form. If the symptom changes, then the symptom bearer changes, and consequently every element and subsystem in the system must also adapt. This means that all members of the system must move from a position of relative security, in which the future is at least somewhat predictable, to a position that is unfamiliar and therefore feels insecure. The new position provides no basis for prediction. Therefore, the homeostatic mechanisms within all of the systems that include or are adjacent to the symptom bearer (in our example, Billy) will resist a change in the symptom bearer. They have adapted to Billy's behavior in some fashion and do not want to be forced to readapt. Of course, this resistance, in most cases, is not conscious or necessarily rational. If it were, counseling would be much simpler and more straightforward. In fact the subsystems are aware, not of their resistance, but only of their good intentions. What is more, these subsystems are important to the symptom bearer and are in almost constant contact with him. The forces opposed to change are tremendously potent. If the symptom bearer is in individual counseling once each week, he is in the system that encourages and reinforces his symptom for the remaining 167 hours of the week. These are formidable odds. Therefore, for many types of problems, it is wiser to counsel the system as a whole and help it to change. If the child's symptoms are a ploy to keep Mother and Father from fighting and therefore divorcing, we believe that treating Billy is far less productive than counseling the couple. Obviously, the counselor's first task is to understand the dynamics of the system and determine the best mode of counseling for each symptom presented. The second task is to sell (persuade, cajole) systemic thinking to a couple or family that has a vested interest in linear thinking. At times, the family or spouse will not come in for counseling; then, of course, the counselor counsels whoever is available, helping them to recognize how the system functions and to "differentiate" from it. Once one is differentiated from the system, one may attempt to help others in the system to do likewise, thus changing the system to a healthier one.

Structuring the First Counseling Session   We recommend that you first introduce yourself to all members of the family present, probably shaking hands and/or briefly asking some history from each of them as well. The counselor needs to be sensitive to their anxiety and fear about this unknown process and unknown person (counselor). Second, the counselor may begin by asking each person to give his or her view of the problem. Start with the person who called to make the appointment, since this person has at least acknowledged the existence of a problem and the need for outside help. Assuming that the person who called was a parent, the second person to be asked would be the other adult (if there is one), then the children with the eldest first. This order attempts to recognize the hierarchy of the family and, therefore, reassures the family that, while the counselor is in charge, he or she will not do anything unexpected or unnecessarily frighten them. During this initial stage of counseling, the counselor is attempting to gather information relative to the following concerns:

1. What is the problem generated by the symptom (Caille, 1982)?
2. What is the symptom?

3. What are the reactions of others to the symptom (Caille, 1982)?
4. When did the symptom begin?
5. What factors contributed to the symptom?
6. What was the couple (family) like before the symptom?

In the third phase of the initial counseling session, the counselor suggests a topic and asks the couple or family to discuss it. The purpose of this exercise is to have the members of the system interact (to "dance"). The counselor watches them interact in order to gain an understanding of the dynamics of the system for the purpose of making a systemic diagnosis. The best way to understand a system is to observe and experience it firsthand. Members of a system, especially one under stress, are so biased by their involvement that they are unable to describe it as it exists. To understand the system, we recommend the counselor evaluate the following five areas:

1. *System dynamics*

   Who talks first?

   Who talks to whom? How does the listener react? How do others react?

   Does someone control the system's discussion? How? What are the reactions?

   What is the power hierarchy in the system? Is there opposition?

   What does the seating arrangement say about the system? (position and distance)

   What messages are communicated nonverbally? By whom? To whom?

   Identify the important triangles. Under stress, who triangulates with whom?

   How adaptive (flexible-rigid) is the family?

   Who triggers a homeostatic mechanism? When? What is it?

2. *Boundary dynamics*

   What are the important subsystems? How do they respond to each other?

   Are boundaries well defined? To what extent is individuality permitted? (enmeshed/disengaged)

   Are generational boundaries appropriate?

   Who speaks for another? Who allows someone to speak for them?

   Who interrupts whom? When?

   Who protects whom? When?

3. *Symptom dynamics*

   Identify the symptom.

   In what way does the symptom work in the system? How does the symptom maintain the family's most familiar traditional pattern?

4. *Family development*

   What stage of the family life cycle corresponds to this system?

   What attitudinal approach, as defined by Carter and McGoldrick (1980), is necessary for completion of the tasks they list? Evaluate the system's progress in this stage.

Evaluate the system's completion of developmental tasks in the previous stages.

5. *Sources of strength*

What are the strengths of the system? How can they be used as a foundation in counseling?

Designing Therapeutic Interventions   Now the counselor needs to describe the functioning of the system to determine possible therapeutic interventions. It is easiest to describe systems using the phrase, "The more that (person A does w), the more (person B does x), and this encourages (A to do y and person C to do z), which invites further reactions from A, B, C, and D . . . and so forth."

The goal of systemic counseling is to help clients make changes in their lives that will maximize their happiness. Since the individual is an integral subsystem of a system, the counselor must help the individual alter her system in a way that maximizes her individual happiness. We recommend Minuchin's (1974) therapeutic style of preserving (possibly establishing) individuation while supporting mutuality. The primary focus is, on the one hand, to enable each person to be an individual; that is, to differentiate self from others and to be able to disagree with and be different from others. At the same time, the focus is also on stressing the importance of belonging to a system and the "complementarity that allow(s) each (member) to 'give in' without feeling he has 'given up' " (Minuchin, 1974, p. 56).

How, then, does a counselor help clients to change? Minuchin (1974) suggests that people change for three reasons. "First, they are challenged in their perceptions of their reality. Second, they are given alternative possibilities that make sense to them. And third, once they have tried out the alternative transactional patterns, new relationships that appear are self-reinforcing" (p. 119). These three points provide a general classification of therapeutic intervention.

The first class of therapeutic interventions challenges the client's perception of reality. This is accomplished when the counselor "sells" systemic thinking rather than linear thinking. One effective way of accomplishing this is by asking the person who is complaining about the other's "faults" or behaviors the question: "What is it that *you* do that encourages her to act in that way?" This introduces the circular nature of cause and effect and is especially useful with couples who are engaged in blaming. It suggests that person A acts as she does partly in response to the encouragement of B's behavior. If person A acts defensively, then person B was perceived as threatening and probably did something to help A perceive that. To introduce triangular systemic thinking, the counselor might ask the third person what she or he feels or thinks and consequently does when he or she sees person A and person B interact. For example, while the mother and father are fighting the counselor might ask little Billy, "I wonder when you listen to your mother and father argue this way what it is you think about." Billy may respond, "It makes me scared that they will hit each other and then get divorced." The counselor can then go back to the parents and ask, "Were you aware that Billy got so frightened when you argued?" At that point the counselor can invite each person to express their thoughts and feelings and open up the communication.

Of course, the counselor could provide the couple with a systemic interpretation such as, "It appears to me that every time you point out a weakness in your wife she reacts by feeling hurt. When she feels hurt, she also feels angry and the more she expresses that, the more you feel maligned and attacked and consequently attack back more strongly. Do you have any thoughts about that?" This systemic interpretation not only educates the clients about their system, but it has the potential for increasing their awareness of themselves and of how they encourage the other person to behave. The counselor then can move them to discuss it and possibly discover a way to express their feelings and thoughts in such a way as to *encourage* the other to hear it and be able to resist being so defensive.

The second general class of therapeutic interventions is psychological education. Here we give our clients information and possible suggestions that were unavailable to them. We might instruct them about child-rearing issues, new behavioral responses to stimuli, techniques (such as relaxation techniques) to use at appropriate times, or ways to differentiate themselves from intrusive parents, friends, or a spouse. One should probably make more than one suggestion at a time to a client so that the client must decide if he or she is ready to change and must choose the technique that will be used.

The third general therapeutic intervention is to have the clients try out a new transactional pattern in the session under the direction and guidance of the counselor. For example, a couple that is arguing about a topic will usually interrupt each other, not listen, and respond in such a way that encourages the other to do the same. The counselor can demonstrate their lack of communication by asking each, in turn, what the other's point of view is After it is stated, instruct the client to ask the spouse if that understanding was correct. If it is ascertained that neither felt understood, in terms of both the content stated and their underlying feelings, the counselor can use the communication skill-training exercises described in this text in Chapter 12. Learning to be empathic toward one's partner accomplishes both (a) appropriate differentiation because each must accept the existence of a differing point of view and (b) a sense of belonging because the other cares enough to try to really understand. We believe that the most important quality of a good relationship is the sense of being understood and accepted by the other person. Acceptance does not mean approval. It means that one person can understand what the other is thinking and/or feeling and can accept it for what it is. Father can accept something believed by Mother about Billy and still not agree with it. However, Mother's belief is not accepted if Father belittles her for having it or undermines her efforts to behave in a way that reflects that belief.

Another intervention that furthers differentiation is to train members to use "I-you" statements. When the counselor notices one person (A) speaking for another (B), she might ask B if A often speaks for her. Then the counselor may help B to tell A, "It makes me feel discounted when you tell people what I think, and I would like you to stop it." This technique states that there is an I-you difference and teaches the discounted members to exert their rights and speak for themselves.

The counselor can use the same basic intervention when one person has the habit of interrupting another, does not look at them when speaking, does not respond to what the other has just said, or tells the other what they "should" do or feel. The counselor generates a transaction that counters this dysfunctional transaction and directs the participants to play it out. After the transaction is effected, the counselor reinforces the transaction, elicits reinforcement from the participants, helps them devise a plan to continue it outside of the session. Such a plan is most effective if all members of the system are involved. Take as an example a family in which the mother speaks harshly to the children, but only the youngest girl (Marge) is hurt by it and as a result cowers. In the session, Marge is encouraged to tell her mother how she feels when she is spoken to in that way, and then Mother, Father, and the siblings all can understand Marge's reaction. Marge is instructed to say to her mother, "It hurts my feelings a lot when you yell at me like that and does not encourage me to get ready on time like you want. Please encourage me differently." The siblings and Father are prepared to help Marge say this at any time they think it is appropriate. Mother is helped with her response and practices it. In this way, the system is activated to help itself change even though the members think they are helping Marge to change. The potential for resistance is minimized but, of course, not eliminated. The next session will begin with the counselor's asking for a report about the exercise, reinforcing the beneficial results, and redesigning any part that did not demonstrate success. Thus the counselor has focused on one basic problem, generated an interaction that will alter the family systemic structure, and reinforced the effects of the change. The family counselor must take steps not to allow the family or couple to overwhelm him with a variety of symptoms that would render him as ineffective as they are. The counselor needs to identify a problem and focus on generating interventions to resolve it until significant progress is made. Only then can counselor and clients move on to the next problem area.

Systemic counseling is counseling with couples or families that recognizes that dysfunction is caused by all of the people involved, not just the person identified as the symptom bearer. In counseling families, the counselor must have a good understanding of systems theory, its application to families, stages of family development and the tasks that need to be mastered in each stage, and finally interventions that fit the problem and help individuals to differentiate themselves from the system without losing their sense of belonging to that system.

Summary

In this chapter we have introduced the concept of multiclient counseling. This can be accomplished with groups of clients who meet special criteria, such as similar problems, equivalent stage of development, or sexual or intellectual similarity. Counseling with couples and with families also permits the counselor to work with several clients simultaneously.

In addition, the following points have been emphasized:

1. The counseling of clients in their familial environment weakens the resistance that inhibits an individual's change by promoting change for all the participants, not just for the person identified as the client.
2. The core counseling skills necessary in individual counseling are just as necessary for working with groups. There are, however, other skills and knowledge needed to work effectively with groups.
3. Family work incorporates a totally new theoretical approach, that of systems theory. It is imperative that all counselors understand this theoretical approach since it is a powerful force that affects clients all of the time and may deter the client from making constructive changes.

References

Altmaier, E. M., and M. Woodward. "Group Vicarious Desensitization of Test Anxiety." *Journal of Counseling Psychology* 28 (1981):467–469.

Archer, J., and J. S. Reisor. "A Group Approach to Stress and Anxiety Management." *The Journal for Specialists in Group Work* 7 (1982):238–244.

Arthur, G. L., P. J. Sisson, and C. E. McClung. "Use of Group Process in Teaching Communication and Life Skills for Law Enforcement Personnel." *The Journal for Specialists in Group Work* 5 (1980):196–204.

Barcai, A. "Normative Family Development." *Journal of Marital and Family Therapy* 7 (1981):353–359.

Beal, E. W. "Divorce and Single Parent Families." In E. A. Carter and M. McGoldrick, eds., *The Family Life Cycle: A Framework for Family Therapy.* New York: Gardner Press, 1980.

Berman, E. M., and H. I. Lief. "Marital Therapy for a Psychiatric Perspective: An Overview." *American Journal of Psychiatry* 132 (1975):583–592.

Boss, P. G. "Normative Family Stress: Family Boundary Changes Across the Life-Span." *Family Relations* 29 (1980):445–450.

Bowen, M. *Family Therapy in Clinical Practice.* New York: Jason Aronson, 1978.

Bratcher, W. E. "The Influence of the Family on Career Selection: A Family Systems Perspective." *American Personnel and Guidance Journal* 61 (1982):87–91.

Caille, P. "The Evaluation Phase of Systemic Family Therapy." *Journal of Marital and Family Therapy* 44 (1982):29–39.

Capuzzi, D., and L. Gossman. "Sexuality and the Elderly: A Group Counseling Model." *The Journal for Specialists in Group Work* 7 (1982):251–259.

Carter, E. A., and M. McGoldrick. "The Family Life Cycle." In E. A. Carter and M. McGoldrick, eds., *The Family Life Cycle: A Framework for Family Therapy.* New York: Gardner Press, 1980.

————, eds. *The Family Life Cycle: A Framework for Family Therapy.* New York: Gardner Press, 1980b.

Cohn, B. "Invited Comment: A Conceptual Model for Group Counseling." *Together* 2 (1977):5–15.

Dinkmeyer, D. C., and J. J. Muro. *Group Counseling: Theory and Practice.* Itasca, Ill.: F. E. Peacock, 1979.

Fenell, D. L., B. Shertzer, and R. C. Nelson. "The Effects of a Marriage Enrichment Program on Marital Satisfaction and Self-Concept." *The Journal for Specialists in Group Work* 6 (1981):83–89.

Gazda, G. *Group Counseling: A Developmental Approach.* Boston: Allyn and Bacon, 1978.

Harris, T. L. "Relationships of Self-Disclosure to Several Aspects of Trust in a Group." *Journal for Specialists in Group Work* 5 (1980):24–28.

Hillman, B. W., and M. Evenson. "Family Enrichment: An Activity Group Process for Multiple Families." *The Journal for Specialists in Group Work* 6 (1981):22–28.

Hipple, J. "Group Treatment of Suicide Clients." *The Journal for Specialists in Group Work* 7 (1982):245–250.

Hodgson, J. W. "Cognitive Versus Behavioral-Interpersonal Approaches to the Group Treatment of Depressed College Students." *Journal of Counseling Psychology* 28 (1981):243–249.

La Greca, A. M., and D. A. Santogrossi. "Social Skills Training with Elementary School Students: A Behavioral Group Approach." *Journal of Consulting and Clinical Psychology* 48 (1980):220–227.

Leak, G. K. "Effects of Highly Structured Versus Nondirective Group Counseling Approaches on Personality and Behavioral Measures of Adjustment in Incarcerated Felons." *Journal of Counseling Psychology* 27 (1980):520–523.

Miller, B. C., and D. L. Sollie. "Normal Stress During Transition to Parenthood." *Family Relations* 29 (1980):459–465.

Minuchin, S. *Families and Family Therapy.* Cambridge: Harvard University Press, 1974.

———, and C. Fishman. *Family Therapy Techniques.* Cambridge: Harvard University Press, 1981.

Morran, D. K. "Leader and Member Self-Disclosing Behavior in Counseling Groups." *The Journal for Specialists in Group Work* 7 (1982): 218–223.

Peteroy, E. T. "Effects of Member and Leader Expectations on Group Outcome." *Journal of Counseling Psychology* 26 (1979):534–537.

Prescott, M. R., and J. D. Morris. "Transition Groups for Divorced and Separated Clients." *The Journal for Specialists in Group Work* 4 (1979):34–39.

Robinson, E. H., III, and E. S. Wilson. "Effects of Human Relations Training on Indices of Skill Development and Self-Concept Changes in Classroom Teachers." *The Journal for Specialists in Group Work* 5 (1980):163–169.

Rogers, C. *Carl Rogers on Encounter Groups.* New York: Harper & Row, 1970.

Rose, G. S., and R. L. Bednar. "Effects of Positive and Negative Self-Disclosure and Feedback on Early Group Development." *Journal of Counseling Psychology* 27 (1980):63–70.

Shamas, R. "Older People and Their Families: The New Pioneers." *Journal of Marriage and the Family* 42 (1980):9–15.

Shertzer, B., and S. C. Stone. *Fundamentals of Counseling.* 3rd ed. Boston: Houghton Mifflin, 1980.

Simone, F. "Adjustment Groups for Single Parents." *The Journal for Specialists in Group Work* 6 (1981):29–34.

Snow, L. S. "Female Sexuality Groups: Growth Workshops for College Women." *The Journal for Specialists in Group Work* 6 (1981):109–114.

Stockton, R., J. E. Barr, and R. Klein. "Identifying the Group Dropout: A Review of Literature." *The Journal for Specialists in Group Work* 6 (1981):75–82.

Stockton, R., and D. K. Morran. "The Use of Verbal Feedback in Counseling Groups: Toward and Effective System." *The Journal for Specialists in Group Work* 5 (1980):10–14.

———. "Feedback Exchange in Personal Growth Groups: Receiver Acceptance as a Function of Valence, Session, and Order of Delivery." *Journal of Counseling Psychology* 28 (1981):490–497.

Wilkie, J. B. "The Trend Toward Delayed Parenthood." *Journal of Marriage and the Family* 43 (1981):583–591.

Zube, M. "Changing Behavior and Outlook of Aging Men and Women: Implications for Marriage in the Middle and Later Years." *Family Relations* 31 (1982):147–156.

CHAPTER 15

Specialized Counseling Concerns

Chapter Organizer

Aim of the Chapter

This chapter will familiarize the reader with the counselor's role in several specialized counseling areas—namely, alcoholism counseling, drug counseling, sex counseling and therapy, holistic counseling, and career counseling.

Chapter Preview

1. Social changes and pressures affect the counseling problems presented to the counselor.
   a. Developmental concerns will remain a major focus for the counselor.
   b. Increasingly, however, the counselor will be confronted by clients under stress and requesting help that might require a specialized therapeutic approach.
2. Alcoholism involves issues of dependency, compulsion, duration, tolerance, and pattern of use.
   a. Impaired social and personal functioning accompanies the disease of alcoholism.
   b. Alcoholism progresses through a series of identifiable stages.
   c. Personal characteristics of alcoholics, including denial, anxiety, anger, manipulation, dependence, and self-centeredness, make them difficult clients to work with.
   d. Treatment models must consider the whole individual once detoxification (if necessary) has taken place.
3. Drug counselors have seen an increase in cross-addicted clients.
   a. A mood altering chemical is a psychoactive drug.
   b. *Set* and *setting* affect the response of the user to a particular chemical.
   c. A full range of treatment and counseling services is required for the alcohol or drug abuser.
4. Sexual dysfunctioning can result from a variety of physical, psychological, and relationship problems.
   a. Responsibility for self is important in healthy sexual functioning.
   b. Permission, limited information, and specific suggestions may be all that is needed by some clients with a sexual concern.
5. Holistic counseling responds to the client's total being—body, spirit, and mind.
6. Career counseling is, by nature, developmental.
   a. Career counseling helps with client awareness, planning, and decision making.
   b. Placement may well be a part of career counseling.

Relevant Questions

The following are several questions to keep in mind while reading this chapter:

1. What are the stages of alcoholism and the signs of each that indicate the presence of the disease?
2. How do *set* and *setting* affect the user of a chemical substance?
3. What are the specific types of sexual dysfunction and how may they be treated?
4. What is holistic counseling? What strategies does it employ?
5. What steps are basic to the career-planning process?

Introduction

Although counseling during the 1970s tended to emphasize developmental concerns rather than problem-centered counseling, counselors in practice were besieged with a variety of concerns that they had not previously encountered. Perhaps the outstanding example was the increased demand for sex counseling and therapy, which stemmed from the changing lifestyles of that decade. Social change alone, and not necessarily social problems, created adjustment problems which the counselor was asked to help resolve. In addition, as people became more aware of the benefits of counseling and therapy, clients presented a full array of behavioral disorders. While counselors will continue to spend the majority of their time on developmental concerns, they need to become familiar with other therapeutic issues and approaches. This chapter presents a brief overview of the therapist's role in alcoholism counseling, drug counseling, sex counseling and therapy, holistic counseling, and career development counseling. The holistic approach to working with individuals stresses the concept of health as a multidimensional mode of living and tries to avoid fragmenting the client.

Alcoholism Counseling

Problems related to alcohol consumption are brought to counselors in greater and greater numbers. It is a medico-psycho-social problem of great magnitude, yet few people are aware of the magnitude. Current estimates of alcoholism range from 6 to 12 percent of the adult population. It is a major health problem in the United States. More than 100 million Americans drink alcoholic beverages, and of these 6–10 million adults and 3 million people under the age of 21 can be classified as alcoholics or problem drinkers; yet less than 10 percent receive help for their alcohol-related problems (Brandsma, 1980). Brisolara (1979) estimates that there are 5 million employed alcoholics, leading to an industrial problem affecting 5 percent of the work force and costing industry over $10.4 billion annually. Alcoholism, left untreated, shortens life expectancy by 10 to 15 years (Connors, 1979, p. 532). At the same time there are a myriad of problems with alcohol use among the elderly (Gross and Capuzzi, 1981).

The families and children of alcoholics must also be considered. There are 7 million people, or one out of 20, under the age of 20, who currently live with an alcoholic (Klemesrud, 1982, p. 44). A study completed in New York in July of 1982 noted that there were 500,000 children in alcoholic families and that they were four times more likely than other children to become alcoholic (Klemesrud, 1982, p. 44). Contrary to stereotype, the alcoholic is not a "stumbling, broken-down, down-and-out Bowery bum," but rather is someone who holds a job, can be found at all socioeconomic levels, in all professions, races, and ethnic groups. It is estimated, for example, that 25 percent of problem drinkers are white collar, 30 percent are blue collar, and 45 percent are professional or managerial (Brandsma, 1980, p. 1).

The alcoholic is a member of a family group, and it is important to remember that not only the alcoholic but the family must be treated. "Research has shown substance abuse treatment to be a remarkably cost-effective social investment. It costs far less to treat substance abuse than to endure the social costs of the associated problems (crime, violence, and so forth)" (Falk et al., 1982, p. 1127).

Definition of Alcoholism

As mentioned earlier, the alcoholic does not fit the "Bowery bum" stereotype that is often held by the public. This stereotype may well be part of the denial system found in the culture at large, for whom alcohol is a problem but who show little acceptance of alcoholism and its related problems.

How can alcoholism be defined? What is the difference between an alcoholic and a problem drinker? Are substance abuse and chemical dependency the same? Key elements in definitions and distinctions among these terms would necessarily address (1) dependency, (2) compulsion, (3) duration, (4) tolerance, and (5) pattern of use. *Substance abuse* involves a pattern of continued use over a sustained period of time that results in impaired personal and social functioning. *Chemical dependency* involves a tolerance to increased amounts of a chemical to achieve a desired effect; in addition, decreasing or terminating the use of the chemical results in the experience of a withdrawal syndrome. Forrest (1978) uses the following definitions:

1. Social drinkers engage in moderate consumption of alcohol, perhaps 2–3 times a week. Intoxication is infrequent.
2. Problem drinkers do not see themselves as excessive drinkers, but are frequently intoxicated. As a result of alcohol consumption, the problem drinker does suffer physically, socially, and economically.
3. Alcoholics are addicted to alcohol and are unable to give up drinking. The alcoholic relies on alcohol to cope with living. Chronic alcoholism indicates a prolonged life-style of intoxication which has led to physical deterioration. (p. 9)

For our purposes alcoholism signifies a loss of the ability to control the intake of alcohol once drinking is initiated before getting intoxicated. Problem drinking is the prolonged, repetitive use of alcohol that has harmful personal and social consequences for the individual.

Stages of Alcoholism The conceptualized model of alcoholism involves a progression of developmental stages. While such stages can be identified, recognizing them does nothing to change the nature and progression of alcoholism.

Peer et al. (1982) identified the stages of alcohol involvement and mood effects as follows:

Stage 1: Alcohol as a mood changer

Moderate use: infrequently intoxicating; user consciously chooses alcohol to change mood; use not noticeable or troublesome to others; no dependency, psychologically or physically.

Stage 2: Alcohol as a coping mechanism

Accelerated use: frequently intoxicating; user unconsciously relying on alcohol as a mood changer; use noticeable and troublesome to intimates and close associates; developing psychological dependency, i.e., anxiety escalates in absence of alcohol.

Stage 3: Alcohol as a need

Pervasive use: predominantly intoxicating; user denies any awareness of habitual reliance on alcohol and is now experiencing impaired consciousness in daily relationships; acute dependency.

Stage 4: Alcohol as survival

Incessant use: chronic intoxication; user denies all reality except the need for alcohol; loss of consciousness occurs for extended periods of time; use noticeable to general public; chronic dependency. (p. 466)

Jellinek (1962), analyzing cases of alcohol addiction, developed a chart of the symptoms and phases of alcoholism. (See Figure 15.1.) Jellinek sees the early phase of alcoholism as characterized by an increasing tolerance of alcohol, the onset of blackouts or memory lapses, frequently thinking about and planning to drink, attempts to avoid calling attention to drinking, and an inability to control drinking after only one drink. The middle phase sees the development of a defense system to justify drinking and to deal with disapproval from others. Mood swings occur; they can fluctuate from guilt and remorse to anger, resentment, and belligerence. It is during this period that attempts may be made to stop drinking just to show self or others that "alcohol is not a problem. I can control it." Social disengagement begins and feelings of isolation set in. Problems develop at home and work that may cause the individual to seek help, but such help is usually not sought for the drinking itself. Drinking becomes prolonged, and physical and psychological changes, such as cirrhosis or brain damage, become apparent. The later phase is characterized by a breakdown of ethical codes, that is, individuals may steal to drink. Emotional extremes may give rise to irrational jealousies or indefinable fears. Trembling and shaking is observable, and

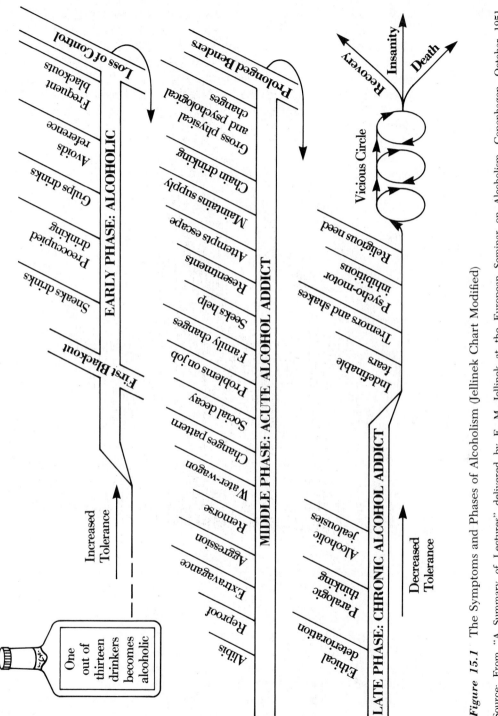

Figure 15.1 The Symptoms and Phases of Alcoholism (Jellinek Chart Modified)

Source: From "A Summary of Lectures" delivered by E. M. Jellinek at the European Seminar on Alcoholism, Copenhagen, October 1951. Copyright by World Health Organization, Geneva. Distributed by the National Council on Alcoholism, New York.

a cycle of drinking is well established. The choices presented at this stage are either recovery or insanity or death. Forrest (1978) raises the "disease" concept of alcoholism. The notion that alcoholism is a disease has become more widely accepted because research findings suggest the strong influences of heredity—the *x* factor—in alcoholism. Concepts of stages and phases of alcoholism mesh easily with the disease concept of alcoholism. While "no actual genetic proof has been found, there is evidence that alcoholism tends to run in families. Studies show that children born of alcoholic parents have about a four-times greater incidence of alcoholism than those whose parents did not abuse the substance. This holds true even among adopted youngsters" (Engelbardt, 1982, pp. 30–31).

Characteristics of the Alcoholic Personality

While there is no "alcoholic personality" that causes alcoholism, it is important for counselors to recognize personality characteristics often associated with alcoholism because of the important role they play in diagnosis and treatment. These characteristics in many cases feed the supports that are used to maintain alcoholism. Edwards and Grant (1977) write that "alcoholics are notorious for denial, rationalization, inconsistency, and ambivalence" (p. 97). Denial allows the alcoholic to refute the idea that drinking has become a problem or that control over drinking has been lost. Since admitting the need for help is a prerequisite to improvement during treatment, denial is usually confronted early in the treatment process. Alcoholic denial may extend beyond the drinking itself and become a more generalized system—for example, denying inadequacy as a spouse, parent, or worker. Forman (1979) feels that manipulation is the dominant factor in the alcoholic's life.

Counselors must recognize that alcoholics by the time they have become active alcohol addicts, have years of successful manipulation of their environment behind them. Generally, they are much more sophisticated at subliminal manipulation than is the counselor. I have seen many seasoned in-the-field counselors so manipulated by the alcoholic's game that they do not even know when, how, or why they are being manipulated. (p. 546)

Anger, anxiety, and periods of depression may be found in everyone, but with the alcoholic these characteristics are more chronic. It is interesting to note that in many cases the alcoholic drinks to mask these feelings but finds (although denying it) that the drinking actually aggravates them. Alcoholics, for example, drink because they feel anxious or depressed but find that the drinking increases their anxiety or depression. The alcoholic's self-centeredness brings with it strong needs for approval and acceptance from others. This need compounds the possibilities of increased anxiety (Will I be accepted?) as well as anger and depression (I am not being accepted to the degree I would like). The strong need for approval and acceptance carries with it dependence on others. This dependency—as a characteristic of the alcoholic—extends so far as the need to be taken care of physically and economically by someone else. In many cases, then, the practicing alcoholic has to have someone "enable" the drinking. Such a dependency may be masked by fluctuating mood swings: dependence gives way to resentment of the dependency, anger, and defiance, which gives way to remorse and dependency. Dependency is a crucial consideration in therapy since it is a basic component of any addictive behavior. Further, the nature of the dependency on others beyond the chemical addiction could determine the forms of therapy. The desirability of bringing in the enabler as a part of the process could necessitate family or marital therapy. The foremost consideration in counseling with the alcoholic is that the person must be sober in order to deal with these characteristics. One final point should be made: This section should not be interpreted to mean that a particular personality type "causes" alcoholism or that alcoholism is representative of a particular personality disorder. In an excellent review of studies of alcoholism, Vaillant and Milofsky (1982) state the following:

[S]tudies suggest that if one controls for antisocial childhood, cultural attitudes toward alcohol use and abuse, for alcoholic heredity, and most especially for the effects of alcohol abuse, then many of the childhood and adult personality variables to which adult alcoholism has traditionally been attributed will appear as carts and not horses. . . . [O]ur findings suggest that even when they employed prospective design, previous investigators may have sometimes erroneously interpreted their data to support the retrospective illusion that alcoholism must be a symptom of personality disorder. (p. 502)

Treatment Models   Treatment models may be broken down into the following categories: the legal model, the medical model, the Alcoholics Anonymous model, and the comprehensive/integrated model.

The Legal Model   The legal model involves attempts to control or reduce alcoholism through legal measures. Prohibition is perhaps the outstanding example of alcohol control by law. Historically, legislation has not been effective in dealing with alcohol use. There is a moral element that often enters into legal measures. Shaw et al. (1978) state, "the temperance movement was trying to stigmatize heavy drinkers as being deliberately degenerate . . . used the term 'inebriate' to refer to someone who could not stop drinking, along with other terms such as 'habitual drunkard' and 'dypsomanic' " (p. 44–45).

The Medical Model   The medical model endorses alcoholism as a disease. It views alcoholism as similar to diseases that cannot be cured but may be arrested with proper treatment and health care. The medical model helped move treatment from a moral/legal arena into a rehabilitative and habilitative one. Detoxification under medical supervision is the most widely accepted component of this particular treatment model today. Critics of the medical model often suggest that the notion of "alcoholism as a disease" allows alcoholics to escape responsibility for their behavior and to be passive throughout the treatment process. It is apparent to us that the "disease concept" may reduce alcoholic self-blame (total escape from self-blame would, of course, only increase the potential for drinking) but does not allow the alcoholic to escape responsibility for seeking treatment and maintaining sobriety. Choosing is always an active process; by its very nature it cannot be passive.

Alcoholics Anonymous Model Alcoholics Anonymous (A.A.) was started in 1935 as a self-help group to minister to the problem drinker and "alcohol-addicted" person. It can be viewed "(1) historically, as an important social movement, (2) as a prime treatment system encompassing annually 'more alcoholics than are seen by the medical profession,' and (3) as a new life model encompassed as an integral component of almost all of the formal inpatient treatment programs" (Smith, 1980, p. 110). The purpose of A.A. is simply stated in its preamble: "Alcoholics Anonymous is a fellowship of men and women who share their experience, strength, and hope with each other that they may solve their common problems and help others to recover from alcoholism. . . . Our primary purpose is to stay sober and help other alcoholics to achieve sobriety." The phenomenal success of A.A. is based on large numbers of recoveries and reunited homes. Indeed, 50 percent of alcoholics "who came to A. A. and made a concerted effort" became sober and retained sobriety, while another 25 percent attained sobriety after a few relapses (Forrest, 1978, p. 113). Pettinati et al. (1982) found that A.A. attendance the first year was related to long-term abstinence, while not attending A.A. the first year after discharge was associated with periodic drinking. Guydish (1982) writes, "Attesting to its effectiveness at a grass roots level is the fact that A.A. groups can easily be found in most cities across the country, and their boast of having helped over 8 million alcoholics. Without government grants, cadres of trained professionals, or corporate bureaucracies, the success of A.A. is wondrous" (p. 399). The goal for treatment by A.A. is sobriety and abstinence from alcohol.

While it is often assumed that A.A. membership involves a religious affiliation, this is not the case. What is called for is a belief in a "higher power." For some this may well involve a spiritual awakening and even a return to organized religion. This element lends itself to philosophical change in the alcoholic's life, which enhances the chance of attaining sobriety. Recognition of the effect on the family has also led to the development of Al-Anon and Alateen programs for spouses and children of alcoholics, respectively. These organizations serve as support, social, and educational groups for family members. Many treatment centers are based solely on the A.A., Al-Anon, Alateen, model; others integrate A.A. into an overall program. For outpatient and private practitioners, A.A. can serve as a major referral resource. Forrest's (1978) comments about A.A. summarize the "fellowship" of A.A. and its importance in recovery:

[W]ithin A.A. the single most potent variable effecting behavior change along the lines of sobriety is that of human relatedness. The hallmark of the alcoholic is interpersonal anxiety. . . . Alcoholics Anonymous provide an interpersonal environment in which the alcoholic can learn and relearn more effective patterns of interpersonal behavior. The emotional climate of A.A. is essentially one of total acceptance. . . . This acceptance and support means being treated as an equal. This in itself is of major significance as most alcoholics have a long developmental history of feelings of inferiority, and inadequacy. (p. 121)

Comprehensive/Integrated Model   It is becoming more widely accepted that the treatment of alcoholism has to involve all potential sources of recovery. The comprehensive/integrated model incorporates the medical and A.A. models within a generalized psychological, educational, and health-care approach to sobriety. Kinney and Leaton (1978) presented a treatment formula

Treatment = individual counseling + client education + family therapy + family education + group therapy + medical care + A.A. + Al Anon + Antabuse + vocational counseling + activities therapy + spiritual counseling + . . .

This particular model calls for the implementation of a holistic approach. The "whole" person has to be treated physically, psychologically, socially, and spiritually. Educational, medical, and therapeutic interventions are integrated into a total program. The comprehensive model includes the following:

Medical detoxification and care
History-taking and diagnosis
Group therapy utilizing affective, cognitive, and behavioral approaches
Individual counseling utilizing affective, cognitive, and behavioral
    approaches
Didactic experiences including lectures and films to facilitate learning
Recreational therapy
Placement and follow-up services
Alcoholics Anonymous, Al Anon, and Alateen
Mental and family therapy
Referral services to community resources

Alcoholism treatment centers often refer to a "revolving door" phenomenon, that is, the individual who comes for treatment—too often just detoxification—leaves the center and keeps returning time after time. Programs, using the holistic approach, are much less likely to see this phenomenon. Further, if the staff observes that a particular treatment modality "enables" the disease for particular clients, they may have to deny that client admittance to that program. Appropriate referral sources may then be used.
    One last point should be addressed in this section—the assertion that

alcoholics may successfully engage in controlled drinking. A major controversy has erupted in health-care fields regarding this position. It has included outcries that the research used to support the "controlled drinking" tenet was insufficient and inadequate (Fields, 1982; Skirball, 1982). Considering alcoholism a progressive disease, and noting the paucity of research to support the "controlled drinking" position, it is apparent that any implementation of this approach is not in the best interests of the recovering alcoholic.

Sacred Heart Center: An Exemplary Program

The November/December 1981 issue of *Alcoholism* gave the highest praise to Sacred Heart Center in Detroit, Michigan. Miller (1981) states:

Sacred Heart isn't just a bleeding one. . . . In 1980 Sacred Heart took [355] hardcore alcoholic unemployables off the welfare rolls, dried them out, made them over and filled them up, placing them in permanent jobs with combined tax-paying salaries totaling [$3,088,900] . . . (p. 9)[1]

Father Quinn's philosophy is "to learn how to live, to learn how to have fun without chemicals." It is a message that has been carried to approximately 20,000 people who have been through the treatment program. Following is a description of the Sacred Heart program.[2]

Sacred Heart Center exists to provide a program of counseling and rehabilitation designed specifically to meet the needs of adult male and female alcoholics.

Intake Clients of Sacred Heart Center are referred from a wide variety of sources in the community at large. After initial client eligibility is established, the beginning of a complete social history is taken to determine the length of affliction, degree of alcoholism, use of other substances, and the existence of any complicating medical, legal, social or mental health problems. As the client is admitted into the detox unit, an assigned counselor completes the social history and begins to work with that person on an individualized treatment plan.

Detoxification A two- to five-day period of observation and treatment is initiated for the client who enters the facility intoxicated or suffering symptoms and sequilae of withdrawal syndrome. The medical director and assisting registered nurse provide primary medical services throughout the week. . . . A continuum of medical care is provided by physicians and nurses throughout the entire length of the rehabilitation program. . . . If, at any time, acute medical complications or contagious diseases are discovered, the client is referred to an acute care facility for appropriate treatment and eventual return to the Sacred Heart Center. . . . Throughout the total rehabilitation process, the doctors and nurses are part of the therapeutic team. Weekly staffings are conducted by the physician and nurse, with the counsel-

---

[1]These brackets indicate 1982 revised data.
[2]Appreciation is expressed for the development of this description to the following staff members at Sacred Heart: Father Vaughan Quinn, Director; Rocco Radice, Administrator; Floyd Lawton, Administrator; James Fleming, Assistant Director; and Betty Lane and Chauncey Smith, Coordinators of Counseling.

ing staff, to review and evaluate the physical condition and progress of each client. Medical recommendations are included in each client's individual service plan.

Initial Therapy After release from detox, approximately one week of intense work is done with the client to promote self-awareness and identification processes, personal problems' assessment and an orientation to the principles and practices of Alcoholics Anonymous as a reality therapy program of specific recovery from alcoholism. A detailed treatment plan, acceptable to both counselor and client, is produced and agreed upon prior to transfer to the advanced treatment facility.

Advanced Therapy After transfer to Memphis, a five- to nine-week course of treatment is implemented that is based on the individualized treatment plan formulated in the initial phase. Advanced therapy is a program of one-to-one, group counseling and didactic experiences which rapidly develop self-awareness through peer interaction, and continues a series of self-assessment and personal problems' inventory sessions designed to lead the client to acceptance of limitations and development of coping skills. Heavy emphasis is placed on dealing with negative feelings and changing self-defeating behaviors by means of specific behavior change objectives detailed in the client's treatment plan.

Supportive and Ancillary Services. Throughout the entire rehabilitation process, each client has access to support services designed to provide necessary activity or meet special needs for the person who lives in the treatment setting. Daily work details are structured into the rehabilitation plan for milieu therapy purposes. An activities coordinator at each facility works to organize a recreation program and to involve all residents in reactivation of constructive leisure time interests. Drivers are employed to meet a host of transportation requirements of residents, the most important being the weekly outside A.A. meetings that introduce and familiarize the client with this most important ongoing self-help resource. Family counseling is available for spouses, close relatives and friends who are still meaningfully involved in the life of the recovering alcoholic. A psychologist is available to provide appropriate testing when necessary. After completion of the rehabilitation program, assistance for regaining former jobs, finding new employment or setting up vocational rehabilitation guidance is available through the Employment Counseling Office. Continued care and supportive living may be offered by referral to halfway houses should this be a need of the client. Sacred Heart's structured follow-up program attempts to maintain contact with former residents for two years from the date of completion of treatment. Regular meetings and activities are scheduled for the departing client, and a full-time follow-up counselor coordinates the activities of this program.

Drug Counseling

It is difficult to determine the degree of drug abuse in the United States today. The compilation of data is complicated by a variety of factors, for example, whether or not to include the misuse of prescribed or over-the-counter medications, the difficulty in acquiring information on the use of illicit drugs, and the movement during the sixties from the use of single drugs to the introduction of the "polydrug" user. The painful realities suggest, however, that drug abuse is increasing. Brill and Winick (1980) note, "For example, the number of active heroin addicts rose from about 50,000 in the mid-1960's to about 500,000 in the mid-1970's. Over the same period the number of people who had used marijuana rose from about 5 million to 43 million" (p. 22). Dacey (1982) notes that about 5 percent of American teenagers are physiologically drug dependent (p. 311). He further notes that of a sample of the class of 1978 the percentages of adolescents who had ever used a particular drug were as follows: 59.2 percent marijuana; 12.0 percent, inhalants; 14.3 percent, cocaine; 1.6 percent, heroin; 9.9 percent, other opiates; 22.9 percent, stimulants; 16.0 percent, sedatives; 17.0 percent, tranquilizers; 93.1 percent, alcohol; and 75.3 percent, cigarettes (p. 311).

Definition of Drug Abuse

A drug is a substance taken to achieve a desired effect, while a mood-altering chemical may be termed a psychoactive drug. Generally, drugs are taken orally, injected, or inhaled and then distributed through the body by the bloodstream. Table 15.1 indicates categories of frequently abused drugs. While we may be able to classify various types of drugs that are abused, many rehabilitation centers report increased frequency of cross-addicted abusers, although counselors can identify a preferred drug of choice.

The effects of drugs are both physical and psychological. Psychological effects are often determined by *set* and *setting.* Set refers to a mind set; that is, if one expects something to happen, it often will regardless of the composition of the drug ingested. What is expected has built in a self-fulfilling prophecy. This idea is supported by research on placebos, or sugar pills, which are reported by predisposed ingestors to have various mood-altering properties, when in fact they have none. The setting, or where the drug is taken, also has some psychological effect. If, for example, a drug is taken with a festive social group, it will appear to have stimulating rather than depressing characteristics. Alcohol, a depressant, is viewed by many to be a stimulant because of the social context in which it is often consumed.

The following terms may be helpful in working with the drug user:

Drug abuse is the misuse of a drug so that a person's physical, emotional, or mental well-being is impaired.

Table 15.1
Categorization of
Abused Drugs

	Depressants			
Sedative-Hypnotic		*Narcotics*	*Stimulants*	*Psychedelics*
Barbiturates		Opium	Caffeine	LSD
Antidepressants or muscle		Morphine	Cocaine	PCP
relaxants		Heroin	Amphetamines	Psilocybin
Marijuana		Codeine		Mescaline

Note: While alcohol is considered in the previous section, it would be classified in the subcategory of sedative-hypnotic.

Drug addiction indicates either a physical or psychological dependence on a drug. In 1964 the World Health Organization felt that because of the misuse of the words *addiction* and *habituation* the term *dependence* was preferable.

Drug dependence "occurs when there is a physical or psychological need, resulting from continuous use. Psychological need occurs when the person feels anxious or irritable when he or she doesn't have the drug. Physical dependence, on the other hand, occurs only when negative physical symptoms result from drug withdrawal, such as vomiting, sweating, muscle tremors, delusions and hallucinations" (Dacey, 1982, pp. 310–311).

Drug tolerance means the individual needs more of a drug to achieve the same desired effect.

Treatment and Counseling

A number of issues have to be considered in the treatment and counseling of drug abusers. First, what are legitimate treatment goals? Is abstinence the end sought? Some would hold that abstinence is an acceptable goal only if there are medical or psychiatric reasons that suggest that drugs not be used. While we can accept this statement in principle, there is some difficulty in determining on a practical level what are legitimate "psychiatric reasons." A conceptual distinction can be made between a "dependent" personality and a "nondependent" personality type. A practical distinction in a counseling is too often based on the client's perception or deception. One client, who was using quaaludes, stated that he had been doing so occasionally for years and was well in control of its use. The therapist later received a call from the client's father who reported that he had thrown the quaaludes down the toilet and discovered his son on hands and knees trying to get them out of the toilet bowl. Client self-report in this case was an inaccurate indicator of the degree of dependency for this adult, male client. If any degree of client dependency is ascertained, abstinence has to be a primary treatment goal.

Second, what areas of the client's life legitimately should be dealt with besides the immediate problem of drug use? It is our belief that clients cannot be segmented for treatment. An evaluation during intake can help determine what problems exist and the nature and scope of treatment. Treatment may even go so far as attempting to get the client to redefine social and cultural relationships that may be supporting drug use.

In dealing with drug abuse, counselors are often asked to provide medical and legal help, to locate adequate living quarters, and to identify social support systems. In addition to providing the full range of counseling and rehabilitation services identified in the section on alcoholism counseling, individual and/or group therapy, family counseling, didactic sessions, medical care, legal help, and job placement are all necessary in working with the drug user.

Sex Counseling and Therapy

Both group and individual counseling have much potential as an aid to healthy sexual functioning. Childhood and adolescent concerns about "normal" development, masturbation, menstruation, and other topics could well be brought up in counseling sessions. The counselor applies counseling skills as he or she might apply them in any other problem area. Regardless of content, counseling goals remain the same: self-exploration, increased self-knowledge, and action or behavior change. The counselor may also provide sex information. In this case the counselor is neither moral nor immoral. The moral obligation is to provide timely and accurate data. This may be classified as sex counseling, whereas sex therapy focuses specifically on a sexual dysfunction.

Types of Sexual Dysfunctioning

A sexual dysfunction involves distress or dissatisfaction with one's sexual functioning. What causes distress for one person may not disturb another; if one partner is distressed, the other may not be. "Rapid" ejaculation or "premature" ejaculation might cause distress for a young man who would like to engage in intercourse for a longer period of time, but not for his partner who may be quite satisfied. Interference with the sexual response cycle (excitement, plateau, orgasm, resolution) could happen at any point in the cycle. Some individuals have difficulty becoming aroused, others may experience difficulty maintaining excitement, and others become aroused but have difficulty reaching orgasm.

More specific categories of sexual dysfunctions have been identified for females as follows:

Orgasmic dysfunction or anorgasmia refers to difficulty in reaching orgasm. Primary anorgasmia indicates that a woman has never experienced orgasm by any means, while situational anorgasmia suggests that a woman who may reach orgasm under one circumstance may not under a different one. Occasional absence of orgasm is usually not stressful for a woman, but consistent anorgasmia may create great concern. While some anorgasmia may be related to a specific partner's sexual dysfunction or poor lovemaking, some women have difficulty reaching orgasm during sexual intercourse with all partners. In some cases situational anorgasmia is caused by relationship problems (for example, fear of letting go with a particular partner) or by psychological ones (experiencing guilt during sexual activity).

Vaginismus is a condition in which there is an involuntary muscular spasm of the vaginal entrance that precludes the introduction of an object into the vagina. In some cases even the thought of penetration will trigger the response. The muscle spasm will close the entrance so tightly that intercourse will be either impossible or quite painful. This response is not voluntary, but is triggered automatically and involuntarily. As Masters and Johnson (1970) point out, "Vaginismus . . . cannot be unreservedly diagnosed by any established interrogative technique. Regardless of the psychotherapist's high level of clinical suspicion, a secure diagnosis of vaginismus cannot be established without the specific clinical support that only direct pelvic examination can provide" (p. 250). Wabrek and Wabrek (1976) note that primary vaginismus is present when the woman "after repeated attempts, has been unable to have intercourse," while secondary vaginismus involves a woman who was able to have intercourse for a period of time, "but either because of dyspareunia [painful intercourse], or some sexual trauma, the muscles around her vaginal opening go into spasm to 'protect' a repeat of the insult" (p. 21). Factors precipitating vaginismus include a history of painful intercourse, strong antisexual feelings or conditioning, and sexual brutality. A reversed conditional response is achieved through the use of dilators of increasing size and other sex therapy techniques, such as sensate focus.

Three types of male sexual dysfunction may be described briefly as follows:

Erectile distress is defined as difficulty in achieving or maintaining an erection. A male with primary erectile distress would never have had or been able to maintain an erection for successful intercourse. Secondary erectile distress describes a condition in a male who at some time had engaged in at least one successful coital experience. The former condition is more severe and less likely to be treated successfully. Physical, psychological, and relationship factors can influence the complex mechanisms that control erection and impair the erectile process.

Premature (early) ejaculation has been identified as ejaculating "too quickly." The definition of "premature" has been difficult since it often uses as a yardstick partner satisfaction and assumes coital orgasmic adequacy by the female. Clinically, this may be a comfortable definition, but practically or under less controlled circumstances the diagnosis is more difficult. Some researchers will define premature ejaculation in terms of seconds (usually 30–60) after intromission into the vagina before ejaculation occurs. This definition ignores partner and self-satisfaction. In some cases premature ejaculation can be clearly identified where ejaculation occurs while the male is still clothed or prior to any direct sexual stimulation of either partner. The squeeze technique is often used with premature ejaculation, but engaging in sex more often also can reduce the concern in this area. The squeeze technique involves the stimulation of the male to full erection and then squeezing the penis which eliminates the urge to ejaculate. After 20–30 seconds the procedure is repeated. The stop-start method approximates this procedure. The male, perceiving that orgasm is approaching, asks the partner to discontinue stimulation. This procedure can then be repeated. Regardless of differences in technique, both approaches help the male to become more aware of sexual feelings and to develop the ability to delay the ejaculatory process.

Retarded ejaculation or ejaculatory inhibition refers to a condition in a male who is able to become aroused, obtain an erection, but is unable to ejaculate. While neuropathy or some drugs can cause this, usually a traumatic experience during intercourse or masturbation is associated with its onset. In many cases it is situational; that is, the male is unable to ejaculate intravaginally but is able to do so by masturbating. McCarthy (1981) feels that there are four areas to be assessed in the treatment of ejaculatory inhibition—namely, sexual attitudes, sexual anxiety, sexual skills, and heterosocial skills—and that treatment of identified problem areas be centered on in therapy.

Some dysfunctions can also be found in both sexes.

Dyspareunia is painful coitus. Various physical causes include vaginal or clitoral inflammations, thin vaginal walls, tight penile foreskin, urethritis, or herpes lesions. If physical reasons are eliminated, emotional, psychological, or relationship problems may be the contributing factors.

Sexual aversion refers to an intense fear or anxiety response, which approaches phobic proportions in a sexual situation. As a result, there is a strong aversive reaction to anything sexual in nature.

Inhibited sexual desire is a persistent and pervasive lack of sexual arousal and desire. This becomes a dysfunction in instances where the individual is stressed by the lack of sexual expression. Rather than a phobic or intense anxiety response, this dysfunction is often described as the result of boredom or disinterest. LaPointe and Gillespie (1979) described a short-term treatment approach for inhibited sexual desire that involved (1) self-definition of the problem, (2) development of bodily awareness, (3) recognition and labeling of sexual feelings, (4) giving permission to thoughts, and (5) developing a positive self-concept. Sensate focus activities, logs, and fantasy work were involved in the process.

It may be of interest, because of the historical significance of their work, to indicate the initial failure rates (IFR) reported by Masters and Johnson in *Human Sexual Inadequacy* (1970, pp. 358–362):

	IFR
Primary erective distress (Impotence)	40.6%
Secondary erective distress	26.3%
Premature ejaculation	2.2%
Ejaculatory incompetence (Retarded ejaculation)	17.6%
Vaginismus	0
Primary orgasmic dysfunction	16.6%

Situational orgasmic dysfunction	22.8%
All males treated	16.9%
All females treated	19.3%

The statistical failure rates approximate 20 percent during the short-term (two-week) rapid treatment program.

Causes of Sexual Dysfunctioning Sexual dysfunctions may result from a variety of physical, psychological, and relationship factors. It is important, however, to remember that the same factors will not lead to dysfunction in others.

Physiological Causes Physical illnesses, ingestion of drugs, infection, and physical well-being can have some impact on sexual activity (see Table 15.2). Occasionally, one may find that sexual dysfunction signals a very serious, otherwise unrecognized, physical problem. Too often a physical ailment is recognized and treated, while the associated sexual difficulties are ignored. Notwithstanding the fact that physical or organic factors contribute to only a small percentage of sexual dysfunctioning, a physical exam by a physician should precede any further sex therapy or counseling in order to rule out such possibilities. Godow (1982) stresses several important points:

Most often sexual functioning is only partially impaired by factors such as diabetes, neurological damage, or use of antihypertensive medication. It is the person's and/or partner's alarmed reactions to this impairment that may lead to complete dysfunction. . . . Thus the medical diagnosis of an organic problem does not necessarily eliminate the possibility that sex therapy may be useful. In general, an organic problem can be ruled out as a contributory factor in sexual dysfunction if the individual's sexual difficulty is situational, that is, if it presents itself in certain situations but not in others. (p. 495)

Psychological Causes Strong negative feelings, such as anger, resentment, fear, disgust, and anxiety, can lead to sexual dysfunction. Fear of rejection, for example, may lead to an avoidance of sex, while anxiety can

Table 15.2 Physiological Factors That May Be Related to Sexual Distress

Diseases	Drugs	Physical Health
Diabetes	Alcohol	Poor nutrition
Prostatis	Heroin	Fatigue
Arthritis	Methadone	Stress
Multiple sclerosis	Tranquilizers	Depression
Diffuse arteriosclerosis		Anemia
Endometriosis		Hormonal changes
Ovarian/uterine cysts and tumors		
Venereal diseases		
Surgical traumas		
Pulmonary disease		
Congestive heart disease		

interfere with the arousal or orgasmic responses. A common cause of anxiety in sexual situations is called *performance anxiety,* or pressure that results from some preconceived notions of sexual adequacy. Performance anxiety can also develop as a result of a sexual "failure." A male, for instance, who has had too much to drink, may be unable to obtain an erection. He approaches the next opportunity with greater anxiety (may even have a drink or two to settle his "nerves") and increases his chances of being unable to have an erection. The anxiety and "fear itself contributes to the very event that is feared" (Godow, 1982, p. 483). Performance orientation and anxiety create another situation, which may be labeled *spectatoring,* or stepping outside of oneself and observing and evaluating one's own performance. The thoughts that occur may be

"Am I good?"
"How am I doing?"
"Is she/he really pleased?"

The problems with spectatoring are twofold. First, it increases anxiety levels, and second, it is a cognitive process that interferes with the emotional responses that add to the enjoyment of the sexual experience. Similarly, anger and resentment serve as destructive forces in the sexual experience. It is very difficult to be open or to engage in sex with someone when you are angry with them. Sexual inhibitions can also contribute to fear in the individual or anger and resentment in the partner. Serious disagreements can arise over oral or anal sex, time or place for sex, sex while the children are awake, and so on. Many of these negative beliefs about sex are instilled during the childhood years and are, in many cases, unrecognized by adults. Those adults may, however, feel the anxiety or guilt that sex brings on—anxiety or guilt that interferes with enjoyable sexual expression. As Godow (1982) points out, "The extent to which persons are alienated from their sexuality on a conscious or unconscious level and the degree to which strong negative emotions have been associated with sexual anatomy, feelings, and actions will directly influence the extent to which sexually destructive conflict and anxiety develops" (p. 481).

Relationship Factors   The most easily recognizable relationship-based factors are sexual ignorance and poor communication. Ignorance can be misinformation or lack of information about sexual matters. Sarver and Murry (1981) found, for example, that high-marital-satisfaction subjects had a higher level of factual sexual knowledge than low-marital-satisfaction subjects. Because of shyness or fear of offending the partner, there is sometimes little or no communication during lovemaking. The combination of sexual ignorance and poor communication can lead to unpleasant feelings and sexual dissatisfaction that may undermine an otherwise happy and compatible relationship.

Frequently, relationship difficulties take the form of a power struggle between partners. The ongoing battle to dominate, consciously or unconsciously, precludes the ability to engage in satisfactory sexual relations. Often humiliation or sexual sabotage is used to undermine the partner's confidence. Unless the interaction is interrupted quickly, it will have devastating effects on the individuals in the relationship.

Principles of Sex Counseling   Maddock and Chilgren (1976) point to some underlying principles of sex counseling regardless of approach:

1. *Responsibility for Self*   "Sex therapy assumes that each partner has the . . . capacity to choose more effective behavior patterns."
2. *Permission to Be Sexual*   Clients can be helped to see sex as a natural function and feel that it is acceptable to be sexually active, to think about and be interested in sex.
3. *Utilization of Re-education Methods*   Clients need adequate and accurate information about sex in a "warm and supportive context."
4. *Increased Awareness*   Communication between partners is increased and made more effective. Each person needs to become more aware of sexual feelings, fantasies and preferences.
5. *Structured Behavior Change*   Sex counseling needs to work toward behavior change. This can be accomplished through specific "homework" or tasks. (p. 372)

Based upon the basic principles of sex counseling, the PLISSIT model, which is a conceptual scheme for the treatment of sexual problems, may be helpful to counselors (Annon, 1976, pp. 1–15). The four levels of handling sexual problems are as follows:

(P)   *Permission*   At this stage the client is given permission to be sexual perhaps through some reassurance that they are "normal." This may "be used to cover a number of areas of concern, such as thoughts, dreams, and feelings, as well as overt behaviors." (p. 5)

(LI)   *Limited Information*   This is viewed as giving clients specific information related to their sexual concern.

(SS)   *Specific Suggestions*   After assessment of the sexual problem, direct attempts are made to help the client change behavior within a "brief therapy" framework.

(IT)   *Intensive Therapy*   For sexual problems that are not amenable to treatment through the aforementioned, more intensive therapy may be necessary.

Because many counselors will deal with their clients' sexual expression at some point in the therapy process, the most effective sex counseling will be integrated throughout counseling. Tegtmeyer (1980) recognized this, for example, in the school counselor's role. She says, "As school counselors become more aware of and receptive to the sociosexual needs of their students and more accepting of their own sexuality, they will help promote a more realistic sexual climate—by acting as models and by offering counseling services and programs" (p. 433). Sexual decision making can be improved through counseling.

Approaches to Sex Counseling

In light of the burgeoning interest in sex counseling and therapy, these areas are sure to change rapidly over the next decade. One can only hope that the debates over differences in counseling and therapy that took place decades ago do not reoccur. Schiller (1976) states, "It is the position of AASECT [American Association of Sex Educators, Counselors, and Therapists] that the quality of the therapeutic process—in terms of establishing rapport, taking a sex history, making a tentative diagnosis, appraising the coping powers of the partners, and working through the sexual problem—is the same for competent sex therapists and sex counselors" (p. 369).

Many traditional approaches, among them rational-emotive therapy and the medical treatment model, have been applied to sex counseling, as have relatively new techniques, for example the use of sex surrogates. Techniques and approaches notwithstanding, the presence of the basic conditions for effective counseling is crucial. Even though the nature of the client's problem is sexual, counselors still need to provide the facilitative conditions of positive regard, warmth, empathy, and genuineness. On this base, a variety of sex counseling techniques and approaches can be effective.

It is important that sex partners learn to communicate openly for many sexual problems are partly the result of inadequate expression of the feelings of each partner. . . . The treatment of sexual dysfunction ideally combines both educational and psychological aspects. (Jones et al., 1977, p. 177)

History-Taking and Round-Table Sex counselors and therapists often use an extensive history-taking as a first step in the therapy process. If cotherapist (male-female) dyads are used, the same-sex counselor begins the history-taking process, followed by the opposite-sex therapist, who concludes the history-taking component. Several valid purposes for history-taking are apparent. First, a complete sex history is obtained from the counselee or the partners in the relationship. In the latter instance history-taking may highlight very obvious contradictions that can be integrated into the process of treatment. Second, the use of opposite-sex cotherapists allows the therapists to note the ease clients feel with counselors of either sex. We often find that clients reveal certain information to one therapist but not to the other. (This by the way does not mean that individual therapists or counselors cannot work with clients' sexual difficulties. Counselors, however, should be aware that their sex may have some impact on the information withheld by or received from the client.) Third, it has been our experience that history-taking is a "safe" way to start counseling sessions that deal with the "emotionally-laden" sexual area. It gives the client "permission" to discuss this sensitive topic. In intense, short-term treatment programs, such as the program at the Masters and Johnson Institute, clients are asked to refrain from sexual activity for a period of time. This may last until the history-taking, physical examination, and round-table are completed. General topics of concern in the history-taking can include:

Sexual activity—frequency and type
Concept of effective sexual functioning
Sexual difficulties
Notions of appropriate sex-role behavior
Chronology and statistics of the relationship
Childhood and adolescent data
Relationships with parents
Social history
Sexual fantasies
Educational background
Sexual attitudes
Sexual communication
Sex education
Emotional openness
Sensual pleasures
Sexual self-esteem
Effects of age on sexual functioning

History-taking is usually followed by a round-table discussion. With both partners in the unit present, the therapists will "mirror" or reflect back what they learned during the history-taking sessions. Round-table is basically a feedback session. Therapists who are working alone can also do this with clients. The therapists will discuss what they have learned about the sexual functioning or dysfunctioning presented by the couple, how it developed, and what maintains it. Particular attention will be paid to communication problems of the couple, including any sexual misinformation acquired by the couple. At this session the client or partners discuss the various areas in greater depth. They may clarify or contradict the information presented by the therapists. During this session therapists have the opportunity to see more fully the clients' interaction with each other.

Sensate Focus   Sensory awareness helps individuals to get in touch with their own senses and feelings of arousal without unnecessary pressures of sexual performance. The focus is on sensation and on receiving and giving pleasure. The couple learns to touch and to communicate what feels good. Various types of lotions and body manipulation may be employed, generally without specific genital touching. Sexual intercourse is to be avoided. While the sensation of touch is emphasized, vision, smell, hearing, and taste may also play a role. The exercise stresses sensual feelings not a "sexual experience." It is a period of relaxation that allows for spontaneous interaction and communication without pressures to perform. Many clients report that they enjoy showering together prior to the exercise as an aid in relaxation. Non-demand pleasuring is the order of the day. Later stages of sensate focus will include breasts and genitalia. The therapists use therapy sessions during this period to discuss the exercises, offer sex information and education, and provide additional insights.

Imagery Methods   Individuals who have difficulty experiencing arousal may be taught to fantasize about sex. The counselor will ask a client who feels guilty, fearful, or anxious about sexual matters to fantasize without having such feelings. Written or pictorial materials may be introduced to encourage fantasy development. Specific exercises incorporate fantasy and guided imagery with relaxation approaches. "Thought stopping," in conjunction with imagery, has the client imagine an anxiety-producing situation; when the client experiences anxiety, the therapist yells "stop." The client can then be taught to practice this subvocally. Desensitization and conditioning procedures are also applicable.

Desensitization Procedures   Systematic desensitization procedures, based on the principles of counter-conditioning, can reduce fear and anxiety in sexual situations. Anxiety reduction is important, since anxiety can inhibit sexual arousal and performance. First, the client is systematically taught to relax. Then a list of sexual behaviors in order of increasing anxiety is presented either verbally or visually to the client. The person is asked to stop imagining the situation and to relax if he or she becomes anxious. The counselor goes through the list until all items are neutralized (Obler, 1977). During the process of therapy, the client may be asked not to engage in certain sexual activities until they have been neutralized. More specifically, desensitization consists of repeatedly presenting items on a list of anxiety-evoking stimuli to the deeply relaxed patient until anxiety is eliminated. The therapist begins with the least threatening item and continues to the next until even the most intense of these stimuli provokes no anxiety in the client. This approach involves (1) learning deep muscle relaxation (DMR), (2) constructing anxiety hierarchies, and (3) combining DMR and items from the hierarchies. Through this process the client learns to reduce or eliminate anxiety evoked in the sexual situation. The alternative is situation avoidance, which can lead to sexual dysfunction. Breathing exercises, positive imagery and biofeedback can aid in obtaining relaxation before physical contact and also provide assessment on arousal changes during therapy procedures.

Other behavioral programs have utilized some of these concepts with other aspects of sexual functioning or dysfunctioning. For example specific masturbation programs, sometimes incorporating the use of a vibrator, have been developed for individuals who feel anxious or uncomfortable in sexual situations (Heiman et al., 1976). Lazarus (1961, 1965) reported successful use of group and individual systematic desensitization with males having sexual difficulties. Self-exploration exercises enable clients to be more aware of basic pleasuring and communication during sex play. At times reading assignments or audio-visual materials help clients to work through feelings of anxiety and to relax and be more comfortable with sexual expression. Sexual assertiveness, being able to make clear their feelings and sexual requests, is taught to clients as a necessary step toward behavior change.

Sexual Surrogates   Sexual surrogates have been introduced in situations where an individual does not have a sex partner. Surrogates develop, in conjunction with the therapist, a program designed to eliminate their client's sexual dysfunction. The surrogate agrees to participate as partner, not as therapist, in carrying out behavioral assignments. The use of surrogates is currently controversial. Because they are paid, surrogates are considered prostitutes in many states. While surrogate therapy has been found helpful, it is difficult to recommend that a counselor encourage an activity that might be considered illegal. Counselors may need to consider alternative treatments for clients without partners (McCarthy, 1980).

Group Approaches to Sex Counseling   Both individual and group approaches can be used in sex counseling. Group situations obviously introduce a number of variables that may complicate the counseling interaction and demand increased skills on the part of the therapist. (See the section on group counseling in Chapter 14.)

Group treatment has proven effective for preorgasmic women (Barbach and Ayres, 1976; Leiblum and Ersner-Hershfield, 1977; Norton and Pion, 1976), males having sexual difficulties (Lazarus, 1961; Zilbergeld, 1975), and couples experiencing sexual dissatisfaction (Baker and Nagata, 1978; Caplan and Caplan, 1979). Groups offer members additional support within a permission-giving framework. Therapists often combine specific behavioral programs, "homework" assignments, and group discussion of feelings to achieve group-member change. In some groups social-skills training—how to ask someone out for a date, for example—has been built into the program.

These are but a few of the approaches being applied in sex counseling. They are diverse and may take from several months to several years to achieve change.

Criticism of Sex Therapy   Most criticism has centered on "sex therapy" per se. There is sufficient research to suggest that sex therapy is somewhat effective, but some criticism may well be legitimate. First, some therapy programs are intensive, short-term formats (serving a select clientele), which may not be practical for most people, and these programs yield inflated success rates. Such results are affected by the selection process—people who can afford it—and by a short-lived enthusiasm in the couple, which allows for some disregard of other relationship problems. Consequently, success rates immediately after therapy are high. Follow-up statistics are needed to provide a more realistic picture of "sex therapy" effectiveness.

A second criticism has centered on the "mechanistic" or "depersonalized" techniques sometimes employed. This particular criticism is unjustified for legitimate programs. Such programs do retain the relationship and personal and interpersonal functioning as the primary focus.

One specific criticism has focused on the results presented by Masters and Johnson and their methodology in the conduct of research:

Masters and Johnson's research is so flawed by methodological errors and slipshod reporting that it fails to meet customary standards—and their own—for evaluation research. . . . From reading what they write it is impossible to tell what the results were. (Zilbergeld and Evans, 1980, pp. 29–30)

While Zilbergeld and Evans criticize the results and the methodology, they do not conclude that sex therapy is ineffective. They see a need for more accurate reporting and better experimental design in sex therapy research, so that practitioners can have better answers as to what will or will not work.

Holistic Counseling for Health and Wellness[3]

Holistic counseling is an evolving concept. It represents counseling's efforts to respond to clients as whole human beings whose potential for personal and interpersonal fulfillment depends on the development of body, mind, and spirit.

When there is undue stress on one or more of these parts our entire self is out of balance. Body, mind, and spirit work together. An ill or distressed physical self will effect an unhealthy mental functioning. One part affects and determines the other. Counseling practices that benefit our cognitive or affective states will in turn enhance our bodily well-being. To engage in holistic treatment, counselors will have to overcome their training, which has been oriented toward dealing with feeling and meaning, and not the body and spirit. *Therapy*, in its full meaning, will have to span a full spectrum of health practices.

The holistic approach recognizes that all counseling practices are of value as long as they promote self-actualization. Exercise, meditation, nutritional guidance, transpersonal approaches, support groups, body therapies, biofeedback training, group therapy, and the like are all valuable tools in the process of holistic counseling. Because of the philosophy that all parts of the self are interconnected and affect one another, the holistic perspective looks deeply for that part of oneself which may be out of tune. A disharmony in spirit may, for example, reflect itself in the symptoms of bodily dysfunction.

Addressing the attainment of wholeness of body, mind and spirit, Bauman et al. (1978) state:

[3]This section on "holistic" counseling was written by Professor James C. Schmidt of Oakland University, Rochester, Michigan.

When we feel pain, we have acted against our essential nature, or against the Unity of all. Unless we connect the pain with its origin, it will be stored in our body-mind and reappear whenever situations similar to the unresolved one arise. Many dreams are vivid reappearances of old conflicts that were incompletely present. What holistic health represents is the acceptance of our entire reality: being in our bodies, owning our feelings, attitudes, and beliefs, being open to relationship and change, and being responsible for every thought, deed, and condition we are involved in. (p. 18)

The practices of the holistic counselor are to facilitate the client's awareness of the connections among the symptoms of the disease and his or her responsibility for its presence as well as its resolution. The holistic approach holds that we determine our personal reality.

Concepts of Holistic Counseling

Behavior and Health   The holistic approach to health and wellness is reflected in the formulation of the Holistic Medical Association, and a new division of the American Psychological Association (Health Psychology). These mental and physical health societies are founded on the knowledge that illnesses are principally caused by the behavior of the individual (for example, poor diet, substance abuse, and so on). Since understanding and changing behavior is the domain of counselors, psychologists, physicians, and social workers, these professionals can join together in the emerging field of Behavioral Health. According to Matarazzo, *"Behavioral health is an interdisciplinary field dedicated to promoting a philosophy of health that stresses individual responsibility in the application of behavioral and biomedical science knowledge and techniques to the maintenance of health and the prevention of illness and dysfunction by a variety of self-initiated individual or shared activities."* (1980, p. 813)

The Mind-Body Connection   Our minds and bodies are intricately connected, each contributing to our total state of health. This whole view of the person has long occupied the center of psychological interest, especially in Germany. Referred to as Gestalt psychology, its concept is to deal with the total person (see Chapter 5). Even further, Gestaltists believe that "the whole is more than the sum of the parts." We can see that a melody is a gestalt of its isolated notes and is valued for its totality. According to Martin and Martin (1982), counselors using a holistic approach with their clients could expect the following to be true:

1. It teaches clients a total sense of personal responsibility.
2. Its effects are immediate and create a better sense of well-being.
3. Wellness rather than the absence of symptoms is the main goal of therapy.
4. All modalities of healing are used.
5. The clients' inner capacity for change has a distinct and clear direction to better health and well-being.
6. Clients can continue patterns that are healthy and significantly decrease problem reoccurrence.

7. Self-discipline is learned and appreciated.
8. Disease prevention is enhanced for clients.
9. Counselors can benefit from all these aspects and be a significant model for clients. (p. 22)

Faith and the Spiritual Dimension   The spiritual dimension of the person seems somewhat more illusive than the mind or body dimensions. Alexander Lowen (1973) defines faith as a quality "of being in touch with oneself, with life, and with the universe. It is a sense of belonging to one's community, to one's country, and to the earth—it is a manifestation of life, an expression of the living force that unites all beings. It is a biological phenomenon and not a psychic creation." (p. 219)

In his study of depression, Lowen observed that the person having faith tends not to become depressed. Faith keeps us moving forward in life, and this is precisely what the depressed person is unable to do (p. 194). Faith cannot be given to the client by a counselor—only shared. In the sharing there is hope that the client's own potential for faith and hope will be sparked. The spiritual dimension is there for everyone who is open to it. Thus, counselors support their clients by encouraging well-being and health rather than illness and disease.

Techniques of Holistic Counseling

Helping Clients Own Responsibility   In making a shift from a remedial/reactive orientation to a proactive/wellness approach, the holistic counselor emphasizes with the client the possibility for controlling his or her own destiny. We all have—to some degree—the opportunity to control our own destiny. We can change or create our lifestyle. Of course this is not necessarily a simple task. What seems to be required is a willingness to "own up" to the responsibility one has for the lifestyle one has been living and, if necessary, choose a more appropriate and healthier one.

When clients own their ability to respond to or create a healthy lifestyle, they develop a strong sense of power and control. It follows then that clients can choose (to a significant degree) to be healthy or ill. Choosing to live a stressful lifestyle and to ignore symptoms of illness (colds, backaches, headaches, insomnia, and the like) for long enough will lead to illness. One may even be surprised to become ill "so suddenly." But it wasn't so sudden at all. It took many years of practiced ignoring.

The following exercise is designed to help counselors to alert clients to their responsibility for their illness and wellness. The client is asked to do the following things:

1. Recall a time you didn't feel well. (Example: I had a cold in January.)
2. What was going on in your life—events and feelings: (I was working two jobs and worrying about bills.)
3. What is your style of illness: Complete the sentence: "When I _____ then I _____ ." (When I don't get enough rest and worry too much, I catch a cold.)

4. Exaggerate your illness until you die of it. What do you die of? (Suffocation, pneumonia.)
5. Write a sentence describing what you do to yourself to become ill. (I make myself sick by pushing too hard and expecting too much from myself.)
6. If you give up this illness, what do you lose? It may be something you very well need! (I lose the excuse to slow down—also the sympathy of my spouse.)
7. How else might you get what you need without having to get sick? (I could spend less and give up the extra job. Also, ask directly for the loving attention I want.)

The client is then guided in becoming aware of his or her healing style:

1. What do you do to heal yourself? (Example: Rest, exercise.)
2. What does healing mean to you? (Taking care of myself—loving myself.)
3. Could your healing be helpful to others as well? (Yes—I would be easier and more fun to live with.)
4. Are you really doing now what you need for wellness? No—I'm going too fast and not exercising or resting.)
5. Think of two or three times when you felt alive and well. (Kept a promise. Did a job well. Walked on the beach.)
6. Picture yourself really well. What one word could describe your picture? (Energetic.)
7. What one thing could you do today to create what is in that picture? (Take a walk in the woods.)

Sum up this exercise by completing this sentence: "When I look at all this I can see I _____ ." (I can see that I can do something about my health—it's up to me!)

Most people tend to ignore their health—until they lose it. Ignoring may even be a means to avoid responsibility. An important goal in all counseling is to help our clients to be aware and responsible for themselves. In the holistic approach, it's the prime goal.

Nutrition and Wellness   For counselors to become totally effective, they need to become totally involved with their clients' whole being. The nutritional dimension is one of several areas in a client's life that may need adjustment. Holistic counselors should legitimately inquire: "What are your favorite foods?" "How many times do you eat during the day and at what times?" "Are you involved in an exercise program?" "What did you eat for breakfast? lunch? dinner?" (Miller, 1980, p. 424)

In summarizing research pointing to nutritional deficiencies as the cause of or contributing factor in emotional distress, Martin and Martin (1982) suggest that the role of the counselor includes

steering clients away from "fast foods," food additives and chemical
pollutants and educating them to read labels

recommending foods including protein, vitamins, minerals, and essential
fats

recommending lean meats and fresh fruits

advising consumption of vegetables and "whole grain" foods

watching the intake of fatty acids

reducing or discontinuing the use of salt, caffeine, sugar, white flour,
hydrogenated fat, food preservatives, coloring agents, and artificial
flavoring

and finally, eating breakfast and taking vitamin/mineral supplements
before or during meals. (pp. 23–24)

Mind and Body Visualization   "The autonomic nervous system con-
nects the mind with every cell in the body. Through the autonomic nervous
system a thought held in the mind affects hormonal balance, blood flow, and
metabolism. Thus thoughts—visualizations—can produce a state in which
disease or health occurs." (Samuels and Samuels, 1975, p. 220) This notion
is supported by the work of Dr. Herbert Benson of Harvard Medical School.
Since the late 1960s, Benson has been studying the body's physiological response to relaxation. In studies using his relaxation techniques for quieting
mental activity, Dr. Benson found a significant lowering of metabolic processes resulting from decreased sympathetic nervous system activity. He
named these physiological changes *the relaxation response.* He believes this
response to be the opposite of the fight-or-flight response. Beary and Benson
(1974) list numerous religious and secular techniques that elicit the relaxation response. Included are autogenic training, progressive relaxation, sen-
tic cycles, cotension, yoga and zen, and transcendental meditation. Through
their visualizations, people are able to create health or disease. Counselors
can guide their clients in the process of visualization that includes images
of health and wellness. As an example clients can be introduced to *autogenic
therapy,* a psychophysiologic technique developed in the 1930s in Germany
by Dr. J. H. Schultz, a psychiatrist and neurologist. In autogenic therapy,
individuals direct themselves to visualize or imagine a healthy or beneficial
process taking place in their body to bring about a state of homeostasis. Clients are advised to concentrate in a passive fashion on the part of their body
they are concerned about and to repeat visually or verbally a given direction
(Luthe, 1969).

An example of an autogenic visualization is found in the work of Dr. Carl
Simonton, a Fort Worth, Texas, radiologist specializing in the treatment of
cancer. Simonton observed that cancer patients experiencing what is referred to as "spontaneous remission" had a consistently positive attitude toward life and toward the possibility of recovery. The individual's attitude
is believed to benefit his or her immunological responses, which in turn de-
stroy the cancer cells. Simply stated, Simonton teaches his patient to peace-

fully relax and to "picture his immune mechanism working the way it's supposed to work, picking up the dead and dying cells. Patients are asked to visualize the army of white blood cells coming in, swarming over the cancer, and carrying off the malignant cells which have been weakened or killed by the barrage of high energy particles of radiation therapy. These white cells then break down malignant cells which are then flushed out of the body. Finally, just before the end of the meditation, the patient visualizes himself well" (Bolen, 1973, p. 20).

Counselors can use the following visualization by Samuels and Bennett (1973) to help a client release images of disease or worry:

[Sit or lie in a relaxed state with your eyes closed. Breathe slowly. Deeply exhale tension and inhale peace and relaxation.] Then let your ideas of all disease symptoms . . . become bubbles in your consciousness. Now imagine that these bubbles are being blown out of your mind, out of your body, out of your consciousness, by a breeze which draws them away from you, far into the distance, until you no longer see them or feel them. Watch them disappear over the horizon.

Now imagine that you are in a place that you love. It may be the beach, in the mountains, on the desert, or wherever else you feel fully alive, comfortable and healthy. Imagine the area around you is filled with bright, clear light. Allow the light to flow into your body, making you brighter and filling you with energy of health. Enjoy basking in this light. (p. 284)

Meditation   Meditation is a useful tool for awakening the client's spiritual dimension. The following 5-4-3-2-1-0 meditation described by Marge Alpern (1980) is an effective counseling technique. The counselor gives these directions:

Sitting up comfortably, take a deep breath and on the exhalation visualize the number 5 being written on a blackboard in front of you as you exhale. Repeat 3 times. Your breathing will slow down as you move to number 4 for three breaths. Then go to 3, 2, 1, 0. At the count of zero, you will feel deeply relaxed. Repeat as necessary; only breathe once lightly, on each number. The zero can then be visualized as:

1. An encircling membrane holding a warm, soft material in which one is floating.
2. A tiny tunnel into the body, entered through the third eye, to relax and heal various parts, exiting again through the third eye.
3. A picture frame for the whole healed body, smiling, happy, loving.
4. As gradually reduced down through the external layers of one's being (one's status, body, mind, emotions, desires) to the very center, the center of pure consciousness. Then expanded out beyond oneself to include the entire universe.
5. Infinite possibilities for your imagination.

Also, while meditating, the client can be guided in visualizing the crown center (top of head) as opening to the total life force in the universe. In so doing, "one is no longer a separate, single independent unit, but one is plugged into and part of the unlimited source of all consciousness and all energy. It is as though your electro-magnetic body were a used up battery, all out of energy, and you plug into the main electric source or current to receive, recharge and revitalize yourself." (pp. 3–4)

Stress Class   Hans Selye, the leading stress researcher, defines stress as "the body's non-specific responses to any demand made upon it" (1974, p. 27). Nobody can escape stress. The list of daily stressors (the internal and external sources of stress) is endless from morning to night. The role of the holistic counselor in stress management is to help clients to recognize when stress is building up to a potentially dangerous level. Client awareness of stress and its symptoms is a key to physical and emotional good health.

Education as prevention of stress illnesses is perhaps most aptly introduced in schools with children and adolescents. Bayerl and Lark (1982), counselor and counseling intern, designed and taught a class on stress and its management in an alternative school in the Ann Arbor (Michigan) Public School System. The objectives of the class included teaching (1) the causes of stress, (2) mind and body reactions to stress, and (3) stress management methods. Among the coping or management methods introduced were use of support groups, problem-solving skills, use of exercise, proper nutrition, and relaxation. Students were encouraged to identify the additional coping mechanisms they have personally used. The counselors found the stress management course useful in promoting student decision-making, problem-solving, health-management, and interpersonal skills.

Time Management   It has often been said that if you control your time, you control your life. In fact, if time controls your life, you have stress. To gain control of your time is, therefore, an effective way to reduce your stress.

Here are some helpful questions for counselors to have clients ask themselves as they begin to think about their use of time:

"How much of my time do I control?"
"Is there some time each day that is my own when I cannot be
    disrupted?"

Even if you work for someone else, there is still some time on the job that you can control or manage. You cannot fulfill your purpose in life through the expectations of others. How are you going to live your own life if you don't control your own time?

Controlling one's time begins with "owning time," actually allowing yourself to be responsible for your use of your time. When we accept the responsibility for controlling our time, then we begin to make it work for us, not against us.

You always hear people complain that they never have enough time. Yet, there are those rare few who manage to get through a tremendous amount of work each day, make major contributions to their communities, and still find time to enjoy family, friends, and possibly a hobby or two. Here are a number of helpful suggestions counselors can give their clients to help them manage their stress through managing their time:

1. *Live in the here and now.* When we finish with the past—incomplete feelings, relationships, or projects—that leaves us free to concentrate 100 percent of our energy and attention on what we want to be doing and enjoying right now. This also means planning for the future, not worrying about it. It seems that 90 percent of our fears and worries are unfounded, yet we spend about 20 percent of our time worrying.

2. *Assign priorities to activities.* Many of us tend to spend most of our time on the trivial things in life and the least amount of time on the vital activities. Consider the following solution: Make a list every day. Divide the things you have to do into three lists. The A list is for the most important. The B's should get done. The C's you can do anytime. Toss out all your C's. Doing the trivial or less important things is often a way of avoiding the more important tasks for which you might lack self-confidence.

Pick out one thing from the A list and do it. Start with something simple, quick, and not likely to give you much trouble, set a time limit, and, finally, don't let perfectionism paralyze you. Get to the B's if you have time. Eventually they either become A's or C's anyway.

3. *Learn to say no.* People who never learn to turn down a request for their time become dump trucks. When you are already overloaded here are three steps to follow:

a. Listen to the person making the request. Let them know you understand what they are saying.
b. Be true to yourself—people actually tend to like and trust people who are honest. If you tell someone no and mean it, they will know they can count on you when you say yes, too.
c. Offer a rain-check if you would be willing to say yes at another time.

Share the load. You are probably getting overloaded, so start getting help. Enlist the aid of others, whether at work or at home. Others often feel good when you give them a share of the action. It also helps if you train others to do what you ask them to do; allow room for mistakes and trust that there is more than one right way to get a job done.

4. *Handle once only.* This one takes some real discipline and practice but saves enormous amounts of time and energy. It requires making a decision, answering a letter, filing a report, and so on, the first time the opportunity presents itself. Reading over a letter then putting it in a pile to be answered at a later time requires one or more *additional* readings in order to respond. Also, delayed responses tend to get longer—it eases our guilt. Stacks of

things to be done lying around distract you from the job you want to concentrate on. When possible, do it now!

One of the major contributions counseling can make to the clients' well-being is in the area of prevention for the promotion of health and wellness of the total person. Holistic counseling, approaching human beings as a unity of body, mind and spirit, holds the promise of reversing the "patch things up" philosophy so prevalent in our society.

Career Development Counseling

Definition of Career Development Counseling   Career development counseling is another area of specialization, one that is gaining importance and recognition. Professionally trained and competent career counselors, using appropriate techniques, can effectively aid clients in their continual development over the life span.

Pietrofesa and Splete (1975) have defined career development as "an ongoing process that occurs over the life span and includes home, school, and community experiences related to an individual's self-concept and its implementation in lifestyle as one lives life and makes a living" (p. 4).

According to Zunker (1981) and Healy (1982), career development counseling deals with all counseling activities related to one's progress through the life stages. The National Vocational Guidance Association (1982) indicated that vocational/career counseling "Consists of those activities performed or coordinated by individuals who have the professional credentials to work with and counsel other individuals or groups of individuals about occupations, careers, life/career, career decision making, career planning, career pathing, or other career development related questions or conflicts" (p. 2).

Career counselors in a variety of human service and business settings have the opportunity to aid persons at various ages and stages in their career development. Of increasing interest are the provision of strategies for coping with adult transitions (Brammer and Abrego, 1981). In addition career counselors can aid clients as they deal with the essentially related concepts of leisure and work, as described by Bolles (1978) and by Blocher and Siegal (1981).

Splete (1978) describes career development counseling as a process in which a counselor aids clients to understand (1) themselves and their environment, (2) career information, (3) career-exploration opportunities, (4) decision-making processes, (5) steps involved in career planning, and (6) factors in employment, training, or educational placement. The starting point in this counseling process depends on the needs and expectations of the *particular client*. Counselors need to determine *with the client* which of their skills, information, and techniques might be of benefit to that client.

Career counselors are expected to be proficient in various competency areas, including interpersonal counseling (Johnson and Johnson, 1982). Six basic competency areas for career counselors were described in the June 1982 issue of the *National Vocational Guidance Newsletter.* They were general counseling skills, information and knowledge of the field, individual and group assessment skills, management and administration skills, implementation skills, and consultation skills.

If the counselor does not have appropriate skills or information, the client should be referred to another counselor. If the counselor has appropriate skills or information, a plan for the counseling process should be agreed on by both the counselor and the client.

Career development counseling can occur in a variety of settings with individuals or with groups. In either situation, the counselor needs to ascertain the client's present self- and career awareness, previous related experiences, ability to make decisions and plans, and capacity to act on occupational or training searches and placements.

Components of Career Development Counseling

The following components of career development are listed consistently in career development programs and seem readily applicable to phases in the counseling process. These components are client self-awareness, client career awareness, client awareness of decision-making processes, client planning, and client placement.

This section provides descriptions of the major counselor activities, a listing of possible techniques, and examples of specific techniques for each component.

Client Self-Awareness   In this component, the counselor helps clients to determine their interests, values, abilities, aptitudes, experiences, and expectations as they relate to career possibilities and relevant training.

Appropriate techniques to enhance client self-awareness include (1) the use of assessment inventories, such as the Strong-Campbell Interest Inventory, Ohio Vocational Interest Survey, Hall Occupational Orientation Inventory, Holland's Self-Directed Search, and the Differential Aptitude Test; (2) the use of client written information, such as job history questionnaire, autobiography, and work experience résumé; (3) the use of computerized programs, such as Discover II, System of Interactive Guidance and Information, and CHOICES; (4) the use of structured activities, such as values-clarification activities, art or music expression, and life-line formation with significant events noted; and (5) the use of various counseling approaches, including: directive, in which the counselor questions and probes to gain information from the client; interpretative, in which the counselor hypothesizes client data based on previous information obtained, possibly through testing; and nondirective, in which the client is helped to express views and opinions without direct questioning.

A technique for enhancing self-awareness would be the use of an autobiography, which can be compiled by a client of almost any age level. This written or taped statement could be reviewed by the counselor and client together to pick out interests and values that might improve client self-awareness and relate this self-awareness to possible occupations and life-styles.

Client Career Awareness   In this component, the counselor helps the client to look at various occupational possibilities, qualifications, skills, expectations, and lifestyles.

Techniques which might be used include (1) the provision of printed information, such as the *Occupational Outlook Handbook, Dictionary of Occupational Titles,* and *Encyclopedia of Careers;* (2) the provision of computerized information, such as Discover II, Computerized Vocational Information System, and Educational and Career Exploration System; (3) the provision of audiovisual information, such as "Bread and Butterflies" films, McGraw-Hill career interviews cassette series, video cassettes, and television and radio programs; (4) the provision of structured activities, such as Bank's Curriculum Careering Workbooks, occupational role-playing, and Singer's Vocational Evaluation System; and (5) the provision of experiences, such as interviews with workers, field trips and job shadowing, and part-time and full-time employment.

An example of a technique to enhance career awareness would be to have clients interview a person in an occupation that interests them. Younger children could interview parents or neighbors regarding skills and abilities needed on their jobs. Adults could interview workers on the job so as to see the environment, as well as to gather information regarding skills needed.

Client Awareness of Decision-Making Processes   In this component the counselor describes and leads the client through various models of decision making. Clients learn one or more methods of making decisions.

Techniques that might be used include (1) Friel and Carkhuff's model, as described in "The Art of Developing a Career"; (2) Peavy's "Counseling Adults for Decision-Making"; and (3) the College Entrance Examination Board's "Deciding" and "Decisions and Outcomes."

For example, the counselor can help the client through a decision-making activity and teach the client how to follow this process in the future. Regardless of the particular model, the following steps seem basic to the decision-making process:

1. Determine the concern to be acted upon.
2. Project possible alternative actions.
3. Review possible consequences of each alternative action.
4. Choose the best alternative at this time.
5. Decide how and when to implement the alternative.
6. Implement it.
7. Evaluate the result of the action.

8. Determine whether a related decision needs to be made now or if further planning is needed.

Client Planning   In this component the counselor aids the client in reviewing self-awareness, career awareness, and decision-making processes as they relate to a client's need to plan a program to further his or her career development.

Techniques which might be used include (1) Friel and Carkhuff's model for systematic, step-by-step planning as described in "The Art of Developing a Career"; and (2) planning for a next step, as facilitated by Daane's Vocational Exploration Group process.

In this area, the counselor would help the client formulate a plan for achieving a goal and teach the client how to follow this process in the future. The following steps seem to be basic to the planning process:

1. Determine a career development goal, such as learning more about the occupation of a robitics technician.
2. Determine steps to be followed in attaining the goal of finding out more about that occupation.
3. Outline these steps in sequence.
4. Determine actions necessary to complete the steps.
5. Determine a timeline for achieving these steps.
6. Set a beginning date and start implementing the plan.
7. Review the plan periodically with the counselor and revise it if appropriate.

Client Placement   In this component, the counselor helps clients place themselves in a job, a training program, or an educational institution. This placement should be as realistic as possible for the client based on the four previous career development elements—self-awareness, career awareness, awareness of decision-making processes, and planning.

Techniques which might be used include (1) helping the client to learn how to interview for a job or how to prepare a résumé; (2) identifying placement offices for the client's use, such as state employment agencies, school or university placement bureaus, and private agencies; (3) showing the client how to find and review employment notices in newspapers and job vacancy bulletins; (4) providing the client with information regarding job requirements and expectations, and educational and training program requirements and expectations; and (5) providing the client with information regarding the effect of a placement on financial rewards, financial costs, and financial aids or support.

For example, the counselor and the client could review employment opportunities in their local area by checking the local newspaper employment sections. The client might then realistically appraise his or her chances of placement in a particular occupation and follow up by applying for a listed job or by looking at other possibilities.

Approaches to Career Development Counseling

Ideally, the career development counselor would aid the client in working with each of these components in sequence. This procedure would lead to the most realistic placement based on the client's knowledge and understanding of self, careers, decision making, and planning. However, where a client begins in this process depends on his or her individual needs and expectations.

Thus, one client might work with the counselor in all five areas; another might concentrate on only one area, such as placement. The amount of work and type of technique also vary according to the age and environment of the client. Super and Knasel (1981) indicate that flexibility in the counselor's approach is appropriate, as many adults need to adapt to the realities of the world of work rather than focus on developmental tasks.

There are a variety of approaches and techniques that can be used by career development counselors. Which ones will be most effective depend on the client or clients, their life stage, and their immediate concerns. Crites (1981) described six career counseling approaches as trait-and-factor, client-centered, psychodynamic, developmental, behavioral, and comprehensive.

Regardless of the approach used or the career development involved, we believe that counselors need to relate their personal skills and professional approaches to the expressed concerns of the client. As in other areas of specialized counseling, the counselor should be thoroughly trained through knowledge acquisition and supervised experience. In that way counselors can most effectively aid clients in need of their career development counseling expertise.

Summary

The most appropriate counseling approach is affected by the client's presenting problem. In some cases additional consideration will have to be given to the identification and treatment of specialized counseling concerns, but in the process the client's total being cannot be ignored.

The major points of this chapter were as follows:

1. A holistic treatment approach is necessary in alcohol and drug centers.
2. There has been no support for a "controlled drinking" paradigm for alcoholics, and the implementation of such a suggestion is not in the best interests of the alcoholic.
3. A total life restructuring may be necessary for the substance abuser.
4. Sex therapy focuses primarily on relationship dimensions.
5. Holistic counseling attempts to maximize development of body, mind, and spirit. It attends to all three areas rather than focusing its attention on the development of just one.
6. Career counseling focuses on developmental transitions and the identification of coping strategies.

References

Alpern, M. *"Body Techniques for Psychotherapists."* Unpublished paper. Bloomfield Hills, Michigan, 1980.

Annon, J. "The PLISSIT Model: A Proposed Conceptual Scheme for the Behavioral Treatment of Sexual Problems." *Journal of Sex Education and Therapy* 2 (1976):1–15.

Baker, L., and F. Nagata. "A Group Approach to the Treatment of Heterosexual Couples with Sexual Dissatisfactions." *Journal of Sex Education and Therapy* 4 (1978) :15–18.

Barbach, L., and T. Ayres. "Group Process for Women with Orgasmic Difficulties." *Personnel and Guidance Journal* 54 (1976):389–391.

Bauman, E., A. Brint, L. Piper, and P. Wright. *The Wholistic Health Handbook.* Berkeley, Calif.: And/Or Press, 1978.

Bayerl, J., and O. Lark. "A Cognitive/Experiential Approach to Teaching High School Students About Stress and Its Management." *Michigan Personnel and Guidance Journal* 14, 1 (1982):11–15.

Beary, J., and H. Benson. "A Simple Psychophysiologic Technique Which Elicits the Hypometabolic Changes of the Relaxation Response." *Psychosomatic Medicine* 36 (1974):119.

Blocher, Donald, and Robin Siegal. "Toward a Cognitive Developmental Theory of Leisure and Work." *The Counseling Psychologist* 9 (1981): 33–44.

Bolen, J. "Meditation and Psychotherapy in the Treatment of Cancer." *Psychic,* July 1973, 1–8.

Bolles, Richard. *The Three Boxes of Life and How to Get Out of Them.* Berkeley, Calif.: Ten Speed Press, 1978.

Brammer, Lawrence, and Philip Abrego. "Intervention Strategies for Coping with Transitions." *The Counseling Psychologist* 9 (1981):19–36.

Brandsma, J. M. *Outpatient Treatment of Alcoholism.* Baltimore: University Park Press, 1980.

Brill, Leon, and Charles Winick. *The Yearbook of Substance Use and Abuse.* Vol. II. New York: Human Sciences Press, 1980.

Brisolara, Ashton. *The Alcoholic Employee.* New York: Human Sciences Press, 1979.

Caplan, R., and S. W. Caplan. "Attitude Change in Couples Involved in a Sexual Therapy Program." *Journal of Sex Education and Therapy* 5 (1979): 37–40.

Connors, John K. "Detecting Alcoholism in Clients." *Personnel and Guidance Journal* 57 (1979): 532–535.

Crites, John. *Career Counseling: Models, Methods, and Materials.* New York: McGraw-Hill, 1981.

Dacey, John S. *Adolescents Today.* Glenview, Ill.: Scott, Foresman, 1982.

Edwards, G., and M. Grant. *Alcoholism.* London: Croom Helm, 1977.

Englebardt, Stanley L. "Are We Teaching Our Kids to Become Alcoholic?" *Families* 2 (1982): 30–33.

Falk, John L., C. R. Schuster, G. E. Bigelow, and J. H. Woods. "Progress and Needs in the Experimental Analysis of Drug and Alcohol Dependence." *American Psychologist* 37 (1982):1124–1127.

Fields, C. M. "Journal Editors Advised to Be Alert to Possibility of Scientific Fraud." *Chronicle of Higher Education,* September 8, 1982, 25, p. 6.

Forman, Stuart I. "Pitfalls in Counseling Alcoholic Clients." *Personnel and Guidance Journal* 57 (1979):546–548.

Forrest, Gary G. *The Diagnosis and Treatment of Alcoholism.* Springfield, Ill.: Charles C Thomas, 1978.

Friel, T. W. *The Art of Developing a Career.* Amherst, Mass.: Human Resource Development Press, 1974.

Godow, Annette G. *Human Sexuality.* St. Louis: C. V. Mosby, 1982.

Gross, Douglas, and Dave Capuzzi. "The Elderly Alcoholic: The Counselor's Dilemma." *Counselor Education and Supervision* 20 (1981):183–192.

Guydish, J. "Substance Abuse and Alphabet Soup." *Personnel and Guidance Journal* 60 (1982):397–401.

Healy, Charles. *Career Development Counseling Through the Life Stages.* Boston: Allyn and Bacon, 1982.

Heiman, J., L. LoPiccolo, and J. LoPiccolo. *Becoming Orgasmic: A Sexual Growth Program for Women.* Englewood Cliffs, N.J.: Prentice-Hall, 1976.

Jellinek, M. E. *Phases of Alcohol Addiction, Society, Culture, and Drinking Patterns.* Pittman and Snyder, 1962. Pp. 356–368.

Johnson, Clarence, and Sharon Johnson. "Competency Based Training of Career Development Specialists or 'Let's Get Off the Calf Path.'" *The Vocational Guidance Quarterly* 30 (1982):327–335.

Jones, K. L., L. W. Shainberg, and C. O. Byer. *Sex and People.* New York: Harper & Row, 1977.

Kinney, J., and G. Leaton. *Loosening the Grip: A Handbook of Alcohol Information.* St. Louis: C. V. Mosby, 1978.

Klemesrud, Judy. "Children of Alcoholics: A Troubled Heritage." *New York Times,* Sunday, October 17, 1982, p. 44.

LaPointe, C., and H. Gillespie. "A Short Term Cognitive and Behavioral Treatment Approach to Sexual Desire Phase Dysfunction." *Journal of Sex Education and Therapy* 1 (1979):35–38.

Lazarus, A. "Group Therapy of Phobic Disorders by Systematic Desensitization." *Journal of Abnormal and Social Psychology* 63 (1961):504–510.

————. "The Treatment of a Sexually Inadequate Man." In J. Fischer and H. L. Gochros, eds., *Handbook of Behavior Therapy with Sexual Problems.* New York: Pergamon, 1977, pp. 568–571.

Leiblum, S., and R. Ersner-Hershfield. "Sexual Enhancement Groups for Dysfunctional Women: An Evaluation." *Journal of Sex and Marital Therapy* 3 (1977):139–152.

Lowen, A. *Depression and the Body.* Baltimore: Penguin Books, 1973.

Luthe, W. *Autogenic Therapy.* Vol. I. New York: Grune & Stratton, 1969.

Maddock, J. W., and R. A. Chilgren. "The Emergence of Sex Therapy." *Personnel and Guidance Journal* 54 (1976):371–374.

Martin, D., and M. Martin. "Nutritional Counseling: A Humanistic Approach to Psychological and Physical Health." *Personnel and Guidance Journal* 61 (1982):21–24.

Masters, W. H., and V. E. Johnson. *Human Sexual Inadequacy.* Boston: Little, Brown, 1970.

Matarazzo, J. D. "Behavioral Health and Behavioral Medicine: Frontiers for a New Health Psychology." *American Psychologist* 35 (1980):807–817.

McCarthy, B. W. "Treatment of Secondary Erectile Dysfunction in Males." *Journal of Sex Education and Therapy* 6 (1980):29–34.

————. "Strategies and Techniques for the Treatment of Ejaculatory Inhibition." *Journal of Sex Education and Therapy* 7 (1981):20–23.

Miller, M. "Cantaloupes, Carrots, and Counseling: Implications of Dietary Interventions for Counselors." *Personnel and Guidance Journal* 58 (1980):421–424.

National Vocational Guidance Association Newsletter 22 (1982):6.

Norton, T., and G. Pion. "A Sexual Enhancement Group for Women." *Journal of Sex Education and Therapy* 2 (1976):35–38.

Obler, M. "Systematic Desensitization in Sexual Disorders." In J. Fischer and H. Gochros, eds., *Handbook of Behavior Therapy with Sexual Problems.* Vol. I. New York: Pergamon, 1977, pp. 59–69.

Peer, Gary G., Ann K. Lindsey, and Patrick A. Newman. "Alcoholism as Stage Phenomena: A Frame of Reference for Counselors." *Personnel and Guidance Journal* 60 (1982):465–469.

Pettinati, H. M., A. A. Sugerman, N. DiDonato, and H. S. Maurer. "The Natural History of Alcoholism Over Four Years After Treatment." *Journal of Studies on Alcohol* 43 (1982):201–216.

Pietrofesa, John, and Howard Splete. *Career Development, Theory and Research.* New York: Grune & Stratton, 1975.

Samuels, M., and H. Bennett. *The Well Body Book.* New York: Random House/Bookworks, 1973.

Samuels, M., and N. Samuels. *Seeing with the Mind's Eye.* New York: Random House, 1975.

Sarver, J. M., and M. D. Murry. "Knowledge of Human Sexuality Among Happily and Unhappily Married Couples." *Journal of Sex Education and Therapy* 7 (1981):23–25.

Schiller, Patricia. "The Sex Counselor and Therapist." *Personnel and Guidance Journal* 54 (1976):369–371.

Selye, H. *Stress Without Distress.* Philadelphia: J. B. Lippincott, 1974.

Shaw, S., A. Cartwright, T. Spratley, and J. Harwin. *Responding to Drinking Problems.* Baltimore: University Park Press, 1978.

Skirball, Richard L. "Substance Abuse." *Personnel and Guidance Journal* 61 (1982):176–177.

Smith, C. M. *Alcoholism—Treatment.* New York: Human Sciences Press, 1980.

Splete, Howard. *Career Development Counseling.* Boulder: University of Colorado (Colorado Career Information System Monograph), 1978.

Super, Donald, and Edward Knasel. "Career Development in Adulthood: Some Theoretical Problems and a Possible Solution." *British Journal of Guidance and Counseling* 9 (1981):192–201.

Tegtmeyer, Virginia. "The Role of the School Counselor in Facilitating Sexual Development." *Personnel and Guidance Journal* 58 (1980):430–433.

Vaillant, G. E., and E. S. Milofsky. "The Etiology of Alcoholism." *American Psychologist* 37 (1982): 494–503.

Wabrek, A. J., and C. J. Wabrek. "Vaginismus." *Journal of Sex Education and Therapy* 2 (1976): 21–24.

Zilbergeld, B. "Group Treatment of Sexual Dysfunction in Men Without Partners." *Journal of Sex and Marital Therapy* 1 (1975):204–214.

———. **and M. Evans.** "A Critical Review of Masters and Johnson's Outcome Research." *Psychology Today* 13 (1980):29–43.

Zunker, Vernon. *Career Counseling—Applied Concepts of Life Planning.* Monterey, Calif.: Brooks/Cole, 1981.

PART V

Professional Issues and Trends

CHAPTER 16

Counseling as a Profession

Chapter Organizer

Aim of the Chapter

This chapter will present views of counseling as a profession and describe areas of professional concern.

Chapter Preview

1. There are seven major areas of professional concern.
   a. The American Association for Counseling and Development (AACD) has put forth ethical standards for the profession.
   b. Legal considerations are important as counselors have no general exemption from criminal law and are subject to civil law. State and local laws can be quite specific and very different. Confidentiality is a critical issue.
   c. Consumer protection can be secured by provision of professional disclosure statements, establishment of a consumers' protective service, implementation of a mechanism that allows clients to evaluate and report on counseling experiences, and use of adequate referral procedures.
   d. Licensure and certification at the state and national levels have been gaining favor. Both are appropriate and needed avenues to professionalism.
   e. Accreditation of training programs has come a long way since 1960. The AACD and its divisions have formulated new standards for counselor education programs. CACREP is the accrediting arm of the AACD.
   f. Organizational involvement is a key to professional development. The AACD is most representative of the counseling profession. The Division of Counseling Psychology of the American Psychological Association and the American Association for Marriage and Family Counselors are appropriate for many counseling professionals.
   g. Burnout is a very real threat for counseling personnel. They must take adequate steps for self-renewal.
2. Professional counselors now have a wide variety of employment settings from which to choose.

Relevant Questions

The following are several questions to keep in mind while reading the chapter:

1. How do you define counseling as a profession?
2. Which professional concern is of most interest to you? Why?
3. How can you work toward the professionalization of counseling?
4. What are your thoughts about involvement in professional organizations?
5. In which counseling setting might you be most comfortable and competent? Why?

Introduction

In Chapter 1, we provided an overview of significant influences on the development of the counseling movement in the United States. We also reviewed various aspects and types of counseling. It was noted that counseling was difficult to define in specific terms that would apply to the many counseling settings and populations. However, there has been increasing pressure on the part of counselors themselves, their professional organizations, and the public to more clearly define counseling as a distinct profession.

This movement toward establishing a clearer professional identity for counselors has been influenced by various sources. One influence has been the increase in the numbers and kinds of employment settings for counselors. Another influence seems to be the need to define professional counseling competencies for various settings in order to better provide the needed types of counseling and to protect the consumers of that counseling. Competencies have been defined and promoted for such specialties as marriage and family counseling and career counseling.

This movement toward professionalism in counseling may also be seen as a normal part of the emergence of a profession. Davis (1981) indicates the professionalization of an occupation follows sequential steps: (1) establishment of a professional association, (2) assertion of a monopoly over a service area, (3) development of ethical standards, and (4) establishment of legislative mandates of certification and licensure while gaining control of training programs and establishing relationships with competing groups.

To help clarify issues that have an impact on the field of counseling and its recognition as a profession, we will present definitions of *profession* and of *counseling*, discuss common concerns of professional counselors and their attempts to resolve them, and review professional counseling settings.

The Counselor as Professional

This section reviews background definitions and descriptions of the terms *profession, counseling* and *counselor.*

The Nature of a Profession

The American Heritage Dictionary (Second College Edition) provides the following definitions of *profession:* "an occupation or vocation requiring training in the liberal arts or the sciences and advanced study in a specialized field; the body of qualified persons of one specific occupation or field" (p. 989). It further defines *professional* as "having great skill or experience in a particular field or activity" (p. 989).

In reviewing past statements regarding a profession from the viewpoint of persons in counseling, we have selected the following as representative.

Ohlsen (1970) indicates that a profession has these following distinctive characteristics:

1. The members of a profession perform unique and clearly defined services. In addition to defining the nature of their services, professionals also define the conditions under which these services can best be provided. When the members of a profession decide that the use of aides will enhance their efficiency, they define the aides' duties and supervise them.
2. The members of a profession define essential professional preparation for their work. Obviously, the unique services to be performed must be clearly defined before adequate professional preparation can be developed.
3. Entry into a profession is based upon a common body of knowledge and skills. Professional preparation stresses intellectual development, the search for new knowledge, and techniques for improving professional practice.
4. A profession controls admission to its ranks. Professional schools and colleges are expected to screen candidates carefully and admit only those who appear to be able to profit from the professional preparation and to qualify for a license when they complete it. Qualifications for a license are usually determined by an examining board drawn from the ranks of the profession. The penalty for practicing without a license is determined by state law.
5. Standards for professional performance are determined by members of the profession. For school counselors this would mean that a school counselor's services could be evaluated only by licensed (or certified) counselors.
6. A profession develops a code of ethics for its members. Furthermore, a profession develops a procedure for clarifying, updating, and enforcing its professional standards. Failure to discipline irresponsible behavior encourages civil agencies to supervise members' behavior.
7. Members of a profession must try to be more concerned about service to society than about income, power, and prestige. Professionals are committed to provide the best service they can offer. When they question their ability to provide the service which a client requires they seek the assistance of qualified consultants and/or refer the client.
8. Members of a profession are given considerable autonomy in practice.
9. Members of a profession must accept responsibility for their judgments. Obviously, this responsibility involves risks, but it also enhances respect and increases autonomy.
10. Members of a profession accept responsibility for growth on the job. This includes both active participation in one's local, state, and national professional organization (in this case, AACD) and keeping up with professional literature and practices. (pp. 159–160)

It is easy to see that characteristics of a profession tend to remain constant over time. In 1982 Boy and Pine clarified and summarized criteria that described a profession:

1. The performance of a service to the public.
2. The possession of a specialized body of knowledge and skill.
3. The requirement of formal preparation.
4. The regulation of admission to practice.
5. The organization into professional groups.
6. Professional autonomy balanced with public accountability.
7. Adherence to a code of ethics. (1982, p. 114)

Recognizing the significance of the previous definitions and descriptions of a profession, we also note the dimension of sequential development in the establishment of a profession. Dugan (1965) lists eight stages of development:

1. establishment and performance of a needed service;
2. development of appropriate programs of preparation;
3. growth in numbers of workers in the specialty;
4. recognition of unevenness in preparation and certification;
5. increasing demand and public expectation for quality in the services performed;
6. recognition of ethical problems;
7. increasing awareness by the emerging profession of the need to examine critically the qualifications and performance of its members;
8. development of standards as guidelines for continuous professional development and strength in meeting its responsible role. (p i)

We believe that counseling, as a profession, has now passed through these eight stages of development and has moved positively to meet the criteria mentioned above. Counseling most definitely is a profession. Counselors need to recognize this and to act in a professional manner so that their clients and the public also recognize this fact.

The Nature of Counseling

Counseling is difficult to define, at least in part because various groups view it differently. We will describe *counsel, counselor,* and *counseling* in terms of the general functions performed by all counselors.

According to *The American Heritage Dictionary* (1982), *counsel* is "An act of exchanging opinions and ideas; advice or guidance; especially as solicited from a knowledgeable person" (p. 330). This same reference defines *counselor* as "a person who gives counsel" and as an "adviser" (p. 330).

Cottingham and Swanson (1976) state that "counseling has been defined in the U.S. Congress (HR 3270, 1975 Session, 94th B Congress) as the 'the process through which a trained counselor assists an individual or group to make satisfying and responsible decisions concerning personal, educational, and career development' " (p. 91).

Our definition of professional counseling, first presented in Chapter 1, bears repeating, as we feel it speaks in a general sense to *all counselors,* regardless of specialty. We define professional counseling as a relationship between a professionally trained, competent counselor and an individual seeking help in gaining greater self-understanding and improved decision-making and behavior-change skills for problem resolution and/or developmental growth. The counseling relationship and skills described in this book follow that definition.

As licensure becomes a more significant issue in the counseling profession, the following definition seems important. The Virginia 1975 licensure law for private practice counselors (as amended in 1976) states: "Professional counselor shall mean a person trained in counseling and guidance services with emphasis on individual and group counseling designed to assist individuals in achieving more effective personal, social, educational and career development and adjustment."

Other descriptions of counselors have included role statements prepared by professional groups and statements of counseling competencies put forth by organizations and groups. In specifying the actual services they perform, counselors meet one of the criteria listed for recognition as a profession. Services have been listed in various role statements, including the AACD's "The Counselor: Professional Preparation and Role" (1964) and the following 1977 AACD publications: "The Unique Role of the Elementary School Counselor," "The Unique Role of the Middle/Junior High School Counselor," and "The Role of the Secondary School Counselor."

Another way to focus on professional standards for counselors has been through the formulation of expected counselor competencies, both in a general sense and as the competencies relate to various groups. Dameron (1980) in *The Professional Counselor: Competencies, Performance Guidelines, and Assessment* lists basic goal statements and related competencies and performance guidelines for all counselors in the following categories: (1) personality characteristics, (2) individual counseling, (3) school counseling, (4) play therapy and family counseling, and (5) group counseling.

One example from Dameron (1980) is "The counselor is a skilled professional who is able to: (1) understand the basic principles of human growth, development, and learning and how they facilitate the learning and counseling process—and demonstrated—by the ability to: (1.1) understand and communicate with clients of different age levels and social maturity" (p. 13).

Specialty groups in counseling, such as the National Vocational Guidance Association, have also presented expected competencies for professionals to demonstrate in their work. These competencies, as described in the *NVGA Newsletter,* are in (1) general counseling skills, (2) information, (3) individual and group assessment, (4) management and administration, (5) implementation of knowledge and skills, and (6) consultation (*NVGA Newsletter,* 1982).

We recognize that various counseling groups need to emphasize skills and competencies that relate to their particular clientele and setting. Yet, as a total group of practitioners committed to providing professional services in counseling, we need to recognize counseling's unique professional identity. We agree with Pate (1980) when he states: "Even though counseling is a profession with strong historical and disciplinary ties to the professions of psychology and education, it is in fact a separate and distinct profession. Counseling must be separate and distinct because psychologists do not accept counselors as part of their profession and counselors do not view themselves as educators in the traditional sense" (p. 523).

It seems apparent to us that counselors can be identified as members of a profession. One way this can be done is through their recognition of professional concerns and their efforts to resolve these concerns.

Concerns of the Professional Counselor

First, we believe that counselors must recognize the professional issues and concerns that affect them in their practice. Second, they need to be proactive in dealing with these issues and concerns. At this time we see the following as major areas of concern for professional counselors:

1. Ethical standards
2. Legal considerations
3. Consumer protection
4. Licensure and certification
5. Accreditation of training programs
6. Organizational involvement
7. Self-renewal: preventing burnout

Ethical Standards   In Appendix A we have reprinted the "Ethical Standards of the American Association for Counseling and Development." Appendix B contains "Ethical Guidelines for Group Leaders." These codes of ethics are self-imposed regulations of behavior, as determined by members of a profession. It is interesting to compare the topics covered in the AACD code and with those covered in the American Psychological Association.

Ethical Standards Topics

AACD		*APA*	
A.	General (member responsibility, behavior, and delivery of services)	1.	Responsibility
		2.	Competence
		3.	Moral and legal standards
B.	Counseling relationship	4.	Public statements
C.	Measurement and evaluation	5.	Confidentiality
D.	Research and publication	6.	Welfare of the consumer
E.	Consulting	7.	Professional relationships
F.	Private practice	8.	Assessment techniques
G.	Personnel administration	9.	Research with human participants
H.	Preparation standards	10.	Care and use of animals

It is the intent of the AACD ethical standards that they reflect on all members of the association as stated in the preamble: "The specification of ethical standards enables the Association to clarify to present and future members and to those served by members the nature of ethical responsibilities held *in common* [*our italics*] by its members."

As these ethical standards are general guidelines, counselors in specialized areas have supplemented them with role statements or specific competency listings for their subgroups. Examples of this would be found in role statements for school counselor and in ethical guidelines for group leaders.

Talbutt (1981) indicates that there are both assets and limitations to having AACD ethical standards. She believes the assets are providing regulations, preventing internal disagreement, and providing protection in case of litigation. Two major limitations noted are the existing conflicts within the standards and the existence of legal and ethical issues not covered by the standards.

One case in particular is noted. Is the counselor's primary responsibility to the client or to the institution where the service is performed? Various statements, in Section B, "Counseling Relationships," are in conflict. Statement 1 reads, "The member's *primary* responsibility is to respect the integrity and promote the welfare of the client." Statement 4 says, "When the client's condition indicates that there is a clear and imminent danger to the client or others, the member must take reasonable personal action or inform responsible authorities."

In addition, statement 2 of this section indicates, "The counseling relationship and information resulting therefrom must be kept confidential. . . ." This relates to the significant issue of confidentiality, which many see as the cornerstone of any counseling relationship. What is a counselor to do? Our response to this question, and to the apparent contradiction of statements 1 and 4, is that the counselor should advise their clients of what they believe the limitations of confidentiality and responsibility to be.

Another concern about a code of ethics is its need to be constantly revised and updated. Onoda (1978) proposed that ethical guidelines on the use of biofeedback be formulated. Sampson and Pyle (1983) indicate that ethical standards should also address the counselor's use of computer-assisted counseling, testing, and guidance systems. As a profession grows, new and emerging ethical concerns need to be recognized and addressed.

We applaud the efforts of AACD and APA in formulating and updating their ethical statements. We believe that counselors should do the following:

1. Be knowledgeable about these standards.
2. Discuss these standards with colleagues, using casebooks, such as Callis's *Ethical Standards Casebook* (1976).
3. Practice the behaviors as outlined.
4. Make suggestions for revisions and additions, as needed in a changing professional world.

Legal Considerations   An organization's ethical standards do not reflect legislation, especially state laws, yet legislation has a tremendous impact on the role of the counselor. This legislation may cover student conduct and dress codes in the schools to the right of minors to have abortions. It is not our intent to discuss all the possible legal influences on counseling practice. We will provide some basic information and refer the reader who needs more detailed information to Huckins's *Ethical and Legal Considerations in Guidance* (1968),

Burgum and Anderson's *The Counselor and the Law* (1975), and Shertzer and Stone's *Fundamentals of Counseling* (1980).

Counselors should note that they have no general immunity from criminal law and are subject to civil law as they perform their duties. While statutes give counselors some general guidelines, state and local laws may be very different and very specific. Counselors need to review their particular procedures as they relate to their state and local laws, as well as to the ethical code.

The issue of confidentiality seems of most concern in the legal area. Shertzer and Stone (1980) state the legal dimensions of a confidential relationship: "(1) There is no disclosure of information, even though it is accurate, to individuals not entitled to it; and (2) material about the relationship entered in written records is accurate, reliable and safeguarded" (p. 386).

There is a question as to who is entitled to information shared in a confidential relationship. Counselors often claim "privileged communication," which, to protect the rights of the client, prevents counselors from revealing in legal proceedings any information given in a confidential relationship. However, states vary in their acceptance of this concept of "privileged communication." Counselors need to establish with their clients what their stance is on providing information in a court of law.

Confidentiality in the area of records is also a thorny issue. A distinction should be made between a counselor's personal notes and an agency's public records. It is now accepted that the agency's records—not the counselor's notes—are open to public inspection.

In 1974, the federal Family Educational Rights and Privacy Act, commonly called the Buckley Amendment, was passed to protect the privacy of individuals. This act withholds federal funds from institutions or agencies that deny parents the right to review records of their children, under 18 years of age, or deny such access to students themselves, if they are over 18 years of age. The initial fear that a great number of requests for these records would be made was not well-founded. However, agencies began reviewing records and culling unnecessary and often subjective material from their files. This was an appropriate behavior. Yet, the issue still remains as to how much and what types of data can be provided without contradicting ethical standards regarding confidentiality.

Counselors can be sued for libel and slander—based on their written or verbal statements about their clients; for invasion of privacy—based on counselor's use and interpretation of personality tests, research studies, and data-processing information; and malpractice—based on the counselor's failure to perform at a recognized level of competence.

Counselors need to be aware of these legal concerns and to protect themselves regarding confidentiality of the counseling relationship and their counseling practices. We agree with Denkowski and Denkowski (1982) when they suggest that counselors do the following:

1. Purchase malpractice insurance, examine any exclusions to that policy, and ask the insurance carrier for a list of local attorneys who specialize in malpractice and may be contacted for consultation.
2. Do not honor third-party blanket consent forms (such as those from insurance companies) but require and answer only specific requests (e.g., do not send an entire client file if it may be sufficient to verify that treatment was provided on specific dates).
3. Restrict access of audio- and videotaped counseling sessions and assure that persons using these materials understand their confidentiality obligations.
4. Make certain that all nontreatment personnel as well as group therapy participants know their confidentiality responsibilities.
5. Do not provide sensitive client information for entry into electronic data storage systems.
6. Formulate contingency plans for dealing with dangerous clients that are derived in consultation with an informed attorney, a local psychiatric hospital, and area law-enforcement personnel. (p. 374)

Consumer Protection   We believe that professional counselors need to make provisions to protect their clients, as consumers of their services. Three approaches to this goal are (1) provision of professional disclosure statements, (2) establishment of a consumers' protective service, and (3) referral to more appropriate counselors and agencies.

Support for professional disclosure statements is found in the AACD "Ethical Standards" in Section A, statement 4, which indicates that counselors should correctly represent their professional qualifications and in Section B, statement 7, which indicates that the client should be informed of the purposes, goals, techniques, rules of procedure, and limitations that may affect the counseling relationship.

The 1980 AACD recommendations for licensure legislation suggest a professional disclosure statement. This statement includes:

The counselor's name, business address and telephone number, philosophy of counseling, formal education and training, competency areas, continuing education, fee schedule, and the name, address and telephone number of the state government agency regulating the practice of counseling. (p. 28)

Winborn (1977) suggests that members of the profession can protect the rights of counseling consumers by informing the clients of the types of counseling services provided and the basic operational procedures used. He has suggested a written format, which would include personal background and qualifications, explanation of the counseling process, and a discussion of the time and fees involved.

Counselors and psychologists in clinical practice often use "informed consent" procedures. These procedures respond to a concern for clients as consumers and a recognition of increasing regulation of clinical practices.

Margolin (1982) suggests that the following types of information be provided to clients before counseling and therapy are started:

a. an explanation of the procedures and their purpose;
b. the role of the person who is providing therapy and his or her professional qualifications;
c. discomforts or risks reasonably to be expected;
d. benefits reasonably to be expected;
e. alternatives to treatment that might be of similar benefit;
f. a statement that any questions about the procedures will be answered at any time; and,
g. a statement that the person can withdraw his or her consent and discontinue participation in therapy or testing at any time. (p. 794)

We propose that all counselors prepare a written self-disclosure statement to share with their clients. This statement should reflect one's *own* professional beliefs and procedures. Gill (1982) provides the following nine questions, which could serve as the basis for one's statement:

1. What do you believe is the purpose of counseling?
2. What do you believe helps people lead more satisfying lives?
3. What should your client expect as a result of counseling?
4. What is your responsibility during counseling?
5. What is the responsibility of your client during counseling?
6. What are the usual methods, strategies, and techniques that you use?
7. For which people, problems, or concerns are you most helpful?
8. Under what circumstances should your client expect referral to another counselor or agency?
9. How do you handle the confidential nature of the counseling relationship? (p. 445)

Potential clients, as a total group, have the right to be informed of counseling services and counselors' qualifications. Swanson (1979) believes that the public should be provided with a counseling directory and consumers' guide. We support his suggestion and feel that the consumers should also have a method of evaluating and reporting on their counseling experiences. In this regard, we agree with Boy and Pine (1982), who propose a Consumer Protective Service that would enable the public to report their reactions and ineffective or unethical counselor behavior. In this way, they feel the public would be served and protected and the professional's qualifications, responsibilities, and behavior would be clearly identified and monitored. Although this procedure would need to be implemented at local and state levels, guidelines could be provided from a national organization such as AACD.

Section B, statement 10 of the AACD Ethical Standards recommends that the counselor avoid initiating the counseling relationship and to terminate it if he or she is unable to be of professional assistance to the client. In either case, the counselor should provide referral information.

Counselors who refer potential clients to other counselors or agencies should be knowledgeable about them. Persons who refer clients to counseling agencies should be able to see such documentation as licensure of the counselors by that state, evidence of their training and degree, and affiliation with reputable professional organizations. We recognize that there are various levels of expertise held by members of all professions and that the vast majority of counselors can do a highly competent job with proper training and supervision. The point to be made is that when counselors offer counseling—at whatever level—they should be competent and able to provide it.

A final caution for counselors who refer clients to other counselors or counseling agencies: When making such referrals, counselors have the obligation to know the new counselor personally or to have visited that agency so that they are certain the referred clients will receive competent professional services.

We believe that all counselors should be actively involved in protecting their prospective clients' rights by providing written self-disclosure statements, establishing a method for client reporting on counseling experiences, and by referring inappropriate clients to appropriate and reputable professionals.

Licensure and Certification
Professional licensure and certification and accreditation of training programs are important concerns of counselors. In this section, we will discuss licensure and certification. Accreditation will be covered next.

Forster (1977) indicated that the counseling profession lacks an effective credentialing process and thus restricts counselors from effectively practicing their profession. He supports the view that licensure, certification, and accreditation are common methods to credential counselors. In this sense, credentialing means "giving a basis for creditability and competence." We equate credentialing with professionalism.

Fretz and Mills (1980) define *licensure* as "the statutory process by which an agency of government, usually of a state, grants permission to a person meeting predetermined qualifications to engage in a given occupation and/or use a particular title and to perform specified functions" (p. 7).

In the AACD brochure on counselor licensure (1980), the following statements are made:

Why Do Counselors Need Licensure?

1. Licensure will give legal standing to the profession of counseling.
2. Licensure will regulate the use of the title "professional counselor" as well as regulating the practice of the profession.
3. Licensure will protect the right of professional counselors to practice their profession.
4. Licensure legislation will establish privileged communications between counselor and client.

5. Licensure will enhance professional identity, credibility, and autonomy.
6. Licensure holds individual practitioners accountable.

What Are the Benefits to the Public?

1. Licensure protects the public's right to be served by qualified counselors.
2. Licensure protects the public's freedom of choice in choosing the services of a helping professional.
3. Licensure will help the public to identify competent counselors since the use of the title "Licensed Professional Counselor" would be protected by law.
4. Licensure would increase public access to the preventive, developmental services offered by professional counselors.
5. Licensure will provide legal recourse for consumers who have been defrauded by untrained or unscrupulous practitioners.
6. Licensure for counselors will be cost-effective for the delivery of mental health services.

The movement toward state legislation for licensure of counselors is substantial, and several states now have licensure laws (Virginia being the first in 1976). Caution is raised, however, by Arbuckle (1977). He suggests that "if licensing is to mean anything, it must be directly related to the professional functions of the person to be licensed, and these, in turn, must be directly reflected in the programs that train and educate the person to be licensed" (p. 582). We believe his concern has been taken into consideration by the formulation of professional statements of competencies and the movement toward accreditation.

We recognize that the national AACD organization has done much to promote licensing efforts. However, counselors need to recognize that licensing is a state activity and requires involvement in the politics of their state legislature. Warnath (1978) indicates that the state organization promoting the bill must have strong support from all segments of its membership. He also mentions that the membership must have full confidence in its legislative committee and that this committee must be in daily contact with the legislative process.

Certification is the credentialing process by which a professional board grants recognition and approval to an individual who has met specific predetermined qualifications prescribed by the profession. This professional certification is voluntary and can be national in scope.

Members of the counseling profession can now be certified as National Certified Counselors. At this writing, there are three certification criteria options. They all require copies of graduate transcripts, written references, completion of a supervised counseling experience, and the passing of a certification examination. Option B does not require documented and endorsed professional counseling experience. This is waived if the applicant has graduated from a training program approved by the AACD Council for Accreditation of Counseling and Related Educational Programs (CACREP).

An overview of this certification process is contained in the application packet:

The National Board for Certified Counselors was initiated as a result of the American Association for Counseling and Development's [AACDs] professional concerns and efforts in the area of credentialing. After several years of investigation and survey of need, it was determined that the time had come for a national certification process for counselors. In 1982, the NBCC was incorporated as an independent, voluntary, not-for-profit organization whose primary purposes are to establish and monitor a national certification system, to identify to professionals and the public those counselors who have voluntarily sought and obtained certification, and to maintain a register of those counselors. This process grants recognition to counselors who have met predetermined NBCC standards in their training, experience, and performance on the NBCC Certification Examination.

By granting certification, it is not the intent of the NBCC to certify counselors for employment nor to impose personnel requirements on agencies and organizations. Rather, it is the intent to provide a national standard that can be used as a measure of professionalism by interested agencies, groups, and individuals. The responsibility for professional integrity and excellence remains with the counselor. It is further intended that national certification will encourage the continuing professional growth and development of National Certified Counselors and advance cooperation among groups and agencies actively involved in the credentialing of counselors and counselor educators.

The NBCC Certification Examination is designed to assess cognitive counseling knowledge. Content is derived from the body of information inherent in counselor preparation programs for the master's degree level and incorporates the following: counseling theory, the helping relationship, group dynamics, processing and counseling, human growth and development, lifestyle and career development, appraisal of individuals, social and cultural foundations, research and evaluation, and professional orientation. We believe that both state licensure of professional counselors and certification of professional counselors by examination are very appropriate and needed approaches to professionalism.

Accreditation of Training Programs

Certainly, appropriate training and educational experiences are needed to prepare counselors to pass certifying examinations and to obtain competencies needed to practice as licensed, professional counselors. An important part of developing counselor education programs is formulating standards for the approval and accreditation of these programs. Section H, "Preparation Standards," of the AACD "Ethical Standards," outlines responsibilities for those training counselors. The last statement indicates that members (counselor educators) should conduct an educational program in keeping with current relevant guidelines of AACD and its divisions.

The Association has been active in developing training program standards since 1960. In 1964, preparation standards by AACD and two of its divisions, the Association for Counselor Education and Supervision (ACES) and the American School Counselor Association (ASCA), were approved. AACD approved "The Counselor: Professional Preparation and Role. A Statement of Policy." ACES approved "Standards for Counselor Education in the Preparation of Secondary School Counselors." ASCA approved "Statement of Policy for Secondary School Counselors," which included a section on professional preparation.

Stoughton (1965) warned that "APGA [AACD] must be alert to potential problems in accreditation. An example is the possibility that in the absence of criteria or procedures for accreditation of programs to prepare college-student-personnel workers, elementary school counselors, and non-school counselors the criteria for secondary school counselor education will become the standard for all counselor education" (p. 15). His comments were prophetic—we are now preparing more non-school-employed counselors than school counselors.

However, efforts to upgrade and revise the preparation standards have continued. In 1972, an ACES commission formulated "Standards for Preparation of Counselors and Other Personnel Specialists," a combined version of the various preparation standards; this was approved by ACES and AACD in 1973. In addition, ACES formulated and approved "Guidelines for Doctoral Preparation in Counselor Education" in 1977.

ACES worked with the National Council for Accreditation of Teacher Education (NCATE), as NCATE approved counselor education programs of study in colleges of education. ACES members were part of the NCATE teams and ACES/AACD guidelines were recognized in NCATE standards. However, nonschool areas of counselor education, such as community mental health counseling, were not reviewed.

During the 1970s, AACD suggested that it, as an organization, approve counselor education programs through the work of its ACES division. ACES moved in this direction and formulated an "Accreditation Procedures Manual for Counselor Education" in 1978 and an "ACES Accreditation Training Manual" in 1979. These manuals, in conjunction with the AACD "Standards for Preparation in Counselor Education" (1979 version), were the basis for self-study by counselor educators and the first ACES/AACD accreditation team visits. The intention of this voluntary accreditation process was to promote high standards of graduate preparation in counselor education. The procedures included self-evaluation and an on-site visit by the accreditation team. Counselor education programs in full or by subarea could receive full approval, provisional approval, or a denial of approval.

In 1980, AACD started the process of establishing an accreditation board, which would be affiliated with AACD and would replace ACES/AACD as the accrediting body. That board became the Council for Accreditation of Counseling and Related Educational Programs (CACREP). CACREP is an independent council created by AACD and its divisions in order to implement standards of preparation in counselor education and related programs. The council works with colleges offering these programs to help them achieve full accreditation status.

Standards for both entry-level and doctoral programs now relate to counselors in general, rather than emphasizing preparation of school counselors. The standards review such areas as the following:

1. Program objectives and evaluation
2. Curriculum characteristics and quality of instruction
3. Sequences of training experiences
4. Program content, including
    a. human growth and development
    b. social and cultural foundations
    c. helping relationships
    d. group work
    e. career development
    f. individual appraisal
    g. research and evaluation
    h. professional orientation
5. Specialized studies
    a. employment counseling
    b. community mental health counseling
    c. school counseling
6. Supervised experiences
    a. laboratory
    b. practicum
    c. internship
7. Program development outreach
8. Responsibilities to students and institutional support for the program

We agree with this increased emphasis on the evaluation and approval of counselor education programs. Hollis and Wantz (1980) identified 475 counselor preparation institutions. Certainly the quality of these programs should meet accreditation standards, not only to properly prepare counselors, but also to ensure that their clients receive professional aid.

We concur with Caulfield and Perosa (1983) that a comprehensive model of counselor education is the preferred mode of preparation. Recognizing that graduates of counseling programs face a changing job market, counselor educators need to adapt their program to meet this need. This adaptation can fit with program approval standards.

A counselor education program should build on a base of common knowledge and theory. After this base of 30–36 credit hours, students could take 18–24 credit hours in their area of specialization. Then supervised internship placements of 12–15 hours could be required. We recognize that this approach lengthens a traditional master's degree program, but we feel it is needed and that different types of certificates and degrees could be awarded at various points in this program, and even expanded to include the doctoral level. Even though the need for this approach is apparent, we recognize that it will take the understanding and support of the institutions' administration and students if it is to be achieved.

Counselor education programs and standards have come a long way since 1960. Revisions and higher standards for accreditation of programs can only help the field of counseling in becoming recognized as credible and professional.

Organizational Involvement

There is no question in our minds that counselors should be actively involved in professional organizations. As we believe the American Association for Counseling and Development is most representative of the counseling profession, we shall provide a brief overview of its thirteen divisions, described in the AACD membership brochure as follows:

1. *American College Personnel Association* (ACPA)
The mission of the American College Personnel Association is to serve professionals who are committed to fostering and promoting student development in higher education. Membership—7,212.

2. *Association for Counselor Education and Supervision* (ACES)
ACES emphasizes the need for quality education and supervision of counselors in all work settings. Membership—3,044.

3. *National Vocational Guidance Association* (NVGA)
NVGA members are concerned with: helping people of all ages find their place in a changing world of work, education, and leisure; helping people to understand themselves better and to cope more effectively with technological and social change; helping members of minority groups and women to overcome barriers to the development of their full potential as human beings and as equals in a work-oriented society. Membership—5,767.

4. *Association for Humanistic Education and Development* (AHEAD)
AHEAD seeks to stress humanism within all phases of education, by exchanging information about humanistically oriented administrative and instructional practices which effect curriculum, and encouraging support of humanistic practices. Membership—1,801.

5. *American School Counselors Association* (ASCA)
ASCA provides a vital common framework for all professionals engaged in public services work. ASCA strives to be proactive to society's human issues as evidenced by concern for, commitment to, and action on behalf of human rights, children's welfare, healthy learning environments, developmental programs, and positive interpersonal relationships. Membership—8,890.

6. *American Rehabilitation Counseling Association* (ARCA)
ARCA links members with a nationwide community of rehabilitation counselors in the public and private sector. It clarifies the role of the rehabilitation counselor, and encourages the establishment of rehabilitation facilities and programs. Membership—2,844.

7. *Association for Measurement & Evaluation in Guidance* (AMEG)
AMEG members plan, administer, and conduct testing programs, provide test scoring services, interpret and use test results, and develop evaluation instruments. Membership—1,461.

8. *National Employment Counselors Association* (NECA)
NECA offers professional leadership to people who counsel in employment and

placement settings or to those employed in related areas of counselor education, research, administration or supervision in business and industry, colleges and universities and federal and state governments. Membership—1,309.

9. *Association for Non-White Concerns in Personnel and Guidance* (ANWC)
ANWC seeks to develop programs specifically to improve ethnic and racial empathy and understanding. Its activities are designed to advance and sustain personal growth and improve educational opportunity for all non-white minorities in this country. Membership—1,442.

10. *Association for Religious and Value Issues in Counseling* (ARVIC)
ARVIC seeks to examine the roles of values, theological, philosophical, and ethical considerations and principles in current counseling and personnel practices and to share this knowledge with colleagues. Membership—1,898.

11. *Association for Specialists in Group Work* (ASGW)
ASGW seeks to assist and further interests of children, youth, and adults by seeking to provide effective services through the group medium, to prevent problems, to provide maximum development, and to remediate disabling behaviors. Membership—2,919.

12. *Public Offender Counselor Association* (POCA)
POCA is concerned with the delivery of effective counseling services to public offenders and is committed to providing leadership in developing public offender counseling as a profession. Membership—600.

13. *American Mental Health Counselors Association* (AMHCA)
The interdisciplinary membership of AMHCA is dedicated to maintaining and improving the quality of mental health counseling in the nation and promoting prevention practices. AMHCA initiated the National Academy of Certified Clinical Mental Health Counselors in February 1979. This voluntary certification system is a "competency based" process of certifying Clinical Mental Health Counselors. Membership—6,770. (AACD, 1980)

The rapid growth of the Association of Mental Health Counselors Division reflects the increasing number of counselors working in this area in public and private agency and clinic settings.

It should be noted that the total AACD membership of 40,983 does not equal the total division memberships, as many AACD members belong to more than one division. The above membership totals were based on the February 28, 1983, AACD Membership Report.

In addition to these thirteen divisions of AACD, counselors may also be interested in belonging to the Division of Counseling Psychology (Division 17) of the American Psychological Association or to the American Association for Marriage and Family Therapy.

Involvement in these organizations allows counselors to affiliate with a professional group and to indicate by their membership their support for the standards and policies of that professional organization. These organizations typically provide such services as professional publications, conferences and workshops, public relations for the profession's counseling services, employment opportunities, and lobbying for political recognition and funding.

Through membership in a professional organization, counselors also gain the opportunity to meet and learn from others in different locations across our country and throughout the world. We encourage counselors to become members of their professional organizations at all levels, so that they can support the efforts of these organizations to better inform the public and governmental funding agencies about the organizations' services and so that they can grow personally and professionally through contacts with other working professionals in their field.

We encourage counselors to contribute to their profession by serving on organization committees, serving as officers, writing for professional journals, and speaking to public groups. Professionals have an obligation to share with their colleagues and encourage their professional growth.

Some criticism has been directed at professional organizations for shutting out those who are not members and, thus, losing touch with activities and issues not discussed within their group. Some of this criticism is justified. We recognize that not all learning and growth occur within professional organizations or, for that matter, in formal training institutions. However, membership in professional organizations is one way for counselors to remain current and actively involved in supporting their profession.

Self-Renewal: Preventing Burnout

We believe that counselors must be alive as persons to be effective as professionals. Recognizing this, counselors can take steps to remain alive and active, personally and professionally.

A common term for the hopelessness and discouragement felt by worn out, disillusioned counselors is *burnout.* Causes of burnout include unreasonable job expectations, unresolved personal conflicts outside of the job situation, conflict, tension and mistrust with fellow employees, doing the same type of tasks with little variety, lack of physical exercise and mental stimulation, and giving much time and effort to the job and/or clients and receiving very little positive response.

There are remedies for burnout. Spicuzza and DeVoe (1982) advocate that counselors join mutual aid groups to obtain new insights and support. Watkins (1983) indicates that counselors can overcome burnout through personal therapy, reserving free and private time for themselves, and through association with healthy, well-adjusted individuals. Baker (1981) proposes that counselors take time to assess their needs and to make and act on plans to deal with these needs.

We agree with Corey (1982) when he states that counselors can take responsibility for themselves and can work to prevent professional burnout. He lists fifteen ways to prevent burnout:

1. Finding other interests besides work.
2. Thinking of ways to bring variety into work.

3. Taking the initiative to start new projects that have personal meaning and not waiting for the system to sanction this initiative.
4. Attending to one's health through adequate sleep, an exercise program, proper diet, and some meditation.
5. Developing a few friendships that are characterized by a mutuality of giving *and* receiving.
6. Learning how to ask for what one wants, though not expecting to always get it, and learning how to deal with not getting what is asked for.
7. Learning how to work for self-confirmation and for self-rewards, as opposed to looking externally for validation and rewards.
8. Playing, traveling, or seeking new experiences.
9. Taking the time to evaluate the meaningfulness of one's projects to determine where personal investment and time will continue to be spent.
10. Avoiding assuming the burden of responsibility that is properly the responsibility of others—for example, worrying more about clients than they are seeming to worry about themselves.
11. Reading, both professional literature and books for fun.
12. Taking new classes or workshops, or attending conferences and conventions to get new perspectives on old issues.
13. Exchanging jobs with a colleague for a short period or asking a colleague to join forces in a common work project.
14. Taking the initiative to form a support group with colleagues to openly share feelings of frustration and to find better ways of approaching the reality of certain job situations.
15. Cultivating some hobbies that bring pleasure. (pp. 287–288)

Boy and Pine (1980) assert that counselors can choose to be optimistic or pessimistic. If they choose optimism, they can endure, cope, manage, and actively change the circumstances of their existence. We agree and believe that those in counseling can promote a professional image by their ability to deal with their everyday concerns in a constructive manner through self-renewal.

Professional Counseling Settings

In this section, we will briefly review types of professional counseling settings. These include public schools, employment agencies, rehabilitation agencies, college career planning and placement centers, private counseling clinics, community counseling centers, college counseling centers, religious settings, business and industry, and hospitals and health clinics.

Counselors are employed in various educational institutions and at all school levels. Public and private school counselors work in elementary, junior high, and senior high schools and help students to deal with educational, personal, and career concerns. Community college and university counselors work with students, and often community adults, in providing career planning and placement as well as personal therapeutic counseling.

Public service centers and private counseling clinics both employ counselors to help clients with a variety of concerns through the use of various techniques, ranging from short-term crisis counseling to long-range in-depth therapy. The type and amount of payment required often determines which service the client will use. An increasing number of mental health counselors are being employed in these types of settings.

Employment counselors work in state employment offices, private and community agencies, and social service agencies. Through interviewing and testing, they help clients review their interests and abilities so that they can gain employment in a satisfactory field of work.

Rehabilitation counselors work with disabled clients to help them with vocational and personal concerns. They counsel in state and local rehabilitation agencies, Veterans Administration offices, special schools, sheltered workshops, hospitals, and other private and public agencies.

Religious leaders serve as counselors in churches and synagogues in aiding individuals and groups in resolving spiritual, educational, economic, and social concerns. They often work in hospital settings as well.

There are increasing numbers of trained counselors employed in health services and related areas. They may work in hospitals, hospices, holistic health centers, and funeral homes. These counselors help clients and their families to deal with cancer treatment and adjustment, terminal illness, and significant loss. Counselors also help clients to establish and maintain positive health practices.

Another setting that is providing more opportunities for counselors is that of business and industry. Businesses are concerned about their workers' problems with low morale, alcohol and drug abuse, family concerns, and financial crises. Many corporations are hiring counselors to work in employee assistance and human resource development programs.

More specific information regarding counselors' work in these settings can be obtained from *The Occupational Outlook Handbook,* compiled by the U.S. Bureau of Labor Statistics. However, persons should be cautious when reviewing occupational information as it tends to become rapidly outdated. We suggest that the most current and realistic information about professional counseling settings can be obtained by visiting those work places and talking to their counselors.

It is important to note that employment opportunities are available in an increasing variety of settings. Professionally competent counselors can apply their generic counseling skills, in combination with specialized techniques appropriate to particular clients in those sites.

Summary

This chapter looked at counseling as a profession by reviewing relevant definitions and professional issues and concerns. Positive approaches to professionalism were presented in the areas of ethical standards, legal considerations, consumer protection, licensure and certification, accreditation of training programs, organizational involvement, and self-renewal. Types of professional counseling settings were noted.

The following points were made in this chapter:

1. Much progress has been made in the counseling profession through the efforts of professional associations and individual counselors.
2. No one approach in itself is sufficient to promote counseling as a profession. What is needed is the involvement of all counselors,

their trainers and supervisors, and their organizations to pursue recognition actively through more rigorous training standards, adherence to ethical standards, and attainment of licensure as counselors.
3. Counselors have the capacity as dedicated professionals to improve their situations and their professional identity.
4. Future counselors will be better prepared and more effective in providing needed and helpful services to their clients as a result of current moves toward increased professionalism.

References

The American Heritage Dictionary of the English Language. Second College Edition. Boston: Houghton Mifflin, 1982.

American Association for Counseling and Development. *Licensure Committee Action Packet.* Falls Church, Va.: APGA publications, 1980.

Arbuckle, Dugald. "Counselor Licensure: To Be or Not to Be." *Personnel and Guidance Journal* 55 (1977):581–585.

Baker, Stanley. *School Counselor's Handbook, A Guide for Professional Growth and Development.* Boston: Allyn and Bacon, 1981.

Boy, Angelo, and Gerald Pine. "Avoiding Counselor Burnout Through Role Renewal." *Personnel and Guidance Journal* 59 (1980):161–163.

———. *Client-Centered Counseling: A Renewal.* Boston: Allyn and Bacon, 1982.

Burgum, Thomas, and Scott Anderson. *The Counselor and the Law.* Washington, D.C.: APGA Publications, 1975.

Callis, Robert, ed. *Ethical Standards Casebook.* Washington, D.C.: APGA Publications, 1976.

Caulfield, Thomas, and Linda Perosa. "Counselor Education—Quo Vodis?" *Counselor Education and Supervision* 22 (1983):178–184.

Corey, Gerald. *Theory and Practice of Counseling and Psychotherapy.* Monterey, Calif.: Brooks/Cole, 1982.

Cottingham, H., and C. Swanson. "Recent Licensure Developments: Implications for Counselor Education." *Counselor Education and Supervision* 16 (1976):84–97.

Dameron, Joseph, ed. *The Professional Counselor: Competencies, Performance Guidelines, and Assessment.* Falls Church, Va.: APGA Publications, 1980.

Davis, Jannar. "Counselor Licensure: Overkill?" *Personnel and Guidance Journal* 60 (1981):83–85.

Denkowski, Kathryn, and George Denkowski. "Client-Counselor Confidentiality: An Update of Rationale, Legal Status, and Implications." *Personnel and Guidance Journal* 60 (1982):371–375.

Dugan, Willis. In John Loughary, ed., *Counseling, A Growing Profession.* Washington, D.C.: APGA Press, 1965.

Forster, Jerald. "What Shall We Do About Credentialing?" *Personnel and Guidance Journal* 55, (1977):573–576.

Fretz, Bruce, and David Mills. *Licensing and Certification of Psychologists and Counselors.* San Francisco: Jossey-Bass, 1980.

Gill, Stephen. "Professional Disclosure and Consumer Protection in Counseling." *Personnel and Guidance Journal* 60, (1982):443–446.

Hollis, Joseph, and Richard Wantz. *Counselor Preparation—1980—Programs, Personnel, Trends.* Muncie, Ind.: Accelerated Development, Inc., 1980.

Huckins, Wesley. *Ethical and Legal Considerations in Guidance.* Boston: Houghton Mifflin, 1968.

Margolin, Gayla. "Ethical and Legal Considerations in Marital and Family Therapy." *American Psychologist* 37, (1982):788–801.

NVGA Newsletter 22 (June 1982):2–3.

Ohlsen, Merle. "Professional Commitment." In William Van Hoose and John Pietrofesa, eds., *Counseling and Guidance in the Twentieth Century.* Boston: Houghton Mifflin, 1970.

Pate, Robert H., Jr. "The Counselor in a Psychological Society." *Personnel and Guidance Journal* 58 (1980):521–524.

Onoda, Lawrence. "Ethical and Professional Issues for Psychologists and Counselors Employing Biofeedback in Counseling Settings." *Personnel and Guidance Journal* 58 (1978):214–217.

Sampson, James P., Jr., and K. Richard Pyle. "Ethical Issues Involved with the Use of Computer-Assisted Counseling, Testing, and Guidance Systems." *Personnel and Guidance Journal* 61 (1983): 283–287.

Shertzer, Bruce, and Shelley Stone. *Fundamentals of Counseling.* 3rd ed. Boston: Houghton Mifflin, 1980.

Spicuzza, Frank, and Marianne DeVoe. "Burnout in the Helping Professions: Mutual Aid Groups as Self-Help." *Personnel and Guidance Journal* 61 (1982):95–99.

Stoughton, Robert. "APGA and Counselor Professionalization." in John Loughary, ed., *Counseling, A Growing Profession.* Washington, D.C.: APGA Publications, 1965.

Swanson, John. "Counseling Directory and Consumer's Guide: Implementing Professional Disclosure and Consumer Protection." *Personnel and Guidance Journal* 58 (1979):190–193.

Talbutt, Lou C. "Ethical Standards: Assets and Limitations" *Personnel and Guidance Journal* 60 (1981):110–112.

Warnath, Charles. "Licensing: Learning the Game of Politics and Compromise." *Personnel and Guidance Journal* 57 (1978):50–53.

Watkins, C. Edward, Jr. "Burnout in Counseling Practice: Some Potential Professional and Personal Hazards of Becoming a Counselor." *Personnel and Guidance Journal* 61 (1983):304–308.

Winborn, Bob. "Honest Labeling and Other Procedures for the Protection of Consumers of Counseling." *Personnel and Guidance Journal* 56 (1977):206–209.

CHAPTER 17

Research and Evaluation in Counseling

Chapter Organizer

Aim of the Chapter
This chapter will give the reader a broader understanding of the importance of research and evaluation in counseling.

Chapter Preview
1. Counseling is a social science and, as such, its effectiveness can be measured.
2. There is a need to conduct counseling research.
   a. The components and dimensions of counseling can be operationally defined.
   b. The proliferation of counseling "gimmickry" presents new challenges.
3. Research is concerned with reaching a solution to a problem or an answer to a question.
4. Action research lends itself to counseling in field settings.
5. There are various problems in conducting research on counseling.
6. Demands for accountability have resulted in an increased emphasis on program evaluation.

Relevant Questions
The following are several questions to keep in mind while reading this chapter:
1. What is the most effective way to evaluate counseling?
2. What is the difference between process and outcome research?
3. What devices can be used in the conduct of counseling research?
4. What evaluation model appears most easily implemented by counselors?

Introduction

Counseling, like education, is a science—a social science. We are not imply-ing that there is no "art" to counseling. Social scientists recognize the fact that human behavior is complex. Human behavior is probably even more difficult to measure in counseling than in education because of counseling's idiosyncratic nature. The results of many studies of classroom interaction are averages of group behavior, whereas the results of studies of counseling must be applicable to individuals and cannot consist of averages. Individuals differ in feelings, attitudes, and experiences, and counseling relationships themselves are unique interactions. Arbuckle (1968) writes:

While there would appear to be an excessive degree of sensitivity on the part of the individual counselors and therapists to any evaluation of their work, there is a very real question about the validity of the means of evaluation that are being used. Thus, while it may be that counselors . . . are not very interested in having the results of their work evaluated, it is equally true that it is rather difficult to an-swer their question to the evaluator, "Are you sure that you have some empirical means by which the results of counseling may be measured?" (p. 430)

Research in counseling, indeed, presents a challenge in trying to arrive at generalizations.

Need for Research and Evaluation in Counseling

There is some question about the need for research in counseling. Sprinthall (1981) notes that counseling practice "has had a long and ambivalent rela-tionship with research" (p. 487). We too often hear the cry that counseling is such a personal endeavor that measurement of effects is impossible. One poet perhaps best sums up negative feelings in general toward empirical science:

> While you and i have lips and voices which
> are kissing and to sing with
> who cares if some one-eyed son of a bitch
> invents an instrument to measure Spring with?
> (e e cummings in *Weaver*, 1964, p. 16)

Cummings questions the measurement of experiences that cannot be opera-tionally defined. The point to be made, of course, is that counseling, its com-ponents and dimensions, *can* be operationally defined, not in the sense of all-or-nothing pronouncements, but rather in light of particular probabili-ties.

Today, perhaps more than ever before, we need research to measure the effects of counseling. Such basic questions as "Does counseling do any good?" and "Who is counseling good for?" need continual answering, because the "faces" of counseling and its methods of application are always changing. Although there is more cumulative research on various aspects of counseling than ever before, there has been a proliferation of approaches to counseling, including "gimmickry," which has far exceeded the amount of relevant and meaningful research. The use of unjustified gimmickry is, unfortunately, widespread.

Research or scientific inquiry in counseling is a method of study "by which, through the careful and exhaustive investigation of all the ascertainable evidence bearing upon a definable problem, we reach a solution to that problem" (Hillway, 1956, p. 5). A question is answered, a hypothesis is accepted or rejected. We are using the term *research* not only to refer to scientific inquiry, which is aimed solely at the advance of knowledge, but also to include the collecting of data that will help in making immediately useful decisions about the counseling enterprise. Without research, or the scientific method, we fall back on the trial-and-error opinions of authority figures, prior experience, or reasoning that is dated or biased. Even the best of authorities can be wrong. It is important for practitioners, not only to conduct research in counseling, but also to disseminate and implement research findings.

Characteristics of Counseling Research

Traditional Characteristics of Research
Generally, seven methodological steps to research studies in the behavioral sciences have been identified. They are as follows:

1. Selection of the problem
2. Problem definition and differentiation, and hypothesis development
3. Data collection
4. Analysis and interpretation of the data
5. Formulation of conclusions
6. Verification of the hypothesis
7. Reporting the research study

Bloom (1956) illustrated the research process schematically (see Figure 17.1).

Furthermore, within the overall process, various characteristics of research have been identified. Best (1959) summarizes five such characteristics:

1. Research involves the acquisition of new data from firsthand sources.
2. Research is expert, systematic, and accurate investigations.
3. Research is logical and objective. . . .

Figure 17.1
Schematic Diagram
of the Research
Process

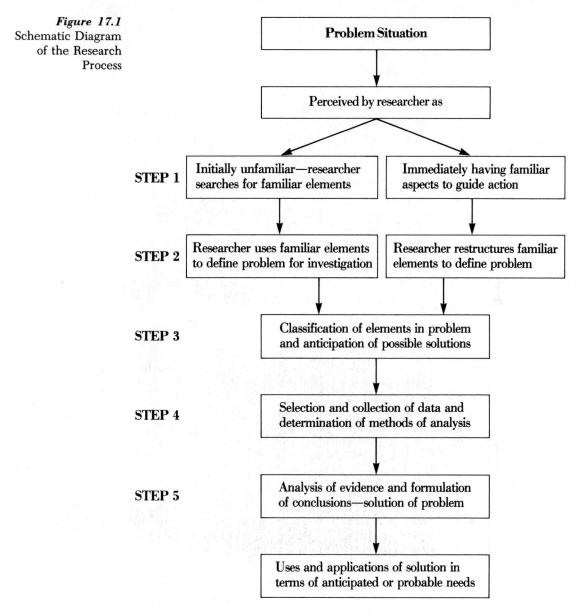

Source: Adapted from *Taxonomy of Educational Objectives: The Classification of Educational Goals: Handbook I: Cognitive Domain* by Benjamin S. Bloom et al. Copyright © 1956 by Longman Inc. Reprinted by permission of Longman Inc., New York.

4. Research endeavors to organize data in quantitative terms. . . .
5. Research is carefully recorded and reported. (pp. 7–8)

Barnes (1964) discusses the following ten characteristics:

1. Research ideas are restricted by the requirement that they be testable.
2. Theories and speculations are closely related to reality.
3. Simplicity in ideas and conceptualizations is the ideal.
4. Research sets out to test, not to prove.
5. The concept of "failure" is an archaic interference in research activities.
6. The potential value of a research project is directly related to the cogency of the questions asked.
7. The methods of research are intentionally devised to prevent the researcher's deluding himself and others.
8. Values play a legitimate and important part in research activities.
9. The methods of analysis, of logical deduction and statistical inference, should fit the limitations inherent in the problem being investigated.
10. The researcher courts recognition through the power of his tested ideas, not through the attractiveness of his rhetoric. (pp. 13–17)

Research, then, involves scientific inquiry and a specific methodological approach. While the above characteristics are acknowledged to be components of more formal research in the behavioral sciences, they are just as applicable to action or field research.

Applied-Action Research

During the past five years, more emphasis has been given to applied research in counseling. Action research comprises research in field settings. Generally, action research turns its attention to the resolution of everyday problems. Practitioners often feel that research has been unresponsive to their practical needs (Minor, 1981, p. 485). Goldman (1976), in fact, questions the value for practitioners of much of the traditional research that has been conducted. He believes that researchers have focused "too narrowly" on the goals and approaches of the physical sciences, even when dealing with "practical problems of a highly intangible nature." He is not questioning, however, the importance of basic research. He is, instead, emphasizing the need for innovative approaches through applied evaluation.

Applied research focuses on immediate application and does not necessarily make any particular contribution to theoretical concepts. It is conducted under field, rather than laboratory, conditions. Findings are considered in terms of local, specific, or idiosyncratic applicability rather than in terms of "universal validity." Both action and traditional approaches to counseling research should complement each other, not negate the worth or the conduct of the other. If practicing counselors are to make a research contribution, it will generally be through an action-research approach. Such research could evaluate specific counseling practices in individualized counseling settings. While the endeavor may be complicated by any number of uncontrollable variables, the results should have many more applications outside of sterile laboratory conditions.

An article by Oetting (1976) suggests the phrase *evaluative research* to refer to immediately useful and practical research. Under the press of everyday problems, decisions need to be made—to do so, typical control, or sampling, procedures may be altered. Small numbers may be studied, but this should be done under "real," rather than laboratory, conditions. Oetting presents an interesting table, comparing characteristics of traditional scientific inquiry with those of evaluative and pseudoevaluative (lacking in rigorous design) research. (See Table 17.1.) In summary, however, it is important to recognize the necessity of both applied and pure research within counseling.

Whereas all these alternatives represent interesting distinctions between different emphases in research, they do not totally erase the overlapping of what is probably best seen as a continuum, nor the generalization that both pure and applied research are essential to the solution of both immediate and long-range problems. There is obvious need for greater cross-fertilization that will benefit both. (Mouly, 1978, p. 43)

Problems in Counseling Research

Both Tyler (1969) and Blocher (1966) identify certain problems in counseling research. The first revolves around the establishment of criteria—aims, goals, or objectives for counseling. Gelso (1979) states, "From the beginnings of psychology, the issue of criterion selection has been a highly complex one. The criterion problem has been a sometimes insurmountable one in counseling and therapy" (p. 19). It is difficult to establish goals that are acceptable to all or even to a majority of counselors. Furthermore, some goals are so vague that they do not lend themselves to research. Blocher (1966) states, "Goals such as developing self-actualization, building up the integrative power of the ego, or reorganizing the patient's self-structure are a bit difficult to translate into observable behaviors" (p. 223). Blocher lists a wide range of criteria to indicate counseling effectiveness.

Social Adjustment Criteria

1. Adjustment, rated by "experts"
2. Reduction in disciplinary offenses
3. Participation in group activities
4. Citizenship grades

Personality Criteria

1. Congruence between self- and ideal-self descriptions
2. Changes on personality tests
3. Ratings of personality change or adjustment

Table 17.1

Comparison of Characteristics of Orthodox Scientific Inquiry and Evaluative Research

	Scientific Inquiry	*Evaluative Research*	*Pseudoevaluative Research*
Purpose	Establish empirical relationships or test theory-derived predictions of relationships	Determine effect of a practical intervention	No clear purpose. May confuse staff activity with goals
Research Controls	Eliminate any crucial alternative explanation of theoretical or empirical importance	At least reduce the number of alternative explanations of practical importance	Crucial, logically and practically important alternative explanations are not dealt with
Sampling	Allows generalization of theory—nature and extent is determined by limits of the theory	Allows generalization of results to the same or similar target groups	Sampling bias is confounded with independent or dependent variables or limits generality so that the results are useless
Independent Variables	Isolation of the effects of each element, single and in combination. Tight control of extraneous variables	May be one or several complex programs where effect of separate elements cannot be determined: Observe for extraneous independent variables	Insufficient information to allow replication of the program
Dependent Variables	Related via constructs to theory. Prior evidence for reliability and validity as an index of the phenomena under investigation	Must be related to intervention goals; at least concurrent or logical evidence for reliability and validity	No logical or empirical relationship to program goals
Results	Observation of systematic deviations from base rates and/or inferential statistics. No conclusions beyond "hard" data. Strong alternative explanations negate results	Both inferential and descriptive statistics may be important. Uses both "hard" and "soft" data to extrapolate beyond present results. Attempts are made to estimate influence of alternative explanations	The statistics used are inappropriate to the data, the design, or the problem. Meaningless relationships are tested. Conclusions not related to data or are used as a vehicle for biases of investigator
Discussion	Focus is on empirical relationships or implications for theory	Focus is on utilization and implications	Reaches no conclusions or only discusses design of future studies
Cost/Benefits	Rarely relevant; inquiry is pursued because of faith in the eventual utility of knowledge	Interacts with interpretation in reaching decisions: Information available to allow estimation of individual and social impact in relationship to staff time, materials, and facilities investment	Potential benefits unclear and costs not estimable

Source: From Oetting, E. R. "Evaluative Research and Orthodox Science: Part I." *Personnel and Guidance Journal* 55 (1976):14. Copyright 1976 American Personnel and Guidance Association. Reprinted with permission.

Vocational Adjustment

1. Specificity of vocational plans
2. Experts' judgments of realism of plans
3. Job satisfaction
4. Persistence in job
5. Promotions on job
6. Amount of earnings

Educational Criteria

1. Increase in grade-point average
2. Correlation between grades and measured aptitude
3. Entrance into college
4. Persistence in college
5. Reduction in scholastic failure
6. Reduction in dropout rate

Other Miscellaneous Criteria

1. Client satisfaction
2. Persistence in counseling
3. Returning to counseling
4. Tendency to use public agencies
5. Self-confidence
6. Optimism about the future

Significant criteria can be identified, and agreed upon, as outcome or process measures of counseling effectiveness. One should keep in mind, however, that "The profession of counseling is concerned with developing methods for solving the real problems of real people. Research that is not relevant to the practice of counseling will offer little toward the development of these methods" (Krumboltz and Mitchell, 1979, p. 50).

A second problem in counseling research has been one of control. It is indeed difficult to identify those changes that occur simply with the passage of time. Counseling change should be significantly greater than any such automatic spontaneous change. The only possible way to consider such differences is through the use of a control group. Yet, it is not easy to come by equivalent control groups. The question can also be raised as to the fairness of giving some persons counseling while others receive none. Future research in counseling must adequately control for counseling self-selection. Simply matching experimental and control groups a priori, without assessment of counseling willingness or readiness, is inadequate.

The third problem, that of contamination, is closely related to the control problem. Contamination can occur from sources outside the study—that is, members of the control group might seek outside assistance, which will contaminate the comparison of results.

There are other obstacles that create problems for counseling research. Here are some of the more common ones:

1. **Observer Bias**   This involves the tendency by researchers to observe consistently and inaccurately. Such bias can be very difficult to overcome when it involves deep-seated beliefs about religion, sex, or race.
2. **The Hawthorne Effect**   The Hawthorne effect simply suggests that attention, in and of itself, affects results. It is similar to the placebo effect, which states that giving a patient a pill, even if it is nothing more than a sugar pill, can help the person feel better. It is necessary to vary the amounts and kinds of observer intervention and measure the resulting effects.
3. **Memory Fallibility**   Measurements of memory of behavior, not of the behavior, lend themselves to inaccuracy. Even the use of records is not particularly accurate.
4. **Trying to Please the Counselor**   Clients will demonstrate in interviews certain types of behavior simply to please the counselor. Such behavior is not continued after counseling termination. Follow-up studies can help to eliminate this difficulty.
5. **Sample Bias**   Any sampling of a population that is not random creates a bias. For example, conclusions about behavior drawn by psychiatrists from their patient subpopulation is biased. Because of such a bias, many generalizations about homosexuality are currently being questioned.
6. **Nonresponse**   Nonresponse bias refers to portions of the sample not available for the study. This problem generally occurs in survey, particularly questionnaire, studies where a portion of the sample does not return the questionnaires. Nonresponders differ from responders, so that the higher the nonresponse rate, the more biased the findings. We have seen studies based on 20-percent questionnaire returns. Such findings are indeed limited, if not useless.
7. **Geographical Variability**   Studies of research in one geographical area may not have much applicability in a different geographical setting. It is well known that urban and rural settings, for example, can account for different results. Differences can also exist, however, among subpopulations within a single city.

Approaches to Counseling Research

Research on the Process and Outcome of Counseling

Research can assess either the process or the outcome of counseling. The former takes into account what is happening during counseling; the latter assesses what has happened as a result of counseling. Shertzer and Stone (1974) write

Process research focuses upon what occurs as counseling proceeds; it generally investigates such factors as shifts in content from session to session by the counselee, the relationship of content to the counselor's remarks, counselee attention on himself versus others, and the like. Outcome research is directed toward assessing the final product of counseling and usually focuses upon such issues as which techniques work best with which counselees, whether counseling was successful, and whether counseling effects were lasting. (pp. 402–403)

Outcome research is crucial in establishing the efficacy of counseling; whereas process research is crucial in assessing the dynamics of the relationship itself.

Descriptive Research in Counseling

Descriptive research describes what currently exists. It "is concerned with conditions or relationships that exist; practices that prevail; beliefs, points of view, or attitudes that are held; processes that are going on; effects that are being felt; or trends that are developing" (Best, 1959, p. 102). It is sometimes called survey research because it is a method of collecting data by surveying, through questionnaires or interviews, a representative sample of some population. Interpretation of the accumulated data, which present a statistical picture of the population studied, is part of descriptive research. The survey method can be used to understand the population under study. Generally, a larger sample can be studied when questionnaires are used. Interviews, on the other hand, offer the advantage of a visual inspection of the interview process. Points where communication was interrupted, shifts in the purposes of the subjects, and logical subrole interaction of either counselor or counselee can be observed.

Percentage of returns is a crucial consideration in survey research. Generalizations based on returns of less than 80 percent are questionable and, furthermore, anything less than 100 percent needs to be qualified. Survey research often presents numerous obstacles to obtaining valid, reliable, and usable data. Hackett (1981) suggests the following:

One way to reduce the problems inherent in all survey data collection methods is through careful attention to the construction of the interview format or questionnaire, including such things as item selection, the phrasing of individual questions, and the sequencing and spacing of questions. In addition, the careful training of interviewers and the pretesting and subsequent refinement of questionnaires will greatly enhance the reliability and validity of survey results. (p. 600)

The case study is another form of descriptive research. A case study attempts to understand a person or group through an intense longitudinal study. Arbuckle (1968) has questioned the use of traditional behavioral research methods here:

Thus, in research with human beings, and their behaviors, a pattern which was set up for things and objects generally has been followed and if the assumption of the behavioral scientist that man is a set of behaviors is correct, then this pattern is reasonable enough. If the assumption is not correct, however, and many believe (do not know) that this is the case, then perhaps some means of research should be devised which will operate on the assumption of the uniqueness of man as a human being, with humanness as his unique quality. (p. 431)

Goldman (1976) suggests conceptualizing the individual as a unit of study and criticizes research that averages data from groups in an attempt to understand individual behavior. An important consideration in case studies is the degree to which the individual or group being examined is typical. Surveys tend to be more quantitative than case studies, while case studies involve a more comprehensive examination of fewer, more typical subjects.

Content analysis involves a systematic examination of records, transcripts, or written documents. Such studies may gather, classify, and evaluate material according to previously established criteria. One common criterion on which to base conclusions is frequency of appearance, for example, the number of times interpretative statements or open-ended questions are used. Prevailing practices, conditions, biases, or errors may be identified through content analysis.

Follow-up studies investigate what happens to an individual once he or she has left counseling. Again, questionnaires or interviews are perhaps the most common tools used in obtaining follow-up data.

Experimental Research in Counseling

Experimental research involves the description, comparison, and analysis of data under controlled conditions. Such research tries to control or eliminate certain variables and their effects during the course of a study. The principal means of accomplishing this is through the single-group, the equivalent-group, or the rotation-group method. In the one-group approach, a single factor is either subtracted or added to the group, and any resulting change is measured. The equivalent-group approach studies two groups of people as much alike as possible under different conditions, whereas the rotational method changes the order of the procedures. The effects on groups are then measured; that is, for one group the control method might come first, while the other group receives the experimental method initially. Both groups then receive the other treatment.

The "tightness" of experimental designs produces much more reliable, valid, and sophisticated results than is possible with research involving other approaches. Gelso (1979), however, stated the "Bubble hypothesis," which "underscores the fact that all experiments are highly imperfect" (p. 12). The nature of counseling necessitates a variety of research designs and procedures, the results of which must be viewed with proper perspective and flexibility.

Evaluation of Counseling Programs

Demands for accountability in public agencies and schools, and by consumers and consumer advocates, place increasing emphasis on evaluating counseling programs.

Recently, significant ideological, theoretical, and operational changes—as well as fiscal crises—have necessitated that counselors be concerned about what they do, under the guise of "accountability pressures." This increasing necessity has brought with it related concerns about to whom should counselors be accountable and, more importantly, how should they be accountable. The major response to these concerns has been for counselors to become involved in program evaluation activities. (Wheeler and Loesch, 1981, p. 573)

The purpose of such evaluations is to determine if counseling programs meet their established goals and objectives.

Characteristics of Program Evaluation

Program evaluation can be defined as the process of identifying, accumulating, and processing data that are useful in formulating program decisions and determining program effectiveness. Evaluation design must be based on program objectives; otherwise it will be haphazard and meaningless. Program objectives will help determine the response to two basic pre-evaluation questions: (1) What types of information will allow for the estimation of program effectiveness? (2) How will the evaluation be conducted? Subsequent decisions can be made as to which components of the program are meeting their objectives and which components should be modified or eliminated. Pietrofesa et al. (1980) summarize important characteristics of any program evaluation:

First, evaluation is more than an occasional judgment of program worth. Rather, it is a systematic process involving several steps that necessarily occur over an extended period of time. Second, the evaluation process requires an initial establishment of program objectives to which accomplishments are later compared. Since the development of these purposes precedes program implementation, systematic program evaluation is an integral part of program development. Third, systematic program evaluation requires comprehensive data collection. Evidence for program accomplishments drawn from multiple sources (e.g., tests, critical incidents, subjective impressions) is more likely to facilitate sound decisions. Finally, program evaluation is characterized by the synthesis of compiled data for the purpose of decision making for program improvement. Evaluation can be viewed as a beginning—judgments of program worth are made so that needed modifications may be identified and advancements realized. (p. 463)

While research can at times be applied and practical, it can also be theoretical and directed toward abstract conceptualizations. Evaluation, on the other hand, is always practical, and related to programmatic concerns. As a result, it has "direct" administrative and supervisory ramifications. While it is not always easy to appreciate the relevance or applicability of research, it is almost impossible to question the relevance of program evaluation. Wheeler and Loesch (1981) write that this is so because evaluation "activities are selected or developed with the idea of immediate utilitarian value as their major characteristic. Thus, at least theoretically, counseling program evaluation activities should be inherently relevant from conception or inception" (p. 574).

Models of Evaluation

Various models have been posited for the evaluation of counseling programs (Stufflebeam et al., 1971; Carr, 1977; Burck, 1978). Each model can serve particular purposes, but they are not mutually exclusive. Proper selection of appropriate evaluation models is predicated upon the identified objectives, the information needed, and the decisions to be reached.

Stufflebeam et al. (1971) identified the *Context-Input-Process-Product* (CIPP) model. Within CIPP there are four types of evaluation, which, by the way, might well be considered in their own right as models of evaluation.

Context evaluation sets the stage for assessing differences between program objectives and results. Was the program successful in accomplishing what it set out to do? Results of this evaluation are used to achieve a "greater congruence between intended and actual program outcomes" (Burck, 1978, p. 183). Stufflebeam et al. (1971) write that context evaluation "determines the specifications for product evaluation" (p. 223).

Input evaluation provides information about the means (for example, facilities, financial support, and personnel) needed to make progress toward program goals. Resource availability and cost effectiveness are determined.

Process evaluation is the continuous assessment of the effectiveness of the design of the program. Stufflebeam et al. (1971) write, "Process evaluation has three main objectives—the first is to detect or predict defects in the procedural design during the implementation stage, the second is to provide information for decisions, and the third is to maintain a record of the procedure as it occurs" (p. 229). Burck (1978) comments that a "good" process evaluation includes "assessment of interpersonal relationships and the monitoring and managing of communications, resources and logistics, and physical facilities" (p. 184). Why the program does or does not work well is a critical issue.

Product evaluation concentrates on effectiveness. "Specifically, product evaluation focuses on the extent to which goals have been achieved," writes Burck (1978, p. 184). Obvious program decisions can be reached at this stage. Program continuance, extension, or elimination may be addressed through product evaluation.

Burck (1978) identified several evaluation models other than CIPP. The first is closely related in format to traditional research. The *research design model* can be used when one wishes to make a decision based on a causal relationship. Some discussion of cause-and-effect may be present; for example, whether relaxation training (deep muscle relaxation—DMR) leads to fewer phobic behaviors. There are five basic steps to this model.

Step 1. Establishing the dependent variable, i.e., in this case the aims and objectives of the program.

Step 2. Formulating the aims and objectives in behavioral terms. This becomes the operational definition.

Step 3. Designing and constructing a test with content validity to measure the behaviorally stated aims that leads to the measurement of the dependent variables.

Step 4. Selecting a group with which to compare the test group, i.e., establishment of the independent variable.

Step 5. Collecting and analyzing the data. (Burck, 1978, p. 182)

The *medical model* of evaluation is not only interested in the analysis of data to measure "intended outcomes" but also in the "side effects" of intervention strategies. For example, one could identify not only the direct and intended results of a weight loss program, but also the possible effects on smoking behavior or the marital relationship. Client affective reactions to the process and program are important in this model.

Economic models are "time-effort systems, effort systems, management information systems, management cost systems, management by objectives, and others" (Burck, 1978, p. 185). Quality and quantity control is greater under this type of model than under others. Identification of the cost effectiveness of intervention variables (that is, the relationship of change effected to dollars spent) forms the basis for an economic model.

The *discrepancy evaluation model* compares what is actually being done with what might be the ideal. Differences between intended and obtained outcomes are sought. A needs assessment is often the starting point for this type of evaluation and provides the baseline data for intended outcomes.

An *adversary model,* although little used, runs along the lines of what might occur in the legal profession. The pros and cons of a particular program are presented. Legal procedure, for example, rules of evidence and argumentation, are followed. Sides are taken and claims and counterclaims are advanced. The reader essentially becomes judge and jury and reaches a decision about the merits of the program.

A *formative-summative evaluation model* was advanced by Scriven (1972). Formative evaluation is part of the development process. There is continual feedback during the process about the development of a product. Answers to questions of content validity, vocabulary level, usability, appropriateness of media, durability of materials, and personnel efficiency are sought. This, then, is an "internal" evaluation attempting to improve the development of the product. Summative evaluation answers questions about the cost effectiveness of the product compared to the competition. This form of evaluation can help consumers make decisions about the merit of the evaluated product. Burck (1978) writes, "Essentially, formative evaluation aims to systematically and consistently improve the program, whereas summative evaluation focuses on determining the overall effectiveness of the program" (p. 187).

Scriven (1972) also introduced a *goal-free evaluation model,* where the evaluator purposely remains unaware of a program's goals and objectives and accumulates data on all of the effects that a program might produce. This is done regardless of the "rhetoric" of intention. The benefit of this type of evaluation may well be that unanticipated effects can be discovered—effects that might have been overlooked if the evaluator was preoccupied with stated goals. Carr (1977) notes, "This form of evaluation pays little attention to goals, but focuses on what actually happened to persons, what they experienced as a totality regardless of what the program's intentions were. This approach enables the counselor to by-pass goal distinctions that are more important at the program proposal stage than they are at the program outcome stage" (p. 115). On the other hand it appears that while goal-free evaluation frees up the investigator from the confines of measuring specific goal-identified attainment, it replaces this limitation with the potentially biasing influence of evaluation based on the evaluator's priorities.

The selection of an appropriate model of evaluation—given the number that exist—is difficult, but it may be accomplished by answering several fundamental questions:

1. What purpose will the evaluation serve? What are the characteristics of the program about to be evaluated?
2. What questions are to be addressed during the evaluation? What conclusions are to be drawn from the questions that are asked?
3. What assumptions underlie the research? Are cause-and-effect relationships to be drawn?
4. Is the evaluation intended for a particular audience?
5. Can the criteria be identified in measurable ways?
6. How can data be derived that will provide answers for the questions asked? Can program costs be assessed? Will the program's competitors be identified and assessed?
7. Do the investigators have the necessary qualifications to conduct the evaluation? (Daniels et al., 1981)

Daniels et al. (1981) provide a meta-model schema of program evaluation. (See Figure 17.2.) It is proposed that such a model will help in the selection of an appropriate evaluation model and in the development of new procedures for future evaluation.

Developing Criteria for Evaluation

Any type of goal-based evaluation carries with it the problems of trying to define goals, objectives, and criteria. Goal-based evaluation focuses on outcomes and compares expected client performance with achieved client outcomes. Goals can be thought of as broad statements of what a program tries to accomplish; objectives focus on quantifiable or measurable elements of the goals; and criteria identify, not only the desired outcome behaviors, but possibly the conditions under which the behaviors may occur and the minimal (quantitative) levels of acceptable performance. The terms *goals* and *objectives* are often used interchangeably, but we conceive of *objectives* as being far more specific. What are legitimate goals and objectives? Part of the difficulty, as mentioned earlier, is that there are no common, universally

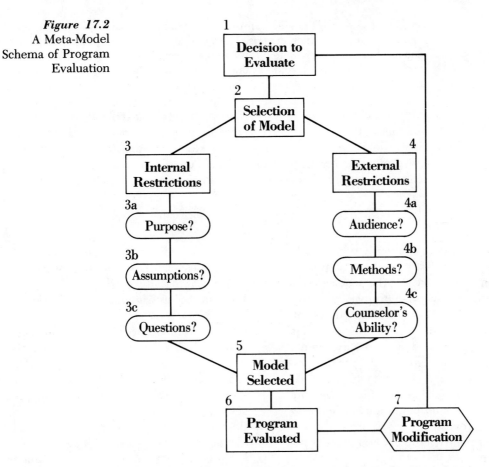

accepted goals for programs in counseling. Value judgments enter into the selection of program goals, the resulting objectives, and eventually the specific criteria to be evaluated. On the other hand, goals can be adequately stated if the counseling staff is committed to program evaluation. As Bardo et al. (1978) remind us, "Program objectives and criteria for success should be determined by the providers and consumers . . . with guides and ideas from outside sources" (p. 208). Such a process would help establish checks and balances on program perspective. Measurement could range from relatively simplistic data, such as the number of clients utilizing a service, to the development of goal attainment scales to assess each client's improvement over a previously identified baseline level.

One further difficulty may exist, however, even after criteria have been identified. That is the difficulty of measurement.

Given goals and objectives for . . . programs, counselors must take the lead in determining specific evaluation criteria. The variable nature of . . . programs does not lend itself to a ready assessment through the use of standardized measures. Therefore, counselors must develop evaluation tools to fit their unique situations. . . . (Bardo et al., 1978, p. 207)

It is perhaps the combination of these elements—the difficulty of identifying and measuring criteria in the face of other demands on counselor time and the lack of counselor training—that makes it most difficult to conduct effective program evaluations. While difficult, it is not an *impossible* task if counselors will recognize the importance of research and evaluation activities.

Summary

Counseling must be continuously subjected to relevant research—research that not only is part of scientific inquiry and the acquisition of knowledge for its own sake (to make a contribution to theory) but research that can also affect everyday practice and decision making. Professionals in the field of counseling cannot afford to (1) be restricted by only utilizing traditionally accepted research methods or (2) allow the field to become dominated by gimmicks that have no substantiation for their purported effectiveness.

The major points of this chapter were as follows:

1. The study of counseling is difficult because of its idiosyncratic nature. Results have to be applicable to individuals, rather than groups. Counseling relationships are unique interactions.

2. Counseling effects are measurable. The basic question "Does counseling do any good?" can be answered.
3. Without research, gimmickry will continue to flower.
4. Certain problems exist in conducting counseling research. It is hard to reach agreement on goals for counseling. Control groups are difficult to establish. Other obstacles include observer bias, sampling, and geographic variability.
5. Research can assess either the process or outcomes of counseling.
6. Program evaluation is essential for determining whether or not counseling programs meet established program goals and objectives.
7. While evaluation is systematic, it is also practical and has a direct impact on administrative decisions.

References

Arbuckle, Dugald S. "Counseling Effectiveness and Related Issues." *Journal of Counseling Psychology* 15 (1968):430–435.

Bardo, Harold, John J. Cody, and **Seymour Bryson.** "Evaluation of Guidance Programs: Call the Question." *Personnel and Guidance Journal* 57 (1978):204–208.

Barnes, Fred P. *Research for the Practitioner in Education.* Washington, D.C.: National Education Association, 1964.

Best, John W. *Research in Education.* Englewood Cliffs, N.J.: Prentice-Hall, 1959.

Blocher, Donald H. *Developmental Counseling.* New York: Ronald Press, 1966, 2nd ed., 1974.

Bloom, Benjamin S., et al. *Taxonomy of Educational Objectives: The Classification of Educational Goals: Handbook I: Cognitive Domain.* New York: Longman, 1956.

Burck, H. D. "Evaluating Programs: Models and Strategies." In Leo Goldman, ed., *Research Methods for Counselors.* New York: Wiley, 1978.

Carr, Rey. "The Counselor or the Counseling Program as the Target of Evaluation." *Personnel and Guidance Journal* 56 (1977):112–118.

Daniels, M. Harry, Robert Mines, and Charles Gressard. "A Meta-Model for Evaluating Counseling Programs." *Personnel and Guidance Journal* 59 (1981):578–582.

Gelso, Charles J. "Research in Counseling: Methodological and Professional Issues." *Counseling Psychologist* 8 (1979):7–36.

Goldman, Leo. "A Revolution in Counseling Research." *Journal of Counseling Psychology* 23 (1976):543–552.

Hackett, Gail. "Survey Research Methods." *Personnel and Guidance Journal* 59 (1981):599–604.

Hillway, T. *Introduction to Research.* Boston: Houghton Mifflin, 1956.

Krumboltz, John D., and Lynda K. Mitchell. "Relevant Rigorous Research." *Counseling Psychologist* 8 (1979):50–52.

Minor, Billy J. "Bridging the Gap Between Research and Practice: An Introduction." *Personnel and Guidance Journal* 59 (1981):485–486.

Mouly, George. *Educational Research.* Boston: Allyn and Bacon, 1978.

Oetting, E. R. "Evaluative Research and Orthodox Science: Part I." *Personnel and Guidance Journal* 55 (1976):11–15.

Pietrofesa, John J., Bianca Bernstein, JoAnne Minor, and Susan Stanford. *Guidance: An Introduction.* Chicago: Rand McNally, 1980.

Scriven, M. "The Methodology of Evaluation." In C. H. Weiss, ed., *Evaluating Active Programs: Readings in Social Action and Education.* Boston: Allyn and Bacon, 1972.

Shertzer, Bruce, and Shelley C. Stone. *Fundamentals of Counseling.* Boston: Houghton Mifflin, 1974.

Sprinthall, Norman A. "A New Model for Research in Service of Guidance and Counseling." *Personnel and Guidance Journal* 59 (1981):487–496.

Stufflebeam, D. L., W. J. Foley, W. J. Gephart, E. G. Guba, R. L. Hammond, H. D. Merriman, and M. M. Provus. *Educational Evaluation and Decision-Making.* Bloomington, Ind.: Phi Delta Kappa, 1971.

Tyler, Leona E. *The Work of the Counselor.* New York: Appleton-Century-Crofts, 1969.

Weaver, W. "The Imperfections of Science." In S. Rappaport and H. Wright, *Science: Method and Meaning.* New York: Washington Square Press, 1964, p. 16.

Wheeler, Paul T., and Larry Loesch. "Program Evaluation and Counseling: Yesterday, Today, and Tomorrow." *Personnel and Guidance Journal* 59 (1981):573–578.

CHAPTER 18

Issues and Trends

Chapter Organizer

Aim of the Chapter

This chapter will present current professional issues and social trends facing counselors in a variety of settings. By re-examining their own values and demands of their job settings, counselors should be able to formulate their own stance regarding each issue and trend.

Chapter Preview

1. Eleven issues pertaining to their professional roles confront counselors today. Among them are role definition, role determinants, training, self-awareness, work with paraprofessionals and volunteers, social concerns, and funding.
2. Fourteen general social trends have significant implications for counselors, their training, and their employment.

Relevant Questions

The following are several questions to keep in mind while reading the chapter:

1. What actions can counselors take to resolve the various issues?
2. Are counselors being effectively trained for their positions?
3. Are counselors fully aware of themselves as they counsel their clients?
4. Is one counseling approach appropriate for all counselors?
5. Can individual counselors provide needed services to all types of clients?
6. Who determines the role and function of a counselor?
7. Should paraprofessionals and volunteers provide counseling services?
8. Should counselors be more actively involved in social issues?
9. Should counselors work with preschool and elementary school children?
10. Should funding for counseling positions be provided through state and federal legislation?
11. Should counselors become more accountable and assertive?
12. Do counselors need more rigorous training programs?

Introduction

This chapter will review some of the issues and trends that are influencing counselors today. As we look at each issue, we ask the readers to ask themselves such personal questions as "Should these things happen?" "Are they appropriate in my job setting (present or future)?" and "What is my position regarding this issue?" As we review the trends, we ask the readers to relate them to their present or projected work situations and to answer for themselves such questions as "Do my counseling procedures take these trends into account?" and "Is there a need for me to better prepare myself for current or future counseling in specific areas?"

Although responses to the following issues may vary according to the perceptions of any one individual counselor and to each particular employment setting, we believe that they are pertinent to the broad majority of counselors in our society today.

Issues Affecting Counseling

1. *How specific should be the role definitions of the various kinds of counselors—such as social workers, psychologists, and school counselors?* Helping professionals often find themselves working with the same clients, sometimes without knowledge of one another's actions. Because role definitions overlap—both in responsibilities and settings—many professional and personal misunderstandings can occur among counselors. But no matter how specific counselor roles are defined, there will always be some activities common to all of them.

It can be helpful for those counselors working with the same clients to meet and determine if a cooperative working relationship is the best approach or if only one counselor, whose professional expertise is most suited to the particular client should conduct the therapy. In other situations, it might be necessary to reevaluate role definitions to see if changes are needed in order to better serve the current needs of a particular population.

Role definitions have a purpose—that of setting guidelines for professional counseling activities and relevant training programs. With these definitions, professionals can better structure their roles as they are in fact practiced in an institutional or societal setting. However, when certain employment situations ask for counseling skills that can be provided by a variety of personnel, general role definitions may not be applicable. For example, many hospitals are now hiring persons to counsel with patients and consult with members of the patients' families. Often counselors and social workers have the same skills for that type of counseling position.

Perhaps counseling roles and services need to be reviewed as to their suitability for a particular employment situation and the client population to be served. We propose that counseling expertise, training, and skills be the appropriate criteria for choosing a counselor, rather than limiting the choice to a stereotypically defined role, which may or may not relate to that specific employment situation.

2. *Who determines the role and functions of a counselor?* Several influences on counselors exist. Role expectations can be stated by their agency or institution or supervisor, by their professional organization, by their clients, and by themselves.

Although it may be helpful for counselors to have role guidelines formulated by professional organizations (the American School Counselors Association or the American Psychological Association), these guidelines might not coincide with their own views, or with the views of the employing institution or their client. Ideally, counselors perform their counseling duties as they personally feel most appropriate under the guidelines of their professional organization, which were accepted by the employing institution.

Realistically, however, counselors frequently must decide for themselves to what extent they will determine their role and to what extent others will determine that role for them. If a particular situation does not allow counselors to work as they wish, they must decide whether to remain in their present position or attempt to find other employment where they would have more autonomy.

3. *Are counselors being effectively trained for their positions?* That knowledge of one's self and of the counseling process is essential in counselor training is accepted by most counselor educators. However, there is disagreement about how much skills training and follow-up supervision (in actual employment settings) is necessary. Some counselor trainers believe that skills training should be instituted at the beginning stages of a training program; others find it more appropriate at the final stages.

We believe that students are best trained to learn about themselves and the counseling process by experiencing realistic counseling throughout the *entire* program. Without practical field experiences and supervision, many counselors-in-training fail to apply effectively the knowledge gained in the classroom and through self-assessment. We recognize that, presently, some training programs are limited to one year's duration. However, we support the movement in training programs to provide more on-site internship experiences for their trainees and to extend their training time to two full years.

As our society constantly changes, our clients' needs change and counselors need to recognize this and to remain current in their practice. Therefore, the necessity of ongoing in-service training for counselors should be recognized. Effective training for counselors will require not only involvement in formal training programs but also participation in ongoing in-service workshops and seminars, in both educational institutions and field settings.

4. *Should counselors be trained in one specific approach or in a manner that builds on generic counseling skills?* Various employment opportunities for counselors require different skills or approaches. Unless a beginning counselor-in-training knows specifically where he or she will work, it seems inappropriate to learn only one counseling approach. We recommend training counselors in the use of generic skills that may be applied in a variety of settings. With the expansion of masters-level training programs to include a second year and more internship experiences, it seems appropriate to provide generic counseling-skills training first and then to concentrate on more specific approaches, as they relate to preferred and possible employment situations at that time.

5. *Is one counseling approach appropriate for all counselors?* Many counselors would automatically reply no to this question and, at the same time, be using an approach just because it was dictated in their training or enthusiastically praised by a persuasive colleague. Counselors need to review their counseling approach, since it might be an inauthentic projection of themselves or inappropriate for their working environment.

Counselor trainers should provide experiences that allow counselors to gain basic helping skills and to determine, through practice and supervision, which counseling approach works best for them—eclectic (parts of several approaches), client-centered, cognitive-behavioral, rational-emotive, behaviorist, or existential.

Counselors must develop an authentic and personalized approach, which recognizes their strengths and how they can relate to the needs of their clients and the counseling environment. They should also be objective in determining the effectiveness of their approach.

6. *Can individual counselors provide needed services to all types of clients?* This issue has been debated widely—on one hand, by those counselors who feel their basic counseling skills can build effective working relationships with any type of client and, on the other, by those counselors who feel that counselors must hold similar values and attitudes and/or have the same type of background as their clients. Nevertheless, all counselors should take into consideration their experiences in urban, rural, or suburban settings and determine if they can be helpful in working with clients from other types of backgrounds.

Dissimilar attitudes and values can often interfere with establishing an effective counseling relationship and hinder the counseling process. If it is true that most counselors in institutional settings (social workers, psychologists, and counselors in schools; therapists, psychologists, and social workers in private clinics and hospitals) hold middle-class values, can they relate to clients with lower- or upper-class values? It is important for counselors to determine whether they can understand and relate effectively to their clients' values.

Counselors must also examine their attitudes toward persons of another race, another sex, another religion, another age generation, and another ethnic background in order to see if they can relate to them, understand them, and effectively counsel them. If counselors find they cannot work well with some individuals, they should state so honestly and try to arrange for another counseling relationship for their clients.

7. *Are counselors fully aware of themselves as they counsel their clients?* As we have mentioned throughout this book, counselor self-awareness and understanding provide the basis for their regard, empathy, and authenticity in the counseling relationship. During training programs and under trainer supervision, counselors-in-training are able to analyze and work with their attitudes, values, and behaviors. There might be a tendency to lose this personal self-awareness in the mechanics of day-to-day counseling and away from the stimulation of a training program. We suggest that counselors set up personal programs of self-evaluation, which would include reviewing perceptions of themselves and their work. Also professional colleagues and former trainers could be asked to help counselors in their self-appraisal. Together, they might review the counselors' goals, expectations, and methods of counseling. Audio- and video-tapes of their counseling activities could facilitate this re-examination of self.

It also might be important for the counselors to see themselves outside of the employment milieu. An opportunity to clarify their thoughts is needed not only to get in tune, but to stay in touch, with their inner self. With counselor burn-out a very real concern, counselors need to take time for themselves to reflect, regroup, and re-examine their present perceptions of self and society. This needed reevaluation of self can be done individually or in concert with other objective helping professionals. Counselors should periodically undertake this type of activity, to benefit not only themselves but also their clients.

8. *Should paraprofessionals and volunteers provide counseling services?* Paraprofessionals can be described as persons who have many of the counseling skills and helping talents of the more formally trained professional counselors. They generally work as paid staff members in an institutional setting under the supervision of a licensed professional counselor. Although disagreements sometimes exist between paraprofessional and professional counselors over such concerns as role definitions, qualifications, pay, and responsibilities, paraprofessionals are needed in the helping professions and can be very effective in many settings.

With structured and systematic training programs, as formulated by Carkhuff (1980) and Brammer (1979) and with close supervision and support by their trainers, paraprofessionals can serve as counselors in many settings by performing such diverse activities as answering phones in a crisis center, doing intake interviews in an employment agency, and aiding students in reviewing and using career development materials.

In many agencies, volunteers are increasingly used to provide counseling services. Two basic reasons explain the use of these nonpaid helpers. One is the cutback in funding for counseling services, which results in the loss of counseling positions. The other is the willingness of many volunteers to provide counseling services for no fee. These volunteers may or may not be trained in the same systematic manner as paraprofessionals.

The real issue here is not whether volunteer services can be helpful, but whether the use of volunteers supports the loss of paid counseling positions. We believe that trained, competent, credentialed counselors have a right to provide their services for pay.

As the mental health needs of our population increase, we must provide more skilled aid for our clients, at all levels and in all settings. For example, some professionally trained counselors cannot work effectively in depressed urban areas or with lower-socioeconomic-class clients. If paraprofessionals or trained volunteers can do this effectively, should we deny clients needed counseling only because these helpers do not hold a particular degree? This is a dilemma, but one that we believe can be solved through proper coordination of all mental health and counseling agencies at national, state, and—particularly—local levels. Provision of needed services entails the understanding and cooperation of counselors from various professional orientations, as well as of those trained paraprofessionals and trained volunteers who work with them and their clients.

While we see paraprofessionals and volunteers as being helpful to clients, we believe that the most effective counseling can be done by competent counselors who have completed rigorous educational and training programs and have demonstrated effective counseling competencies.

9. *Should counselors be more actively involved in social issues?* In this book, our definition of counseling focuses on the one-to-one interpersonal relationship between a professionally trained counselor and an individual seeking help. If it is true that individuals can be aided through the counseling process, should counselors also work to influence the social, economic, and political factors which in fact cause many of the clients' personal concerns?

We believe that counselors must not only understand the world outside the counseling office, but become active in it. Changing values in our society in such areas as sexuality, the roles of women and minorities, drug usage, and military service affect the clients we see daily. Thus, it is incumbent upon us to understand our society and its influence on our clients. To become active in the political and social arena is another issue. Is the fact that we are counselors enough in itself to impel social activity on our parts?

Many counselors are involved in activities that support or challenge major governmental policies and practices. Counselors are taking stands on such issues as defense spending, the nuclear arms freeze, draft registration, protection of civil liberties, ecology, funding for abortions, and provision of benefits for the unemployed and the aging. We recognize there are different viewpoints on all of these issues. Yet, counselors have the right, as concerned individuals, to work for their beliefs.

In aiding clients to live better in our society, counselors can and should be involved in activities to change the environments and influences impinging on their clients. However, they need to look closely at their activities and ask themselves whether they honestly feel this type of social involvement is appropriate for them. Whether or not they choose to become more socially and politically involved is their choice, but they should understand their reasons for whatever they decide.

10. *Should counselors work with preschool and elementary school children?* Critics of counseling programs involving preschool and elementary school children have charged that the counselors' time, effort, and pay could be better used elsewhere. While it is true that youngsters at these ages are not as independent as adults and are most influenced by their families and their environments, much can be done by counselors to assist children in becoming socially, emotionally, personally, and academically adept. The development of positive and adequate self-concepts in these children can be aided through the counselors' work with them—individually and in conjunction with their family members and their teachers.

Many of the counseling procedures used with younger children involve structured activities that provide success experiences for them. All children, not just those diagnosed as having academic or emotional difficulties, can benefit from learning about themselves and others through programs like Dinkmeyer's DUSO-R (Developing Understanding of Self and Others) (1983).

We look at counseling with preschool and elementary school children as an effective way to work with them in a positive manner that is developmentally related to their current and future mental health. Many concerns that surface in adulthood may be identified and dealt with at this younger age level through various counseling activities. Youngsters at the preschool and elementary school levels deserve as much, if not more, counseling than is provided to secondary school students, adults, and senior citizens in our society.

11. *Should funding for counseling positions be provided through state and federal legislation?* Financial support for counseling positions in public agencies and schools has been a crucial issue for some time. Taxpayers are being asked to provide more money for school support and for financing public counseling agencies. At the same time, many counselors have been forced out of their positions and entire programs eliminated due to the lack of funding. Some maintain that our nation does not have its spending priorities in order in that it spends so much on military and business support and so little on social programs, including counseling services.

Whatever the reason, it appears that financial support by governments has not been what it should have been. Yet, some funding has been provided. For example, Peck and Jackson (1976) report that educational leaders in Florida were able to focus the attention of their state legislature on needed financial aid for elementary school counselors. Funding was increased from $2.8 million (1972–73) to $7.9 million (1974–1975) because these counselors proved their worth under careful evaluation. Another example of support is Public Law 94-482, which was passed by the U.S. Congress in October of 1976 and authorized the appropriation of $20 million for each of the fiscal years of 1978 and 1979 to aid guidance and counseling programs.

In recent years, the major cuts in funding of social and educational programs have cost many counselors their jobs. However, with current governmental emphasis on the fields of engineering and science, technological employment in business, industry and the military, and job retraining, counseling positions related to these areas may be receiving funding support.

Various counseling organizations—for example, the American Association for Counseling and Development (AACD)—lobby for funding support for counseling positions in community and school settings. An AACD task force has recommended that "any legislation dealing with the technology question must address the central role which professional counselors play in advising students in their career development, assisting teachers and administrators in curriculum improvement and creating awareness in parents and youth about the employment needs of the business, industrial and defense establishment which utilize high technology. The counselor and strengthened guidance and counseling programs provide a structure for this to occur" (*Guidepost*, 1983, p. 1).

AACD's Government Relations Committee is actively involved in lobbying for a variety of legislative actions at the national level. Some areas of concern are the reauthorization of the Vocational Rehabilitation Act and a proposed American Defense Education Act. AACD also sponsors workshops on political education training and legislative involvement.

We believe that counselors need to work for state and federal funding for counseling programs, either individually or as members of professional organizations. However, the outcomes of counseling must not be dictated by the guidelines or restrictions accompanying the funds. Counselors must allow clients to make their own decisions and act independently of any governmental implication or directive. Counselors should not be placed in a position of "selling their clients' souls" to obtain funding for their counseling positions and programs.

Trends Affecting Counseling

This section will discuss some general trends in our society that affect counselors and their work as well as trends in counseling services. As the readers review these trends, they need to ask themselves, "Are my counseling procedures relevant to current and future needs, as indicated by these trends?" and "Do I need further information or training to help me in better serving clients influenced by these trends?" All counselors must continually assess themselves and their ability to deal with present and future influences on their clients.

1. *Our society has become very mobile, both in terms of residence and job continuity.* People move from one residence to another with increasing frequency. These moves may result from personal dissatisfaction with a particular job or location, lack of employment opportunities in an area, or job transfer. Furthermore, people are moving between urban, suburban, and rural settings. There is a definite population transfer from the Northeast and Midwestern sections of our country to the Southeast and the Southwest. The fact that whites are leaving cities in increasing numbers has implications for counselors working in urban areas. Counselors may need to ask themselves, "Do I have the understanding and ability to successfully aid clients in a particular location?"

No longer do people make a single career choice and remain in one job for their entire working life. Job changes, whether horizontal or vertical, are frequent and are accepted by both employers and employees. Often, people look for personal and professional satisfaction in their jobs or look for a change in employment. The desire to find self-satisfaction in a job is often countered by the necessity of just having a job in poor economic times. This conflict creates a dilemma for many workers who want their employment to relate to personal interests or values yet cannot find occupations that match these interests. Thus job change and mobility relate directly to the next trend discussed.

2. *Career counseling is assuming renewed importance in the counseling field.* Career development counseling has long been associated with the concept of career maturity and developing a career pattern based on career exploration, understanding, and decision making. Career development theorists and researchers, such as Super and Knasel (1981), are now beginning to emphasize the concept of career adaptability as part of one's career development. This relates to the idea of career transitions, especially as they seem appropriate for middle-aged job changers.

Our changing employment world reflects the increased use of high technology and automated equipment. Robots and computers often replace workers. One example is the use of robots, rather than assembly line workers, in painting newly manufactured automobiles. With this type of job displacement, there is a definite need for worker retraining. Compounding this problem is the fact that the overall number of unskilled and semiskilled jobs is being reduced.

Career counselors will be much more in demand to help all persons of working age to review career options as they are involved in retraining programs and in assessing possible career transitions. Counselors are needed to help clients with these career concerns.

3. *Family structure and relationships are changing.* The status of the family as a traditional and unalterable institution has changed. There are more

divorces and separations occurring in our society. More remarriages are also taking place. In many situations, divorce and remarriage may be better for both the adults and their children. Counselors are often called on to aid clients in discussing alternatives to their current family situation and in making decisions that affect them and their family members.

Today there is a movement to involve counselors with appropriate background and training as "divorce mediators." The use of counseling skills in divorce situations can often pave the way for continuing or follow-up counseling to aid these clients in adapting to new situations.

In many instances, divorce and remarriage means moving to a new location and establishing new and frequently confusing relationships with step-children, new in-laws, and family friends. Counselors can also provide help for the increasing number of one-parent families, especially those where the one parent is the father. Counseling can benefit children, as well as adults, in reaffirming their self-worth and in dealing with the feelings of guilt that often accompany a change in the family situation.

Within families themselves, there has been less contact with older generations. This may be due to greater physical distances between the families or to difficulties in communication patterns between the generations. In any event, older family members are not as available as they once were to work with and aid their children and grandchildren. Often, older neighbors in the family's location serve as pseudo grandparents.

The fact that more wives and mothers are working than ever before influences relationships within families. In the past being the money provider meant being the head of the household. As a result, men have often been greatly disturbed when their wife earned more than they or when they were unemployed and the wife was the sole financial support of the household. Acceptance of this type of relationship, nevertheless, has been growing.

Parental authority seems to be challenged by children and young adults more frequently and at earlier ages than previously. Some of this may be due to the change of the legal adult age status to 18, and some may be due to a growing laxity on the part of parents in trying to establish and maintain discipline in their home. Whatever the cause of these conflicts, there seems to be a growing demand on the part of clients for counseling and related training programs regarding marriage, family, and parental concerns.

4. *Counseling services are more accepted by the public.* In the past, many people felt that those who were in counseling had something drastically wrong with them, that they were not capable of handling their own problems, and that this in itself was a sign of weakness. However, more and more people are using counseling services as a method of helping themselves and their families. Counselors have become more available to help clients deal with their own personalities and actions, their educational and career plans, their marriage and family relationships, and their employment opportunities.

Clients have increasingly used public counseling agencies regarding legal and medical concerns. Insurance companies, such as Blue Cross–Blue Shield, have encouraged client use of public and private licensed counseling clinics by providing payments for these counseling services. Some businesses have established counseling centers for their employees to aid them in resolving personal problems, which may impair their working effectiveness. In addition, businesses are establishing Employee Assistance Programs. These programs most often coordinate referrals to private and public counseling services, which aid workers with such problems as alcohol and drug abuse. In schools, parents, teachers, and administrators have continued to recognize the value of counselors in aiding students from kindergarten through college. Pretrial juvenile diversion programs have been instituted by the courts and enforcement agencies. Yet, these counselors have been hampered by the lack of adequate funding. As more people regard mental health as important to themselves and their society, the more accepted and needed counseling becomes.

5. *Counseling is being provided in an increasing variety of settings.* As mentioned above, the acceptance of counseling services is increasing. One reason for this is that these services are being offered in an increasing variety of settings—locations that are more convenient for the clients and, thus, often less threatening than formal, institutional, "clinic-type" settings.

Centers for community activities have provided new locations for counselors. Churches and other religious buildings have been and are being used to provide many community services, including counseling. Storefront public counseling agencies place themselves in the center of their clients' environments. Community centers, which service the needs of senior citizens and retirees, also offer counseling services.

More hospitals are providing counseling services by chaplains, social workers, and hospital staff counselors. These counselors work with patients, their families, and hospital staff—often in the patients' rooms. Agencies such as the American Cancer Society often provide counselors, who visit clients in their homes or in hospital settings.

Young adults are offered counseling services in coffee houses and informal youth centers. Crisis centers and "hot lines" have provided immediate counseling in all types of communities. New and varied counseling programs have been provided for public offenders, for those in jails and on probation.

While recognizing that the traditional formal setting and institutional locations are appropriate to many clients, we applaud the movement of counselors to new locations, "where the action is" for many clients in our diverse population.

6. *Counselors are providing services to an increasing variety of sub-groups within our society.* As counseling opportunities increase in settings outside of our public schools and as training programs prepare more agency and

adult counselors, a greater variety of subgroups within our society are requesting counseling services.

As the number of elderly citizens in our country increases, the field of gerontology gains more attention. Counselors are finding themselves more and more in demand by senior citizens and retirees. Concerns of these clients may include physical health, financial obligations, legal difficulties, relationships with their children and relatives, and employment or service opportunities.

Another counseling concern for many in our population is significant loss. Counselors are working increasingly with terminally ill patients in hospices, in hospitals, and in their homes. Families of these clients are also becoming more involved in counseling, both before and after the death of a family member.

Counselors have become involved to a greater degree with preschool children and their parents. Much of this counseling benefits the parents, as they expand their knowledge of child growth and development and are better able to help their children prepare for school and for life. Families with children at any age are also using counseling as a means to resolve family conflicts and to improve communication patterns within the family.

A subgroup within our society that has received an increasing amount of counseling attention includes those with drug and alcohol problems. Many private and public clinics using a variety of approaches have been established to work directly with this group of clients. The handicapped are also demanding more counseling aid. In particular, physically and emotionally handicapped citizens are helped to adapt to society and employment.

Various ethnic groups, such as blacks and Latinos, have requested counseling services directed to their populations. Many counselors, paraprofessionals, and peer counselors work with these groups in their homes and community centers. Women's groups, whose members have had concerns about their lives and career changes, have increasingly involved counselors. Consciousness-raising and assertiveness-training, although at first geared to women's groups, have now been provided to groups of men as well.

7. *Counselors are working within more narrowly defined areas of concern.* As the previous trend indicated, there are a variety of counseling services needed by diverse groups. Although counselors have been considered generalists who work with personal, emotional, social, and career concerns of all their clients, we find that there is a trend toward specialization on the part of many counselors to meet the specific needs of their clients, either individually or in groups.

There is an increased focus on providing counseling for our aging population. Senior citizens often need specialized counseling regarding retirement plans, financial matters, and housing. Coping with the illness and the death of a family member is not confined to one age group. Counselors are following the guidelines of specialists, such as Kübler-Ross, in working with distressed clients.

Clients with specific concerns about marriage and divorce are able to locate counselors who specialize in these matters. Some family counselors now specialize in such areas as child abuse. Also, many professionals now specialize in counseling rape victims.

The areas of career development and job placement are receiving much attention from some counseling specialists. Clients are asking for help in reviewing their aptitudes and interests and in decision making in regard to career opportunities and employment realities. As part of total career development, the use of leisure time has become more important. Counselors who are able to help clients look at this aspect of their life may find yet another area of specialization.

Anxieties about one's sexuality, sexual development, and performance have led to specialized counseling services that deal with such physical and emotional concerns. Also, there are services that provide counseling to help clients break such habits as smoking, drinking, and disturbed eating patterns. The concept of healthy lifestyle is the focus of holistic counselors.

The examples provided here indicate that some particular knowledge, information, and expertise may be needed to deal with certain clients' concerns. If counselors do not have the necessary information or skills required to deal with a unique concern, they should be ready to refer the client to a counselor who does specialize in that area.

8. *Counselors are being asked to be more accountable for their services.* With the decrease in funding for public agency and school counseling programs, there has been an increased demand for counselors to be held accountable for their activities and to demonstrate their effectiveness. Accountability may range from a detailed accounting of the number of clients seen to a listing of how many students were placed in a college or job setting after high school graduation. Progress reports of counseling effectiveness in clinic settings are also being requested by insurance agents, such as Blue Cross–Blue Shield.

This trend toward accountability has promoted the specialization of some counselors, since it is easier to evaluate attainment of a specific goal. More and more counselors are presenting their services to clients in the form of systematic and programmed approaches—again, for an easier evaluation of activities carried out and progress made.

No longer can counselors speak in generalities when discussing their services. Goal formation and stipulation, as well as performance objectives, are being presented by counselors as justification for their services. We do not disagree with an explicit definition of counseling goals, expectations, and techniques, as long as the client is in agreement. As a matter of fact, this approach might help counselors to be realistic about what they promise clients and themselves.

Further support for this notion of accountability is given in the guidelines provided with governmental or agency funding for counseling. Often a grant is given only after counselors have indicated what their goals are, what techniques will be used, and how the success of their project will be evaluated. Such stipulations are understandable. However, counselors must guard against counseling clients to meet funding goals rather than appropriate goals for the client. Counselors can be asked to be accountable, but they need to remember they are as accountable to their clients and themselves as they are to an institution's regulations or a funding agency's requirements.

9. *Counselors are becoming more directive and assertive.* This trend is directly related to counselor accountability. We believe that counselors are becoming less inclined to allow clients to proceed at their own pace and make decisions based on self-insight and self-understanding.

In a sense, this trend indicates that counselors are more willing to follow a model that moves clients through exploration and understanding to *action,* where action can be observed in behavioral terms and, thus, demonstrate the counselors' effectiveness. This movement toward greater action-orientation might entail greater use of behavioral counseling techniques, such as behavior modification, that changes can be tabulated and seen. This trend is also reflected in research regarding counseling. Much less research is being reported regarding respect, authenticity, and empathy, and more research describes specific counseling techniques and skills.

Counselors are becoming more assertive and less passive, both individually and in professional groups. This action may result from attempts to preserve jobs in the face of agency cutbacks or declining school enrollments. It may come about because counselors are more willing to take stands regarding social and political issues.

Whatever the reason, we applaud the efforts of counselors to speak out in support of their jobs and the worthiness of counseling itself. If we believe in the value of our services and the client gains they make possible, there is no choice but to share these successes with others. The promotion of ourselves and the counseling profession is not unethical; it is appropriate behavior in behalf of our profession.

10. *Counselors are working as consultants and as change agents.* Whether or not counselors should become more active in social issues, there is no question that many counselors in varying job settings are presently working to benefit clients in ways that extend beyond the traditional one-to-one counseling relationship.

As consultants, counselors often work with a third person or a group of people in discussing their clients and ways of aiding them. This can effectively supplement the work done in a one-to-one counseling relationship. This is especially true when clients, such as elementary school children, can benefit from a change in their environment and/or a change in the behavior of significant adults who interact with them. Consulting can aid clients, when others such as teachers and parents are able to share insights with counselors. Individual counseling and consulting activities can supplement one another. Jones and Stewart (1980) and Splete (1982) have described models for consultants to use in promoting organizational change. Often, a counselor serves as an external consultant acting in cooperation with a member of the organization, who serves as the internal consultant.

Counselors have also been working with larger groups and organizations in communities. Lewis and Lewis (1977) indicate that community counseling can be done in any institution or agency setting. This type of counseling tends to foster more cooperation and understanding among counselors from various settings. In addition to providing counseling services and training programs, community counselors are aiding in community planning and development and in formulating and promoting community action for change. This role of the counselor, as a change agent in institutions and communities, is still being developed and more research and experimentation in this area will be helpful in defining the most successful approaches for the counselor.

We believe that work as consultants and change agents can be appropriate for current and future counselors and their clients, especially as they provide additional benefits for those involved with counselors in individual counseling relationships.

11. *Group counseling, as a technique, is being increasingly accepted and used by counselors.* As group counseling has been widely advocated and adopted, an ever-increasing number of counselors are accepting it as an economical use of their time and as an effective way of aiding their clients. The goals of aiding clients to become self-understanding and self-acceptant and to develop self-direction and self-responsibility are the same in both individual and group counseling.

There are additional benefits for many clients who participate in group counseling. These include having the chance to help others as well as oneself, to try out new behaviors with the group and gain their feedback and support, and to gain the understanding and acceptance of members of the group. Thus, individuals can use the group setting as a place to work on their own concerns. While providing guidelines for group counseling, Kottler (1983) indicates that differing facilitative factors impact on an individual's growth in a group. Many approaches and techniques of group counseling and therapy have been promoted. We suggest that counselors be trained in approaches that are appropriate to their needs and their work settings before engaging in any type of group work. If they do not function well as group leaders, they should not work as group counselors.

It should be remembered that not all clients will benefit from group counseling sessions. Counselors have the obligation to meet with clients who are potential group members and discuss the group procedures, so that the clients themselves can decide wisely if they should join.

Often group counseling participants find that individual counseling might be as appropriate or more appropriate for their needs. Counselors might review the various types of counseling available to their clients and then decide with the clients which might be best for them. It could well be that those clients presently in individual counseling might be effectively aided through group counseling or through a combination of group and individual counseling. In effect, group counseling may no longer be considered a trend, but a relatively well established approach.

12. *Counselors are training others in the use of counseling and related skills.* Rather than being the only provider of counseling skills, formally trained counselors are teaching others basic counseling and helping skills. Teachers, parents, students, paraprofessionals, and community helpers are among those being trained by counselors.

Carkhuff (1980) has advocated the use of a systematic training model to teach helping skills to all types of populations. He has demonstrated its effectiveness through its use by counselors who have been trained to teach others. In many instances, students have learned counseling skills in order to serve as peer counselors in school and community settings. Parents have also been trained by counselors in basic helping skills that allow them to communicate more effectively with their children and with their marriage partners. Gordon (1975) has provided models for effective communication for parents, teachers, administrators, and students.

Counselors who work with paraprofessionals and volunteers have trained them in basic counseling skills, such as attending, listening, and responding, and in methods of formulating and implementing community action projects. Brammer (1979), and Lewis and Lewis (1977) have provided information and methodology for counselors to use in training these helpers.

It is important that counselors carefully select these participants for training in counseling skills and that they continue to aid these helpers after their training by follow-up activities and supervision in field settings. These helpers, whether youths or adults, need to be accepted by counselors and regarded as members of the total mental health team in our society.

13. *Computerized technology and audio-visual aids will be increasingly used by counselors.* Counselors have often tried to be encyclopedias of information by providing their clients with data about educational and occupational opportunities, employment openings, referral agencies, and other counseling programs. Counselors have often been burdened with the clerical duties of record keeping, storage, and retrieval. Automation has aided and will continue to aid counselors in dealing with these tasks.

In many institutions, record keeping has been a tremendous problem, and often counselors have been charged with personally maintaining all of their clients' records. Computers now have the capability of storing and retrieving basic data about clients. Granted that the counselors' confidential material should not be stored in the computer's data bank, much pertinent information about clients can be readily stored and retrieved. We see that more and more institutions are using computerized data banks for information storage and record keeping.

Information regarding educational and occupational opportunities and current employment openings is now available in the form of films, cassettes, and computer printouts as well as at computer terminals that have access to computerized programs. Microcomputers also provide this information in personalized formats.

State employment agencies use computerized programs to predict employment trends and provide current job openings for their clients. As more of these programs are developed, there will be a need to coordinate these various programs and to share educational and career information and data among various agencies and institutions.

Computerized programs, such as the Computerized Vocational Information Systems (CVIS) and the Educational Career Exploration System (ECES), provide current data to clients as they review possibilities for themselves in terms of their personal backgrounds, the educational and training requirements for occupations, and the current and future employment outlook. Microfilm information, as used in the Vital Information for Education and Work (VIEW) program, films, and audio and video cassettes can provide basic information for clients. Microcomputer programs, such as DISCOVER II and SIGI, allow clients to access information that can be discussed and interpreted with counselors in individual or group sessions.

It should be noted that computers, films, and cassettes cannot do the counseling. Counselors may find that demands for their time increase due to the use of these programs by clients. Clients need to work with counselors in discussing the information gained and its personal relevance to them. Individual and group counseling supplement the use of this technology by clients.

In addition to using computers and related technology for such tasks as keeping records and providing information, counselors are finding that the use of audio- and videotapes with clients has been effective. A pioneering effort of this type of procedure, Interpersonal Process Recall, is described by Kagan et al. (1965); the counselor and client review video-tapes of their counseling sessions and share and explore further concerns based on these reviews.

As our technology continues to develop, further applications to the counseling profession, its services, and the actual counseling process itself will be found. Counselors will need to stay informed about these developments and to use technological aids that are appropriate for their clients and their situations.

14. *Counselor training and preparation programs will be extended and become more rigorous.* The increasing demand for counseling services and growing emphasis on counselor accountability put pressure on counselor training programs to produce high quality counselors who can meet increasingly higher standards and qualify for licensure. We applaud the efforts of counselor training programs to meet this need.

The background of prospective counselors admitted to counselor training programs is increasingly reflecting more undergraduate work in the behavioral sciences and, in many instances, an undergraduate degree in guidance or in human resources development. With this type of background, more can be expected of graduate students in counselor training programs.

Masters programs are being extended from one year to two. This longer time frame allows more emphasis on the attainment and practice of basic counseling skills. Counselors-in-training are taking more counseling techniques, process, and practicum courses. The increased length of the program also provides for extended internship hours under professional supervision.

We feel that counselors-in-training should have the option to specialize in certain areas in the latter part of this extended program. For example, potential counselors could develop extended expertise in marriage and family counseling, career counseling, health services counseling, or counseling the aging.

Support for this movement is being provided by the AACD's accreditation of counselor education programs and its National Board for Certified Counselors examination, for which counselors need extensive graduate school preparation. This trend toward more rigorous counselor training can only benefit our profession and the clients it serves.

Summary

In this chapter we have reviewed eleven issues and fourteen trends facing counselors at this time. Several issues are related to present trends in our society and the counseling field.

We see counselors becoming more active and involved in meeting the needs of clients in various ways and in a greater number and variety of settings. Counselors are confronted with some difficult decisions regarding (1) funding for their programs, (2) provision of effective counseling services in the mental health field at *all* levels, and (3) cooperation among counselors in various settings.

Our society continues to change in terms of its employment opportunities for counselors and related expectations of counselors. The general public is more accepting of counseling services and will be asking for more of them. Along with this increased demand will come expectations for more action on the part of counselors and for constructive behavioral change on the part of the clients.

Now, more than ever, it is a good time for counselors to prove themselves by providing effective services to their clients. Each individual counselor needs to recognize the current issues and trends in our society, especially as they relate to his or her own personal position and action in response to them.

Counselors do have a significant impact on our society and its citizens. We can continue to aid others in the future as we remain in touch with our colleagues, our clients and their worlds, ourselves, and the ever present influences of current issues and trends. Through our counseling activities, which respond to our various clients and our changing society, we can grow personally and professionally to meet the exciting and demanding challenges that are part of the daily world of counseling.

The major points of this chapter were as follows:

1. Counselors need to determine their own roles as role definitions structure counselor activities.
2. Counselor training needs to include self-awareness and knowledge of and experience in generic and specific counseling approaches and techniques.
3. Counselors need to be aware of the potential counseling services of paraprofessionals and volunteers.
4. Counselors should be knowledgeable about social issues and the need for funding for counseling programs.
5. Increasing population shifts and new patterns in job mobility and change need to be recognized by counselors.
6. Career counseling is assuming renewed importance.
7. Counseling is becoming more accepted by the public.
8. Counselors are working in a variety of settings with a variety of clients.
9. Counselors are becoming more accountable, more assertive, and are working more with specific areas of client concern.
10. Counselors are working as consultants and trainers.
11. Counselors are increasingly using group work and computerized technology.
12. Counselor preparation and training programs are extending the amount of time required and are formulating higher standards for their students.

References

American Association for Counseling and Development. "Funding Support for Counselors." *Guidepost* (1983):1.

Brammer, Lawrence. *The Helping Relationship, Process and Skills.* Englewood Cliffs, N.J.: Prentice-Hall, 1979.

Carkhuff, Robert. *The Art of Helping.* Vol. IV. Amherst, Mass.: Human Resource Development Press, 1980.

Dinkmeyer, Donald. *Developing Understanding of Self and Others.* Rev. ed. Circle Pines, Minn.: American Guidance Service, Inc., 1983.

Gordon, Thomas. *Parent Effectiveness Training.* New York: Plume Books, New American Library, 1975.

Guidepost. APGA Newsletter, vol. 25, no. 10, January 27, 1983, p. 1.

Jones, Michael, and Norman Stewart. "Helping the Environment Help the Client: A Sequenced Change Process," *Personnel and Guidance Journal* 58 (1980):501–506.

Kagan, Norman, David Krathwohl, and William Farquhar. *Interpersonal Process Recall: Stimulated Recall by Videotape.* Educational Research Series, No. 24. East Lansing: Michigan State University, 1965.

Kottler, Jeffrey. *Pragmatic Group Leadership.* Monterey, Calif.: Brooks/Cole, 1983.

Lewis, Judith, and Michael Lewis. *Community Counseling, A Human Services Approach.* New York: Wiley, 1977.

Peck, Hugh, and Billie Jackson. "Do We Make a Difference? A State Education." *Elementary School Guidance and Counseling* 10 (1976):171–176.

Splete, Howard H. "Consultation by the Counselor." *Counseling and Human Development* 15 (1982):1–7.

Super, Donald, and Edward Knasel. "Career Development in Adulthood: Some Theoretical Problems and a Possible Solution," *British Journal of Guidance and Counseling* 9 (1981):192–201.

APPENDICES

Appendix A   Ethical Standards

American Association for Counseling and Development

Preamble
The Association is an educational, scientific, and professional organization whose members are dedicated to the enhancement of the worth, dignity, potential, and uniqueness of each individual and thus to the service of society.

The Association recognizes that the role definitions and work settings of its members include a wide variety of academic disciplines, levels of academic preparation and agency services. This diversity reflects the breadth of the Association's interest and influence. It also poses challenging complexities in efforts to set standards for the performance of members, desired requisite preparation or practice, and supporting social, legal, and ethical controls.

The specification of ethical standards enables the Association to clarify to present and future members and to those served by members, the nature of ethical responsibilities held in common by its members.

The existence of such standards serves to stimulate greater concern by members for their own professional functioning and for the conduct of fellow professionals such as counselors, guidance and student personnel workers, and others in the helping professions. As the ethical code of the Association, this document establishes principles that define the ethical behavior of Association members.

Section A: General
1. The member influences the development of the profession by continuous efforts to improve professional practices, teaching, services, and research. Professional growth is continuous throughout the member's career and is exemplified by the development of a philosophy that explains why and how a member functions in the helping relationship. Members must gather data on their effectiveness and be guided by the findings.

2. The member has a responsibility both to the individual who is served and to the institution within which the service is performed to maintain high standards of professional conduct. The member strives to maintain the highest levels of professional services offered to the individuals to be served. The member also strives to assist the agency, organization, or institution in providing the highest caliber of professional services. The acceptance of employment in an institution implies that the member is in agreement with the general policies and principles of the institution. Therefore the professional activities of the member are also in accord with the objectives of the institution. If, despite concerted efforts, the member can-

Source: AACD Code of Ethics, approved by Executive Committee upon referral of the Board of Directors, January 17, 1981. Reprinted by permission of the American Association for Counseling and Development.

not reach agreement with the employer as to acceptable standards of conduct that allow for changes in institutional policy conducive to the positive growth and development of clients, then terminating the affiliation should be seriously considered.

3. Ethical behavior among professional associates, both members and nonmembers, must be expected at all times. When information is possessed that raises doubt as to the ethical behavior of professional colleagues, whether Association members or not, the member must take action to attempt to rectify such a condition. Such action shall use the institution's channels first and then use procedures established by the state Branch, Division, or Association.

4. The member neither claims nor implies professional qualifications exceeding those possessed and is responsible for correcting any misrepresentations of these qualifications by others.

5. In establishing fees for professional counseling services, members must consider the financial status of clients and locality. In the event that the established fee structure is inappropriate for a client, assistance must be provided in finding comparable services of acceptable cost.

6. When members provide information to the public or to subordinates, peers or supervisors, they have a responsibility to ensure that the content is general, unidentified client information that is accurate, unbiased, and consists of objective, factual data.

7. With regard to the delivery of professional services, members should accept only those positions for which they are professionally qualified.

8. In the counseling relationship the counselor is aware of the intimacy of the relationship and maintains respect for the client and avoids engaging in activities that seek to meet the counselor's personal needs at the expense of that client. Through awareness of the negative impact of both racial and sexual stereotyping and discrimination, the counselor guards the individual rights and personal dignity of the client in the counseling relationship.

Section B:
Counseling
Relationship

This section refers to practices and procedures of individual and/or group counseling relationships.

The member must recognize the need for client freedom of choice. Under those circumstances where this is not possible, the member must apprise clients of restrictions that may limit their freedom of choice.

1. The member's *primary* obligation is to respect the integrity and promote the welfare of the client(s), whether the client(s) is (are) assisted individually or in a group relationship. In a group setting, the member is also responsible for taking reasonable precautions to protect individuals from physical and/or psychological trauma resulting from interaction within the group.

2. The counseling relationship and information resulting therefrom must be kept confidential, consistent with the obligations of the member as a professional person. In a group counseling setting, the counselor must set a norm of confidentiality regarding all group participants' disclosures.

3. If an individual is already in a counseling relationship with another professional person, the member does not enter into a counseling relationship without first contacting and receiving the approval of that other professional. If the member discovers that the client is in another counseling relationship after the counseling relationship begins, the member must gain the consent of the other professional or terminate the relationship, unless the client elects to terminate the other relationship.

4. When the client's condition indicates that there is clear and imminent danger to the client or others, the member must take reasonable personal action or inform responsible authorities. Consultation with other professionals must be used where possible. The assumption of responsibility for the client(s) behavior must be taken only after careful deliberation. The client must be involved in the resumption of responsibility as quickly as possible.

5. Records of the counseling relationship, including interview notes, test data, correspondence, tape recordings, and other documents, are to be considered professional information for use in counseling and they should not be considered a part of the records of the institution or agency in which the counselor is employed unless specified by state statute or regulation. Revelation to others of counseling material must occur only upon the expressed consent of the client.

6. Use of data derived from a counseling relationship for purposes of counselor training or research shall be confined to content that can be disguised to ensure full protection of the identity of the subject client.

7. The member must inform the client of the purposes, goals, techniques, rules of procedure and limitations that may affect the relationship at or before the time that the counseling relationship is entered.

8. The member must screen prospective group participants, especially when the emphasis is on self-understanding and growth through self-disclosure. The member must maintain an awareness of the group participants' compatibility throughout the life of the group.

9. The member may choose to consult with any other professionally competent person about a client. In choosing a consultant, the member must avoid placing the consultant in a conflict of interest situation that would preclude the consultant's being a proper party to the member's efforts to help the client.

10. If the member determines an inability to be of professional assistance to the client, the member must either avoid initiating the counseling relationship or immediately terminate that relationship. In either event, the member must suggest appropriate alternatives. (The member must be knowledgeable about referral resources so that a satisfactory referral can be initiated). In the event the client declines the suggested referral, the member is not obligated to continue the relationship.

11. When the member has other relationships, particularly of an administrative, supervisory and/or evaluative nature with an individual seeking counseling services, the member must not serve as the counselor but should refer the individual to another professional. Only in instances where such an alternative is unavailable and where the individual's situation warrants counseling intervention should the member enter into and/or maintain a counseling relationship. Dual relationships

with clients that might impair the member's objectivity and professional judgment (e.g., as with close friends or relatives, sexual intimacies with any client) must be avoided and/or the counseling relationship terminated through referral to another competent professional.

12. All experimental methods of treatment must be clearly indicated to prospective recipients and safety precautions are to be adhered to by the member.

13. When the member is engaged in short-term group treatment/training programs (e.g., marathons and other encounter-type or growth groups), the member ensures that there is professional assistance available during and following the group experience.

14. Should the member be engaged in a work setting that calls for any variation from the above statements, the member is obligated to consult with other professionals whenever possible to consider justifiable alternatives.

Section C: Measurement and Evaluation

The primary purpose of educational and psychological testing is to provide descriptive measures that are objective and interpretable in either comparative or absolute terms. The member must recognize the need to interpret the statements that follow as applying to the whole range of appraisal techniques including test and nontest data. Test results constitute only one of a variety of pertinent sources of information for personnel, guidance, and counseling decisions.

1. The member must provide specific orientation or information to the examinee(s) prior to and following the test administration so that the results of testing may be placed in proper perspective with other relevant factors. In so doing, the member must recognize the effects of socioeconomic, ethnic and cultural factors on test scores. It is the member's professional responsibility to use additional unvalidated information carefully in modifying interpretation of the test results.

2. In selecting tests for use in a given situation or with a particular client, the member must consider carefully the specific validity, reliability, and appropriateness of the test(s). *General* validity, reliability and the like may be questioned legally as well as ethically when tests are used for vocational and educational selection, placement, or counseling.

3. When making any statements to the public about tests and testing, the member must give accurate information and avoid false claims or misconceptions. Special efforts are often required to avoid unwarranted connotations of such terms as *IQ* and *grade equivalent scores.*

4. Different tests demand different levels of competence for administration, scoring, and interpretation. Members must recognize the limits of their competence and perform only those functions for which they are prepared.

5. Tests must be administered under the same conditions that were established in their standardization. When tests are not administered under standard conditions or when unusual behavior or irregularities occur during the testing session, those conditions must be noted and the results designated as invalid or of questionable validity. Unsupervised or inadequately supervised test-taking, such as the use of tests through the mails, is considered unethical. On the other hand, the use of instruments that are so designed or standardized to be self-administered and self-scored, such as interest inventories, is to be encouraged.

6. The meaningfulness of test results used in personnel, guidance, and counseling functions generally depends on the examinee's unfamiliarity with the specific items on the test. Any prior coaching or dissemination of the test materials can invalidate test results. Therefore, test security is one of the professional obligations of the member. Conditions that produce most favorable test results must be made known to the examinee.

7. The purpose of testing and the explicit use of the results must be made known to the examinee prior to testing. The counselor must ensure that instrument limitations are not exceeded and that periodic review and/or retesting are made to prevent client stereotyping.

8. The examinee's welfare and explicit prior understanding must be the criteria for determining the recipients of the test results. The member must see that specific interpretation accompanies any release of individual or group test data. The interpretation of test data must be related to the examiner's particular concerns.

9. The member must be cautious when interpreting the results of research instruments possessing insufficient technical data. The specific purposes for the use of such instruments must be stated explicitly to examinees.

10. The member must proceed with caution when attempting to evaluate and interpret the performance of minority group members or other persons who are not represented in the norm group on which the instrument was standardized.

11. The member must guard against the appropriation, reproduction, or modifications of published tests or parts thereof without acknowledgment and permission from the previous publisher.

12. Regarding the preparation, publication and distribution of tests, reference should be made to:

a. *Standards for Educational and Psychological Tests and Manuals,* revised edition, 1974, published by the American Psychological Association on behalf of itself, the American Educational Research Association and the National Council on Measurement in Education.

b. The responsible use of tests: A position paper of AMEG, APGA, and NCME. *Measurement and Evaluation in Guidance,* 1972, 5, 385–388.

c. "Responsibilities of Users of Standardized Tests," APGA, *Guidepost,* October 5, 1978, pp. 5–8.

Section D: Research and Publication

1. Guidelines on research with human subjects shall be adhered to, such as:

a. *Ethical Principles in the Conduct of Research with Human Participants,* Washington, D.C.: American Psychological Association, Inc., 1973.

b. Code of Federal Regulations, Title 45, Subtitle A, Part 46, as currently issued.

2. In planning any research activity dealing with human subjects, the member must be aware of and responsive to all pertinent ethical principles and ensure that the research problem, design, and execution are in full compliance with them.

3. Responsibility for ethical research practice lies with the principal researcher, while others involved in the research activities share ethical obligation and full responsibility for their own actions.

4. In research with human subjects, researchers are responsible for the subjects' welfare throughout the experiment and they must take all reasonable precautions to avoid causing injurious psychological, physical, or social effects on their subjects.

5. All research subjects must be informed of the purpose of the study except when withholding information or providing misinformation to them is essential to the investigation. In such research the member must be responsible for corrective action as soon as possible following completion of the research.

6. Participation in research must be voluntary. Involuntary participation is appropriate only when it can be demonstrated that participation will have no harmful effects on subjects and is essential to the investigation.

7. When reporting research results, explicit mention must be made of all variables and conditions known to the investigator that might affect the outcome of the investigation or the interpretation of the data.

8. The member must be responsible for conducting and reporting investigations in a manner that minimizes the possibility that results will be misleading.

9. The member has an obligation to make available sufficient original research data to qualified others who may wish to replicate the study.

10. When supplying data, aiding in the research of another person, reporting research results, or in making original data available, due care must be taken to disguise the identity of the subjects in the absence of specific authorization from such subjects to do otherwise.

11. When conducting and reporting research, the member must be familiar with, and give recognition to, previous work on the topic, as well as to observe all copyright laws and follow the principles of giving full credit to all to whom credit is due.

12. The member must give due credit through joint authorship, acknowledgment, footnote statements, or other appropriate means to those who have contributed significantly to the research and/or publication, in accordance with such contributions.

13. The member must communicate to other members the results of any research judged to be of professional or scientific value. Results reflecting unfavorably on institutions, programs, services, or vested interests must not be withheld for such reasons.

14. If members agree to cooperate with another individual in research and/or publication, they incur an obligation to cooperate as promised in terms of punctuality of performance and with full regard to the completeness and accuracy of the information required.

15. Ethical practice requires that authors not submit the same manuscript or one essentially similar in content, for simultaneous publication consideration by two or more journals. In addition, manuscripts published in whole or in substantial part, in another journal or published work should not be submitted for publication without acknowledgment and permission from the previous publication.

Section E: Consulting   *Consultation* refers to a voluntary relationship between a professional helper and help-needing individual, group or social unit in which the consultant is providing help to the client(s) in defining and solving a work-related problem or potential problem with a client or client system. (This definition is adapted from Kurpius, DeWayne. Consultation theory and process: An integrated model. *Personnel and Guidance Journal,* 1978, 56.)

1. The member acting as consultant must have a high degree of self-awareness of his/her own values, knowledge, skills, limitations, and needs in entering a helping relationship that involves human and/or organizational change and that the focus of the relationship be on the issues to be resolved and not on the person(s) presenting the problem.

2. There must be understanding and agreement between member and client for the problem definition, change goals, and predicated consequences of interventions selected.

3. The member must be reasonably certain that she/he or the organization represented has the necessary competencies and resources for giving the kind of help that is needed now or may develop later and that appropriate referral resources are available to the consultant.

4. The consulting relationship must be one in which client adaptability and growth toward self-direction are encouraged and cultivated. The member must maintain this role consistently and not become a decision maker for the client or create a future dependency on the consultant.

5. When announcing consultant availability for services, the member conscientiously adheres to the Association's *Ethical Standards.*

6. The member must refuse a private fee or other remuneration for consultation with persons who are entitled to these services through the member's employing institution or agency. The policies of a particular agency may make explicit provisions for private practice with agency clients by members of its staff. In such instances, the clients must be apprised of other options open to them should they seek private counseling services.

Section F:
Private Practice

1. The member should assist the profession by facilitating the availability of counseling services in private as well as public settings.

2. In advertising services as a private practitioner, the member must advertise the services in such a manner so as to accurately inform the public as to services, expertise, profession, and techniques of counseling in a professional manner. A member who assumes an executive leadership role in the organization shall not permit his/her name to be used in professional notices during periods when not actively engaged in the private practice of counseling.

The member may list the following: highest relevant degree, type and level of certification or license, type and/or description of services, and other relevant information. Such information must not contain false, inaccurate, misleading, partial, out-of-context, or deceptive material or statements.

3. Members may join in partnership/corporation with other members and/or other professionals provided that each member of the partnership or corporation makes clear the separate specialities by name in compliance with the regulations of the locality.

4. A member has an obligation to withdraw from a counseling relationship if it is believed that employment will result in violation of the *Ethical Standards.* If the mental or physical condition of the member renders it difficult to carry out an effective professional relationship or if the member is discharged by the client because the counseling relationship is no longer productive for the client, then the member is obligated to terminate the counseling relationship.

5. A member must adhere to the regulations for private practice of the locality where the services are offered.

6. It is unethical to use one's institutional affiliation to recruit clients for one's private practice.

Section G:
Personnel
Administration

It is recognized that most members are employed in public or quasi-public institutions. The functioning of a member within an institution must contribute to the goals of the institution and vice versa if either is to accomplish their respective goals or objectives. It is therefore essential that the member and the institution function in ways to (a) make the institution's goals explicit and public; (b) make the member's contribution to institutional goals specific; and (c) foster mutual accountability for goal achievement.

To accomplish these objectives, it is recognized that the member and the employer must share responsibilities in the formulation and implementation of personnel policies.

1. Members must define and describe the parameters and levels of their professional competency.

2. Members must establish interpersonal relations and working agreements with supervisors and subordinates regarding counseling or clinical relationships, confidentiality, distinction between public and private material, maintenance, and dissemination of recorded information, work load and accountability. Working agreements in each instance must be specified and made known to those concerned.

3. Members must alert their employers to conditions that may be potentially disruptive or damaging.

4. Members must inform employers of conditions that may limit their effectiveness.

5. Members must submit regularly to professional review and evaluation.

6. Members must be responsible for inservice development of self and/or staff.

7. Members must inform their staff of goals and programs.

8. Members must provide personnel practices that guarantee and enhance the rights and welfare of each recipient of their service.

9. Members must select competent persons and assign responsibilities compatible with their skills and experiences.

Section H:
Preparation
Standards

Members who are responsible for training others must be guided by the preparation standards of the Association and relevant Division(s). The member who functions in the capacity of trainer assumes unique ethical responsibilities that frequently go beyond that of the member who does not function in a training capacity. These ethical responsibilities are outlined as follows:

1. Members must orient students to program expectations, basic skills development, and employment prospects prior to admission to the program.

2. Members in charge of learning experiences must establish programs that integrate academic study and supervised practice.

3. Members must establish a program directed toward developing students' skills, knowledge, and self-understanding, stated whenever possible in competency or performance terms.

4. Members must identify the levels of competencies of their students in compliance with relevant Division standards. These competencies must accommodate the para-professional as well as the professional.

5. Members, through continual student evaluation and appraisal, must be aware of the personal limitations of the learner that might impede future performance. The instructor must not only assist the learner in securing remedial assistance but also screen from the program those individuals who are unable to provide competent services.

6. Members must provide a program that includes training in research commensurate with levels of role functioning. Para-professional and technician-level personnel must be trained as consumers of research. In addition, these personnel must learn how to evaluate their own and their program's effectiveness. Graduate training, especially at the doctoral level, would include preparation for original research by the member.

7. Members must make students aware of the ethical responsibilities and standards of the profession.

8. Preparatory programs must encourage students to value the ideals of service to individuals and to society. In this regard, direct financial remuneration or lack thereof must not influence the quality of service rendered. Monetary considerations must not be allowed to overshadow professional and humanitarian needs.

9. Members responsible for educational programs must be skilled as teachers and practitioners.

10. Members must present thoroughly varied theoretical positions so that students may make comparisons and have the opportunity to select a position.

11. Members must develop clear policies within their educational institutions regarding field placement and the roles of the student and the instructor in such placements.

12. Members must ensure that forms of learning focusing on self-understanding or growth are voluntary, or if required as part of the education program, are made known to prospective students prior to entering the program. When the education program offers a growth experience with an emphasis on self-disclosure or other relatively intimate or personal involvement, the member must have no administrative, supervisory, or evaluating authority regarding the participant.

13. Members must conduct an educational program in keeping with the current relevant guidelines of the Association and its Divisions.

Appendix B   Ethical Guidelines for Group Leaders

Preamble   One characteristic of any professional group is the possession of a body of knowledge and skills and mutually acceptable ethical standards for putting them into practice. Ethical standards consist of those principles which have been formally and publicly acknowledged by the membership of a profession to serve as guidelines governing professional conduct, discharge of duties, and resolution of moral dilemmas. In this document, the Association for Specialists in Group Work has identified the standards of conduct necessary to maintain and regulate the high standards of integrity and leadership among its members.

The Association for Specialists in Group Work recognizes the basic commitment of its members to the Ethical Standards of its parent organization, the American Personnel & Guidance Association and nothing in this document shall be construed to supplant that code. These standards are intended to complement the APGA standards in the area of group work by clarifying the nature of ethical responsibility of the counselor in the group setting and by stimulating a greater concern for competent group leadership.

The following ethical guidelines have been organized under three categories: the leader's responsibility for providing information about group work to clients, the group leader's responsibility for providing group counseling services to clients, and the group leader's responsibility for safeguarding the standards of ethical practice.

A.   Responsibility for Providing Information About Group Work and Group Services

A-1. Group leaders shall fully inform group members, in advance and preferably in writing, of the goals in the group, qualifications of the leader, and procedures to be employed.

A-2. The group leader shall conduct a pre-group interview with each prospective member for purposes of screening, orientation, and, in so far as possible, shall select group members whose needs and goals are compatible with the established goals of the group; who will not impede the group process; and whose well-being will not be jeopardized by the group experience.

A-3. Group leaders shall protect members by defining clearly what confidentiality means, why it is important, and the difficulties involved in enforcement.

A-4. Group leaders shall explain, as realistically as possible, exactly what services can and cannot be provided within the particular group structure offered.

A-5. Group leaders shall provide prospective clients with specific information about any specialized or experimental activities in which they may be expected to participate.

Source: Published by the Association for Specialists in Group Work (ASGW), a division of the American Association for Counseling and Development. Approved by the ASGW Executive Board, November 11, 1980. Reprinted by permission of the American Association for Counseling and Development.

A-6. Group leaders shall stress the personal risks involved in any group, especially regarding potential life-changes, and help group members explore their readiness to face these risks.

A-7. Group leaders shall inform members that participation is voluntary and that they may exit from the group at any time.

A-8. Group leaders shall inform members about recording of sessions and how tapes will be used.

B. Responsibility for Providing Group Services to Clients

B-1. Group leaders shall protect member rights against physical threats, intimidation, coercion, and undue peer pressure insofar as is reasonably possible.

B-2. Group leaders shall refrain from imposing their own agendas, needs, and values on group members.

B-3. Group leaders shall insure to the extent that it is reasonably possible that each member has the opportunity to utilize group resources and interact within the group by minimizing barriers such as rambling and monopolizing time.

B-4. Group leaders shall make every reasonable effort to treat each member individually and equally.

B-5. Group leaders shall abstain from inappropriate personal relationships with members throughout the duration of the group and any subsequent professional involvement.

B-6. Group leaders shall help promote independence of members from the group in the most efficient period of time.

B-7. Group leaders shall not attempt any technique unless thoroughly trained in its use or under supervision by an expert familiar with the intervention.

B-8. Group leaders shall not condone the use of alcohol or drugs directly prior to or during group sessions.

B-9. Group leaders shall make every effort to assist clients in developing their personal goals.

B-10. Group leaders shall provide between-session consultation to group members and follow-up after termination of the group, as needed or requested.

C. Responsibility for Safeguarding Ethical Practice

C-1. Group leaders shall display these standards or make them available to group members.

C-2. Group leaders have the right to expect ethical behavior from colleagues and are obligated to rectify or disclose incompetent, unethical behavior demonstrated by a colleague by taking the following actions:

(a) To confront the individual with the apparent violation of ethical guidelines for the purposes of protecting the safety of any clients and to help the group leader correct any inappropriate behaviors.

(b) Such a complaint should be made in writing including the specific facts *and dates* of the alleged violation and all relevant supporting data. The complaint should be forwarded to:

The Ethics Committee,
c/o The President
Association of Specialists in Group Work

Two Skyline Place, Suite 400
5203 Leesburg Pike
Falls Church, Virginia 22041

The envelope must be marked "CONFIDENTIAL" in order to assure confidentiality for both the accuser(s) and the alleged violator(s). Upon receipt, the President shall (a) check on membership status of the charged member(s), (b) confer with legal counsel, and (c) send the case with all pertinent documents to the chairperson of the ASGW Ethics Committee within ten (10) working days after the receipt of the complaint.

(c) If it is determined by the Ethics and Professional Standards Committee that the alleged breach of ethical conduct constitutes a violation of the "Ethical Guidelines," then an investigation will be started within ten (10) days by at least one member of the Committee plus two additional ASGW members in the locality of the alleged violation. The investigating committee chairperson shall: (a) acknowledge receipt of the complaint, (b) review the complaint and supporting data, (c) send a letter of acknowledgement to the member(s) of the complaint regarding alleged violations along with a request for a response and relevant information related to the complaint and (e) inform members of the Ethics Committee by letter of the case and present a plan of action for investigation.

(d) All information, correspondence, and activities of the Ethics Committee will remain confidential. It shall be determined that no person serving as an investigator on a case have any disqualifying relationship with the alleged violator(s).

(e) The charged party(ies) will have not more than 30 days in which to answer the charges in writing. The charged party(ies) will have free access to all cited evidence from which to make a defense, including the right to legal counsel and a formal hearing before the ASGW Ethics Committee.

(f) Based upon the investigation of the Committee and any designated local ASGW members one of the following recommendations may be made to the Executive Board for appropriate action:

1. Advise that the charges be dropped.

2. Reprimand and admonishment against repetition of the charged conduct.

3. Notify the charged member(s) of his/her right to a formal hearing before the ASGW Ethics Committee, and request a response be made to the Ethics Chairperson as to his/her decision on the matter. Such hearing would be conducted in accordance with the APGA Policy and Procedures for Processing Complaints of Ethical Violations, "Procedures for Hearings," and would be scheduled for a time coinciding with the annual APGA convention. Conditions for such hearing shall also be in accordance with the APGA Policy and Procedures document, "Options Available to the Ethics Committee, item 3."

4. Suspension of membership for a specified period from ASGW.

5. Dismissal from membership in ASGW.

Appendix C   General Relaxation Instructions

Begin by getting as comfortable as you can.* Settle back comfortably. Just try to let go of all the tension in your body. Now take in a deep breath. Breathe right in and hold it (five-second pause). And now exhale. Just let the air out quite automatically and feel a calmer feeling beginning to develop. Now just carry on breathing normally and just concentrate on feeling heavy all over in a pleasant way. Study your own body heaviness. This should give you a calm and reassuring feeling all over (ten-second pause). Now let us work on tension and relaxation contrasts. Try to tense every muscle in your body. Every muscle: your jaws, tighten your eyes, your shoulder muscles, your arms, chest, back, stomach, legs, every part just tensing and tensing. Feel the tension all over your body—tighter and tighter—tensing everywhere, and now let it go, just stop tensing and relax. Try to feel this wave of calm that comes over you as you stop tensing like that. A definite wave of calm (ten-second pause).

Now I want you to notice the contrast between the slight tensions that are there when your eyes are open and the disappearance of these surface tensions as you close your eyes. So while relaxing the rest of your body just open your eyes and feel the surface tensions which will disappear when you close your eyes. Now close your eyes and feel the greater degree of relaxation with your eyes closed (ten-second pause) all right, let us get back to the breathing. Keep your eyes closed and take in a deep, deep breath and hold it. Now relax the rest of your body as well as you can and notice the tension from holding your breath. Study the tension. Now let out your breath and feel the deepening relaxation—just go with it beautifully relaxing now. Breathe normally and just feel the relaxation flowing into your forehead and scalp. Think of each part as I call it out—just relaxing—just letting go, easing up, eyes and nose, facial muscles. You might feel a tingling sensation as the relaxation flows in. You might have a warm sensation. Whatever you feel I want you to notice it and enjoy it to the full as the relaxation now spreads very beautifully into the face, into the lips, jaws, tongue, and mouth so that your lips are slightly parted as the jaw muscles relax further and further. The throat and neck relaxing (five-second pause), shoulders and upper back relaxing, further and further, feel the relaxation flowing into your arms and to the very tips of your fingers (five-second pause). Feel the relaxation in your chest as you breathe regularly and easily. The relaxation spreads even under your armpits and down your sides, right into the stomach area. The relaxation becomes more and more obvious as you do nothing but just give way to the pleasant serene emotions which fill you as you let go more and more. Feel the relaxation—stomach and lower back all the way through in a warm, penetrating, wavy, calm and down your hips, buttocks, and thighs to the very, very tips of your toes. The waves of relaxation just travel down your calves to your ankles and toes. Feel relaxed from head to

*Source: Arnold A. Lazarus, *Behavior Therapy & Beyond* (New York: McGraw-Hill, 1971), pp. 273–75. Reprinted by permission.

toe. Each time you practice this you should find a deeper level of relaxation being achieved—a deeper serenity and calm, a good calm feeling.

Now to increase the feelings of relaxation at this point what I want you to do is just keep on relaxing and each time you exhale, each time you breathe out for the next minute, I want you to think the word *relax* to yourself. Just think the word *relax* as you breathe out. Now just do that for the next minute (one-minute pause). Okay, just feel that deeper relaxation and carry on relaxing. You should feel a deeper, deeper feeling of relaxation. To even further increase the benefits, I want you to feel the emotional calm, those tranquil and serene feelings which tend to cover you all over inside and out, a feeling of safe security, a calm indifference—these are the feelings which relaxation will enable you to capture more and more effectively each time you practice a relaxation sequence. Relaxation will let you arrive at feeling a quiet inner confidence—a good feeling about yourself (five-second pause). Now once more feel the heavy sensations that accompany relaxation as your muscles switch off so that you feel in good contact with your environment, nicely together, the heavy good feeling of feeling yourself calm and secure and very, very tranquil and serene.

Now we can deepen the relaxation still further by just using some very special stimulus words. Let's use the words *calm* and *serene*. What I would like you to do is to think these words to yourself twenty times or so. Don't bother to count. Approximately twenty or thirty times just say to yourself *calm* and *serene* and then feel the deepening—ever, ever deepening—waves of relaxation as you feel so much more calm and serene. Now you just do that: take your time, think of the words and feel the sensation over and over (pause of about one minute). Good.

Now I am going to count backward from 10 to 1. At the count of 5 I would like you to open your eyes, and then by the time I reach 1, just kind of stretch and yawn and then you can switch off the recorder and just go back and relax on your own. Okay, now counting backward: 10, 9, 8, 7, 6, 5, open your eyes 4, 3, 2, and 1. Now just stretch and kind of yawn and then slowly get up and switch off the recorder and then you can go back and carry on relaxing as long as you wish.

Author Index

Subject Index

Suppression, 80
Sympathy, vs. empathy, 233, 237
Systemic thinking, 393–395. *See also* Family systems
System of Interactive Guidance and Information (SIGI), 431, 499
Systems counseling, 390–395
Systems theory, 383–387, 390

T-groups, 371–372
"Talking cure," 78. *See also* Psychoanalysis
Task groups, 372–373, 380
Taylor Manifest Anxiety, 248
Termination, 47, 223–224, 247, 296–298
  in group counseling, 382–383
  of initial interview, 266–269
Tests, 15, 347–351
  assessment, in career counseling, 431
  interpretation of, 350–351
  purposes of, 348
  Rorschach, 131, 248
  selection of, 348–350
Themes, identifying, 286–287, 321–322
Therapeutic approaches, 74–75, 431, 486. *See also* Counseling, theories of
Therapeutic interventions, in systemic counseling, 393–395
Therapeutic relationship, *see* Counselor-client relationship
Therapy, *see* Counseling; Psychotherapy
"Thought stopping," in sexual counseling, 420
Threat, coping with, 166–169
"Ties," Adlerian, 87–88
Time
  being on, 203, 261
  management of, 428–430
"Topdog"/"underdog" split, 117–118

Topic change, by client, 246
Training, counselor, 75, 196–197, 204–206, 212, 225–227, 313, 485–486, 499–500
  accreditation of, 453–456
  standards for, 455–456
  videotapes in, 206, 224, 487
  see also Counselor-trainees
Trait-and-factor theory, 126, 127–132, 157
  evaluation of, 132
  goals of, 129–130
  theoretical beginnings of, 127–128
  therapeutic process in, 130–132
  view of individual in, 128–129
Transaction(s), in transactional analysis, 93, 96–97
Transactional analysis, 73, 76–77, 92–101, 121
  evaluation of, 101
  goals of, 98
  theoretical beginnings of, 92–93
  therapeutic process in, 99–100
  view of individual in, 93–98
Transactional patterns, 394–395
Transference, 84, 106, 293–396
Transparency
  client, 217, 220
  counselor, 216–218, 220
Triangles, in systems theory, 384, 393
Trust, in counseling relationship, 200–201
Two-chair method, in Gestalt counseling, 118

Unconscious, concept of, 79, 83, 85
Unemployment, vocational counseling and, 15–16
"Unfinished" business, 116, 118
Universalization, in groups, 377

Vaginismus, 412–413
Validation, in groups, 376–377

Value judgments, 272, 479
Values, in counseling, 33–35, 131, 133, 146, 199–200, 486
Values clarification, 33, 352
Verbal patterning, 287–290
Verbal responses, and acceptance, 202
Video- and audiotapes, 449, 499
  in training, 206, 224, 487
Visualization, mind-body, 426–427
Vital Information for Education and Work (VIEW), 499
Vocational Bureau of Boston, 14
Vocational counseling, 265
  sex bias in, 47–48
  societal changes and, 15–16
  see also Career development counseling
Vocational guidance movement, 14
Vocational Rehabilitation Act, 490
Volunteers, as counselors, 487–488, 498
Volunteers vs. nonvolunteers, in research, 50
von Ehrenfels, Christian, 114

Warmth, in counseling, 190, 194, 196
Weight loss, counseling program for, 329–330, 362
Wellness, 424, 425–426
Wertheimer, Max, 114
Wholeness, concept of, 383–384, 422
Williamson, E. G., 127–128, 129–130, 131
Women, 87, 88, 492
  as clients, 31, 43, 47–48, 60, 61, 223–224
  as counselors, 25, 29, 30–31
Women's groups, 494
Women's liberation, 212
Working through, in psychoanalysis, 85
Worth, feelings of, 150–151, 156

Reader Response Form

We would like to find out what your reactions are to *Counseling: An Introduction,* Second Edition. Your evaluation of the book will help us respond to the interests and needs of the readers of future editions. Please complete the form and mail it to College Marketing, Houghton Mifflin Company, One Beacon Street, Boston, MA 02108.

1. We would like to know how you rate our textbook in each of the following areas:

	Excellent	Good	Adequate	Poor
a. Selection of topics	___	___	___	___
b. Coverage of theory	___	___	___	___
c. Order of topics	___	___	___	___
d. Writing style/readability	___	___	___	___
e. Explanation of concepts	___	___	___	___
f. Art	___	___	___	___
g. Design	___	___	___	___

2. Please cite specific examples that illustrate any of the above ratings.

_____

_____

_____

3. Describe the strongest feature(s) of the book.

_____

_____

_____

4. Describe the weakest feature(s) of the book.

_____

_____

_____

5. What other topics should be included in this text?

_____

_____

_____

6. What recommendations can you make for improving this book?

_____

_____

_____